Clinical Assessment of Child and Adolescent Personality and Behavior

Clinical Assessment of Child and Adolescent Personality and Behavior

Third Edition

Paul J. Frick

University of New Orleans, New Orleans, LA, USA

Christopher T. Barry

University of Southern Mississippi, Hattiesburg, MS, USA

Randy W. Kamphaus

Georgia State University, Atlanta, GA, USA

Springer

Paul J. Frick
University of New Orleans
New Orleans, LA
USA
pfrick@uno.edu

Christopher T. Barry
University of Southern Mississippi
Hattiesburg, MS
USA
christopher.barry@usm.edu

Randy W. Kamphaus
Georgia State University
Atlanta, GA
USA
rkamphaus@gsu.edu

ISBN 978-0-387-89642-7 e-ISBN 978-1-4419-0641-0
DOI 10.1007/978-1-4419-0641-0
Springer New York Dordrecht Heidelberg London

Library of Congress Control Number: 2009926176

Printed on acid-free paper

Springer is part of Springer Science+Business Media (www.springer.com)

To my inspiration, Vicki, Josh, Jordan, and Jacob (PJF)

To my "home team," Tammy and Andersen (CTB)

To the memory of my parents, Richard and Nancy Kamphaus (RWK)

CONTENTS

Part II
Assessment Methods

Chapter 6
Self-Report Inventories 101

Chapter 7
Parent and Teacher Rating Scales 141

Chapter 8
Behavioral Observations 189

Chapter 9
Peer-Referenced Assessment 211

Chapter 10
Projective Techniques 225

Chapter 11
Structured Diagnostic Interviews 253

Chapter 12 Assessing Family Context 271

Chapter 13 History Taking 299

Chapter 14 Adaptive Behavior Scales 315

Part III Advanced Topics

Chapter 15 Integrating and Interpreting Assessment Information 339

Chapter 16 Report Writing 357

Chapter 17 Assessment of Attention Deficit Hyperactivity and Disruptive Behavior Disorders 377

Chapter 18 Assessment of Depression and Anxiety 413

Chapter 19 Assessment of Autism Spectrum Disorders 437

PREFACE

Psychologists offer an increasing variety of services to the public. Among these services, psychological assessment of personality and behavior continues to be a central activity. One main reason is that other mental health professionals often do not possess a high level of competence in this area. When one views psychologists who serve children and adolescents, psychological, assessment seems to take on an even greater role. It follows, then, that comprehensive and enlightened graduate-level instruction in assessment should be a high priority for educators of psychologists who are destined to work with youth.

This book is an outgrowth of our efforts to improve our own instruction of child and adolescent assessment skills. We found that existing textbooks were not serving us well. Most of them were encyclopedic, edited volumes that were (1) uneven in the quality across chapters and/or (2) not geared either in format or level of presentation for beginning graduate instruction. The few single- or co-authored volumes available tended to lack the breadth of coverage we deemed necessary. Some focused largely on theoretical issues related to psychological testing, with minimal discussion of practical applications and use of specific tests. Others focused solely on summaries of individual tests, without reviewing the theoretical or empirical context within which to use the tests appropriately. Hence, this volume reflects our desire to provide a more helpful tool for instruction - one that provides a scientific context within which to understand psychological testing with children and adolescents and that translates this scientific context into practical guidelines for using individual tests in clinical practice.

Among our specific objectives for this volume are the following:

- To focus on measures specifically designed to assess the emotional, behavioral, and social functioning of children and adolescents
- To provide current research findings that enable students to draw heavily on science as the basis for their clinical practice
- To help in the translation of research into practice by providing specific and practical guidelines for clinical practice
- To include a broad coverage of assessment methods from a variety of theoretical, practical, and empirical traditions
- To systematically compare tests and assessment methods using research findings, reviews, and our own synthesis of positions
- To provide a readable volume that would enhance the interest and retention of students through the use of numerous

case examples, tables, research notes, and other "boxes" containing practical advice

In writing a readable text that goes beyond a cursory survey of available instruments, we were faced with the difficult task of determining what specific instruments to include in the book. As we struggled with this decision, we eventually chose several selection criteria. Our main criterion for inclusion was a test's ability to serve as an exemplar of some specific type of assessment instrument or theoretical approach to assessment. In many cases we looked for "prototypes" that we thought would highlight some key points to the reader that could then be used in evaluating other assessment instruments not covered specifically in the text. Other criteria included a test's popularity or our estimate of a new test's potential impact on the field. Granted, this decision- making was highly subjective, but we strove to be analytic and to limit to the extent possible our personal feelings and biases. Fortunately, several external anonymous reviewers of earlier drafts of the text helped us to be more objective.

A final point that should be clearly outlined is our basic orientation to psychological assessment. We feel that the goal of psychological assessment is the measurement of psychological constructs and, for clinical practice, measurement of psychological constructs that have important clinical implications, such as documenting the need for treatment or the type of intervention that is most appropriate. For an individual child the constructs that need to be assessed will vary from case to case and depend on the referral question. But what is important from this conceptualization is that our view of psychological assessment is not test-driven but construct-driven. Without exception, assessment techniques will measure some constructs well and other psychological dimensions less well. Another important implication from this view of testing is that it is critical that assessors become familiar with and maintain familiarity with research on the constructs they are trying to assess. In short, the most critical component in choosing a method of assessment and in interpreting assessment data is understanding what one is trying to measure.

In this volume, we have focused on the measurement of psychological constructs that emphasize a child's emotional, behavioral, and social functioning. There is still a great debate over definitional issues in this arena of psychological functioning in terms of what should be called "personality," "temperament," "behavior," or "emotions," with distinctions usually determined by the level of analysis (e.g., overt behavior vs. unconscious motivational processes), assumed etiology (e.g., biologically determined vs. learned), or proven stability (e.g., transient problems vs. a stable pattern of functioning) (see Frick, 2004; Martin, 1988). Unfortunately, people often use the same terms with very different connotations. In writing this text, we tried to avoid this debate by maintaining a broad focus on "psychological constructs," which often vary on the most appropriate level of analysis, assumed etiology, or stability. This definitional variability adds a level of complexity to the assessment process because assessors must always consider what they are attempting to measure in a particular case and what research suggests about the best way of conceptualizing this construct before they can select the best way of measuring it. It would be much easier if one could develop expertise with a single favorite instrument or a single assessment modality that could be used in all evaluations to measure all constructs. Because this is not the case, psychologists must develop broad-based assessment expertise. Hence, our overriding objective in writing this volume is to provide the breadth of coverage that we feel is needed by the psychologist in training.

We have organized the text into three sections consistent with our approach to teaching. Part I provides students with an introduction to the psychological knowledge base necessary for modern assessment practice including historical perspectives; measurement science; research in developmental psychopathology; ethical, legal, and cultural issues; and the basics of beginning the assessment process (e.g., planning the evaluation, rapport building). Part II gives students a broad review of the specific assessment methods used by psychologists, accompanied by specific advice regarding the use and the strengths and weaknesses of each method. In Part III we help students perform some of the most sophisticated of assessment practices: integrating and communicating assessment results and infusing assessment practice with knowledge of child development and psychopathology. We think that, on completion of this volume, and a similar one covering aspects of cognitive assessment (Kamphaus, 2001 and in press), that the student psychologist has the background necessary for supervised practicum experiences in the assessment of children and adolescents.

Paul J. Frick
Christopher T. Barry
Randy W. Kamphaus

Part I

Basic Issues

CHAPTER 1

Historical Trends

Chapter Questions

- Who were the major innovators in the field of personality assessment?
- How were these innovations extended to the assessment of children and adolescents?
- What is meant by the terms *personality* and *behavior*?
- What is meant by the terms *objective* and *projective* personality assessment?
- Who conducted the seminal research and coined the terms *internalizing* and *externalizing behavior* problems?

Personality assessment is a process that most individuals engage in throughout their lives (Martin, 1988). Mothers label their children as happy, cranky, or similarly shortly after birth, and often in utero (e.g., active). The musings of Alfred Binet about the personality of his two daughters are typical of observations made by parents. He described Madeleine as silent, cool, and concentrated, while Alice was gay, thoughtless, giddy, and turbulent (Wolf, 1966).

Adolescents are keenly aware of personality evaluation as they carefully consider feedback from their peers to perform their own self-assessments. Personality assessment is also prized by the business community, in which human resources personnel consult with managers and others to gauge the effects of their personality on coworkers and productivity.

Early personality assessment emphasized the assessment of enduring traits that were thought to underlie behavior or, in modern terminology, latent traits. Kleinmuntz (1967) described personality as a unique organization of factors (i.e., traits) that characterizes an individual and determines his or her pattern of interaction with the environment. Thus, personality structure is commonly thought to be a result of multiple individual traits interacting with one another, and with the person's environment.

P.J. Frick et al., *Clinical Assessment of Child and Adolescent Personality and Behavior*,
DOI 10.1007/978-1-4419-0641-0_1,

Definitions of Terms in Personality Assessment

Traits

A *trait* is often conceptualized as a relatively stable disposition to engage in particular acts or ways of thinking (Kamphaus, 2001 and in press). A child, for example, may be described by her parents as either shy or extroverted. The shy (introverted in psychological terms) child may tend to cope with stressful situations by withdrawing from social contact, whereas the extrovert readily approaches social situations. For parents and psychologists alike, these traits are often thought to have value for predicting human behavior, because of the presumption of trait stability across time and, in many cases, environments. In fact, because of trait stability, parents may take special precautions to ensure that the shy child adapts well to the social aspects of attending a new school by asking one of their child's friends who attends the same school to accompany the child on the first day. Similarly, a stable tendency to be shy or introverted should manifest itself in numerous social situations such as interactions in the neighborhood, at church, and in ballet class. Personality traits, then, are characterized by longitudinal and situational stability, not unlike other enduring characteristics of a person such as intelligence, height, and activity level.

The Big Five Personality Traits (Factors)

In 1961, Tupes and Christal discovered five factors of personality that appeared in the reanalysis of numerous data sets from scales of bipolar personality descriptors. These central personality traits have subsequently become the focus of an extensive research effort, including the development of tests designed to assess the constructs. One of the well known scales used to identify the "big five" in adults is the NEO Personality Inventory (NEO-PI; Costa & McCrae, 1985).

Although commonly referred to as "factors" because of their origins in factor analysis, they are prototypical examples of traits with the requisite characteristic of presumed stability. The big five factors are typically identified by bipolar comparisons that are summarized in Table 1.1. These factors are often assessed using forced-choice item formats in which adjectives are used as personality descriptors. This item format is in direct contrast to the more commonplace true/false item format that is typical of many psychological tests.

Table 1.1 Early Descriptions of the Big Five Personality Dimensions (Goldberg, 1992)

Factor I – Surgency (or introversion–extroversion)
Unenergetic vs. energetic
Silent vs. talkative
Timid vs. bold
Factor II – Agreeableness (or pleasantness)
Cold vs. warm
Unkind vs. kind
Uncooperative vs. cooperative
Factor III – Conscientiousness (or dependability)
Disorganized vs. organized
Irresponsible vs. responsible
Negligent vs. conscientious
Factor IV – Emotional stability (vs. neuroticism)
Tense vs. relaxed
Nervous vs. at ease
Factor V – Culture, intellect, openness, or sophistication
Unintelligent vs. intelligent
Unanalytical vs. analytical
Unreflective vs. reflective

Commercially available instruments such as the NEO-PI have provided new opportunities to study and refine these constructs. Given the amount of research and development in this area, the big five personality factors could eventually have a substantial impact on the field of child and adolescent personality assessment. With some noteworthy exceptions (e.g., Lynam et al., 2005) however, big five research has largely been focused on adult populations.

Temperament

A concept related to personality is *temperament*, which also emphasizes the measurement of specific traits that are hypothesized as underlying behavior across settings. In this regard, Goldsmith and Rieser-Danner (1990) observed, "most researchers consider temperament to be the behavioral manifestation of biologically influenced processes determining both the infant's characteristic response to the environment and his or her style of initiating behavior" (p. 250). Therefore, some researchers distinguish temperament from personality based on the presumed biological basis of temperament, whereas personality is thought to be formed by a dynamic interplay of biological and social factors over development (Frick, 2004; Martin, 1988). Predictably, much of the research on temperament is conducted with infants and young children. In this conceptualization, personality may be viewed as being superimposed on a person's temperamental foundation. This distinction between temperament and personality, however, is not universally agreed upon.

Behavior

In contrast to temperament and personality trait assessment, the assessment of behavior focuses on the measurement of observable behaviors, although recently the definition has been broadened to include cognitions as a type of behavior. For most purposes, Martin (1988) provides a useful definition of behavior.

> When applied psychologists speak of behavior, they are usually referring to that range of human responses that are observable with the naked eye during a relatively brief period of time in a particular environment. This conception of behavior rules out biochemical and neurological events, for example, because they are not observable by the unaided eye. Behavior is differentiated from traits or dispositions because the latter may only be seen if behavior is aggregated over relatively long periods of time and in a number of environmental contexts. Classical examples of observed behaviors of interest to child psychologists include tantrum behavior among young children, aggressive interactions with peers, attempts at conversation initiation, and so forth (p. 13).

There are, therefore, several distinguishing features of behavioral assessment methods that differentiate them from trait assessment measures. First, behavioral assessment methods have a different theoretical foundation and associated set of premises. Behavioral assessment methods draw heavily on the theory and research tradition of operant conditioning as exemplified by the work of B. F. Skinner (Skinner, 1963). This research tradition also emanates primarily from laboratory research, as opposed to clinical practice; thus, it is often considered to be more empirically based.

Second, behavioral assessment methods are distinguished from medical models of assessment more than are trait-based methods. The medical model assumes that symptoms are caused by underlying conditions, and it is the medical condition that must be measured, diagnosed, and treated to remove the symptoms (see Chap. 3 for a more extended discussion of the medical model). In direct contrast, behavioral assessment emphasizes the measurement and treatment of the symptoms or behavior itself, and makes no assumptions regarding underlying cause.

Third, behavioral assessment places a premium on the assessment of discrete behaviors. For example, behavioral assessment may emphasize the measurement of finger tapping while completing seatwork in school, as opposed to aggregating several behaviors to form a test or scale with several items that measure "motor activity" in the classroom. This situation is changing, however, with the work of Thomas Achenbach, Keith Conners, Cecil Reynolds, and others (see Chap. 7), all of whom began combining behaviors into dimensions of behavior that may or may not differ from trait-based assessment methods.

As we suggested in the preface, we think that it is premature to reify any of these approaches as the ultimate method for assessing children's psychological adjustment. We merely seek progress in our methods and theories. This cautious approach seems warranted as the distinctions between the methods have become blurred as the science of assessment emerges. Furthermore, we think that each approach may be more or less helpful for answering particular assessment questions. Clearly, some of the questions directed at psychologists are trait-based, whereas others require the measurement of distinct behaviors. For example, a parent who asks, "Will my child ever become more outgoing like his sister?" is asking for trait assessment, but the parent who queries, "How can I get him to stop wetting the bed?" may require behavioral assessment expertise.

Early History of Personality Assessment

Formal personality measures emerged as a logical outgrowth of other efforts to measure individual differences, most notably the experimental methods of Wundt, Galton, and others (Chandler, 1990). Of the early assessment luminaries, Sir Francis Galton is one of the most notable. Although well known for his intelligence measurement contributions, he also studied the measurement of "character." In order to introduce the utility of personality measurement, Galton (1884) recounted the personality test invented by Benjamin Franklin as a crude form of personality measure. The scale was described in the tale of "The Handsome and Deformed Leg," in which Franklin recounts how his friend tested people so as to avoid those who, "being discontented themselves, sour the pleasures of society, offend many people, and make themselves everywhere disagreeable" (p. 9). This friend sought to diagnose such pessimistic individuals by showing them an attractive leg and a malformed one. If the stranger showed more interest in the ugly leg, the friend became suspicious and subsequently avoided this person. Franklin astutely identified this "test" as a grotesque but, nevertheless, an effective personality assessment device. Galton concluded: "The other chief point that I wish to impress is, that a practice of deliberately and methodically testing the character of others and of ourselves is not wholly fanciful, but de-serves consideration and experiment" (p. 10).

Intelligence tests, acknowledged as the first fruits of the psychometric movement, reached prominence early in the twentieth century with the introduction of the original Binet and Simon scale and numerous variants (Kamphaus, 2001 and in press). A lesser known fact is that Alfred Binet developed some intelligence test items that resembled stimuli used 30 years later in apperceptive techniques for assessing personality (DuBois, 1970). Test development activity also received a boost from the World War I effort, when ability testing became widespread (Kamphaus, 2001 and in press). Thus, it is no coincidence that the first formal and widely used measures of personality were developed about this same time.

Robert S. Woodworth

The Woodworth Personal Data Sheet was published in 1918 as a result of the surge of interest in testing potential soldiers. Woodworth developed a list of 116 questions about daydreaming, worry, and other problems. Some sample items from the Woodworth Personal Data Sheet (Woodworth, 1918) include:

> Do people find fault with you much?
> Are you happy most of the time?
> Do you suffer from headaches and dizziness?
> Do you sometimes wish that you had never been born?
> Is your speech free from stutter or stammer?
> Have you failed to get a square deal in life?

The examinee responded to each question with "yes" or "no" (French & Hale, 1990).

According to French and Hale (1990), the Woodworth Personal Data Sheet served as the foundation for the development of the Thurstone Personality Scale and the Allport Ascendance-Submission Test, among others. DuBois (1970) described the Personal Data Sheet as "the lineal ancestor of all subsequent personality inventories, schedules and questionnaires" (p. 94).

The Personal Data Sheet was an important practical innovation because, prior to this time, all military recruits suspected of having mental health disorders, stress disorders in particular, had to be identified by being interviewed by trained interviewers. The Personal Data Sheet allowed for the screening of large numbers of recruits without the time and expense of using huge cadres of interviewers (Kleinmuntz, 1967).

Thus, it was not basic research on personality or employee selection that led to the eventual popularity of personality testing. Instead, it was the need for diagnosis created by World War I which provided considerable evidence of the need for personality tests. The successful World War I and then later World War II applications of psychological testing proved that psychology could make practical contributions to society by identifying, accurately and time-efficiently, those in need of mental health services.

After World War II the mental health needs of citizens, veterans in particular, were the focus of greater attention. In the postwar years, the U.S. Veteran's Administration began to hire psychologists in large numbers to diagnose and treat veterans suffering from significant emotional disturbance. Psychologists brought their psychometric expertise to bear again by contributing new methods to the diagnostic process. The increased need for postwar mental health services, therefore, created the fertile ground in which personality testing flourished. As Kleinmuntz (1967) noted, "The most popular personality tests of the past 30 years grew out of the need to diagnose or detect individuals whose behavior patterns were psychopathological" (p. 10). The use of personality tests after the first and second world wars expanded beyond diagnosis into many areas including counseling, personnel selection, and personality research (Kleinmuntz, 1967).

Projective Techniques

The central assumption underlying projective testing is that the use of less well-defined stimuli that are prone to a variety of interpretations will encourage clients to reveal information that they otherwise would not share in response to direct questioning (Chandler, 1990). Given that test stimuli (e.g., ink blots) or questions were not clearly linked to known personality traits, projective testing depended heavily on the explicit or implicit personality theory that was favored by the test developer. Theory was necessary to determine the underlying nature or cause of the projected thoughts, emotions, or behaviors.

The most popular theory of the post-World War I era was psychodynamic personality theory as espoused by Sigmund Freud (1936) and others. Psychodynamic personality theory provided a useful theoretical framework for the development of projective assessment measures due to the concepts of repression, projection, and other constructs that are entirely consistent with the use of atypical test stimuli for identifying personality traits (see Chap. 10 for a more extended discussion of the basic assumptions of the projective technique).

Association Techniques

The use of association techniques, such as word association methods, for assessment purposes can be traced as far back as the work of Aristotle (DuBois, 1970). In relatively recent history, Sir Francis Galton began studying association techniques as early as 1879. Galton's contribution to the study of association was his introduction of scientific rigor to the enterprise. He used experimental methods to study association methods, including quantitative scaling of the results (DuBois, 1970).

Subsequently, Kraepelin, Wundt, Cattell, Kent, and Rosanoff studied the associations of patients and research participants to word lists, recording such variables as response time and type of association. The latter names, Kent and Rosanoff, may be least familiar to many readers because the other names are linked with the illustrious history of intellectual assessment. Kent and Rosanoff made their contribution solely to the study of associations by developing a list of 100 stimulus words and systematically recording the associations of 1,000 normal subjects (DuBois, 1970). This effort represents an important initial attempt at developing norms to which researchers and clinicians could compare the responses of clinical subjects.

The renowned psychoanalyst Carl Jung made extensive use of association techniques for the study of personality. In an address at Clark University in 1909, he described his research efforts in detail and provided some insight into the types of interpretations commonly made of these measures. Jung described his association word list as *a formulary*. His list consisted of 54 words including *head*, *to dance*, *ink*, *new*, *foolish*, and *white*. According to Jung (1910), normality could be distinguished from psychopathology with this formulary using variables such as reaction time and response content. In his speech, he provided a transcript of the responses of a normal individual and of a "hysteric." A sampling of their associations to the formulary follows:

Stimulus	Normal	Hysterical
To sin	Much	This is totally unfamiliar to me, I do not recognize it
To pay	Bills	Money
Bread	Good	To eat
Window	Room	Big
Rich	Nice	Good, convenient
Friendly	Children	A man

As noted previously for other measures, reaction time to the stimulus words was also interpreted by Jung. He gave a glimpse of one such interpretation in the following quote:

> The test person waives any reaction; for the moment he totally fails to obey the original instructions, and shows himself incapable of adapting himself to the experimenter. If this phenomenon occurs frequently in an experiment, it signifies a higher degree of disturbance in adjustment (p. 27).

These early word association methods set the stage for the development of other association (projective) techniques, such as the Thematic Apperception Technique and Rorschach's test, both of which used pictures in lieu of word lists to elicit associations.

Thematic Apperception Test

The Thematic Apperception Test (TAT) of Henry A. Murray constitutes a prototypical example of a projective device. Charles E. Thompson summarized the central tenet of the projective approach in the following quote taken from his 1949 adaptation of Murray's TAT.[1]

> If the pictures are presented as a test of imagination, the subject's interest, together with his need for approval, can be so involved in the task that he forgets his sensitive self and the necessity of defending it against the probing of the examiner, and, before he knows it, he has said things about an invented character that apply to himself, things which he would have been reluctant to confess in response to a direct question (p. 5).

The TAT is unique among projective measures in that it has traditionally been interpreted qualitatively, even though quantitative scoring methods are available (Kleinmuntz, 1967). Murray's original approach to TAT scoring was entirely qualitative and psychoanalytically based. He proposed the following categories for analyzing the characteristics of the stories given by the subject (Murray, 1943).

1. *The Hero.* This is the person with whom the subject seems to identify. The hero may share characteristics such as age, gender, occupation, or other features with the subject that aid identification. The hero's traits should be evaluated to determine the self-perceptions of the subject including superiority, intelligence, leadership, belongingness, solitariness, and quarrelsomeness.
2. *Needs of the Hero.* Needs may include those for order, achievement, and nurturance.
3. *Environmental Forces.* Factors that affect the hero and these are also referred to as *press.* An example would involve scoring aggression if the hero's property or possessions were destroyed in a story.
4. *Outcomes.* The success of the hero and the hero's competencies are assessed by evaluating the outcomes of stories.
5. *Themas.* Themas assess the interplay of needs and presses, and they reveal the primary concerns of the hero.
6. *Interests, Sentiments, and Relationships.* For this aspect of scoring the examiner records the hero's preferences for topics.

Murray's qualitative scoring system for the TAT is a classic example of systems that dominated the early interpretation of projective devices. Numerous quantitative scoring systems followed Murray's original work as exemplified by scoring systems eventually developed for Rorschach's test.

The Rorschach

Hermann Rorschach (1884–1922) was a major figure in Swiss psychiatric research who began his work as a physician in 1910. He married a Russian colleague who became his comrade and collaborator (Morgenthaler, 1954). He served as a physician in a hospital in Herisau until his death from complications of appendicitis in 1922. His death was

[1]Thompson's modification is identical to the original TAT with the exception that African American figures are used as characters on the stimulus cards. Thompson found that African Americans did not respond optimally to the original TAT pictures. In fact, one of his patients asked if he could imagine that the people in the pictures were "colored," and if he could make up some stories about "colored people."

described as a critical blow to Swiss psychiatry. In a 1954 eulogy to Dr. Rorschach, published in the English translation of his original work, Morgenthaler attempted to describe Rorschach for future generations.

> Flexibility of character, rapid adaptability, fine acumen, and a sense for the practical were combined in Hermann Rorschach with a talent for introspection and synthesis. It was this combination which made him outstanding. In addition to this rare nature, which tempered personal emotional experience with practical knowledge, he possessed sound traits of character most valuable in a psychiatrist. Most important of these were an unerring tendency to search for the truth, a strict critical faculty which he did not hesitate to apply to himself, and a warmth of feeling and kindness. (p. 9)

Rorschach's approach to personality assessment was novel in many respects. The test stimuli used were inkblots placed on paper that was then folded in half. Rorschach was not, however, interested in the content of the subject's response to the inkblots. Rather, he was interested in the form of the response (or its *function*). Some functions of interest included the number of responses, perception of color or movement, and perception of the whole vs. the parts. These and other characteristics of Rorschach responses continue as part of modern scoring systems (see Chap. 10).

Rorschach first offered his method as an experiment. His original sample is described in Table 1.2. He expressed a desire for larger sample sizes but noted that the number of experiments was limited because the stimulus figures were damaged by passing through hundreds of hands.

Rorschach's legacy, his original inkblots, and many of the associated scoring criteria remain influential as the test continues to enjoy popularity. Several scoring systems have been offered for the Rorschach, with the Exner Comprehensive System (Exner & Weiner, 1982) contributing most to the continuing usage of the instrument.

Table 1.2 Rorschach's Original Research Sample

Sample	N
Normal, educated	55
Normal, uneducated	62
Psychopathic personality	20
Alcoholic cases	8
Morons, imbeciles	12
Schizophrenics	188
Manic-depressives	14
Epileptics	20
Paretics	8
Senile dements	10
Arteriosclerotic dements	5
Korsakoff and similar states	3

Source: Adapted from Rorschach (1951).

Sentence Completion Techniques

Sentence completion techniques are venerable personality assessment methods of the association tradition that can trace their roots to Payne (1928). The sentence completion method, however, obtained a substantial boost in popularity because of its use by the U.S. Office of Strategic Services (OSS), the forerunner of the Central Intelligence Agency (CIA). Henry Murray was the coordinator of a sophisticated OSS assessment effort. About 60 military assessment stations, staffed by American psychologists, were situated in the USA and abroad to screen recruits for sensitive and dangerous assignments. Some of the methods used in this ambitious program are described in the following quote from DuBois (1970):

> In one of the stations near Washington, recruits in fatigue uniforms assumed a false identity and developed a cover story, which the staff members during the three-day stay endeavored to break. The procedures described in a comprehensive report (OSS, Assessment Staff, 1948) were varied: casual conversations,

> searching interviews, the sentence completion test, questionnaires about health and working conditions and personal history, conventional aptitude tests such as map memory and mechanical comprehension, and a number of situational tests (p. 111).

After World War II, the sentence completion technique continued to enjoy some favor among psychologists. The well-known Rotter Incomplete Sentences Blank was published in 1950 (Rotter & Rafferty, 1950). Sentence completion methods have a lengthy history of use with children and adolescents as well. They enjoyed worldwide use in countries such as Finland, Germany, Denmark, India, Japan, and Taiwan (Haak, 1990).

Projective Techniques for Children

The use of projective techniques with children dates back to the early part of the twentieth century when Florence Goodenough began to study children's human figure drawings (DuBois, 1970). Goodenough noted, as did others, that children's drawings were affected by their emotionality. The typical paradigm for drawing techniques has been to have the child draw a picture of a person. Traditionally, the content of the drawings has been interpreted as a measure of child adjustment and personality. Some aspects of content that were extensively studied for adults included (Swensen, 1968):

Size of the person depicted
Placement on the page (bottom, top, corner, etc.)
Stance (vertical, horizontal, balanced, etc.)
Line quality (heavy, light, etc.)
Shading
Erasures
Omissions (missing body parts)
Distortion (poor proportion of body parts)

Various interpretations have been associated with these and other content variables over the years. Heavy lines, for example, have been associated with assertive and aggressive individuals and light lines have been viewed as being indicative of passive individuals (Koppitz, 1968). Swensen (1968) found such interpretations to be highly unreliable. The most reliable and valid interpretive approach involved making general judgments about the mental health status of the individual based on the overall quality of the drawing, rather than specific content interpretations (Cummings, 1986).

The TAT, among other projective methods, has also been adapted by many for use with children and adolescents. One of the most well-known TAT adaptations is the Children's Apperception Test (CAT) (Bellak & Bellak, 1949b), designed for ages 3–10. The CAT consists of ten pictures with animals as stimuli in contrast to the TAT's depictions primarily of people. The Rorschach has also been widely used with children, and several compendiums of child responses have been published to aid interpretation (e.g., Ames, Metraux, Rodell, & Walker, 1974).

The proper interpretation of children's projective responses remains a topic of debate. Indeed, the degree to which children obey the *projective hypothesis* has been questioned. Chandler (1990) elucidates the nature of the projective hypothesis as follows:

> *Projection*, in common usage, means to cast forward. In this sense, *projection* implies a direct extension of psychological characteristics onto the outer world. But *projection* also has a specific meaning within psychoanalytic theory. Freud (1936) used the term to refer to the process that occurs when the ego, faced with unacceptable wishes or ideas, thrusts them out onto the external world as a means of defense. In projection the individual attributes his or her own thoughts and actions to someone else. Thus, if one's own faults or feelings are unacceptable to

> the ego, they may be seen as belonging to someone else; in the process, the material may become distorted or remain partially repressed. From such a perspective, projective material would not be seen as direct representation of aspects of the personality, certainly not with the sort of one-to-one correspondence that the first meaning of projection implies (p. 57).

For adults as well as children, the process of projection still rests primarily on a theoretical rather than empirical foundation. In the absence of data to support the projective hypothesis, psychologists have focused on the use of psychometric methods to assess the reliability of obtained scores and the validity of score inferences. This shift to the accumulation of psychometric evidence for measures is reflected best in the work of Exner. In the 1960s, John Exner began a research program designed to take the best of the Rorschach scoring systems and incorporate their features into a comprehensive system (Exner & Weiner, 1982). Further, a standard method for scoring responses on the test has led to scores that have proven to be reliable and, as a result, has set the stage for direct tests of the validity of various interpretations that can be made from them. The application of psychometric standards to projective measures is a clear departure from a long history of qualitative analysis and interpretation. The efforts of Exner and others have set a new course for projective measures in that they are increasingly held to the same standard as tests of intelligence, adaptive behavior, and "objective" personality assessment methods.

Objective Tests

Although we acknowledge that the distinction between projective and objective testing is an oversimplification, it is nevertheless useful for pedagogical purposes. Objective methods can be differentiated from projective tests in several ways. First, objective methods are often considered to be atheoretical and/or empirical. As opposed to requiring the examiner to use theory to interpret results, the results often derive their meaning from empirical procedures, such as matching a person's results to those of a clinical sample. Second, objective methods are not likely to be based on psychodynamic theory. Hence, the results of objective measures are often considered to be less useful for providing insight into the dynamics of an individual's interactions with the world. Third, objective methods take greater advantage of measurement science for the development of tests. Issues of item selection, reliability, and validity are often emphasized in the test manuals.

Minnesota Multiphasic Personality Inventory (MMPI)

Until the advent of the MMPI, projective techniques reigned supreme. In a 1961 survey of tests used by psychologists in the USA, the MMPI was the only nonprojective measure mentioned among the top ten most used tests. Of the top ten tests, five were intelligence tests and four were projective measures (Sundberg, 1961). A confluence of circumstances, including the expansion of clinical psychology practice during and after World War II, and the emergence of an extensive research base led to almost immediate acceptance of this self-report personality inventory (Kleinmuntz, 1967). Further, the MMPI was one of the first tests to gain popularity with others outside of the mental health professions (see Box 1.1). However, this popularity led to significant friction and disagreements over the relative merits of the MMPI, and its objective methods, compared with the popular projective techniques. This tension is reflected in the comments of Paul Meehl that are summarized in Box 1.2.

The MMPI (Hathaway & McKinley, 1942) differed from its predecessors (such

Box 1.1

Sample Items from 1960s MMPI Spoofs

Personality testing eventually became popular enough to warrant derision by members of Congress, well-known humorists such as Art Buchwald, and others. Some of these alternate MMPI items were published in a 1965 issue of *American Psychologist* (p. 990) to poke fun at this method of personality assessment.

> When I was younger I used to tease vegetables.
>
> I think beavers work too hard.
>
> I use shoe polish to excess.
>
> When I was a child I was an imaginary playmate.

Box 1.2

Meehl on Science and Technics

Paul Meehl is considered one of the founders of modern personality assessment and diagnostic practice. His 1973 collection of selected papers published by the University of Minnesota Press provides a unique glimpse of the genius of an astute clinician. In the following quote, Dr. Meehl discusses the tension between science and practice in psychology and takes a stance against theoretical dogmatism:

> Doubtless every applied science (or would-be science) presents aspects of this problem to those working at the interface between science and technics, as is apparent when one listens to practicing attorneys talking about law professors, practitioners of medicine complaining about medical school teaching, real engineers in industry poking ambivalent fun at academic physicists, and the like. So I do not suggest that the existential predicament of the clinical psychologist is unique in this respect, which it certainly is not.
>
> But I strongly suspect that there are few if any fields of applied semiscientific knowledge in which the practitioner with scientific interests and training is presented *daily* with this problem in one guise or another, or in which its poignancy, urgency, and cognitive tensions are so acute. I am aware that there are *some* clinical psychologists who do not experience this conflict, but I have met, read, or listened to very few such during the thirty years since I first began working with patients as a clinical psychology trainee. Further, these rare exceptions have seemed to me in every case to be either lacking in perceptiveness and imagination or, more often, deficient in scientific training and critical habits of mind.
>
> When I encounter a hard-nosed behaviorist clinician who knows (for sure) that Freud's theory of dreams is 100 percent hogwash and is not worth five hours of his serious attention; or, toward the other end of the continuum, when I converse with a devoted Rorschacher who knows (for sure) that the magic inkblots are highly valid no matter what the published research data indicate-I find both of these attitudes hard to understand or sympathize with (p. viii).

as the Personal Data Sheet) in at least one fundamental way. It was one of the first tests to use an empirical approach to objective personality test development. Most tests of the day used a priori or rational–theoretical approaches (Martin, 1988). Rational approaches, as the name implies, depend heavily on the test author's theory of personality for many aspects of test construction, including item development and scoring methods. On the other hand, empirical approaches make greater use of empirical data to make such decisions (see Chap. 2 for a more detailed discussion of this distinction).

The MMPI used an item selection method called *empirical criterion keying* (Anastasi &

Urbina, 1998). Simply stated, this method involved selecting items that meet an empirical criterion. In the case of the MMPI, items were selected if they were able to routinely differentiate clinical groups from samples of "normal" subjects, and distinguish clinical groups from one another. For example, items for the Psychasthenia scale (a scale designed to assess anxiety-related problems such as obsessions and fears) were selected based on a clinical group of 20 cases, the results of which were compared with "normals" and other clinical groups to identify items that best differentiated the target clinical group from the others.

The original version of the MMPI consisted of 550 statements printed on separate cards. The cards were separated by the patient into three categories: true, false, and cannot say. The first MMPI clinical scales were linked to the major diagnostic nosology of the day (Kleinmuntz, 1967), which is another factor that contributed to its popularity. The ten clinical scales of the original version included are provided in Table 1.3. The MMPI has undergone many changes since its inception, with the most recent edition entitled the MMPI-2. In fact, some of the scale names (e.g., Psychasthenia) had fallen into disuse at about the time of original publication (Kleinmuntz, 1967). A chronology of MMPI developments is listed next and a thorough discussion of this important measure is provided in Chapter 6.

MMPI Version	Publication Date
MMPI	1942
MMPI-2	1989
MMPI-A (Adolescent)	1992

TABLE 1.3 The Original Scales from the MMPI

Clinical scales
Hypochondriasis
Depression
Hysteria
Psychopathic deviate
Masculinity–Femininity
Paranoia
Psychasthenia
Schizophrenia
Hypomania
Social Introversion
Validity scales
Question scale
Lie scale
F scale
Correction scale

SOURCE: Kleinmuntz, 1967.

The "Children's MMPI"

Not surprisingly, the MMPI profoundly influenced child assessment practice including the development of the Personality Inventory for Children (PIC) in the 1950s. The PIC was based on a pool of 600 items; hence, it was comparable in length to the MMPI. A central difference between the MMPI and the PIC was the informant. The PIC was not a self-report measure. Instead, a parent rated the child's behavior. Lachar (1990) gave the following rationale for this decision:

> Selection of the parents as the source of PIC test responses helps overcome two of the major obstacles posed by requesting the referred child or adolescent to respond to numerous self-report descriptions in order to obtain a multiple-scale objective evaluation. The majority of children seen by mental health professionals in a variety of settings appear for such an evaluation because of their noncompliant behaviors and/or documented problems in academic achievement, most notably in the development of reading skills. Therefore, it seems unlikely that a technique requiring such children to read and respond to a large set of self-descriptions will find broad acceptance in routine clinical practice (p. 299).

The scales of the PIC were derived using factor-analytic methods. Thus, the PIC, like the MMPI, was developed with a heavy emphasis on empirical methods (see Chap. 6). In the 1960s, empirical methods of test development were also applied to the development of other types of child assessment devices.

Rating Scales

Parent and teacher ratings of children's behavior and emotions trace their roots to the assessment of adult psychopathology in hospital settings. Conceptualized as one type of observational method, rating scales were developed in the 1950s for use by nurses and other caretakers who worked closely with patients for extended periods of time. One of the first such measures was the Wittenborn Psychiatric Rating Scales (1955). According to Lorr (1965), the scales were designed for recording currently observable behavior and symptoms in hospitalized mental patients. The Wittenborn could be completed by a social worker, psychologist, psychiatrist, nurse, attendant, or other individual familiar with the patient's day-to-day behavior. The original scale consisted of 52 symptoms that were combined to yield 9 scores for acute anxiety, conversion hysteria, manic state, depressed state, schizophrenic excitement, paranoid condition, paranoid schizophrenic, hebephrenic schizophrenic, and phobic compulsive. An item assessing withdrawal included the following options:

> No evidence of social withdrawal
> Does not appear to seek out the company of other people
> Definitely avoids people

The Wittenborn was used for diagnostic purposes as well as for the design and evaluation of treatment (Kleinmuntz, 1967). Reviewers of the day found many reasons to recommend the Wittenborn, including a thorough research base (Eysenck, 1965) and easy administration and scoring (Lorr, 1965). There was considerable concern, however, about overlapping scales. The hebephrenic schizophrenic and schizophrenic excitement scales correlated at .88 and the paranoid condition and paranoid schizophrenic scales correlated at .79. On the basis of these data, Eysenck (1965) and Lorr (1965) recommended that these scales be combined to reflect this overlap.

Other rating scales of adult psychopathology for use in inpatient settings included the Hospital Adjustment Scale (McReynolds, Ballachey, & Ferguson, 1952) and the Inpatient Multidimensional Psychiatric Scale (Lorr, 1965), a rating of symptomatology completed by the clinician after a diagnostic interview. Such measures probably fell into decline for many reasons, one of the most prominent being the deinstitutionalization movement of the 1970s. These instruments did, however, clearly demonstrate the utility of ratings of behavior as practical and useful assessment tools. These scales set the stage for the development of parent and teacher rating scales of child behavior.

Internalizing and Externalizing Dimensions

Research into the diagnosis of child psychopathology led to increased attention to the use of rating scales for child diagnosis. In a 1978 article in *Psychological Bulletin*, Thomas Achenbach and Craig Edelbrock introduced many clinicians to the terms *internalizing* and *externalizing* psychological disorders of childhood. These dimensions, or types of child psychopathology, were based on an extensive empirical analysis (typically using factor analysis) of parent and teacher behavior problem rating scales. Children experiencing adjustment difficulties of the internalizing variety have also been described as over-controlled, with problems of inhibition, anxiety, and, perhaps, shyness (Edelbrock, 1979). On the other hand, children with externalizing problems have been described as undercontrolled with difficulties such as aggression, conduct problems, and acting-out behavior (Edelbrock, 1979).

These two dimensions of child psychopathology trace their roots to the work of Peterson (1961), who labeled the syndromes as *conduct problem* (externalizing) and *personality problem* (internalizing). The veracity of the broad internalizing and externalizing categorizations of child psychopathology is supported by many factor-analytic investigations of both parent and teacher rating scales alike (Edelbrock, 1979). The utility of these behavioral distinctions was also demonstrated in an early study of 163 consecutive referrals to a child psychiatry outpatient department (Cohen, Gotlieb, Kershner, & Wehrspann, 1985). Children were classified as externalizers and internalizers based on the Achenbach Child Behavior Checklist (CBCL; a parent report form) and the Teacher Report Form (TRF) (see Chap. 7). The resulting analyses uncovered distinct differences between the two groups, particularly on the Teacher Form. Internalizers were found to be more intelligent, better readers, less egocentric, and they used more adaptive means of coping with stressful situations. Internalizers were also generally rated as being less disruptive than externalizers.

Numerous independent research studies, many of which have been conducted internationally (Ivanova et al., 2007), have demonstrated strong factor-analytic support for these two types of child behavioral adjustment. This preponderance of evidence, supported by other types of validity evidence, has resulted in these factors serving as the foundation for the development of many teacher and parent rating scales, most notably the Achenbach Child Behavior Checklist (Achenbach, 1991b) and the Behavior Assessment System for Children (BASC-2; Reynolds & Kamphaus, 2004). Furthermore, the terms *internalizing* and *externalizing* are now a part of psychologists' everyday parlance when discussing child behavior problems.

The Diagnostic and Statistical Manual of Mental Disorders Diagnostic Systems

Diagnostic systems have had a profound impact on child assessment by defining symptoms and other diagnostic indices that have subsequently been incorporated into various assessment methods. The most obvious link exists between the various editions of the *Diagnostic and Statistical Manual of Mental Disorders* (currently *DSM-IV-TR;* American Psychiatric Association, 2000) and structured interview methods designed to assess symptomatology associated with various *DSM* diagnostic categories (see Chap. 11). Given this interdependence, a thorough knowledge of the nature of the *DSM* and its variants is prerequisite to the study of child assessment.

As mental disorders became recognized as conditions worthy of medical treatment, the need for diagnostic systems became more pressing. Consistent diagnosis was necessary for communication among clinicians and for the conduct of epidemiological research and other scientific investigations. The American Medico-Psychological Association (now the American Psychiatric Association) began efforts to standardize diagnostic procedures in 1917. The first diagnostic manual, a classification of mental disease, was produced by the American Psychiatric Association in conjunction with the U.S. Census Bureau (Widiger, Frances, Pincus, Davis, & First, 1991).

The first edition of the *DSM* (*Diagnostic and Statistical Manual*) appeared in 1952. Part of the impetus for the creation and frequent updating of the *DSM* has been provided by the *International Statistical Classification of Diseases, Injuries, and Causes of Death* (*ICD*). The *ICD*, currently *ICD-11*, is published by the World Health Organization. The *DSM* has been revised both to coordinate with the *ICD* and to add criteria for conditions that are of concern to US clinicians, and delete conditions that are not apparent in the USA (Widiger et al., 1991). The *DSM* has also been revised because of a desire to make the diagnostic categories more evidence-based. Prior to the development of the *DSM-III*, the system was based primarily on the expert judgment of a relatively small number of clinicians. The *DSM-II*, for example, was finalized after review by 120 psychiatrists in February of 1967 (Widiger et al., 1991).

The *DSM-IV* (APA, 1994) was based on a more comprehensive research base than any of its predecessors. According to Widiger et al. (1991), three research methods have formed the empirical cornerstone for the development of *DSM-IV*.

1. *Literature reviews*: Comprehensive reviews of the research were completed to advise the various committees charged with proposing diagnostic criteria for conditions. These reviews were seen as a way to mitigate against biases on the part of some committees (Widiger et al., 1991).
2. *Data reanalyses*: Existing data sets were made available to the *DSM-IV* committees supported by funding from the John D. and Catherine T. MacArthur Foundation. According to Widiger et al. (1991), these data set reanalyses allowed the committees to evaluate the validity of current diagnostic algorithms and pilot-test new proposals for making diagnoses.
3. *Field trials*: These studies were particularly useful for testing the reliability and validity of diagnostic categories (Widiger et al., 1991).

TABLE 1.4 Chronology of Diagnostic Systems Developed Under the Auspices of the American Psychiatric Association

1917	Classification of Mental Disease
1933	Standard Classified Nomenclature of Disease
1952	Diagnostic and Statistical Manual of Mental Disorders I (DSM-I)
1968	Diagnostic and Statistical Manual of Mental Disorders II (DSM-II)
1980	Diagnostic and Statistical Manual of Mental Disorders III (DSM-III)
1987	Diagnostic and Statistical Manual of Mental Disorders III-Revised (DSM-III-R)
1994	Diagnostic and Statistical Manual of Mental Disorders IV (DSM-IV)
2000	Diagnostic and Statistical Manual of Mental Disorders IV-Text Revision (DSM-IV-TR)

The *DSM-IV-TR*, because of its greater reliance on empirical methods, has had an even more substantial impact on the personality assessment process (see Chap. 3). The chronology of the *DSM* is provided in Table 1.4.

IDEA and Special Education

The 1974 Education of Handicapped Children's Act, better known as Public Law 94–142 (IDEA), and its reauthorization, the Individuals with Disabilities Education Improvement Act (IDEIA), mandated special education and related services for children classified as having an emotional disturbance. As a result, some method had to be developed to define child problems and determine children's eligibility for special education services. Under IDEA, and the subsequent IDEIA with few substantive changes, the classification of severe emotional disturbance was defined as follows:

> The term means a condition exhibiting one or more of the following characteristics over a long period of time and to a marked degree which adversely affects school performance: (a) an inability to learn which cannot be explained by intellectual, sensory, or health factors; (b) an inability to build or maintain satisfactory relationships with peers and teachers; (c) inappropriate types of behavior or feelings under normal circumstances; (d) a general pervasive mood of unhappiness or depression; or (e) a tendency to develop physical symptoms or fears associated with personal or school problems (Federal Register, 1999).

With its passage in the 1970s, this law effectively mandated US public schools to identify and serve children with behavioral or emotional problems, many of which had previously been educated in a variety of settings, including residential treatment programs or state mental hospitals. Consequently, these laws expanded school-based diagnostic practices to include evaluation for the presence of "emotional disturbance," just as had been more commonly done for developmental and learning disorders. These federal mandates also enhanced the popularity of rating scales (particularly teacher ratings) as assessment methods of choice in many school systems.

The IDEA nosology of emotional disturbance (the word *severe* has now been removed) has long been the target of criticisms that it is invalid, restrictive, or otherwise flawed (Forness & Kritzer, 1992). Bower (1982), the recognized developer of the conceptual basis of the IDEA diagnostic categories, raised similar questions about the system. He noted that:

> Section ii [which excludes the socially maladjusted from the IDEA act] is, one would guess, a codicil to reassure traditional psychopathologists and budget personnel that schizophrenia and autism are indeed serious emotional disturbances on the one hand, and that just plain bad boys and girls, predelinquents, and sociopaths will not skyrocket the costs on the other hand. It is clear what these modifications and additions were intended to do. It is perhaps not clear what such public policy and fiscal modifications do to the conceptual integrity of the definition and the nature and design of its goals (p. 56).

Despite such controversy, the IDEA classification system remains as the "gold standard" nosology when determining child eligibility for oft-costly special education and related services.

Constructs (Dimensions) vs. Categories

The measurement problems associated with categorical diagnostic systems such as the DSM are well known (Kamphaus & Campbell, 2006), and the advantages of using dimensional methods are recognized as well. Achenbach and McConaughy (1996), for example, noted that the yes/no nature of categorical methods does not necessarily account for children whose problems vary in degree or severity. As a result, the nexus between normality and psychopathology cannot be well understood with categorical methods, since most high prevalence problem behaviors of childhood, such as inattention and hyperactivity, are not classifiable when below diagnostic threshold levels. Substantial evidence is emerging to suggest that child behavior problems such as inattention, hyperactivity, depression, and conduct problems, in fact, fall along continua in the population (Hudziak et al., 1998; Scahill et al., 1999).

As a result, dimensional classification methods have demonstrated their usefulness in the study of psychopathology. For example, dimensional approaches have demonstrated more predictive validity than categorical approaches (Fergusson & Horwood, 1995), as well as statistical reliability (Cantwell, 1996). Such methods also minimize the need for clinical judgment and inference (Haynes & O'Brien, 1988), provide greater sensitivity to the presence of comorbid conditions (Caron & Rutter, 1991), and have the ability to depict multiple symptom patterns in a given individual simultaneously (Cantwell, 1996). Furthermore, the use of dimensional, person-oriented approaches to identify subtypes or clusters of individuals may lead to more efficient, streamlined subtype-specific intervention and prevention services (Achenbach, 1995; Bergman & Magnusson, 1997). The overlap and tensions between categorical and dimensional classification methods will be elucidated throughout this text. It is important to do so because a merger of these methodologies is likely in the DSM-V and other future diagnostic systems (Rounsaville et al., 2002).

Future Trends

The pace of change in personality assessment is ever hastening. There is increasing interest in the development of new child assessment methods, providing clinicians with a wide array of assessment options. In 1990, Tuma and Elbert (1990) identified test development and research trends that remain true to the present day.

> It is apparent that personality assessment is undergoing rapid development in all areas: projective, objective, and behavioral assessment; clinical interviewing and informal assessment; and environmental assessment. The developments outlined above encompass observable behavior, structured and unstructured use of tests and interviews, and assessment of broad- and narrow-band aspects of personality, all within the context of a person's situation/environment. Thus, in spite of various criticisms and some apparent decrease in the use of personality assessment instruments (*they were referring to projective devices primarily*), all indications point to vigorous activity in the area that promises to continue." (p. 23; italics added).

In the past, the technology of personality assessment has been viewed as lagging behind other areas of assessment, such as intelligence and achievement testing (Martin, 1998). This conclusion is no longer true. New measurement science rigor is being applied to the development of behavioral rating scales, interview methods, and diagnostic systems. Two trends of the past few decades are continuing; relatively less emphasis on training in projective methods (Belter & Piotrowski, 1999) and increased use of rating scales (Archer & Newsom, 2000). In fact, a veritable explosion in the creation and publication of behavior rating scales alone necessitated creation of this, our third edition of this text.

Chapter Summary

1. Personality is typically considered to be composed of traits, a more enduring set of characteristics of the individual.
2. Formal personality measures emerged as a logical outgrowth of other efforts to measure individual differences, most notably the experimental methods of Wundt, Galton, and others.
3. The Woodworth Personal Data Sheet was published in 1918 as a result of the

surge of interest in testing potential soldiers.

4. The needs for diagnosis created by World War I and World War II provided con-sider-able impetus for the development of personality tests.
5. A major assumption underlying projective testing is that the use of stimuli that are prone to a variety of interpretations will encourage clients to reveal information that they otherwise would not share in response to direct questioning.
6. The Rorschach test stimuli were originally inkblots placed on paper that was then folded in half.
7. The use of projective techniques with children dates back to the early part of this century, when Florence Goodenough began to study children's human figure drawings.
8. The MMPI was one of the first tests to use an empirical approach for personality test development and used an item selection method called *empirical criterion keying*.
9. The use of informant rating scales for the assessment of child psychopathology traces its roots to the assessment of adult psychopathology in hospital settings.
10. In a 1978 article in *Psychological Bulletin*, Achenbach and Edelbrock introduced the terms *internalizing* and *externalizing* when referring to psychological disorders of childhood.
11. The first edition of the *DSM* (*Diagnostic and Statistical Manual*) appeared in 1952.
12. The most recent edition of the manual, the *DSM-IV-TR*, is based on a more comprehensive research base than any of its predecessors.
13. The 1974 Education of all Handicapped Children's Act, better known as Public Law 94–142, and its reauthorization, the Individuals with Disabilities Education Improvement Act (IDEIA), have mandated special education and related services for children classified as emotionally disturbed.

CHAPTER 2

Measurement Issues

Chapter Questions

- What type of information is yielded from a T-score?
- How does skewness affect scaling decisions?
- How has factor analysis been used to develop personality tests and diagnostic schedules?

Users of instruments assessing personality and other aspects of behavioral, emotional, and social functioning should have a thorough understanding of measurement principles. The discussion that follows, however, hardly qualifies as thorough because measurement instruction is not the purpose of this book. This chapter merely points out some of the most important measurement concepts for conducting assessments of youth.

We assume that the user of this text has had, at a minimum, undergraduate courses in statistics, tests and measurements, as well as at least one graduate-level measurement course. If a user of this text is not acquainted with some of the principles discussed here, then a statistics and/or measurement textbook should be consulted. There are a number of excellent measurement textbooks available, including Anastasi and Urbina (1998) as well as Allen and Yen (1979). The reader is also referred to the *Code of Fair Testing Practices in Education* (Joint Committee on Testing Practices, 2004) for a discussion of the appropriate procedures for test development, test selection, scoring, interpretation, and communication of results.

This chapter begins by defining the nature of the tests that assess psychological constructs. Then, a review of basic principles

P.J. Frick et al., *Clinical Assessment of Child and Adolescent Personality and Behavior*, DOI 10.1007/978-1-4419-0641-0_2, © Springer Science+Business Media, LLC 2010 of statistics and measurement is presented, including topics ranging from measures of central tendency to factor analysis. The last part of the chapter introduces measurement issues that are specific to the use and interpretation of personality tests and similar instruments.

Defining Personality Tests

There is a plethora of methods, including tests, designed to assess similar-sounding psychological constructs, including personality scales, behavior rating scales, and diagnostic schedules. The available personality measures differ to such an extent that they can be subtyped in order to clarify their psychometric properties. A definition for a psychological test, taken from an early, well-known personality assessment text, may be a good starting point. Kleinmuntz (1967) defines a psychological (including personality) test by observing, "A psychological test is a standardized instrument or systematic procedure designed to obtain an objective measure of a sample of behavior" (pp. 27–28). This rather broad definition provides a useful starting point for conceptualizing the great variety of measures available.

The central characteristic of this definition is the notion of standardization of behavioral sampling. *Standardization* has at least two meanings: *standardization* in the sense of collecting a sample for the purpose of norm referencing and *standardization* as administration of the measure according to a consistent set of rules. Most of the measures discussed in this volume fit the first notion of standardization in that they are norm-referenced. That is, these measures use norm groups for gauging a child's performance in comparison to some reference group. Furthermore, the principle of administration structure or consistency applies to all of the measures in this text. For example, respondents should complete the measure in an environment free of distractions and should clearly comprehend the response-format (e.g., true/false, frequency ratings, etc.) and time frame (e.g., the last 6 months) referenced by the test. Standardized procedure emanates from experimental psychology, where laboratory control is central to obtaining reliable and valid results (Kamphaus, 2001). Similarly, in the case of personality assessment, standardized administration procedure is necessary to produce reliable and valid measurements of behavior.

All psychological tests take a sample of behavior from which the findings are subsequently generalized (Anastasi & Urbina, 1998). This ability to generalize findings is the central strength of psychological tests and is probably the reason for their widespread use. Without these tests, psychological measurement would be impractical because of the time and expense required. Of course, a sample can always be in error, a fact that should always be considered when interpreting results (Dahlstrom, 1993).

Types of Tests

How does one identify an instrument that assesses personality or behavioral, social, and emotional functioning? Personality tests have traditionally attempted to assess personality traits such as introversion, agreeableness, and anxiety. As noted in Chap. 1, traits are usually considered to be relatively stable characteristics of the individual (Martin, 1988). For children and adolescents, such characteristics may be similarly conceptualized under the term *personality traits* or, typically for younger children, *temperament*. Research has clearly indicated that individual differences in a variety of personality domains in youth are measurable (see Shiner & Caspi, 2003), and relatively stable (e.g., Durbin, Hayden, Klein, & Olino, 2007; Hampson, Andrews, Barckley, & Peterson, 2007).

Rating scales, one of the most popular child assessment methods, may fall into yet another category of test called diagnostic schedules (Kamphaus et al., 1995). Kamphaus et al. define a diagnostic schedule as a specialized psychometric method that provides a structured procedure for collecting and categorizing behavioral data that correspond to diagnostic categories or systems. A diagnostic schedule, then, is not designed to assess a trait, but rather to diagnose a syndrome. How does one identify a diagnostic schedule? One clue is the source of the item pool. The Children's Depression Inventory (CDI; Kovacs, 1992) is a popular measure of childhood depression that used the *DSM* as its item source. It was designed to assess the symptoms of depression in order to assist with making the diagnosis of depression. It was not designed to assess a stable personality trait or temperament but rather to allow the examiner to make the diagnosis of depression with confidence. In fact, a cut score that indicates the possible presence of clinical depression is often used for interpreting scores (Kovacs).

However, adding further complexity to understanding how rating scales fit within the array of tools available for clinical assessments is the fact that many widely used rating scales cannot be considered diagnostic schedules. For example, although the Behavior Assessment System for Children-2 (BASC-2; Reynolds & Kamphaus, 2004) assesses clinically relevant domains for youth (e.g., hyperactivity, aggression, depression, anxiety), elevated scores on those domains do not necessarily mean that the individual being assessed meets the criteria for a corresponding diagnosis. Such rating systems routinely have items that do not directly map onto the diagnostic criteria. Rather, the content of these scales may be indicative of aspects of the young person's functioning that may lend themselves to recommendations for intervention, as well as help signal a diagnosis or impairment in a particular domain. Furthermore, some rating scales may blend the elements of personality tests and diagnostic schedules, making sound clinical judgment essential in drawing the most sound conclusions from the data collected. The primary purpose of the assessment (e.g., diagnostic clarification vs. identifying areas of behavioral, social, or emotional concern) should guide the selection of diagnostic schedules and/or behavior rating scales. Further, we would argue that if given a choice, clinicians should initially seek tools that provide a broad screening of a variety of possible problems rather than narrowing in too quickly on a specific diagnosis.

Mash and Hunsley (2005) have articulated the problems with considering a focus on specific diagnoses as synonymous with psychological assessment:

> "Although formal diagnostic systems…provide one alternative for framing the range of disorders and problems to be considered, there is no need to limit the range of problems to those detailed in a diagnostic system. Refraining from excessive reliance on formal diagnostic systems is warranted given the well-documented shortcomings in the nature and development of such systems (e.g., Beutler & Malik, 2002; Mash & Dozois, 2003; Scotti, Morris, McNeil, & Hawkins, 1996) and the lack of evidence that such diagnostic systems provide the best way to match a treatment to a child (Bickman, 2002)" (p. 368).

Despite these concerns, diagnostic schedules or checklists may still play a critical role in helping to address a referral question and make treatment recommendations that are diagnostically-relevant (e.g., classroom accommodations for a child who meets criteria for ADHD). Diagnostic schedules have evolved from behavioral assessment methods, as has the *DSM*, which now emphasizes the tally of behaviors (symptoms) in order to make a diagnostic decision. Personality tests and many rating scales, on the other hand, are rooted in the psychometric tradition in which such tests are designed to assess traits across a continuum. While such instruments may not lead directly to a diagnostic decision, as noted above, they can play other important roles by identifying traits that have implications for the course or prognosis of a disorder, or even for treatment.

While diagnostic schedules are practical for making diagnostic decisions, such measures have limitations for studying the nature of individual differences or for contributing to other important aspects of the assessment process. These limitations are inherent in diagnostic schedules because they often lack a clear theoretical basis or evidence of a priori defined trait(s) that can be supported with construct validity evidence. Therefore, the emergence of diagnostic schedules as the instruments of choice for much of assessment practice is evidence of the profound impact of behavioral-based diagnostic systems on psychometric test development, particularly over the last decade or two, as well as the (real or perceived) need to provide diagnoses as a result of all assessments due to managed health care.

Appropriate conclusions that could be drawn based on diagnostic schedules include statements like the following:

- Tonya suffers from major depression, single episode, severe.
- Tony exhibits nearly enough symptoms to be diagnosed as having conduct disorder.
- Traci has attention problems that are worse than those of 99% of the children her age.

Alternatively, conclusions that could be offered based on psychometric tests of personality or behavioral, emotional, or social functioning could include:

- Allison shows evidence of poor adaptability to new situations and changes in routine, which puts her at risk for school adjustment problems.
- Patrick's high score on the sensation seeking scale warrants consideration as part of his vocational counseling and educational planning.
- Maria's somatization tendencies reveal the need for counseling in order to reduce her frequency of emergency clinic visits.
- Andersen's apparent signs of depression indicate a need for further evaluation and intervention.

A central difference between these interpretive statements is that those made based on diagnostic schedules are dependent on diagnostic nosologies. A variation of this premise is the third statement exemplifying diagnostic-based conclusions, which may result from a norm-referenced behavior rating scale that has a scale devoted to inattention. Such norm-based information can typically be gleaned from personality tests or other rating scales as well. The interpretive statements made based on psychometric tests, however, can be offered independently of diagnosis. These conclusions are based on the measurement of traits or tendencies that may or may not represent diagnostic symptoms or signs, and yet, these conclusions contribute substantially to the assessment process.

Widely used rating scales such as those to be discussed later in this volume have several scales with the same name as a diagnostic category such as depression or anxiety. At the same time, such measures are scaled similarly to traditional personality tests with standard scores based on norms.

Although research is emerging on this issue (e.g., Ferdinand, 2008; Kerr, Lunkenheimer, & Olson, 2007), generally speaking, we do not know the extent to which these scales demonstrate the stability associated with traits or the diagnostic accuracy of the *DSM* system. Their popularity for clinical practice, however, continues to increase due to their cost effectiveness and time efficiency. Furthermore, rating scales allow for the rapid and accurate identification of domains of deviant behavior that may require diagnosis or treatment (Hart & Lahey, 1999).

In this volume, the term *personality test* will occasionally be used generically to apply to personality trait measures, diagnostic schedules, syndrome scales, and related measures, always assuming that the reader is aware of the distinctions between subtypes of measures.

Scores, Norms, and Distributions

Types of Scores

In this section, some of the basic properties of score types are reviewed, with particular emphasis on the T-score standard score metric and its variants. The properties of these scores will be highlighted in order to encourage psychometrically appropriate score interpretation.

Raw Scores

The first score that the clinician encounters after summing item scores is usually called *a raw score.* Raw scores, on most tests, are simply the sum of the item scores. The term *raw* is probably fitting for these scores in that they give little information about a child's performance as compared to his or her peers. Raw scores are not particularly helpful for norm-referenced interpretation. Raw scores merely identify the number of behaviors or symptoms present, not how deviant this amount of symptomatology is from the norm nor how impairing it is for the individual.

Norm-Referenced Scores

Personality test interpretation often focuses on *norm-referenced interpretation,* the comparison of children's scores to some standard or norm. For the purposes of assessing psychological constructs, scores are usually compared to those of children the same age. Norm-referenced achievement tests, by contrast, may compare children's scores to those of others in the same grade, and college admission counselors may compare an incoming student's GPA to that of freshmen who entered the year before.

Norm referencing is of importance in personality and behavioral assessment because it allows the clinician to gauge deviance, which is often central to the referral question. Parents who refer a child for a psychological evaluation often have norm-referencing in mind. They ask questions such as "Is her activity level normal for her age?" or "Everyone says he is just a boy, but fire setting isn't normal, is it?" Norm-referencing allows the clinician to answer such questions objectively. The remaining scores discussed in this section are norm-referenced scores that allow the clinician to make these important comparisons.

Standard Scores

The *standard score* is a type of derived score that has traditionally been the most popular for psychometric test interpretation. Standard scores convert raw scores to a distribution with a set mean and standard deviation and with equal units along the scale (Anastasi & Urbina, 1998). The typical standard score scale used for personality tests and behavior rating scales is the T-score, which has a mean of 50 and standard deviation of 10. Another popular standard score that is coming into more frequent use for personality test interpretation has the mean set at 100 and the standard deviation at 15, similar to the IQ metric (see Table 2.1). Because they have equal units along the

Table 2.1 Standard Score, T-Score, Scaled Score, and Percentile Rank Conversion Table

Standard Score M = 100 SD = 15	T-Score M = 50 SD = 10	Scaled Score M = 10 SD = 3	Percentile Rank	Standard Score M = 100 SD = 15	T-Score M = 50 SD = 10	Scaled Score M = 10 SD = 3	Percentile Rank
160	90		99.99	128	69		97
159	89		99.99	127	68		97
158	89		99.99	126	67		96
157	88		99.99	125	67	15	95
156	87		99.99	124	66		95
155	87		99.99	123	65		94
154	86		99.99	122	65		92
153	85		99.98	121	64		92
152	85		99.97	120	63	14	91
151	84		99.96	119	63		89
150	83		99.95	118	62		88
149	83		99.94	117	61		87
148	82		99.93	116	61		86
147	81		99.91	115	60	13	84
146	81	19	99.89	114	59		83
145	80		99.87	113	59		81
144	79		99.84	112	58		79
143	79		99.80	111	57		77
142	78		99.75	110	57	12	75
141	77		99.70	109	56		73
140	77	18	99.64	108	55		71
139	76		99.57	108	55		69
138	75		99	107	55		67
137	75		99	106	54		65
136	74		99	105	53	11	65
135	73	17	99	104	53		62
134	73		99	103	52		57
133	72		99	102	51		55
132	71		98	101	51		52
131	71		98	100	50	10	50
130	70	16	98	99	49		48
129	69		97	98	49		45

(Continues)

Table 2.1 (Continued)

Standard Score M = 100 SD = 15	T-Score M = 50 SD = 10	Scaled Score M = 10 SD = 3	Percentile Rank	Standard Score M = 100 SD = 15	T-Score M = 50 SD = 10	Scaled Score M = 10 SD = 3	Percentile Rank
97	48		43	68	29		2
96	47		40	67	28		1
95	47	9	38	66	27		1
94	46		35	65	27	3	1
93	45		33	64	26		1
93	45		31	63	25		1
92	45		29	63	25		1
91	44		27	62	25		1
90	43	8	25	61	24		.49
89	43		23	60	23	2	.36
88	42		21	59	23		.30
87	41		19	58	22		.25
86	41		17	57	21		.20
85	40	7	16	56	21		.16
84	39		14	55	20	1	.13
83	39		13	54	19		.11
82	38		12	53	19		.09
81	37		11	52	18		.07
80	37	6	9	51	17		.06
79	36		8	50	17		.05
78	35		8	49	16		.04
78	35		7	48	15		.03
77	35		6	48	15		.02
76	34		5	47	15		.02
75	33	5	5	46	14		.01
74	33		4	45	13		.01
73	32		3	44	13		.01
72	31		3	43	12		.01
71	31		3	42	11		.01
70	30	4	2	41	11		.01
69	29		2	40	10		.01

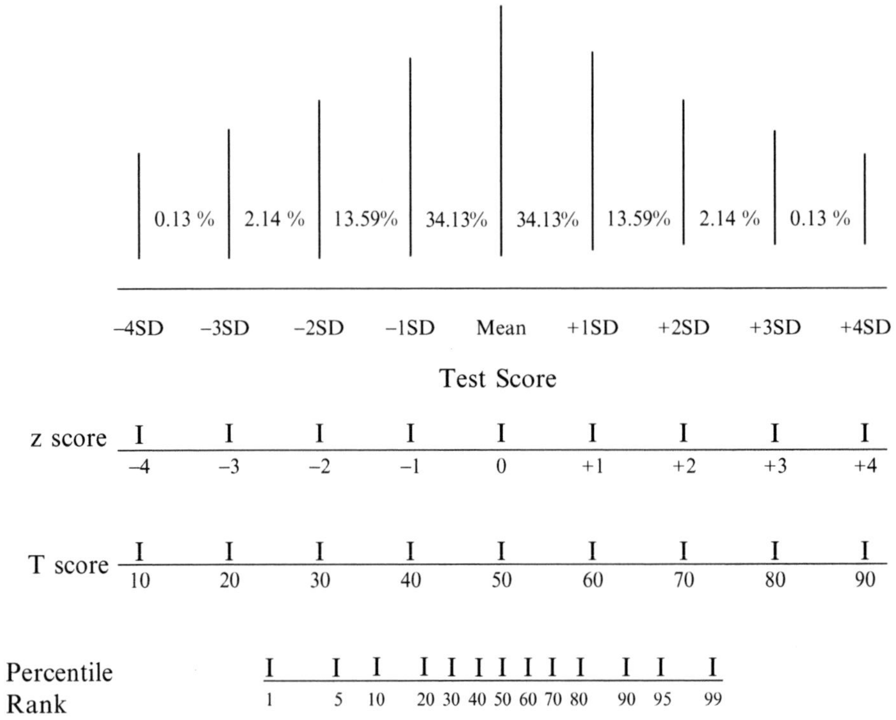

FIGURE 2.1
A normal distribution of scores

scale, standard scores are useful for statistical analyses and for making comparisons across tests. The equal units (or intervals) that are characteristic of standard scores are shown for various standard scores and percentile ranks in Table 2.1. This table may also be useful for converting a score from one scale to another. In the T-score metric, the distance between 20 and 30 is the same as that between 45 and 55.

Standard scores are particularly useful for test interpretation because they allow for comparisons among various subscales, scales, and composites yielded by the same test, allowing the clinician to compare traits. In other words, standard scores allow the clinician to answer questions such as "Is she more anxious than depressed?" thus facilitating profile analysis. Most modern personality tests use T-scores.

In a normal distribution (a frequently untenable assumption in personality and behavior assessment, as is shown in a later section), a normalized standard score divides up the same proportions of the normal curve. However, because many scales on syndrome measures in particular are heavily skewed (the most frequent scenario is that most individuals are not experiencing psychopathology and a few are, resulting in positive skewness), some test developers opt for the use of linear T-scores. Linear T scores maintain the skewed shape of the raw score distribution, which means that the same T-score on different scales may divide up different portions of the norming sample. Specifically, 50% of the norming sample may score below a linear T-score of 50 on the Anxiety scale, whereas 55% of the norming sample may score below a linear T-score of 50 on the

Aggression scale. Essentially, then, the use of linear T-scores makes the relationship of percentile ranks to T-scores unique for each scale.

Percentile Ranks

A percentile rank gives an individual's relative position within the norm group. Percentile ranks are very useful for communicating with parents, administrators, educators, and others who do not have an extensive background in scaling methods (Kamphaus, 2001). It is relatively easy for parents to understand that a child's percentile rank of 50 is higher than approximately 50% of the norm group and lower than approximately 50% of the norm group. This type of interpretation works well so long as the parent understands the difference between the percentile rank and the percent of items passed.

Figure 2.1 shows that percentile ranks have one major disadvantage in comparison to standard scores. Percentile ranks have unequal units along their scale. The distribution in Fig. 2.1 (and in Table 2.1) shows that the difference between the 1st and 5th percentile ranks is larger than the difference between the 40th and 50th percentile ranks. In other words, percentile ranks in the middle of the distribution tend to overemphasize differences between standard scores, whereas percentile ranks at the tails of the distribution tend to underemphasize differences in performance (Kamphaus, 2001).

Here is an example of how confusing this property of having unequal units can be. A clinician would typically describe a T-score of 55 as average. When placed on the percentile rank distribution, however, a T-score of 55 corresponds to a percentile rank of 69 in a normal distribution of scores (see Table 2.1). The percentile rank of 69 sounds as though it is higher than average. Examples such as this clearly show the caveats needed when dealing with an ordinal (unequal scale units) scale of measurement such as the percentile rank scale. It is important to remember that the ordinal properties of the scale are due to the fact that the percentile rank merely places a score in the distribution. In most distributions, the majority of the scores are in the middle of the distribution, causing small differences between standard scores in the middle to produce large differences in percentile ranks.

Uniform T-scores

A uniform T-score (UT) is a special type of T score that was used for development of the MMPI-2 norms (Tellegen & Ben-Porath, 1992). This derived score is a T-score like all other normalized standard scores with the exception that it maintains some (but not all) of the skewness of the original raw score distributions. The UT is like a normalized T-score in that the relationship between percentile ranks and T-scores is constant across scales, and it resembles a linear T-score metric in that some of the skewness in the raw score distribution is retained. The problem of a lack of percentile rank comparability across scales is described by Tellegen and Ben-Porath (1992) in reference to the MMPI-2:

> "For example, the raw score distribution of Scale 8, Schizophrenia (Sc), is more positively (i.e., right-) skewed than that of Scale 9, Hypomania (Ma). This means that a linear T-score of, say, 80 represents different relative standings on these two scales in the normative sample. For women in the MMPI-2 normative sample, the percentile values of a linear T-score of 80 are 98.6 for Scale 8 and 99.8 for Scale 9; for men, the corresponding values are similar, 98.6 and 99.7" (p. 145).

In order for the UT scale score to have the properties of percentile rank comparability across scales and reflection of raw score distribution skewness, the UT-score is based on the average skewness value across all of the clinical scales (Tellegen & Ben-Porath, 1992). This approach meets the objectives outlined by the developers, but it relies on the assumption that the skewness of the MMPI-2 clinical scales is similar. There is, however, evidence that some MMPI-2 clinical scales (e.g., Hypochondriasis and Schizophrenia) are far more skewed than others (see Tellegen & Ben-Porath). It appears that the UT is a compromise metric that meets test development objectives while, at the same time, not addressing completely the issue of different skewness across scales. More research and clinical experience with the UT metric is necessary to determine whether or not this method should be adopted by other test developers.

Norm Development

Sampling

Norm development is one area in which the technology of personality and behavioral assessment has generally lagged behind that of intelligence or achievement testing (Martin, 1988). Intelligence tests, for example, have routinely collected stratified national samples of children to use as a normative base. Stratification is used to collect these samples in order to match, to the extent possible, the characteristics of the population at large. Common stratification variables include age, gender, race, geographic region, community size, and parental socio-economic status (SES; Kamphaus, 2001). These variables are used presumably because they are related to score differences. Of these widely used stratification variables, SES is known to produce the most substantial score differences on intelligence measures (Kamphaus). The precedent, then, is set for the norming of personality and behavioral assessment tools.

This precedent, however, has not been followed in several important respects. Until recently, many relatively popular personality scales have not done a good job of stratifying their samples. Some norming samples do not control for geographic region, and others fail to control for SES. The result is a normative standard of unknown utility. While poor norming is less likely to be tolerated in intelligence and academic achievement assessment, it is less frequently criticized or even noted in discussions of personality assessment. We will, however, note the characteristics of norming samples in subsequent sections of this text. This is important because users of personality and behavior tests should know the characteristics of a test's norming sample in order to make the best decisions and gauge the amount of confidence to place in the obtained scores.

Intelligence, achievement, and adaptive behavior tests typically feature interpretation based on a national norm sample. In contrast, a national normative standard has often not been offered for personality tests. A substantial number of personality tests offer only local norms, a subset of the national normative sample. Local norms answer different questions than do national norms. Hence, their potential utility has to be evaluated prior to test selection and interpretation.

Local Norms

Local norms, or norms based on a specific population in a specific setting or location, may sometimes be more useful than national norms, particularly in terms of their relevance for the clinician's work, and in some cases, recency relative to national norms (Elliott & Bretzing, 1980; Petersen, Kolen, & Hoover, 1989). In order for local norms to be meaningful, however, the range of their usefulness must be defined clearly.

Regardless of the use of local or national norms, typical norm-referenced questions of interest to psychologists are diagnostic ones. Common questions might include:

- Does Lindsey have attention-deficit/hyperactivity disorder?
- Is Jose clinically depressed?
- Is Stephanie more anxious than other children her age?

One of the goals of diagnostic practice is consistency, which is fostered by the publication of diagnostic criteria. Consistent methods of diagnosis allow clinicians to communicate clearly with one another. If, for example, Dr. Ob Session in Seattle says that a patient is suffering from conduct disorder, then Dr. Sid Ego in Atlanta will know what to expect from this adolescent when he enters his office for follow-up treatment.

National norms similarly promote consistency. If a clinician concludes that a child has clinically significant attention problems based on a deviant score on an inattention scale, then others may reasonably conclude that this child has attention difficulties that are unusual for her age. Popular tests, however, may offer different local norms that can hamper consistent communication. Similarly, local norms also will be less generalizable to the general population of children who do or do not meet criteria for a particular diagnosis. The clinician must then balance these disadvantages of local norms with the potential for local norms to be more relevant to the population with which he/she works.

Gender-Based Norms

Personality and behavior measures are unusual in that gender-referenced (local) norms are sometimes offered by test developers. This practice is unusual in comparison to other domains of assessment where, although significant gender differences exist, national combined gender norms are typically the only ones provided. Specifically, intelligence, academic achievement, and adaptive behavior scales produce mean score differences between gender groups, but local norms by gender are rarely offered. Why then are gender local norms commonly offered for personality tests? Tradition could be the most parsimonious explanation.

When comparing a child to his or her gender group, the effects of gender differences in behavior are removed. Another way of expressing this is to say that, when gender norms are utilized, roughly the same proportion of boys as girls is identified as having problems. Because, for example, boys tend to have more symptoms of hyperactivity than girls (*DSM-IV*, APA, 1994), the use of gender local norms would erase this difference in epidemiology. Gender norm-referencing would identify approximately the same percentage of girls and boys as hyperactive, such that a boy would require more severe symptomatology to be identified as elevated on hyperactivity relative to other boys. Depression is another example of how gender norms may affect diagnostic rates. Much evidence suggests that girls express more depressive symptomatology than boys in adolescence (Weiss & Weisz, 1988). The use of gender norms for a depression scale would result in the same number of adolescent boys as girls exceeding a particular cut score, whereas general national norms would retain the known greater prevalence among adolescent girls.

Are gender local norms a problem? Not so long as clinicians are clear about the questions they are asking. A gender norm question would be "Is Traci hyperactive when compared to other girls her age?" whereas a national norm question would be "Is Traci hyperactive in comparison to other children her age?" General national norms are preferred when a diagnostic question is asked. An example of a diagnostic question is, "Does Frank have enough symptoms of depression to warrant a diagnosis?" The *DSM-IV* diagnostic criteria do not have differing thresholds for boys, so a gender norm would be inappropriate.

Age-Based Norms

Because there are substantial differences across age groups, intelligence and academic achievement tests routinely offer norms separately by age groups, typically using age ranges of 1 year or less. By contrast, age ranges as large as 5–7 years are frequently used for personality tests. This tradition of articulating norms for larger age groups may be attributable to personality traits often having smaller normative samples than intelligence and achievement tests and a lack of age group differences in personality and behavior characteristics (Martin, 1988). Some data suggest that the latter explanation may be more appropriate. That is, differences between adjacent age groups are often insignificant for behavior rating scales, whereas more meaningful differences only occur over longer developmental periods (e.g., Reynolds & Kamphaus, 2004).

Clinical Norms

A more unique norm group is a sample of children who have been previously diagnosed as having a mental health problem. This clinical norm-referenced comparison can answer questions such as:

- How aggressive is Sheila in comparison to other children who are receiving psychological services?
- Are Tonya's psychotic symptoms unusual in comparison to other children who are referred for psychological evaluation?

There is not a clear precedent for the development of clinical norms. The relevant demographic stratification variables have not been identified, making it difficult to judge the quality of clinical norms. Should clinical norms, for example, attempt to mimic the epidemiology of childhood disorders including 10% depression cases, 5% ADHD cases, and so on? Should norms attempt to match the epidemiology of specific disorders within child clinic-referred populations (i.e., include mostly externalizing disorders)? Should norms be offered separately by diagnostic category to offer a more exact comparison? Or should attempts be made to address each of these issues?

Until such standards emerge, clinicians should seek clinical norms that are at least well-described. A clear description of the sample will allow the clinician to determine if the clinical norm group has the potential to answer questions of interest. For example, the clinician who works in an inpatient setting may have more interest in a clinical sample of inpatients, whereas others may prefer that clinical norms be based on a referral population. If the clinical norm group for a test is not well-described, the clinician cannot meaningfully interpret the norm-referenced comparisons.

The *normal curve* refers to the graphic depiction of a distribution of test scores that is symmetrical (normal), resembling a bell. In a normal distribution, there are a few people with very low scores (these people are represented by the tail of the curve on the left in Fig. 2.1), a few with very high scores (the tail on the right), and many individuals with scores near the average (the highest point in the curve).

When a distribution is normal or bell-shaped, as is the case in Fig. 2.1, the standard deviation always divides up the same proportion. Specifically, ±1 standard deviation always includes approximately 68% of the cases in a normal distribution, and ±2 standard deviations always include approximately 95% of the cases. The normal curve is also sometimes referred to as the normal probability, or Gaussian curve.

Normal distributions, however, cannot be assumed for personality tests or behavior ratings. While intelligence and academic tests often produce near-normal distributions, personality tests often produce skewed distributions. Examples of skewed distributions are shown in Figs. 2.2 and 2.3. The distribution depicted in Fig. 2.2 is negatively skewed; a positive skew is shown in Fig. 2.3. A mnemonic for remembering the distinction between positive and negative skewness is to note that the valence of the skewness applies to the tail, when positive is on the right and negative is on the left.

It is understandable that diagnostic schedules and syndrome scales such as behavior rating scales produce skewed distributions. After all, only a small proportion of the population is experiencing a particular disorder at some point in time, and the majority of individuals are free of such symptomatology (positive skew). On the other hand, it is quite likely that the distributions for many adaptive skills or behaviors would be negatively skewed, in that the majority of the population would possess high levels of such skills, particularly with age (c.f., Sparrow, Cichetti, & Balla, 2005).

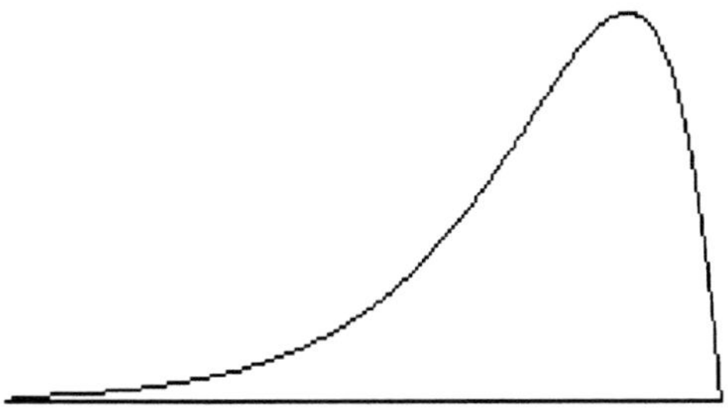

FIGURE 2.2
A hypothetical example of a negatively skewed distribution of scores

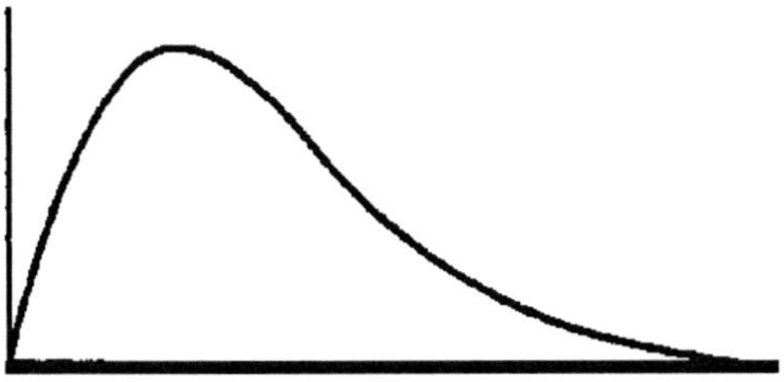

FIGURE 2.3
A hypothetical example of a positively skewed distribution of scores

The often skewed distributions obtained for personality measures, particularly diagnostic schedules, produce more controversy regarding scaling methods. If, for example, a distribution is heavily skewed, should normalized standard scores (which force normality on the shape of the standard score distribution regardless of the shape of the raw score distribution) or linear transformations (which maintain the shape of the raw score distribution) be used? Petersen et al. (1989) maintain that "usually there is no good theoretical reason for normalizing scores" (p. 226), and we concur with this opinion.

What differences does the scaling method make (i.e., normalized versus linear transformations)? The primary difference is in the relationship between the standard scores (T-scores) and percentile ranks yielded by a test. The positively skewed distribution shown in Fig. 2.3 is a good example of how this relationship can be affected. If this distribution was normalized (i.e., forced normal by converting raw scores to normal deviates and then the normal deviates to T-scores), then a T-score of 70 will *always* be at the 98th percentile. If linear transformations were used for the scale distribution shown in Fig. 2.3, then the corresponding percentile rank would most certainly be something other than 98. Clearly the type of standard score used for scaling a test affects diagnostic and, perhaps, treatment decisions. If normalized standard scores were used for a positively skewed scale (e.g., one measuring conduct problems), then potentially more children would be identified as having significant problems. On the other hand, normalized standard scores make the clinician's job easier by fostering interpretation across scales. Herein lies the debate: Is the interpretive convenience of normalized standard scores worth the trade-off in lack of precision?

Clinicians will find that many tests use normalized standard scores (usually expressed in a T-score metric) even when clear evidence of significant skewness exists. We suggest that readers note the scaling method used by tests discussed in this volume as they consider the strengths and weaknesses of each measure.

Reliability

The *reliability* of a test refers to the degree to which test scores are free from measurement error and includes the presumed stability, consistency, and repeatability of scores for a given individual (AERA, APA, NCME, 1999).

The reliability of a personality test is expressed by the computation of a reliability coefficient, which is a special type of correlation coefficient. One essential difference between a reliability coefficient and a correlation coefficient is that reliability coefficients are typically not negative, while negative correlation coefficients are eminently possible. Reliability coefficients range, then, from 0 to +1. Reliability coefficients represent the amount of reliable variance associated with a test. In other words, a reliability coefficient is not squared, as is the case with correlation coefficients, to calculate the amount of reliable variance (Anastasi & Urbina, 1998). For example, the reliable variance of a test with a reliability coefficient of .90 is 90%, an unusually easy computation!

The error variance associated with a test is also easy to calculate. It is done by subtracting the reliability coefficient from 1 (perfect reliability). Taking the previous example, the error variance for a test with a reliability coefficient of .90 is 10% (1 - .90).

The sources of measurement error, while potentially crucial for interpretation, are often not specified, leaving the psychologist to engage in speculation. Error may result from changes in the patient's attitude toward assessment or cooperation, malingering, rater biases, patients' health status, subjective scoring algorithms, or item content that is incomprehensible to the examinee, among other factors.

For this reason, it is important to consider statistics that document both the reliable and error variance of a scale or test. In addition, multiple reliability coefficients and error estimates based on classical and modern test theory methods are necessary to guide clinical and research practice. Logically, then, it follows that no single estimate of reliability or error discussed in this section is adequate to support routine use of a test of assessment procedure.

Test–Retest Method

A popular method for computing the stability of personality test scores is the test-retest method. In this method the same test, for example the MMPI-A, is administered to the same group of individuals under the same or similar conditions over a brief period of time (typically 2–4 weeks). The correlation between the first and second administrations of the test is then computed, yielding a test-retest reliability coefficient that is optimally very close to 1.0. Of course, the importance of such reliability depends on the construct being assessed. If clinicians seek to assess changes in specific, discrete behaviors as a result of an intervention, for example, then test-retest reliability becomes less of a concern. On the other hand, if a clinician seeks to evaluate what are presumably relatively stable indicators of behavioral functioning or personality, the test-retest reliability of the measure becomes paramount.

Internal Consistency Coefficients

Another type of reliability coefficient typically reported in test manuals is an internal consistency coefficient. This estimate differs from test-retest or stability coefficients in that it does not directly assess the stability of the measure of personality over time. Internal consistency coefficients assess what the name implies-the average correlation among the items in a test or scale. In other words, this index of reliability assesses the homogeneity of the test item pool. Internal consistency coefficients are inexpensively produced, since they only require one administration of the test. Typical formula used for the computation of internal consistency coefficients include split-half coefficients, Kuder Richardson 20, and Coefficient (or Cronbach's) Alpha.

On occasion, there are differences between internal consistency and test-retest coefficients that can affect test interpretation. A test may, for example, have a relatively poor internal consistency coefficient and yet a strong test-retest coefficient (Kamphaus, 2001). Because internal consistency coefficients are imperfect estimates of stability coefficients, both types of coefficients should be recorded in the manual for a test (AERA, APA, NCME, 1999). It is then up to the professional making use of the test to determine if the reliability is suitable for the purpose for which the tool is to be used.

Variables that Affect Reliability

Clinicians who use personality or behavior tests should recognize factors that can affect reliability. Some factors that the clinician should keep in mind when estimating the reliability of a test for a particular child include the following:

1. Reliability can differ for different score levels. A test that is very reliable for emotionally disturbed students is not necessarily as reliable for nondisabled students without research evidence to support its use (AERA, APA, NCME, 1999).
2. Reliability can suffer when there is a long interval between assessments (Nitko, 1983).
3. Reliability can be affected by rater or child characteristics such as age, reading level, and fatigue. Reliability of personality measurement, for example, may drop if the child does not understand the test items.
4. Analogously, error may be introduced if a poor translation of a test is used.

Reliable Specific Variance

Subtest specificity is the amount of reliable specific variance that can be attributed to a single subtest or scale. Kaufman (1979) popularized the use of subtest specificity in clinical assessment as a way of gauging the amount of confidence a clinician should have in conclusions that are based on a single subtest. In effect, knowledge of subtest specificity makes clinicians more cautious about drawing conclusions based on a single scale.

A reliability coefficient represents the amount of reliable variance associated with a scale. An example would be an anxiety scale taken from a larger battery of 13 tests, all of which are part of a major personality test battery. The anxiety scale has a test-retest reliability coefficient of .82. On the surface, this test appears reliable. If this scale produces the child's highest score, the examiner may wish to say that the child has a problem with anxiety. The examiner can then make this statement with confidence because the test is relatively reliable, right? Not necessarily. As Kaufman (1979) points out, the conclusion being drawn by the clinician is about some skill, trait, or ability (in this case, anxiety) that is specific or *measured only by this one scale.* The reliability coefficient, on the other hand, reflects not just reliable specific variance but also reliable shared variances. Subtest specificity is typically computed in the following way (Kamphaus, 2001):

1. Compute the multiple correlation (R) between the scale in question and all other scales in the battery, and square it (R^2). This computation yields the amount of reliable shared variance between the scale in question, in this case anxiety, and the other scales in the battery.
2. Subtract the squared multiple correlation coefficient from the reliability coefficient, or r_{tt}. If R^2= .30, .82 - .30 = .52. This formula yields the reliable specific variance.
3. Compare the amount of reliable specific variance (.52) to the amount of error variance (1 – .82 = .18). If the reliable specific variance exceeds the error variance by .20 or more, then the scale is considered to have adequate specificity for interpretive purposes. By convention, if the reliable specific variance exceeds the error variance by .19 or less, then the test lacks specificity, and it should be cautiously interpreted. If the reliable specific variance does not exceed the error variance, then interpretation of the scale is ill-advised.

Standard Error of Measurement

The standard error of measurement (SEM) gives an indication of the amount of error associated with test scores. In more technical terms, the SEM is the standard deviation of the error distribution of scores. The reliability coefficient of a test is one way of expressing the amount of error associated with a test score in order to allow the user to gauge the level of confidence that should be placed in the obtained scores. An examiner may report a personality test score for a child as being 63 with a test-retest reliability coefficient of .95. This practice, however, is unorthodox and clumsy. The typical practice is to report a test score along with the test's standard error of measurement, as is frequently done for opinion polls conducted by the popular media (e.g., the error rate or margin of error of this poll is...). The standard error of measurement is simply another way of reflecting the amount of error associated with a test score.

In classical test theory, if a child were administered a personality test 100 times under identical conditions, he or she would not obtain the same score on all 100 administrations. Rather, the child would obtain a distribution of scores that approximates a normal curve. This error distribution would have a mean. The mean of this theoretical distribution of scores is the child's true score. *A true score is a theoretical construct that can only be estimated.* This error distribution, like other distributions, not only has a mean, but it can also be divided into standard deviations. In an error distribution, however, instead of being called a standard deviation, it is called the SEM. As one would predict, then, in this error distribution of scores ±1 SEM divides up the same portion of the normal curve (68%) as does a standard deviation, and ±2 SEMs divide up the same proportion of the error distribution (95%) as ±2 standard deviations do for a normal distribution of obtained scores.

Confidence Bands

A confidence band is a probability statement about the likelihood that a particular range of scores includes a child's true score. As is done with opinion polls, clinicians use the SEM to show the amount of error, or unreliability, associated with obtained scores. Obtained scores are then banded with error. "Banding" is frequently accomplished by subtracting 1 SEM from, and adding 1 SEM to, the obtained score. If, for example, the child obtained a T-score of 73 on the Reynolds Child Depression Scale (RCDS; Reynolds, 1989), one could apply the theory of standard error of measurement to band this score with error. For the total RCDS sample, the standard error of measurement rounds to 4 T-score points. Given that ±1 SEM includes approximately 68% of the error distribution of scores, the clinician could then say that there is a 68% likelihood that the child's true score lies somewhere in the range of 69–77. An examiner who wanted to use a more conservative ±2 SEMs could say that there is a 95% probability that the child's true score lies somewhere between 65 and 81. Confidence bands can be obtained for a variety of levels if one knows the SEM of the scale. Some manuals include confidence bands at the 68%, 85%, 90%, 95%, and 99% levels.

Construct Validity

Validity is defined as "the degree to which accumulated evidence and theory support specific interpretations of test scores entailed by proposed uses of a test" (AERA, APA, NCME, 1999, p. 184). There are a number of different ways of evaluating the validity of a test. Some of the more common types of validity evidence will be discussed in this section. Validity is the most important psychometric characteristic of a test. A test can be extremely well normed and extremely reliable and yet have no validity for the assessment of personality. One could, for example, develop a very good test of fine motor skill, but if one tried to make interpretations about someone's personality from this test, such interpretations would not be valid. That is, validity is essentially an issue pertaining to the uses of a test and the interpretations that one seeks to make from test results.

Virtually every aspect of a test either contributes to or detracts from its ability to measure the construct of personality or behavior, or, in other words, its *construct validity*. Construct validity is the degree to which a test measures some hypothetical construct. As such, the construct validity of a personality test cannot be established based on a single research investigation or the study of only one type of validity (e.g., factor analysis). Construct validity is based on the long-term accumulation of research evidence about a particular instrument, using a variety of procedures for the assessment of validity.

Based on the information provided in the previous paragraphs, it is clear that a statement that a test is valid or invalid is inappropriate. Instead, certain interpretations can have more or less evidence to support their validity and the accumulation of evidence in support of these interpretations is always ongoing (AERA, APA, NCME, 1999).

Content Validity

One of the reasons that many people would disagree with using a test of vocabulary knowledge as a measure of personality is that it does not appear to possess valid content. *Content validity* refers to the appropriate sampling of a particular content domain. Content validity has been most closely associated with the development of tests of academic achievement (Anastasi & Urbina, 1998). Typically, procedures for the establishment of content validity are judgmental (Petersen, Kolen, & Hoover, 1989).

Personality test developers have often relied on empirical test development methods, in which items are assigned to scales based on statistical properties only (such as factor loadings, to be discussed later), and many manuals do not provide a clear indication of the source of items. In some cases, the item source is clear, such as with the Children's Depression Inventory (CDI; Kovacs, 1991), where items were based on accepted diagnostic nosologies such as the *DSM*. Even in such cases, however, personality test developers usually do not go to the lengths of other test developers to document adequate sampling of the content (or psychopathology) domain. Few personality tests or behavioral rating scales, for example, use panels of experts to develop item content.

Problems with regard to content validity may be identified as cases of construct underrepresentation or construct irrelevance. A depression scale may suffer construct underrepresentation, for example, if it lacks both cognitive (e.g., excessive self-deprecation) and vegetative symptoms of depression (e.g., problems sleeping). In this scenario, it may be said that there are not enough items on the scale that are known to be "indicators," or symptoms of depression, resulting in questionable content validity.

The reader will note in later chapters that construct irrelevant items are a more serious problem in behavior assessment. This problem is likely to occur when only empirical methods are used to construct scales and select items for scales (i.e., factor analysis). Examples of construct irrelevance are listed in Chap. 17 as they relate to the assessment of ADHD. In comparison to some others, ADHD is a well-studied condition with a widely agreed-upon set of symptoms (e.g., motor hyperactivity and inattention). What if, however, an item such as "My child is adopted" was placed on an inattention scale of a parent rating scale? As is noted in Chap. 17, such an item would likely be identified as a source of construct irrelevant variance for this scale, a source that would lead to a less valid assessment of attention problems for the child undergoing evaluation.

In our view, construct irrelevance and construct underrepresentation are likely to become problems at the item selection stage of test development. We, therefore, caution test users to carefully review the process of item selection and scale construction for each test that they utilize. By doing so, we think that clinicians will be better able to judge the implications of test content for interpretation.

Criterion-Related Validity

Criterion-related validity assesses the degree to which tests relate to other tests in a theoretically appropriate manner. There are two kinds of criterion-related validity: concurrent and predictive.

Concurrent Validity

This type of validity stipulates that a test should show substantial correlations with other measures to which it is theoretically related. One of the important criteria for the evaluation of personality or behavior measures since their inception has been that they show a substantial correlation with other indicators of psychopathology, such as well-validated tests or clinicians' ratings or diagnoses. The typical concurrent validity investigation involves administering a new behavior rating scale and an existing well-validated measure of psychopathology to a group of children. If a correlation of .20 is obtained, then the concurrent validity of the new test would be in question. A .75 correlation, on the other hand, would be supportive of the validity of the new test.

Predictive Validity

Predictive validity refers to the ability of a test to predict (as shown by its correlation) some later criterion. This type of research investigation is conducted very similarly to a concurrent validity study, with one important exception. The critical difference is that in a predictive validity study the new personality test is first administered to a group of children, and then sometime in the future-perhaps two months, three months, or even six years-a criterion measure (such as clinicians' ratings of adjustment) is administered to the same group of children (see Verhulst et al., 1994).

Correlations with Other Tests

One can use correlations with other tests to evaluate the validity of a behavior or personality test. In a sense, this method is a special type of concurrent validity study. The difference is that the correlation is not between a personality measure and some criterion variable, such as clinicians' ratings of adjustment, but between a personality test and a measure of the same construct, another personality measure. For example, if a new test of anxiety is published, it should show a substantial relationship with previous measures, but not an extremely high relationship (Anastasi & Urbina, 1998). If a new personality test correlates .99 with a previous personality test, then it is not needed, as it is simply another form of an existing test and does not contribute to increasing our understanding of the construct of personality. If a new anxiety scale correlates only .15 with existing well-validated anxiety scales, it is also likely not to be a good measure of personality. New personality tests should show a moderate to strong relationship with existing tests, yet contribute something new to our understanding of the construct of interest.

Convergent/Discriminant Validity

Convergent validity is established when a scale correlates with constructs with which it is hypothesized to have a strong relationship. Discriminant validity is supported when a personality measure has a poor correlation with a construct with which it is hypothesized to be unrelated. These types of validity may be important to consider if there are no existing, well-normed, or relatively recent measures of a construct. That is, one may not be able to judge the criterion-related validity of a measure because no other suitable measures of that particular construct exist. Of course, convergent and discriminant validity are important indicators of validity for existing/established measures as well.

If one were assessing the convergent and discriminant validity of a measure of anxiety, one would expect high correlations with other measures of anxiety and moderate correlations with other measures of depression, given the well documented association between anxiety and depression (Klein et al., 2005). However, one would expect only minimal correlations between anxiety and measures of learning problems, thus providing support for its divergent validity.

Factor Analysis

Factor analysis is a popular technique for validating modern tests of personality that traces its roots to the work of the eminent statistician Karl Pearson (1901). Factor analysis has become increasingly popular as a technique for test validation. A wealth of factor-analytic studies dates to the 1960s when computers became available. Factor analysis is difficult to explain in only a few paragraphs. Those readers who are interested in learning factor analysis need a separate course on this technique and a great deal of independent reading and experience. A thorough discussion of factor-analytic techniques can be found in Gorsuch (1988). An introductory-level discussion can be found in Anastasi & Urbina (1998) and Kamphaus (2001).

Factor analysis is a data reduction technique that attempts to explain variance in the most efficient way. Most scales or items included in a test correlate with one another. It is theorized that this correlation is the result of one or more common factors. The purpose of factor analysis is to reduce the correlations between all scales (or items) in a test to a smaller set of common factors. This smaller set of common factors will presumably be more interpretable than all of the scales in a personality test battery considered as individual entities.

Factor analysis begins with the computation of an intercorrelation matrix showing the correlations among all of the items or scales in a test battery. Most studies of behavior or personality tests use item intercorrelations as input. These intercorrelations then serve as the input to a factor-analytic program that is part of a popular statistical analysis package.

The output from a factor analysis that is frequently reported first in test validation research is a factor matrix showing the factor loading of each subtest on each factor. *A factor loading* is, in most cases of exploratory factor analysis, the correlation between a scale and a larger factor.[1] Factor loadings range from -1 to +1 just as correlation coefficients do. Selected factor loadings for the MMPI-A factor analysis of the standardization sample (Butcher et al., 1992) are shown in Table 2.2. A high positive correlation between a scale and a factor means the same thing as a high positive correlation between two scales in that they tend to covary to a great extent. One can see from Table 2.2 that the Hysteria scale is highly correlated with Factor 1, for example, and that Mania is not highly correlated with Factor 1, but it is highly correlated with Factor 2.

Once the factor matrix, as shown in Table 2.2, is obtained, the researcher must label the obtained factors. This labeling is not based on statistical procedures, but on the theoretical knowledge and perspective of the individual researcher. For the MMPI-A, there is general agreement as to the names of the factors. The first factor is typically referred to as general maladjustment and the second as overcontrol. The third and fourth factors are named after the scales with the highest loadings on each: social introversion and masculinity-femininity (Butcher et al., 1992).

Test developers often eliminate scales or items based on factor analyses. They also commonly design their composite scores based on factor-analytic results. This process was not followed in the development of the MMPI-A, as this test was developed long before the ready availability of factor-analytic procedures. Although the MMPI-A appears to be a four-factor test, it produces 10 clinical scale T-scores, and no composite scores corresponding to the four obtained factors are offered. More recently developed tests, such as the CBCL, made heavy use of factor analytic methods in the development of scale and composite scores (see Chap. 7).

Generally, consumers of factor-analytic research seek comparability between the factors and composite scores offered for interpretation. If there is, for example, a one-to-one relationship between the number of factors found and the number of composite scores produced, then the validity of the composite scores is likely enhanced.

Confirmatory Factor Analysis

The procedures discussed thus far are generally referred to as *exploratory factor-analytic procedures*. A newer factor-analytic technique is called *confirmatory factor analysis* (Kamphaus, 2001). These two factor-analytic procedures differ in some very important ways. In exploratory factor analysis, the number of factors to be yielded is typically dictated by the characteristics of the intercorrelation matrix. That is, the number of factors selected is based on the amount of variance that each factor explains

[1]When orthogonal (independent or uncorrelated) rotation techniques are used (and these techniques are very frequently used in test validation research), the factor loading represents the correlation between the subtest and a factor. This is not the case when oblique or correlated methods of factor analysis are used (Anastasi & Urbina, 1998).

TABLE 2.2 Selected MMPI-A Factor Loadings

	Factors			
	1 General Maladjustment	2 Social Overcontrol	3 Introversion	4 Masculinity Femininity
Hs	.77	.09	.31	.05
D	.69	−.23	.51	−.08
Hy	.88	−.15	−.22	−.15
Pd	.71	.28	.21	.19
Mf	.08	.01	.07	−.84
Pa	.70	.19	.23	.25
Pt	.52	.39	.67	.06
Sc	.61	.38	.53	.36
Ma	.31	.78	−.04	.33
Si	.19	.10	.91	.02

NOTE: These are varimax rotated factor loadings.
SOURCE: Adapted from Butcher et al., 1992.

in the correlation matrix. If a factor, for example, explains 70% of the variance in the correlation matrix, then it is typically included as a viable factor in further aspects of the factor analysis. If, on the other hand, the factor only accounts for 2% of the variance in a factor matrix, then it may not be included as a viable factor.

In confirmatory factor analysis, the number of factors is not dictated by data, but rather by the theory underlying the test under investigation. In confirmatory factor analysis, the number of factors is selected a priori, as well as the scales that load on each factor (Keith, 1990). The primary test in confirmatory factor analyses is the correspondence (i.e., fit) between the factor structure dictated a priori and the obtained data. If there is a great deal of correspondence between the hypothesized structure and the obtained factor structure, then the validity of the personality test is supported (hence the term *confirmatory*) and the theory is confirmed. If, for example, a researcher hypothesized the existence of four factors in a particular personality test, the confirmatory factor analysis will test how well the data from a specific sample conform to this hyopothesized test structure.

Thorough confirmatory factor-analytic studies use a variety of statistics to assess the fit of the hypothesized factor structure to the data. These statistics may include a chi-square statistic, goodness-of-fit index, adjusted goodness-of-fit index, or root mean square residual (RMR). Several statistics are desirable for checking the fit of a confirmatory factor analysis because all of these statistics have strengths and weaknesses. The chi-square statistic, for example, is highly influenced by sample size (Glutting & Kaplan, 1990).

Cluster Analysis

Similarly to factor analysis, cluster analysis attempts to reduce the complexity of a data set. In factor analysis, it is typical to try to reduce a large number of variables (e.g., items) to a smaller set. In cluster analysis, researchers are most often interested in grouping individuals (as opposed to variables) into groups of people who share common characteristics. Ward's (1963) hierarchical agglomerative method is one example of a popular cluster-analytic technique.

Several steps are common to cluster-analytic techniques, including the following:

1. Collect a sample of individuals who have been administered one test yielding multiple scores or a battery of tests.
2. For each variable (e.g., depression scores), compute the distance between each pair of children.
3. These distances between each individual on each variable are then used to produce a proximity matrix. This matrix serves as the input for the cluster analysis in the same way that correlation or covariance matrices are used as input in factor analysis.
4. Apply a cluster-analytic method that sorts individuals based on the distances between individuals that were plotted in the proximity matrix. In simple terms, clustering methods in this step match individuals with the smallest distance between individuals on a particular variable.
5. This sorting process continues until groups of individuals are formed that are homogeneous (i.e., have profiles of scores of similar level and shape).
6. Just as in factor analysis, the researcher has to decide next on the number of clusters that is the most clinically meaningful. Statistical indexes are provided as an aid to the researcher in this step.

Cluster-analytic techniques are useful in psychopathology research for identifying subtypes of disorders or for designing diagnostic systems (Borgen & Barnett, 1987). Cluster-analytic techniques have frequently been applied to identify subgroups based on their performance on a particular personality measure (e.g., LaCombe et al., 1991).

In a series of investigations, Kamphaus and colleagues have used cluster analysis of large data sets to identify children with *subsyndromal* behavior problems (Huberty, Kamphaus, & DiStefano, 1997; Kamphaus, Huberty, DiStefano, & Petoskey, 1997; Kamphaus et al., 1999). These studies of elementary school children suggest that there are numerous children with profiles suggestive of functional impairment in school or at home who, nevertheless, are either not diagnosed or do not meet accepted diagnostic criteria. Thus, these cluster analyses helped to classify children without mental health diagnoses but who may require prevention or treatment.

Sensitivity and Specificity

Identification of a diagnosis is one of the primary reasons for conducting an evaluation. A test that is to be used for such a purpose should possess evidence of *sensitivity*, or the ability to identify true positives (i.e., the percentage of children who actually have the disorder). A prototypical study might involve administering an electronic measure of inattention to a group of children with ADHD and a group without any psychiatric diagnoses ("normals"). In this type of investigation, electronic measures of inattention often demonstrate good sensitivity by correctly identifying the vast majority of cases of ADHD, a finding that then triggers investigation of *specificity*. Specificity refers to the relative percentage of true negatives, or the correct identification of individuals who do not have the disorder as not having the disorder. This same measure of inattention may also identify only 50% of the nondiagnosed sample as "normal." Therefore, it may have demonstrated good sensitivity but inadequate specificity (i.e., a high rate of false positives). Electronic measures of inattention often produce results of this nature. In an exhaustive review of the literature on such measures, Riccio and Reynolds (2003) have found that, while sensitivity is typically good, evidence of specificity is often poor.

In a later chapter, we will observe that the standards for this type of sensitivity and specificity have been raised considerably by the most recent *Standards for Educational and Psychological Testing* (AERA, APA, NCME, 1999). Now tests must demonstrate the ability to differentiate among diagnostic categories-not just *between* a diagnostic group and normality. Unfortunately, few test manuals provide evidence of this nature and many journal articles test only the relatively easy distinction between some condition and normality. The clinician, however, routinely has the more difficult task of differentiating among diagnostic categories. Again, electronic measures of inattention have not shown good evidence of diagnostic group differentiation. In fact, Riccio and Reynolds (2003) concluded that when children with a number of problems are included, the proportion of children correctly classified drops significantly.

More recent work has focused on the development of an evidence-base that will improve problem specificity, or the ability to distinguish particular problems from each other (Mash & Hunsley, 2005). Clinicians routinely are faced with this task which is also often considered "differential diagnosis." The call for a larger more sound evidence base also raises awareness of *positive predictive power* (i.e., the ability of an item to correctly identify a child with a particular problem) and *negative predictive power* (i.e., the ability of an item to correctly identify a child without a problem; Pelham, Fabiano, & Massetti, 2005). More research on these issues can only serve to assist in clinical decision making, but increased evidence will still not replace clinical judgment in integrating information from a variety of sources that have varying degrees of validity.

Threats to Validity

Readability

An obvious, but easily overlooked, threat to validity is the lack of ability of the parent, teacher, or child to understand the personality test items. While concern is often expressed about the ability of children to read test items, parents may also have difficulty due to limited educational attainment or cultural or linguistic differences. Harrington and Follett (1984) found that most tests available at the time they conducted their study failed to address the issue in their test manuals. They provide several suggestions to the practitioner for screening informants in order to guard against readability serving as a threat to validity.

For parents, Harrington and Follett recommend having examiners read the test instructions for the informant and paraphrase. Children can be asked to read some items from the beginning, middle, and end of the instrument aloud so the examiner can gauge the child's reading skill.

Related to this point is the problem of *translational equivalence* or the degree to which a translation of a test is equivalent to its original language form (AERA, APA, NCME, 1999). Evidence of translational equivalence should be offered to reassure the test user that a threat to validity is not present.

Response Sets

A response set is a tendency to answer questions in a biased fashion, thus masking the true feelings of the informant. These response sets are often mentioned, and addressed in construction and interpretation, in some personality tests .

The *social desirability response set* is the tendency of the informant to respond to items in a socially acceptable way (Anastasi & Urbina, 1998). Some personality tests include items and scales to assess the potential effects of such a response set.

"I like everyone that I meet" might be an item on such scales. The *acquiescence response set* is the tendency to answer "true" or "yes" to a majority of the items (Kaplan & Saccuzzo, 1993). A third response set is called *deviation*, and it comes into play when an informant tends to give unusual or uncommon responses to items (Anastasi & Urbina, 1998).

Guarding Against Validity Threats

Personality and behavior tests often include other validity scales or indexes in order to allow the examiner to detect validity threats. Some tests include fake bad scales, which assess the tendency to exaggerate problems. Computer scoring of personality tests has allowed for the inclusion of consistency indexes. One such index allows the examiner to determine if the informant is answering questions in a predictable pattern. A consistency index might be formed by identifying pairs of test items that correlate highly. If an informant responds inconsistently to such highly correlated items, then his or her veracity may be suspect.

Examiners often also conduct informal validity checks. One quick check is to determine whether or not the informant responded to enough items to make the test result valid. Another elementary validity check involves scanning the form for patterned responding. A form that routinely alternates between true and false responses may reflect a patterning of responses.

One way to limit the influence of response sets is to ensure that informants are clear about the clinician's expectations. Some clients may also need to take the personality test under more controlled circumstances. If an examiner has reason to believe, for example, that a child is oppositional, then the self-report personality measure may best be completed in the presence of the examiner.

Utility

As described earlier, clinical utility is the "next frontier" in evidence-based assessment. By the time an assessment instrument is well-known and widely used in clinical settings, it usually has demonstrated adequate reliability and construct validity. However, as Mash and Hunsley (2005) describe, the question of utility or whether the instrument provides "psychologists with the kinds of information that can be used in ways that will make a meaningful difference in relation to diagnostic accuracy, case formulation considerations, and treatment outcomes" (p. 365) remains. This concept can also be applied to the inclusion of a particular informant in the assessment process.

In short, a rating scale, for example, may be a valid indicator of depression, but its utility indicates how valuable that particular rating scale is for an assessment of depression relative to other measures and relative to the cost (monetary and time) involved in administering it. Validity, including incremental validity (i.e., the improved assessment decision as a result of adding a measure), is a necessary condition for utility, and establishing such validity evidence for an assessment tool, and especially an entire assessment battery, is arduous. Nevertheless, various forms of validity evidence are likewise not sufficient for demonstrating utility. Ultimately, in addition to cost effectiveness, the clinician must take into account the assessment's role in translating to effective intervention and subsequent positive change for a child (Mash & Hunsley, 2005).

Calls to examine the clinical utility of assessment are not entirely recent (e.g., Hayes, Nelson, & Jarrett, 1987). However, give the current state of affairs, our discussion of utility is necessarily brief. As the move toward evidence-based assessment becomes strengthened by a larger collection of empirical research and improved communication about assessment strategies, future volumes will hopefully be well poised to take on a detailed review of evidence on clinical utility.

Conclusions

Knowledge of psychometric principles is crucial for the proper interpretation of personality tests. As psychometrics become more complex, clinicians have to become increasingly sophisticated regarding psychometric theory. Because personality assessment technology has generally lagged behind other forms of child assessment, knowledge of psychometric theory must be considered more often by the clinician when interpreting scores.

Some personality tests, for example, do not include basic psychometric properties such as standard errors of measurement in the manual. Such oversights discourage the user from considering the error associated with scores, which is a basic consideration for scale interpretation. Omissions like this one are rare in academic and intelligence assessment. The application of the SEM is merely one example of the psychometric pitfalls to be overcome by the user of personality tests. This chapter ends, however, on an optimistic note. Newer tests and recent revisions are providing more evidence of validity and test limitations in their manuals.

Chapter Summary

1. A T-score is a standard score that has a mean of 50 and standard deviation of 10.
2. A percentile rank gives an individual's relative position within the norm group.
3. In order to select a representative sample of the national population for any country, test developers typically use what are called *stratification variables.*
4. *Local norms* are those based on some more circumscribed subset of a larger population.
5. The *reliability* of a test refers to the degree to which its scores are repeated over several measurements.
6. The *standard error of measurement* (SEM) is the standard deviation of the error distribution of scores.
7. *A confidence band is* a probability statement about the likelihood that a particular range of scores includes a child's true score.
8. The *reliability* of a test may differ for various score levels.
9. *Construct validity* is the degree to which tests measure what they purport to measure.
10. *Factor analysis* is a data reduction technique that attempts to explain the variance in a personality or behavior test parsimoniously.
11. In *cluster analysis* researchers are most often interested in grouping individuals (as opposed to variables) into clusters that share common behavior or traits.
12. Personality tests and behavioral rating scales often include other validity scales or indexes in order to allow the examiner to detect validity threats.
13. *Sensitivity* refers to the ability of a test to identify true positives and *specificity* to the ability of a test to identify true negatives.
14. *Clinical utility* concerns how well a particular tool provides necessary information and does so in a unique and cost-effective manner relative to other tools (or informants).

Chapter 3

Classification and Developmental Psychopathology

Chapter Questions

- Why is understanding the basic research on children's and adolescents' emotional and behavioral functioning important to clinical assessment?
- How are classification and assessment related?
- What are some of the models used for the classification of the emotional and behavioral functioning of children and adolescents?
- What are some of the advantages and dangers of classification?
- What are some of the most important implications of the basic research in the field of developmental psychopathology for the clinical assessment of children and adolescents?

Science and Assessment

A basic assumption underlying the writing of this text is that, to be competent in the clinical assessment of children and adolescents, much more knowledge is required than being able to simply administer tests, this being the easier part. Many other crucial areas of expertise are necessary for appropriately selecting the tests to be administered and for interpreting them after administration. One such area of expertise was the focus of the previous chapter: an understanding of the science of measuring psychological constructs. However, a more basic level of knowledge is needed for using measurement theory appropriately. That is, one must have a thorough understanding of the nature of the phenomenon being measured before determining the best method for measuring

P.J. Frick et al., *Clinical Assessment of Child and Adolescent Personality and Behavior*,
DOI 10.1007/978-1-4419-0641-0_3,

it. In particular, the constructs of interest discussed in this chapter are the emotional and behavioral functioning of youth. The first hint at the importance of this basic understanding of psychological constructs was made in the previous chapter on psychometrics. It should have become clear that good psychometric properties are not absolutes. They depend on the nature and characteristics of the *specific* psychological construct being assessed. For example, childhood depression is frequently characterized by multiple episodes of depression interspersed with periods of normal mood (Kovacs, 2001). Therefore, high stability estimates over lengthy time periods should not be expected. In fact, if such stability occurs, then one is measuring something that is not an episodic depression.

In addition to appropriately utilizing psychometric theory, understanding the nature of the phenomenon to be assessed is crucial to almost every aspect of a clinical assessment, from designing the assessment battery and selecting the tests, to interpreting the information, and communicating it to the child and parent. For these reasons, science and clinical practice are inextricably linked. There are many areas of basic research that enhance an assessor's ability to conduct psychological evaluations, but we have selected two that we feel are the most critical to the clinical assessment of children and adolescents. First, a thorough understanding of the theories that guide the different models of classification are necessary because the framework used to define and classify psychological functioning determines how one designs and interprets an assessment battery. Secondly, the clinical assessment of children must be conducted in the broad context of developmental psychopathology.

Developmental psychopathology refers to an integration of two scientific disciplines: child development and child psychopathology. The integration rests on the basic assumption that the most appropriate way to view the emotional and behavioral functioning of children, both normal and problematic, is within a comprehensive framework that includes the influence of developmental processes (Rutter & Garmezy, 1983). A noted developmental psychopathologist, Judy Garber, summarized her views on this field as being "concerned with both the normal processes of change and adaptation, and the abnormal reactions to stress or adversity, as well as the relationship between the two" (Garber, 1984, p. 30). Thus, developmental psychopathology is a framework for understanding children's emotions and behaviors that has many implications for the assessment process.

It is beyond the scope of this book to provide an intensive and exhaustive discussion of classification theories, or the many important findings in the field of developmental psychopathology. Instead, this chapter illustrates the criticality of these two knowledge areas to the assessment process, and also provides a basic framework for applying this knowledge to the assessment of children and adolescents. The discussion that follows highlights some of the issues in both areas that we feel have the most relevance to the assessment process.

Classification

Classification refers to the process of placing psychological phenomena into distinct categories according to some specified set of rules. There are two levels of classification. One level of classification is the method of determining when a psychological functioning is abnormal, deviant, and/or in need of treatment, while the second level of classification is the method of distinguishing among the different dimensions or types of psychological functioning. Thus, clinical assessment is considered partly, as a process of classification. It involves (1) determining whether some areas of psychological functioning in a child and adolescent are pathological and need treatment and (2) determining the types of pathology that may be present. Alternatively, according to Achenbach (1982) "assessment and classification are two facets of what should be a single process: assessment aims to identify the distinguishing features of individual cases; taxonomy (classification) is the grouping of cases according to their distinguishing features" (p. 1). Therefore, understanding the issues involved in classification is essential to clinical assessment.

The first issue involves acknowledging that any classification system of psychological functioning will be imperfect. Psychological phenomena do not fall into specific categories of normal and abnormal, or into clear, non-overlapping dysfunction types. This seems to be especially true with children; there is often no clear demarcation of when a dimension of behavior should be considered normal and when it should be considered pathological. Further, there is often a high degree of overlap among the various forms of psychopathology in children. Finally, any classification system is only as good as the research used to create it. As the research advances, so should the classification system.

Therefore, any system of classification is bound to be imperfect. Due to this imperfection, many experts have argued against the need for any *formal* classification system. Instead, they argue that psychological functioning should be assessed and described idiosyncratically for each individual person. That is, each person is a unique individual whose psychological functioning should simply be described in ways that maintain this uniqueness without comparing it with that of other individuals or fitting it into artificial categories. This argument has an intuitive appeal given the complexity of human nature. However, there are several compelling arguments for the need for *good* classification systems, in spite of the fact that even the best system will be imperfect.

The Need for Classification Systems

Communication

The main purpose of classification systems is to enhance communication among professionals (Blashfield, 1984; Quay, 1986). A classification system defines the rules by which psychological constructs are defined. In the absence of such a system, psychological constructs are defined by idiosyncratic rules developed by each professional, and one cannot understand the terminology used by a professional unless the rules employed in defining the terms is understood. For example, the term *depression* is a psychological construct that has several meanings in the psychological literature on children. It can refer to Major Depressive Episodes, as defined by the Diagnostic and Statistical Manual of Mental Disorders, Fourth Edition-Text Revision (*DSM-IV-TR*; APA, 2000). In contrast, it can also refer to elevations on a rating scale of depression (Curry & Craighead, 1993), or to a set of responses on a projective technique (Exner & Weiner, 1982). The concept of masked depression is used to describe the belief that many childhood problems (e.g., hyperactivity, enuresis, learning disabilities) are the result of an underlying depressive state (Cytryn & McKnew, 1974). Not surprisingly, each of these definitions identifies a different group of children.

Thus, simply saying that a child exhibits depression does not communicate much to another professional unless there is further explanation on how this classification was made. On the contrary, if one states that the child meets the criteria for Major Depression according to the *DSM-IV-TR* system, then a classification is said to be made using a system with clearly defined rules. Also, another professional will then have a clear idea of how depression is defined, even if he or she does not agree with the *DSM-IV-TR* system. However, this communication requires precision in the use of terms. In this example, using the term *Major Depression* would be misleading, and actually impair the communication, if the term was used without ensuring that the *DSM-IV-TR* criteria were met (e.g., based on responses from a projective technique).

Documentation of Need for Services

Classification systems allow for the documentation of the need for services. This encompasses documenting the need for special educational services for a child, determining the need for mental health services within a given catchment area, attempting to determine appropriate staffing patterns within an institution, or documenting the need for services to third-party payers (e.g., insurance companies). These uses of the classification systems have been the most controversial because the imperfections inherent in the existing systems can lead to very deleterious outcomes for many people. For example, a child can be denied services by a school or payment for the services by an insurance company can be denied if the child's problems do not fit into the classification system being used. Unfortunately, the task of documenting need is inextricably linked to classification because it requires some method of differentiating between those in need of services and those that are not in need of services. The solution is not to eliminate the classification systems, but instead (1) to develop better systems of classification that more directly predict the need for services and (2) to educate other professionals on the limitations of the classification systems, so that they can be used more appropriately for documenting the need for services.

Dangers of Classification

Due to the reasons already stated, it is generally accepted that explicit classification systems are needed. However, users of the classification systems must be aware of the dangers and limitations of such systems. Because clinical assessment is a process of classification, the clinical assessor must be especially cognizant of these issues. Many of these dangers can be limited if classification systems are used appropriately. Therefore, in the discussion that follows, we have tried to not only outline the dangers of classification but also to present practices that minimize or eliminate potentially harmful effects.

Because psychological phenomena, and the persons they represent, do not fall neatly into categories, one loses information by attempting to fit people into arbitrary categories. People within the same category (e.g., Major Depression) share certain characteristics (e.g., depressed mood, loss of interest in activities, disturbances in sleep, impaired concentration), but there also exist many differences among persons within a category (e.g., the number of depressive episodes, whether the depression started after the death of a relative). The shared characteristics should provide some important information about the persons in the category (e.g., prognosis, response to treatment), else the classification becomes useless. However, given the loss of information inherent in any classification grouping, classification should not be considered the only information necessary for an adequate case conceptualization. Instead, any classification, whether it is a diagnosis or an elevation on a behavior rating scale, should be one part of a larger description of the case. This approach allows one to take advantage of the positive aspects of formal classification (e.g., enhanced communication); yet, it acknowledges the limits of such systems and integrates classification into a broader understanding of the case. In this book, case studies that illustrate this approach are provided. In each case, diagnoses or other methods of classification are integrated into a more complete clinical description of the child being assessed.

A second danger of classification systems is that they foster the illusion of a clear break between normal and psychopathological functioning. For example, if the classification is based on an elevation on a rating scale (over a T-score of 70), it gives the illusion of a dramatic difference between children with T-scores of 69 (not classified) and children with T-scores of 70 (classified). Stating that this is an illusion does not imply that all psychological traits are on a continuum with normality, because some are clearly not. For example, in Jerome Kagan's work with behaviorally inhibited children, there seem to be a number of qualitative differences between children with behaviorally inhibited temperament and those without this temperament (Kagan & Snidman, 1991). However, if one was using a measure of behavioral inhibition with some cut-off for classifying inhibition (e.g., a T-score of 65), there may be some children close to this threshold (e.g., T-scores of 60–64) who were not classified due to imperfections in the measurement technique (Ghiselli, Campbell, & Zedeck, 1981). Therefore, whether the illusion of a clear break is due to a normally distributed trait or due to measurement error, it is still an illusion.

A third danger of classification is the danger of stigmatization associated with the psychological labels, often the end result of classification. How strong the effect of labeling is on psychological functioning is not clear from research. There is no evidence to suggest that the act of labeling creates significant pathology through a self-fulfilling prophesy. However, it is also clear that labels can affect how others, either lay persons (e.g., Snyder, Tanke, & Berscheid, 1977) or clinicians (Rockett, Murrie, & Boccaccini, 2007), interact with children who have been diagnosed with certain mental health problems. Given this potential danger, classificatory terms (labels) should be used cautiously and only when there is a clear purpose for doing so (e.g., when it influences treatment considerations). Also, when such terms are used, great efforts should be made to clearly define the meaning of the term to avoid misinterpretations. And, finally, terms should be worded to emphasize the classification of a psychological construct and not classification of the person. For example, it is better to use the phrase "a child with conduct disorder" rather than stating "a conduct disordered child".

Evaluating Classification Systems

Thus far, we have argued that classification systems are necessary despite the potential dangers and misuses. However, this is only the case for good classification systems. If a classification system tells little about a person, then nothing is gained in terms of communication, and all the dangers (e.g., loss of information, stigmatization) are maintained. Therefore, it is essential to critically evaluate any system of classification and, even within a system, to evaluate the individual categories.

As discussed in the previous chapter, while illustrating the association between classification and assessment, one finds that evaluation of classification systems is similar to the evaluation of assessment and procedures, in general. Specifically, the primary considerations for evaluating a system are its reliability and the validity of interpretations derived from it (Quay, 1986). In terms of reliability, a user of a system must be able to make classifications consistently, such as over short time periods (test-retest reliability) or between two independent users who make the classification (interrater reliability). In order for classification systems to be reliable, the rules of classification must be simple and explicit. However, reliability is important primarily because it limits the validity of a classification system. Therefore, the validity of a system is of paramount importance. Classification must allow for some valid interpretations to be made. That is, classification must mean something. It should tell something about the causes of the child's emotional or behavioral problems or the likely course of the problems. Most importantly, it should tell whether the child needs treatment, and if so, what type of treatment.

Models of Classification

So far, our discussion of classification systems has been on issues that transcend any single type of classification system. The uses of a system, the dangers inherent in classification, and the methods of evaluating systems are all pertinent, irrespective of the model on which a system is based. However, there are several different theoretical models on which a classification system can be based. *A model* is a specific framework for viewing classification, such as whether abnormal behavior is viewed as a statistical deviance ("Is this level of functioning rare in the general population?") or in terms of its functional impairment ("Does it affect a person's adaptive functioning?"). The theoretical model of a system will determine the rules of classification. As will become evident, the different types of assessment techniques discussed in this book were designed to provide information about the different models of classification. The following sections will review two general models of classification that have strongly influenced the classification of children and adolescents, and have had a major influence on the types of assessment procedures that have been developed.

Medical Models

The first major model of classification, the medical model, was largely derived from clinical experience with disturbed children and adolescents (Achenbach, 1982; Quay, 1986). In this type of classification, a diagnostic entity is assumed to exist, and the system defines the characteristics that are indicative of this diagnosis. The approach is called a *medical model* approach because it assumes there is a disease entity, or a core deficit, which is the disorder. It then defines the symptoms that are indicative of the presence of the disorder.

There are two primary characteristics of the medical model approach to classification. First, because of the emphasis on a core deficit, medical model systems differ dramatically depending on the theory or theories used to define the deficits considered to underlie the psychological disorders. That is, medical model systems are strongly influenced by the theory of abnormal behavior espoused by the system, such as psychodynamic theories or biological theories. Second, because of the emphasis on a pathological core (e.g., the disease entity), medical model systems typically make sharp distinctions between disordered and non-disordered individuals. There is typically an underlying assumption that there are qualitative differences between individuals with and without a disorder.

Multivariate Approaches

The second major approach to classification that has been extremely influential in the clinical assessment of children has been labeled the multivariate statistical (Quay, 1986) or the psychometric approach (Achenbach, 1982). In this approach, multivariate statistical techniques are used to isolate interrelated patterns of behavior. Therefore, unlike the clinically derived syndromes that are defined by theory and clinical observations, behavioral syndromes are defined by the statistical relationship between behaviors or their patterns of covariation. In this approach, behaviors form a syndrome if they are highly correlated with each other, and there is no necessary assumption of a pathological core to underlie the symptoms, as is the case in medical models of classification.

TABLE 3.1 An Example of a Multivariate Classification System

Externalizing			**Internalizing**		
Inattention	**HI/ODD**	**CD**	**Social Anxiety**	**Depression**	**SAD/Fears**
Disorganized	Interrupts others	Fights	Timid/shy	Sad	Upset over separation
Distractible	Stubborn	Spreads rumors	Not self-confident	Low energy	Worried about parent
Forgetful	Loud	Bullies	Nervous in groups	Anhedonia	Afraid to leave house
Sloppy/messy	Noisy	Steals			
Daydreams	Talks a lot	Lies			

NOTE: Dimensions are based on a series of exploratory and confirmatory factor analyses of caretaker ratings of 1,358 children and adolescents of ages 4–17 (Lahey et al., 2004). Behaviors listed are just examples and not the complete list of items used in the factor analyses. *HI* hyperactivity-impulsivity, *ODD* oppositional defiant disorder, *CD* conduct disorder, *SAD* separation anxiety disorder.

In addition to being based on statistical covariation, the psychometric approach is also different from medical models of classification because it emphasizes quantitative distinctions rather than qualitative distinctions. Once behavioral syndromes are isolated through statistical analyses, a child's level of functioning along the various dimensions of behavior is determined. Behavioral syndromes are conceptualized along a continuum, from normal to deviant. Interpretations are typically made by comparing an individual case to a representative normative sample, and choosing some level of functioning as being so rare in the average population that it should be considered deviant. Classifications are thus based on how a child falls into a certain dimension of functioning (e.g., anxiety/withdrawal) relative to some comparison group (e.g., compared to other children of the same age group).

In Table 3.1, we provide an example of a multivariate approach to the classification of childhood emotional and behavioral functioning reported by Lahey et al. (2004). This system was based on a series of exploratory and confirmatory factor analyses of caretaker ratings of 1,358 children and adolescents of ages 4–17. It shows six dimensions of behavior that can be subsumed under two broad dimensions of Externalizing and Internalizing problems.

Classification in the Future: An Integration of Medical and Multivariate Approaches

These two basic approaches to classification are important for clinical assessment because the design of assessment instruments is often consistent with one of these basic approaches. More importantly, the interpretation of assessment instruments is basically a process of classification. Therefore, it is often guided by these models or some variation of them. The clinical assessor should be aware of the issues involved in the classification generally, and the advantages and disadvantages of these two models of classification specifically, to aid in the interpretation of assessment measures.

Research has indicated that both the medical and the multivariate models have flaws that make their exclusive use problematic (see Quay, 1986). For example, the dependence of medical model approaches on theory has led to many "disorders" being created with little support from research. Also, the medical model approach, with its emphasis on qualitative distinction, masks a continuum with normality that seems most appropriate for understanding many dimensions of functioning. In contrast, the multivariate approach with its dependence on statistical analyses in the absence of clear theory has resulted in syndromes that are hard to generalize across samples and with different sets of symptoms. Also, while some psychological phenomena in children and adolescents are best conceptualized on a continuum with normality, there are others that may fit with more qualitative distinctions (e.g., Kagan & Snidman, 1991; Lahey et al., 1990) and are not captured well by the multivariate approach.

As a result, future classifications should look towards an integration of the approaches. For example, clinical diagnoses can be improved by conducting multivariate analyses to see if the covariation of symptoms for the diagnosis is supported (e.g., Frick, et al., 1993; Lahey et al., 2004). However, there are other ways in which the correspondence between statistically derived syndromes and the clinically derived diagnoses can be explicitly tested (e.g., Eiraldi, Power, Karustis, & Goldstein, 2000), thereby improving the validity of both the approaches and leading to classification systems that accommodate the diverse nature of psychological constructs. In the following section, we provide an overview of one of the most commonly used classification systems, the *Diagnostic and Statistical Manual of Mental Disorders*, which is published by the American Psychiatric Association. Although initially this system of classification was based largely on a medical model system of classification, more recent revisions have attempted to capture the best characteristics of the two major classification approaches.

Diagnostic and Statistical Manual of Mental Disorders, Fourth Edition (DSM-IV; APA, 1994 & DSM-IVTR; APA, 2000)

The *DSM* approach to defining psychiatric disorders has undergone dramatic changes in its many revisions since its first publication in 1952. The biggest change came with the publication of its third revision in 1980. In the first two editions, the definition of disorder was clearly based on a medical model approach to classification. The definition assumed an underlying pathological core, and the conceptualization of the core was largely based on psychodynamic theory. In the third edition, there was an explicit switch from a medical model view of disorders and a dependence on the psychodynamic theory. In the third and subsequent editions, a functional approach of viewing disorders was used in which mental disorders were defined as "a clinically significant behavioral or psychological syndrome or pattern that occurs in an individual and is typically associated with present distress (e.g., a painful symptom) or disability (i.e., impairment in one or more important areas of functioning), or with a significantly increased risk of suffering, death, pain, disability, or important loss of freedom." (p. xxxi, American Psychiatric Association, 2000).

Another major change in the third edition, also maintained in subsequent revisions, is an increase in the level of specificity with which disorders are defined. In the first two editions of the manual, disorders were often poorly defined, leading to problems of obtaining high levels of reliability in the diagnostic classifications (Spitzer & Cantwell, 1980). In contrast, later revisions include more detailed diagnostic definitions with explicit symptom lists, which have led to an increase in the reliability of the system (e.g., Spitzer, Davies, & Barkley, 1990). To illustrate this change, the *DSM-II* (APA, 1968) definition of Hyperkinetic Reaction of Childhood is contrasted with the analogous *DSM-III-R* definition of Attention-Deficit Hyperactivity Disorder in Box 3.1.

As a result of these changes, the most recent revision of the manual (*DSM-IV*; APA, 1994) has characteristics of both the medical and multivariate models of classification. For example, its functional approach to defining disorders, which does

Box 3.1

A Comparison of *DSM-II* and *DSM-III-R* Diagnostic Criteria

DSM-II: Hyperkinetic Reaction of Childhood (Adolescence)

This disorder is characterized by overactivity, restlessness, distractibility, and short attention span, especially in young children; the behavior usually diminishes in adolescence. If this behavior is caused by brain damage, it should be diagnosed under the appropriate non-psychotic *organic brain syndrome*.

DSM-III-R: Attention-Deficit Hyperactivity Disorder

Note: Consider a criterion met only if the behavior is considerably more frequent than that of most people of the same mental age.

A. A disturbance of at least 6 months during which at least eight of the following are present:
   1. Often fidgets with hands or feet or squirms in seat
   2. Has difficulty remaining seated when required to do so
   3. Is easily distracted by extraneous stimuli
   4. Has difficulty awaiting turn in games or group situations
   5. Often blurts out answers to questions before they have been completed
   6. Has difficulty following through instructions from others (not due to oppositional behavior or failure of comprehension), e.g., fails to finish chores
   7. Has difficulty sustaining attention in tasks or play activities
   8. Often shifts from one uncompleted activity to another
   9. Has difficulty playing quietly
   10. Often talks excessively
   11. Often interrupts or intrudes on others, e.g., butts into other children's games
   12. Often does not seem to listen to what is being said to him or her.
   13. Often loses things necessary for tasks or activities at school or at home (e.g., toys, pencils, books, assignments)
   14. Often engages in physically dangerous activities without considering possible consequences (not for the purpose of thrill seeking), e.g., runs into street without looking

B. Onset before the age of 7.

C. Does not meet criteria for a Pervasive Developmental Disorder.

SOURCES: *Diagnosis and Statistical Manual of Mental Disorders, Second Edition*, American Psychiatric Association, 1967 and *Diagnosis and Statistical Manual of Mental Disorders, Third Edition, Revised*, American Psychiatric Association, 1987. Reproduced with permission of the publisher.

not assume a pathological core, is consistent with the multivariate approach to classification. Also, many of the disorders are based, at least in part, on the patterns of symptom covariation, which is the hallmark of multivariate models (e.g., Frick, et al., 1994). In contrast to the multivariate approach, *DSM-IV* definitions classify disorders into discrete categories, which is more consistent with the medical model approach, although many of the cut-offs were empirically determined rather than being based purely on theoretical considerations (Lahey, et al., 1994).

One of the major changes in *DSM-IV* from its predecessors is the emphasis on users having access to the basic research underlying the various diagnostic categories. For example, in the manual, each disorder is initially introduced by summarizing the current research on its basic characteristics, associated features like age, gender, and cultural trends, prevalence, course, and familial pattern (APA, 1994). These introductory descriptions were enhanced in a later version of the manual: the Diagnostic and Statistical Manual of Mental Disorders, Fourth Edition, Text Revision (*DSMIV-TR*; American Psychiatric Association, 2000).

In this revision, no changes were made to the basic structure and diagnostic criteria for the individual disorders, nor were any disorders added or deleted. Instead, work groups were formed to identify any errors or omissions in the introductory material for each disorder, and to provide additional material to enhance the description of the disorders and their basic characteristics, if these could be justified by a review of the relevant research. In addition, the publication of the *DSM-IV* and *DSM-IV-TR* were accompanied by the publication of a number of edited volumes called "*DSM-IV* Source Books" (e.g., Widiger et al., 1994) that provide more extended reviews of the research that led to the diagnostic criteria included in these manuals. As such, these most recent revisions of the *DSM* have tried to enhance the ability of users of this system to gain access to the research findings related to the disorders included in the manual.

DSM-IV maintained the multiaxial system of classification that was initiated in *DSM-III*. As discussed previously in this chapter, a major disadvantage of any classification system is its inability to capture all relevant dimensions of a person's functioning within a single given category or diagnosis. For a broader view of classification, *DSM-IV* specifies several dimensions of functioning (axes) that are relevant to understanding a person's functioning. Specifically, Axis I (Clinical Disorders) and II (Personality Disorders/Mental Retardation) are fairly typical of other classification systems and comprise the major categories of mental disorders. Box 3.2 provides a summary of the Axis I and Axis II diagnoses that are most relevant for children and adolescents. However, *DSM-IV* includes three other dimensions on which a child can be classified. Axis III allows the system user to indicate any physical disorder that is potentially relevant for the understanding or managing of a case. Axis IV allows for a reporting of the psychosocial and environmental stressors that may affect the diagnosis, treatment, and prognosis of mental disorders in Axes I and II. Axis V provides a scale to indicate the highest level of adaptive functioning (psychological, social, and occupational/educational) that is currently being exhibited or the highest level of adaptive functioning that has been exhibited within the past year. Clearly, this multiaxial approach of *DSM-IV* is not sufficient to take the place of an adequate case formulation. However, it highlights the need to place diagnoses in the context of many other important aspects of a person's psychological functioning.

Box 3.2

A Summary of DSM-IV Axes I and II Diagnoses Relevant to Children and Adolescents

Intellectual	Mental Retardation	*Emotional*	Bipolar Disorders (I & II)*
Learning	Mathematics Disorder		Cyclothymia*
	Disorder of Written Expression		Adjustment Disorder with Depressed Mood*
	Reading Disorder		
	Language and Speech	*Identity*	Gender Identity Disorder of Childhood
	Expressive Language Disorder		
	Mixed Receptive-Expressive Language Disorder		Reactive Attachment Disorder of Infancy or Early Childhood
	Phonological Disorder		
	Stuttering		
	Selective Mutism	*Physical (Eating)*	Anorexia Nervosa*
Motor Skills	Developmental Coordination Disorder		Bulimia Nervosa*
			Pica
			Rumination Disorder
Pervasive Developmental	Autistic Disorder	*Physical (Motor)*	Tourette's Disorder
	Rhett's Disorder		Chronic Motor or Vocal Tic Disorder
	Childhood Disintegrative Disorder		Transient Tic Disorder
	Asperger's Disorder		Stereotypic Movement Disorder
Behavioral	Attention-Deficit Hyperactivity Disorder		
	Oppositional Defiant Disorder	*Physical (Elimination)*	Encopresis
	Conduct Disorder		Enuresis
Emotional (Anxiety)	Separation Anxiety Disorder	*Physical (Somatic)*	Somatization Disorder*
	Generalized Anxiety Disorder*		Conversion Disorder*
	Panic Disorder*		Pain Disorder*
	Agoraphobia*		Hypochrondriasis*
	Social Phobia*		Body Dysmorphic Disorder*
	Obsessive Compulsive Disorder*		
	Post-Traumatic Stress Disorder*		Adjustment Disorder with Physical Complaints*
	Adjustment Disorder with Anxious Mood*	*Psychosis*	Schizophrenia*
		Substance– Related Disorders	Alcohol (Amphetamine, Cannabis, etc.) Dependence*
Emotional (Mood)	Major Depression*		
	Dysthymia*		

*Denotes disorders that have the same criteria for children and adults.

NOTE: The selection of disorders most relevant to children and adolescents and the grouping of disorders were made by the authors and not by DSM-1V.

Developmental Psychopathology

As mentioned earlier, the overriding principle of developmental psychopathology is that children's emotional and behavioral functioning must be understood within a developmental context (Rutter & Garmezy, 1983). Therefore, it follows that the *assessment* of children's emotional and behavioral functioning must also be conducted within a developmental framework. Such themes as understanding behavior in a developmental context and conducting assessment within a developmental framework are broad principles that have several important specific implications for the assessment process.

Developmental Norms

First, a developmental approach recognizes that a child's emotional and behavioral functioning must be understood within the context of developmental norms. To be specific, there are numerous behaviors of children that are common at one age, but relatively uncommon at others. For example, bedwetting is quite common prior to age 5, and even at age 5, it is present in 15 - 20% of children (Doleys, 1977; Walker, Milling, & Bonner, 1988). Similarly, childhood fears tend to be quite common, and the types of fears that are most common show a regular progression with child development (Campbell, 1986). For example, separation anxiety is not uncommon in infants toward the end of the first year of life (Bowlby, 1969), whereas fears of the dark and imaginary creatures are quite common in preschool and school-age children but decrease in prevalence with age (Bauer, 1976).

These are just a few of the many development-related changes in the prevalence of specific child behaviors. Knowledge of these developmental changes in behavior is crucial to clinical assessment because the same behavior may be developmentally appropriate at one age but indicative of pathology at another. Therefore, assessment of children and adolescents must allow development-based interpretations. The critical nature of these interpretations implies that selection of assessment techniques must be based, at least in part, on the availability of age-specific norms. Further, given the rapid developmental changes experienced by children and adolescents, comparisons must be made within fairly limited age groups. Whereas for adults using a comparison group that spans the ages from 25 to 35 may be justifiable, a comparison group for children that spans the ages 5–15 would be meaningless, given the many changes in development that are subsumed within this period. Because the normative information provided by an assessment instrument and the appropriate use of norm-referenced information by the assessor are critical components to the clinical assessment of children, these issues are discussed in great detail throughout this book.

Developmental Processes

Unfortunately, many assessors believe that simply comparing the assessment information with age norms is all that is needed to take a developmental approach to child and adolescent assessment. This is a much too limited view of development, and how can it be applied to understanding both normal and pathological outcomes in children. A developmental approach is a "process-oriented" approach. Put simply, this means that any developmental outcome, be it a normal personality dimension or a problematic behavioral pattern, is the end result of an interaction of numerous interrelated maturation processes (e.g., socioemotional, cognitive, linguistic, biological).

This process-oriented approach has several important implications for how assessors conceptualize what they are trying to assess and how they go about doing it.

First, given the interrelated nature of the maturation processes, this approach recognizes that a focus on any single type of developmental process will provide only a limited, and sometimes misleading, understanding of a child's psychosocial functioning. For example, understanding the family environment of a child with behavioral problems will only provide a limited perspective on how these behavioral problems developed without considering the child's temperament, which may make the child more difficult to raise. Such transactional relations among developmental processes necessitate that an assessor design batteries that assess the many different types of processes and take into consideration the potential transactional relations among these processes when interpreting the testing results.

Second, the process-oriented developmental approach recognizes that the same developmental process (e.g., a permissive rearing environment) may result in different outcomes (e.g., some children who are creative, others who are dependent, and others who are antisocial), leading to a concept called "multifinality". The complementary concept is "equifinality" and refers to the possibility that the same outcome (e.g., antisocial behavior) can result from very different developmental processes among individuals (e.g., very strong emotional reactivity leading to strong, angry and aggressive reactions or weak emotional reactivity leading to problems in the experience of empathy and guilt). The implications for the assessment process are that the assessors need to expect that the same personality pattern or psychopathological condition may result from very different processes across individuals, and assessment batteries need to be designed to assess these "causal pathways." This, in fact, may be one of the most critical concepts in a developmental psychopathological approach to assessment because it places the assessment process in the important role of uncovering the unique causal pathway that leads to a child's current functioning so that interventions can be better tailored to the unique needs of the child (see, e.g., Frick, 2006).

Third, how the various processes unfold over development leads to specific "tasks" that may make certain behaviors more likely to occur at certain points in development. These unique demands, or "developmental tasks," lead to many of the age-related changes in children's emotions and behaviors discussed previously. Comparing a child's behavioral or emotional functioning to the developmental norms can help determine whether the child's functioning is deviant compared to other children who are experiencing similar developmental demands. However, simply comparing a child's behavior to developmental norms and determining whether or not the child's functioning is deviant compared to other children of the same age does not allow the assessor to determine whether (1) the child's problems should be considered an exaggeration of the normal maturational processes operating at that development stage or (2) the child's problems should be considered as a qualitative deviation from normal development (i.e., not consistent with the specific demands of that developmental stage), with the latter often being indicative of a more severe pathological process.

These two different interpretations of deviations from developmental norms can be illustrated in the assessment of conduct problems in children and adolescents. Research has documented an increase in the acting-out behavior for both boys and girls that coincides with the onset of adolescence (e.g., Offord, et al., 1989). The first implication of this finding is that the assessment of adolescent conduct problems should be based on a comparison with the adolescent norms, so that age-specific deviations can be determined. However, to interpret these age-specific deviations, it is also helpful to realize that an increase in acting-out behavior in adolescence is consistent with the identity formation process outlined in Erik Erikson's psychosocial theory of personality development (Erikson, 1968). Specifically, Erikson characterizes adolescence as a time when youths are struggling with the development of an individual identity, one that is separate from their parents. Rebellion and questioning of authority are manifestations of adolescents' rejection of parental and societal values, as they struggle to develop their unique identity. Understanding this process allows for an additional interpretation when one documents deviations from age norms. If a youth exhibits developmentally deviant levels of conduct problems for the first time in adolescence, the conduct problems may be best conceptualized as an exaggeration of a normal developmental process (e.g., identity development). In contrast, a preadolescent child who exhibits deviant levels of conduct problems is showing a behavior that seems more qualitatively different from what is expected from normal developmental processes. It may, therefore, be an indication of more severe pathology. This is consistent with research, indicating that conduct problems that have onset in adolescence are more likely to be transient, whereas conduct problems with a prepubertal onset tend to be more severe and chronic (Moffitt, 2003).

Stability and Continuity

Issues regarding the stability of childhood behavioral and emotional functioning are important from a developmental perspective to psychopathology. These complex issues have important implications for the assessment process. The basic issue of stability is not unique to the assessment of children and adolescents, but has been a long-standing controversy in psychological assessment throughout the life span. For example, many have questioned the concept of personality, because it implies a consistency of behavior over place and time that is often not apparent in human behavior (Mischel, 1968). This issue is more relevant to children than adults because childhood behavior seems to be less stable over time and situation, making the concept of personality in children even more controversial. Our view of the debate, which is similar to the view of many other theorists (e.g., Buss, 1995; Martin, 1998), is that the concept of personality can be useful if conceptualized appropriately, but dangerous if viewed wrongly.

For example, many measures of children's behavior or other aspects of personality show much less stability in children than do analogous constructs in adults. Specifically, Roberts and DelVeccio (2000) reported a meta-analysis of 152 longitudinal studies assessing the average stability of personality traits in different age groups over a 6–7-year period. They reported that the average stability coefficient for children and adolescents was 0.31, compared to 0.54 for young adults, 0.64 for middle-aged adults, and 0.75 for adults over the age of 50. These findings are not surprising given the rapid developmental changes that occur in childhood. However, the findings have important implications for the interpretation of personality measures in children. Specifically, interpretations of dispositional characteristics must be made cautiously in children so that there is no implication of strong stability over time, unless data are available to support such an interpretation. Given that the data are lacking in most cases, the term *personality* may be misleading for many domains of child behavior.

Although we feel that this caution is warranted, there are also several ways in which this general statement must be qualified. First, there is clearly some continuity in children's behavior, and the degree of stability (or instability) seems to be dependent on the domain of behavior being assessed. For example, research generally indicates that externalizing behaviors (e.g., hyperactivity, aggression, antisocial behavior) tend to be more stable over time than internalizing behaviors (e.g., fears, depression) (e.g., Frick & Loney, 1999; Ollendick & King, 1994). Therefore, interpretations of the stability of behavior must be dependent on the dimension of behavior that is of interest.

In addition, aggregates of behaviors (behavioral domains) tend to be more stable than discrete behaviors. For example, Silverman and Nelles (1989) reported on the 1-year stability of mothers' reports of fears in their children between the ages of 8 and 11. Over the 1-year study period, there was only a 10% overlap between Time 1 and Time 2 in the ten specific objects or situations that mothers reported as eliciting the most fear in their children. However, the correlation between the absolute number of fears was quite high. Although the specific types of fears were not stable over the study period, the level of fears was stable. Some have argued that aggregation allows one to pick up generalized response tendencies that are not captured by discrete behaviors (Martin, 1988). However, this increase in stability through the aggregation of behaviors can also be conceptualized from basic measurement theory. It has consistently been shown that increasing the number of items on a measure of a trait also increases its reliability (Ghiselli et al., 1981). Hence, the increased stability may be a function of a more reliable method of measurement.

Finally, stability can be affected by whether one is viewing the developmental outcome or the processes that may have led to this outcome. For example, the type of adjustment problem may be episodic, as in the case of depression, but the factors that led to this problem, such as problems in emotional regulation, may continue even after the depression has remitted and could place the child at risk for other adjustment problems in the future. As such, depression may not appear stable, but the problems in emotional regulation are stable (Keenan, 2000). Again, this illustrates the relevance of the process-oriented approach to assessment that is consistent with the developmental psychopathology framework. This framework illustrates the importance of not simply assessing the developmental outcomes (e.g., psychopathological conditions), but also assessing the various interacting processes that lead to these outcomes.

Situational Stability

Explicit in the developmental psychopathological perspective is a transactional view of behavior. That is, a child's behavior influences his or her context and is also shaped by the context. As a result, one expects a high degree of situational variability in children's behavior based on the differing demands present across situations.

Providing some of the best data on this issue, Achenbach, McConaughy, and Howell (1987) conducted a meta-analysis of 119 studies that reported correlations between the reports of different informants on children's and adolescents' (ages $1^{1/2}$ to 19 years) emotional and behavioral functioning. The correlations between different types of informants (e.g., parent-teacher) were fairly low, averaging about 0.28. This low correlation is not a good indicator of cross-situational specificity by itself, because reduced correlations could also be due to the individual bias of different informants rather than to actual differences in a child's behavior across settings. However, the mean correlations between informants who typically observe the child in similar situations (between two parents or two teachers) were generally much higher, averaging about 0.60. The relatively low correlations (0.28 vs. 0.60) across the informant types compared to those within the informant types serve as a more relevant indicator of the high variability in children's behavior across settings.

These findings by Achenbach et al. (1987) were replicated in a later meta-analysis by Renk and Phares (2004). Also, the modest correlation among ratings from different informants may not be limited to only children or adolescents. For example, the average correlation between the adult's ratings of their own personality and the ratings that their spouse make of them only show an average correlation of 0.39 (McCrae, Stone, Fagan, & Costa, 1998). Thus, in general, the correlation between different raters of a person's personality and behavior across different informants appears to be quite modest across the age range. Achenbach et al. (1987) highlight several important implications of these findings to the assessment process. These are summarized in Box 3.3.

In addition, there are several issues on cross-situational specificity that are analogous to those discussed on the stability of childhood behavior. First, like stability, the low correlations across situations may depend on the type of behavior being assessed. Specifically, externalizing problems tend to show higher correlations across informants than internalizing problems (Achenbach et al., 1987; Renk & Phares, 2004). Second, the situational specificity of behavior may be a function of whether or not aggregated domains of behavior are studied, or whether discrete behaviors are studied. For example, Biederman, Keenan, and Faroane (1990) compared the reports of both the parent and teacher on the symptoms of attention deficit disorder (ADD). Individual symptoms showed an average correlation across home and school settings of about 0.20. In contrast, on a diagnostic level there was a much higher agreement. There was a 90% probability of a teacher reporting enough symptoms to reach a diagnosis of ADD if the child was diagnosed by parents' report. Similar to the findings on stability, this suggests that, although individual behaviors (symptoms) may show a high level of specificity across situations, the broader construct (diagnosis) of aggregated behaviors seems to show greater consistency across situations.

Comorbidities

Comorbidity is a medical term that refers to the presence of two or more diseases that occur simultaneously in an individual. This term has also been applied in the psychological literature to denote the presence of two or more disorders, or two or more problematic areas of adjustment co-occurring within the same individual. There can be several reasons for comorbidity. For example, comorbidity can involve the co-occurrence of two independent disorders, two disorders having a common underlying etiology, or two disorders having a causal relation between themselves (Kendall & Clarkin, 1992). Unfortunately, research in most areas of psychology has not allowed for a clear delineation of the various causes of comorbidity among psychological problems.

Despite this inadequate understanding of the causes of comorbidity, this concept is important for the clinical assessment of children, for it is clear that comorbidity is the rule, rather than the exception, in children with psychological difficulties (Bird, Gould, & Staghezza, 1993). Specifically, children's problems are rarely circumscribed to a single problem area; instead, children tend to have problems in multiple areas of adjustment. For example, in children with severe conduct problems, 50%–90% have a co-occurring ADD, 62% have a co-occurring anxiety disorder, 25% have a learning disability,

Box 3.3

Research Note: Meta-Analysis of Cross-Informant Correlations for Child/Adolescent Behavioral and Emotional Problems

As noted in the text, Achenbach et al. (1987) conducted a meta-analysis of 119 studies that reported correlations between different informants on children's and adolescents' emotional and behavioral functioning. The meta-analysis included studies that correlated ratings of parents, teachers, mental health workers, observers, peers, and self-report ratings. The overall findings suggested that correlations between different types of informants (e.g., parents and teachers) are fairly low, averaging about 0.28, indicating a high degree of variability in the report of a child's emotional and behavioral functioning across different types of informants. The correlations were higher when calculated between similar informants (e.g., between two parents or between two teachers), averaging about 0.60. This suggests that the low correlations between different informants may be at least partially due to differences in children's behavior in different settings, rather than to idiosyncratic methods of rating behavior across informants.

The authors of this meta-analysis discuss several important implications of their findings to the clinical assessment of children.

1. "The high correlations between pairs of informants who see children in similar settings suggest that data from a single parent, teacher, observer, etc. would provide a reasonable sample of what would be provided by other informants of the same type who see the child under generally similar conditions" (p. 227).
2. "In contrast, the low correlations between different types of informants suggest that each type of informant provides substantially unique information that is not provided by other informants. The high degree of situational specificity poses a specific challenge to clinical assessments intended to categorize disorders according to fixed rules" (p. 227), such as the *Diagnostic and Statistical Manual of Mental Disorders-Fourth Edition, Revised* (APA, 1994). Such systems specify symptoms that must be judged present or absent, and the low correlations across settings suggest that in most cases the presence or absence will depend on the setting.
3. As a result of the high degree of specificity, clinical assessments of children should obtain information from different informants who see the child in different settings. "In such assessments, disagreement between informants' reports are as instructive as agreement because they can highlight variations in judgments of a child's functioning across situations" (p. 228). In Chap. 15, we discuss the issues involved in deciding how to interpret these variations in reports of a child's or adolescent's emotional and behavioral functioning.

SOURCES: Achenbach, T. M., McConaughy, S. H., & Howell, C. T. (1987). Child/adolescent behavioral and emotional problems: Implications of cross-informant correlations for situational specificity. *Psychological Bulletin, 101*, 213–232.

and 50% have substantial problems in peer relationships (see Frick & O'Brien, 1994; Strauss et al., 1988). Similar rates of comorbidity are found in many other types of child psychopathology.

Research attempting to understand comorbidity in childhood psychopathology has had a major impact on our understanding of the causes of several childhood disorders (e.g., Hinshaw, 1987). However, comorbidity also has a more immediate impact on the clinical assessment of children and adolescents. In a special issue of the *Journal of Consulting and Clinical*

Psychology (Kendall & Clarkin, 1992), several articles highlighted the unique treatment needs of children with various types of comorbid psychopathological conditions. The high degree of comorbidity and its importance to the design of effective treatment programs makes the assessment of comorbid conditions crucial in the clinical assessment of children and adolescents.

Because of the importance of comorbidity, most clinical assessments of children and adolescents should be comprehensive. Specifically, assessments must cover multiple areas of functioning so that, not only are the primary referral problems assessed adequately, but potential comorbid problems in adjustment are also assessed. In general, the clinical assessment must be designed with a thorough understanding of the high degree of comorbidity present in child psychopathology and the most common patterns of comorbidity that are specific to the referral question.

Practical Implications for Assessment

Although we have tried to summarize some of the major findings in the field of developmental psychopathology that have particular relevance to clinical assessment, sometimes it is difficult to translate research into guidelines for practice. The following is a summary of some of the major implications of the findings discussed in this section applied to the clinical assessment of children and adolescents. These implications are expanded and applied to specific situations throughout this book.

1. A competent assessor needs to be knowledgeable in several areas of basic psychological research to competently assess children and adolescents. In addition to competence in measurement theory, knowledge of developmental processes and basic characteristics of childhood psychopathology is also essential.
2. Children's behaviors and emotions must be understood within a developmental context. Therefore, an important characteristic of assessment instruments for children is their ability to provide developmentally sensitive normative comparisons. On a more general level, appropriate interpretations of test scores, even if they are based on age-specific norms, should be guided by a knowledge of developmental processes, and their effect on a child's behavioral and emotional functioning.
3. Children's behavior is heavily dependent on the contexts in which the child is participating. Therefore, assessments of children must be based on multiple sources of information that assess a child's functioning in multiple contexts. In addition, an assessment of the relevant aspects of the many important contexts in which a child functions (e.g., at school, at home, with peers) is crucial in understanding the variations in a child's behavior across settings.
4. Most assessments of children must be comprehensive. This is necessary because of the need to adequately assess the many important situational contexts that influence a child's adjustment. Children often exhibit problems in multiple areas of functioning that span emotional, behavioral, learning, and social domains. Effective treatments must be based on the unique strengths and weaknesses of the child across these multiple psychological arenas.

Conclusions

The main theme of this chapter and, in fact, of this entire text, is that appropriate assessment practices are based on the knowledge of the basic characteristics of the phenomena being assessed. As a result, the competent assessor is knowledgeable not only in test administration but is also well versed in psychometric theory, child development, and childhood psychopathology.

Clinical assessment can be conceptualized as a process of classification. Therefore, understanding the issues involved in classifying psychological functioning is important. Formal classification systems are needed to promote communication between professionals, to utilize research for understanding individual cases, and to document the need for services. However, classification systems can also be quite dangerous if they are poor systems or if they are not used appropriately.

Two models of classification have had a great influence on our understanding and assessment of children's emotional and behavioral functioning: clinically-derived medical models and statistically-derived multivariate models. Understanding the basic assumptions of these approaches to classification, and understanding the advantages and disadvantages of each are important for interpreting the assessment information.

Being knowledgeable about basic research within the field of developmental psychology is also crucial in conducting and interpreting psychological assessments of children and adolescents. This research illustrates the importance of conducting and interpreting assessments within a developmental context, the importance of understanding the stability and situational specificity of children's psychological functioning, and the importance of comorbidity in childhood psychopathology. These research findings have many practical applications to the assessment process; these applications are discussed throughout this text.

Chapter Summary

1. To be competent in the clinical assessment of children and adolescents, one must be knowledgeable about the current research base on emotional and behavioral disorders.
2. *Classification* refers to a set of rules that delineates some levels or types of psychological functioning as pathological and places these significant areas of pathology into distinct categories or along certain dimensions.
3. Appropriately developed and competently used classification systems can aid in communication among professionals, in applying research to clinical practice, and in documenting the need for services.
4. Poor classification systems or inappropriately used classification systems can foster an illusion of few differences among individuals within a given category, can foster an illusion of a clear break between normality and pathology, and can lead to stigmatization.
5. Medical model approaches to classification assume an underlying disease entity, and tend to classify people into distinct categories.
6. Multivariate approaches base classification on patterns of behavioral covariation and tend to classify behavior along continuous dimensions, from normality to pathology.
7. The *Diagnostic and Statistical Manual of Mental Disorders, Fourth Edition Text Revision* (APA, 2000) is one of the most commonly used classification systems with characteristics of both medical model and multivariate approaches.
8. Developmental psychopathology provides a framework for understanding the adjustment of children and adolescents.
9. Based on this framework, assessments must be conducted with a knowledge of age-specific patterns of behavior, with a knowledge of normal developmental processes, and with consideration of issues regarding the stability of behavior over time and across situations.
10. Because research has shown that children with problems in one area of

adjustment typically have problems in multiple areas, most assessments of children need to cover multiple domains of functioning.

11. Because research has shown that children's behaviors are heavily dependent on the contexts in which they occur, clinical assessments must assess a child across multiple contexts and assess the characteristics of the most important contexts in which a child functions.

CHAPTER 4

Standards and Fairness

CHAPTER QUESTIONS

- Are professional guidelines available for the assessment of individuals from diverse cultural, linguistic, ethnic, economic and other backgrounds?
- Why is it problematic to use the phrase, "valid test?"

The majority of problems that occur in applied clinical assessment are due not to inherent flaws in the tests, but to the inappropriate use of tests, and misinterpretation of their results, by clinicians (Anastasi, 1992). Test misuse is primarily due to substandard practice by clinicians, just as most auto accidents are caused by driver error and not by the car per se. Even a widely used and accepted test can become a tool for disserving a client. And these cases of misuse are common, and include misuses ranging from incorrect scoring to interpretations of scores that have not been shown to be valid by several independent research studies (Eyde et al., 1993). Consequently, psychological assessment practice has long been governed by peer-developed guidelines and standards that have proliferated and become more explicit and sophisticated as the field matures (AERA, APA, NCME, 1999). This chapter is devoted to providing an executive summary of some of the major publications in this area, especially those developed by relevant learned societies. It also provides guidance for practice based on some of the most widely cited ethical principles, test standards, regulations, and recent treatises that give suggestions for assessing diverse clientele. (A self examination for enhancing retention of these issues is given in Box 4.1.)

P.J. Frick et al., *Clinical Assessment of Child and Adolescent Personality and Behavior*,
DOI 10.1007/978-1-4419-0641-0_4, © Springer Science+Business Media, LLC 2010

Box 4.1

Ethics and Standards Self-Examination Checklist

Periodic completion of this checklist may serve as a quick reference for the clinician to cue adherence to optimal practice methods.

Principle/Guideline Questions

1. Do I have adequate training to use the tests/methods that I plan to use?
2. How might the individual's background-cultural, linguistic, social, economic, or otherwise-affect the planning of my evaluation or the interpretation of my results?
3. Are the tests that I am using validated for the specific purposes that I have in mind?
4. Are there particularly unreliable scales that I should refrain from interpreting?
5. Have I received informed consent and assent prior to initiating the evaluation?
6. Will I provide feedback to the client or to the others concerned, such as the child's parents, teachers, or pediatrician?
7. Did I adequately protect patient privacy?
8. Do I have written permission to share confidential information with concerned parties?
9. Whom do I need to assist with in this examination-a translator, patient, social worker, community member, etc.?
10. Have I consulted a professional colleague regarding questionable issues as needed?

Use and Misuse

There are many elements of competent test usage. According to one empirical study of test usage, there are exactly 86 of them (Eyde et al., 1993). These competencies range from "accepting responsibility for competent use of the test to "not making photocopies of copyrighted materials" to "restricting test administration to qualified personnel." In their unique casebook, Eyde and her colleagues assembled 78 case studies of test "misuse," accompanied by instructional questions and documentation of each violation of the 86 elements. This work represents a unique effort to document the relationship between clinician behavior and assessment practices that makes it a recommended reading for students of assessment. Furthermore, the vignettes provide ample evidence that guidelines and standards are necessary for promoting optimal assessment practices.

APA Ethical Principles of Psychologists

Virtually every professional organization adopts some ethical responsibility for its members. An initial step is the development and dissemination of ethical principles for the members of the organization. Many organizations also adjudicate ethical complaints against members made by the public or others.

Psychology has a long history of involvement in test development and assessment practice, resulting in the frequent use of the term *psychometrics*. Hence, the ethical standards published by the American Psychological Association (APA) are among the most well known sets of ethical principles promulgating standards for assessment practice. This section presents some of the relevant APA principles and provides sample applications of their use. These standards provide helpful guidance regarding the restriction of test use from a professional context only, requirements for evidence or scientifically-based test interpretation, restriction of test use to qualified persons, adherence to relevant testing guidelines and standards of practice, proper and full explanation of test results, and maintaining the security of test items and other content that may make the test useless if released to the general public.

It can be challenging to maintain the security of test content given the access to records by many sources, and numerous requests from parents, lawyers, or patients themselves to see the actual record forms used for the evaluation. Some internet sites provide sample items that are analogous to items found in popular tests, such as the MMPI-2. However, for the most part, test item content can be shielded from would-be test takers. When faced with questions about test security, it has commonly been considered a good practice to a) explain the problems associated with release if items have the ability to practice psychological assessment with others, or b) agree to release test record forms only to other qualified professionals, to interpret them appropriately for the person making the request. These two responses are an oversimplification of the various request types and potential responses, suggesting that consultation with colleagues will be considered wise under these circumstances.

Test Standards

The *Standards for Educational and Psychological Testing* (AERA, APA, NCME, 1999) discuss in great detail the many issues introduced by the ethical principles. In fact, this volume should be part of every psychologist's library, and it would serve as a useful adjunct to this or any other textbook dealing with clinical assessment.

This latest version of the test standards is ambitious, and includes chapters on validity, reliability, test development, scales and norms, test administration, scoring and reporting, supporting documentation for tests, fairness, rights of test takers, testing individuals from diverse linguistic backgrounds, testing individuals with disabilities, responsibilities of test users, psychological testing, educational testing, employment testing, and program evaluation and public policy. These standards are well-articulated and thorough, which portends that they are influential in court proceedings and forensic work, formation of public policy, and, hopefully, in the assessment training of psychologists and other users of tests (Kamphaus, 1998).

One of the vital points presented by the test standards is that it is incorrect to use the phrase "the validity of the test," because it cannot be concluded that a particular test is valid for all children under all assessment situations (AERA, APA, NCME, 1999). The validity of a test should be gauged properly in relation to every assessment situation in which it may be put to use. Clinicians who assess children's personalities must, therefore, learn how to use more than one personality test well in order to validly assess children, families, institutions, or systems. A small sampling of some of the important aspects of psychological test use and validation are given in the following excerpts from the test standards.

Evidence-Based Interpretation

Given the scope and complexity of the standards, only a few of them can be summarized here. Of course, there is always some loss of content when one summarizes an original source. Therefore, again, the reader is advised to read the original standards. Also, the Test Standards should be a required study for all doctoral programs in psychology, as is currently the case for relevant ethical standards.

While it is understood that it is simplistic to say that a test is valid or not valid, it is, therefore, also incorrect to consider a particular test interpretation to be valid for all children being evaluated. First, test developers must present a rationale for each intended interpretation for their test

(AERA, APA, NCME, 1999). This rationale must include documentation of validity evidence and theory relevant to the interpretation in a "comprehensive summary" (Standard 1.1; AERA, APA, NCME, 1999). In addition, although test developers are required to produce such evidence, individual psychologists have to evaluate the quality of the evidence, as it relates to specific circumstances.

With regard to validity, the following standards are also offered (paraphrased from AERA, APA, NCME, 1999).

1. Uses and interpretations of test scores, intended populations of application, and the construct(s) assessed must be clearly stated by the test developer. (Standard 1.2)
2. Users should be cautioned not to interpret tests in a manner inconsistent with the available evidence. (Standard 1.3)
3. Psychologists must justify and collect evidence for an interpretation of a test that is not justified. (Standard 1.4)
4. Validity of study samples should be described in detail. (Standard 1.5)
5. Procedures for selecting the test content should be specified. (Standard 1.6)
6. If experts are used in the test design, their roles and credentials should be described in detail. (Standard 1.7)
7. A rationale should be offered for interpretation of items or item subsets when such interpretations are advised by the developer. (Standard 1.10)
8. The relationships among scores within a test should be supported with evidence. (Standard 1.11)
9. A rationale and scientific evidence should be provided for all interpretations of score differences and profiles. (Standard 1.12)
10. The conditions under which validity evidence was gathered should be described. (Standard 1.13)
11. The relationship between a test and scores on other measures should be theoretically consistent. (Standard 1.14)
12. When statistical adjustments, such as those for restriction of range, are made, both adjusted and unadjusted values should be given. (Standard 1.18)
13. If a test is used to recommend alternative treatments, evidence of differential treatment outcomes should be provided when feasible. (Standard 1.19)
14. When unintended consequences of test use occur, test invalidity should be ruled out as a cause for such consequences. (Standard 1.24)

With regard to psychologists, the following standards are given.

1. Psychologists should limit their assessment practice to the use of tests that are qualified by training. (Standard 12.1)
2. Psychologists should refrain from making biased interpretations that serve as special interests. (Standard 12.2)
3. Tests should be selected only if they are suitable for the characteristics of the patient. (Standard 12.3)
4. Evidence must be provided if it is suggested that an interpretation can be made based on combinations of test scores. (Standard 12.4)
5. Tests used in combination to make a diagnosis must show adequate validity (sensitivity and specificity), and the psychologist must meet the user qualifications required to interpret the tests involved. (Standard 12.5)
6. Psychologists should choose tests for differential diagnosis only if evidence shows that the test can differentiate between clinical samples of interest, not just between a clinical sample and the general population. (Standard 12.6)

7. When a test is used to help make a diagnosis, the diagnostic category must be carefully defined. (Standard 12.7)
8. Psychologists must ensure that psychometrists who work under their supervision are adequately trained. (Standard 12.8)
9. Psychologists should describe the testing procedures in a language understandable by the patient. (Standard 12.10)
10. Confidentiality of the results should be maintained consistent with legal and ethical requirements. (Standard 12.11)
11. Psychologists should use a setting and equipment necessary to obtain valid results. If this setting is not available, the test should also be administered under optimal conditions when possible for comparison purposes. (Standard 12.12)
12. Psychologists should be familiar with the reliability and validity of evidence of each test they use, and they should provide a logical and coherent analysis of the results that support their inferences. (Standard 12.13)
13. Qualitative information, such as background information and observations, should be considered when making test interpretations. (Standard 12.14)
14. The quality of actuarial or computer-based interpretations and the norms on which they are based should be evaluated for their quality. (Standard 12.15)
15. Psychologists should not imply that a relationship exists between test results and prognoses or treatment outcomes unless evidence is available for patients who are similar to the patient being evaluated. (Standard 12.16)
16. Interpretations that suggest how a patient will perform on other measures or outcomes should be supported by evidence of criterion-related validity. (Standard 12.17)
17. Psychologists should base their interpretations on several sources of data, test results, or other evidence, and they should be cognizant of the theory, empirical evidence, and limitations of each test used. (Standard 12.18)
18. Construct irrelevant factors (e.g., motivation, response sets, health factors, suboptimal testing conditions) should be considered as an alternative explanation for a set of test results. (Standard 12.19)
19. Normally, psychologists should discuss the results with the patient in a language that he or she can understand. (Standard 12.20)

One reason for delineating these two sets of standards is to give the reader an appreciation of their scope, which is truly impressive. Awareness of the scope of the standards should alert psychologists that a compliance with these standards requires dedicated effort and self monitoring.

A few themes in these standards deserve elaboration. First, interpretation must be evidence-based and, when it is not, the fact should be made known to all consumers of the results. We suggest that psychologists ask themselves a few questions about a test interpretation in order to encourage compliance with the standards. If we conclude, for example, that a child has depression, our self-monitoring questions could include:

1. On what assessment results do we base this interpretation?
2. Do the structured interviews and self-report measures have adequate evidence of reliability, sensitivity, and specificity?
3. Is this scientific evidence based on adolescent samples with similar demographics (e.g., sex, age, ethnicity, geographic region, language, etc.)?
4. Is this evidence based on studies that use clinical control samples in addition to comparisons with the general population?

5. Are the scales and interviews free of construct-irrelevant variance (e.g., "threatens others," which is not a core symptom of depression but is an indicator of aggression)?
6. Is there an evidence of construct under-representation (e.g., scale does not include any "vegetative" symptoms of depression)?
7. Are the procedures for developing diagnostic interview and scale content described and are reasonable?
8. Were the interview results, test findings, patient background/history, and other evidence integrated into a coherent rationale for the diagnosis?
9. Could there be an alternate explanation for the conclusions drawn by the construct-irrelevant variance (e.g., child was coached on the content of some test items)?
10. What is the definition of *depression (e.g., DSM-IV* diagnostic criteria)?
11. Is a classification or diagnostic decision made only to receive insurance reimbursement or other remuneration, financial or otherwise?
12. Have these results been shared with the client in a manner that he or she can fully understand?
13. Has confidentiality of the clients' results been maintained?

Of course, a different set of questions may be posed for non-diagnostic interpretations such as prognosis, treatment, or program evaluation.

The issue of confidentiality is worth additional comment. Rights to privacy continue to be threatened due to changes in health insurance practices and increasing access to electronically stored information, among other factors (Alderman & Kennedy, 1995).

Standards for Privacy of Individually Identifiable Health Information have been issued by the U.S. Department of Health and Human Services (Federal Register: December 28, 2000, volume 65, number 250). These standards are remarkable in at least three ways: (1) They specifically include records of psychologists who provide "qualified psychologist services"; (2) Psychotherapy notes that are "separated from the rest of the individual's medical record" are generally excluded from release, including release to the patient; (3) A patient may be denied access to his or her medical record if

> "a licensed health care professional has determined, in the exercise of professional judgment, that the access requested is reasonably likely to endanger the life or physical safety of the individual or another person." (p. 82823)

These medical record release standards are, therefore, reflective of some of the vicissitudes of mental health care. The exclusion of psychotherapy notes from the medical record shows a high regard for the sensitivity of such information. For the purposes of this text, however, it should be noted that psychotherapy notes are not de-fined to include the "results of clinical tests," "diagnosis," and so on.

With regard to the other aspects of the medical record that may include psychological test and assessment results and interpretations, a psychologist may also deny access if the "protected health information" makes reference to another individual who may suffer harm if information is released. Finally, release may be denied to the patient's personal representative, if the provider thinks that harm may occur. Of course, a patient may ask for a review of any denial request and certain exclusions (e.g., criminal activities) from this denial provision are stipulated. However, these regulations appear to give psychologists some discretion regarding the release of patient records.

BIAS and Cultural Competence

Test Bias

The perception that bias is inherent in psychological tests has spurred many challenges and accusations (Kamphaus, 2001). A review of some of the major technical issues follows.

Mean Score Differences

Most definitions of test bias do not usually consider the issue of mean score differences as a meaningful test of bias (Reynolds & Kaiser, 1990). Instead, important questions related to the validity of a personality test's inferences across groups forms a test of bias. In this approach to bias, an evidence of the *construct validity* for a personality test score inference differing across groups exist. Numerous studies have addressed these technical issues. For the purpose of this chapter, the definition of test bias offered by Reynolds and Kaiser is most appropriate.

> "Test bias refers in a global sense to *systematic* error in the estimation of some true value for a group of individuals. The key word here is *systematic;* all measures contain error, but this error is assumed to be random unless shown to be otherwise." (p. 624)

Given this definition, one would expect score differences to indicate genuine differences in behavior or personality, if the test works the same way (i.e., measures the same constructs in a valid way) for various groups. An interesting finding with regard to ratings of child behavior is that few mean differences exist between cultural and linguistic groups even for tests developed primarily for use in the United States. Crijnen, Achenbach, and Verhulst (1997), for example, found remarkably small differences between groups for parent ratings using the Child Behavior Checklist. They studied the results for 13,697 children and adolescents from 12 cultures including China, Israel, Sweden, German, Jamaica, and the United States. Their results have a striking similarity across culture, including similarities in cross-sectional changes associated with age. They also noted that sex differences were invariant across cultures:

> With no significant exceptions, boys obtained higher externalizing scores but lower internalizing scores than girls. This gender difference in the kinds of problems that parents report might thus be a "cultural universal"... (p. 1276).

Several aspects of this study were corroborated for four cultural groups, for both parent and teacher ratings in a study by Kamphaus et al. (2000). This investigation evaluated the differences between U.S. Anglo, U.S. African American, U.S. Hispanic, and Colombian (Medellin) samples for both parent and teacher ratings from the BASC. Kamphaus et al. also found that differences were small between groups for both parent and teacher ratings, and sex differences were consistent regardless of cultural/linguistic groups.

Taken together, these studies, and many others, revealed that differences among racial, ethnic, cultural, and linguistic groups for behavior problem measures are relatively small, a trend that stands in contrast to other realms of testing (i.e., intelligence and academic achievement) with large differences (Kamphaus, 2001). And, while sex differences are relatively small for cognitive measures (i.e., intelligence), they are greater for child behavior problem measures. While interesting, however, these studies of mean score differences do not serve as clear indices of bias.

Content Validity Bias

Content validity was one of the first areas of investigation of test bias. This search for bias is understandable given that a frequent bias concern is usually directed at item content that seems inappropriate or, perhaps, even offensive to a group of individuals. Again, a very helpful definition of content validity bias can be taken from Reynolds and Kaiser (1990):

> "An item or subscale of a test is considered to be biased in content when it is demonstrated to be relatively more difficult for members of one group than for members of another in a situation where the general ability level of the groups being compared is held constant and no reasonable theoretical rationale exists to explain group differences on the item (or subscale) in question." (p. 625)

Numerous procedures have been proposed for assessing bias in individual items, but the logic behind item bias detection techniques is fairly simple (Kamphaus, 2001). The fundamental aspect of most statistical methods that assess bias across cultural or gender groups is to match the groups on an overall score level, which is the first step in the procedure. If, for example, one was looking for gender bias in a pool of personality test items, one would first match boys and girls on their overall test score, be it standard or raw score. So, if one wanted to evaluate biased items in the MMPI-A, for example, one would first statistically group the cases, with perhaps all the boys and girls with f-scores above 90 on a particular scale as one group, those between 80 and 89 as another group, those between 70 and 79 as a third group, and so on (it should be noted, however, that this is not the exact procedure used by most item bias techniques but an oversimplification of such procedures). Subsequently, some statistical test of significance is applied to check if, within these various score groups, there are still significant differences in response to the items of one group or another.

This discussion relates to another item bias detection technique: judgmental bias reviews. The procedure used by some publishers is to have groups of individuals review the items carefully. This procedure ensures that members of a number of cultural groups review the items to determine not only the potential bias, but also the items that may be inappropriate for various cultural groups. There is, however, much disagreement between judgmental reviews of items and statistical analyses of bias. It appears that statistical analyses of bias are more reliable (Reynolds and Kaiser, 1990). In an investigation of judgmental bias reviews for intelligence test items, Sandoval and Mille (1979) compared the ratings of 45 WISC-R items by 38 African American, 22 Mexican American, and 40 undergraduate students. This study found that minority and non-minority judges did not differ in their ability to identify the culturally biased items. The conclusions of Sandoval and Mille were that: (1) Judges are not able to detect items that are more difficult for a minority child than for a Caucasian child, and (2) the item selection for minority children by judges of ethnic background did not show any difference.

Item bias, however, may be subtle and difficult to detect. Canino and Bravo (1999) cite an example of a problem with content equivalence on the Diagnostic Interview Schedule for Children (DISC; Shaffer et al., 2000). They found that, initially, it was difficult to translate items regarding seasonal depression into Spanish. Later it was found that even successful translation of the symptoms was of no value because seasonal depression never occurred for the children in sunny Puerto Rico.

Construct Validity Bias

A workable definition of construct validity bias by Reynolds and Kaiser (1990) reads as:

> "Bias exists in regard to construct validity when a test is shown to measure different hypothetical traits (psychological constructs) for one group or another, or to measure the same trait but with differing degrees of accuracy" (p. 632).

The most popular method used for the study of construct validity bias is factor analysis. Numerous researchers have used similar procedures. The central characteristic of these procedures is to conduct factor analyses separately for various cultural and gender groups, and determine if a similar factor structure is yielded for each group. The most popular procedure for assessing agreement between factor structures across groups is a coefficient of congruence, which is interpreted similar to a correlation coefficient.

Lachar and Gruber (1994) provide an example of this method for the Personality Inventory for Youth (see Chap. 6). They conducted factor analyses separately by gender and ethnicity, and then compared the factors yielded separately for the groups. Their findings were similar to those for ability tests (Kamphaus, 2001) in that correlations between the obtained factors were uniformly *high*, in the low 0.90 at their worst.

Predictive Validity Bias

The final type of bias that has received a great deal of attention is predictive validity bias. A working definition of predictive validity bias is

> "A test is considered biased with respect to predictive validity if the inference drawn from the test score is not made with the smallest feasible random error or if there is constant error in an inference for prediction as a function of membership in a particular group". (p. 638) (Reynolds & Kaiser, 1990)

The issue of predictive or criterion-related validity is that these coefficients should not differ significantly across cultural or gender groups. One of the typical procedures in this research literature is to compare the predictive validity coefficients across groups. A study might compare the ability of a depression measure to predict future adjustment for various groups, for example.

If different predictive validity coefficients were obtained for two or more groups, the results would be called *slope bias*. In order to understand the concept of slope bias, it is helpful to recall how correlation coefficients are learned in introductory statistics courses. Such procedures are typically taught by having the students collect data on two variables and plot the scores of a group of individuals on these two variables. This plot results in a scatter plot. Then students compute a correlation coefficient and draw a line of best fit through the scatter plot. This line of best fit is a visual representation of the slope. A correlation coefficient (predictive validity coefficient) of 0.90 would produce a slope that is very different from that obtained with a correlation coefficient of 0.30. Consequently, this form of bias in prediction is often referred to as slope bias.

Summary Comments on Bias

While psychometric evidence of test bias can be found, little compelling evidence of bias is found for various groups residing in the United States (Figueroa, 1990). As a result, the focus has now changed to implicate test misuse as the major contributing factor to improper assessment of individual and groups of children. This misuse, however, includes more than individuals. Government, school district, or other entities may, for example, create unwise policies that inadvertently produce biased and untoward outcomes for children, such as imposing strict cut-off scores that affect assessment and conceptualization of the case.

Fairness

The term *fairness* refers to "… the principle that every test taker should be assessed in an equitable way" (AERA, APA, NCME, 1999, p. 175). Some issues related to achieving this objective are discussed in this section. The renewed focus on test use comes at a time when psychologists are seeking to improve test use for various linguistic and cultural groups. Cultural plurality has posed a challenge to assessment and diagnostic practice since the early days of the mental tests. The testing movement was forced early on to change tests and testing practice in the United States because of the tremendous influx of new immigrants. Between 1901 and 1910, over nine million immigrants entered the United States-more immigrants than the combined populations of New York, Maryland, and New Hampshire in 1900 (French & Hale, 1990). One component of the initial appearance of the Wechsler scales as an alternative to the Stanford-Binet monopoly of the time was the fact that Wechsler included a performance scale that could be used with some success with non-English speakers (Kamphaus, 2001).

Little has changed since the days of mass migration to the United States. In many ways, psychologists have used the same strategies for dealing with clients from diverse cultures. A popular approach involves adapting existing assessment instruments. The Thompson adaptation of the TAT for adults of African American heritage during the 1930s is one of the early examples of such attempts. Psychologists with multi-cultural expertise should be able to adequately assess the needs of a child from a culture that may differ from their own, even if test instruments that are not specifically designed for the child's culture are the only ones available.

A study by Malgady and Costantino (1998) highlighted the need for developing new cultural competencies. They evaluated the effects of language and ethnicity of the clinician on diagnostic decision making, using Spanish-dominant adult patients of Puerto Rican and Dominican descent. These patients were then seen by board-certified psychiatrists and clinical psychologists for diagnostic interviews. Patients were matched on *DSM-IV* diagnosis and divided into four interview language and clinician assessment groups: English only/non-Hispanic clinician; Spanish only/Hispanic clinician; English only/Hispanic clinician; Bilingual/Hispanic clinician. Several of the Malgady and Costantino's results are noteworthy. First, they found no differences in the diagnoses or symptoms between psychiatrists and psychologists. Symptom severity was highest among patients interviewed in Spanish by a bilingual interviewer. Symptom severity was rated lowest when a patient was interviewed in English by an Anglo clinician. While concern has been expressed that a clinician who does not share ethnicity and language with a patient will pathologize (Cohen & Kasen, 1999), these results suggest that it is also possible that such a mismatch between patient and clinician could lead to failure in identifying psychopathology, which could exacerbate the symptoms of those denied access to treatment. Either way, research does suggest a need for broader training of clinicians in multi-cultural competencies.

Emic Versus Etic Perspectives

An *emic perspective* refers to behavior that is considered specific to a culture, whereas an *etic perspective* presupposes that much of the behavior and laws of psychology are applicable cross-culturally. Anastasi (1992) proposes that both perspectives are valid by theorizing that learned behavior may be culture-specific (emit) but that the "laws of learning" apply cross-culturally (etic). She hypothesizes further that hierarchical models of personality may be most useful in studying their behavior, as is the case for studies on intelligence when supporting evidence can be found for a "g" factor and for specific traits (e.g., spatial ability) at lower levels of the hierarchy. There is, for example, evidence that several temperament traits can be identified cross-culturally (Martin, 1988).

Inappropriate, ill-informed, or insensitive interpretations may also be made of the "clinical" data. An examiner may conclude that a 13-year-old girl of Asian heritage is socially introvert, shy, and perhaps in need of assertive training because of her behavior during an interview with a male clinician. She may have been demure and made no eye contact. The examiner may draw such a conclusion despite the fact that she appeared friendly and outgoing when she was observed on the school playground and seemed to interact openly with her family members. This client may not, in fact, be pathologically shy; rather, she may be adhering to a prohibition against making eye contact with a male because of cultural values that suggest that this is a sexually seductive behavior (or an indication of a lack of respect) that is deemed inappropriate for her (Hasegawa, 1989). In this case, the clinician was simply ignoring relevant data, and the clinician's lack of familiarity with the child's culture resulted in an erroneous interpretation.

The clinician, however, must also remember the importance of individualizing interpretation. Within a cultural group, variability can be substantial (Zuckerman, 1990). It may be assumed by some that Vietnamese and Chinese children have similar values due to early Chinese domination and the inculcation of Vietnamese culture with Confucian ethics. There have also been other influences on this culture that may affect a child's behavior, including European Roman Catholicism, brought by the French conquest of 1958, the influence of U.S. culture from the Vietnam War, and Buddhist influences from neighboring Cambodia (Huang, 1989). Classifying children by race, culture, or language background is an appealing approach for researchers and clinicians alike that is fraught with errors, primarily due to the tendency to overgeneralize a particular group of people (Zuckerman, 1990).

Inclan and Herron (1985) cite the "culture of poverty" as another subculture that may affect a variety of groups. This "culture" is formed by a clash between those who have achieved material wealth and prosperity and those who struggle to achieve economic parity with little hope of doing so. Children reared in a culture of poverty possess identifiable characteristics: an orientation to present time, inability to delay gratification, impulsivity, sense of predetermined fate, resentment of authority, alienation and distrust of others, and lack of emphasis on rigor, discipline, and perseverance (Inclan & Herron, 1989). They note that some impoverished parents of adolescents may be assessed by a therapist as being too rigid and controlling their youngsters at a time when parents should be giving their children more freedom. It is possible, however, that poor parents may be all too familiar with the culture of poverty and may be seeking control, not for its own sake, but rather to ensure that their child or adolescent does not fall prey to the negative consequences of the behavior associated with that culture (Inclan & Herron, 1989).

These examples demonstrate the need for clinicians to develop an enlarged knowledge base in order to deal effectively with their referral population. Just as clinicians need to have knowledge of behavioral principles, psychometrics, child development, child psychopathology, and physiological psychology to conduct an evaluation competently, it is increasingly clear that they must know the history, culture, and language of their community extremely well in order to not use assessment procedures inappropriately, and to avoid making naïve and inappropriate interpretations.

Guidelines for Assessing Children from Diverse Backgrounds

Resources for assessing children from diverse groups are now more readily available (e.g., Dana, 1999; Geisinger, 1992). Two developments that can assist practitioners are (1) the availability of guidelines from blue ribbon panels and committees and (2) the increasing availability of formal measures of acculturation.

Numerous sets of guidelines provide specific advice for the psychologist who is unsure of what procedures to use in questionable situations. The *Guidelines for Providers of Psychological Services to Ethnic, Linguistic, and Culturally Diverse Populations* give specific and helpful advice to the clinician seeking to carry out a competent evaluation of a child for whom cultural/social/linguistic issues loom large (see www.apa.org).

A good example of the guidance to be gained from such publications deals with the frequently occurring situation of a language difference between the examiner and the child or other family members. Guideline 6a suggests that a cascade of three options applies to the examiner faced with such a case: (1) Refer the child to a clinician who can communicate in the client's preferred language; (2) if this is not possible, use a translator who also possesses professional training; and, lastly, (3) one is advised to use a paraprofessional from the community to translate. Moreover, the next guideline, 6b, highlights the potential threat to validity of using a translator who has a dual relationship with the client (e.g., a grandparent).

Assessing Acculturation

The previously discussed guidelines for considering cultural and linguistic issues hint at the need to more carefully assess an individual's level of adoption of the so-called "dominant culture," which, of course, could change from one neighborhood to the other. The guidelines indicate the need to collect information, such as the number of generations of residence within the dominant culture, number of years of residence, dominant language fluency, community resources, and so on. This data collection is an informal means of assessing level of acculturation. There are, however, more formal (some are quantifiable) methods for assessing acculturation. In fact, it has been argued that the ready availability of such measures warrants their routine use in assessment practice (Geisinger, 1992).

Marin (1992) defines the constructs relevant to assessing ethnic identity and acculturation. He cites three components of ethnic identity: (1) "birth and gestational history, (2) culture-specific behaviors and practices (e.g., language), and (3) culture-specific attitudes that include adherence to a culture's values and norms as well as in-group and out-group attitudes" (p. 236). The process of acculturation is defined as "... changes in individuals that are produced by contact with one or more cultural groups" (p. 237). Several instruments are now available for assessing the ethnic identification of individuals and the degree to which acculturation has taken place.

Dana (1993) provides a detailed compendium of measures of acculturation and identification with a particular culture. Some of these scales are listed below.

African American Measures

Developmental Inventory of Black Consciousness (DIB-C; Milliones, 1980)

Racial Identity Attitude Scale (RIAS; Helms, 1986)

African Self-Consciousness Scale (ASC; Baldwin & Bell, 1985)

Asian American Measures

Ethnic Identity Questionnaire (EIQ; Masuda, Matsumoto, & Meredith, 1970)

Hispanic American Measures

Acculturation Rating Scale for Mexican Americans (ARSMA; Cuellar, Harris, & Jasso, 1980)

Children's Acculturation Scale (Franco, 1983)

Cuban Behavioral Identity Questionnaire (CBIQ; Garcia & Lega, 1979)
Hispanic Acculturation Scale (HAC; Marin et al., 1987)
Children's Hispanic Background Scale (CHBS; Martinez, Norman, & Delaney, 1984)
Cultural Life Style Inventory (Mendoza, 1989)
Multi-dimensional Scale of Cultural Differences (MSCD; Olmedo, Martinez, & Martinez, 1978)
Multi-cultural Experience Inventory (MEI; Ramirez, 1984)
Behavioral Acculturation Scale (BAS; Szapocznik, Scopetta, & Aranalde, 1978)
Bicultural Involvement Questionnaire (BIQ; Szapocznik & Kurtines, 1980)

Conclusions

The child psychologist of today has to become steeped in various ethical, legal, professional, language and cultural issues, and standards of practice that face the profession. It is necessary for the practitioner to seek this knowledge through experiences during graduate school and beyond. Continuous professional development is especially important in order to achieve fairness in the assessment process. Knowledge of cultural, linguistic, technology change, and other effects on assessment remains in its infancy, thus portending considerable change in the future.

Chapter Summary

Some of the APA ethics principles of relevance to assessment include

1. Evaluation, diagnosis, or intervention in a professional context, competence and appropriate use of assessments and interventions, limiting use of psychological tests to qualified professionals, and maintenance of test security.
2. The *Standards for Educational and Psychological Testing* (AERA, APA, NCME, 1999) provide a rich resource for maintaining standards of practice.
3. While psychometric evidence of content-, construct-, or criterion-related validity test bias can be found, little compelling evidence of bias is found for various groups residing in the United States. As a result, the focus has now changed to implicate test misuse as the major contributing factor in improper assessment of children.
4. The renewed focus on test use comes at a time when psychologists are seeking to improve test use for various cultural and linguistic groups.
5. The emic perspective refers to behavior that is thought to be specific to a culture, whereas the etic perceptive presupposes the behavior theory and laws of psychology that are applicable cross-culturally.
6. The *Guidelines for Providers of Psychological Services to Ethnic, Linguistic, and Culturally Diverse Populations* give specific and helpful advice to the clinician seeking to carry out a competent evaluation of a child for whom cultural/social linguistic issues provide threats to test validity.
7. There are now formal and quantifiable methods for assessing acculturation.

CHAPTER 5

Planning the Evaluation and Rapport Building

Chapter Questions

- Why is it important to carefully plan an evaluation?
- What information is necessary for planning a focused clinical assessment?
- What are some of the important considerations in determining whether or not a child should be tested and who should do the testing?
- What is a scientific approach to testing?
- What is rapport and why is it more difficult to develop in the clinical assessment of children and adolescents than in many other clinical endeavors?
- How can informed consent be considered a rapport-building strategy?
- What are some of the important strategies that can aid in developing rapport with children and adolescents?

Non-specifics in Clinical Assessment

A recurrent theme in this text is that an assessor needs to have knowledge of several areas of basic research to appropriately select and interpret psychological tests for children and adolescents. In this chapter, we consider another area of competence crucial to clinical assessment that goes beyond knowing how to administer specific tests. It is rather difficult to discuss this competence in objective terms because it relates to difficult topics for research and, as a result, there is only limited objective data to guide this practice. Instead, much in this chapter is guided by clinical experience, not just our own experience, but the experience of other practicing

P.J. Frick et al., *Clinical Assessment of Child and Adolescent Personality and Behavior*,
DOI 10.1007/978-1-4419-0641-0_5, © Springer Science+Business Media, LLC 2010

psychologists who have written in this area.

This chapter deals with setting an appropriate context in which testing takes place. This is not simply the physical context of testing, but the activities of the assessor that allow the clinical assessment to achieve its goals. Many of the issues discussed involve clinical skills that are difficult to teach, but often require refinement based on practical experience in testing children and adolescents. However, an analogy can be made with the literature on psychotherapy. Many useful guides for practicing clinicians have been published that deal with the non-specifics of psychotherapy. The term non-specifics has been used to refer to several contextual factors, within which the psychotherapy techniques take place, such as the relationship between therapist and client or the process by which a therapist engages a client in a therapeutic setting (Karver, Handlesman, Fields, & Bickman, 2006). In this chapter, we attempt to deal with the non-specifics in the clinical assessment of children and adolescents.

One critical component of setting an appropriate context for an evaluation is careful planning. In the following section, we discuss a basic framework for designing clinical assessments for children and adolescents. Within this basic framework, however, evaluations must be tailored to the needs of the individual case. The critical developmental issues, the most relevant areas of adjustment to be assessed, and the most important elements of a child's or adolescent's environment will all vary from case to case. As a result, it is inappropriate to develop specific guidelines for designing evaluations. Instead, in this section we attempt to provide a framework for designing assessments that can be tailored to most assessment situations.

Clarifying the Referral Question

A crucial part of planning any evaluation is having enough information, prior to beginning the testing, to make at least some initial decisions on the structure and content of the assessment process. This is not to say that the assessment process should be so structured from the outset that changes after testing is underway are not possible. However, obtaining crucial information before the first testing session enhances the likelihood that one will provide a focused and appropriate assessment. Almost every testing agency, whether clinic, school, hospital, or private practitioner, has some established intake process that provides preliminary information on the child or adolescent being tested. There is no single best way to structure the intake procedure. However, there are some pieces of information that should be obtained routinely in any intake process, in addition to any basic information (e.g., name, address, phone number, insurance coverage) that is required by the agency.

Purpose of Testing

The most important piece of intake information for planning an evaluation is the intended purpose of the evaluation. A major flaw in many clinical assessments is a lack of focus. From the outset, an evaluation should have clearly specified goals and objectives. As discussed previously, it is erroneous to think in terms of an assessment technique or battery being valid or invalid. Results of the evaluation can be valid for *specific interpretations*. Therefore, what interpretations one anticipates making at the end of the evaluation should guide the selection of tests for the assessment battery. For example, if an assessment is primarily intended to determine school placement, then the focus of the evaluation will not be to determine whether or not a psychiatric diagnosis is warranted, but to determine whether or not the child meets the eligibility requirements of the school system. The assessor may feel that more information is needed to make appropriate recommendations to meet a child's psychological and educational needs than is required by these criteria. However, enough information to determine the eligibility should be part of the assessment, if this is the primary referral question. In our experience, it is not uncommon for an otherwise sound and competently conducted evaluation to be useless for the specific purposes for which a child was referred.

There are many other examples showing how the intended use of the assessment information determines the measures to be used. This may be as broad as defining what areas need to be covered for a certain purpose (e.g., some residential treatment centers require a personality assessment prior to acceptance) to as specific as requiring certain tests (e.g., some school systems require specific tests to be given for special education placement). The assessor should not give a test that, in his or her professional judgment, is inappropriate for a particular use or is inappropriate for a particular client. However, if, at the time of referral, the intended use of the assessment is clarified and there is some question as to how appropriate certain requirements are for a given case, the assessor can attempt to address these issues before beginning the evaluation.

Often the person or agency referring a child or adolescent for testing is not sure how the test results will be used. Instead, the child is referred because the agency is unsure of the nature of a child's problem (or even whether there is a problem), and the referrer is unsure of what can be done to help the child. There are many variations on this theme, but, in essence, the goal of the assessment is to diagnose the source of a child's difficulty and to make treatment recommendations based on this diagnosis. In Chap. 3, we discussed many important issues in making diagnostic decisions. However, Martin (1988) provides a succinct and practical analysis of the specific goals involved in diagnosis. These are to (1) predict future behavior, (2) differentiate between abnormal and normal behavior, (3) make differential diagnoses, and (4) delineate individual differences in competencies and disabilities. Martin also provides some interesting recommendations for planning the evaluation to maximize the reliability of the diagnostic process. These are summarized in Box 5.1.

Description of Referral Problems

In addition to understanding the purpose of the testing referral, it is also important to obtain an initial description of the difficulties that a child is experiencing that led to the referral. One of the reasons that clinical assessments are so fascinating is that, if done right, the assessment is a type of scientific inquiry. Based on the intake information, the assessor should have some initial hypotheses for understanding a given case that will be tested during the evaluation. These hypotheses will guide the initial planning of the evaluation and initial test selection. As in any good scientific endeavor, we must be clear of the data that would support and those that would not support the various hypotheses. In contrast to many other scientific enterprises, however, the hypotheses can, and should, change during the investigation.

Box 5.1

Planning the Evaluation to Enhance Reliability

In our chapter on psychometric theory, we discussed reliability as a key concept in understanding the psychological measurement. Reliability is often considered as a property of individual tests. However, Martin (1988) discusses several issues in planning an assessment battery that can maximize the reliability of the information that is obtained. Key to Martin's approach is his conceptualization of four primary sources of error variance that can affect the reliability of measurement of children's social and emotional functioning:

(1) Temporal variance – changes in behavior over time
(2) Source or rater variance – differences in information due to characteristics of the informant
(3) Setting variance – differences due to different demand characteristics across settings
(4) Instrument variance – unreliability inherent in individual instruments

Martin uses the basic concept in measurement theory to describe how these sources of error variance can be controlled in an assessment. Specifically, the primary method of controlling error variance and increasing reliability is through *aggregation*. As the length of a test increases, the reliability of the scores increases. Thus, to control the temporal variance, repeated measurements on several occasions should be obtained. Similarly, to reduce source and setting variance, information should be obtained from multiple sources and across multiple settings. The implication of these psychometric considerations is the need for a comprehensive evaluation.

The final source of error variance in Martin's scheme is the *instrument variance*. Like the other sources of variance, aggregating information across instruments is a crucial method for increasing reliability. However, this is only the case if additional tests provide reliable information. If one adds unreliable tests to a battery, then aggregation actually *decreases* the reliability of the battery. Clinicians, who have a favorite test that they use in the batteries, will often justify their use of the test, even if it has been proven unreliable, by the statement "I only use it as one part of a more comprehensive battery." This is clearly better than using the test in isolation. However, adding a piece of unreliable information will only reduce the reliability of the aggregated information. In a separate publication, Martin (1982) gives the example of three umpires calling a baseball game. If one of the umpires is blind, his calls will only serve to reduce the reliability of the calls made by the entire umpiring team. The moral of the story: Aggregation only increases the reliability of the information obtained if the individual tests are selected to enhance reliability.

SOURCE: Martin (1988). *Assessment of Personality and Behavior Problems Infancy through Adolescence.* New York: Guilford Press.

As data accumulate on a case and it becomes clear that initial impressions of a case were wrong, the assessor must revise the assessment accordingly. To employ this scientific approach to clinical assessment, enough preliminary information on a child's functioning must be obtained prior to starting the evaluation, so that initial hypotheses can be formed. A case example that utilizes this approach is provided in Box 5.2.

Box 5.2

A Scientific Approach to Clinical Assessment: A Case Example

Joshua is a 10-year-old boy who was referred to the outpatient psychiatry department of a large inner-city pediatric hospital for testing. The intake worker determined that Joshua was being referred by his parents because he was in danger of failing the fifth grade. According to the intake information, Joshua was having great difficulty paying attention in class and completing assignments. He was also described as being excessively fidgety and restless. The intake information indicated that these school problems were new this school year. He had been an A\B student in the four previous school grades, which made his current poor performance especially puzzling.

Based on this information, several initial hypotheses were formulated. It could be that similar problems were experienced in the past grades but they had just increased in severity in the fifth grade; in which case, dispositional causes were possible such as an attention deficit disorder and/or a learning disability. Alternatively, if this recent onset was supported in the evaluation (through interviewing parents about past school performance, obtaining school records, interviewing past teachers), it may be that Joshua had experienced or was experiencing some type of newly occurring stressor (e.g., parental divorce, sexual abuse) that was resulting in the deterioration in behavior. The evaluation was designed to test these initial hypotheses.

Interestingly, during the assessment of potential stressors, Joshua's mother reported that he had been involved in an automobile accident during the summer prior to entering the fifth grade. He had sustained a closed head injury and had lost consciousness for several minutes. He was released from the hospital with no noticeable effects of the injury. After obtaining this information, another hypothesis became possible. Joshua might have sustained neurological damage from the accident that was affecting his behavior. As a result, he was referred for a neurological exam, which uncovered neurological damage that seemed to be the most likely cause of his behavioral difficulties. Although the initial hypotheses were not correct, this illustrates how a scientific approach to hypothesis testing can be useful in structuring the assessment process.

Designing the Evaluation

We concluded Chap. 3 by providing several guidelines for clinical assessments of children that followed from research in developmental psychopathology. In this section, we take these research-based guidelines and use them to develop practical considerations in designing clinical assessments of children. Once again, these recommendations are designed to provide a generic framework that can be tailored to the needs of the individual case.

Developmental Considerations

From the discussion of developmental psychopathology provided in Chap. 3, it is clear that assessments of children's emotional and behavioral adjustment need to be sensitive to a number of important developmental issues. First, a basic tenet of developmental psychopathology is the importance of taking a "process-oriented" approach to conceptualizing children's adjustment. As a result, it is important that clinical assessments not only involve a standardized and comprehensive assessment of a child's behavioral and emotional adjustment, but it is also important that they include an assessment of the developmental processes (e.g., temperamental tendencies, family context) that may be related to the child's current pattern of adjustment. This more comprehensive assessment requires that assessors maintain a current knowledge of the research related to the type of problems they encounter in their evaluations, so that they have an adequate understanding of the processes that may be involved in the development of these problems.

This research provides the assessor with some initial hypotheses regarding the problems that led to a child's referral for testing. Measures are selected so that these hypotheses can then be tested in the evaluation. For example, there is research to suggest that there are distinct subgroups of children with conduct problems, some of whom react very strongly to peer provocation and emotional stimuli, and some of whom show a lack of reactivity to emotional cues, leading them to ignore the potential consequences of their behavior on others (Frick, 2006). Solely assessing the child's level and severity of conduct problems and making a diagnosis of "Conduct Disorder," without assessing the child's affective and interpersonal style, would not allow one to distinguish between these different subgroups that may require different approaches to treatment (Frick & McMahon, 2008).

Secondly, it is important for the psychologist to consider the developmental stage of the child to be assessed in designing an assessment battery. For example, it is important, when selecting tests for a battery, to determine whether the tests provide good norm-referenced scores for the developmental stage of the child or adolescent being assessed. Because this is so important, a significant focus of the later chapters (which provide reviews of specific testing instruments) is on the description of the instruments' norm-referenced scores. It is evident from these reviews that the adequacy of these scores can vary across developmental stages (e.g., having a very limited normative sample for older adolescents). In addition to specific tests, some testing modalities may be more or less appropriate depending on the developmental level of the child. For example, in the chapter on structured interviews, we discuss research suggesting that the child self-report format on these interviews may be unreliable before age 9.

Determining the Relevant Psychological Domains

A fairly ubiquitous finding in research on childhood psychopathology is the high degree of overlap or comorbidity in problem behaviors (Jensen, 2003). That is, children with problems in one area of emotional or behavioral functioning are at high risk of having problems in other areas of emotional or behavioral functioning, as well as problems in social and cognitive arenas. In addition, a key assumption to a developmental approach to understanding children's adjustment is that all outcomes are influenced by multiple interacting processes. As a result, most evaluations of children and adolescents must be fairly comprehensive to ensure that all areas that could be relevant to treatment planning are assessed. In planning an evaluation, one should consider the most likely comorbidities associated with the referral problem and the most likely factors that can lead to such problems, and design the evaluation to provide an adequate assessment of these areas. From the referral information, one may also gather some clues as to how intensive the assessment of these potentially important domains should be.

For example, consider a referral of a 7-year-old boy who is having significant problems of being disorganized, being very impulsive, and having difficulty staying in his seat. An initial hypothesis may be that the child has attention-deficit hyperactivity disorder (ADHD), and an evaluation is designed to test this hypothesis and to test the many different processes (e.g., poor executive functioning) that could lead to this disorder (see Chap. 17). In addition, from research on ADHD one knows that approximately 30% of children with the disorder have a co-occurring learning disability (Frick & Kimonis, 2008). Therefore, one needs to determine how this comorbidity can be assessed. However, in the initial intake, the child's mother states that her son has no real problems academically, other than losing his assignments frequently, and, in fact, he has only made two B's on his report cards since entering school. Based on this piece of information, one may decide not to conduct an intensive evaluation of a potential learning disability unless, during the course of the evaluation, some evidence of learning problems is discovered.

Screening of Important Contexts

Research has indicated that children's behavior is strongly influenced by factors in their psychosocial environment. Therefore, an important consideration in planning an evaluation is determining the aspects of a child's environment being assessed (e.g., teaching styles of specific teachers, affective tone of family interactions) and the assessment methodology (e.g., naturalistic observations, behavior rating scales). However, the relevance of context will vary from child to child. The intake information should provide enough information so that an evaluation can be planned, in which (1) informants from each of a child's relevant contexts provide information on the child's functioning and (2) the contexts that seem to have the most impact on a child's functioning can be assessed in greater detail.

One of the most influential contexts for the majority of children is the family. A chapter in this text (Chap. 12) is devoted to the assessment of a child's family environment. However, what constitutes a family for a child is becoming increasingly diverse, and the intake can yield some preliminary information on the family structure (e.g., marital status of parents, degree of contact with non-resident parents, other adult caretakers in the home) that provides the assessor with some clues as to the best method of structuring an evaluation of the family context.

Practical Considerations in Designing an Evaluation

In an important clinical endeavor like psychological testing that can have important consequences for a child, one does not like to consider mundane factors such as time and expense in designing the evaluation. Clearly, these factors should not outweigh what is in the best interest of the child being tested. However, sometimes these factors are unavoidable and often expediency is in the best interest of the child. For example, an adolescent who has an impending court date for a juvenile offense may need to have an evaluation completed before this date to help in determining the most appropriate placement and the most appropriate services. One should take care not to be so influenced by expediency that treatment decisions are misguided by poor assessment results. But one must consider what can be meaningfully obtained within the available time frame, and possibly make as part of the outcome of the evaluation a recommendation for the additional testing that might be beneficial as time allows.

How much to weigh cost and time constraints will vary from case to case. However, we feel that one should ask the following two questions in designing any evaluation:

1. What is the essential information needed to answer the referral question(s)?
2. What is the most economical means of obtaining this essential information without compromising the usefulness of information?

To Test or Not to Test

When a child is referred for testing, an important question that should be asked is whether or not an evaluation is in the child's best interest. We feel that simply because an evaluation is requested by someone is not sufficient reason to conduct the evaluation. A professional must make the decision as to whether or not an evaluation is likely to benefit the child or adolescent. Often this question is ignored for financial reasons. If you don't do the evaluation, you don't get paid. However, we feel that a clinical assessor has the ethical obligation to estimate the potential benefit of the evaluation to the child and then convey this determination to the referring agency.

There can be several reasons why an evaluation would not be in a child's best interest. For example, a child's parent may seek multiple evaluations because the parent does not agree with the findings of previous evaluations. We feel that second opinions are not inappropriate in many cases. However, if this is not considered carefully, a child may be subjected to numerous intrusive evaluations that are not necessary and the evaluator may inadvertently reinforce a parent's denial of a child's special needs. Alternatively, the person referring a child or adolescent may have unrealistic expectations from what an evaluation can accomplish, or the reason for the evaluation may be insufficient to justify performing the evaluation. An example that illustrates both of these issues is a child who is referred by a parent to determine his future sexual orientation.

Even if one determines that a child or adolescent may benefit from an evaluation, one must also question whether or not the assessor is the appropriate person to conduct the evaluation. The appropriateness of an assessor may simply be a matter of one's competence, either because of unique characteristics of the child (e.g., age, culture) or because of the specific nature of the referral question. Assessors must hold closely to the principle noted in the Standards for Educational and Psychological Testing published jointly by the American Educational Research Association, American Psychological Association, and National Council on Measurement Education that "test users should not attempt to interpret the scores of test takers whose special needs or characteristics are outside the range of the user's qualifications" (Standard 11.3, p. 114).

In addition to competence, a clinical assessor must also question whether or not personal reasons might prevent him or her from conducting an objective evaluation. For example, an examiner may have a personal relationship with a child or family that might interfere with the ability to objectively administer and interpret tests. Alternatively, the assessor may have personal issues related to the referral problem that might prevent him or her from being able to competently perform the evaluation. For example, a psychologist who himself is dealing with memories of a past sexual abuse may not be able to conduct an evaluation of another sexual abuse victim because he is unable to transcend his own issues related to the abuse. There are no specific guidelines for determining when personal issues would interfere with an evaluation. Our point is to suggest that assessors should routinely question whether or not they are appropriate to conduct an evaluation, and they should consult with colleagues if there is any question regarding their ability to competently conduct the evaluation.

Rapport Building

There is no aspect of the assessment process that is as difficult to define and to teach as the concept of rapport. However, rapport is a critical component of testing children and adolescents (Fuchs & Fuchs, 1986), although it is rarely discussed in child assessment texts (e.g., Achenbach & McConaughy, 1987; Ollendick & Hersen, 1993) or in administration manuals for tests designed for children (see Fuchs, 1987). The *Longman Dictionary of Psychology and Psychiatry* (1984) defined *rapport* as "a warm, relaxed relationship that promotes mutual acceptance, e.g., between therapist and patient, or between teacher and student. Rapport implies that the confidence inspired by the former produces trust and willing cooperation in the latter" (p. 619). To paraphrase and apply this definition to the testing situation, *rapport* refers to the interactions between the assessor and the person being assessed (client) that promote confidence and cooperation in the assessment process. Rapport building is not something that is done at the outset of testing and then forgotten. Instead, it is a process that evolves throughout the entire assessment endeavor (Barker, 1990; Sattler, 1988).

The importance of rapport is not specific to psychological assessment; it is a critical concept in most clinical endeavors. There are several recommendations that can be drawn from other clinical situations that apply equally well to child testing. For example, Phares (1984) described the basic elements of establishing rapport in psychotherapeutic relationships as "having an attitude of acceptance, understanding, and respect for the integrity of the client" (p. 195). Phares goes on to point that this attitude is not synonymous with establishing a state of mutual liking but is more related to a clinician's ability to convey to the client a sincere desire to understand his or her problems, and to help him or her to cope with them. This general attitude of the assessor is the basic component of establishing rapport with the client. As a result, our specific recommendations are designed to foster this attitude in testing situations.

While the importance of rapport is not confined to the psychological assessment of children and adolescents, there are several unique aspects to the assessment of youth that make rapport building a complicated process in this context. First, the clinical assessment of children typically involves many people (e.g., child, parent, and teacher) who have varying levels of understanding of the assessment process, and who possess varying levels of motivation for the assessment. Therefore, the assessor must be skilled in enlisting and fostering the cooperation of many different participants. The issue of motivation is especially salient in the evaluation of youth because children and adolescents are often not self-referred. Children are often referred for evaluations because their behavior causes problems for significant others in their environment (Frick & Kimonis, 2008). Therefore, enlisting their cooperation and trust is a critical, but often difficult, process. Later in this chapter we provide examples of how testing can be presented to children and adolescents in ways that foster the establishment of a working relationship.

A second factor that complicates the development of rapport in testing situations is the presence of severe time limitations. In many, if not most, testing situations the assessor has limited time for rapport building with all participants. Often testing is confined to one or several discrete testing periods and testing starts early in the first session. This is quite different from the many other clinical contexts, such as the psychotherapeutic context, in which there is likely to be more flexibility in the time allowed for developing rapport prior to the initiation of some clinical intervention.

Based on this discussion, it is evident that establishing rapport in the typical assessment situation for children and adolescents involves enlisting the cooperation of *multiple participants* to divulge personal and sometimes distressing information, despite a potential *lack of motivation* and despite the fact that the testing must be completed within a *limited time frame*. It is obvious from this description that rapport building is not always an easy task in clinical assessments of youth. Therefore, it is important to outline the important considerations in the development of rapport in clinical assessments of children and adolescents.

Informed Consent

We view informed consent in two ways in this book. The first, which is the more traditional way, is to view it as a legal and ethical right of the recipients of any psychological service. The assessor has the responsibility of ensuring that informed consent is provided for the assessment. However, we also view informed consent in a second way: as a basic element of rapport building. As discussed previously, a fundamental element in developing rapport is expressing a respect for the individual participating in the evaluation. There is no more basic way of conveying respect than by placing great importance on the informed consent process.

In Chap. 4, we discussed the legal requirements of obtaining informed consent from a child's legal guardian. However, the assessor can communicate a sincere respect for the child's guardian by spending a great deal of time reviewing all the testing procedures in very clear and specific terms, by discussing the limits of confidentiality in sensitive terms, by clearly reviewing the intended uses of the test results, and by allowing and encouraging the parents to ask questions about these issues. In essence, the assessor should convey to the parent that the consent procedures are not just a legal formality, but are intended as the first step in establishing a collaborative effort between the parent and assessor. Also, there is no greater damage to the development of rapport than a parents' *perception* that some procedures were used without his or her full knowledge and consent.

The need to transcend legal requirements is even more important with the child. With the view that minors may not be competent to make decisions regarding their need for certain medical or psychological procedures, like psychological testing, the right to informed consent generally rests with a child's parent or legal guardian. Unfortunately, many assessors take this to mean that a child does not have the right to have procedures explained to him or her in understandable language. Although in some situations we agree that a child may not have the right to refuse participation in an evaluation, we feel that *in all situations*, irrespective of a child's age, the assessor should explain to the child all the procedures that he or she will undergo as part of the testing. Clearly, the degree of depth and sophistication of this explanation should be made in recognition of the possible fears about the evaluation that a child or adolescent might experience and with recognition of his or her varying levels of motivation. Boxes 5.3–5.5 provide examples of how testing procedures can be explained to children and adolescents of various ages in ways that enhance the establishment of rapport.

Discussing testing with the child or adolescent is critical for conveying respect towards the child, and helps enlist the child as a collaborative participant in the process. It reduces the feeling of the child that the testing is being done to him or her rather than for or with him or her. Also, many children arrive for testing with substantial

Box 5.3

Explaining Testing to a 5-Year-Old Boy

We have argued that all children should have testing procedures explained to them in terms that are understandable given their developmental level. This is a crucial aspect of developing rapport with a child. However, many beginning clinical assessors have difficulty describing testing in terms comprehensible to young children and fail to recognize some of the fears and motivations that children bring to the evaluation. The following is an example of an explanation of procedures that is given to a 5-year-old boy referred to a private psychologist for testing.

> "Hello, Johnny. My name is Dr. Test. I'm not the type of doctor you come to when you're sick, like with a stomachache or headache, but I'm the type of doctor who likes to get to know kids better, like how they feel about some things and how they act sometimes. So what I'm going to do today is find out a lot more about you. I'm going to ask you to draw some pictures for me and tell me about them. I also have some pictures and I want you to make up stories about them. And then, I have a bunch of questions about how you feel about certain things that I'm going to help you answer. We will have to work pretty hard together but I think it will be fun, too. We're going to take a lot of breaks and please let me know if you need to stop and go to the bathroom. Now, your mom and dad have already been telling me a lot about you and I'm also going to be talking to your teacher at school. After I do this, I'm going to take what you tell me, and what your parents and teacher tell me and try to get a good picture of what you're like, how you feel about things, all the things you're doing well, and anything you might need help in. And then I will talk to your parents and to you about what I find and let you know if there is anything that I can suggest that might help you."

This explanation is designed to be an example of the types of terms and phrasing that can be used in explaining psychological procedures to very young children. As can be seen from the content of the explanation, we feel that in this age group, one of the most important sources of anxiety is the fear of the unknown. Therefore, we try to let the child know that the procedures will be pretty innocuous (e.g., answering questions, drawing). Obviously the actual content of the description will depend on the procedures that are planned. But we feel strongly that *all* procedures to be used should be explained to the child, albeit in a language that is understandable.

Also, to illustrate the level of explanation, the discourse was presented in a narrative form. In actual practice it is helpful to involve the child in the discussion by asking simple questions (e.g., Do you like to draw?) and encouraging him or her to ask you questions if there is anything he or she does not understand. This helps the child feel more respected and valued in the assessment process. Finally, we often find it helpful in this age group to present this information in the presence of the child's parent(s). When children see that their parents are comfortable with the procedures, they often develop a greater sense of comfort themselves.

---

misconceptions about what the testing will entail (e.g., thinking that the psychologist is going to operate on their brain or that they will be punished for being bad). Simply spending time to clearly review why the child is being tested, what the child should expect during testing, and what will happen with the test results helps to eliminate possible misconceptions and reduce unnecessary anxiety.

Box 5.4

Explaining Testing to a 10-Year-Old Girl

Older, pre-adolescent children often have a better understanding of the basic nature of the testing situation than do younger children. However, the procedures should still be explained in very clear and simple terms to ensure that there are no misconceptions. In this age group, we find that the explanation must be sensitive to the potential threat to a child's self-concept that the testing may present. One of the major emotional tasks during the pre-adolescent period is the development of a sense of mastery and a sense of competence. Testing can be a threat to a child in these areas for several reasons. First, just the term "testing" conveys the possibility of failure. Secondly, the child may have been implicitly or explicitly told that the reason for the testing is to see "what's wrong with you." The explanation of testing in this age group should be sensitive to these issues. Here, we provide a sample explanation to a 10-year-old girl referred for a comprehensive evaluation.

> "Jessica, I want to explain exactly what we are going to be doing together today, and give you a chance to ask me any questions you may have. Your parents were concerned about some of the problems you have been having at school and they wanted to know if there was anything more they could be doing to help you. In order for me to answer this question, I have to find out a lot more about you-what you like to do, how you feel about different things, what things you're good at, what things you might not be so good at. To do this, we are going to do a lot of different things together. First, I am going to ask you to do some reading and math problems with me. Then I will ask you to fill out some questionnaires that will tell me how you feel about different things, how you get along with kids in your class, and how you see your family. Finally, I am going to show you some pictures and ask you to tell me some stories about them. Before we start each of these activities, I will tell you what we're going to do and how to do each thing. I promise to give you a chance to ask me any questions you have about each task. I have already talked to your mother about how things go at home and I am going to ask your teacher to fill out a questionnaire about how she sees you at school. After I get all the information, I should understand you a little better and I will then talk about what I found with you and your parents. Jessica, it is very important that you understand that I'm not looking for things that are wrong with you. My guess is that you are like most kids. You have things that you're good at and some things that you're not so good at, and that there are things you like and other things you don't like. I am just trying to get a good picture of all these different parts of you."

Box 5.5

Explaining Testing to an Adolescent

There are several crucial issues that one must keep in mind when explaining testing to an adolescent. First, adolescents spend a great deal of energy trying to convince people that they are no longer children. Therefore, one must be very careful not to come across as condescending to them. Secondly, because of the importance of peers in adolescence, adolescents are very concerned with fitting in. Coming in for psychological testing may be viewed as a threat to this by making them feel different from other adolescents. Therefore, the explanation should attempt to normalize the testing as much as possible. Thirdly, privacy is

(Continues)

Box 5.5 (Continued)

a major issue for adolescents. In testing, adolescents may be asked many personal questions. They must be warned of these questions and informed as to how the information from the testing will be conveyed to other people. This is very threatening to most adolescents, and the explanation should be sensitive to this issue. Fourth, a majority of adolescents referred for testing do not see the need for such testing and don't want to be there. A major flaw we often see in presenting testing to adolescents is that the assessor tries to cajole the adolescent into being happy to be there and into appreciating the potential benefits of testing. Clearly, the potential benefits of testing should be discussed with the adolescent in an attempt to enhance motivation. However, this often has a minimal effect on motivation, and often one must simply acknowledge to the adolescent that you understand that he or she is not happy about being there but, if you work together, you will get through it quickly and relatively painlessly. The following is a sample explanation of psychological testing provided to a 16-year-old male.

"Jeff, I want to explain what we will be doing today and, please, feel free to ask me any questions about what I say. You probably know that your parents are concerned about your behavior. They have seen some changes in you recently and they want to know if they can do something more to help you. I understand that you are not wild about being here, but if we work together, maybe we can see if there is anything that I can recommend to help you or at least put your parents' minds at ease. But if we're going to get anything out of this we have to work together. I work with a lot of people of your age who don't want to be here at first, but end up getting a lot out of the experience. I will start by just asking you about some of the things that have been going on with you lately to get your view on things. I have already talked to your parents about their views of what's going on. I also have some questionnaires for you to complete about your feelings, your behaviors, and your attitudes. Some of these questions are pretty personal, but they are important for me to get a better understanding of you. After the testing, I will summarize the results in a report and go over it with you and your parents. At that time we can discuss anything that I think may help you."

Building Rapport with the Child

As mentioned previously, the child is often not the one seeking an evaluation but is usually referred by some significant adult who feels that the child or adolescent needs the testing. Therefore, the motivation of the child for the evaluation is often low. Another reason for low motivation is that the child often realizes, or has been explicitly told, that the evaluation is prompted by problems either at home or school. As a result, the child is legitimately concerned about the outcome of the evaluation (i.e., getting into more trouble). In addition, the testing situation is often unique in most children's experiences. Children have had a few similar experiences, and therefore they often have little idea of what to expect in the testing situation. Finally, the many developmental stages that characterize childhood and adolescence imply that assessors must be familiar with development to be able to tailor their rapport-building strategies to the unique needs of children at various stages.

We have already mentioned that rapport building is a process that evolves throughout testing. It starts at the very first contact between the assessor and the child. When an assessor greets a child, the assessor should (1) use a warm, friendly, and interesting tone, (2) be sure to greet the child by name (don't simply greet the child's parents), and (3) introduce him- or herself using his or her title (e.g., Dr., Ms., Mr.). This last recommendation is a subject of considerable debate by practicing psychologists (Barker, 1990). However, we feel that using a title is important in the time-limited, task-oriented assessment situation because it sets the stage that you are a professional (albeit a caring, friendly, and respectful one) who will be working with the child, and not a friend who will play with the child.

After informed consent, many authors recommend a period of time for discussing innocuous and pleasant topics, such as the children's hobbies, pets, friends, or other interests (Barker, 1990). For younger children, some authors even recommend a period of play to allow the children to become more accustomed to the examiner. In our experiences, such rapport-building strategies should be used cautiously and sparingly. For many children, the assessor may be perceived as simply delaying the inevitable by using these strategies. This could have the paradoxical effect of increasing their anticipatory anxiety. In our experience, one of the best rapport-building strategies is to begin the assessment tasks quickly, so that the child begins to realize that the procedures will not be as bad as they imagined.

Periods of play before the evaluation are especially problematic if structured testing is to follow. Young children often have difficulty switching from unstructured to structured tasks (Perry, 1990). Therefore, it is usually best when testing preadolescent children to start with the more structured parts of the evaluation (e.g., rating scales, structured interviews) rather than starting with less structured tasks (e.g., projective drawing tests). This is not only because of the greater difficulty in switching from unstructured to structured tasks, but also because the structured tasks have clearer demand characteristics. That is, it is usually quite clear to children what is expected of them on these tasks and this, in turn, helps the children become more comfortable in a situation that is different from anything they have experienced in thepast.

Box 5.6 provides a summary of some additional rapport-building strategies for use with children that were proposed by Barker (1990) in his book on interviewing children

Building Rapport with the Parent

There are also some unique considerations in building a working relationship with a child's parents. Of course, the importance of rapport with parents will depend on the degree of their involvement in the testing. However, in most situations their involvement will be substantial. Although many evaluations are conducted at the request of a parent, there are also many situations in which a child is referred by others (e.g., school, court), and, in these situations, building rapport with the child's parent is critical. Under these circumstances, the assessor must allow the parent to express his/her views on the need for evaluation prior to the testing process. The assessor need not necessarily agree with these views, but the assessor should convey to the parents a sincere interest in understanding their views in order to build a working relationship with them.

Even for parents who have initiated the referral for testing, the assessor should be aware of the potential threat to a parent's self-esteem that many testing situations present. For many parents, acknowledging that their child might have some type of disability is quite traumatic and can evoke a sense of failure. Also, parents often struggle with guilt blame for

Box 5.6

Rapport-Building Strategies

Barker (1990), in his book on conducting clinical interviews with children and adolescents, discussed several helpful strategies for establishing rapport. These can be summarized as follows:

1. A critical basis for rapport building is an assessor's communication style. The assessor who is able to adopt a warm, friendly, respectful, and interested communication style is more likely to develop a good working alliance with a child.
2. The assessor's physical appearance can also enhance rapport. Overly formal dress can make a child feel ill at ease.
3. Assessors should attempt to conform his or her posture, movements, speed of speech, voice tone and volume, etc. to the style of the person being tested. This should be done sensitively and unobtrusively.
4. Assessors should tailor their vocabularies to match the vocabularies of the person being tested. Few things impede the establishment of rapport as much as repeatedly using words and expressions that are unfamiliar to those with whom you are speaking.
5. Respect the views of those you are testing. This does not necessarily mean agreeing with or approving of the views expressed.
6. Occasionally the assessor should adopt a one-down position. To reduce the intimidation that children sometimes feel with experts, the assessor can sometimes ask a child, from a position of ignorance, about something with which a child has expertise, such as video games, television shows, or soccer.
7. Taking time during the testing to talk of experiences and interests that the assessor and child have in common can also increase the trust between the assessor and the child.

Barker (1990) also emphasizes that the development of rapport is continuous throughout the testing process. "Rapport can always be developed further; the reverse is also possible. Although it is certainly true that once it is well established, rapport can withstand a lot of stress, it nevertheless can be damaged or even destroyed at any time if continuing attention is not paid to maintaining it" (p. 35).

SOURCE: Barker (1990). *Clinical Interviews with Children and Adolescents.* New York: Norton.

their child's problems and may be concerned that testing will confirm their potential role in their child's difficulties. An assessor should be sensitive to these dynamics and allow the parents to express their concerns at some point during the testing. Additionally, the parents should be supported in their role of getting help for their child. For example, an assessor might tell the parents how lucky their child is to have parents who care enough to obtain help for him or her, and not just let things get worse. This helps to reframe the testing situation as one that could increase the parents' self-esteem, rather than one that is a threat to their self-concept.

Several reasons were given for starting with structured tasks in testing children in an effort to enhance rapport. In our experience, the opposite is true in rapport building with parents. Even prior to obtaining specific background information from a parent, it is important to let the parent discuss his or her concerns about the child in an unstructured format. The unstructured clinical interview is discussed in more detail in a later chapter. However, having such an interview at the start of the evaluation conveys to the parent (1) a genuine concern with his or her perceptions of their child's adjustment and (2) that the evaluation will be personalized for the individual child. If parents are immediately asked to fill the rating scales or administer a structured interview as part of a standard evaluation, they often develop the impression that the assessor is more interested in administering tests than in actually understanding their child's needs. As one would expect, such an impression is very damaging to the development of rapport.

Building Rapport with Teachers

It is becoming increasingly clear that evaluations of children must involve information from teachers (Loeber, Green, & Lahey, 1990). The degree of teachers' involvement varies considerably depending on the focus of the evaluation. However, many assessors who are not used to working in school settings find themselves ill-equipped to collaborate with teachers to conduct psychological evaluations (Conoley & Conoley, 1991).

In the introduction to the concept of rapport, we defined the basic ingredient to rapport building as exhibiting an attitude of respect towards the client or informant. Although many psychologists work hard in respecting and developing rapport with parents and children, often this respect is lost when dealing with other professionals, such as teachers. A key to demonstrate this attitude is by respecting the importance of teachers' time. Scheduling phone calls during teacher's planning times, eliminating all but the most essential work for the teacher, and always personally thanking the teacher for his or her efforts in the evaluation are very simple, yet important, rapport-building strategies.

If a teacher is sent assessment material for completion (e.g., rating scales), it is important for the assessor to call the teacher and personally request the teachers' participation in the evaluation, acknowledging and thanking the teacher for his or her efforts, rather than simply sending the material to the teacher via the child, parent, or mail. Such a call is a professional courtesy that greatly enhances the collaborative effort. It sets the tone for the teacher being involved in the evaluation as a valued professional who has much to offer in the assessment of the child.

Conclusions

In this chapter, some non-specifics of the clinical assessment of children were discussed. That is, a successful evaluation is not simply a matter of appropriately administering and interpreting psychological tests. It is also dependent on an assessor's ability to provide an appropriate context in which the testing takes place.

The first major issue discussed was the importance of good planning. A good evaluation is focused and goal-oriented. The purpose of the evaluation and the intended uses of the assessment results will have a major impact on how the assessment is structured. Enough information should be available prior to actual testing so that the assessor has some initial hypotheses to be tested in the evaluation.

The second part of the chapter is focused on rapport-building strategies with all participants in the evaluation. Developing a collaborative, respectful, and trusting working relationship is crucial to a successful evaluation. Being able to develop rapport is a skill that often takes years of practical experience to develop fully. However, in this chapter we have tried to highlight some of the important issues in rapport building with children and adolescents of various ages. We have also tried to make some practical recommendations that address these issues.

Chapter Summary

1. The first step in planning an evaluation is to clarify the reason for referral, both in terms of the purpose of testing and the types of behavior that led to the referral.
2. Two important decisions that a clinical assessor should make prior to starting any evaluation is whether or not a formal evaluation is warranted and whether he or she is the most appropriate person to conduct the evaluation.
3. In addition to competently administering tests, clinical assessors must create an appropriate environment within which the evaluation can take place.
4. Building rapport with a child refers to developing a collaborative and supportive relationship with the child for the purpose of conducting the evaluation.
5. Building rapport with other important people who will be involved in the evaluation (e.g., parents, teachers) is also critical to the assessment process.
6. A thorough and sensitive informed consent procedure can play a major role in showing respect to the child client, and his or her parents and thereby can greatly aid in the establishment of rapport.
7. An explanation of the testing procedures with a child must be sensitive to a large number of motivational and developmental issues.

Part II

Assessment Methods

Chapter 6

Self-Report Inventories

Chapter Questions

- What are the strengths and limitations of self-report measures for child and adolescent assessments?
- What are some of the key differences between omnibus measures and single domain measures?
- How does the MMPI-A differ from its adult counterpart?
- Which of the self-report measures possesses good evidence of content validity?
- What are validity scales and how can they be used to interpret self-report measures?

Omnibus Personality Inventories

The use of self-report inventories with children is a relatively new phenomenon. It was heretofore commonly believed that children could not accurately report on their own feelings, perceptions, and behaviors. As a result, parent and teacher reports have routinely been preferred over the use of self-report inventories in child personality assessment. One of the first popular child assessment instruments, for example, the Personality Inventory for Children (PIC; Wirt et al., 1984), resembled a "junior" MMPI. It included a large item set similar to

P.J. Frick et al., *Clinical Assessment of Child and Adolescent Personality and Behavior*,
DOI 10.1007/978-1-4419-0641-0_6, © Springer Science+Business Media, LLC 2010

the MMPI, and the name conveys similarities to omnibus personality inventories. Yet, the PIC was, and is (PIC-2; Lachar & Gruber, 2001) a *parent* rating scale.

As a result, many of the omnibus scales described in this chapter are relatively new. This is a result of the growing consensus that at least older children and adolescents can provide useful information about their feelings and behavior. However, as with any assessment tool, there are limitations to the reliability, validity, and usefulness of any self-report measure, and these limitations should be taken into account when designing an assessment battery and interpreting its results.

Unfortunately, all of the complexity of using and interpreting omnibus self-report inventories cannot be conveyed in one chapter. Most of the inventories discussed herein have entire volumes devoted to their interpretation. The following discussion serves primarily as an introductory guide for studying the larger literature that is available for an instrument. The eventual user of any of the omnibus inventories discussed will have to spend considerable time with the test manuals and additional readings and seek supervised interpretation practice. What has become more clear in recent research is that despite their relative lack of validity for the assessment of very young children, self-report inventories can provide invaluable information as to the youth's perception of his/her functioning and the factors that ameliorate or exacerbate his/her problems.

Whether or not a self-report inventory has a place in a psychological assessment will depend on many factors, including the client's developmental level, presenting problem, and the purpose of the assessment. This chapter in no way represents an exhaustive review of the self-report inventories available. Instead, we have reviewed what appear to be the most widely used and/or well-researched measures. In addition, although the appropriate uses of self-report measures are highlighted, there are limitations to any assessment technique. For self-report rating scales in particular, one must consider the client's comprehension of items and the potential for response sets including socially desirable response tendencies. The instruments reviewed below vary in the degree to which they have appeared to take these factors into account. Therefore, the burden rests with the clinician to select tools that will answer the referral question in a legitimate, comprehensive, and cost-effective manner (Table 6.1).

Behavior Assessment System for Children Self-Report of Personality (BASC-2-SRP; Reynolds & Kamphaus, 2004)

The Behavior Assessment System for Children, 2nd edition-Self-Report of Personality (BASC-2-SRP; Reynolds & Kamphaus, 2004) is based closely on its predecessor, albeit with some unique features. For example, the BASC-2 includes a college report form for students aged 18–25. Our discussion, however, will focus on the child version (SRP-C) for ages 8–11 and the adolescent version (SRP-A), which is normed for ages 12–21. Interested readers should consult the BASC-2 manual (Reynolds & Kamphaus) for a discussion of the development of the unique college student report version. As with the previous version of this instrument, the BASC-2-SRP is the component of the BASC-2 that attempts to gauge the child's perceptions and feelings about school, parents, peers, and his or her own behavioral problems. The estimated minimum reading level of the SRP is the third grade. The SRP may also be read to children in order to ensure comprehension of the items. According to its authors, it takes approximately 20–30 min to administer.

Scale Content

The SRP includes 16 scales: 12 clinical and 4 adaptive. The scales were developed using a combination of rational, theoretical,

TABLE 6.1 Overview of Self-Report Inventories

Inventory	Ages	Content	Reading Level	Time to Administer	Norm Sample	Reliability	Validity	MI
Behavior Assessment System for Children, 2nd edition (BASC-2; Reynolds & Kamphaus, 2004)	8–11; 12–21; 18–25	139–185 items; Emotional symptoms index, inattention/hyperactivity, internalizing problems, school maladjustment, personal adjustment; 3 validity scales; 12 clinical scales, 4 adaptive scales, 4 optional content scales	3rd grade	20–30 min	E	Internal consistency (good); 4–8 week test–retest (good)	Good relations with similar tools; support for factors	E
Achenbach Youth Self-Report (YSR; Achenbach & Rescorla, 2001)	11–18	112 items; Internalizing, Externalizing, Competence; 8 scales	5th grade	15–20 min	G	Internal consistency (good); 7 month test–retest (moderate); interrater (low to moderate)	Good validity (clinical vs. non-clinical groups); limited info. on relations with other tools	E
Minnesota Multiphasic Personality Inventory-Adolescent (MMPI-A; Butcher et al., 1992)	14–18	478 items; 10 clinical scales; 6 validity scales; 15 content scales; 6 supplementary scales; 28 Harris-Lingoes scales; 3 Si scales	5th–6th grade	90 min	G	Internal consistency; test–retest; content scales better reliability than clinical scales	Item overlap detracts from content validity; scores do not match 4 factor solution found in research	P

(Continues)

TABLE 6.1 (Continued)

Inventory	Ages	Content	Reading Level	Time to Administer	Norm Sample	Reliability	Validity	MI
Conners 3rd Edition, Self-Report (Conners-3; Conners, 2008a)	8–18	59 items; 39-item short form; 3 validity scales, 6 empirical scales, 1 rational scale, 5 *DSM-IV-TR* symptom scales	3rd grade	20 min	E	Internal consistency and test–retest (good)	Good evidence of criterion-related and discriminant validity	E[a]
Personality Inventory for Youth (PIY; Lachar & Gruber, 1994)	9–18	270 items, 80 item screener; 9 clinical scales (several subscales); 4 validity scales	3rd–4th grade	30–60 min	G	Internal consistency; test–retest; good reliability but lower for subscales	Good validity (clinical vs. non-clinical groups); some support for criterion-related validity	G

Note: Norm sample evaluated as E = excellent, G = good; MI = degree of enhancement of muti-informant assessment; E = Excellent, G = Good, P = Poor
[a]We view the Conners-3 as providing an excellent means of assessment of externalizing problems; however, if an extensive assessment of internalizing or learning difficulties is desired, the Conners Comprehensive Behavior Rating Scales (CBRS; Conners, 2008b) is recommended.

and empirical approaches to test development. Based on relatively low reliabilities of some SRP scales on the original BASC and preliminary analyses comparing SRP versions with different response formats, the authors developed the BASC-2-SRP to include both True-False items and Frequency-based items (i.e., Never, Sometimes, Often, Almost Always). Items from the original BASC were reviewed, particularly for reliability and developmental appropriateness. Scales were defined based largely on the original version, items were retained or new items developed based on these definitions, and covariance structure analysis was used to enhance the homogeneity of scale content (Reynolds & Kamphaus, 2004). The SRP includes scales that are typical of self-report measures (e.g., anxiety, depression), as well as some that are relatively unique (e.g., self-reliance, locus of control; see scale definitions in Table 6.2). The BASC-2 system also includes critical items that indicate clinically significant problems that warrant further follow-up assessment.

Five composites were constructed for the SRP using factor analysis: Emotional Symptoms Index; Inattention/Hyperactivity; Internalizing Problems; Personal Adjustment; and School Problems. The Inattention/Hyperactivity composite includes the Attention Problems and Hyperactivity scales. The School Maladjustment composite includes the Attitude Toward School and Attitude Toward Teacher scales. The Personal Adjustment composite assesses self-perceived personal strengths and includes the four adaptive scales (i.e., Relations with Parents, Interpersonal Relations, Self-esteem, and Self-reliance). The Internalizing composite consists of the remaining six scales (i.e., Atypicality, Locus of Control, Social Stress, Anxiety, Depression, and Sense of Inadequacy) The ESI represents the scores for the six scales with the highest loadings on an unrotated first factor (i.e., Social Stress, Anxiety, Depression, Sense of Inadequacy, Self-esteem reversed scored, and Self-reliance reverse scored). According to the authors, this index is "the most global indicator of serious emotional disturbance" (p. 81).

An additional feature, new to the adolescent version of the BASC-2-SRP, is the inclusion of four content scales: Anger Control, Ego Strength, Mania, and Test Anxiety. These scales were formed via a combination of rational and empirical methods and include some items that are part of other SRP scales and other items that are not part of another scale. These scales are considered optional and are not part of the hand scoring of the BASC-2 (Reynolds & Kamphaus, 2004). Obviously, research is needed regarding the usefulness of these scales in clinical assessments, but they may very well represent important constructs heretofore not assessed.

Administration and Scoring

The SRP is available in three administration formats: a scannable form, a carbonless hand-scored form, and a computer-scorable form. The SRP has a reasonable administration time, given that there are 139 items on the SRP-C and 176 items on the SRP-A. Although efforts were made to keep the item stems brief and at a third grade reading level, some young people may still have difficulty using the SRP. This and other self-report inventories are not recommended for use with children with significant cognitive deficits or severe reading problems. Oral administration or the use of the available audiotape for the SRP is possible, but the child with comprehension problems may still have a great deal of difficulty with this procedure.

Validity Scales

The BASC-2-SRP includes three validity scales, as well as two indexes that alert the clinician to response patterns or inconsistency in responses (i.e., the Response Pattern Index and Consistency Index, respectively). The three validity scales are

TABLE 6.2 BASC-2-SRP Scale Definitions

Scale	Definition
Anxiety	Feelings of nervousness, worry, and fear; the tendency to be overwhelmed by problems
Attention Problems	Tendency to be easily distracted and unable to concentrate more than momentarily
Attitude to School	Feelings of alienation, hostility, and dissatisfaction regarding school
Attitude to Teachers	Feelings of resentment and dislike of teachers; beliefs that teachers are unfair, uncaring, or overly demanding
Atypicality	The tendency toward bizarre thoughts or other thoughts and behaviors considered "odd"
Depression	Feelings of unhappiness, sadness, and dejection; a belief that nothing goes right
Hyperactivity	Tendency to report being overly active, rushing through work or activities, and acting without thinking
Interpersonal Relations	The perception of having good social relationships and friendships with peers
Locus of Control	The belief that rewards and punishments are controlled by external events or other people
Relations with Parents	A positive regard for parents and a feeling of being accepted by them
Self-Esteem	Feelings of self-esteem, self-respect, and self-acceptance
Self-Reliance	Confidence in one's ability to solve problems; a belief in one's personal dependability and decisiveness
Sensation Seeking	The tendency to take risks and seek excitement
Sense of Inadequacy	Perceptions of being unsuccessful in school, unable to achieve one's goals, and generally inadequate
Social Stress	Feelings of stress and tension in personal relationships; a feeling of being excluded from social activities
Somatization	The tendency to be overly sensitive to, experience, or complain about relatively minor physical problems and discomforts

NOTE: From Reynolds & Kamphaus (2004).

patterned after those found in the Minnesota Multiphasic Personality Inventory (MMPI) tradition (see below). These scales provide a variety of checks on the validity of a child's results. The *F Index* is designed to indicate if a respondent may have answered in an overly negative (i.e., "fake bad") manner. The *L Index* does the opposite in that it evaluates a tendency to respond in an overly positive manner. The *V Index* on the SRP consists of nonsensical items (e.g., "I have never been to sleep") that, if endorsed, would likely indicate carelessness or lack of cooperation. The Response Pattern Index (available in the computer scoring program) assesses the degree to which an item response is the same as the response to the previous item. For example, marking "True" for 15 items in a row would yield a higher number in this Index and would suggest that the respondent indicated "True" regardless of item content. The Consistency Index (also available in the computer scoring program) is based on response patterns to items that should be answered similarly. The authors also point out that the change to a mixture of True-False and Likert-type response formats on the new version of the SRP may also help safeguard against response sets (Reynolds & Kamphaus, 2004). It is still quite possible, however, to have the SRP invalidated by a response set or lack of cooperation. The validity indexes should be examined at the outset of interpretation; further, the clinician should examine for himself/herself response patterns that do not seem to fit the other evidence provided about a case. In particular, a child or adolescent might present himself/herself in an unrealistically favorable light, given referral concerns (i.e., that is, nearly all T-scores on the clinical scales are below 50; see Box 6.1).

Box 6.1

An Example of Fake Good Response Set

Self-report inventories, despite the best efforts of test developers, always remain susceptible to response sets. In the following case example, the BASC-2-SRP was utilized.

Bethany is a 14-year-old girl who was admitted to the inpatient psychiatric unit of a general hospital with a diagnosis of Major Depression following threats of suicide. Bethany's parents reportedly divorced two years ago. She currently lives with her mother and sees her father about once a month. Bethany does not have any siblings. Her mother reported that Bethany tends to isolate herself at home and seems sad and irritable most of the time. Bethany is currently in the eighth grade, and her school attendance during this year has been poor. She has been suspended from school on numerous occasions this year, including for getting into fights with peers, refusing to follow teachers' directions, and damaging school property. Her grades are reportedly poor, although her mother indicated that she used to make mostly "As" and "Bs" until this year. In addition, it was reported that Bethany has a history of problems concentrating at school.

Bethany was talkative during the diagnostic interview, yet it appeared that she was trying to portray herself in a favorable light, as she endorsed very few symptoms. When asked about hobbies, for example, she said that she liked to read. When questioned further, however, she could not name a book that she had read.

According to her mother, Bethany's family history is significant for depression on both her maternal and paternal side. Bethany's father reportedly had difficulty in school.

Bethany's results show evidence of a social desirability response set. On the L-scale of the SRP, Bethany obtained a raw score of 12 which is in the Extreme Caution range. Furthermore, all but one of her clinical scale scores were lower than the normative T-score mean of 50, and all of her adaptive scale scores were above the normative mean of 50. In other words, the SRP results suggest that Bethany is well-adjusted which is inconsistent with her reported current functioning and background information.

This example clearly indicates the need to consider all evidence gathered rather than strictly relying on the results of any one assessment strategy. Her SRP scores were:

Scale	T-Score
Clinical Scales	
Attitude to School	43
Attitude to Teachers	39
Attention Problems	44
Hyperactivity	40
Sensation Seeking	39
Atypicality	40
Locus of Control	38
Somatization	37
Social Stress	40
Anxiety	32
Depression	42
Sensation Seeking	51
Sense of Inadequacy	42
Adaptive Scales	
Relations with Parents	51
Interpersonal Relations	56
Self-Esteem	55
Self-Reliance	59

Norming

The SRP was normed on a national sample of 1,500 children aged 8–11 and 1,900 adolescents aged 15–18. Equal numbers of boys and girls were included within each age group (i.e., 8–11; 12–14; 15–18). Based on the occurrence of age group differences on many subscales, these age groups were used in the development of T-scores (i.e., separate T-score distributions were used for 8–11-year olds from 12–14-year olds). Reynolds and Kamphaus (2004) report that "Within each sex at each age grouping, the General norm samples were matched to targeted US population estimates taken from the March 2001 *Current Population Survey* (Current Population Survey, 2001)" (p. 116–117). The matched variables were socioeconomic status, race/ethnicity variable and geographic region. The authors also considered the presence of emotional and behavioral problems in the General norm sample relative to the proportion of youth with such problems in the general population.

The SRP offers clinical norms for a sample of 577 children and 950 adolescents selected from an unspecified number of special education classrooms and mental health settings throughout the United States. Data presented by the authors show good correspondence to the general United States population for the General norm group on the demographic variables considered. In addition, the Clinical norm group showed variability in race/ethnicity, geographic region, and age for each category (i.e., Learned Disability, ADHD, other; Reynolds & Kamphaus, 2004). As with the previous version of the SRP, separate gender norms were also devised. The purpose of this procedure was to reduce any sex differences in T-scores on the various scales and composites. Such norms may be of interest if the clinician wants to consider the severity of a child's problems relative to others of the same sex. However, in most assessment situations, the question is regarding the degree of problems relative to the overall population of same-aged children, which would suggest the use of norms that include both boys and girls (Reynolds & Kamphaus, 2004).

Reliability

The reliability of the SRP scales is good as indicated by a variety of methods. Median internal consistency coefficients are generally in the .80s (see Table 6.3). Test-retest coefficients taken between 4 and 8 weeks later are generally in the .70s. As shown in Table 6.3, the lowest internal consistency

TABLE 6.3 BASC-2-SRP Median Internal Consistency Coefficients

Scale	Coefficient
Anxiety	0.86
Attention Problems	0.78
Attitude to School	0.82
Attitude to Teachers	0.79
Atypicality	0.83
Depression	0.86
Hyperactivity	0.76
Interpersonal Relations	0.79
Locus of Control	0.78
Relations with Parents	0.87
Self-Esteem	0.82
Self-Reliance	0.70
Sensation Seeking	0.70
Sense of Inadequacy	0.79
Social Stress	0.83
Somatization	0.67
Median	0.80
Composites School Problems	0.85
Inattention/Hyperactivity	0.84
Internalizing Problems	0.96
Personal Adjustment	0.89
Emotional Symptoms Index	0.94

was for the Somatization scale, which may make sense in that this scale consists of physical symptoms which may not be highly interrelated.

Validity

The BASC-2 manual provides an extensive report of exploratory and confirmatory factor analyses of the SRP items. Three factors were initially found, with Attention Problems and Hyperactivity loading on the Internalizing Problems factor; however, a four-factor solution with these two scales included as a separate factor was judged superior. This factor structure is shown in Table 6.4. The school maladjustment factor remains a relatively unique contribution of the BASC self-report. The personal adjustment factor is also unique in that it provides a multidimensional assessment of adaptation or potential strengths. The implications of this composite for long-term prognosis are unclear, however.

Table 6.4 BASC-2-SRP Factors and Scale Members

School Maladjustment
Attitude to School
Attitude to Teachers
Sensation Seeking (adolescent only)
Internalizing Problems
Anxiety
Depression
Locus of Control
Sense of Inadequacy
Somatization
Social Stress
Personal Adjustment
Relations with Parents
Interpersonal Relations
Self-Esteem
Self-Reliance
Inattention/Hyperactivity
Attention Problems
Hyperactivity

The criterion-related validity of the SRP was evaluated by correlating it with the Achenbach Youth Self-Report, the Conners-Wells Adolescent Self-report Scale, Children's Depression Inventory, Revised Children's Manifest Anxiety Scale. Notably, research on the correlations between the adolescent version of the BASC-2 and the MMPI-A has not yet been conducted.

In general, the SRP scales correlated highly (i.e., r = .65 and higher) with analogous scales from the Achenbach Youth Self-report, whereas the correlations were generally moderate between the SRP-A and the Conners-Wells Adolescent Self-report Scale. Interestingly, the Depression scale of the SRP showed only modest correlations with the Children's Depression Inventory subscales and total score (i.e., r = .09–.42) for the child version of the SRP. However, the adolescent version of the SRP demonstrated much more congruence with the correlation coefficients ranging from .39 to .69. The Anxiety scale of the SRP demonstrated generally moderate correlations with the Revised Children's Manifest Anxiety Scale (i.e., r = .31 to .60 for the SRP-C; r = .33 to .49).

The original BASC was the focus of a number of investigations of the correlates of its scales in varied populations and for varied purposes (e.g., basic research questions on child functioning; treatment outcome research; see Kamphaus & Frick, 2005 for a review). However, to date, very few such investigations have used the BASC-2 system. The BASC-2 manual provides initial results on the correlates of the SRP scales; however, much more research is needed, particularly with clinical populations to help provide further understanding of the information garnered from these scales.

Interpretation

Although the composites of the SRP have some factor-analytic evidence to support their validity, there is little evidence as to the validity and utility of the composites. The composites may very well provide parsimonious and clinically relevant information, but such studies simply have not been conducted yet. In the BASC-2 manual, the authors provide results indicating that the Internalizing Composite and Emotional Symptoms Index show morderate to strong correlations with virtually all scales and composites from the Achenbach Youth Self-report. The Inattention-Hyperactivity composite showed correlations with the ADHD-oriented scales on the Achenbach and on the Conners-Wells Adolescent Self-report Scale that were $r = .54$ and higher. However, given the relative lack of research to date and the difficulty in interpreting these composites given their varied content (see Table 6.4), until further research studies are available, initial efforts at SRP interpretation should focus on the scale level. Examples of such interpretations are provided in Box 6.2. The scales of the BASC-2, and by extension, the original BASC, are better understood because the scale contents have some rational, theoretical, and research basis.

Many items from the original BASC-SRP were retained or slightly altered for the BASC-2-SRP (see Reynolds & Kamphaus, 2004), which lends some confidence in scale interpretation for the clinician with experience using the previous version. Item-level factor-analytic results provide one empirical clue to the meaning of SRP scales. Some of the items with the most substantial factor loadings on each scale are identified in Table 6.5. These symptoms can be linked to background information in order to interpret SRP results with greater certainty. However, the elevations of SRP scales may also lead the clinician to follow-up on issues that might not have been raised during the gathering of background information.

We propose the following steps in interpreting the SRP (which can be applied to other omnibus rating scales as well: (1) check validity scales; (2) check critical items if available; (3) determine which scales are elevated; (4) examine the items that appeared to lead to scale elevations.

Some caution is needed in keeping a focus on interpretation at the scale level. In particular, scales may have intuitive appeal and some relevant content, but questionable reliability would hamper the validity of interpretations garnered based on unreliable scales. The reliability estimates shown in Table 6.3 can help a clinician gauge the level of confidence in scale-level interpretations for the BASC-2-SRP.

Strengths and Weaknesses

The BASC-2-SRP is a potentially useful tool in child and adolescent assessment. The BASC-2-SRP has numerous strengths that make it a viable option for use with children and adolescents. Notable strengths include:

1. A broader age range than is typically available for omnibus inventories designed to obtain self-report from children.
2. Unique scales that are relevant to the milieus of children, such as attitude toward teachers and school and parent-child relations
3. A normative sample that is well-described and seems appropriately reflective of the US population as of 2001.
4. Good reliability estimates (see Reynolds & Kamphaus, 2004)
5. Ease of administration and scoring.
6. Items account for heterogeneity of behaviors and symptoms within domains (McMahon & Frick, 2005).

Box 6.2

A Sample Case Illustrating the Interpretation of the BASC-2-SRP

Farrah is a 14-year-old high school freshman who was recently discharged from a psychiatric inpatient unit, where she was hospitalized for suicidal statements and severe cutting behaviors.

Farrah presented for the evaluation with depressed mood and flat affect. She cried several times during the evaluation. She complained about her difficulty getting along with her mother and the fact that she rarely hears from her father. Farrah reportedly had behavioral problems at school since a very young age and tends to interact with peers of whom her mother does not approve. She has had a recent increase in physical complaints and has missed several days of school this year because of those complaints.

Farrah's BASC-2-SRP results were consistent with background information: T-scores and brief descriptions of her results for elevated scales are below

Depression 80

This finding is consistent with observations during the evaluation and background information suggesting recent suicidality and increased anhedonia.

Sense of Inadequacy 74

Farrah expressed a lack of confidence about her ability to do well in school and succeed in other tasks. Her grades this year have been mostly "Ds" and "Fs," and she has a history of getting into trouble at school. However, her measured intellectual functioning and academic achievement are in the High Average range, suggesting that her lack of confidence regarding schoolwork may be unrealistic.

Attention Problems 68

Farrah's reports of difficulty concentrating on the BASC-2 are consistent with her reported problems concentrating in general and her relative inattentiveness during test.

Attitude to School 74

Farrah appears to have low self-efficacy regarding school, and she reports that school is boring.

Attitude to Teacher 71

During interview, Farrah described her teachers as uncaring and as having unrealistic expectations.

Locus of Control 76

During an interview, she reported that she is unfairly blamed for things at home and at school and that her mother's expectations are too high – reports that are consistent with her reports on the BASC-2.

Somatization 86

Farrah reportedly complains of nausea and headaches frequently. These complaints appear to be independent of her anti-depressant medication regimen and also seem to be a strategy for her to avoid going to school.

Social Stress 75

Farrah reported that she usually feels uncomfortable around others, including people her own age. She also reported feeling lonely most of the time for the last two years.

Relations with Parents 28

This adaptive scale score is low and fits with Farrah's long history of parent-child enmity.

Self-Esteem 30

Farrah views herself as less attractive than others and does not see herself as having any particular strengths.

TABLE 6.5 SRP Key Symptoms as Indicated by Items with the Highest Factor Loadings per Scale

Scale	Key Symptoms
Anxiety	Nervousness, being bothered by little things, worry, fear
Attention Problems	Trouble paying attention, getting in trouble for not paying attention
Attitude to School	Not caring about school, feelings of wanting to quit school, expressions of school hatred, expressions of boredom at school
Attitude to Teachers	Feeling that teachers are unfair, feeling that teacher is not proud of him/her, report that teacher gets mad at him/her for no reason
Atypicality	Hearing voices/things that others cannot, feeling like someone is watching, seeing things.
Depression	Feeling that does nothing right and that life is getting worse, feeling that nothing goes his/her way.
Hyperactivity	Is told by others to be still, having trouble sitting still, feeling like has to move around
Interpersonal Relations	Feeling that nobody likes respondent (reverse scored), feeling that others hate to be with him/her (reverse scored), being made fun of by others (reverse scored)
Locus of Control	Complains of being blamed for things that he or she can't help or didn't do, people get mad at respondent for no reason
Relations with Parents	Parents listen to what respondent says, parents are proud of him/her, parents trust him/her
Self-Esteem	Wishes he/she were different (reverse scored), respondent likes the way he or she looks
Self-Reliance	Says that he or she is dependable and is good at making decisions
Sensation Seeking	Likes it when dared to do something, likes to ride in a car going fast
Sense of Inadequacy	Fails even when trying hard, wants to do be better but is unable, has difficulty keeping mind on school work
Social Stress	Feels left out, feels that others find things wrong with him/her, people find things wrong with him/her
Somatization	Complains of stomach upsets, nausea, and dizziness

7. Availability of a range of derived scores and norms for general, clinical, and gender-referenced samples.
8. Inclusion of validity scales that are intuitive.
9. Expanded, user-friendly manual.
10. A clear link between teacher and parent rating scales (BASC-2-PRS and BASC-2-TRS) which enhances its use in multi-informant assessment.

To date, notable weaknesses of the BASC-2-SRP are:

1. Lack of research regarding this version of the BASC and the improvements made from the original BASC-SRP
2. Limited criterion-related validity evidence, particularly for the adaptive scales
3. Lack of case studies in the manual
4. Lack of validity evidence for the validity scales
5. An excessive number of Self-Esteem scale items that deal with self-perceptions of personal appearance which is also a concern raised about the previous version of the SRP (Hoza, 1994)

Achenbach System of Empirically Based Assessment Youth Self-Report (YSR; Achenbach & Rescorla, 2001)

The Youth Self-Report (SRP; Achenbach & Rescorla, 2001) is one component of the larger set of assessment instruments offered within the Achenbach System of Empirically Based Assessment that includes a parent rating scale, a teacher rating scale, an observation scale, and other measures. The YSR is designed for ages 11 through 18, and obtains adolescents' reports about their own competencies and problems in a format similar to that of the parent CBCL and teacher TRF, discussed in the next chapter. As with their predecessors, the most recent measures in the Achenbach system have considerable content overlap, which can be both an advantage and disadvantage of this system, depending on what the clinician is seeking from behavioral rating scales.

An additional form covers the ages of 18–30 entitled the Young Adult Self-Report (YASR; Achenbach, 1997). The YASR content is similar to that of the YSR with noteworthy differences such as scales for substance use and some unique adaptive functioning scales (e.g., Friends, Education, Job, etc.). In light of the developmental periods of focus in this text, the YASR will not be discussed in detail here, but an introduction may be found at http://www.aseba.org/products/yasr.html.

Scale Content

Composite scores reflecting externalizing and internalizing dimensions and a total composite are offered. The following clinical scales contribute to these composites.

Withdrawn/Depressed- preferring to be alone, shy, sulks, sad, lacking energy, etc.

Somatic Complaints- nausea, headaches, dizziness, etc.

Anxious/Depressed- crying, fears, nervous, suicidal ideation, etc.

Rule-Breaking Behavior- lying, substance abuse, truancy, stealing, etc.

Aggressive Behavior- teasing others, arguing, fighting, destruction of property, etc.

Included in the Total Composite but not the Internalizing or Externalizing composites are the following:

Social Problems- jealous of others, teased by others, clumsy, etc.

Thought Problems- strange behaviors, hoarding objects, sleeping less, hallucinatory experiences, etc.

Attention Problems- failing to finish assignments, immature, impulsivity, daydreaming, etc.

Scales referred to as Social Competence are also included that assess participation in a variety of activities (e.g., sports) and social interactions (e.g., friendships).

The clinical scales are empirically-derived via factor analysis, and the competence scales are rationally derived. Critical items (e.g., harming self, setting fires, etc.) are also available on this version of the YSR. In addition, six DSM-Oriented scales are available for the YSR. These scales were formed based on psychiatrists' impressions of items (see Achenbach, Dumenci, & Rescorla, 2001) that theoretically map on to the DSM-related domains being assessed (i.e., Affective Problems, Anxiety Problems, Somatic Problems, Attention/Hyperactivity Problems, Oppositional Defiant Problems, Conduct Problems). Research has supported the structure of the syndrome scales of the YSR across over 20 cultures (Ivanova et al., 2007).

Administration and Scoring

The YSR is designed to be self-administered and requires approximately 15–20 min (Achenbach & Rescorla, 2001). The YSR uses a three choice response format: "Not True, Somewhat/Sometimes True, and Very True or Often True." Some items also provide space for additional information such as, for example, "Describe:" following "I store up too many things I don't need."

Templates are used for hand-scoring, and computer scoring is also available. An integrative computer program can be used to compare results for several raters (e.g., a parent, two teachers, and the YSR), and this option is discussed in great detail by Achenbach and Rescorla (2001). The level of comparability facilitates the study of inter-rater agreement in clinical or research settings and aids in clinical interpretation of converging evidence and discrepancies in reports of the child's functioning.

Norming

The design of the YSR norming sample attempted to mimic the national population of school children for ages 11 through 18 in terms of SES, geographic region, and ethnicity. The sample included 1,057 youth, 52% of whom were boys. Children who had reports of mental health, substance abuse, or special education services were excluded, thus making this a "normal" sample rather than a "normative sample. Most participants (i.e., 53%) were from a middle SES background, whereas 16% were from lower SES homes. The sample was 60% White, 20% African American, 8% Latino, and 11% Mixed or Other. From these statistics, both African Americans and individuals identifying as Latino(a) appear to be underrepresented (Current Population Survey, 2001). Approximately 40% of participants were from the southern part of the United States with the Northeast, Midwest, West each being represented by approximately 20% of the sample participants (see Achenbach & Rescorla, 2001).

The derived T-scores for the YSR are normalized, which results in changing the shape of the raw score distribution (i.e., reducing skewness). Furthermore, the T-score distributions are truncated, which limits the range of low scores on the clinical scales and high scores on the competence scales. For example, T-scores for the clinical scales were not allowed to be articulated below a value of 50. The transformation to reduce skewness and truncated score range both serve to make the T-score distribution for the YSR different from original sample results. The intent of this approach is to aid in interpretation of strengths and difficulties across domains. However, this lack of reflection of sample characteristics in the T-scores makes them of dubious value for research purposes in particular. For most research questions, raw scores would likely be more appropriate than normalized T-scores.

Reliability

Internal consistency estimates are reasonable for the clinical scales falling between .71 and .89. The internal consistencies of the composites are all above .90. Internal consistency estimates are somewhat lower for the competence scales (see Achenbach & Rescorla, 2001).

Short-term (i.e., approximately one-week interval) test-retest coefficients are generally good, with only the Withdrawn/Depressed scale having a coefficient below .70. Seven-month test-retest coefficients were adequate with coefficients generally in the .50 range. Coefficients for the Withdrawn/Depressed scale and Somatic Complaints scale were somewhat lower.

Validity

The YSR manual does not report evidence of criterion-related validity, particularly in regards to the correspondence between the YSR and other measures of emotional and behavioral functioning.

Some differential validity data are presented, with the scales of the YSR consistently differentiating between clinic-referred and non-referred youth. Exceptions to this differential validity were the

DSM-Oriented Anxiety Problems and Somatic Problems scales. The ability of the YSR to differentiate among clinical groups is not addressed. Achenbach and Rescorla (2001) indicate that differential validity is the driving force behind content selection for the current YSR and its predecessors. The most recent YSR has six items that differ from the items in the previous YSR. Generally speaking, the validity evidence reported in the manual concerning the YSR is minimal. However, the previous version of the YSR enjoys a great deal of validity evidence from independent researchers. In addition, in light of the close item correspondence between the two versions, one can surmise that support for the validity of the earlier YSR can be taken as providing some support for the current YSR, particularly the problem scales.

A study by Thurber and Hollingsworth (1992) compared YSR results with the results of several other measures (e.g., California Personality Inventory and Beck Depression Inventory) in a factor-analytic investigation. The sample for this study included 102 adolescent inpatients. Support for the existence of the internalizing and externalizing dimensions was found, as these factors converged with measures of similar constructs to form recognizable factors. Of interest was an additional finding that the Externalizing Scale may be affected by a tendency to respond in a socially desirable way and deny problems. The Internalizing Scale also showed some sensitivity to response sets in that it was affected somewhat by minimizing symptoms (Thurber & Hollingsworth, 1992). Brown (1999) likewise found that "high-risk" adolescents tended to underreport behavior problems when school records and police reports were used as external criteria. Adolescent reports tended to agree with other reports for "more positively oriented items." These findings should be taken into account when interpreting self-report results and should be combined with corroborating evidence in drawing conclusions.

In contrast, Sourander, Helstelae, and Helenius (1999) found that Finnish adolescents reported significantly more problems than their parents, and girls reported more distress, especially internalizing problems, than boys. These authors concluded that many adolescents may not be receiving appropriate mental health services because their problems go unrecognized by their parents.

A criterion-related validity study by Handwerk, Friman, and Larzelere (2000) compared the YSR to the NIMH Diagnostic Interview Schedule for Children (DISC). They compared DISC and YSR results to behavior in a treatment program and, generally speaking, found no differences between diagnostic groups formed by using either instrument. Similar results have also been found for the YSR in comparison to the DISC Version 2.1 (Morgan & Cauce, 1999).

More validity studies exist for various cultural groups on the previous version of the YSR. Reliability and factorial validity of the YSR have been found to be comparable to North American findings in the Netherlands (de Groot, Koot, & Verhulst, 1996), Switzerland (Steinhausen & Metzke, 1998), Japan (Kuramoto et al. 1999), and Spain (Abad, Forns, Amador, & Martorell, 2000).

Research has led to the conclusion, given that sex differences appear very consistently on the YSR, that sex is a more important consideration in predicting psychopathology than demographic factors such as age or nationality (Steinhausen & Metzke, 1998). However, unlike the teacher and parent report measures of the Achenbach system, the YSR does not include gender-specific norms.

A predictive validity study of the previous YSR was conducted in Finland, where 121 adolescents were administered the YSR at age 14 or 15 and followed up to ages 20 and 21 (Aronen, Teerikangas, &

Kurkela, 1999). YSR problems were good predictors of adult symptomatology. Of equal interest are the findings that internalizing symptoms were better predictors and that self-report was more predictive than parent report. Results such as these specifically support the practical utility of the YSR, and they suggest that self-report technology should be used with all children and adolescents with adequate reading comprehension.

Interpretation

The Achenbach manual provides some case studies, yet it does not provide interpretive guidance. This omission is remedied to some extent by the existence of other articles on the YSR and by its amenability to general interpretive approaches such as those described earlier in this chapter.

A strength of the Achenbach approach to scale construction is the ease with which interpretations can be made across informants because of the close item correspondence on the different forms. As mentioned above, Achenbach and Rescorla (2001) detail the approach by which statistical comparisons across informants may be made. To the extent that informants agree on the presence of a problem, the clinician may be more confident that a problem warranting attention exists.

However, it is possible to be too heavily influenced by indexes of agreement in the interpretive process. For example, one might require agreement across raters to make diagnostic or other decisions. We prefer to consider each rater as a valuable source of information that may be diagnostically or otherwise valuable for case conceptualization in its own right, when combined with other information. To illustrate, if a clinician requires parental agreement for a self-report finding, a child or adolescent may be denied needed services (Sourander et al., 1999). Youth may be rich and valid sources of information about their emotional and behavioral functioning (Aronen et al., 1999; Barry et al., in press).

Convergence across informants has merits for answering a referral question and making recommendations. However, we also hold to the philosophy that different raters make unique contributions to the understanding of a child's referral difficulties (see Chap. 15) and that disagreement among informants is not necessarily indicative of a measurement problem.

Strengths and Weaknesses

The YSR has several strengths:

1. Brief administration time
2. A large research base on its closely-related predecessor
3. Research conducted with individuals representing many cultures and norms from a number of cultural groups
4. A large base of experienced users
5. Considerable item overlap with its parent and teacher report counterparts, which aids in cross-informant interpretation
6. A helpful Web site with information for administration, purchasing, interpretation, and user discussion is available at http://www.aseba.org/products/ysr.html

Weaknesses of the YSR include:

1. Little assessment of school-related problems
2. Limited assessment of adaptive competencies
3. The absence of validity scales
4. Limited construct validity evidence to date for the current YSR.
5. Direct comparisons of norm sample demographics to US population are not provided; however, African Americans and Latino(a)s appear to be under-represented.

Minnesota Multiphasic Personality Inventory-Adolescent (MMPI-A; Butcher et al., 1992)

The Minnesota Multiphasic Personality Inventory-Adolescent (MMPI-A; Butcher et al.) has strong roots in the original work of Hathaway and McKinley (1940), and the authors of MMPI-A tried to maintain continuity with the original work (Butcher et al.). This objective was achieved, as all of the clinical and validity scales were retained. In addition, the MMPI-A includes content scales (discussed below) which may be useful for addressing many clinical questions of interest. The MMPI-A is designed for youth aged 14–18.

Scale Content

Knowledge of the history, rationale, psychometric properties, and item content of the MMPI-A clinical scales is important for proper interpretation. Consequently, each of the featured clinical scales is discussed in turn.

Scale 1, Hs: Hypochondriasis. Items for this scale were originally developed to identify respondents with a history of symptomatology characteristic of hypochondriasis (Butcher et al., 1992). Items of this scale assess topics such as nausea, vomiting, upset stomach, sleep problems, chest pain, numbness, muscle twitching, bodily tenderness, dizziness, weakness, and lack of general feeling of wellness.

Scale 2, D: Depression. Hathaway and McKinley (1942) described this measure as an index of general dissatisfaction with one's life, including feelings of discouragement, hopelessness, and low morale. Item content includes appetite changes, health worries, anhedonia, work problems, tension, constipation, increased swearing, concentration problems, sleep problems, withdrawal, teasing animals, low self-confidence, low self-esteem, worry at bedtime, crying easily, decreased reading comprehension, weight change, and impaired memory, among other things. The item content of this scale is diverse, reaching far beyond diagnostic criteria for depression such as those included in the *DSM* and likely contributes to mediocre internal consistency reliability coefficients.

Scale 3, Hy: Hysteria. According to Butcher et al. (1992), this scale consists of 60 items that were originally selected to identify individuals who respond to stress with hysterical reactions that include sensory or motor disorders without an organic basis. Some of the item content includes poor appetite, fatigue, cold extremities, decreased work productivity, nausea and vomiting, urges to curse, poor concentration, disturbed sleep, health concerns, chest pain, unhappiness, difficulty persuading others, muscle twitching, irritability, worry about contracting diseases, dysfunctional relationships with family members, concern about others' opinion, and dislike of school. Like D (scale 2), this item pool is very diverse, resulting in mediocre internal consistency coefficients. It should also be noted that the first three scales of the MMPI-A share considerable item overlap.

Scale 4, Pd: Psychopathic Deviate. This scale was originally constructed based on the responses of individuals with histories of lying, stealing, sexual promiscuity, and alcohol abuse (Butcher et al., 1992). Furthermore, high scores on this scale are associated with family, legal, and school difficulties (Butcher et al.). Item content includes loss of interest in daily activities, a desire to leave home, feeling misunderstood, feeling used, poor concentration, having unusual experiences, history of trouble because of sexual behavior, history of stealing, unhappiness, disapproval by family members, winning arguments, inability to tolerate ridicule, regretting actions, admissions of misbehavior, history of school disciplinary action, feeling like someone is out to get him/her, and weight changes. For the most part, this is the first scale with item content that is distinctive from the first three.

Scale 5, Mf Masculinity-Femininity. This scale was originally developed on a sample of adult men, described by Hathaway (1956) as "male sexual inverts" (Butcher et al., 1992). Presumably, males with high scores are more feminine, and women with clinically significant scores are thought to have more masculine interests. Item content includes topics such as lack of interest in mechanics magazines, reluctance to incriminate oneself, a desire to be of the opposite gender, interest in love stories and poetry, sensitive feelings, lack of interest in forest ranger work, being a soldier or hunter, expressing the need to argue to make a point, attending few parties, dislike for wagering, interest in gardening and cooking, maintaining a diary, fear of snakes, worry, and talks about sex. This scale is, to say the least, unique, and, by most current understanding, out of step with the times. Therefore, it is not particularly useful for clinical interpretation.

Scale 6, Pa: Paranoia. This scale is designed to assess paranoid symptomatology. The scale includes item content such as feelings of persecution, having evil thoughts, feeling misunderstood, emotional lability, feeling possessed by evil spirits, unhappiness, sensation seeking, distrust of others, crying easily, feeling as though one is being followed or poisoned by someone, ideas of reference, and history of legal trouble.

Scale 7, Pt: Psychasthenia. This scale assesses anxiety, particularly a tendency to worry obsessively. The item content of Scale 7 includes health worries, loss of interest in activities, having shameful thoughts, emotional lability, poor concentration, fatigue, unhappiness, low self-esteem, feelings of regret, guilt, impaired reading comprehension, impaired memory, worry, restlessness, excitability, fear of speaking in front of others, being easily embarrassed, impatience, counting unimportant things, rumination, and overreaction to failure. This scale has many items in common with scales 2, 3, and 8.

Scale 8, Sc: Schizophrenia. This scale was designed to identify patients with diagnoses of various forms of psychosis (Butcher et al., 1992). Scale 8 items sample content such as lack of interest in daily activities, having unwanted thoughts, desire to leave home, poor concentration, bizarre experiences, stealing, feelings of persecution, avoidance of others, day-dreaming, muscle twitching, urges to do something socially unacceptable, changes in speech pattern, decreased reading comprehension, impaired memory, blackout spells, fear of losing control, impaired balance, restlessness, difficulty initiating activity, excitability, numbness, de-creased taste sensitivity, sexual preoccupations, impaired relationships with parents and other family members, loneliness, lack of intimacy, impatience, and feelings of unreality. This scale shares many items with scales 2, 3, and 7. It is a long scale with 77 items, making item overlap with other scales a central characteristic. Its high correlations with other scales are discussed in a later section. Some of the items that differentiate this scale from others have to do with impaired social relationships and poor reality contact.

Scale 9, Ma: Hypomania. This scale assesses a tendency toward excitability and includes items assessing tension, desire to leave home, crying spells, urges to do something socially unacceptable, indecision, sensation seeking, racing thoughts, feelings of persecution, lack of fear of heights, blackout spells, occasional ability to make decisions very easily, self-righteousness, restlessness, satisfaction with personal appearance, sweatiness, excitability, excessive thirst, and admiration for cleverness even if it is criminal.

Scale 10, Si: Social Introversion. Si score elevations are produced by content such as failure to face crises or problems, poor concentration, poor sociability, unhappiness, fear of ridicule, lack of interest in parties, easily losing arguments, low sensation seeking, change in speech pattern, distrust of others, indecision, shyness, difficulty with small talk, brooding, concerns about personal appearance, embarrassment in front of groups, failure to initiate conversation, difficulty making friends, loneliness, envy of others' successes, and low self-esteem.

Content scales are a relatively unique feature of the MMPI that were developed differently from the original clinical scales. Whereas empirical approaches, including empirical criterion keying, were used for the development of the original scales, content scales depend more on a rational/theoretical approach to test development (Williams et al., 1992) in which scale content considers both empirical factor loadings and homogeneity of content within scales.

The first step in the content scale development process was to select 22 content categories based on a review of the adult experimental version (the predecessor to the MMPI-2). In the second step, a total of three raters assigned items from the adult experimental form to the 22 categories (Williams et al., 1992). A group consensus was reached on the assignments, and some items were discarded. A total of 21 content scales remained after this step. In the next step, correlations and reliability indices were used to enhance the reliability and homogeneity of each scale. The fourth stage involved another "rational review" of the items in response to the aforementioned statistical data. Some scales were renamed and some dropped at this stage. In the fifth and final step, items that correlated higher with a scale of which they were not a member were removed. The result was 15 MMPI-2 content scales for the adult measure (Williams et al., 1992).

These same procedures were applied to the development of the MMPI-A content scales, with the MMPI-2 content scales serving as the foundation. Items were added and removed, and some new scales were developed (Williams et al., 1992). This step resulted in the retention of the majority of the MMPI-2 content scales for adolescents and the addition of three scales-Alienation, Low Aspirations, and School Problems. Descriptions of the MMPI-A content scales are shown in Table 6.6.

There are also six supplementary scales on the MMPI-A (Butcher et al., 1992):

Anxiety (A): distress, discomfort, conformity, being upset by social situations.

Repression (R): tendency toward submissiveness and conventionality, avoidance of conflict

MAC-R, MacAndrew Alcoholism Scale-Revised: substance abuse problems, willingness to take risks, extraversion

Alcohol/Drug Problem Acknowledgement

(ACK): items that directly refer to drug and alcohol use

Alcohol/Drug Problem Proneness (PRO): stimulus seeking, negative peer group influence, rule-breaking, negative attitudes toward achievement

Immaturity (IMM): orientation to the present instead of future, lack of insight, hostility, self-centeredness

Administration and Scoring

The MMPI-A is unusually long (i.e., 478 items) compared to other self-report inventories designed for children and adolescents, which calls for special administration guidelines. In total, the MMPI-A takes approximately 90 min to administer, and some adolescents may have to take the test in more than one session (Butcher et al., 1992). Furthermore, because many adolescents require supervision during the administration of these scales, considerably more examiner time may be required. Substantial administration time savings, however, can be gained by using

Table 6.6 MMPI-A Content Scales

Scale	Description
Anxiety (A-anx)	Includes excessive worry, problems sleeping, problems concentrating, tension
Obsessiveness (A-obs)	Unreasonable worry, rumination, difficulty making decisions, reports that others are impatient with them, regret
Depression (A-dep)	Includes frequent crying, fatigue, self-deprecating thoughts, hopelessness
Health Concerns (A-hea)	Physical complaints including nausea, dizziness, constipation, difficulty hearing, headaches
Alienation (A-aln)	Feeling disliked and misunderstood by others, feeling that others are out to get them, preferring to be alone
Bizarre Mentation (A-biz)	Strange thoughts and experiences, hallucinations, paranoia
Anger (A-ang)	Starting fights, cursing, destroying things, irritability, impatience with others
Cynicism (A-cyn)	Mistrust of others, feeling that others are unfair, feeling that others are jealous
Conduct Problems (A-con)	Stealing, lying, disobeying rules, shoplifting, being disrespectful toward others
Low self-esteem (A-lse)	Feeling unattractive, lacking self-confidence, feelings of uselessness
Low Aspirations (A-las)	Dislike of studying and reading, giving up quickly, difficulty starting tasks
Social Discomfort (A-sod)	Shyness, avoidance of others, dislike of crowds or social gatherings
Family Problems (A-fam)	Family discord, feeling that one cannot depend on family members, jealousy, limited family communication
School Problems (A-sch)	Poor grades, negative attitudes toward teachers, suspensions, truancy, belief that school is a waste of time.
Negative Treatment Indicators (A-trt)	Negative attitudes toward doctors and mental health professionals, feeling that faults and bad habits cannot be overcome, unwillingness to face problems

From Butcher et al. (1992).

a computerized adaptive administration format (Forhey, Handel, & Ben-Porath, 2000). In fact, time savings of 50–123 items may be possible, with research suggesting no significant differences in average scale scores or in the distributions of scale scores (Hays & McCallum, 2005).

Checks on the adolescent's reading comprehension level are also required. Readability analyses of individual items show readability at approximately the fifth to sixth grade level in most cases. However, when in doubt, an examiner may ask the child to read some items aloud to get some sense of the child's ability to comprehend the item content. The validity checks provide another useful alert to possible readability problems.

Validity Scales

The MMPI series has a long tradition of the use of validity indexes which is reflected in the adolescent version. Brief descriptions of the validity scales follow (Butcher et al., 1992):

Cannot Say (?). This scale is comprised of the total number of items that the respondent either failed to answer or endorsed as both true and false. If there are a large number of items fitting this description, the clinician should attempt to ascertain the reason (e.g., carelessness, discomfort, difficulty with comprehension, defiance).

LIE (L). This scale is intended to detect naive attempts by adolescents to put themselves in an overly favorable light.

F, Fl, and F2 (Infrequency). The F scale is the antithesis of the L scale in that it assesses the tendency of individuals to place themselves in an unfavorable light, or "fake bad." Items were selected for this scale if they were endorsed in their deviant direction by less than 20% of the normative sample.

K (Defensiveness). According to Butcher et al. (1992), "This scale was designed originally to identify adults in psychiatric settings who displayed significant degrees of psychopathology, but produced profiles that were within normal limits" (Meehl & Hathaway, 1946, p. 40). Butcher et al. (1992), however, suggest that an MMPI-A profile should not be invalidated solely on the basis of an elevated K score, particularly if used with individuals who are not in a restrictive mental health or psychiatric setting.

VRIN (Variable Response Inconsistency). The VRN scale consists of pairs of items that have either similar or opposing item content. The score yielded by the VRIN scale reflects the number of item pairs answered inconsistently. A high score may reveal a careless response style on the part of the client.

TRIN (True Response Inconsistency). This scale is analogous to the VRIN scale in that it is made up of pairs of items. It differs in that the TRIN scale consists solely of items with opposite content. An elevated score may reveal an acquiescence response set, or the tendency for the test subject to indiscriminately answer True to the items. Conversely, a low TRIN score may reveal non-acquiescence.

Some validity evidence exists to support the use of MMPI-A validity scales; a strength of these scales relative to similar scales from other measures. The L and K scales have been shown to be reasonably good at assessing symptom underreporting (Baer, Ballenger, & Kroll, 1998; Stein & Graham, 2005). Validity scale cut scores had to be lowered somewhat to detect a fake good response set when evaluating adolescents in a correctional facility (Stein & Graham, 1999). The F, Fl, F2, and VRIN scales were best for assessing random responding for a sample of 354 adolescents (Archer & Elkins, 1999).

Norming

The MMPI-A was normed in eight states in the continental United States on 1,620 adolescents. One state, however (Washington), contributed only 14 cases to the norming.

The distribution of the sample by variables such as gender, age, grade, and parental education and occupation are given in the manual. These variables were not, however, used as stratification variables in order to match US Census or other criteria as is common for clinical test instruments. The Hispanic population, for example, is clearly under-sampled, constituting only 2.2% of the female sample and 2.0% of the male sample, which is smaller than the sample of Native American children. However, a great deal of subsequent research on the MMPI-A has been conducted with Hispanic individuals, increasing the confidence one can have in using this instrument with Hispanic clients (see

Butcher, Cabiya, Lucio, & Garrido, 2007). Similarly, the SES distribution may be skewed toward higher levels of SES than the national population. The authors noted that, "This rough classification of occupations suggests that mothers and fathers are described by many children as having professional and managerial occupations, while relatively low percentages are recorded for the homemaker and unskilled" (Butcher et al., 1992, p. 13). The age distribution of the sample is also highly variable. At age 18, only 42 male cases and 45 female cases were collected.

The small sample at age 18 may contribute to flawed estimates of psychopathology. A study by Shaevel and Archer (1996) revealed that 18-year olds scored substantially differently on the MMPI-A and MMPI-2. More evidence of pathology was obtained on the MMPI-2 with correspondingly lower validity scale values. Differences in T-scores between the two instruments were sometimes as high as 15 points for the same scales.

At the opposite end of the age range, one study of an inpatient population of 13-year olds found little difference in scores in comparison to a matched group of 14-year olds (Janus, de Groot, & Toepfer, 1998). Another investigation found little effect of demographic variables on MMPI-A T-scores (Schinka, Elkins, & Archer, 1998). However, Archer (2005) discussed the tendency across several samples for symptom endorsement on the MMPI-A to be inversely correlated with age.

The norm sample also included 193 individuals who had received mental health services, leading to a relatively large proportion of adolescents who do not appear elevated on the MMPI-A (Archer, 2005). However, removing these individuals and recalculating norms does not appear to change the pattern of results a great deal (Hand, Archer, Handel, & Forbey, 2007).

The US clinical normative sample consisted of 420 boys and 293 girls. All of the clinical cases were taken from the Minneapolis area (Butcher et al., 1992). Further details regarding the clinical sample can be found in Williams et al. (1992). The majority of cases (i.e., 71% of the boys and 56% of the girls) were undergoing treatment in alcohol/drug units (Williams et al., 1992), suggesting that the clinical sample could be reconceptualzied to more accurately reflect the preponderance of substance abuse cases.

Reliability

There are distinct scale differences in the internal consistency estimates for the MMPI-A (see Table 6.7). Some of the clinical scales (e.g., Hs, Pt, Si) have respectable estimates. In direct contrast, some of the scales have internal consistency estimates that raise questions about their content. The desirability of including a scale that possesses more error than reliable variance is not clear. The Mf coefficients of .43 (boys) and .40 (girls) are the worst of those reported. The Pa, D, and Ma scales are also less reliable than most of the scales described in this chapter.

Internal consistency estimates for the validity scales range from unacceptably low to impressively high, with most being moderate (.70s and .80s). According to Butcher et al. (1992), the lowest coefficients were obtained for the L scale, where coefficients ranged from .53 in the female clinical sample to .64 in the male normative sample. In contrast, the F scale produced coefficients ranging from .81 (female clinical sample) to .90 (male normative sample).

The internal consistency estimates for the "content" scales of the MMPI-A are generally better than those for the original clinical scales (see Table 6.7). The A-dep scale coefficients are considerably better than those of the original D scale, ranging from a low of .80 for the normative sample of boys to a high of .89 for the clinical sample of girls (see Butcher et al., 1992).

The lowest internal consistencies of the content scales are produced by the A-las

TABLE 6.7 MMPI-A Median Internal Consistency Reliability Estimates

Clinical Scale	Boys (*N = 805*)	Girls (*N = 815*)	Content Scale	Girls and Boys
Scale 1, Hs	.78	.79	A-anx	.80
Scale 2, D	.65	.66	A-ohs	.74
Scale 3, Hy	.63	.55	A-dep	.83
Scale 4, Pd	.63	.68	A-hea	.82
Scale 5, Mf	.43	.40	A-aln	.74
Scale 6, Pa	.57	.59	A-biz	.75
Scale 7, Pt	.84	.86	A-ang	.72
Scale 8, Sc	.88	.89	A-cyn	.80
Scale 9, Ma	.61	.61	A-con	.73
Scale 10, Si	.79	.80	A-lse	.74
			A-las	.61
			A-sod	.78
			A-fam	.82
			A-sch	.70
			A-trt	.76
			A	.89
			R	.53
			MAC-R	.48
			ACK	.66
			PRO	.69
			IMM	.82

Note: From Butcher et al. (1992).

scale, which has coefficients ranging from .55 to .66. These coefficients, however, are better than those of the MF clinical scale.

Some of the supplementary scales are also plagued by poor reliability estimates. The revised MacAndrew (MAC-R) scale yields a median coefficient of .48, which is, again, lower than most of the scales cited in this chapter. This lack of reliability also makes the MAC-R scale difficult to validate because reliability is a necessary condition for validity. The MMPI-A manual cautions that a cut-off raw score of 28 on the MAC-R may result in false positives; the existence of such poor reliability estimates makes one question the reliability of any cut score or, for that matter, the inclusion of the scale. Reliability coefficients in the .40s are typically not seen as adequate for clinical decision making.

If one orders all of the MMPI-A clinical and content scales by their reliability estimates, some implications for interpretation become clear. Scales can be grouped by reliability coefficients with guidance for interpretation as shown:

This reliability-based interpretive hierarchy is, of course, overly simplistic because the validity of these scales is not equivalent for all purposes. The hierarchy, however, is useful in that there is a relation between reliability and validity. The four scales with median coefficients below .60 are less likely to be the beneficiaries of substantial validity evidence, as will be noted in the next section.

Good Reliability (median coefficient .80)
Scale 7, Pt
Scale 8, Sc
A-anx
A-dep
A-cyn
A-hea
A-fam
A

Adequate Reliability (median coefficient = .70 to .79)
Scale 1, Hs
Scale 10, Si
A-obs
A-aln
A-biz
A-ang
A-con
A-lse
A-sod
A-sch
A-trt

Poor Reliability (median coefficient = .60 to .69)
Scale 2, D
Scale 3, Hy
Scale 4, Pd
Scale 9, Ma
A-1as
ACK PRO

Inadequate Reliability (median coefficient .59)
Scale 5, Mf
Scale 6, Pa
R
MAC-R

For the MMPI-A, the preceding charts suggest that the clinician could have more confidence in the information obtained from the content scales than the clinical scales. The higher internal consistency reliability of the content scales may very well be an artifact of the sometimes substantial item overlap in the clinical scales. In light of this issue, for clinical scale elevations, caution must be taken to determine what sorts of symptoms led to the elevations.

As is typical for such scales, test-retest coefficients differ from internal consistency estimates. Test-retest coefficients are somewhat more difficult to interpret, however, because it is unclear whether or not some scales measure traits that theoretically should be stable over at least short periods of time. Regardless, test-retest data can be of value when gauging changes from one evaluation to another.

One scenario might involve an adolescent who was hospitalized with paranoid ideation that was reflected by a high T-score (78) on the Pa scale. It is conceivable that this individual would obtain a lower score of 61 on re-test prior to discharge two weeks after the initial assessment. One interpretation of these results is that treatment has been effective. Another interpretation is that Pa scale results are relatively unstable (r = .65) and that the T-score of 78 was spuriously high or the 61 was erroneously low. These test-retest data do provide an alternative hypothesis for this score difference that, in this case, may have implications for discharge planning. In such a scenario, when MMPI-A results may not be well-corroborated by other clinical findings, more careful outpatient follow-up may be warranted to ensure that paraniod ideation has abated significantly enough so as to not adversely affect functioning in school or other settings.

Overall, the reliability estimates for the MMPI-A are more variable than might be expected. Such variability requires a more discerning user who evaluates the reliability of results on a scale-by-scale basis, which would not be necessary with more uniform reliability coefficients. It is also noteworthy that the new content scales appear to be more reliable on average than the original clinical scales. The user may more confidently assume that the content scales possess adequate reliability.

Validity

An important fact to keep in mind when interpreting the factor structure of the MMPI-A is the extent of item overlap (Archer, Belevich, & Elkins, 1994). The clinical scales were designed with many overlapping items that serve to strengthen the correlation between the scales. Item 31, for example, is included on six scales (2, 3, 4, 7, 8, 10). An analogous situation would be to have some WISC-IV items included on several subtests or composites. It is difficult to imagine, but what if several Block Design items were allowed, because of their correlations with the Verbal Comprehension subtests, to be included in calculations of the Verbal Comprehension Index? Such a move would probably be greeted by skepticism, causing clinicians to wonder about the distinction between the Verbal Comprehension and Perceptual Reasoning Indexes.

Analogously, scales 7 (Pt) and 8 (Sc) correlate highly with one another at .85 for females and .83 for males (Butcher et al., 1992). As might be expected, these scales both "load" highly on the first factor. However, these scales have 17 items in common, which parsimoniously explains the similar factor loadings of these scales. This validity evidence is potentially important in that it warns against routinely interpreting these scales as measures of distinct constructs, traits, or symptom clusters.

An early factor analysis of the MMPI-A revealed four factors: general anxiety, overcontrol or repression, the Si (third factor) and Mf (fourth factor) scales (Butcher et al., 1992). This factor solution reported in the manual is highly similar for both males and females.

The general anxiety factor accounts for the vast majority of the variance in the correlation matrix. Factor 1 is marked by loadings for the Hs, D, Hy, Pd, Pa, Pt, and Sc scales. Based on these results, this factor looks like a measure of general distress.

The second (overcontrol) factor is identified by loadings for L and K for males and Ma for females. The Si factor is clear-cut for both genders, whereas the Mf factor is clear-cut for males only.

Another factor analysis of the same normative sample produced somewhat different findings, with 14 factors being yielded from an exploratory factor analysis at the item level and 8 factors when conducted at the scale level (Archer et al., 1994). A factor analytic study of the MMPI-A content scales, based on normative samples, suggested that the 15 content scales could represent two latent variables-"general maladjustment" and "externalizing tendencies" (McCarthy & Archer, 1998). A single factor solution, on the other hand, may be more appropriate for girls.

Other Validity Studies

There is a wealth of external validity evidence for the MMPI-A clinical and content scales. The reader will note, however, that this evidence re-quires cross-validation; therefore, much of it is difficult to interpret.

For example, the A-dep (Depression content scale) was correlated with several criteria/variables for the normative and clinical samples. Correlations with these criteria ranged from a low (considering the absolute magnitude of the correlation) of −.18 with grades in school and outstanding personal achievement to a high of .24 for increase in disagreements with parent(s). The correlations between a high A-dep score and suicidal ideation/gestures and history of depression were .23 and .22 (Williams et al., 1992). By comparison, the A-anx (Anxiety) scale correlated .23 with a history of depression, and the A-lse (Low Self-Esteem) also correlated .26 with depression history. The majority of the external validity coefficients seem to be in the range of .20 to .30. The authors suggest several reasons for these results and numerous methodological caveats, including the appropriateness of the criterion measures, sample sizes, composition of the clinical samples, and other factors (Williams et al., 1992). It has also been suggested that the A-dep and A-anx content scales simply do not discriminate well between the anxiety and depression constructs (Arita & Baer, 1998).

The A-cyn (Cynicism) and the A-trt (Negative Treatment Indicators) scales produced little external validity data to support their use (Butcher et al., 1992; Williams et al., 1992). The A-sch (School Problems) fared better than most by producing 44 significant correlations with meaningful external criteria in the normative sample.

Over the years, several studies have been conducted to assess the ability of the MMPI-A to discriminate between levels of symptomatology, diagnostic categories, and so forth. One such study has evaluated the ability of the MMPI-A to differentiate three patterns of substance abuse (behavioral undercontrol, absence of behavioral undercontrol, and behavioral undercontrol and overcontrol) for a sample of 180 "substance abusers" (Gallucci, 1997). Several scales were needed to predict group membership at a 79% correct classification rate including MAC-R, D, Pd, Ma, Hy, Alcohol/Drug Problem Proneness, and Alcohol/Drug Problem Acknowledgment. Still another investigation used the MMPI-A to differentiate adolescent criminal offenders who had violent infractions (Hicks, Rogers, & Cashel, 2000). The MMPI-A was predictive of total number of infractions, and Pd was associated more with violent infractions. Archer and Slesinger (1999) investigated the relationship between three MMPI-A suicidal ideation items and score profiles. The three items were associated with higher clinical scale T-scores in general. Finally, with regard to group differentiation validity, Cumella, Wall, and Kerr-Almeida (1999) used the MMPI-A to discriminate between cases of anorexia and bulimia. There are two findings of interest: (1) the MMPI-A did not differentiate the groups as well as the older MMPI, and (2) bulimia patients differed from anorexia patients across content, supplemental, clinical, and validity scales suggesting different symptoms underlying these disorders.

An additional two studies have made direct comparisons between the MMPI-A and projective (i.e., Rorschach) and rating scale (i.e., Achenbach CBCL and TRF) measures. Archer and Krishnamurthy (1997) compared the utility of the MMPI-A and Rorschach (Exner's Comprehensive System) for distinguishing between Conduct Disorder and depression. In short, the MMPI-A did a better job of predicting diagnostic status with the Rorschach contributing only two variables that accounted for a small proportion of variance in a depression diagnosis, and none to a Conduct Disorder diagnosis. The Rorschach results contributed no significant variance to the prediction beyond that contributed by either the D or A-dep scales. The MMPI-A A-con, A-cyn, and IMM scales were the only predictors of Conduct Disorder diagnosis.

Despite decades of research and use by clinicians, the MMPI-A as a valid and useful measure in adolescent assessment is not completely understood. Archer (2005) has provided a summary of much of the work on the MMPI-A. In his summary, which is highlighted in Box 6.3, Archer promotes an understanding of

Box 6.3

Understanding MMPI-A Results in a Developmental Framework

Archer (2005) provided a review of MMPI/MMPI-A research that sought to demonstrate how the MMPI-A can contribute to knowledge of adolescent development. In doing so, Archer also highlights some issues to consider when interpreting the results of an MMPI/MMPI-A and making clinical decisions and recommendations. He emphasizes nine key points. The following is a brief summary of those points:

1. "Generalizing adult findings to adolescents is frequently inappropriate" (p. 258). Quite simply, when adult norms are used with adolescents, even with available statistical corrections, adolescents tend to score in an elevated fashion
2. "MMPI [MMPI-2] items are more effective in discriminating normal from abnormal functioning for adults than [MMPI-A items are] for adolescents" (p. 260).
3. "Maturational influences have profound effect on adolescents' (and adults') MMPI responses" (p. 261). To illustrate this point, Archer presents data showing a decrease in adolescents' MMPI-A raw scores throughout the teen years. In contrast, cross-sectional data reviewed by Archer show an increase in scores on the MMPI-2 Hypochondriasis scale (Hs) with age.
4. In general, "it is considerably more difficult to discriminate normal from abnormal functioning among adolescents than adults" (p. 263). Archer notes that many adolescents in clinical settings produce profiles with few, if any, elevations. Ironically, as Archer points out, this pattern may exist because many adolescents in the non-clinical norm sample may have endorsed a relatively high number of items.
5. "The expression of psychopathology has many similarities across age groups (p. 263). That is, despite notable developmental influences on item endorsement, the underlying implications of MMPI profiles for adolescents or adults do not appear to differ greatly.
6. "Acting out is the ubiquitous defense mechanism among adolescents" (p. 265). To support this notion, Archer reports the lower frequency of L and K scale elevations for adolescents than for adults as well as the relative commonality of adolescent clinical profiles that involve the Psychopathic Deviate (Pd) scale.
7. "Adolescents in the juvenile justice and mental health systems are often similar" (p. 265) based on MMPI-A responses.
8. "Given the fluid nature of symptomatology during adolescence, long-term predictions based on MMPI-A findings are ill-advised" (p. 267). Such a statement should be made about the results of any currently available assessment tool for child or adolescent personality, emotional functioning, or behavioral functioning.
9. A turbulent view of adolescence proffered by many early theories of adolescent development "receive substantial support from the MMPI/MMPI-A" (p. 267). This conclusion is drawn based on the relatively high symptom endorsement by adolescents on the MMPI-A and the lack of evidence indicating that such results are predictive of long-term psychological difficulty. In other words, adolescents may, as a group, experience significant problems that warrant attention, but in many cases, these difficulties are fortunately transient in nature.

adolescent response patterns on the MMPI-A (and thus, evidence regarding potential psychopathology) within a developmental framework.

Interpretation

The MMPI-A manual and subsequent literature (e.g., Archer, Krishnamurthy, & Stredny, 2007) supplies several aids to interpretation. Considerable psychometric information is available, including reliability and factor-analytic validity information. The potential import of reliability information for interpretation was outlined earlier. Similarly, factor-analytic data can help clinicians understand MMPI-A results.

If an adolescent obtains high score elevations on all of the clinical scales save Si and Mf, for example, then the client is producing a high factor 1 score. This client, consistent with the factor-analytic research, is showing a high level of general anxiety or distress. This result may not be of particular import for differential diagnosis, but it is a sensible and predictable finding in light of factor-analytic results.

Furthermore, the MMPI-A, as with its adult counterpart, includes Harris-Lingoes scales which are subscales that may help the clinician determine what types of items led to a clinical scale elevation. For example, The Depression (D) scale includes five Harris-Lingoes subscales (i.e., Subjective Depression, Psychomotor Retardation, Physical Malfunctioning, Mental Dullness and Brooding).

The previous description of scale item content can also be most useful for understanding scale elevations. The MMPI-A manual (Butcher et al., 1992) also provides a list of items and their scale membership (Table E-1), which can be useful for scale interpretation.

Some questions to ask oneself when interpreting the MMPI-A could include:

- How does an adolescent get a high score on this scale? What are the behaviors, perceptions, and feelings assessed by this scale (i.e., the item content)?
- How reliable are the scales that I wish to interpret as being of some clinical value in this case?
- Is there a content scale analogue that is more reliable and potentially more valid (e.g., D versus A-dep) than the clinical scale?
- What does the pattern of scale elevations suggest in terms of factor-analytic research?
- How is this scale reflective of nontest-based clinical symptomatology?
- Does external validity evidence exist (e.g., differential validity studies) to support or refute my interpretation of this scale?
- Has the validity study been independently replicated?

Interpretation of the MMPI is also supported by practical and thorough books on the topic (e.g., Archer, 1997) as well as numerous work-shops and other continuing professional development opportunities. The MMPI-A literature, while not nearly as extensive as that of the MMPI-2, is expansive. A specific example of this range of resources is a guide devoted singularly to the use of the MMPI system in forensic work (Pope, Butcher, & Seelen, 2000).

A sample case (Box 6.4) on the following page illustrates briefly how MMPI-A scale elevations can be used in conjunction with other assessment information to aid diagnostic decisions and in determining the primary target(s) of intervention.

Strengths and Weaknesses

The MMPI-A's long history is simultaneously its greatest asset and liability. On the one hand, the volumes of MMPI research guide practice. In direct contrast, the original clinical scales are incongruent with modern research on child and adolescent psychopathology and test development methods. The continually expanding research base and new scale development ensures that the MMPI will enjoy continued popularity and utility. It is, after all, a unique self-report measure.

Box 6.4

A Sample Case Using the MMPI-A

Michael is a 16-year-old high school junior He was referred for an evaluation because of recently increased anxiety symptoms that have interfered with his social interactions and functioning at school. More specifically, Michael has experienced some increased concerns with cleanliness or organization at home, and he has has begun to avoid social situations for fear of experiencing noticeable anxiety in front of others. Michael also has a history of depression, according to his mother, which has included a trial of antidepressant medication about three years ago. Medication was discontinued after a couple of months because his symptoms had diminished.

Michael currently lives with his parents and his 11 year-old brother. He reportedly gets along well with his family, and he has historically performed well academically until the current school year when his grades have gone from "As" and "Bs" to "Bs," "Cs," and "Ds."

Michael was cooperative and attentive throughout the test session. He appeared motivated to do well. No speech, visual, auditory, or motor abnormalities were noted.

Michael demonstrated tendencies toward perfectionism and anxiety during intelligence testing. During the arithmetic subtest he began to tremble and remarked, "I feel nervous." He was visibly nervous (i.e., hands shaking, voice cracking) when faced with relatively difficult items. He also seemed perfectionistic in his response style as evidenced by his unwillingness to give up on difficult items. Michael also displayed depressed affect during a clinical interview, although he did smile on occasion. Michael's intellectual test findings were all within the High Average range. Likewise, all of his achievement subtest scores were in the High Average range. These findings are consistent with his educational history.

On the MMPI-A, Michael indicated moderate levels of depressive symptoms and a tendency to isolate himself socially. He was self-described as shy, which is consistent with his mother's report. Content scale elevations on the Social Discomfort and School Problems scales are consistent with referral concerns. More specifically, he reported being uncomfortable in social situations, has difficulty interacting with others, and avoids social events. In regards to problems at school, Michael indicated that he does not care about doing well at school and that school is boring. Structured interviews with Michael indicate that these issues are relatively recent. However, his mother expressed concern that Michael has had a tendency to lose interest in activities such as school and social outings over the last few years.

The Depression (D) clinical scale was somewhat elevated. Michael indicated that he has feelings of inadequacy and worthlessness. Also, on the MMPI-A, Michael acknowledged having lost interest in activities and losing sleep due to worry. The reports of Michael and his mother on structured interviews indicate that he meets diagnostic criteria for Dysthymic Disorder. Since childhood, Michael reportedly has had periods of crying easily, difficulty making decisions, feelings of inadequacy, a lack of enjoyment from praise or rewards, and feeling that he is not as good as other people. He recently has experienced increasingly depressed mood, difficulty sleeping, and avoidance of activities.

His social anxiety and negative attitudes about school have apparently been recent developments that do not warrant a diagnosis at this time but should receive clinical attention.

The findings of this evaluation support the need for intervention at this time. Michael continues to demonstrate depressive symptoms. In addition, he is beginning to exhibit some anxiety in social situations which are interfering with his desire to interact with others and his enjoyment of school. A possible

(Continues)

Box 6.4 (Continued)

focus of psychotherapeutic interventions may be on the self-deprecating nature of his cognitions and anxiety during social interactions.

Scale	T-score
L	56
F	54
K	49
Hs	48
D	67
Hy	58
Pd	51
Mf	33
Pa	52
Pt	55
Sc	58
Ma	48
Si	65
Content Scale Elevations	
Social Discomfort (A-sod)	72
School Problems (A-sch)	71

The MMPI-A is likely to continue to remain as one of the most widely used adolescent measures of personality in the world. Claiborn (1995) concluded:

Strengths of the MMPI-A include:

1. Its familiarity to a large group of devoted users
2. The existence of a number of valuable validity scales
3. Interpretive flexibility because of the numerous scales
4. A thorough evaluation of the adolescent's self-appraisal due to the variety of items presented
5. The availability of numerous books, chapters, and empirical articles devoted to MMPI interpretation, many of which offer highly sensible interpretive guidance

Potential weaknesses of the MMPI-A include:

"Its flaws are relatively minor, correctable, and enormously outweighed by the strengths of the inventory. Clearly, the MMPI-A was developed with a great deal of care, expertise, and sensitivity to the problems of adolescents and the needs of practitioners who work with them" (p. 628).

1. Retention of scales that have not been well-supported by validity evidence
2. Retention of scales that lack internal consistency (Black, 1994)
3. Failure to incorporate factor-analytic evidence into the test development process (e.g., consideration of composite scores or clarifying how scales measure differing traits or problems despite the fact that they load on the same factor)
4. Duplicating items on different scales which produces high intercorrelations, thus bringing into question the distinctiveness of measurement of individual constructs (Kline, 1995)
5. Lack of a complete description of the normative sample and little evidence that the sample matches well a particular population (e.g., US Census bureau statistics)
6. Length of the MMPI-A relative to other self-report inventories, making the practicality of administering the MMPI-A an issue.

In spite of the extraordinary amount of MMPI research available, much remains to be done. The majority of the available research is based on adult samples. However, we refer the reader to the work of Archer and colleagues (e.g., Archer, 2005; Archer, Handel, & Lynch, 2001; Archer & Krishamurthy, 1994) who have greatly contributed to the body of knowledge regarding MMPI-A validity and interpretation.

Conners, 3rd Edition, Self-Report (Conners-3 SR; Conners, 2008a)

The Conners-3 SR (Conners, 2008a) is the most recent addition to a rating scale system with a long history of research and clinical use. However, despite this long history, a self-report instrument had largely been considered experimental until the most recent revision of the Conners rating scale system. The Conners-3 self-report rating scale consists of 59 items which are written at approximately a third grade reading level. A 39-item Short Form also exists.

It takes approximately 20 min to complete the Long Form of the Conners-3 SR. The inclusion of a standard self-report form makes the Conners system competitive with other well-known rating scale systems highlighted in this chapter. It should be noted that the Conners-3 SR includes extensive assessment of externalizing problems, particularly ADHD, with screening of anxiety and depression. Depending on the referral issue, this design may be either ideal or less-than-ideal for the clinician.

We focus on the Conners-3 rather than its companion rating scale system, the Conners Comprehensive Behavior Rating Scales (CBRS; Conners, 2008b), because the Conners-3 is relatively unique in its extensive evaluation of externalizing problems. The CBRS self-report form (for ages 8–18) provides an assessment of several areas of behavioral, emotional, and academic functioning and is desirable if the clinician needs information in more domains than externalizing problems.

Scale Content

The Conners-3 includes four content scales: Hyperactivity/Impulsivity, Inattention, Aggression, Family Relations, and Learning Problems. There are five *DSM-IV-TR* Symptom scales (i.e., ADHD, Combined Type; ADHD Inattentive; ADHD Hyperactive-Impulsive, ODD, and CD). As noted above, the Conners-3 SR includes screening items for depression and anxiety, as well as impairment items for home, school, and social relationships. Like the BASC, the Conners-3 includes critical items that may signal the need for further follow-up. The critical items on the SR are specific to severe conduct problems. Consistent with its predecessors, the Conners-3 includes a brief ADHD Index. This scale is based on items that best differentiate ADHD from nonclinical samples. New to the Conners-3 are three validity scales: Positive Impression (or "fake good"), Negative Impression ("fake bad"), and the Inconsistency Index. Lastly, the Conners-3 SR includes an open-ended item assessing "strengths/skills." Overall, the Conners-3 scales and the existence of the validity scales are in line with the current state-of-the-art in rating scale systems, as well as providing perhaps more detailed assessment of externalizing symptoms than is typical for other rating scales.

Administration and Scoring

The Conners-3 SR is designed for use with youth ages 8–18. Responses are made on a four-point scale, where 0 = not at all true (never, seldom), and 4 = very much true (very much true, very frequent). The time frame for responses is the last month prior to the assessment. Both hand scoring and computer scoring are available as are secure Internet administration and scoring.

The profile form that is included with the response form is used to convert raw scores to T-scores. The T-scores for the Conners-3 are linear T-scores, meaning that the scales maintain their distributions when converted to T-scores. Male and female norm-referenced scores are obtained separately. In addition, each age has separate norms. The T-scores shown on the available profile forms are truncated such that T-scores below 40 are not specified. Detailed step-by-step scoring procedures are available in the Conners-3 manual (Conners, 2008a).

Norming

The normative sample of 1,000 cases was collected mostly in the United States, with "a limited amount of data" (Conners, 2008a; p. 139) collected in Canada. Recruitment was targeted to approximate the ethnic/racial distribution of the population according to US Census statistics. Data presented in the Conners-3 manual indicate that accurate representation across ethnic groups was attained. Only 8% of cases came from the western part of the United States, indicating some underrepresentation of this region. The majority (i.e., 70%) of cases in the normative sample of the SR had parents with at least some secondary education.

Equal numbers of girls and boys were included in the normative sample at each age. As noted above, norm-referenced T-scores are provided separately for boys and girls, which does limit interpretation to sex-only comparisons.

Reliability

Internal consistency coefficients for SR are good for both the content scales and *DSM* symptom scales. Specifically, coefficients were all above .80 in all age groups across genders, with the exception of the Conduct Disorder scale for girls with coefficients ranging from .74 to .79 and the Aggression scale for 8 and 9-year-old girls (i.e., .75). Two to four week test-retest reliabilities were also good, with coefficients all .71 and higher (Conners, 2008a).

Validity

Factor analysis was used extensively in development of the Conners-3. Exploratory and confirmatory factor analyses support a four-factor model (i.e., Family Relations, Learning Problems, Aggression, and Hyperactivity/Impulsivity; Conners, 2008a). Thus, these content scales are considered empirically-derived, whereas the Inattention scale is considered theoretical/rational. The SR content and *DSM* scales show moderate to high intercorrelations and moderate correlations with analogous scales from the Conners-3 parent and teacher rating scales.

Criterion-related validity was demonstrated through correlations with other rating scales. Specifically, correlations between scales on the Conners-3 SR were moderately to highly correlated with analogous scales on the BASC-2-SRP and Achenbach YSR. The one exception was a non-significant negative relation between the Relations with Parents (higher scores indicate better relations) scale on the BASC-2-SRP and the Family Relations (higher scores indicate worse relations) scale of the Conners-3 SR for younger children (ages 8–11). This relation was significant and negative for older youth (ages 12–18).

Discriminant validity for the SR is also supported based on comparisons of clinical and general populations. In particular, the Learning Problems, Inattention, Hyperactivity/Impulsivity, and Aggression scales all differentiated not only the clinical sample from the general sample, but they also tended to differentiate among individuals within the clinical sample. For example, scores on the Aggression scale were higher for individuals diagnosed with disruptive behavior disorders than individuals with other diagnoses. This pattern was also the case for the Family Relations scale. The *DSM* scales also fared well in these analyses.

It should be noted that the above information pertains to the Long Form of the Conners-3 SR in particular. Reliability and validity evidence of the Short and Index forms are similarly good (see Conners, 2008a).

Interpretation

Conners (2008a) provides a clear recommended approach to interpretation of the SR and other scales in the Conners-3 family. This approach is well-aligned with the approach recommended in this text. First, the validity scales should be examined as to the potential usefulness of the responses. The next interpretation should occur at the scale level followed by a consideration of the overall "profile" or pattern of elevations. Then, item-level responses should be examined, including the anxiety and depression screening items, the items on elevated content or *DSM* scales, critical items, and strength/skills items. Lastly, reports from the SR should not stand-alone in an assessment but instead should be integrated with other information.

Strengths and Weaknesses

Some of the strengths of the Conners-3 SR are:

1. Good initial validity evidence.
2. User-friendly manual that assists with scoring and interpretation.
3. Availability of empirically-derived, rational, and *DSM*-oriented scales.
4. Thorough coverage of externalizing symptomatology
5. Availability of a Short Form for efficiency
6. Availability of validity scales.

Some characteristics that may be considered weaknesses are:

1. Limited assessment of internalizing problems.
2. Limited assessment of adaptive functioning.
3. Limited independent validity research to date.

Personality Inventory for Youth (PIY; Lachar & Gruber, 1994)

The Personality Inventory for Youth (PIY; Lachar & Gruber, 1994) has its roots in the well-known Personality Inventory for Children, which is designed as a parent rating scale (see Chap. 7). The PIY consists of 270 True-False items designed to assess emotional and behavioral adjustment, school adjustment, family characteristics and interactions, and academic ability in children aged 9 through 18 years (Lachar & Gruber, 1994). The PIY offers a substantial array of scales designed to assess these issues.

Scale Content

The PIY features four broad-band factor scales; Externalizing/Internalizing, Cognitive Impairment, Social Withdrawal, and Social Skills Deficit. The Externalizing/Internalizing factor includes several scales, whereas the other three factors each include the scale of the same name. The scales and subscales of the PIY are:

- Cognitive Impairment
  - Poor Achievement & Memory Inadequate Abilities
  - Learning Problems
  - Impulsivity and Distractibility
  - Brashness
  - Distractibility & Overactivity
  - Impulsivity
- Delinquency
  - Antisocial Behavior Dyscontrol
  - Noncompliance
- Family Dysfunction
  - Parent-Child Conflict
  - Parent Maladjustment
  - Marital Discord

Reality Distortion
  Feelings of Alienation
  Hallucinations & Delusions
Somatic Concern
  Psychosomatic Syndrome
  Muscular Tension & Anxiety Preoccupation with Disease
Psychological Discomfort
  Fear & Worry Depression
  Sleep Disturbance
Social Withdrawal
  Social Introversion Isolation
  Social Skill Deficits
Limited Peer Status Conflict with Peers

The PIC item pool served as the basis for developing items for the PIY (Lachar, 1999). In fact, only a few new items were added. The vast majority (i.e., about two-thirds) of PIY items are adapted from the PIC. We raise the question regarding item content because it is surprising to see a self-report measure that does not produce familiar scales or composites (not subscales) for constructs such as depression and anxiety. The authors explain (p. 34 of the Technical Guide) that they combined these scales in order to measure "emotional distress." The scale is labeled "Psychological Discomfort." The lack of clear operational definitions for Psychological Discomfort, Cognitive Impairment, Dyscontrol, and other scales and subscales hinders interpretation, and the clinician should pay close attention to the item content within scales and subscales in making interpretations.

Interpretation could be hindered because an idiosyncratically defined scale cannot be interpreted with the assistance of the vast research associated with a well-researched construct such as depression. If a well-researched construct is defined and assessed (e.g., hyperactivity), then the user can obtain information about diagnosis, prognosis, course of treatment, and so forth from the behavioral sciences at large-, rather than solely relying on the research base for a specific measure such as the PIY. The content of the PIY is, in many ways, broad and unique, but experience with administering and interpreting the PIY would be necessary for successfully articulating the meaning of a client's scale elevations and making appropriate decisions.

Validity Scales

Four validity scales are also featured. The PIY Validity (VAL) scale is intended to assess the presence of inattentive, oppositional, or provocative responses (e.g., responding "True" to "My teachers are trying to poison me."). The Inconsistency (INC) scale indicates if a protocol was answered haphazardly. In other words, the INC scale gauges the respondent's consistency on similarly worded items. Dissimulation (FB) measures the tendency of the informant to fake bad or malinger. Finally, the Defensiveness (DEF) scale provides an index that may reflect a fake good or a social desirability response set (Lachar & Gruber, 1994). A study of the validity of these scales found that they detected inconsistent and overly positive or negative responding as intended (Wrobel et al., 1999).

Administration and Scoring

The PIY is a 270-item inventory in a True-False format. It takes approximately 30–60 min to administer. The PIY manual (Lachar & Gruber, 1994) provides several helpful guidelines for administration. The manual suggests, for example, that the examiner explain the directions to the examinee, even though the directions are included in the Administration Booklet, in order to ensure compliance and enhance rapport. The administration requires two components, the booklet, and WPS Autoscore™ Answer Forms.

A single "template" is included in the answer form. The examiner adds rows and columns in order to obtain raw scores. These scores are then converted to gender-based T-scores. The PIY does not offer combined norms by gender as an interpretive option. Both PC and mail-in computer-scoring services are also available.

Abbreviated Form

The PIY also includes an 80-item abbreviated form which consists of the first 80 items of the full PIY. In addition, a unique feature within the abbreviated PIY is a 32-item classroom screening tool (CLASS) that assesses for difficulties in classroom adjustment (Lachar, 1999).

Norming

The PIY normative sample consists of 2,327 regular education students tested in 1991–1992 in five states. The sample was stratified to meet US Census Bureau statistics for ethnicity, parental educational level (SES), and community size. In addition, the marital status of the parent(s) was also considered. There was a slight under-sampling of African American children. An additional norming sample of 1,178 cases was collected to produce clinical norms. These cases were collected from 50 facilities serving a variety of inpatients and outpatients.

Reliability

Internal consistency coefficients are available for the PIY for both the normative and clinical samples (see Table 6.8 for data on the clinical samples). The reliabilities of the scales for the clinical sample are generally good, producing a median of .85. The median reliability for the subscales is lower, at .73. In fact, for the clinical sample, eight of the internal consistency coefficients fall below .70. The internal consistency coefficient for the learning problems scale, for example, was the lowest, at .44.

TABLE 6.8 PIY Scales and Internal Consistency Reliabilities for the Clinical Samples

Scales and Subscales	Internal Consistency Coefficient
Cognitive Impairment	.74
Poor Achievement and Memory	.65
Inadequate Abilities	.67
Learning Problems	.44
Impulsivity and Distractibility	.77
Brashness	.54
Distractibility and Overactivity	.61
Impulsivity	.54
Delinquency	.92
Antisocial Behavior	.83
Dyscontrol	.84
Noncompliance	.83
Family Dysfunction	.87
Parent–Child Conflict	.82
Parent Maladjustment	.74
Marital Discord	.70
Reality Distortion	.83
Feelings of Alienation	.77
Hallucinations and Delusions	.71
Somatic Concerns	.85
Pychosomatic Syndrome	.73
Muscular Tension and Anxiety	.74
Preoccupation with Disease	.60
Psychological Discomfort	.86
Fear and Worry	.78
Depression	.73
Sleep Disturbance	.70
Social Withdrawal	.80
Social Introversion	.78
Isolation	.59
Social Skill Deficit	.86
Limited Peer Status	.79
Conflict with Peers	.80

Note: Adapted from Table 46 in Lachar and Gruber (1994).

The 7–10 day test-retest coefficients for the clinical sample are also good at the scale level, with a median of .82. The median coefficient at the subscale level was again lower, at .73. At the subscale level, a total of seven subscales yielded test-retest coefficients of .70 or less. The lowest coefficient was .58 for the Impulsivity subscale, and the highest was .88 for the Antisocial Behavior and Dyscontrol subscales (Lachar & Gruber, 1994).

The manual also reports useful estimates for the standard error of measurement for each scale and subscale in T-score units. The typical SEM at the scale level is about 4 or 5 T-score points for the test-retest estimates.

Validity

The major argument presented for content validity of the PIY is that the items were derived from the PIC-R item pool. Lachar and Gruber argue that any validity evidence already gathered for the PIC-R lends indirect support for the validity of the PIY. However, it is worth noting that because items on the PIY are necessarily self-referent and items on the PIC are necessarily not, data regarding the PIC cannot be extrapolated toward understanding response tendencies on the PIY. In regards to adolescent self-reports of psychological constructs, it is unclear why the PIY does not include any items directly relevant to high-incidence syndromes of childhood such as depression and anxiety.

Several criterion-related validity studies are included in the manual. A study of 152 adolescents produced very modest relations between the PIY and the original MMPI clinical scales. Among the highest correlations were Reality Distortion and MMPI Schizophrenia (r = .66), and Psychological Discomfort and Psychasthenia (r = .65). The majority of correlations were in the .20 to .50 range, and many of the correlations were not statistically significant.

Another study correlated the PIY with the State-Trait Anxiety Inventory and the Reynolds Adolescent Depression Scale for 79 cases.

These data allow for the evaluation of the criterion-related validity of the PIY Psychological Discomfort scale and its component subscales. The correlations ranged from modest to strong. The State-Trait correlated .51 and the Reynolds .70 with the PIY Psychological Discomfort scale, suggesting that this scale may measure more depressive than anxiety symptomatology, although indicators of both constructs appear to be part of the Psychological Discomfort scale. It is difficult to summarize the wealth of data included in these studies in the limited space available here. The clinician who is seriously interested in the PIY would be served well by reading the criterion-related validity studies included in the manual very carefully prior to interpreting the scales and subscales.

Several samples were also used to assess the factor invariance of the PIY by gender and ethnicity (Lachar & Gruber, 1994). The results were generally supportive of the hypothesis of factor invariance across groups, although cross-validation with independent samples should be sought before drawing definitive conclusions.

An additional study supported the relevance of PIY items for detecting peer-related problems. Wrobel, Lachar, and Wrobel (2005) found that PIY scales constructed of items indicative of peer problems and peer withdrawal were significantly related to analogous peer-reported items. Another study in Bilingual adolescents supported the correspondence between the English version of the PIY and a Spanish version of the instrument (Negy, Lachar, & Gruber, 2001).

Interpretation

A five-step interpretive system for the PIY is offered by the authors (Lachar & Gruber,

1994). The first step involves assessing the validity of the obtained results using the four validity scales and a review of the completed form.

The second interpretive step suggests identifying primary profile elevations. A primary scale elevation is defined as a clinical scale with a T-score of 60 and subscale member of this same scale with a T-score of at least 65 for the majority of scales, although this cut score varies. These primary scale elevations may identify the diagnostic issues most likely to require additional attention and/or study.

The third interpretive step pertains to secondary scale elevations. These significant profile elevations are defined as scales that exceed the clinical cut score that are not accompanied by corresponding subscale scores that exceed the clinical cut score. In addition, subscales that exceed the cut score (without a corresponding high scale score) are also interpreted in this step. These secondary scale elevations may reveal mild problems, issues linked to the primary area of concern (e.g., social problems secondary to one's externalizing behaviors), and/or frequently occurring personality characteristics (Lachar & Gruber, 1994).

Step four includes tallying and interpreting items labeled as critical. This extensive list is intended to identify items that suggest clinical issues that should be examined in greater detail (Lachar & Gruber, 1994).

The last interpretive step is probably the most crucial-the integration of PIY results with other findings. The complexity of this interpretive step cannot be overstated. Our suggested approach for integrating information is described in detail in Chap. 15.

The PIY manuals provide detailed interpretive guidance that is grounded in scientific evidence. Cut scores and many decision rules are based on careful investigations of clinical samples. The chapter of case studies included in the administration and scoring manual should also be highly valued by users.

Strengths and Weaknesses

The PIY is clearly the result of a thorough and thoughtful test development process as is duly noted in reviews of the instrument. Destefano (1998), for example, concluded:

> "Given the shortcomings of projective testing and parent report for this age group, the PIY is a welcome addition to clinical assessment batteries for children of ages 9 through 18" (p. 757).

Marchant and Ridenour (1998) also have high praise for the PIY: "Seldom does a self-report instrument enter the field with the background of the PIY" (p. 758). These reviews also offer some caveats that are of interest to potential users.

We wish to add two caveats. First, we suggest that PIY users study the item content of the clinical scales, rather than relying on scale labels, in order to develop an understanding of the constructs being measured and assess their correspondence to similar constructs in the child psychopathology literature. Second, we caution users that virtually all of the extant PIY research to date was generated by members of the PIY authorship and research team. We hope that more independent investigations will be forthcoming to cross-validate, extend, and clarify the current findings.

Some specific strengths of the PIY include that:

1. The PIY is supported by a thorough set of manuals that give considerable statistical data, guidelines for interpretation, and case studies.
2. The PIY appears to assess a broad spectrum of child and adolescent behavior.
3. The PIY is part of a comprehensive assessment system that includes both parent and teacher reports.
4. The PIY interpretive system is thoughtful and helpful.

5. Computer scoring options are available for the PIY, which enhances its practicality.

Some potential weaknesses of the PIY may include:

1. Evidence of content validity is not compelling. Some of the item placements on scales do not seem consistent with rational/theoretical approaches to test development, which are gaining favor in personality assessment.
2. The use of norm-referenced scores at age 9 seems questionable given the small norming sample at this age (i.e., $N = 70$ for the regular education sample) (Lachar & Gruber, 1994).
3. The subscales should likely be used with caution for clinical purposes, or not used by the inexperienced PIY user, until further reliability studies are conducted (Destefano, 1998).
4. The PIY has a limited research base outside of studies published by the developers.

Single Construct Personality Inventories

In addition to an ever-growing body of omnibus self-report rating scales, a number of single construct or single domain scales exist. These scales are typically oriented toward older children and adolescents and toward an additional assessment of internalizing problems. Some examples of these scales are reviewed in later chapters when we discuss the assessment of specific constructs.

Given the need to approach assessment comprehensively, particularly in regards to assessing for comorbidity, we recommend first administering interviews and rating scales that evaluate a variety of domains. As information indicates problems in a particular domain or that more information on a construct would aid in decision-making and recommendations, well-validated single construct inventories may be useful.

Conclusions

The current state of self-report personality assessment continues to improve. In particular, a variety of assessment systems have developed methods that allow for relatively easy interpretation across self-, parent-, and teacher-reports. Personality assessment through self-report ratings continues to lag behind assessment of intelligence and achievement testing in many ways. Subscale reliabilities are often still too low to support diagnostic decisions. In some cases, they are too low to support hypothesis generation. Only a few of the instruments discussed herein have been empirically checked for item bias, and few have used modern statistical methods such as structural equation modeling and latent trait methodology as is commonly done for intelligence and achievement tests.

Improvements have been made in norming and the inclusion of reliability and validity data in test manuals. Some of the noteworthy contributions have been the extended age range and expansion of adaptive competencies on the BASC-2-SRP, the identification of correlates of profiles for the PIY, the history of numerous cross-cultural studies with the YSR, the extensive assessment of various externalizing problems on the Conners-3, and the burgeoning validity evidence for the MMPI-A content scales. Psychologists clearly have more and better options than in years past, and youth self-report of emotional, social, and behavioral functioning is valuable for obvious reasons. Still, much validity evidence remains to be gathered, particularly with so many measures being relatively new to the market. Relatively few validity studies are available for some of these scales. Much more evidence will have to be gathered for all measures in order to approximate the higher standards of practice required today and to develop a truly evidence-based approach to assessment.

Chapter Summary

1. Until recently, parent and teacher reports have routinely been preferred over the use of self-report inventories in child personality assessment.
2. Decisions to use self-report inventories should be based, in part, on the child's developmental level, the constructs being assessed, and the purpose of the assessment. In general, older children are more useful informants. Self-reports of covert conduct problems and internalizing symptoms may be particularly informative.
3. The SRP is one of many components of the BASC-2. The SRP attempts to gauge children's perceptions and feelings about school, parents, peers, and their own behavior problems.
4. Five composites are available for the SRP: the Emotional Symptoms Index (ESI), Inattention/Hyperactivity, Internalizing Problems, School Maladjustment, and Personal Adjustment.
5. The SRP includes three validity scales.
6. The SRP was normed on a national sample of 1,500 children and 1,900 adolescents.
7. The reliability of the SRP scales is good as indicated by a variety of methods.
8. Until clinical experience and further research studies are available, initial efforts at SRP interpretation should focus on the scale level rather than the composite level because these item pools have some rational, theoretical, and research basis.
9. Relatively few independent studies have been conducted with the most recently updated YSR. However, numerous studies have demonstrated that the previous version of the YSR produces similar scores across cultures and consistent sex differences across cultures.
10. The YSR does not include validity scales. However, it includes an assessment of clinical and adaptive domains that are relevant for most purposes of child assessment.
11. The MMPI-A has ten clinical scales, eight validity scales, and several empirically-based content scales.
12. The MMPI-A is unusually lengthy is comparison to other self-report inventories designed for children and adolescents. This length entails special administration guidelines.
13. There are distinct differences in the internal consistency estimates for the MMPI-A, with many adequate scales and some that are below minimum standards.
14. Factor analysis of the MMPI-A reveals four factors: the first two are labeled general anxiety and overcontrol or repression, and the third and fourth factors are composed solely of the Si and Mf scales, respectively.
15. The self-report form of the Conners-3 is a recent addition to a long-standing rating scale system.
16. The Conners-3 SR has good initial validity evidence. It offers an extensive assessment of ADHD and disruptive behaviors but a limited assessment of internalizing problems.
17. The PIY manual provides considerable interpretive guidance.
18. The PIY used the PIC item pool (see Chap. 7) as its source of items.
19. A number of single domain self-report rating scales, particularly for internalizing problems, are in existence. Examples of these instruments are discussed in later chapters.

Chapter 7

Parent and Teacher Rating Scales

Chapter Questions

- How reliable are parent and teacher ratings of child behavior problems?
- What domains of behavior are assessed by parent and teacher rating scales?
- How are parent and teacher rating scales used in the typical psychological evaluation?
- Why are teachers important sources of information about a child's emotional and behavioral adjustment?
- To what extent do parents and teachers agree in their ratings of children and adolescents?
- What factors influence this agreement?
- What factors should play a role in the use and selection of parent and teacher rating scales?

Evaluating Children via Parent Ratings

It has long been recognized that children are often less-than-accurate reporters of their own behavior. Furthermore, children may not have sufficient reading or oral expression skills for self-report purposes (Lachar, 1990). Problems with underreporting and response sets have always been well-recognized by clinicians and, to some extent, have been documented by research (see previous chapter). These concerns about child self-reports have undoubtedly contributed to the popularity of parent rating scales. Furthermore, the parental perspective is often invaluable when conceptualizing a case; that is, because children are often referred for an evaluation because of a parent's concerns, information on the parent's perspective of a child's problems is critical.

P.J. Frick et al., *Clinical Assessment of Child and Adolescent Personality and Behavior*,
DOI 10.1007/978-1-4419-0641-0_7,

Parent ratings of child behavior possess additional advantages, including brevity and cost efficiency (Hart & Lahey, 1999). The time-efficient nature of parent ratings makes it easy to collect additional information about child behavior. Given the importance of parental influence on child behavior, parental perceptions of behavior should routinely be collected in clinical assessments.

Today, the commonly used parent rating scales routinely provide a broad coverage of problems. For example, while the unstructured interview may allow the clinician to carefully evaluate a specific area of functioning, other important behavioral problems or areas of concern may be missed (Witt, Heffer, & Pfeiffer, 1990). Parent or other caretaker ratings also foster objectivity and clarity in the assessment process. Because of the behavioral specificity of the typical item content of these measures, parents are required to operationally define their concerns and provide specific and objective ratings of hyperactivity, depression, nervousness, and the like (Witt et al., 1990).

All rating scales, including parent ratings, can be influenced by bias and rater response sets (Witt et al., 1990). Even biased reporting, however, can be of value. If, for example, parent ratings provide very different results when compared to the ratings of others, the clinician can develop some important insights into the child's family functioning. If a child's father rates his son as having significantly more behavioral problems than the mother, the clinician can explore the dynamics behind the ratings. A straightforward explanation may be that the father is doing the majority of the child care. This information could be important to acquire if the presumption had been that the child's mother was providing most of the caretaking.

Factors Influencing Parent Ratings

As discussed in more detail in Chap. 15, research has indicated that parental, specifically maternal, distress may influence the ratings of child functioning in a negative way. Although the issue of whether or not maternal distress is directly influential on the ratings of a child's symptoms is far from settled, it stands to reason that stressful home environments would be positively correlated with parent reports of child symptoms.

The construct being evaluated and the child's developmental level are two additional factors that may influence parents' reports. Teachers have traditionally been considered superior to parents as reporters of a child's ADHD-like symptoms (Loeber, Green, & Lahey, 1990; Loeber et al., 1991; Tripp, Schaughency, & Clarke, 2006). However, parents are still considered necessary and useful in providing information about inattention and hyperactivity (Tripp et al., 2006) and in documenting the effects of treatment for ADHD (Biederman, Gao, Rogers, & Spencer, 2007). In addition, parents may be in a unique position to understand the antecedents of a child's disruptive behaviors, as they can observe their child more closely than a teacher who works with several children simultaneously. Parents have also been discussed as particularly important observers and informants of child anxiety and depression (Klein, Dougherty, & Olino, 2005; Silverman & Ollendick, 2005).

As reviewed by De Los Reyes and Kazdin (2005), research has reached mixed conclusions about the degree to which the child's age influences agreement in ratings across informants. Parents, in particular, may be useful informants of a child's functioning throughout childhood and adolescence, although there may be discrepancies between their reports and the reports of others. The information used in conjunction with parent reports may vary with age. More specifically, parents are obviously vitally important sources of information for young children in such areas as conduct problems, whereas the children themselves would not be reliable (and thus, not valid) informants. Teachers, however, could offer useful perspectives of the young child's social, academic, and behavioral functioning. For adolescents, parents may still provide valid and useful information, but their knowledge of the child's conduct and behavior problems may be more limited, as the behaviors may sometimes occur outside of the parent's awareness. The adolescent – provided that he or she is willing to provide such information – would be the most knowledgeable informant of these behaviors, and the teacher's contribution would also presumably diminish.

Finally, parent ratings are more likely to attribute the child's problems to dispositional factors in the child, whereas youth self-reports are more likely to indicate the family environment as a factor in need of intervention (see De Los Reyes & Kazdin, 2005). Thus, informants (including parents, teachers, and children) may base their ratings of a child's functioning on the attributions that they make regarding the genesis and maintenance of the child's problems.

That parent ratings may be influenced by factors that are not necessarily directly tied to the child's actual functioning does not render parent ratings questionable. Instead, it calls to mind the many potential variables to consider in understanding the child's presenting problems – an understanding that is critical for case conceptualization and subsequent recommendations for intervention.

Evaluating Children via Teacher Ratings

Although teachers have traditionally been considered an important source of information about children's academic performance, they have not often been used in the assessment of children's behavioral and emotional functioning. However, knowing how a child behaves in the classroom is important for several reasons. First, school is a setting in which the child spends several hours a day. Therefore, a child's adjustment to the school setting can have a dramatic impact on his or her overall psychological functioning. Second, the multiple demands of the school environment (e.g., to stay seated, to follow the demands of adults, to interact with classmates) present many challenges to the child— challenges that may not be present in other settings. Third, the demands of the school setting change as a child progresses through school (e.g., demands for organization, the importance of social acceptance). Therefore, understanding school-related problems that are unique to a given period can provide clues to specific problems in adaptation that a child or adolescent might experience.

On the basis of these considerations, there is increasing interest in assessing a child's behavioral and emotional functioning in the school setting. Given the many advantages of behavior rating scales, such as time-efficiency and objectivity, it is not surprising that the primary assessment instruments for children's school behavior have been teacher-completed behavior rating scales. In addition to suggestions for appropriate use of rating scales in general discussed previously, there are several considerations for interpreting information from teachers that warrant special attention.

Factors Influencing Teacher Ratings

As described above for parents, the usefulness of teacher information may vary depending on what type of behavior is being assessed. Teachers are often considered the best source of information about a child's attention problems and overactivity because they have the opportunity to observe the child in a situation that demands sustained attention and inactivity. In contrast, teachers' ratings tend to be less useful in assessing many types of antisocial behavior that are unlikely to occur in the school environment (e.g., setting things on fire, being cruel to animals) or for internalized types of problems that may not be readily observable in the classroom setting (Loeber et al., 1991).

The usefulness of teacher information may also vary according to the age of the child. Children in early elementary school frequently have one teacher who observes a child across several class periods, if not the entire school day. In contrast, high school teachers frequently have students for one class period during the day. Therefore, the usefulness of information may decrease as a child advances in school and contact with any single teacher decreases (Edelbrock et al., 1985).

A final issue in interpreting teacher rating scales is understanding the frame of reference or standard used by teachers. As discussed previously (e.g., Piacentini, 1993), a number of characteristics of a rater can influence his or her judgment of the intensity, quality, and/or frequency of a child's behavior. In the case of teacher ratings, a characteristic of teachers that can influence their ratings is their experience with many children of the same age. Experience allows the teacher to make some internal normative comparison of a child's behavior with the behavior of other children the teacher has taught. This internal norm is a double-edged sword. It often gives the teacher a unique perspective of knowing both the individual child and the behaviors that are age-appropriate. However, some teachers, such as teachers who work in special education classrooms, may have a skewed base of comparison that could influence their ratings. That is, their ratings of a child's behavior may be influenced by a comparison of the child with other disturbed children.

Despite these cautions and limitations, we feel strongly that teacher ratings are an essential element of a comprehensive clinical assessment of children's behavioral and emotional functioning. Carlson and Lahey (1983), in an early review of teacher ratings, reported that most of the teacher rating scales available at that time suffered from significant psychometric problems in development and inadequate norming. As a result, the available scales were severely limited in their usefulness for clinical evaluations. Fortunately, since that 1983 review, there have been numerous advances in the teacher rating scales and the emergence of new scales, with many of the inadequacies of earlier scales eliminated or greatly reduced.

Overview of Omnibus Parent and Teacher Rating Scales

Parent and teacher rating scales are not interchangeable and, with the seemingly exponential growth of such instruments, psychologists have to make many decisions about the utility of various measures. This chapter attempts to aid the clinician in decision making by providing an overview of the variety of scales available, with particular attention devoted to defining the strengths and weaknesses of each measure. Writing such a chapter requires selectivity. Hence, if a scale is not mentioned in this chapter, it should not be construed as a judgment of the quality of the scale. As with our chapter on self-report rating scales, we have attempted to review those instruments that are widely used and/or part of a long-standing system of rating scales used for child and adolescent assessment. This broad overview of the various scales is not designed to replace information provided in the technical manuals that accompany these instruments, to be reviewed by any user of the scales. Optimally, however, the principles applied to evaluating parent and teacher rating scales in this chapter can be used by psychologists to evaluate other scales as well.

The parent and teacher rating scales reviewed in this chapter are highlighted in Tables 7.1 and 7.2, respectively. Commonly used omnibus measures that assess many different domains, as opposed to single construct measures, are the focus. Although these scales are discussed in isolation to balance clarity and specificity, it should be recalled that they are often part of larger multimethod assessment methods that are discussed in various chapters of this book. The integration of components and information from different informants and methods is discussed in the context of interpretation in Chap. 15 and in subsequent chapters that address specific syndromes.

Behavior Assessment System for Children, 2nd Edition (BASC-2)

Parent Rating Scale (PRS)

The BASC-2 Parent Rating Scale (BASC-2-PRS; Reynolds & Kamphaus, 2004) is part of the larger BASC system. The PRS was published concurrently with the SRP (discussed in Chap. 6) and TRS (see below) as well as other components of the BASC assessment system (Reynolds & Kamphaus, 2004). The PRS has three forms composed of similar items and scales that span the preschool (2–5 years), child (6–11 years), and adolescent (12–21 years) age ranges. The PRS takes a broad sampling of a child's behavior in home and community settings.

Content

As with its predecessor, the BASC-2-PRS was developed using both rational/theoretical and empirical means in combination to construct the individual scales. The benefit of this approach is that the resulting scales have relatively homogenous content. The uniqueness of the scales was also enhanced by not including items on more than one scale. Table 7.3 provides item examples for each scale. There are four composites: Externalizing Problems, Internalizing Problems, Adaptive Skills, and a Behavioral Symptoms Index that includes some internalizing and externalizing scales (i.e., Atypicality, Attention Problems, Hyperactivity, Aggression, Depression, and Withdrawal).

Two types of scales are included at each age level: clinical and adaptive. Clinical scales of the PRS are designed to measure behavior problems much like other measures discussed below in that behavioral excesses (e.g., hitting others) are the focus of assessment. The PRS also includes critical items that are thought to warrant follow-up or clinical attention in their own right. These items (e.g., "Has a hearing problem.") are not necessarily indicative of the most severe pathology; instead, they may be worthy of further questioning or recommendations by the clinician. The adaptive scales measure behaviors (e.g., compliments others) or skills that are associated with good adaptation to home and community (see Table 7.3).

TABLE 7.1 Overview of Parent Rating Scales

Inventory	Ages	Content	Reading Level	Time to Administer	Norm Sample	Reliability	Validity	MI
Behavior Assessment System for Children, 2nd edition (BASC-2; Reynolds & Kamphaus, 2004)	2–5; 6–11; 12–21	134–160 items; Behavioral Symptoms Index, Adaptive Skills, Internalizing Problems; 3 validity scales; 9 clinical scales, 5 adaptive scales; 7 optional content scales	4th grade	10–20 min	E	Internal consistency (good); 1–7 week test–retest (good); Interrater (moderate to high)	Moderate to high with similar tools; Support for factors	E
Achenbach Child Behavior Checklist (CBCL; Achenbach & Rescorla, 2000; Achenbach & Rescorla, 2001)	1½– 5; 6–18	100–113 items; Internalizing, Externalizing, Competence; 8 problem scales; 6 DSM-oriented scales	Not given	15–20 min	G	Internal consistency (good for school age version); 1 week test–retest (good); interrater (moderate for preschool version; good for school age version)	Good validity (clinical vs. nonclinical groups); limited info. on relations with other tools; limited info. on current version	E
Child Symptom Inventory-4 (Gadow & Sprafkin, 1998) ESI/CSI/ASI	3–5; 5–12; 12–18	97 items corresponding to 17 disorders	Not given	10–15 min	F	Internal consistency (moderate to good); Test-retest; content (moderate to good)	Content derived from DSM criteria; Evidence of construct validity (good)	G

(Continues)

Table 7.1 (Continued)

Inventory	Ages	Content	Reading Level	Time to Administer	Norm Sample	Reliability	Validity	MI
Conners 3rd Edition, Parent Rating Scale (Conners-3; Conners, 2008a)	6–18	110 items; 43-item short form; 3 validity scales; 6 empirical scales; 1 rational scale; 5 *DSM-IV-TR scales*	4th–5th grade	20 min	E	Internal consistency, 2–4 week test–retest, and interrater reliability all good	Good evidence of criterion-related and differential validity	E[a]
Personality Inventory for Children, 2nd edition (PIC-2; Lachar & Gruber, 2001)	5–19	275 items, 96 item short form; 9 clinical scales (several subscales); 3 validity scales	4th grade	40 min	E	Internal consistency; test–retest; interrater; Good reliability, somewhat lower for subscales	Validity (based on teacher and self-reports of same system); lack of research on relations with other criteria	G

Note: Norm Sample evaluated as E = Excellent, G = Good, F = Fair; MI = Degree of enhancement of multi-informant assessment; E = Excellent, G = Good; ESI = Early Symptom Inventory; CSI = Child Symptom Inventory; ASI = Adolescent Symptom Inventory.

[a]We view the Conners-3 as providing an excellent means of assessment of externalizing problems; however, if an extensive assessment of internalizing or learning difficulties is desired, the Conners Comprehensive Behavior Rating Scales (CBRS; Conners, 2008b) is recommended.

TABLE 7.2 Overview of Teacher Rating Scales

Inventory	Ages	Content	Reading Level	Time to Administer	Norm Sample	Reliability	Validity	MI
Behavior Assessment System for Children, 2nd edition (BASC-2; Reynolds & Kamphaus, 2004)	2–5; 6–11; 12–21	100–139 items; Behavioral Symptoms Index, Adaptive Skills, Externalizing Problems, Internalizing Problems, School Problems; 3 validity scales; 10 clinical scales, 5 adaptive scales, 7 optional content scales	Not given	10–20 min	E	Internal consistency (good); 1–9 week test–retest (good); interrater reliability (good with exception of Somatiz)	Moderate to high relations with similar tools; Support for factors	E
Achenbach Teacher Rating Form (TRF; Achenbach & Rescorla, 2000; Achenbach & Rescorla, 2001)	1½–5; 6–18	100–113 items; Internalizing, Externalizing, Adaptive Functioning; 8 problem scales; 6 DSM-oriented scales	Not given	15–20 min	G	Internal consistency (good); 7 month test–retest (moderate); interrater (low to mode-rate)	Good validity (clinical vs. nonclinical groups); limited info. on relations with other tools	E
Child Symptom Inventory-4 (Gadow & Sprafkin, 1998) ESI/CSI/ASI	3–5; 5–12; 12–18	77 Items corresponding to 13 disorders	Not given	10 min	F	Test–retest; limited evidence available	Content derived from DSM criteria; Classification rates match well with epidemiology	E
Conners 3rd Edition, Teacher Rating scale (Conners-3-T; Conners, 2008a)	8–18	115 Items; 39-item short form; 3 validity scales, 6 empirical scales, 1 rational scale, 5 *DSM-IV-TR* symptom scales	4th–5th grade	20 min	G	Internal consistency and test–retest reliability (good). Interrater reliability (moderate to good)	Good evidence of criterion-related and differential validity	E[a]

(Continues)

Table 7.2 (continued)

Inventory	Ages	Content	Reading Level	Time to Administer	Norm Sample	Reliability	Validity	MI
Student Behavior Survey (SBS; Lachar, Wingenfeld, Kline, & Gruber, 2000)	5–18	102 items; Academic Resources, Health Concerns, Emotional Distress, Unusual Behavior, Social, and Aggression composites	Not given	10–15 min	E	Good reliability (internal consistency; test–retest)	Good convergent validity for most scales; DBD scales do not overlap fully with DSM criteria; Limited validity evidence for some scales	F

Note: Norm Sample evaluated as E = Excellent, G = Good; MI = Degree of enhancement of multi-informant assessment; E = Excellent, G = Good, F = Fair; ESI = Early Symptom Inventory; CSI = Child Symptom Inventory; ASI = Adolescent Symptom Inventory; DBD = Disruptive Behavior Disorder.
[a]We view the Conners-3 as providing an excellent means of assessment of externalizing problems; however, if an extensive assessment of internalizing or learning difficulties is desired, the Conners Comprehensive Behavior Rating Scales (CBRS; Conners, 2008b) is recommended.

Table 7.3 BASC-2-PRS Scale Definitions and Key Symptoms as Indicated by Items with the Highest Factor Loadings Per Scale

Activities of Daily Living	Skills associated with performing everyday tasks; "Acts in a safe manner", "Sets realistic goals", "Attends to issues of personal safety"
Adaptability	Ability to adapt to changes in the environment; "Adjusts easily to new surroundings", "Adjusts well to changes in family plans", "Recovers quickly after a setback"
Aggression	Tendency to act in hostile or threatening manner; "Is cruel to others", "Loses temper too easily", "Annoys others on purpose"
Anxiety	Tendency to be nervous, fearful, or worried; "Worries about making mistakes", "Worries about what other children think", "Is nervous"
Attention Problems	Tendency to be easily distracted or have difficulty concentrating; "Has a short attention span" "Listens carefully" (reverse scored); "Is easily distracted"
Atypicality	Tendency to behave in odd manner; "Acts strangely." "Says things that make no sense", "Seems out of touch with reality"
Conduct Problems	Tendency to engage in antisocial and rule-breaking behavior; "Breaks the rules"; "Deceives others"; "Gets into trouble"
Depression	Feelings of unhappiness, sadness, or stress; "Is negative about things", "Says 'I don't have any friends'", "Seems lonely"
Functional Communication	Ability to communicate ideas and express oneself clearly; "Communicates clearly", "Responds appropriately when asked a question", "Accurately takes down messages"
Hyperactivity	Tendency to be overly active and act without thinking; "Acts out of control", "Interrupts others when they are speaking", "Disrupts other children's activities"
Leadership	Possessing skills needed to accomplish goals, ability to work with others; "Gives good suggestions for solving problems", "Is creative", "Is a 'self-starter'"
Social Skills	Having the skills necessary to interact successfully with peers and adults; "Encourages others to do their best", "Offers to help other children", Congratulates others when good things happen to them"
Somatization	Tendency to be sensitive to, and complain about, minor physical ailments; "Complains about health"; "Gets sick"; "Complains of being sick when nothing is wrong"
Withdrawal	Tendency to avoid others; "Makes friends easily" (reverse scored), "Avoids other children", "Quickly joins group activities" (reverse-scored)

Note: Adapted from Tables 7.7 and 10.3 of the BASC-2 manual (Reynolds & Kamphaus, 2004).The clinical norms may be especially important when assessing a child in a residential setting to be able to compare him or her to others with relatively severe difficulties. That is, it may be understood that a child is functioning poorly compared to most other children his/her age (i.e., elevations on general norms), but it may be informative to consider how the child functions (e.g., "How severe are his conduct problems?") in comparison to other children with emotional and behavioral difficulties for treatment planning purposes.

Each of the parent forms of the BASC-2 includes seven optional content scales: Anger Control, Bullying, Developmental, Social Disorders, Emotional Self-control, Emotional Self-control, Executive Functioning, Negative Emotionality, and Resiliency. As with the BASC-2-SRP (see Chap. 6), the content scales for the BASC-2-PRS were constructed via theoretical and empirical methods. These scales were developed based on current theoretical perspectives about important domains of youth functioning (Reynolds & Kamphaus, 2004). There exists very little research on these scales, yet their labels and item content are intriguing and warrant further investigation of their reliability, validity, and clinical utility. Initial analyses indicate that the PRS content scales possess adequate (i.e., 0.70 and higher) internal consistencies (Reynolds & Kamphaus, 2004).

Administration and Scoring

The PRS uses a four-choice response format (i.e., never, sometimes, often, almost always) with no space allowed for parent elaboration. According to the authors, the scale takes about 10–20 min for parents to complete.

A variety of derived scores and interpretive devices are offered. Linear T-scores are available for all scales and composites, meaning that the original distributions for these indices in the norming sample were maintained. Other scores available include percentile ranks, confidence bands, and statistical methods for identifying high and low points in a profile. Both hand-scoring and computer entry scoring are available for the PRS.

Norming

PRS provides three norm-referenced comparisons depending on the questions of interest to the clinician. Some examples of questions and their implications for norm group selection include the following.

Question	Norm Group
Is Daniel inattentive in comparison to children of the same age?	General national sample
Is Daniel inattentive in comparison to a large sample sample of children who are currently diagnosed and receiving treatment?	Clinical national sample
Is Daniel inattentive in comparison to boys of the same age?	Male national

These various norm-referenced comparisons are more than are typically offered for such scales. The general national norming sample is advised as the starting point for most purposes (Reynolds & Kamphaus, 2004). Of course, as just noted, depending on the question, the clinician may opt for gender-specific or clinical norms. Gender-specific norms may be useful in trying to convey a child's current level of functioning to others, such as parents. In other words, one might present the child's scores relative to the general population and then emphasize how the child compares to other boys/girls on areas of concern in order to provide a more complete picture. However, too much information may cause confusion for some parents. Gender-based norms may also help answer some specific research questions (i.e., correlates of inattention and hyperactivity among girls and among boys).

The general norm sample for the PRS included 1,200 preschoolers, 1,800 children, and 1,800 adolescents. Cases were collected at test sites in 40 states. Across age groups, the PRS sample closely matches US Census statistics (Current Population Survey, 2001) in terms of sex, race/ethnicity, and socioeconomic status (SES). The norming sample also represents a good fit to census data on geographic region (see

Reynolds & Kamphaus, 2004 for more details). The clinical norming sample for the PRS included responses from 1,975 parents, with most cases being classified as having a learning disability or ADHD.

Reliability

The median reliability coefficients provided in the manual suggest good evidence for the reliability of the individual scales and composites. All scales and composites have median reliability estimates of 0.80 and above, with the exception of the Activities of Daily Living and Atypicality Scales. The BASC-2 manual also provides information on 1–7-week test-retest reliability and interrater reliability between parents. Test-retest reliability coefficients were 0.70 and higher, with the exception of Depression for the preschool form which was .66. Interrater reliability was generally good, with coefficients in the same range, with the exception of Aggression on the preschool and child forms (i.e., 0.59 and 0.58, respectively) and Anxiety on the preschool form (.56).

Validity

The PRS appears to have a broad content coverage. The PRS assesses a variety of externalizing behavior problems (McMahon & Frick, 2002) and has an expanded assessment of adaptive skills. In addition, the PRS enjoys considerable factor analytic support for a three factor model consisting of externalizing problems, internalizing problems, and adaptive skills. The strongest measures of the externalizing factor are the Aggression, Conduct Problems and Hyperactivity. The Internalizing factor is marked by loadings by the Atypicality, Depression, Anxiety, Somatization, and Withdrawal scales. Adaptive skills scales that load highly on this factor include Activities of Daily Living, Functional Communication, Leadership, and Social Skills.

Some of the secondary loadings for the scales may also have implications for interpretation. Specifically, the factor-analytic data suggest that the following profiles are reasonable:

- Poor Adaptive Skills with Attention Problems
- Good Adaptive Skills with Anxiety
- Internalizing Problems accompanied by Poor Adaptability

Criterion-related validity analyses produced consistent associations between the PRS and other parent rating scales. This pattern particularly holds for the composites and for the externalizing problem scales. Generally, the internalizing problem scales (e.g., Anxiety, Depression, Somatization) show moderate correlations with analogous scales from other measures (see Reynolds & Kamphaus, 2004).

Interpretation

The same logical interpretive steps that were outlined for the BASC-SRP (discussed in Chap. 6) also apply to the BASC-PRS. Briefly, the clinician should:

1. Assess validity using validity indexes and informal means (e.g., inspect for a high number of items with no response).
2. Inspect critical items and follow-up as appropriate.
3. Interpret scores on scales and composites, with particular attention to elevations (T-scores of 65–70 and higher) on clinical scales and low scores (T-scores of 35 and below) on adaptive scales.
4. Attend to items that appeared to have led to scale elevations (or low adaptive scores).
5. Integrate score with information from other informants.
6. Integrate data with information from other assessment tools (e.g., interview,

behavioral observations, intelligence testing).
7. Set objectives for treatment/intervention

As was the case with the SRP, we again recommend a focus on interpretation at the scale level, as the reliabilities of the PRS scales are generally good, and elevations on scales are more specifically informative than would be the case for elevated composite scores.

The original PRS enjoyed a great deal of research support and research use. There is quite limited information available to date on the BASC-2-PRS. Nevertheless, the combined rational and empirical approach to scale development has intuitive appeal for use in clinical situations. Clinicians are still urged to keep abreast of the research literature discussing the strengths and limitations of any assessment tool.

Strengths and Weaknesses

The BASC-2-PRS has a number of apparent strengths and weaknesses as follows:

The strengths of the PRS are:

1. Good psychometric properties based on the information reported in the BASC-2 manual.
2. A variety of scales that may be useful for differential diagnosis (e.g., Attention Problems vs. Hyperactivity, and Anxiety vs. Depression).
3. The availability of validity scales and critical items.
4. An expanded group of norm-referenced adaptive scales

Among the weaknesses of the PRS are:

1. A response format that does not allow parents to provide additional detail about their responses
2. Cross-informant and cross-scale comparisons not as readily made as on other measures, as different forms (e.g., parent vs. self-report) include different item content and scales
3. Limited research on the latest edition of the PRS.

Teacher Rating Scale (TRS)

The BASC-2 Teacher Rating Scale (BASC-2-TRS; Reynolds & Kamphaus, 2004) allows the clinician to gather information on a child's observable behavior from the child's teacher and place that information in the context of other information obtained in the overall BASC system (e.g., self-report scale, parent rating scales, classroom observation system). As with the PRS, there are three forms of the BASC-2-TRS: preschool (ages 2–5), child (6–11), and adolescent (12–21). The three forms contain behavioral descriptors that are rated by the teacher on a four-point scale of frequency, ranging from "Never" to "Almost Always." The three forms have 100 items for the preschool version and 139 for both the child and adolescent versions.

Content

As with the other BASC-2 rating scales, the items of the BASC-2-TRS were chosen to measure multiple aspects of a child's personality and behavior. The TRS includes both positive (adaptive) and pathological (clinical) dimensions. For the most part, the BASC-2-TRS has maintained the content areas of the original BASC. The only scale additions to the current version of the TRS were the Functional Communication scale for all age groups and the Adaptability scale for the adolescent version. The BASC-2-TRS consists of five composites (i.e., Behavioral Symptoms Index, School Problems, Externalizing Problems, Internalizing Problems, Adaptive Skills) across all age ranges, with 11 scales in the preschool version and 15 scales in the child and adolescent versions. The scales grouped into the composites – except for the Behavioral Symptoms Index which includes the Hyperactivity, Atypicality, Depression, Aggression, Attention Problems, and Withdrawal scales – are provided in Table 7.4. The TRS also has the same optional content scales as those provided for the PRS (see above). Because these are a new feature of the BASC-2, very limited information is available on their psychometric properties or clinical utility.

The content coverage of the BASC-2-TRS scales has several unique features relative to other teacher rating scales. First, it provides comprehensive coverage of several areas of adaptive behavior. Second, the current version of the TRS continues the strategy of including separate scales for motor hyperactivity and attention problems, which aids in the differentiation of subtypes of Attention-Deficit Hyperactivity Disorder (Vaughn, Riccio, Hynd, & Hall, 1997). Third, there are separate scales for anxiety, depression, and withdrawal, which aid in the assessment of emotional difficulties. Fourth, the BASC-2-TRS includes items that screen for learning problems that often accompany emotional and behavioral problems in children.

Table 7.4 Composites and Scales of BASC-2-TRS

Composite	Scales
Externalizing Problems	Aggression Hyperactivity Conduct Problems
Internalizing Problems	Anxiety Depression Somatization
School Problems	Attention Problems Learning Problems
Adaptive Skills	Adaptability Functional Communication
	Leadership
	Social Skills
	Study Skills

Administration and Scoring

The BASC-TRS takes approximately 10–20 min to complete. The cover of the record provides instructions to the teacher for completing the form and space for recording background information about the child and teacher (e.g., age, gender, type of class, length of time in class). Both hand scoring and computer scoring are available. Norm tables in the BASC manual are provided so that any of four sets of norms can be used: general, male, female, and clinical (see above for discussion of the uses of these different types of norms). Both T-scores and percentile ranks are listed for each set of norms, with linear T-scores again being utilized for the TRS. As with the other BASC-2 rating scales, the BASC-2-TRS scoring sheet highlights critical items (e.g., "I want to kill myself") that are clinically important or that warrant further follow-up.

Norming

The norming group included 1,050 preschoolers, 1,800 children (ages 6–11), and 1,800 adolescents (ages 12–21) with equal sex distributions in all age groups. Respondents were recruited from sites throughout the USA. As described previously, the sampling procedures for obtaining the normative sample were designed to closely mirror US Census statistics in terms of race/ethnicity, SES, and geographic region, and this goal was accomplished (see Reynolds & Kamphaus, 2004). Details regarding the 1,779-member clinical sample for the TRS are also provided in the BASC-2 Manual.

Reliability

The manual for the BASC-2-TRS (Reynolds & Kamphaus, 2004) provides evidence on three types of reliability: internal consistency, test-retest reliability, and interrater reliability. With very few exceptions, the scales of the BASC-2-TRS proved to be quite reliable in the normative sample.

More specifically, internal consistency coefficients tended to average well above 0.80 across all age groups, and all were 0.75 or higher. Similarly, test-retest reliability over one to nine weeks was high, with the exception of the Anxiety scale, with coefficients ranging from 0.64 for the adolescent version to 0.77 for the adolescent version. Still, these coefficients are adequate. Finally, the consistency of ratings between two teachers was tested in samples of preschool-age children ($n = 74$), school-age children ($n = 38$), and adolescents ($n = 58$), with moderate reliability estimates emerging across age group samples (median coefficients of 0.69, 0.60, and 0.52, respectively). Correlation coefficients tend to be somewhat higher for externalizing than for internalizing problems consistent with past research (Achenbach, McConaughy, & Howell, 1987). It is also worth noting that the coefficients tended to be lower for adolescents, which may be associated with the limited contact an individual teacher may have with students of that age group. Interrater agreement for Somatization ($r = 0.25$), Withdrawal ($r = 0.24$), and Atypicality ($r = 0.31$) was particularly low for teacher ratings of adolescents.

Validity

The TRS is closely, but not exactly, aligned with the item content of the PRS. However, the TRS has additional scales (i.e., Study Skills, Learning Problems) that seem particularly valid for use with a teacher rating scale. The BASC-2 manual provides factor analytic support for the construct validity of the scales and composites of the TRS. In addition, initial research on the TRS shows generally high correlations with analogous scales from other teacher rating scales. However, the correspondence to analogous scales is somewhat lower for internalizing types of problems than for the indices of externalizing problems (see Reynolds & Kamphaus, 2004). One notable finding was the lack of a correlation (i.e., $r = .03$) between the TRS Somatization scale and the Somatic Complaints scale of the Achenbach Teacher Report Form. A significant limitation of the latest version of the TRS is the very limited research on its validity and utility outside of what was conducted by the developers.

Interpretation

The BASC-2-TRS includes validity scales that provide a useful and efficient first point of interpretation. More specifically, it contains a "fake bad" index (F), which helps to assess the possibility that a teacher rated a child in an overly negative pattern. Therefore, interpretation of this scale, in particular, should be the first step in the interpretative process, keeping in mind that a high score on the F index may actually indicate significantly problematic functioning. Therefore, this validity index should be interpreted in the context of other assessment data. The Consistency Index and the Response Pattern Index available for the TRS (as are available for the PRS and SRP) provide another initial point of interpretation. Critical items should be reviewed promptly, because these items tend to be clinically important indicators that deserve careful follow-up assessment.

The reliability estimates at the scale level of the TRS are good; therefore, we again recommend focusing interpretation mainly at the scale, rather than composite, level since more specific information is available through the TRS scales. Interpretations at the item level must be made quite cautiously because of the low reliability of individual items. It is often informative to see which items led to a child's or adolescent's elevation on a given clinical scales. For example, it may be informative for a child with an elevation on the Adaptability scale to determine if this elevation was largely due to problems specifically within the interpersonal domains or due to more general problems in adapting to changes in routine. Finally, interpretation at the scale level for the parent form is a viable early step in interpretation (see above); therefore, interpretation at the scale level of the TRS facilitates integration of information across parent and teacher ratings. In addition, considering individual items within elevated scales on both rating forms may help determine the source of consistencies and inconsistencies across parent and teacher ratings, further informing case conceptualization and recommendations.

Strengths and Weaknesses

Like its predecessor and its companion parent rating scale, the BASC-2-TRS has a number of strengths and weaknesses. Notable strengths include:

1. It is part of a multimethod, multi-informant system that aids in a comprehensive clinical evaluation with item content that covers important problematic and adaptive domains of classroom behavioral and emotional functioning.
2. The assessment of adaptive functioning is enhanced on this version of the TRS.
3. The preschool age range of the BASC-2-TRS is expanded from the age range available from the original TRS.
4. The BASC-2-TRS has a large nationwide normative sample on which norm-referenced scores are based, allowing for one to confidently make many norm-referenced interpretations of scores.

Weaknesses of the BASC-2-TRS include:

1. The limited research base for the current edition.
2. The relatively lower correlations between internalizing scales on the TRF and analogous scales from other teacher rating scales.
3. The different item content across informants, especially with the SRP, makes integration of BASC-2 information somewhat more challenging.

A sample case using the BASC-2-PRS and BASC-2 TRS is provided in Box 7.1.

Achenbach System of Empirically Based Assessment (Achenbach & Rescorla, 2000, 2001)

Parent Report: Child Behavior Checklist (CBCL)

The Child Behavior Checklist (CBCL; Achenbach, 2001) and its predecessors have a long history of prominence in child assessment. The CBCL scale is the product of an extensive multiple-decade research effort, and it has a distinguished history of research usage. The current version of the CBCL is much like its predecessors with some item changes, response format changes, and the introduction of DSM-Oriented scales (see below; see Achenbach & Rescorla, 2001).

The CBCL is part of an extensive system of scales including teacher rating (TRF), self-report (YSR), and classroom observation measures. The newest version of the CBCL (Achenbach & Rescorla, 2001) has two separate forms: one for ages 1½–5 and the other for children of ages 6–18.

The development of the CBCL and its revisions reflects the author's belief that parent reports are an important part of any multi-informant system of child evaluation. In Achenbach's (1991) own words:

> Parents (and parent surrogates) are typically among the most important sources of data about children's competencies and problems. They are usually the most knowledgeable about their child's behavior across time and situations. Furthermore, parent involvement is required in the evaluation of most children, and parents' views of their children's behavior are often crucial in determining what will be done about the behavior. Parents' reports should therefore be obtained in the assessment of children's competencies and problems whenever possible (p. 3).

Box 7.1

Sample Case Using the BASC-2 PRS and TRS

Johnny was referred for a psychological evaluation by his mother because of his academic difficulties and distractibility. He is a 12-year-old sixth-grader. Johnny has reportedly had trouble completing schoolwork since the first grade. Johnny was retained in the second grade because of poor work completion and academic progress. He was reportedly placed in special education in the third grade in a learning problem class. He was reportedly placed in a regular class again in the fourth grade. A psychological evaluation conducted at the end of the fourth grade resulted in the conclusion that he was a "slow learner," according to his mother. This year, he is again having difficulty concentrating, and he rarely completes his assignments. Academic progress is still unacceptable to his mother and teachers.

Johnny's developmental milestones were slightly delayed. He still reportedly has problems drawing and using scissors. Last year, he was diagnosed with juvenile diabetes, according to his mother. His family psychiatric history is significant for depression (mother), and Johnny's father reportedly had difficulty academically when he was in school.

Johnny was exceedingly cooperative during the evaluation. He addressed the examiner politely and would occasionally answer questions by saying "yes sir." He had considerable difficulty comprehending instructions on an intelligence test. He was reluctant to admit to not knowing an answer, and he worked extremely slowly. The test session had to be conducted over two days because of his slow response style.

He responded impulsively to items on occasion. He also wiggled in his seat and frequently looked around the room and asked questions of the examiner. His full scale IQ score in this evaluation was 85. His achievement test scores were similarly in the Low Average range.

His BASC-2-PRS (completed by his mother) and BASC-2-TRS (completed by his current teacher) results are highly consistent with background information.

Hyperactivity
$T = 63$ (parent report)
$T = 60$ (teacher report)

The reports of relatively mild levels of hyperactivity are consistent with Johnny's history which indicates no history of disruptive or impulsive behaviors.

Attention Problems
$T = 76$ (parent)
$T = 77$ (teacher)
The parent and teacher reports of significant attention problems (e.g., has trouble concentrating, is easily distracted, daydreams) is consistent with reports of Johnny's difficulties dating back to the first grade.

Somatization
$T = 67$ (parent)
$T = 63$ (teacher)
Mild to moderate concerns in the area of Somatization appear to be related to Johnny's history of diabetes and its attendant difficulties.

Learning Problems
$T = 72$ (teacher)
Johnny's teacher reported significant learning problems for Johnny, indicating concerns in all academic areas. It was recommended that he be further evaluated through a Response to Intervention (RTI) procedure at his school, and services available to him should be planned accordingly.

Adaptability
$T = 39$ (parent)
$T = 32$ (teacher)

Functional Communication
$T = 30$ (parent)
$T = 32$ (teacher)
Johnny's mother and teacher reported concerns with his ability to adjust to changes in plans and to adequately communicate his need for help. These difficulties may interfere with his academic performance.

Johnny's results were strikingly similar for both teachers and parents. The diagnosis of ADHD, Predominantly Inattentive Type was made based on Johnny's history as reported by his mother and teacher during interviews and based on these scores on the PRS and TRS.

Content

The CBCL includes 100 items for the preschool version and 113 items for the school age version. Responses are made on a three-point scale (i.e., Not True; Sometimes/Somewhat True; Very True/Often True).

The CBCL syndrome scales are primarily empirically derived, with substantial use of factor-analytic methods. The CBCL scales were also derived separately by gender and age group (see Achenbach & Rescorla, 2000, 2001). Throughout the test development process, the CBCL developers also emphasized the derivation of scales that were common across raters (e.g., parents and teachers). The CBCL parent and teacher scales have closely matched items and scales that make it easier for clinicians to make cross-informant comparisons. Sample item content from the CBCL scales is shown in Table 7.5.

TABLE 7.5 Sample Content of CBCL (6–18-Year-Old Version) Syndrome Scales

Anxious/Depressed: Cries a lot, is fearful, feels too guilty, talks of suicide

Withdrawn/Depressed: Would rather be alone, shy/timid, sad

Somatic Complaints: Feels dizzy, constipated, has headaches, nausea

Social Problems: Dependent, lonely, gets teased, prefers to be with younger kids

Thought Problems: Cannot get mind off of certain thoughts, sees things, stores things, strange behavior

Attention Problems: Cannot concentrate, daydreams, impulsive, cannott sit still

Rule-breaking Behavior: Drinks alcohol, lacks guilt, breaks rules, sets fires, prefers to be with older kids

Aggressive Behavior: Argues a lot, destroys others' things, gets in fights, mood changes, attacks people

From Achenbach & Rescorla (2001).

The item content for the preschool (ages 1½–5) version of the CBCL is notably different from the version for 6–18-year olds, with somewhat different syndrome scales. The syndrome scales for the 1½–5-year-old version are Emotionally Reactive, Anxious/Depressed, Somatic Complaints, Withdrawn, Sleep Problems, Attention Problems, and Aggressive Behavior (Achenbach & Rescorla, 2000).

On both versions, there is a Total Problems score (the most global score available on the CBCL) as well as composites for Internalizing Problems and Externalizing Problems (see Achenbach & Rescorla, 2000, 2001). The CBCL also includes competence scales (except for the preschool version) that are designed to discriminate significantly between children referred for mental health services and non-referred children (Achenbach & Rescorla, 2001).

DSM-Oriented scales were formed based on experts' ratings (see Achenbach, Dumenci, & Rescorla, 2001) of how well the items fit DSM criteria for relevant disorders or groups of disorders (e.g., Major Depression and Dysthymia for the Affective Problems scale). For the school-age version of the CBCL, the DSM-Oriented scales are Affective Problems, Anxiety Problems, Somatic Problems, Attention/Hyperactivity Problems, Oppositional Defiant Problems, Conduct Problems. The five DSM-oriented scales on the preschool version of the CBCL are Affective Problems, Anxiety Problems, Pervasive Developmental Problems, Attention Deficit/Hyperactivity Problems, and Oppositional Defiant Problems. The DSM-Oriented scales are a new feature to the Achenbach system and were designed to more closely align scores that were available from these instruments to current diagnostic nomenclature.

Administration and Scoring

The CBCL is easily administered in 15–20 min. The CBCL is somewhat unique in that adaptive behavior is assessed with a combined fill-in-the-blank and Likert scale response format. In addition, some of the problem behavior items require the parent to elaborate on or describe the problem endorsed. This format is advantageous in that it allows the parent to respond in an open-ended format. Clinicians can gain access to qualitative information of value using this format. Open-endedness, however, also has a disadvantage: It may extend administration time and requires more decision making on the part of the parent.

Hand scoring and computer scoring are available for the CBCL. The CBCL offers normalized T-scores as the featured interpretive scores. Percentile ranks are also provided. T-scores are available for all scales and three composites: Externalizing, Internalizing, and Total. T-scores are now also offered for the Competence scales.

The advantages and disadvantages of using normalized versus linear T's are debatable (see Kline, 1995). On the one hand, the advantage of comparable percentile ranks across scales was recognized by the MMPI-A author team (see Chap. 6). Normalized scores, however, clearly change the shape of the many skewed raw score distributions forcing the T-score distribution to take a shape that it does not actually take in the general population (see Chap. 2). In addition, the reporting of T-scores on the CBCL is truncated for the Syndrome and DSM-Oriented scales such that low scores are reported simply as $T \leq 50$. For the Competence scales, the distribution is truncated above a T-score of 65 and below a T-score of 35.

Norming

The norming of the school age CBCL is based on a national sample of 1,753 children aged 6 through 18 years. This sample was collected in 40 states and the District of Columbia (Achenbach & Rescorla, 2001). Relevant stratification variables such as age, gender, ethnicity, region, and SES were recorded in an attempt to closely match US Census statistics on these variables. The respondents were mothers in 72% of the cases and fathers in 23% of the cases (5% of the cases used "others"). Sixty percent of the respondents were classified as White, with Hispanics appearing to be somewhat underrepresented (9%). Fifty-one percent of cases were from a middle SES background, 33% were from an upper SES background, and 16% were from a lower SES background. Forty percent of respondents were from the southern part of the USA (see Achenbach & Rescorla, 2001). From this sample, separate norms were developed for ages 6–11 and 12–18, with each of these groups further delineated by gender.

The norming sample for the preschool CBCL version for ages 1½–5 was also recruited in an attempt to match US Census statistics on the same variables. This sample consisted of 700 respondents (76% mothers, 22% fathers, 2% "others"). Fifty-six percent of respondents were White, 21% African American, 13% Latino, and 10% Mixed or Others. In the preschool norming sample, 33% of respondents were from an upper SES background, 49% from middle SES, and 17% from a lower SES background. Again, 40% of these respondents were from the southern USA (Achenbach & Rescorla, 2000).

Children were excluded from the sample if they had "received mental health or special education classes during the previous 12 months" (Achenbach & Rescorla, 2001, p. 76). Separate clinical norms are not offered for the CBCL.

Reliability

The CBCL has good evidence of reliability with internal consistency coefficients ranging from 0.78 to 0.97 on the Syndrome scales, 0.72 to 0.91 on the DSM-oriented scales, and somewhat lower internal consistency on the

Competence scales (i.e., 0.63 to 0.79; Achenbach & Rescorla, 2001). On the preschool version of the CBCL, the internal consistency coefficients for the Syndrome scales and composites ranged from 0.66 to 0.95. For the DSM-Oriented scales, internal consistencies ranged from 0.63 to 0.86 (Achenbach & Rescorla, 2000). The data from a test-retest study for a sample of 73 (*mean* interval = 8 days) children yielded coefficients ranging from 0.80 for the Anxiety DSM-Oriented scale to 0.93 for the DSM-Oriented Conduct Problems scale on the 6–18-year-old version (Achenbach & Rescorla, 2001). For the preschool CBCL (n = 68), 8-day test-retest reliabilities were good, ranging from 0.74 for the Attention-Deficit/Hyperactivity Problems DSM-Oriented scale to 0.92 for the Sleep Problems scale (Achenbach & Rescorla, 2000).

A two-year stability study of 67 children yielded coefficients ranging from 0.45 for Somatic Problems to 0.81 for Aggressive Behavior for the school age CBCL. Twelve-month test-retest coefficients for the preschool version (n = 80) ranged from 0.52 for two of the DSM-Oriented scales to 0.62 for the Anxious/Depressed Syndrome Scale. These coefficients are indicative of strong reliability in light of the lengthy interval and the expected natural instability in some of these areas over time. Lastly, mother–father interrater agreement on the CBCL was generally good on the school age version with all coefficients except the Activities scale being 0.63 or higher. The interrater agreement on the preschool version was lower, with coefficients ranging from 0.48 to 0.67 (see Achenbach & Rescorla, 2000).

Validity

Much of the validity evidence reported by the authors of the CBCL focuses on the ability of the scale to differentiate clinical from nonclincal samples. Results of these analyses indicated good differential validity across scales for both boys and girls. As noted in Chap. 2, however, evidence of differential validity must now also show differentiation between clinical samples. To date, such evidence is lacking for the latest versions of the CBCL.

The factor structure of the CBCL continues to raise some conceptual issues regarding the content validity of the scales. For example, it is unusual for depression and anxiety items to be included on the same scale. In addition, the Attention Problems scale includes items that appear more indicative of hyperactivity and impulsivity than inattention (see Table 7.5). High scores on these scales still require a great deal of clinical judgment as to what characteristics led to the high scores and should be the focus of further attention.

Validity studies as well as basic and applied research investigations using the previous versions of the CBCL are legion. Although the research base of the current CBCL is not as well-established, some evidence on its validity is promising. For example, the preschool version of the CBCL has been found to be useful in screening for Autism Spectrum Disorders based on the Withdrawal and Pervasive Developmental Problems scales (Sikora et al., 2008), and the CBCL has been touted for its ability to screen for a variety of problem areas and its strong convergent and divergent validity (Scholte, Van Berckelaer-Onnes, & Van der Ploeg, 2008). However, the correspondence of the DSM-Oriented Anxiety scale on the CBCL to *DSM* criteria for anxiety disorders has been called into question (Ferdinand, 2008). Clearly, more research is needed on the latest rating scales in the Achenbach system, but just as clearly, the CBCL has enjoyed and continues to enjoy a great deal of empirical support.

Interpretation

Interpretation of the CBCL is bolstered by many articles by Achenbach and colleagues devoted to its clinical use dating to McConaughy and Achenbach's (1989) informative work on this subject. The CBCL user is fortunate to have many interpretive resources available.

More specifically, McConaughy and Achenbach (1989) provide an assessment methodology for the identification of severe emotional disturbance in the schools. Their multi-axial empirically based assessment model proposes five axes for such assessment situations: (1) parent reports (Achenbach, CBCL), (2) teacher reports (Achenbach Teacher Report Form), (3) cognitive assessment, (4) physical assessment, and (5) direct assessment of the child (i.e., Achenbach Direct Observation Form and Youth Self-Report). McConaughy and Achenbach assist the psychologist working in schools further by linking each CBCL scale to the accepted criteria for severe emotional disturbance. High scores on the Anxious/Depressed scale may, for example, indicate the presence of a general pervasive mood of unhappiness, which, in turn, may qualify a child as severely emotionally disturbed and document eligibility for special education and related services. Of course, these examples fit best with previous versions of the CBCL and are only as useful as their degree of correspondence with eligibility categories used by school systems.

For interpreting the CBCL specifically, because there are no established validity scales and because there are some scales that include heterogeneous content, we recommend more attention to item-level interpretation than we have for other measures. That is, the clinician should pay close attention to scale elevations and draw most conclusions at the scale level; however, it would behoove practitioners to determine any concerning aspects of the parent's item response style that would render the protocol invalid. Additionally, interpretation should not stop at the scale level. Rather, one should inspect the items that led to the scale elevations to determine the best way to describe the child's difficulties. Fortunately, the scoring methods available for the CBCL make linking item responses to scale elevations a straightforward process.

Strengths and Weaknesses

The CBCL has many strengths that continue to make it a popular choice for clinicians. Noteworthy strengths include:

1. An ever-growing research base on the current CBCL, as well as a wealth of validity research on its predecessors.
2. Its popularity among professionals which facilitates communication about its results
3. Several writings that provide interpretive guidance above and beyond that provided by the manual
4. Improved approach to assessing competence and available of new DSM-Oriented scales that are aligned to *DSM* criteria.
5. Some response flexibility in that parents are asked to elaborate on their answers to some items.

Weaknesses of the CBCL include:

1. Lack of validity scales which are now common among behavioral rating scales.
2. Lack of close correspondence between the empirically derived scales and common diagnostic criteria (e.g., *DSM;* Hart & Lahey, 1998)
3. Heterogeneous content within some scales.

The CBCL continues to be a preferred choice of many child clinicians because of its history of successful use and popularity with researchers. The continuing development of the CBCL database bodes well for its future. The most recent versions of the CBCL would benefit from research aimed at assessing the construct validity of its scales, particularly the DSM-Oriented scales which were not part of the previous CBCL. Such research efforts are necessary to define further the degree of confidence that a clinician can place on specific scales for making differential diagnostic decisions.

Teacher Report: Teacher Report Form (TRF)

The Achenbach Teacher Report Form (TRF; Achenbach & Rescorla, 2001) is designed to be completed by teachers of children between the ages of 6 and 18 for the school-age version and between 1½ and 5 for the preschool version which is labeled the "Caregiver-Teacher Report Form" (Achenbach & Rescorla, 2000). The item content of the TRF is very closely matches the CBCL item content.

Content

The school age version of the TRF includes several background questions (e.g., "How long have you known this pupil?" "How well do you know him/her?"), a teacher's rating of a child's academic performance, and a four-item screening of a child's adaptive behavior with scoring on a 1–7 scale (e.g., "How hard is he/she working?" "How appropriately is he/she behaving?" "How much is he/she learning?" "How happy is he/she?"). The preschool TRF includes the same background questions but does not include the other items. These background questions have associated norms and fall under the "Adaptive Functioning" domain of the TRF. The major portion of the TRF consists of 100 items for the preschool version and 113 items for the school age version. These items describe problematic behaviors and emotions that the teacher rates as being Not True, Somewhat True/Sometimes True, or Very True/Often True of the child. The problem behavior items cover a broad array of both internalizing (e.g., anxiety, depression, somatic complaints) and externalizing (antisocial behavior, aggression, oppositionality) behaviors. As with the CBCL, the TRF now includes DSM-Oriented scales (6 for the school age version; 5 for the preschool version). The only scale difference is that the TRF does not include a Sleep Problems scale.

Administration and Scoring

The TRF takes approximately 15–20 min to complete. The instructions to the teacher are printed on the front of the answer sheet. Scoring of the TRS can be done by hand using the TRF Profile Sheets with separate profile sheets available for boys and girls. However, a computer-scoring system is available that greatly facilitates scoring by automatically calculating raw scale scores and converting them to norm-referenced scores appropriate for the child's age and gender.

Both the Profile Sheets and the computer-scoring program provide raw scores and norm-referenced scores for several scales. As with the CBCL, a Total Problem score, which is an overall indicator of a child's classroom adjustment, and two broadband scores consisting of Internalizing and Externalizing behaviors are included. These broad dimensions are further divided into the eight Syndrome scales.

The TRF allows for raw scores on all scales to be converted to T-scores and percentile ranks based on the standardization sample. The T-scores are normalized standard scores. That is, the raw score distributions are transformed to a normalized distribution. This procedure allows T-scores on all scales to have similar distributions and corresponding percentiles based on the assumptions of a normal distribution. However, as noted previously for the CBCL, this transformation assumes that the dimensions assessed by the scale *should* be normally distributed in the general population, an assumption that is questionable because most children tend to cluster in the normal end of the distribution. Norm-referenced scores are based on gender and age-specific norms. In addition, as with the CBCL, T-scores on the TRF are truncated, such that the lowest score provided is ≤ 50.

Norming

The norming sample for the school-age version of the TRF consisted of 2,319 children, 72% of whom were White. Fourteen percent were identified as African American, and 7% were identified as Latino; thus, both ethnic minority groups appear to be underrepresented in this sample. The TRF normative sample appears to be geographically representative. Thirty-eight percent of children in this sample were from an upper SES background, 46% from a middle SES background, and 16% from a low SES background.

For the preschool version, the norming sample consisted of 1,192 children. This sample was geographically diverse, but only 10% of the sample came from a lower SES background. The sample represented Whites and African Americans well (i.e., 48% and 36%, respectively), with only 8% of the sample identifying as Latino.

For both versions of the TRF, the normative sample excluded children who had received mental health or special education services within the preceding 12 months. Therefore, as with the other rating scales in the Achenbach system, the sample should be considered a normal comparison group, rather than one that is normative and representative of the general population.

Reliability

Achenbach and Rescorla (2000, 2001) provide three types of reliability information on the TRF. Internal consistency estimates were provided for the Syndrome and DSM-Oriented scales. Coefficients indicated good internal consistency, ranging from 0.72 to 0.95. For the preschool version, coefficients were quite variable, ranging from 0.52 for Somatic Complaints to 0.96 for the Aggressive Behaviors scale. Test-retest reliability over an average of a 16-day interval is presented on a sample of 44 children in the age range of 6–18. The test-retest coefficients were generally high (i.e., 0.80s and higher), with the exception of the Withdrawn/Depressed scale ($r = 0.60$) and the Affective Problems scale ($r = 0.62$). Four-month test-retest reliability was variable, ranging from 0.31 (Affective Problems) to 0.72 (Hyperactivity-Impulsivity). The 8-day test-retest reliability for the preschool version of the TRF was somewhat variable, ranging from a coefficient of 0.57 for Anxiety Problems to 0.91 for Somatic Complaints (the scale with the lowest internal consistency). Three-month test-retest reliability for the preschool TRF was variable with coefficients ranging from 0.22 for Somatic Complaints to 0.71 for Emotionally Reactive.

Correlations between ratings from two different teachers are provided for 88 children (Achenbach & Rescorla, 2001). The correlations were modest across scales, with the mean coefficient for the full sample being 0.49 for the Competence scales, 0.60 for the Syndrome scales, and .58 for the DSM-Oriented scales. Similar analyses for 102 preschoolers revealed an overall mean coefficient of 0.62, with a range of 0.21 (Somatic Complaints) to 0.78 (Aggressive Behavior).

Validity

There is relatively limited validity information available for the current versions of the TRF. The validity data reported in the manuals (Achenbach & Rescorla, 2000, 2001) mainly focus on the ability of the scales to differentiate non-referred from clinical samples within gender. The TRF scales generally show such differential validity. However, the Somatic Complaints scale of both versions does not appear to consistently differentiate the two groups (Achenbach & Rescorla, 2000, 2001). As noted above, validity studies for the BASC-2-TRS demonstrated good correspondence with the TRF, especially for externalizing problems. An exception was the lack of correlation between scales on each form assessing somatic complaints. Research has supported the predictive validity of the TRF at age three in predicting problems, especially externalizing problems, at age five (Kerr et al., 2007). The TRF, like the CBCL, was based heavily on its well-researched predecessor. There is a wealth of research on the previous versions of the TRF which supports its validity in (1) differentiating clinic-referred children from non-referred children, (2) correlating with classroom observations of children's behavior, and (3) correlating with independent clinical diagnoses (see Achenbach, 1991; Casat, Norton, & Boyle-Whitesel, 1999; Piacentini, 1993).

Interpretation

Information on the reliability and validity of the adaptive functioning component of the TRF is lacking; therefore, interpretations of these scales should be done very cautiously, if at all. Subsequently, although it may be useful to next consider the TRF Total Problems score and composites, more specific information can be gleaned from interpretations of the eight syndrome scales and the six DSM-Oriented scales. The reliability of these scales (with the exception of the Somatic Complaints scale) is good. However, because the initial development of the TRS item pool was done in an attempt to be atheoretical, the item content of the TRS scales tends to be more heterogeneous than other rating scales that used a more explicit guiding theory for scale development. For example, the Attention Problems scale consists of items traditionally associated with inattention (e.g., difficulty concentrating) but also includes items associated with immaturity, overactivity, poor school achievement, and clumsiness. Therefore, it is imperative that the items that led to a clinical scale elevation be reviewed to understand the meaning of the elevation. For example, a child may show an elevation on the Attention Problems scale because of problems with immaturity, clumsiness, or academic problems, or a child may have an elevation due to problems of inattention and/or hyperactivity. However, because of the unreliability of individual items, this item-level analysis should be conducted only when there is an elevation on the clinical scale. The Attention-Deficit/Hyperactivity Problems DSM-Oriented scale can be quite helpful in this type of scenario as it is more closely aligned with characteristics indicative of ADHD.

Interpretation of the Thought Problems scale on both the TRF and CBCL deserves several cautionary notes. This scale has an especially heterogeneous content, consisting of items describing obsessions (e.g., "Cannot get mind off certain thoughts"), compulsions (e.g., "Repeats acts over and over"), fears (e.g., "Fears certain animals, situations, or places"), and psychotic behaviors (e.g., "Hears sounds or voices that are not there"), many of which are fairly ambiguous (e.g., strange behavior, strange ideas). For this scale, it should be apparent that item level interpretation and integration with other information collected during the assessment are crucial before drawing conclusions.

One final note is in order for interpreting TRS scales. Because the norm-referenced scores of the TRS are based on a normal sample and not a normative sample, it is recommended that a more conservative cut-off score be used than would be the case for other rating scales. Any elevations, regardless of the degree of elevation, should still be considered in conjunction with other assessment results (e.g., parent report, self-report, history, observations, etc.). The sample case that follows gives a brief example of an interpretive approach to the CBCL and TRF (Box 7.2).

Box 7.2

Sample Case Using the CBCL and TRF

Doug is an 11-year-old, fifth-grade boy who was referred for an assessment because of parental and teacher concerns about his school performance. He is suspected of having significant attention problems. Doug also has significant trouble in peer and other relationships. He often fights and argues with peers, resulting in his often playing by himself.

Doug has a history of significant medical difficulties. He is reportedly the product of an at-risk pregnancy. Although he reportedly reached most developmental milestones within normal age limits, he has a history of motor delays. In second grade, he was diagnosed with muscular dystrophy. He does not tolerate many foods well, and consequently, his appetite is poor.

In the first grade, Doug was diagnosed with a learning disability in reading. He is in a resource special education program. He is described by his teacher as having significant social difficulties. He is reportedly often disrespectful toward teachers and peers. His grades deteriorated significantly toward the end of the last academic year. His teachers consider him to be a capable underachiever with behavior problems such as inattention, excessive talking, fighting, arguing, and poor work completion.

Doug's performance on intelligence and achievement testing indicate that his cognitive functioning is consistent with what would be expected for his age, whereas his writing and reading skills were slightly below what would be expected for his age.

Doug's ratings from the CBCL and TRF completed by his mother and teacher reflect the multitude of his difficulties as follows:

Scale	Mother/Teacher (T)
Withdrawn/Depressed	70/61
Somatic Complaints	91/64
Anxious/Depressed	79/55
Social Problems	80/75
Thought Problems	79/67
Attention Problems	78/69
Rule-Breaking Behav.	73/76
Aggressive Behav.	85/65

Comparisons across these two raters, behavioral observations, and background information indicate that Doug is experiencing difficulties in a number of behavioral, emotional, and social domains. In particular, reports by Doug's mother and teacher of his tendency to daydream, his difficulty sustaining attention, his impulsive behavior, and his restlessness, as well as the fact that such behaviors were reported for Doug at an early age, suggest that he meets criteria for a diagnosis of Attention-Deficit Hyperactivity Disorder (ADHD)- Combined Type. Ratings on the CBCL and TRF Attention-Deficit/Hyperactivity Problems scale also indicated significant problems with behaviors related to ADHD. In addition, Doug's reported argumentativeness, disrespect toward others, and tendency to break rules at home and at school indicate that he meets criteria for Oppositional Defiant Disorder as well. Some concerns regarding depression were also reported, particularly by Doug's mother. However, these issues do not warrant another diagnosis, but they do warrant continued monitoring and some interventions.

Indications of thought problems were not corroborated by other findings. The problems reported by Doug's mother on this scale (e.g., trouble sleeping, cannot't get his mind off certain things) seemed particularly tied to his reported problems with depression.

CBCL and TRF Social Problems scores were corroborated by reports of his difficulty getting along with others. Doug's social interaction skills are in need of intervention.

Although the CBCL and TRF clearly indicate some areas of concern and in need of intervention, this case also highlights the need, more pressing in a case like this, to complement the CBCL and TRF with other assessment strategies. In this case, background information was particularly important for corroborating rating scale information and indentifying treatment objectives.

Strengths and Weaknesses

The TRF remains one of the most widely used of the teacher-completed behavior rating scales. In addition to its popularity and familiarity with a large number of professionals, the strengths of the TRF include:

1. The large research literature on the TRF and its predecessors which demonstrates good correspondence between the TRF and other indicators of child functioning, particularly on externalizing behaviors.
2. The inclusion of DSM-Oriented scales aids the clinician in interpreting teacher reports in terms of diagnostic categories.
3. A larger normative sample than was available for the previous versions of the TRF.

Some weaknesses of the TRF include:

1. An underrepresentation of Hispanics in the normative sample.
2. The exclusion of children with mental health or special education services in the normative sample, indicating that such children are not represented.
3. The questionable reliability and validity of the Somatic Complaints scale.
4. A relatively limited assessment of adaptive functioning.

Child Symptom Inventory-4 (CSI-4)

Parent and Teacher Report Checklists

The Child Symptom Inventory-4 (CSI-4; Gadow & Sprafkin, 1998) is a standardized rating scale designed to assess the symptoms of over a dozen childhood disorders. This content is unique from other rating scales in that it is the only omnibus rating scale whose entire content is explicitly tied to the diagnostic criteria specified in the *DSM-IV* (American Psychiatric Association, 1994). Therefore, its content reflects the research that went into developing these diagnostic criteria, which is excellent for some disorders but more suspect for others especially for children (Widiger et al., 1998).

The CSI-4 has both parent and teacher report versions that contain analogous scale content, which enhances its usefulness for comparing and combining ratings across informants. The CSI-4 was designed for use with children of ages 5–12, but there is an analogous Adolescent Symptom Inventory-4 for youth ages 12–18 (ASI-4; Gadow & Sprafkin, 1998) that has both parent and teacher versions and an adolescent self-report checklist, the Youth Symptom Inventory-4 (YSI-4). As part of the same system, the Early Childhood Inventory-4 (ECI-4; Gadow & Sprafkin, 1997) assesses *DSM-IV* symptoms in preschool children of ages 3–5.

The content of these forms is mostly identical; however, they also each include some domains that may be particularly developmentally relevant. For example, the ASI-4 includes assessments of Antisocial Personality Disorder, Anorexia, and Bulimia. The ESI-4 omits items screening for psychosis but includes items for Selective Mutism, Reactive Attachment Disorder, sleep problems, and elimination problems.

A fairly unique aspect of this system is the inclusion of a symptom checklist specifically for ADHD (ADHD-SC4). This inventory includes 50 items that assess the core symptoms of inattention and hyperactivity as well as other areas of interest related to ADHD. More specifically, the ADHD-SC4 includes a Peer Conflict scale to assess the social difficulties that often accompany ADHD and a Stimulant Side Effects Checklist as a means to monitor side effects of medication a child may be taking for the management of his/her ADHD symptoms.

Content

The CSI-4, because of its explicit link to the *DSMIV* system for classifying mental disorders (Table 7.7), covers many symptom domains that are not assessed by other rating scales (e.g., tic disorders), especially symptoms of more severe types of childhood psychopathology (e.g., Obsessive-compulsive Disorder, PosttraumaticStress Disorder, schizophrenia, autism, Asperger's Disorder). As a result, the CSI-4 may be especially useful in the assessment of more severely disturbed children. The items on the CSI-4 were designed to approximate symptoms from the *DSM-IV* with rephrasing done to eliminate jargon, to emphasize observable behavior, rather than making inferences about internal processes, and to eliminate descriptions of frequency (e.g., "often" acts without thinking). The CSI-4 is fairly long (i.e., 97 items for the parent form, 77 items for the teacher form), but the scales are grouped according to each individual diagnosis and, as a result, the whole scale need not be given. Instead, symptoms of certain disorders can be selected based on the specific purpose of the evaluation (e.g., Frick, Bodin, & Barry, 2000).

Administration and Scoring

The 97 items on the CSI-4 are rated on a 0 ("Never") to 3 ("Very Often") scale. Like other rating scales, quantitative scale scores corresponding to each diagnostic category (e.g., Conduct Disorder) can be determined by simply summing the ratings across items, and this score is called the "symptom severity" index. However, a "symptom count" score can be used to more closely approximate the *DSM-IV* method of considering symptoms as either present or absent. Using this method, any item rated as being present "Often" or "Very

TABLE 7.6 Prevalence of *DSM-IV* Disorders in a Normal Sample using the CSI-4 Screening Criteria

	Parent Checklist		Teacher Checklist	
DSM-IV Category	**Boys**	**Girls**	**Boys**	**Girls**
Attention-Deficit Hyper.	(*n* = 134)	(*n* = 129)	(*n* = 662)	(*n* = 661)
Inattentive	6.4	2.4	11.2	4.2
Hyperactive-Impulsive	4.1	3.2	3.5	0.5
Combined	4.1	0.8	4.7	1.2
Oppositional Defiant	9.2	7.0	6.3	1.8
Conduct	6.8	2.3	3.5	1.1
Generalized Anxiety	3.7	2.3	0.8	0.8
Separation Anxiety	3.0	3.1		
Schizophrenia	0.0	0.0	0.0	0.0
Major Depression	0.0	0.0	0.0	0.0
Dysthymia	2.2	0.0	0.8	0.6
Autism	0.7	0.8	0.4	0.3
Asperger's	0.0	0.0	0.0	0.0

Often" is considered to indicate the presence of the symptom, and any item rated as "Never" or "Sometimes" is considered to indicate the absence of the symptom.

Norming

The normative sample of the CSI-4 included 552 parent ratings (272 boys, 280 girls) and 1,323 teacher ratings (662 boys and 661 girls) in three states (Gadow & Sprafkin, 2002). The children were elementary school-age. Children receiving special education services were not included, making this sample a normal rather than normative sample.

In addition to being somewhat geographically limited, there was great overrepresentation of Caucasian children, particularly for the teacher rating sample, with that sample being 95% Caucasian, 2.8% African American, and 0.7% Hispanic. Because of these limitations in the CSI-4 normative samples, norm-referenced interpretations should only be made very cautiously. However, because the CSI-4 was not designed primarily to be used as a norm-referenced instrument but instead was designed as a screener for *DSM* diagnoses, the more critical psychometric consideration is its reliability and validity for this purpose.

Reliability

One study reporting on the reliability of the parent CSI-4 found moderate to good internal consistency for both symptom-severity scores and symptom-count scores (Sprafkin et al., 2002). More specifically, internal consistency coefficients ranged from a low of 0.45 for the symptom-severity index for schizophrenia to 0.92 for symptom severity of ADHD-Predominantly Inattentive Type. Four-month test-retest reliability coefficients ranged from 0.35 for Major Depression to 0.88 for ADHD Predominantly Hyperactive-Impulsive Type, with all but two coefficients being 0.65 or higher (Sprafkin et al.).

Relatively limited information on the reliability of the teacher version of the CSI-4 is available. For example, the CSI-4 manual describes test-retest reliability for the ADHD and ODD categories during a medication trial for children with behavioral problems. One-week test-retest coefficients for these two diagnoses averaged 0.62 for ADHD and 0.90 for ODD (Gadow & Sprafkin, 1998).

Validity

There are several pieces of evidence for the validity of the CSI-4 as a screener for *DSM-IV* diagnoses in school-aged children. First, the prevalence of the diagnoses, based on the symptom-count scoring method of the CSI-4 in the norm sample, seemed to approximate those found in community samples of children using structured diagnostic interviews (Frick & Silverthorn, 2001). These estimates, computed separately for boys and girls, are provided in Table 8.4. Second, when these prevalence estimates were compared to a clinic-referred sample of school-aged children, the prevalence of *DSM* diagnoses was higher in the clinic-referred sample for almost all diagnoses. The exceptions were ADHD Hyperactive/Impulsive Type for both boys (7.5% clinic vs. 4.1% norms) and girls (4.7 vs. 3.2%), Asperger's Disorder for both boys (2.7 vs. 0%) and girls (1.3 vs. 0%), and Schizophrenia for boys (1.1 vs. 0%). The primary concern is the finding for the one ADHD subtype, because the failure to find significant differences for the latter two disorders seems largely due to the very low base rate of these disorders in both samples.

Third, and probably most importantly, Gadow and Sprafkin (1998) reported on a clinic-referred sample of 101 referrals (between the ages of 6 and 12 years) to an outpatient child psychiatry service, in which they tested the correspondence between CSI-4 diagnostic cut-offs and clinical diagnoses made by mental health professionals. In general, the sensitivity and specificity rates for the disorders assessed by the CSI-4 generally indicated quite good correspondence with clinical diagnoses. This correspondence was especially good when parent and teacher ratings were combined, such that a disorder was considered present if either the parent or teacher ratings led to a CSI-4 screening diagnosis. For this multi-informant composite, the Sensitivity rates ranged from 0.87 to 1.00, and the specificity rates range from 0.40 to 0.92. For example, a diagnosis of Generalized Anxiety Disorder (GAD) showed a sensitivity rate of 0.93 indicating that, of those in the sample who had a clinical diagnosis of GAD, 93% crossed the screening cut-off for a diagnosis on the CSI-4. The specificity rate of 0.71 indicates that, of those without the diagnosis of GAD in the sample, 71% did not cross the screening cut-off on the CSI-4.

Sprafkin and colleagues (2002) found good convergent validity for the CSI domains (parent form) based on their relations with the CBCL Syndrome scales. Of note, virtually all CSI domains were moderately correlated with the Anxious/Depressed scale of the CBCL, which may speak more to the general distress nature of that CBCL scale than the lack of discriminative validity of the CSI domains. They also concluded that the CSI-4 is a good screener of a variety of child disorders based on the high correct classification rates found in their sample.

In a separate study, the teacher form of the CSI-4 showed similarly good diagnostic accuracy with diagnoses made from structured interviews and moderate relations with parent ratings (Gadow et al., 2004).

It should be noted that the research on the parent and teacher forms of the CSI-4 far outpaces the research available on their companion measures, the ESI-4 and ASI-4. However, this issue is of less concern given the highly similar framework under which these measures were developed and the true intent of these measures (i.e., to screen for symptoms included in a widely used diagnostic nosology).

Interpretation

Although the CSI-4 content is designed to correspond to the symptoms of *DSM-IV* disorders, the authors of the scale are very clear in stating that the scale should never be used in isolation to make diagnoses (Gadow & Sprafkin, 1998). Instead, the CSI-4 is a screener that could indicate the need for a more complete diagnostic assessment. Rather than being a significant limitation, it highlights some very important uses of the CSI-4. As mentioned in Chapter 3, there is a great deal of overlap and co-occurrence among the various forms of childhood disorders. The CSI-4 provides an efficient way of screening for a large number of potential comorbidities that can allow for a more focused and intensive assessment in the specific areas of concern indicated by this screening. Also, such a screening, because it is time- and cost-efficient, may be quite beneficial for defining smaller samples at high risk for psychopathology from larger non-referred samples (see Frick et al., 2000).

Given the fairly substantial limitations in the normative samples for the CSI-4 and its companion measures, norm-referenced interpretations are not recommended. Instead, the symptom-count method of scoring is recommended to provide the best approximation of *DSM-IV* disorders. Although the normative data suggest that the symptom-severity method of scoring is somewhat more reliable, it is not as consistent with the structure of the *DSM* criteria that relies on the presence or absence of symptoms to make diagnoses. Also, without good normative data, it is difficult to judge when symptom severity should be considered "significant," unless one is simply trying to make relative comparisons between groups of children. In addition, the symptom-count method provides a very easy method for combining information from multiple informants, which as the available data clearly suggest also provides the best correspondence to clinical diagnoses. Specifically, a symptom can be considered present if endorsed by any informant (e.g., either teacher or parent), and the rate of symptomatology based on this multi-informant procedure can be compared to *DSM-IV* criteria (see Piacentini, Cohen, & Cohen, 1992).

Strengths and Weaknesses

Strengths of the CSI-4 system include:

1. Its uniqueness in attempting to assess content that directly corresponds to *DSM-IV* classifications of childhood psychopathology.
2. Efficiency in gaining diagnosis-relevant information.
3. Good correspondence with clinical diagnoses, especially when using both parent and teacher informants.

Weaknesses of note include:

1. The lack of a large normative base; thus, norm-referenced interpretations should not be made from this rating scale system.
2. A relative lack of research, particularly on the ESI-4 and ASI-4, as well as the self-report component of this system.

The CSI-4 and its related measures offer a potentially useful component to child assessment, particularly when preliminary diagnoses are needed for reimbursement/insurance purposes. However, as the authors note, the CSI-4 (or any other assessment technique) should not be used as the sole criterion for making a clinical diagnosis. Instead, such decisions must be based on a combination of many sources of information.

Conners, 3rd Edition (Conners-3)

Parent Rating Scale

The Conners-3 (Conners, 2008a) Parent Rating Scale (Conners-3-P) is the most recent revision to a widely used behavior rating scale system. The Conners Parent Rating Scale is designed similarly to the BASC and Achenbach systems in that it includes a number of clinically relevant domains for which normative scores are derived. The parent rating scale is designed for ages 6 through 18. The Long Form contains 110 items and the Short Form contains 45 items. There is also a 10-item Global Index form. The Conners-3-P takes 10–20 min to complete, depending on which form is used. The following discussion will focus on the Long Form.

As noted in Table 7.1, we recommend the Conners Comprehensive Behavior Rating Scales (Conners, 2008b) for an assessment that covers externalizing, internalizing, and academic issues. However, as the information below indicates, the Conners-3 is unique in its detailed evaluation of ADHD and other externalizing issues.

Scale Content

The Conners-3-P includes five empirically-derived scales: Hyperactivity/Impulsivity, Executive Functioning, Learning Problems, Aggression, and Peer Relations. An Inattention scale developed theoretically is also available, as are five *DSM-IV-TR* Symptom scales for each of the Disruptive

Behavior Disorders (i.e., 3 ADHD subtypes, ODD, and CD). The Conners-3-P includes screening items for depression and anxiety, as well as impairment items for home, school, and social relationships. Like the BASC, the Conners-3 includes critical items that may signal the need for further follow-up. These critical items are particularly geared toward severe conduct problem behaviors (e.g., uses a weapon, is cruel to animals). Consistent with its predecessors, the Conners-3 includes a brief ADHD Index. This scale is based on items that best differentiate ADHD from nonclinical samples. As described in Chap. 6 for the Conners-3 SR, the Conners-3-P has three validity scales: Positive Impression (or "fake good"), Negative Impression ("fake bad"), and the Inconsistency Index. These scales are new to the Conners system. Two open-ended questions regarding other concerns and particular strengths/skills are also included. Detailed information on the generation and selection of items is provided in the Conners-3 manual (Conners, 2008a).

Administration and Scoring

The Conners-3-P uses a four-choice response format where 0 = not at all true (never, seldom), and 4 = very much true (very often, very frequently). A Spanish translation is available. Both hand scoring and computer scoring are available. Raw scores are transformed to linear T-scores, meaning that each scale maintains its natural distribution in the conversion to norm-referenced scores. Separate norms are used for boys and girls, as is the case for the other versions of the Conners-3. Norms are also computed by age.

Norming

The normative sample of 1,200 cases was collected mainly in the USA, with a small number of cases coming from Canada. Recruitment of the normative sample was aimed at reflecting US Census data regarding ethnicity/race. Data reported by Conners (2008a) indicate that the normative sample closely reflects the Census statistics. This representativeness is a notable improvement over previous versions of the Conners rating scale, in that the previous samples were predominantly Caucasian. As noted for the Conners-3 SR, the Western USA appears to have been somewhat underrepresented. The majority of the parents (63.5%) in the normative sample had at least some post-secondary education. A clinical sample of 718 participants was also collected for validation purposes, with over 35% of that sample being diagnosed with ADHD or one of its subtypes.

Reliability

Internal consistency coefficients for the content and *DSM* scales of the Conners-3-P are all 0.80 and higher, and many are 0.90 and higher for the overall sample. The Peer Relations scale for girls had somewhat lower coefficients (i.e., 0.72 for 6–9-year olds; 0.78 for 10–13-year olds) Two to four week test-retest coefficients were good (i.e., all higher than .70). Interrater reliability for the parent form was also good, with adjusted *r*s all 0.74 and higher for the content and *DSM* scales (see Conners, 2008a).

Validity

Because the content scales were empirically-derived, it is not surprising that confirmatory factor analyses supported the five-factor model for those scales. All intercorrelations among content and *DSM* scales were moderate to high in magnitude (i.e., ranging from 0.36 to 0.98). Correlations with analogous scales from the teacher and self-report forms of the Conners-3 were all moderate (i.e., *r*s = 0.49

to 0.67). Criterion-related validity was demonstrated through moderate to high correlations between Conners-3-P scales and analogous scales from the BASC-2-PRS, CBCL, and BRIEF (see Conners, 2008a). The associations between the Conners-3 and CBCL were particularly high. Differential validity evidence also indicates that the Conners-3-P was successful in distinguishing both a general population sample and within clinical samples. That is, scores on scales such as those tied to ADHD tended to be elevated for clinical groups relative to non-clinical groups and higher for individuals with ADHD relative to others within a clinical population. The correct classification rate based on content and *DSM* scale elevations were also relatively high (i.e., 57 to 86%). More validity evidence for the Short Form and the Indexes are available in the manual (Conners, 2008a).

Interpretation

As discussed in Chap. 6, Conners (2008a) provides a clear step-by-step approach for interpreting ratings on the various forms of the Conners-3. This approach involves (a) examining the validity scales; (b) evaluating scale elevations; (c) examining the overall profile of scores (i.e., determining the constructs that seem to be represented across elevations); (d) item-level interpretation, including critical items and screener items; and (e) integration with other assessment information.

Strengths and Weaknesses

Some of the strengths of the Conners-3-P are:

1. The improved representativeness of normative sample
2. Availability of complementary teacher and self-report forms that provide a comprehensive assessment of externalizing problems
3. Good initial reliability and validity evidence
4. Brevity of Short and Index Forms

Some characteristics that may be considered weaknesses are:

1. Limited assessment of internalizing problems and adaptive functioning (an issue that is addressed through use of the Conners CBRS)
2. Uniform negative wording of items, which may result in a negative response set
3. A lack of available validity research conducted by persons other than the developers

Teacher Rating Scale

The Teacher Rating Scale in the Conners-3 system is very similar to the parent rating scale. In fact, the teacher ratings scale and parent rating scale include the same scales. The Long Form of the teacher rating scale is slightly longer than that of the parent rating scale (i.e., 115 items), whereas the Short Form is slightly shorter (i.e., 41 items). Two 10-item Hyperactivity Index forms are also available. The following discussion will focus primarily on the Long Form of the Conners-3-T. As with the self-report and parent forms of the Conners-3, we discuss the Conners-3-T because of its relatively unique focus on ADHD and behavioral problems. The companion teacher rating scale from the Conners CBRS (Conners, 2008b) provides a more extensive assessment of broader domains of functioning. Therefore, the selection of one set of rating scales versus the other in the Conners family should be dictated by the purpose of the evaluation.

Content

The Conners-3-T has some item overlap with the Conners-3 parent rating scale, but there are also unique items in each form. The same four-point response scale used for the self-report and parent-report versions of the Conners-3 is also used for the teacher-report scale. As noted above, the scales are the same as those for the parent rating scale, including validity scales, impairment items, and critical items.

Administration and Scoring

The Conners-3-T can be completed in 10–20 min, or less if the Short Form is used. The Conners-3-T has both hand-scoring and computer-scoring formats that allow for easy calculation of norm-referenced scores. As with the self-report and parent report forms, only sex-specific T-scores can be calculated. The scores are Linear T-scores and are based on each age group, which allows it to capture potential variability in discrete developmental stages.

Norming

The norming process for the Conners-3-T was essentially the same as that used for the Conners-3-P and Conners-3 SR. Specifically, the norming sample for the Conners-3-T consists of 1,200 teachers from throughout the USA, with a few respondents from Canada. Recruitment was aimed at a sample that would reflect U.S. Census data on ethnicity/race. The students rated by teachers in the norming sample do appear to match the Census data on ethnicity/race (Conners, 2008a). However, the sample appears to be somewhat skewed toward middle to high SES – based on parent education – as 76.9% of the students rated by teachers in the norming sample had parents with at least some post-secondary education. Almost as many cases came from Canada as came from the western USA in the Conners-3-T norming sample.

Reliability

Internal consistency coefficients for the teacher report version Conners-3 were quite high. Specifically, the coefficients for each of the content and *DSM* scales were 0.90 or higher, with the exception of the Conduct Disorder scale (0.77). Two- to four-week test-retest reliability coefficients were also good, ranging from 0.72 to 0.83 (see Conners, 2008a). Lastly, and perhaps particularly importantly for teacher ratings, interrater reliability coefficients for pairs of teacher raters were moderate to high. The Peer Relations and Oppositional Defiant Disorder scales had the lowest adjusted coefficients (i.e., 0.52 and 0.55, respectively), whereas the Hyperactivity/Impulsivity and Conduct Disorder scales had the highest coefficients (i.e., 0.77). It should be noted that the lower coefficients from these analyses may reflect less-than-ideal rater agreement, or they may reflect real differences in a child's behavior from one classroom context to another. Additional analyses, particularly in determining whether teacher agreement might change as a function of the child's age, are needed.

Validity

Factor analyses revealed a four-factor solution for the Conners-3-T: Hyperactivity/Impulsivity, Aggression, Peer Relations, and a combined Learning Problems/Executive Functioning scale. Conners (2008a) also found support for considering the Learning Problems/Executive Functioning as consisting of two subscales consisting of items intended to load on a Learning Problems and an Executive Functioning scale. As noted above, the Conners-3-T scales were moderately correlated with the same scales from the parent and self-report versions. The scales on the Conners-3-T were all moderately interrelated. Criterion-related validity for the Conners-3-T was supported through moderate to high correlations between Conners-3-T scales and analogous scales on the BASC-2-TRS, Achenbach TRF, and BRIEF Teacher Form. Similar to the parent version of the Conners-3, the teacher version demonstrated good differential validity in that scales were elevated for individuals from a clinical sample relative to a general sample, and scale scores tended to differ within the clinical sample in intuitive ways. For example, ADHD scale scores tended to be higher for youths diagnosed with ADHD than for youths with other difficulties who did not have ADHD diagnoses (see Conner, 2008a).

Interpretation

At the very least, the Conners-3-T appears to be useful as a screening for problems in classroom adjustment, particularly in terms of learning or externalizing problems, and as part of a comprehensive assessment battery. The recommended approach for interpreting the Conners-3-T mirrors that described for the Conners-3 SR and Conners-3-P.

Strengths and Weaknesses

The strengths of the Conners-3-T include:

1. Content that allows for an extensive assessment of ADHD symptoms and other behavioral problems.
2. Good correspondence across scales on the parent and teacher versions, which facilitates comparisons in a multi-informant assessment.
3. The presence of several short screening scales which may be more feasible for many teachers.

Apparent weaknesses of the Conners-3-T include:

1. Minimal assessment of depression and anxiety, as well as adaptive functioning. The Conners CBRS should be used if extensive assessment of these domains is desired.
2. Lack of research on reliability and validity conducted by persons other than the developer.
3. The normative sample is not quite as diverse as that for the parent and self-report forms of the Conners-3, yet it is still diverse in terms of race/ethnicity.

Personality Inventory for Children-2 (PIC-2); Student Behavior Survey (SBS)

Parent Report *PIC-2*

The Personality Inventory for Children-2 [(PIC-2); Lachar & Gruber, 2001] is based closely on its predecessor, the PIC-R (Wirt, Lachar, Klinedinst, & Seat, 1990). The original development of the PIC followed closely on the heels of the MMPI, with much of the early development work taking place in the 1950s. The PIC-2 is a 275-item rating scale designed for use with parents of children between the ages of 5 and 19 years (Lachar & Gruber, 2001).

Scale Content

The PIC-2 scales, although revised, have a long clinical history. The PIC-2 includes scales that were developed via a mixture of empirical means with considerable use of external validation techniques and scales developed through rational/ theoretical approaches.

Many changes and improvements have been made in the PIC-2 scales. Content overlap was either reduced or eliminated between scales, item-total correlation had to be high, and validity scales were added (Lachar & Gruber, 2001). Scale content was also better articulated with that of the PIY in order to enhance score comparisons. A Spanish translation was developed as well. The PIC-2 also includes a 96-item short form (the first 96 items of the Standard Form) called the "Behavioral Summary."

An overview of the PIC-2 clinical scales is provided in Table 7.7. In addition to these scales, the PIC-2 provides three validity scales (i.e., Inconsistency, Dissimulation, and Defensiveness) and critical items.

TABLE 7.7 PIC-2 Clinical Scales, Subscales, and Internal Consistency Coefficients

Cognitive Impairment (r = 0.87)

Inadequate Abilities (r = 0.77)

Others think my child is talented

My child seems to understand everything that is said.

Poor Achievement (r = 0.77)

It is hard for my child to make good grades.

Reading has been a problem for my child.

Developmental Delay (r = 0.79)

At one time my child had speech difficulties.

My child could ride a tricycle by the age of 5.

Impulsivity and Distractibility (r = 0.92)

Disruptive Behavior (r = 0.91)

My child jumps from one activity to another.

My child cannot keep attention on anything.

Fearlessness (r = 0.69)

My child will do anything on a dare.

Nothing seems to scare my child.

Delinquency (r = 0.95)

Antisocial Behavior (r = 0.88)

My child has been in trouble with the police.

My child has run away from home.

Dyscontrol (r = 0.91)

When my child gets mad, watch out!

Many times my child has become violent.

Noncompliance (r = 0.92)

My child often breaks the rules.

My child tends to see how much he/she can get away with.

Family Dysfunction (r = 0.87)

Conflict among members (r = 0.83)

There is a lot of tension in our home.

Our family argues a lot at dinner time.

Parent Maladjustment (r = 0.77)

One of the child's parents drinks too much alcohol.

The child's parents are divorced or living apart.

Reality Distortion (r = 0.89)

Developmental Deviation (r = 0.84)

My child often gets confused.

My child needs protection from everyday dangers.

Hallucinations and Delusions (r = 0.81)

My child thinks others are plotting against him/her.

My child is likely to scream if disturbed.

Somatic Concern (r = 0.84)

Psychosomatic Preoccupation (r = 0.80)

My child is worried about disease.

My child often has an upset stomach.

Muscular Tension and Anxiety (r = 0.68)

Recently my child has complained of chest pains.

My child often has back pains.

Psychological Discomfort (r = 0.90)

Fear and Worry (r = 0.72)

My child will worry a lot before starting something new.

My child is often afraid of little things.

Depression (r = 0.87)

My child has little self-confidence.

My child hardly ever smiles.

(Continues)

TABLE 7.7 (continued)

Psychological Discomfort (r = 0.90)
Sleep Disturbance/Preoccupation with Death (r = 0.76)
My child's sleep is calm and restful.
My child thinks about ways to kill himself/herself.
Social Withdrawal (r = 0.81)
Social Introversion (r = 0. 78)
My child is usually afraid to meet new people.
Shyness is my child's biggest problem.
Isolation (r = 0.68)
My child does not like to be close with others.
My child often stays in his/her room for hours.
Social Skill Deficits (r = 0.91)
Limited Peer Status (r = 0.84)
My child often brings friends home. (reversed)
My child is very popular with other children. (reversed)
Conflict with Peers (r = 0.88)
My child seems to get along with everyone. (reversed)
Other children make fun of my child's ideas.

NOTE: From Lachar & Gruber (2001).

Administration and Scoring

It takes a parent about 40 min to complete the 275 true–false statements of the PIC-2. All administrations require at least two components, an administration booklet and hand-scoring or computer-scoring answer sheets. The hand-scoring process involves the use of four forms with a Critical Items Summary Sheet as an option. The use of either PC or mail-in computer scoring limits the number of components to only two (administration booklet and answer sheet).

Norming

The norming sample included 2,306 children in the kindergarten through 12th grades. The normative sample appears to represent 1998 US Census data – which were the data available at the time of the PIC-2 norming – well in terms of ethnicity, parents' education level, and geographic region of residence.

Linear transformations of T-scores were utilized. The range of derived scores is limited to T-scores based only on within-sex comparisons. Therefore, as alluded to in the discussions of other tests, one is not able to determine how a child's behavior compares to that of children in general. Percentile ranks are also not available.

Reliability

Internal consistency coefficients for the scales are for the most part acceptable and are shown in Table 7.7. The results of one-week test-retest studies are also generally supportive (see Lachar & Gruber, 2001). Interrater reliability between mothers and fathers was generally very good, with coefficients mostly 0.75 and higher for non-clinic-referred children. One exception was the Somatic Complaints scale and its subscales, with coefficients of 0.49 to 0.54 (Lachar & Gruber, 2001).

Validity

Several types of validity evidence are reported in the PIC-2 manual including criterion-related, differential diagnosis, and factorial validity. Factors corresponding to the Externalization, Internalization, Social Adjustment, and Total composite scores are described.

The relations between PIC-2 scores and external indicators of adjustment are described in detail in the manual (see Lachar & Gruber, 2001). Some of the indicators include teacher SBS and child self-report PIY ratings. Unfortunately, such studies, by being limited to the PIC "family" of measures, do not allow clinicians to determine the degree to which PIC-2 results will differ from CBCL, BASC-2, MMPI-A, or other results. Evidence of this nature is important, as clinicians often use multiple measures and frequently have to describe their findings in comparison to previous evaluation results. The extent of PIC-2 criterion-related validity evidence to be found in the manual is sometimes difficult to discern. Considerable reference is made to SBS and PIY validity studies.

Children with diagnoses in the clinical samples were used to compare PIC-2 results for several diagnostic groups using MANOVAs. Many significant effects were found. However, sensitivity, specificity, and other typical indices of diagnostic accuracy are not provided.

As is the case with the PIY, independent evidence of validity is difficult to obtain at this time. Several aspects of validity remain to be assessed in order to support clinicians' use of the scale. First priority for further validation is to assess the criterion-related validity of the PIC-2 with widely used scales, such as the CBCL and BASC-2 PRS because many clinicians will be faced with having to interpret PIC-2 results in tandem with these measures.

Interpretation

Chapter 3 of the PIC-2 manual provides considerable guidance to the user. In fact, the sheer amount of tabular information presented is potentially overwhelming. The frequency of item endorsements for various samples, for example, is presented for each scale. The value of such information is questionable because it is based on the assumption that an item response is a reliable and valid indicator of some construct, which is a dubious assumption. Nevertheless, the manual provides numerous useful case studies and correlates of profiles. In addition, the meaning of various T-scores for the individual scales is thoroughly described in an additional set of tables. Clinicians will probably find these descriptions of T-score outcomes to be valuable for deriving score meaning.

Otherwise, we reiterate our recommended sequential approach to interpretation (i.e., checking validity scales, critical items, scale elevations, subscale elevations, relevant item endorsements, considering primary vs. secondary concerns, integration with other information).

Strengths and Weaknesses

PIC-2 strengths include:

1. A thorough manual by Lachar and Gruber (2001) that summarizes important studies of scale development.
2. A great variety of subscale scores that may be of value for specialized uses.
3. The inclusion of valuable interpretive guidance in the manual.
4. Norming sample that closely matches census data at the time of the scale's development.

Weaknesses of the PIC-2 may include:

1. Test length.
2. A lack of criterion-related validity studies and shortage of validity studies independent of the test developers.
3. Limited score options (i.e., absence of general norm-referenced comparisons and percentiles).

The PIC-2 represents a significant upgrade of the PIC-R. The most important improvements are a reduction of item overlap between scales and the collection of new norms. Both independent validation research and clinical experience are necessary to determine the ultimate utility of the scale.

Teacher Report: The Student Behavior Survey

The Student Behavior Survey (SBS; Lachar, Wingenfeld, Kline, & Gruber, 2000) is the teacher version of the rating scale system that includes the parent-completed PIC-2 youth self-report PIY. As a result, SBS rounds out a rating scale system with a long and distinguished history in the assessment of children and adolescents by providing a source of information on a child's classroom adjustment based on teacher report. The SBS is not as long as its parent-report and self-report siblings, containing 102 items that are rated on a four-point Likert scale. This rather moderate length allows most teachers to complete the form easily in 15–20 min. The scale has normative information for children of ages 5 through 18.

Content

Despite being developed to complement the PIC-2 and PIY scales, the SBS was not beholden to the item content of the parent-report and self-report scales. Instead, the content of the SBS was developed based on teacher endorsements of statements that seem to reflect important dimensions of classroom adjustment. The content of the SBS can be divided into three major categories. The first category is Academic Resources, which contains four subscales: Academic Performance (eight items), Academic Habits (thirteen items), Social Skills (eight items), and Parent Participation (six items). These subscales are adaptive scales focusing on potential strengths of the child in the academic environment, and therefore, items on these subscales are worded in a positive direction. The second category is Adjustment Problems, which includes seven subscales: Health Concerns (six items), Emotional Distress (fifteen items), Unusual Behavior (seven items), Social Problems (twelve items), Verbal Aggression (seven items), Physical Aggression (five items), and Behavior Problems (fifteen items). These two areas include the main clinical scales of the SBS focusing on emotional, social, and behavioral areas of concern for the child's classroom adjustment.

The third section is a Disruptive Behavior Disorders category that includes three subscales: Attention-Deficit Hyperactivity (16 items), Oppositional-Defiant (16 items) and Conduct Problems (16 items). As the names of the subscales imply, these scales were developed to provide a screening for the major disruptive behavior disorder categories specified in the *DSM-IV*. However, the individual items were not specifically developed to tap *DSM* criteria. Instead, three clinicians chose items from the existing 102-item pool that were judged to be most indicative of the *DSM-IV* criteria, a similar approach to that employed for the Achenbach measures (discussed earlier). This procedure led to some criteria not being assessed (e.g., "Is spiteful and vindictive") and other items included that are not part of the *DSM* criteria (e.g., "Demonstrates polite behavior and manners" reverse-scored). This issue is especially relevant to the Conduct Problems scale, which is fairly divergent from the content of the *DSM-IV* definition of Conduct Disorder, including such items as "uses drugs or alcohol" and "preoccupied with sex."

Administration and Scoring

The items on the SBS are grouped according to their subscales, such that the 8 items for the Academic Performance subscale are items 1 through 8, the 13 items for the Academic Habits subscale are items 9 through 21, and so on. In addition, the subscale titles document this explicit grouping to the teacher raters. This is a somewhat unique format in that other rating scales have items for the subscale intermixed throughout the scale. There could be both positive and negative consequences of this format. For example, it makes scoring much easier and reduces the likelihood of clerical errors in computing raw scores, because it is readily apparent which items are included on each subscale. Also, it makes inspection of items that led to subscale elevations a very simple process. Alternatively, it opens the possibility that teachers may be influenced by the name of the construct (e.g., social skills) and rate children according to their overall perceptions of a child's adjustment for that domain rather than basing their ratings on their perceptions of the individual behaviors. For example, a teacher who views a child as socially unskilled may rate items under that heading as more problematic than if he or she was not explicitly informed about the overall domain being assessed.

However, there is no empirical evidence that this item format affects ratings in any systematic way, and as mentioned previously, it greatly simplifies the scoring process. There are two "Auto-Score" forms for the SBS: one for children of ages 5–11 and one for adolescents of ages 12–18. Raw scores are simply computed by summing the ratings within each of the 11 subscales included in the Academic Resources and Adjustment Problem domains. Between the two sides of the ratings is carbon paper that copies ratings on only those items that correspond to the three disruptive behavior subscales. Raw scores are based on a sum of these items as well. These 14 raw scores are then transferred to a cover Profile page with separate columns for boys and girls. These profiles reflect a conversion to T-scores and show the relative elevations among subscales based on this norm-referenced score. Importantly, the conversions and profiles can only be computed for separate male and female norms, and not for both sexes combined.

Norms

The primary normative sample for the SBS includes 2,612 children from regular education classrooms from 22 schools in 11 states. The sample was fairly evenly divided between boys and girls and had substantial representation at each year of age from 5 to 18. Also, the regional breakdown, parental educational level, and ethnic composition (e.g., 70% Caucasian, 15% African American, 10% Hispanic American) was fairly representative of US Census Bureau statistics (see Lachar et al., 2000). The one relatively minor exception was the somewhat high rate of college graduates in this norm sample (i.e., 35 vs. 26.9% cited for the US Census).

One of the unique features of the SBS is that, in addition to the regular education norm sample on which T-score conversations were based, the manual also reported on a large referred sample (n = 1,315) that obtained teacher ratings on children from 41 different sites in 17 states in the USA. These children included those in special education classes, those referred to both inpatient and outpatient mental health clinics, and those referred to juvenile justice facilities. This large sample allows for a comparison of the psychometric properties of the SBS in both a large normal sample of children and in a large disturbed sample. Overall, each of the SBS scales differentiated the referred and normal samples with Cohen's d ranging from 0.23 (Parent Participation) to 0.98 (Academic Performance; see Lachar et al., 2000).

Reliability

The information provided in the manual (Lachar et al., 2000) on the reliability of the SBS is exemplary. Internal consistency estimates for the 14 subscales across both the normal and referred samples ranged from 0.85 to 0.95, indicating uniformly excellent internal consistency. Test-retestcorrelations are provided for four samples of children ranging in age from 5 to 18 and with retest intervals ranging from 2 to 30 weeks. Again, all scales showed quite good temporal stability, with the test-retest of the Unusual Behavior scale over a 20-week period in adolescents being the only index to be somewhat low (i.e., $r = 0.29$). A third type of reliability, inter-rater agreement, was tested in two samples of 30 children, one sample including fourth and fifth grade regular education students and a second sample including children (ages 5–12) receiving special education services. The correlations between two teacher ratings across these samples ranged from 0.44 to 0.91, with most indexes being above 0.70.

Validity

The dimensionality of the SBS was tested in a way that was somewhat different from that reported for other behavioral rating scales. That is, rather than conducting a factor analysis on the individual items, the item-subscale correlations were compared for each item's correlation with the dimension it is purported to assess and its correlations with other dimensions. While this method led to rationally derived scales that were fairly homogeneous in content, the decision as to whether an item is "more strongly" associated with the dimension it is purported to measure is somewhat subjective in the absence of factor analysis. For example, "Blames others for own problems" is correlated 0.79 with the Behavior Problems subscale on which it is included, but it is also correlated 0.76 with the Verbal Aggression subscale, 0.61 with the Physical Aggression subscale, and 0.54 with the Social Problems subscale. The most problematic in this regard are the three Disruptive Behavior Scales, on which many items load equally high on all three dimensions, although this is likely due to the nature of the criteria they were designed to assess, which tend to be substantially overlapping (Frick et al., 1994).

The manual of the SBS (Lachar et al., 2000) provides (1) the correlations of the SBS subscales with clinician ratings of adjustment problems in 129 primarily clinic-referred children, (2) the correlations among SBS scores and parent- and self-report ratings using the PIC-2 and PIY, and (3) the correlations between the SBS and an early version of the Conners Rating Scale for teachers (see also Pisecco et al., 1999; Wingenfeld, Lachar, Gruber, & Kline, 1998).

In general, these correlations support the convergent validity of the SBS scales, but like most rating scales, the divergent validity was less clear. That is, the SBS subscales were often correlated with the other scales designed to measure similar constructs (i.e., convergent validity), but they were also correlated with other dimensions of maladjustment as well. For example, the Emotional Distress subscale was significantly correlated with clinician ratings of psychological discomfort ($r = 0.55$), but this subscale was also highly correlated with the ratings of disruptive behavior ($r = 0.44$). Again, this pattern is common for ratings of children's adjustment because children with problems in one area often have problems in many other areas of adjustment as well, and raters may also demonstrate response sets in that a child rating negatively in one area is rated similarly in other areas. One notable weakness uncovered in these validity analyses was for the Unusual Behavior subscale, which seemed to be more strongly associated with measures of disruptive behaviors and ADHD than with more severe psychopathology or reality distortion. For example, it was correlated 0.40 with clinician ratings of disruptive behavior but 0.25 with clinician ratings of serious psychopathology. Similarly, the Unusual Behavior subscale was correlated at 0.41 with parent ratings of impulsivity and distractibility on the PIC-2, but at 0.27 with the Reality Distortion subscale of the PIC-2.

One additional set of validity analyses provided in the manual were comparisons between groups of children either diagnosed with Disruptive Behavior Disorders by clinicians or children elevated on the Hyperactivity Index in an earlier version of the Conners Rating Scale compared to control children. As would be expected, the Social Problem subscale, the three behavior problem subscales, and the disruptive behavior disorder subscales all differentiated children with behavior problems from control children. Also as expected, the academic resources subscales tended to be lower in groups of children with behavioral problems, with the exception of the Parent Participation subscale.

Interpretation

Within the tradition of the PIC-2, which, in turn, was based on the MMPI tradition, the manual of the SBS provides a very detailed step-by-step interpretative guide (Lachar et al., 2000). First, the manual recommends examining items for response adequacy, including ensuring that there are only a few missing responses. The one exception noted in the manual is that many teachers above the early elementary school grades may have difficulty completing the Parent Participation scale because they are less likely to converse with parents on a regular basis (Lachar et al., 2000). Also, it is important to note that, unlike the PIC-2 and PIY, there are no validity indexes on the SBS designed to help in detecting potential threats to the quality of the teacher ratings. Second, and the main focus of the interpretative approach in the manual, is a description of the characteristics that are often associated with children who score in a given range on each subscale.

These interpretive guidelines were developed by correlating the T-scores on the SBS subscales with descriptors provided by clinicians (n = 379), parents (n = 425), and students (n = 218). Descriptors are provided for T-scores below 40 for the academic resources subscales and for (1) T-scores between 60 and 70, and (2) T-scores above 70 for the adjustment problems scales. The authors note that the descriptors for the higher elevations (above 70) should be considered more definitive than those between 60 and 70. The authors clearly note, however, that all interpretations, even those above 70, should be considered only as "interpretative hypotheses," and additional information (e.g., from parent report, child self-report, and clinical observations) should be used to better determine if these hypothetical descriptors are appropriate for a given case.

Strengths and Weaknesses

The strengths of the SBS include:

1. Content that includes a number of adaptive dimensions of classroom adjustment and a rather comprehensive assessment of conduct problems, including separate subscales for verbal and physical aggression, and a general Behavior Problems subscale.
2. Fairly homogeneous subscale content, which greatly enhances the interpretation of scale elevations, as does the very easy-to-use, step-by-step interpretive guidelines, which provide the most common characteristics for children with specific scale scores.
3. A large and representative norm sample.
4. The evidence for subscale reliability using both community and clinic-referred samples is exemplary.

All of these characteristics make the SBS a very useful tool for obtaining teacher ratings of classroom adjustment.

Weaknesses of the SBS include:

1. Limited research on the validity of the SBS scales and subscales

2. A lack of cross-validation in other samples of the interpretative descriptors provided for children who score in a specific range on each subscale need to be cross-validated.
3. The heterogeneous content of the Unusual Behavior subscale includes some items related to inattention (e.g., "Daydreams") and some vague behaviors (e.g., "Behavior is strange and peculiar"). Early evidence suggested that it is more associated with disruptive behavior dimensions than with indexes of more severe psychopathology and thought disturbances.
4. The lack of direct correspondence between the three disruptive behavior disorder subscales and *DSM* criteria. This is especially true for the Conduct Problems scale, which appears quite divergent from the criteria for Conduct Disorder. In addition, there is no evidence for how well the specific SBS subscales (e.g., Attention-Deficit Hyperactivity) correspond to specific *DSM-IV* diagnoses (e.g., ADHD). As a result, the usefulness of SBS as a screener for specific *DSM* disorders has not been established.

In addition to these issues, it is worth noting that while SBS was developed to be part of the assessment system that includes the PIC-2 and PIY (reviewed previously) the item content and scale structure of the SBS is substantially different from these other scales. The result is a tool that is very relevant for assessing children's classroom functioning. However, it also makes it more difficult to integrate information from the different informants. A case example with PIC-2 and SBS data follows (Box 7.3).

Box 7.3

Sample Case Using the PIC-2 and SBS

Ricky is a 7-year-old boy who was referred for an evaluation by his teacher because of concerns about inattention, overactivity, and poor peer interactions. Ricky was reportedly born at home without the benefit of any medical attention

Most of Ricky's developmental milestones were delayed, especially language. According to his mother, he did not speak his first words until the age of 2 years. He has reportedly demonstrated some improvements in language since beginning speech therapy at age 4.

According to his mother, as a toddler, Ricky began demonstrating significant behavioral problems including frequent temper tantrums, overactivity, and oppositional behavior. Such behavioral concerns continued when Ricky began school. He has a history of getting in trouble at school due tobecause of overactivity and defiance toward his teachers.

Throughout the evaluation, Ricky demonstrated a short attention span and a high level of motor activity. He did not sit still and was easily distracted by other objects in the room. When he was unable to testing objects and toys in the waiting room with him, Ricky displayed tantrum behavior (e.g., kicking and crying).

Ricky's cognitive assessment results indicated overall functioning in the Low Average range, with his verbal skills being in the Borderline range. Tests of his achievement in reading and math indicated slightly below average achievement relative to his same-aged peers.

PIC-2 Scale elevations were as follows:

Impulsivity/Distractibility	*T* = 80
Delinquency	*T* = 82
Family Dysfunction	*T* = 75
Social Skill Deficits	*T* = 68

(Continues)

Box 7.3 (Continued)

SBS Scale elevations were as follows:

Academic Habits (adaptive)	*T* = 33
Social Skills (adaptive)	*T* = 32
Emotional Distress	*T* = 71
Social Problems	*T* = 67
Unusual Behavior	*T* = 63
Verbal Aggression	*T* = 80
Physical Aggression	*T* = 72
Behavior Problems	*T* = 82
Attention-Deficit/Hyperactivity	*T* = 73
Oppositional Defiant	*T* = 73

On rating scales, both Ricky's mother and teacher reported significant concerns regarding inattention, overactivity, impulsivity, and externalizing behaviors. These behavioral concerns have apparently been present for some time. Furthermore, based on background information as well as ratings by Ricky's mother and teacher, Ricky's behavioral problems are causing impairment in his relationships with others and his ability to perform required tasks in the classroom. Therefore, diagnoses of Attention-Deficit/Hyperactivity Disorder (ADHD)-Combined Type and Oppositional Defiant Disorder are warranted. The elevation on the SBS Emotional Distress scale is consistent with reports that Ricky gets upset easily and throws tantrums in the classroom. The slight elevation the Unusual Behavior scale of the SBS completed by Ricky's teacher appears consistent with attention problems in that she reported that he daydreams and seems disoriented. In addition, Ricky's mother indicated concerns regarding a high level of conflict in the home, particularly between Ricky and his parents. This conflict appears to also be related to Ricky's behavioral problems, particularly his defiance.

Recommendations for Ricky included parental consultation with a mental health specialist to address his behavioral problems, consultation with a physician regarding a possible medication trial for his ADHD symptoms, and classroom accommodations to help minimize the impact of Ricky's behavioral concerns and inattention on his academic and social functioning. The results of parent and teacher rating scales in this case highlight the dissimilar structure of the PIC-2 and SBS. However, similar information can still be gleaned from these rating scales that can aid in case conceptualization and recommendations.

Sample Impairment-Oriented Scales

As can be determined from the previous review, omnibus rating scales can provide invaluable information about a variety of domains of child functioning. This information, however, tends to describe functioning in terms of severity of problems and/or frequency of problems. Rating scales typically stop short of providing an indication as to what extent the problems interfere with the child's functioning. Information on impairment is often left to the clinician to infer based on interview or other information. However, this information is no less important for case conceptualization and treatment planning. In addition to assessing for impairment via structured or unstructured interviews, one may employ an inventory to gather such information in a time-efficient manner and then follow-up accordingly. A brief discussion of some such inventories follows.

Home Situations Questionnaire (HSQ) and School Situations Questionnaire (SSQ)

The content of the Home Situations Questionnaire (HSQ; Barkley & Edelbrock, 1987) and the School Situations Questionnaire (SSQ; Barkley & Edelbrock, 1987) is markedly different from the other rating scales reviewed in this chapter. Rather than having items that describe different types of child behaviors, these measures include situations (e.g., while playing alone, when visitors are in the home, during individual desk work, at recess, on the bus) in which a child may have problems. That is, the HSQ and SSQ were not designed to assess specific behaviors but to assess specific situations in which problem behaviors can occur. Therefore, these measures provide an indication of the specific situations in which the child may demonstrate particular difficulty or impairment.

Both measures were designed to be completed in the same manner. The respondent (parent or teacher) rates whether or not the child has any problem in a given situation and then rates the severity of the problem on a 1–9 scale. These measures may be used with a variety of clinical problems, as the respondent can be directed to respond as to whether or not the child "has problems" in the situations provided.

The psychometric development of both measures is limited. Normative information is available from Altepeter and Breen (1989) as well as Barkley and Edelbrock (1987). However, norm-based comparisons may not represent the best use of these tools. Factor analyses have revealed four factors for the HSQ (i.e., Non-Family Transactions, Custodial Transactions, Task-Performance Transactions, and Isolate Play) and three factors for the SSQ (i.e., Unsupervised Settings, Task Performance, and Special Events; Altepeter & Breen, 1989).

The HSQ has demonstrated good test-retest reliability and internal consistency (Altepeter & Breen, 1989). The number of problems and mean severity rating of the HSQ have been found to be related to ratings of impulsivity and hyperactivity (Altepeter & Breen, 1989). Test-retest reliability of the SSQ in a sample of 119 regular education children was estimated at 0.68 for the number of problem situations and 0.78 for the mean severity score (Barkley & Edelbrock, 1987). Also, inter-rater agreement for the SSQ was tested in a sample of 46 students ages 8–17. The correlation between teachers was 0.68 for the number of problem situations and 0.72 for the mean severity score (Danforth & DuPaul, 1996). Barkley and Edelbrock (1987) reported numerous significant correlations between the SSQ and rating scale measures of externalizing behavior problems and evidence that the SSQ differentiates children with ADHD from children without ADHD. However, for both the HSQ and SSQ criterion-related validity evidence is more difficult to operationalize, as these measures have a different focus than ratings of symptoms or problems. Still, situations in which the child has difficulties, as indicated on the HSQ and SSQ, can assist the clinician in appropriately designing and prioritizing intervention strategies.

Child Global Assessment Scale (CGAS)

Another example of an assessment of impairment takes a different approach. The Child Global Assessment Scale (CGAS; Shaffer et al., 1983) is an adaptation of an adult scale designed to assess overall level of impairment at home, in school, or with friends. The scale extends from a low of 1 (extremely impaired) to a high of 100 (no impairment). A parent, teacher, or interviewer is asked to rate the child on this scale where deciles are accompanied by a descriptor (e.g., 51–60, "some noticeable problems"). Previous studies have demonstrated some evidence of reliability and validity. A cut score is commonly used in studies of child psychopathology (e.g., CGAS 70 or below identifies a clinical case).

The CGAS was used as one of the criteria for validating the *DSM-IV* criteria for the diagnosis of ADHD (Lahey et al., 1994). Lahey and colleagues used a CGAS score of 60 or less as an indication of significant impairment associated with symptoms of ADHD. A noteworthy finding of this study was the differential results for the parent and teacher CGAS scores. The parent CGAS scores were significantly related to symptoms of hyperactivity/impulsivity but not to inattention. Teacher CGAS scores were not significantly related to hyperactivity/impulsivity problems. These same teacher scores were, however, related to ratings of academic problems. The Lahey et al. investigation then used the relation between teacher and parent CGAS scores and inattention symptoms to shape the DSM-IV criteria for inattention problems associated with ADHD.

The psychometric properties of the CGAS have been well-studied (see review by Schorre & Vandvik, 2004). Of course, the accuracy of CGAS ratings (as is the case for all ratings) depends heavily on the rater's knowledge of the child's functioning in a variety of spheres (Weissman, Warner, & Fendrich, 1990). Can parents, for example, validly rate school and peer functioning as is required by the CGAS? Schorre and Vandvik (2004) call for increased consistency in how clinicians assess and then rate impairment. Certainly consistency in conceptualizing constructs such as attention problems or depression aid in communication and treatment planning. Such could also be the case for assessing impairment caused by these problems.

An additional consideration is whether the best approaches to assessing impairment are already embedded in rating scales such as those reviewed in this chapter. For instance, a study by Bird et al. (1990) found a strong association between CGAS scores and the Total T-score of the CBCL. The most impaired group had a mean Total T of 70, the next most impaired group had a mean of 67, the next group produced a mean of 59, and the no-diagnosis group mean was 53 (Bird et al.). Clinical elevations on standard rating scales may, then, provide an indicator of impairment. However, Mash and Hunsley (2005) concluded that "Assessments of children and adolescents need to focus not only on specific disorders and problems but also on specific impairments that may occur in the absence of a diagnosable disorder" (p. 368). Therefore, it is quite likely and important that measures of impairment will see increasing use in clinical assessment practice (Bird, 1999).

Conclusions

Parent and teacher rating scales are now common methods for assessing child problems. The quality of parent and teacher rating scales has improved considerably in recent years. Routinely, scales have national normative samples and provide expansive information about their reliability and validity. In essence, rating scales provide a time-efficient and reliable method for obtaining assessment information from parents and teachers.

We focused primarily on global scales that assess multiple domains of functioning because the nature of childhood problems is such that dysfunction in one domain is often associated with problems in other areas of functioning. Our review of rating scales was not intended to be exhaustive but was designed instead to focus on some of the most commonly used scales and to illustrate what we feel are some crucial areas to consider in evaluating scales for use in a clinical assessment. Also, our overview was not intended to replace a careful reading of the technical manuals of these scales but to highlight some of the important features of the scales that might influence their use in clinical assessments.

Furthermore, the ECBI (Box 7.4) is an example of a parent rating scale that could

Box 7.4

Assessing Change

Assessment of change is important in clinical practice, particularly in light of increasing calls for accountability for the delivery of health care. Throughout this text, our focus is primarily on assessment as a mechanism to provide an answer to an initial referral question and treatment recommendations. Quite obviously, however, assessment is an ongoing process throughout treatment as well. If for no other reason, assessment of change should be routine because research has shown that such evaluations lead to better fidelity to evidence-based treatments, and ultimately, to better treatment outcomes (Lambert et al., 2003).

Some considerations of assessment tools as useful for answering referral questions may not apply to assessments of change. Demonstration of utility for intervention planning and assessment is a tricky endeavor since psychometric evidence of validity is not clearly applicable to questions of treatment progress. A measure designed for evaluating change, for example, may not need norms. Consequently, the quality of the norming sample is not relevant. Moreover, a rating scale that assesses a child's tendency toward problems in various areas may not be sensitive to changes over a short period of time. Furthermore, it may not be necessary to interpret total scores if one is interested only in change in the individual behaviors. Perhaps ironically, good test-retest reliability may be *undesirable* in the assessment of session-to-session change. Therefore, ratings scales of the nature discussed in this chapter may not be suitable for assessing change – at least not in the short-term.

Clinicians may wish to assess change through instruments that they develop for use with a specific client with a specific treatment plan. Such strategies, if true to the treatment targets, would have strong validity and utility. However, to the extent that standardized measures can be used, a larger evidence base on meaningful ways to assess change will develop. The Eyberg Child Behavior Inventory (ECBI; Eyberg & Ross, 1978) is an instrument that has a long history of use for evaluating treatment results. It should be noted, however, that its usefulness for assessing particular constructs is not well supported.

The ECBI is a 36-item parent rating scale designed to assess behavior problems for children of age 2 through 17 years (Eyberg & Ross, 1978). Each item is rated in two ways: (1) a Likert-type scale that is used for marking frequency, and (2) a dichotomous scale that the parent uses to identify if the issue is in fact a problem.

The ECBI has been used as a measure of conduct-problem behaviors (Burns & Patterson, 1990), and it does possess some advantages, including the fact that it provides an indication of both frequency and severity for individual behavior problems, which is not common for parent rating scales. This characteristic may make the scale particularly useful for planning and evaluating treatment. The ECBI also produces total scores for both the frequency (Intensity) and severity (Problem) measures.

The available research suggests that the ECBI is an example of an instrument that *may* be useful for identifying treatment objectives for children referred for disruptive behavior problems and for evaluating response to treatment. Certainly, it was ahead of its time in its amenability to evaluations of change. When the ECBI is used for other purposes, such as norm-referenced assessment of constructs, research to date does not reveal significant evidence of construct validity (using the term as outlined by Anastasi, 1988). The ECBI is an excellent example of a scale that has some value only in the hands of the well-informed clinician who applies the scale only in circumstances where it possesses empirical strengths.

We recognize that the preponderance of our attention is devoted to other forms of assessment rather than assessment of change. Nevertheless, an increased research base on individualized as well as large scale approaches to evaluating treatments is imperative. We have every reason to believe that discussions of evidence-based assessment will also include assessments of treatment progress (e.g., Mash & Hunsley, 2005).

be used to evaluate change. The Outcomes Questionnaire-45 (OQ-45) is a questionnaire that has been used as a means to provide therapists with feedback from adult clients as often as after every session (Okiishi et al., 2006). The suitability and feasibility of such an approach with parents/child clients and in many clinical settings is uncertain. Therefore, it is likely the case that the clinician is routinely left to evaluate change, whether formally or informally. This strategy has the advantage of being executed by someone trained to define and detect the problems of focus. It has the disadvantage of being utilized by the very person or persons trying to implement and demonstrate the effectiveness of their therapeutic strategies. Research has increasingly addressed the implications of this approach (e.g., Lambert et al., 2003), but relatively little is known. Far less is known about the teacher assessment of changes in behavioral and emotional functioning during and following interventions. An exception would be single-case designs tracking behavioral changes resulting from classroom interventions; many times, these interventions are evaluated by school psychologists or other mental health professionals.

Chapter Summary

1. Concerns about child self-reports and practicality have made parent and teacher rating scales commonplace in modern child assessment practice. These tools tend to be a very efficient means of gathering clinically relevant information.
2. Research has indicated that the construct being evaluated and the child's developmental level influence ratings provided by parents and teachers and even the usefulness of such ratings.
3. The Behavior Assessment System for Children (BASC-2) Parent Rating Scales (PRS) and Teacher Rating Scales (TRS) have three forms of similar items that span the preschool (2–5), child (6–11), and adolescent (12–21) age ranges. The PRS takes a broad sampling of a child's behavior in home and community settings, whereas the TRS does the same for the school setting.
4. The PRS and TRS were developed using both rational/theoretical and empirical means in combination to construct the individual scales.
5. The BASC-2 measures include a relatively comprehensive assessment of adaptive functioning.
6. The Achenbach CBCL and TRF and their predecessors have long been considered one of the premier rating scale measures of child psychopathology.
7. The CBCL and TRF continue to be a preferred choice of many child clinicians because of its history of successful use and popularity with researchers.
8. The CBCL and TRF now include DSM-Oriented scales that are more closely aligned to *DSM* criteria than the Syndrome scales of both measures.
9. The CSI-4 is unique in its content being explicitly tied to the diagnostic criteria in *DSM-IV.* Thus, it provides a screening of severe forms of childhood psychopathology in a time-efficient manner.
10. The Conners-3-P and Conners-3-T are designed for ages 6 through 18. They both provide an extensive assessment of externalizing problems and have good reliability and validity evidence thus far.
11. The PIC-2 is a 275-item rating scale designed for use with parents of children between the ages of 5 and 19 years. Its companion teacher rating scale, the SBS, has 102 items and is designed to complement the parent report PIC-2 and self-report PIY.
12. PIC-2 and SBS subscales were derived via rational and empirical means.

Therefore, they have fairly homogeneous scale content which enhances interpretation.

13. The SBS in particular includes an assessment of several areas of adaptive classroom functioning
14. A new trend in parent and teacher rating scales is the development of scales that focus on the degree of impairment associated with a child's problems in adjustment. Examples of such measures are the Home Situations Questionnaire (HSQ) and School Situations Questionnaire (SSQ). More research is needed on these instruments. Nevertheless, they represent a significant improvement, particularly since the lack of assessment of impairment has been a historic weakness of rating scales.

Chapter 8

Behavioral Observations

Chapter Questions

- Why have direct observations often been considered the standard by which other assessment techniques are judged?
- What are some of the characteristics of behavioral observations that limit their usefulness in many clinical situations?
- What are the basic components of observational systems?
- What are some examples of observational systems that might be used as part of a clinical assessment of children and adolescents?

Direct observation of a child's or adolescent's overt behavior has held a revered status in the clinical assessment of youth. Frequently, the validity of other methods of assessment is judged by their correspondence with direct observations of behavior. In fact, behavioral observation is often viewed as synonymous with the practice of behavioral assessment (Shapiro & Skinner, 1990). There are two primary reasons for this importance provided to direct observations. First, as the term *direct* implies, observations of behavior are not filtered through the perceptions of some informant. Instead, the behaviors of the child are observed directly. As we have discussed in the chapters on behavior rating scales, information provided by others in the child's environment or by the child himself or herself can be influenced by a host of variables and biases. This increases the complexity of interpreting these types of assessment by requiring assessors to account for these influences in their interpretations. Therefore, direct observations of behavior eliminate a great deal of the complexity in the interpretive process. Second, direct observations of behaviors frequently allow

P.J. Frick et al., *Clinical Assessment of Child and Adolescent Personality and Behavior*,
DOI 10.1007/978-1-4419-0641-0_8,

for the assessment of environmental contingencies that are operating to produce, maintain, or exacerbate a child's behavior. For example, direct observations can assess how others respond to a child's behavior, or they can detect environmental stimuli that seem to elicit certain behaviors. By placing the behavior in a contextual framework, behavioral observations often lead to very effective environmental interventions.

To illustrate this potential of behavioral observations, Carroll, Houghton, Taylor, West, and List-Kerz (2006) conducted a study of 58 students (ages 8 to 11) in which two students, one with Attention Deficit Hyperactivity Disorder (ADHD) and one with no disorder, were observed for 40 min. As would be expected, the children with ADHD showed more off-task behavior. However, the observational system documented "triggers" to this off-task behavior. Nearly, half of the off-task behaviors of students with ADHD could be attributed to environmental distractions, and over a quarter were preceded by specific teacher behaviors.

While these characteristics of behavioral observations make their use an important component of many clinical assessments, we feel that the importance of direct observation is sometimes overstated. Like any assessment technique, direct observations have several limitations. One of their major limitations is that direct observations are often expensive and time consuming, if one is to obtain high-quality information. Because of their cost, many assessors simply eliminate this source of information from their assessment battery. Alternatively, assessors may attempt less rigorous observations than are appropriate. For example, an assessor may observe a child interacting on a playground for a 20-min period and record the child's behavior in a narrative form, without clearly specifying what behaviors will be observed or how they will be recorded. These informal observations are dangerous if the assessor is unaware of the severe limitations and potential biases in the data that are collected and, instead, interprets the data as if they were objective (see Harris & Lahey, 1982a).

Another result of the costliness of direct observations is that the development of many observational systems has ignored basic psychometric considerations (Hartmann, Roper, & Bradford, 1979). In the previous chapters on rating scales, we focused a great deal of attention on the psychometric properties of scales such as the different types of reliability that have been established, the information on the validity of the scales, and the normative base with which to compare scores. Because of cost factors, few observational systems have established their reliability or validity in multiple samples. An even more widespread problem for observational systems is the lack of a representative normative sample that would allow for a comparison of a child's scores with those from the general population. As we have discussed in earlier chapters, having norm-referenced scores is crucial in the clinical assessments of children and adolescents, given the rapid developmental changes they are experiencing.

Even if one were to use an observational system in the most sophisticated manner, direct observations are still limited by (1) the reactivity of the observational setting, (2) difficulties in obtaining an adequate sample of behaviors, and (3) an inability to detect internal events such as cognitions and emotions. *Reactivity* refers to a well-documented phenomenon that a person will change his or her behavior when it is being observed (Kazdin, 1981; Mash & Terdal, 1988). As a result, the sample of behavior may not be as objective as one would hope. There is a significant amount of research on factors that influence the degree of reactivity that results from direct observations (Harris & Lahey, 1982b; Kazdin, 1981). For example, the age of the child can affect the degree of reactivity, with preschool children showing less reactivity to observation than older children

(Keller, 1986). Also, steps can be taken to reduce reactivity during observation such as allowing the child time to get used to (habituate to) the observational setting and reducing the conspicuousness of the observational system (Keller, 1986). But, even under optimum conditions, reactivity is still likely to affect the results of the assessment to some degree.

Another liability of direct observations is the difficulty of obtaining an adequate sample of behaviors. There are several facets to this issue. The first issue involves ensuring that the sample of behavior is obtained under the most ecologically valid conditions; that is, under conditions that will generalize to other times and situations. Although the issue of ecological validity is most important for observational systems that use contrived (analog) conditions (e.g., observing the child in a clinic playroom), it is also important in selecting the natural setting most appropriate for conducting the observation. The second issue is that, even if one selects the best setting, one must ensure that a large enough time frame is used, so that behaviors will be representative and generalizable to other times and settings. In the previous example of a child being observed in a playground setting for a 20-min period, it cannot be determined how typical a child's behavior was during this observational period. He or she may have had an especially good or especially problematic day on the playground. A third issue, which encompasses both the selection of settings and adequacy of the observational period, is the difficulty in assessing many behaviors that are very infrequent (e.g., cruelty to animals, hallucinations, panic attacks) or by nature covert (e.g., stealing, lying). In most cases, one would not ethically want to contrive a situation that would prompt such behaviors, and the behaviors are often too infrequent to be observed naturally occurring in the child's environment.

A final issue in the use of behavior observations is the fact that observations are limited to the assessment of overt behaviors. They do not provide a means for assessing the cognitive, affective, and motivational components of a child's functioning (Mash & Terdal, 1988). This does not negate the importance of having a good assessment of a child's overt behavior in making diagnostic and treatment decisions. However, it has become increasingly clear that overt behavior is only one piece of a complex puzzle. Research in several areas of child psychopathology has supported the importance of intrapsychic variables for both assessing (e.g., Frick, 2006) and treating (e.g., David-Ferdon & Kaslow, 2008) children and adolescents.

In summary, direct observations are affected by some factors that often preclude their use in many clinical settings and limit the usefulness of the data obtained. We spent a great deal of time reviewing the factors that affect behavioral observations, not because of a bias against this form of assessment, but because we have found that assessors sometimes ignore these issues. We feel that a clinical assessor should be aware of these issues in deciding whether or not direct observations should be included in an assessment battery and should consider these issues when interpreting observational data. However, these limitations should not be considered any greater than those associated with other assessment techniques, and the limitations must be weighed against some very important advantages of direct observation (e.g., elimination of reporter bias and ready translation into environmental interventions). Direct observations can be an integral part of many assessment batteries but, as is the case for all assessment techniques, they also have limitations in the information they provide in isolation.

In the following section, we discuss basic issues in the development and use of observational systems. As was mentioned earlier in this chapter, many clinical assessors use informal observational techniques in their assessment battery without establishing a well-defined system. Unfortunately, the information obtained from such systems is difficult to interpret. Unlike rating scales, there are few standardized observational systems that are readily available for clinical use that have well-established psychometric properties. Therefore, the next section focuses on basic considerations in designing an observational system for one's own clinical use. Following this discussion, some examples of observational systems that are commercially available or that have been used in research are reviewed.

Basics of Observational Systems

Defining Target Behaviors

The basic components of observational systems can be broken down into the what, where, how, and by whom of the system. The first part of developing a system of direct observation involves defining *what* behaviors one wishes to observe. Defining the behaviors of interest first involves deciding on the level of analysis one wishes to use (Barrios, 1993). Specifically, the level of analysis can be at the level of isolated behaviors, at the level of constellations of behaviors (syndromes), or at the level of interactions within a social unit. As an example of the social unit level of analysis, many observational systems allow for the recording of how a child behaves in response to parental behavior and how a parent responds to a child's behavior (Gelfand & Hartmann, 1984). Also, the example given previously demonstrates an observational system that focuses on behaviors by fellow students and teachers that can influence the on-task behavior of a student with ADHD (Carroll et al., 2006). Because these systems allow one to document events (stimuli) that elicit a behavior and responses to the behavior that may help to maintain or increase it, this level of analysis provides important information on potential targets of intervention. An example of a simple antecedent-behavior-consequence (A-B-C) type of observation is provided in Box 8.1. From this example, it is clear that recording antecedents and consequences allows one to determine the sequence of events within which a behavior is embedded.

After the level of analysis is chosen, one must operationally define what behaviors, what constellation of behaviors, or what antecedents/consequences will be observed within this window. These definitions are made prior to beginning a direct observation and must be specified in objective and understandable terms in order to reduce the potential for bias and increase the reliability of the observation. Some examples of target behaviors used in observational systems are described in Table 8.1.

The target behaviors in Table 8.1 are simply lists of behaviors from several domains that can be assessed by observational systems. In order to be reliable, coding systems must have very explicit definitions of each behavior. This is necessary to reduce the possibility that the observer will use subjective and idiosyncratic definitions of the behaviors, thereby making interpretations from the observations difficult. Without such definitions the primary advantage of direct observations, objectivity, is severely compromised. One would think that behaviors such as those in Table 8.1 are easy to define and that simple definitions would lead to different observers being able to code the same behavior in the same way. Decades of research have found that this is not true. To reliably code behaviors, one must develop very detailed definitions. Box 8.2 provides an example of a very detailed definition of behavior from a frequently used coding system.

Box 8.1

A Hypothetical Example of Simple A-B-C Observational System of an 8-Year-Old Boy (B)

Time/Setting	Antecedent	Behavior	Consequence
8:30/Math class-copying from board		B takes pencil from another child	Child ignores him
	Child ignores him	B tears paper on child's desk	Child tells teacher and teacher reprimands B
	Teacher reprimands B	B sulks	Teacher allows B to erase board
8:35/Math class-doing seatwork		B leaves seat to sharpen pencil	Teacher asks B to raise hand to leave seat
		B raises hand	Teacher continues to work with other student
	Teacher ignores B	B gets out of seat and pulls on teacher's shirt to get attention	Teacher scolds B for leaving seat and places name on board
	Teacher puts B's name on board	B starts to cry	Child teases B
	Child teases B	B tries to hit other child	B sent to office
8:55/Math class-completing seat work	B returns to class	B sullen and refuses to work	Teacher allows B to collect assignments

TABLE 8.1 Examples of Target Behaviors from Several Behavioral Domains

ADHD (Carroll et al., 2006)	**Conduct Problems (Patterson, 1982)**	**Social Competence (Dodge, 1983)**	**Depression (Kazdin, 1988)**	**Autism (Lord, Rutter, DiLavore, & Risi, 1999)**
Off task	Noncompliance	Solitary play	Talking	Asking for help
Fidgeting	Destructiveness	Cooperative play	Playing alone	Symbolic play
Inappropriate talking	Aggressive play	Smiling	Negativism	Taking turns
Gazing around	Insults/threats	Compliments	Frowning	Reciprocal play
Out of seat	Aggression	Rule making	Complaining	Telling a sequential story
Loud talking	Arguing Teasing	Turn taking	Whining	

Box 8.2

Criteria for "Whine" from the Dyadic Parent–Child Coding System

Definition

A whine consists of words uttered by the child in a slurring, nasal, high-pitched, falsetto voice.

Examples

When can we go home?
Mommy, I hurt my finger.
I have to go to the bathroom. This is too hard.
I don't want to play this anymore.

Guidelines

1. The voice quality of the word or phrase is the primary distinguishing element for coding whine.
2. Each whined sentence constitutes a separate whine. Whined phrases separated from one another by a pause of 2 s or longer are coded as separate whines.

Examples:

Child: I have a headache. I want to go home. (2 whine)
Child: I don't like the red blocks... 2-s pause... and I don't like the Legos. (2 whine)
Child: Please let me take it home... 2-s pause... Please. (2 whine)

3. The content of the word or phrase may be anything except smart talk.

Examples:

I don't like this anymore.	(whine)
I hate you.	(smart talk)
I feel sick.	(whine)
You make me sick.	(smart talk)
You hurt my feelings.	(whine)
You're a jerk.	(smart talk)

4. Whining is a verbal behavior and can occur simultaneously with a nonverbal deviant child behavior (destructive or physical negative child).

Decision Rules

1. When uncertain as to whether the child's voice quality is actually a whine or normal voice quality, do not code whine.
2. When uncertain as to whether a child's verbalization is a whine, smart talk, or a cry, code whine.
3. When uncertain as to whether the deviant behavior is a whine or a yell, code yell.

Source: Summarized from the manual for the Dyadic Parent–Child Interaction Coding System (Eyberg & Robinson, 1983) with the authors' permission.

Setting

Once the target behaviors are defined, the next decision is to determine *where* to observe these target behaviors. Naturalistic observations involve observing the child in his or her natural setting (e.g., in the classroom, at home). The kind of behaviors of interest (e.g., social interactions during free play) often determines what natural setting is best to conduct the observation (e.g., on the playground). In its purest form, naturalistic observations involve placing no constraints on a child's behavior other than those naturally occurring in the observational setting. However, sometimes it is necessary to place some restrictions on the observational setting to enhance the quality of the observations. For example, an observer who is in the home of a child to observe parent–child interactions may need to place some constraints on the child and parents to ensure that there are sufficient opportunities to observe interactions during the observational session. For example, one may wish to place restrictions that parents and children must stay in the same room and that there is no talking on the telephone, working on a computer, playing video games, or watching TV. Another example is an observational system designed to observe a child's anxious behavior. The observer may wish the teacher to "create" a situation that seems to lead to anxiety in the child, such as being called on in class or taking a test, in order to observe the child's response.

In Box 8.3, we provide an example of a study by Ostrov and Keating (2004) in which observations of aggressive behavior of preschool children were observed in both free play and during several structured interactions. Both types of observations were conducted in a naturalistic setting (i.e., the child's school). The use of different observational situations within the same study allowed the authors to determine the types of settings in which aggression is most likely to occur.

Naturalistic observations are often preferred because they generally provide more ecologically valid data. However, time and cost constraints may prevent one from conducting a naturalistic observation. For many clinical assessments, it is often impossible for the assessor to make several

Box 8.3

An Observational Study of Preschool Aggression

Ostrov and Keating (2004) reported a study of aggression in preschool children using naturalistic observations in the child's school setting. This study provides a good example of two common types of naturalistic observational techniques, one in which no restrictions are placed in the natural setting (i.e., free play) and one in which the situation is structured (i.e., coloring task). The study involved 46 children (mean age of 64 months) in rural preschools.

What: The observation coding system focused behaviors in four main categories: (1) *physical aggression:* hitting, pushing, pulling, punching, forcibly taking objects; (2) *verbal aggression:* teasing, calling mean names, verbal threats of harm, insults; (3) *relational aggression:* excluding from play group; spreading rumors, withdrawing friendship; telling lies; ignoring peer; (4) *number of male and female playmates:* number of children of each sex the observed child directly interacted.

Where: Free play observations were conducted during regularly scheduled free play periods in large indoor playrooms, in classrooms, and outdoors on the playground. For the coloring task, pairs of children were given a series of three pictures to color. However, the potential for mild conflict was introduced by providing one colorful crayon and one white one.

How: Each observational session was 10 min and every instance of the specified behaviors were coded. Each child was observed for five sessions. Behavioral counts were summed across observational periods to determine a score in each of the four behavioral categories.

By Whom: Observers were three female and one male undergraduate students who were trained on the observational system. Prior to conducting observations, observers were introduced to the teacher and students and they spent a few days in the classroom to let the students adjust to their presence.

Results: Boys exhibited more physical aggression but girls displayed more relational aggression. Aggression was less overall and these gender differences were less pronounced during the coloring task. However, there was fairly high stability in a child's level aggression across contexts.

Summarized from: Ostrov, J. M., & Keating, C.F. (2004). Gender differences in preschool aggression during free play and structured interactions: An observational study. *Social Development, 13,* 255–277.

home visits to observe a child or adolescent interacting with his or her parents. Also, for some behaviors, there may not be a way of obtaining unobtrusive observations in a child's natural environment. As a result, the level of reactivity would be so high that the data would be meaningless. In addition to these more practical considerations, sometimes there is a need to exert more control over the situation than is possible in a natural setting. For example, one may wish to observe a child's activity level in a free play situation by determining how many times a child passes from one part of a room to another. To code this reliably, one can divide the room into sections with tape and then code the number of times a child crosses over a tape divider (Milich, 1984). This type of control (e.g., dividing the playroom into grids) may not be feasible in a child's natural environment.

For these reasons, it is sometimes necessary or desirable to conduct analog observations in a laboratory or clinic. *Analog* refers to the creation of a contrived setting that approximates the natural environment. Dividing a clinic playroom into grids to observe a child's activity level is one example of an analog setting. However, the key to these observations is how well the analog situation approximates the natural environment. Staying with our example, it would be imperative that the playroom be similar to a play area that a child would be in outside of the clinic (e.g., with age-appropriate toys available). There are many other examples of analog settings for behavioral observations, but each involves the basic component of simulating a child's natural environment in a clinic setting.

Sometimes it is not feasible to have the clinic setting approximate the natural setting. In these cases, children may be asked to imagine themselves in a situation, and their behavior is observed in this role-play situation. An area in which role play observations have been frequently used is the assessment of children's social competence (e.g., Bornstein, Bellack, & Hersen, 1977; Dodge, McClaskey, & Feldman, 1985). For example, Dodge et al. (1985) had children pretend that they were in certain social situations and then pretend that the assessor was another child. An explicit coding system was developed to code the degree of social competence of a child's behavior in each of the imagined situations. An example of one of the role-play situations used in this study is included in Box 8.4.

Data Collection

The next stage in developing an observational system is to determine *how* one will code the target behaviors in the selected setting. There are several data collection methods that can be used, with the method of choice depending on the characteristics of the behaviors of interest. Although there are many variations of these basic data collection methods, the techniques can be largely placed into three categories: Event Recording, Duration Recording, and Time Sampling.

Event Recording

Event recording is the simplest of the data collection methods. It involves recording the number of times that a target behavior occurred during preset intervals or during an entire observational session. This method was illustrated in the study of preschool aggression described in Box 8.3 (Ostov & Keating, 2004). Due to its simplicity, event recording is the most frequently used method of direct observation. However, to use event recording, target behaviors must have discrete beginnings and endings, such as hitting another child, raising one's hand, and asking to play a game (Shapiro, 1987). In contrast, behaviors that are continuous and persist for long periods of time are more difficult to code using event recording because it

Box 8.4

A Role-Play Situation from the Dodge Study of Social Competence

Situation #2

Let's pretend that I'm playing blocks with some of my friends after lunch. We're building a really neat house. You come in the schoolroom and see us. Pretend that you really want to play blocks with us. what do you do and say?

a. Was the child role playing?
b. How competent was the response? Score:
   8-Complimentary or evaluative remark with a re-quest to play: "Boy, that's neat. Can I play?"

6—A simple request to play: "I'd ask, May I please play?"

4—Rhetorical question or evaluative remark: "What are you doing?" or "That's neat."

2—Suggestion for different activity: "Want to play a game?"

0—Aggressive responses: "I'd knock the blocks over", "I would say nothing or sit down at desk without speaking": "I do'nt know what to do", or no answer.

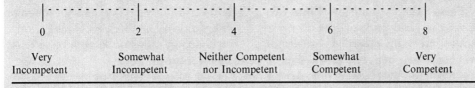

0	2	4	6	8
Very Incompetent	Somewhat Incompetent	Neither Competent nor Incompetent	Somewhat Competent	Very Competent

Reproduced with permission of authors from the Scoring System for Child Role Plays: Role Playing Criteria used in Dodge, K. A., McClaskey, C. L., & Feldman E. (1985). Situational approach to the assessment of social competence in children. *Journal of Consulting and Clinical Psychology, 53*, 344–353.

is difficult to distinguish the occurrence of one incident from the next. Examples of such continuous behaviors are off-task behavior, talking out loud, and engaging in solitary play. Event recording is especially useful for recording behaviors that occur only briefly and for recording low-frequency behaviors that only occur once or twice in an observational period, such as swearing or hitting another child (Keller, 1986; Shapiro, 1987).

Duration Recording

For some assessments, it may be more important to know how long a behavior occurs rather than the frequency of the behavior. In duration recording, the observer records the length of time from the beginning to the end of an instance of behavior. Duration and event recording can be combined to provide an even richer source of information (Shapiro, 1987). For example, in observing the temper tantrums of a young child, it may be helpful to record not only the frequency of tantrums within a given period, but to also record the duration of each tantrum episode.

Time Sampling

In both event and duration recording techniques, all instances of the behaviors are recorded during the observational period.

However, some behaviors occur too frequently to obtain accurate counts, or there are no clear beginning or end points to the behaviors, which prevents effective event and duration recording. For these types of behaviors, the observation period can be divided into predetermined intervals, and the behaviors are simply coded as being either present or absent during each interval. Therefore, rather than yielding an exact count of the number of times that a behavior occurred during the observational period, time sampling allows one to determine the proportion of intervals in which the behavior occurred.

Shapiro (1987) reviews three types of time-sampling techniques. In *whole-interval* recording one codes a behavior as present only if it occurs throughout a time interval. For example, an observational period in a child's classroom can be broken down into 20-s intervals and the number of intervals in which the child remained on task for the entire interval is recorded. In *partial-interval* recording, one records whether or not a behavior occurred at any time during the interval. Shapiro gives the example of a teacher dividing the day into 15-min segments and noting whether or not certain behaviors occurred during each segment. A final type of time sampling is *momentary* recording, in which one records whether a behavior was present or absent only during the moment when a time interval ends. For example, when observing the degree of social withdrawal of a child, one may divide an observational period into 60-s intervals and record whether or not a child was engaged in interactions with other children at the end of each interval.

Selecting the Observers

After determining what behaviors will be observed, where the observations will take place, and how the observations will be conducted, one still must determine *who* is best suited to conduct the observation. Having someone who is in the child's natural setting (e.g., teacher or parent) conduct the observation is often useful in naturalistic observations because it helps to maintain unobtrusiveness. However, it is often difficult to teach people in the child's natural environment how to use a coding system and to ensure that it is being used appropriately.

In order to exert more control over the observational methodology, many observational systems require rigorously trained and monitored observers. Barrios (1993) provides a summary of steps required in training and monitoring observers (see Table 8.2). As one can see from this summary, using specially trained observers is quite costly. Such stringent methodology is feasible only when a large number of children are being observed with the same observational method. Therefore, this methodology may not be optimal in many clinical settings.

One type of observation that is frequently used in clinical assessments involves training a person to observe his or her own behavior. The same steps of selecting target behaviors, determining the setting for the observation, and determining how the target behaviors will be recorded are followed. However, in *self-monitoring* the child is trained to record his or her own behavior. Although self-monitoring has been used largely with adults, children have used self-monitoring systems to monitor such diverse behaviors as classroom attending, class attendance, talking out in class, room cleaning, aggression, and inappropriate verbalizations (Mash & Terdal, 1988).

One method of self-monitoring that has begun to receive some attention in research is the use of electronic diaries. That is, with the advent of small computers and personal digital assistants (PDAs), children and adolescents can be taught to

TABLE 8.2 Steps in Training and Monitoring Observers

Step	Description
Orientation	Informing observers of the importance of objective assessment in the understanding and treating of childhood disorders. Informing observers of their duties and responsibilities, in particular their independent, unbiased, and faithful recording of the behavior of interest.
Education	Instructing observers in the response definitions and recording scheme through the use of written materials, filmed illustrations, and live demonstrations.
Evaluation	Assessment of observers' knowledge of the response definitions, coding system, and recording scheme through the use of written and oral examinations. Representation of materials until observers are thoroughly acquainted with all aspects of tracking and recording of the behaviors of interest.
Application	Graduated implementation of the observation system across a range of situations, beginning with analog ones and ending with actual setting of interest. Transition from one situation to the next contingent upon observers achieving a criterion level of agreement and accuracy.
Recalibration	Assessment of the accuracy and agreement of observers' recordings in the setting of interest. Identification and correction of any breakdowns in the fidelity of observers' recordings.
Termination	Questioning observers as to the merits of the observation system. Informing observers of their contributions to the understanding and treating of the behaviors of interest. Reminding observers of the need to maintain confidentiality.

Reproduced with permission from Barrios (1993). Direct observation. In T. H. Ollendick and M. Hersen (Eds.), Handbook of child and adolescent assessment (pp. 140–164). Boston: Allyn & Bacon.

carry a small PDA which cues the child to respond to certain prompts and questions. This allows the child to record responses in real time (i.e., when it is actually occurring). For example, Whalen et al. (2006) had 52 children (mean age of 10.58) report on their moods, behaviors, and social contexts every 30 min during nonschool hours. The children carried a PDA that beeped every 30 min to signal it was time to respond to certain questions. The children's responses were saved in the PDA for later analyses. Twenty-seven of the children were diagnosed with ADHD and the results showed that these children had more behavioral problems, negative mood, and conflict with parents.

Research suggests that children can self-monitor their behavior accurately if they are trained appropriately, have a clear and simple observational system, have an outside monitor of the accuracy of their recording, and are reinforced for the accuracy of their recording (Keller, 1986). The advantages of self-monitoring are that it is cost effective and is less intrusive than many other forms of behavioral observation. However, research clearly suggests that children change their behavior as they become more aware of it through self-monitoring (Keller, 1986; Shapiro, 1987). Whereas this change in behavior may be a beneficial aspect of self-monitoring in a treatment program, this reactivity limits the usefulness of self-monitoring as a means of obtaining objective information on a child's behavior for assessment purposes.

Examples of Observational Systems

In contrast to behavior rating scales, there are few observational systems that are widely used, have standardized procedures, and are readily available for clinical use. In this section, we review some notable exceptions. The goal of this overview is not to provide an exhaustive list of observational systems but to provide a carefully selected list of observational techniques that vary in terms of target behaviors, settings of observation, method of data collection, and degree of training needed to reliably use the observational system. We feel that, even if one does not choose to use one of the specific systems discussed here, these systems provide concrete examples of some of the issues discussed in this chapter and therefore can serve as a guide for the development and use of other observational systems. Also, some additional observational systems that focus on a specific areas of adjustment are reviewed in other chapters.

Achenbach System of Empirically Based Assessment: Direct Observation Form and Test Observation Form

The ASEBA system of assessments contains two observational systems. The first is the Direct Observation Form (DOF; Achenbach, 2001) which is designed for use with children and adolescents ages 5 to 14. It provides a method of coding observations in academic classrooms and other group activities. The Test Observation Form (McConaughy & Achenbach, 2004) is designed for use with children and adolescents ages 2 to 18 and allows for the coding of behavioral observations during the individual administration of standardized ability and achievement tests. Both of these systems are part of the ASEBA system and are designed to be interpreted in conjunction with the parent, teacher, and child self-report versions of the ASEBA, all of which have been discussed in previous chapters.

The DOF is designed to provide a direct observation of a child in a classroom or group setting during a 10-min period. There are three parts to the DOF. First, the observer is asked to write a narrative description of a child's behavior throughout the 10-min observational period, noting the occurrence, duration, and intensity of specific problems. Second, at the end of each minute the child's behavior is coded as being on- or off-task for 5 s. Third, at the end of the 10-min period, the observer rates the child on 96 behaviors that may have been observed during the observational period using a 4-point scale (from 0 = behavior was not observed to 3 = definite occurrence of behavior with severe intensity or for greater than 3 min duration).

The 96 problem behaviors on the DOF have a high degree of item overlap with the behaviors rated on the parent and teacher rating scales of the ASEBA system. Therefore, the DOF is nicely suited for a multimodal assessment of a child's or adolescent's emotional and behavioral functioning. Like the other parts of the ASEBA system, the DOF can be used to calculate a Total Problem score, which is a sum of the ratings of all 96 problems, two broadband scales (Internalizing and Externalizing), and six narrowband scales (Withdrawn-Inattentive, Nervous-Obsessive, Depressed, Hyperactive, Attention-demanding, Aggressive) (Achenbach, 2001). The DOF does report norms from a relatively small sample of 287 nonreferred children (Achenbach, 2001).

There is evidence that the DOF can be used reliably by observers with minimal training. Inter-observer correlations have been calculated on the Total Problems scale in several samples. Correlations between observers range from .96 in a residential treatment center (Achenbach, 1986) to .92 in a sample of boys referred for special services in school (Reed & Edelbrock, 1983) to.75 in a sample of outpatient referrals to a child psychiatry clinic (McConaughy, Achenbach, & Gent, 1988). Inter-observer correlations for the On-task scores were .71, .71, and .88 in the three samples, respectively. Reed and Edelbrock (1983) reported inter-observer reliability in their sample of 25 boys for a selected set of individual items from the DOF. In general, most items showed high inter-observer correlations (most above .80), with the exceptions of Nervous, high-strung, or tense (.20); Picks nose, skin, or other parts of body (.52); and Compulsions, repeats behavior over and over (.53).

Reed and Edelbrock (1983) reported that the Total Problems scale and On-task scores from the DOF correlated in expected directions with teacher ratings of total problems and adaptive behaviors. In addition, the DOF Total Problems scale and On-task scores have been shown to differ in normal and disturbed children (McConaughy et al., 1988; Reed & Edelbrock, 1983). In terms of discriminating within disturbed children, the evidence for the DOF is less clear. McConaughy et al. (1988) reported that the Total Problems, On-task, and Externalizing scores differentiated children classified with internalizing or externalizing problems. However, the internalizing scale of the CBCL-DOF did not demonstrate discriminant validity in this study.

The TOF is designed to rate children's behavior during an individual standardized testing session. It has 125 items that are rated on a four point scale (0 = "no occurrence" – 3 = "definite occurrence with severe intensity or 3 or more minutes duration"). Items are rated by the examiner immediately after the testing session. Like the DOF, the TOF has a strong overlap in items with other measures in the ASEBA system. Thus, a Total Problem, an Internalizing, and an Externalizing composite can all be obtained from the TOF. Also, it includes five narrow band scales: Withdrawn/Depressed, Language/Thought Problems, Anxious, Oppositional, and Attentional Problems.

The TOF has a normative sample of 3,943 children between the ages of 2 and 18, most of which were obtained during the standardization of the Stanford-Binet Intelligence Scales-5th Edition (Roid, 2003). In general, the TOF scales show good test-retest reliability (.53–.87) over a period of 10 days, adequate interrater reliability (.42–.73), and good internal consistency (.74–.94) (McConaughy, 2005). Scores on the TOF are moderately correlated with corresponding parent completed ASEBA (.27–.43) and teacher completed ASEBA (.26–.38) scales (McConaughy, 2005). Also, the TOF scales have differentiated children with ADHD from normal control children (McConaughy, 2005).

In summary, the TOF and DOF are both time-efficient observational systems that require minimal observer training and fit into a multimethod assessment system. Both observational systems have information showing some basic levels of reliability. They both also provide norm-referenced scores, although the sample for the DOF norms is very limited. Also, both systems have proven to be useful for discriminating normal from clinic-referred children. However, their ability to differentiate within children with emotional and behavioral problems is less clear.

Behavioral Assessment System for Children-Student Observation System

The BASC-2-Student Observation System (BASC-2-SOS; Reynolds & Kamphaus, 2004) is a commercially available, short (15-min) observational system that is designed for use in a classroom setting. It is part of the comprehensive BASC-2 system, which includes parent and teacher behavior rating scales and a child self-report form, all of which have been discussed in previous chapters. The BASC-2-SOS defines 65 specific target behaviors that are grouped into 13 categories (4 categories of positive/adaptive behaviors and 9 categories of problem behaviors). The 13 categories and examples of target behaviors in each category are provided in Table 8.3.

Table 8.3 Behavioral Categories from the Student Observation System of BASC2 Category/Definition

Category/Definition	Example of Specific Behaviors
Response to Teacher/ Lesson (appropriate academic behaviors involving teacher or class)	Follows directions Raises hand Contributes to class discussion Waits for help on assignment
Peer Interaction (appropriate interactions with other students)	Plays with other students Interacts in friendly manner Shakes hand with other student Converses with others in discussion
Work on School Subjects (appropriate academic behaviors that student engages in alone)	Does seatwork Works at blackboard Works at computer
Transition Movement (appropriate nondisruptive behaviors while moving from one activity to another)	Puts on/takes off coat Gets book Sharpens pencil Walks in line Returns material used in class
Inappropriate Movement (inappropriate motor behaviors that are unrelated to classroom work)	Fidgeting in seat Passing notes Running around classroom Sitting/standing on top of desk
Inattention (inattentive behaviors that are not disruptive)	Daydreaming Doodling Looking around room Fiddling with objects/fingers
Inappropriate Vocalization (disruptive vocal behaviors)	Laughing inappropriately Teasing Talking out Crying
Somatization (physical symptoms/complaints)	Sleeping Complaining of not feeling well
Repetitive Motor Movements (repetitive behaviors that appear to have no external reward)	Finger/pencil tapping Spinning an object Body rocking Humming/singing to oneself
Aggression (harmful behaviors directed at another person or property)	Kicking others Throwing objects at others Intentionally ripping another's work Stealing
Self-Injurious Behavior (severe behaviors that attempt to injure one's self)	Pulling own hair Head banging Biting self Eating or chewing nonfood items
Inappropriate Sexual Behavior (behaviors that are explicitly sexual in nature)	Touching others inappropriately Masturbating Imitating sexual behavior
Bowel/Bladder Problems (urination or defecation)	Wets pants Has bowel movement outside toilet

From C. R. Reynolds and R. W. Kamphaus (2004). Behavior assessment system for children – 2nd Edition (BASC-2). Circle Pines, MN: American Guidance Services.

The BASC-2-SOS was designed to be completed during a 15-min observation of the child in an academic classroom.

The behaviors during the observation are coded in three parts. In Part A, each of the 65 behaviors are rated as being "Not Observed," "Sometimes Observed" or "Frequently Observed." Also, any behavior judged to be disruptive is noted. Part B uses a momentary time-sampling approach in recording data. The 15-min observational period is divided into 30 intervals. At the end of each 30-sec interval the child's behavior is observed for 3-sec. A checklist allows the observer to mark each category of behavior that occurred during the 3-sec observation interval. In Part C, the observer is asked to describe the teacher's interactions with the student, focusing on contingencies in the classroom that may be influencing the child's behavior.

The BASC-2-SOS is a simple and time efficient observational system that assesses, through direct observation, many behaviors that are crucial for the clinical assessment of children and adolescents. It is one of the few direct observational systems commercially available. Also, the BASC-2-SOS has an electronic coding format in which behavioral observations can be recorded directly into a PDA device.

However, the BASC2-SOS lacks a number of crucial psychometric elements. First, there is no information on the reliability of the system provided in the manual. Establishing inter-observer agreement is a crucial component in developing an observational system, to ensure that observations are objective and relatively free from bias. Second, there are no norms for the BASC-2-SOS, so norm-referenced interpretation of scores is not possible. Third, there is limited information on the validity of BASC-2SOS, such as whether or not the BASC-2-SOS code categories correlate with clinically important criteria (e.g., diagnoses, behavior rating scales, response to intervention). Lett and Kamphaus (1997) reported that scores on the BASC-2-SOS did differentiate children with ADHD from normal control children. However, the limited information on the psychometric properties of the BAS-2-SOS greatly limits its potential contribution to many clinical assessments.

Behavioral Avoidance Tests

Behavioral Avoidance Tests (BATs) have been used to observe a person's behavioral response to anxiety-producing stimuli since the early 1900s (Jersild & Holmes, 1935). Although there are many different versions of BATs (e.g., Morris & Kratochwill, 1983; Van Hasselt, Hersen, Bellack, Rosenblum, & Lamparski, 1979), they all involve exposing the child or adolescent to some feared stimuli (e.g., animal, dark, stranger, heights, blood), then requiring the child to approach the feared stimuli in graduated steps.

BATs provide explicit and objective criteria for observing a child's behavioral reaction to the feared stimulus, such as how closely the stimulus is approached, the number of steps in the gradual approach that are taken, or the time spent touching or handling the phobic stimulus. In quantifying these responses to anxiety-producing stimuli, BATs provide a measure of the severity of a child's anxiety and can help document changes brought about by interventions (Vasay & Lonigan, 2000).

Southam-Gerow and Chorpita (2007) provide a good summary of the advantages and disadvantages of BATs. They describe the primary disadvantage of BATs as the absence of a single standardized BAT. Instead, there have been numerous different BATs developed that vary widely on the number of steps in the graduated approach, the types of instructions given to the child, and how the feared stimulus is presented. As a result, it is impossible to compare the findings across studies and therefore it is impossible to develop a significant body of knowledge on the reliability, validity, and normative base for any of the BATs. In addition, a hallmark of the BATs is the rigorous control over how the feared object is presented to the child and how the child approaches it. This degree of control may prevent the behavior observed in the contrived setting from generalizing to the child's natural environment. One final limitation of BATs is that they are most commonly used to assess specific fears and are more difficult to design for assessing more generalized anxiety (Vasay & Lonigan, 2000).

On the positive side, however, BATs are relatively simple and time efficient in their administration. Many of the BATs have been shown to have good inter-observer agreement with minimal observer training and to be sensitive to treatment effects (Barrios & Hartmann, 1988; Southam-Gerow & Chorpita, 2007). Also, scores from BATs are correlated with subjective ratings of fear and with phobia diagnoses (Vasay & Lonigan, 2000). Most importantly, they provide one of the only methods of assessing the behavioral components (i.e., a child's avoidance of a feared stimulus) of childhood anxiety.

Conflict Negotiation Task

The Conflict Negotiation Task was designed to assess peer interactions, especially those interactions that may be associated with childhood depression (Rudolph, Hammen, & Burge, 1994). Children are observed with an unfamiliar partner of the same age and gender. The system uses a task involving three points of potential conflict of interest between the child and his or her partner. First, child dyads are placed in a situation in which they are to build structures with colored blocks to match either of two models. They are informed that whoever constructs an identical model would win a prize. The dyad is given a set of blocks to share but the number of blocks is only sufficient to build one complete model. Second, after 10 min of observation, the dyad is asked to decide on how to distribute two prizes of unequal value. Third, the dyad participates in a 5-min interview and the child who received the less valuable prize is allowed to choose a new one.

The interactions during this task are coded by trained observers. Using an event recording system, behaviors are rated on a seven-point scale (0 = not at all present; 4 = moderately present; 7 = to a large degree present) and all ratings are scaled such that high scores indicate more negative peer interactions. The behaviors are grouped into four composites. Two composites are related to broad dimensions of social behavior displayed by the child being assessed. Conflict-resolution competence includes persistence in problem-solving efforts, positive assertiveness, positive conflict management, and general social competence. Emotional regulation includes conflict exacerbation, positive affect, and negative affect. The third composite consists of a dyadic quality code based on ratings of conflict or friction within the dyad, collaboration, problem-solving competence of the dyad, and mutuality/reciprocity. Finally, a peer response code is based on the ratings of the peer's behavior toward to the assessed child, including general response valence (negative or positive) to the target child, discomfort and embarrassment in response to the target child, and emotional state at the end of the interaction.

Rudolph et al. (1994) reported on the use of this system in a sample of 36 children (20 girls and 16 boys) between the ages of 7 and 13. The four composites from this observational system showed very high correlations between raters (.88 to .92) and the behaviors within each composite were highly intercorrelated (.82 to .97). Most importantly, when the 36 children were divided into those high on a measure of depression and those low on this measure, depressed children were rated as significantly less competent on all four of the composites. Specifically, children high on depression were observed to be significantly worse in their conflict-resolution competence, in their emotional regulation, in mutuality and cooperation during the interaction, and in the negative valence placed on the interactions by their partners (e.g., their partner being more uncomfortable in the interactions). The authors point out that these data support the contention that children who score high on depression have significant interpersonal difficulties. Furthermore, the findings suggest that observational systems of children's interactions with peers can be useful for assessing important aspects of these social difficulties.

Dodge's Observation of Peer Interactions

Dodge (1983) developed a direct observation system that also assesses several components of peer interactions. However, this observation system focuses on behaviors associated with acceptance in a peer group. Dodge developed his system in a sample of 5-, 6-, 7-, and 8-year-old boys. Children were observed in 60-min play groups of eight boys each by three observers who were stationed behind a one-way mirror. The boys wore numbered T-shirts to aid in quick identification by the observer. Each observer coded the behaviors of one boy for a 6-min period and then coded a second child according to a prearranged schedule.

There were 18 target behaviors of five types that were defined for the observation system (see Table 8.4). A complex event recording system was used for the observations. Each time a target behavior was observed, the observer coded the time, the context (structured vs. unstructured), the target behavior observed, and the peer target (number of child). Observers received extensive training over a 4-week period and, with this training, the observational codes showed quite high inter-observer agreement (Dodge, 1983). Across the 18 target behaviors, 15 behaviors showed inter-observer agreement of 65% or better.

TABLE 8.4 Target Behaviors in the Dodge Observational System of Peer Interactions

Behavior Category	Target Behaviors
Solitary active	Solitary play Watching peers On-task behavior Off-task behavior
Interactive play	Cooperative play Aggressive play Inappropriate play (e.g., standing on table)
Verbalizations	Social conversations with peers Norm-setting statements (e.g., rule making) Hostile verbalizations (e.g., insults, threats) Supportive statements (e.g., compliments, offers of help) Exclusions of peers from play Extraneous verbalization (e.g., laughs, cheers)
Physical contact with peers	Hits Object possession (e.g., grabbing an object from peer) Physically affectionate behavior (e.g., holding hands, hugging)
Interactions with adult	Social conversation with adult leader Reprimanded by adult group leader

From K. A. Dodge (1983). Behavioral antecedents of peer social status. Child Development, 54, 1386–1399.

The three behaviors that showed poor inter-observer agreement were watching peers, norm-setting statements, and supportive statements.

Family Interaction Coding System

One of the most common uses of behavioral observations is to observe parent–child interactions, especially those associated with childhood conduct problems (Frick & Loney, 2000). For example, Patterson and colleagues at the Oregon Social Learning Center have developed a direct observational system designed to assess children's conduct problems in the home and to assess the interactional patterns in which the conduct problems are often embedded. The Family Interaction Coding System (FICS; Patterson, 1982) is composed of 29 code categories that include both child behaviors and parental reactions to the child behaviors. These categories are summarized in Table 8.5. The goal of the FICS was to observe children interacting with family members in natural home settings. However, as described by Patterson (1982), several restrictions had to be made in the home for the observational sessions. Specifically, to use the FICS, all family members must be present during the pre-arranged observation times with no guests present, and the family is limited to being present in two rooms of the house. There can be no telephone calls out (only brief answers to incoming calls) and no TV. Finally, there is to be no talking to the observers during coding.

TABLE 8.5 Target Behaviors in the Family Interaction Coding System

Approval	High rate[a]	Physical negative[a]
Attention	Humiliate[a]	Physical positive
Command	Ignore[a]	Receive
Command negative[a]	Laugh	Self-stimulation
Compliance	Noncompliance[a]	Talk
Cry[a]	Negativism[a]	Tease[a]
Disapproval[a]	Normative	Touch
Dependency[a]	No response	Whine[a]
Destructiveness[a]	Play	Yell[a]

Reproduced with author's permission from G. R. Patterson (1982). Coerceive family process. Eugene, OR: Castalia.

[a]Denotes aversive behaviors that are included in the Total Aversive Behavior (TAB) score.

The FICS was designed to have data coded continuously and to provide a sequential account of the interactions between a child and other family members. The behavior of the child and the person(s) with whom the child interacts are coded in sequence. After initial coding, many of the child's behaviors are summarized in a rate-per-minute variable that combines both frequency and duration of the behavior. However, the most frequently used score from the FICS is the Total Aversive Behavior (TAB) score which is a sum of the number of aversive behaviors which occurred during the observational session.

Patterson (1982) describes a moderate level of inter-observer agreement for most code categories of the FICS, with the categories of Negativism and Self-Stimulation showing the most questionable levels of agreement. One week test-retest reliability of the TAB was studied in a sample of 27 boys and was found to be quite high (.78). The TAB was also found to discriminate between families of children referred for behavior problems and nonreferred families and has proven to be sensitive to family-focused treatment for children's conduct problems (Patterson, 1982). Although most of the individual code categories of the FICS can be coded consistently by two observers, psychometric information is generally limited to the global index of aversive behavior, the TAB.

In summary, the FICS is an example of an observation system designed to assess a child's behavior in the home environment and to assess parent–child interactional patterns in which the behavior is embedded. The FICS is generally most useful for younger children (10 and under). Also, most of the psychometric information available for the FICS is for the aversive behaviors assessed by the TAB. This is not as severe a limitation as one might think, however, given that these aversive behaviors have proven to be quite important to understanding and treating children with conduct problems (Patterson, 1982).

Structured Observation of Academic and Play Settings

Milich, Roberts, and colleagues (Milich, 1984; Milich, Loney & Landau, 1982; Roberts, Ray, & Roberts, 1984) developed an observational system (Structured Observation of Academic and Play Settings [SOAPS]) to assess behaviors associated with ADHD in a clinic playroom analog setting. In this system, a clinic playroom is designed with age-appropriate toys, four tables, and a floor divided into 16 equal squares by black tape. The child is placed in two situations. Free Play involves the child being placed alone in the room and allowed to play freely with the toys. The Restricted Academic Playroom Situation involves the child being requested (1) to remain seated, (2) to complete a series of academic tasks, and (3) not to play with any of the toys.

Each observational situation lasts for 15 min. A combination of event recording and time sampling is used in this observation system. Event recording is used to determine the total number of grids crossed for the entire observational period. That is, the number of times that a child moves completely from one square of the divided room into another is counted. Event recording is also used to determine the number of times the child shifts his or her attention from one task to another during the entire observational period. A 5-sec time sampling procedure is used to observe other target behaviors. These include the proportion of 5-sec intervals that the child is out of his or her seat, fidgeting, noisy, and on task. In addition, a 5-sec time sampling is used to determine the number of intervals that the child was observed touching forbidden toys. Also during the academic task, the number of items completed is recorded.

This observational system is useful in clinical assessments of ADHD for a number of reasons. First, it is a relatively easy to use observational system. As a result, high inter-observer reliability has been obtained for most categories with minimal observer training. Second, categories from this system have been correlated with clinicians' diagnoses of ADHD, they have differentiated ADHD children from aggressive and other clinic-referred children (Milich et al., 1982), and they have been relatively stable over a 2-year period (Milich, 1984). Third, a modified version of this task has been shown to be sensitive to treatment with stimulant medication (Barkley, 1988).

Conclusions

In this chapter, we have attempted to summarize both the advantages and disadvantages of direct observations of behavior as part of a comprehensive clinical assessment. Although there are some limitations, direct observations are a useful component to many assessment batteries. Probably the biggest limitation to the clinical utility of direct observations is the time and cost involved in conducting behavioral observations appropriately. We have attempted to outline some of the major considerations in developing and using observational systems so that clinical assessors can (1) evaluate existing observational systems appropriately, (2) develop their own observational systems as needed, and (3) recognize limitations in the data provided by observational systems that are not developed and used in a sound manner.

We concluded this chapter by providing an overview of several existing observational systems. This overview was not meant to be exhaustive. The observational systems included were specifically chosen to provide examples of the various domains of behavior that observational systems can assess, the different settings in which observations can be conducted, and the various methodologies that can be employed. Two of the systems are commercially available (ASEBA-DOF/TOF; BASC-2-SOS) and cover a broad array of behaviors. The other systems reviewed focus on more narrowly defined dimensions of behavior such as anxiety, social interaction, aggression, or ADHD. Whether or not a clinical assessor chooses to use these specific systems, we feel that concrete examples of observational systems help to illustrate the unique contribution that behavioral observations can make to an assessment battery.

Chapter Summary

1. Direct observations of children's and adolescents' behavior are an important part of an assessment because they provide an objective view of behavior that is not filtered through an informant.
2. Direct observations are also helpful in assessing environmental contingencies that affect a child's behavior.
3. Direct observations also have a number of limitations:
   a. Conducting observations in a way that provides valuable information is often an expensive and time-consuming process.
   b. Because of the cost of obtaining observations, the development of observational systems often has ignored basic psychometric considerations such as testing the reliability of the system or developing an adequate normative base.
   c. Even well-developed observational systems are subject to reactivity. That is, persons change their behavior when they are aware of being observed, which reduces the validity of the observations.
   d. Other factors affecting the validity of observational systems include the difficulty in observing an adequate sample of behavior and the inability to observe internal events.
4. The basic components of observational systems include:
   a. What-defining target behaviors to be observed.
   b. Where-selecting the most appropriate setting in which to observe the behavior
   c. How-determining how the target behaviors will be coded
   d. Who-determining who should observe the target behaviors
5. In defining target behaviors, one must consider the level at which behaviors will be defined and then clearly define the behaviors to be observed.
6. Observations conducted in a child's natural environment have greater ecological validity but allow less control over the observational setting than observations conducted in a laboratory or analog setting.
7. There are three basic ways in which behaviors can be recorded in an observational system:
   a. Event recording-the number of times a behavior occurred is recorded.

   b. Duration recording-the length of time from the initiation to the desistance of a behavior is recorded.
   c. Time sampling-behaviors are recorded as to whether or not they have occurred during preset time intervals.
8. Observations can be conducted by outside observers, people in a child's environment (e.g., parents, teachers), or by the child or adolescent himself or herself.
9. The ASEBA-DOF and ASEBA-TOF are two observational systems that can be used in conjunction with other components of the ASEBA system.
   a. The DOF allows for a direct observation of a child's classroom behavior during three to six 10-min observational periods.
   b. The TOF allows for a direct observation of a child's behavior during individual standardized testing, and it has strong normative data.
   c. Both the DOF and TOF have evidence supporting their reliability and for differentiating referred from nonproblem children.
10. The BASC-2-SOS is an observational system used to assess classroom behavior that can be integrated with other assessment components of the BASC-2 system.
    a. It specifies 65 target behaviors and uses a momentary time-sampling procedure for observations.
    b. There is no normative information nor is there any information on the reliability or validity of this observational system.
11. BATs allow one to observe a child's response to anxiety-provoking stimuli.
12. Observational systems have also been developed to assess peer interactions, parent–child interactions, and behaviors associated with ADHD.

CHAPTER 9

Peer-Referenced Assessment

Chapter Questions

- What contributions can peer-referenced techniques make to clinical assessments of children and adolescents?
- What are some ethical concerns in the use of peer-referenced assessments?
- What are the different types of peer-referenced assessments?
- What do sociometric exercises measure and why might this be an important component of clinical assessments?
- Besides social status, what other areas of a child's behavioral, emotional, and social functioning can be assessed by peer nomination techniques?

Peer-referenced assessment strategies are assessment techniques in which a child or adolescent's social, emotional, or behavioral functioning is assessed by obtaining the *perceptions of the child's peers*. One of the most common types of peer-referenced assessment is the sociometric assessment, in which the child's acceptance in or rejection by his or her peer group is determined. We discuss sociometric techniques in more depth later in this chapter. However, sociometric assessment should not be considered synonymous with peer-referenced assessment. There are many aspects of a child's adjustment, not just peer social status, that can be usefully assessed through the perceptions of a child's peers. A sampling of the most common psychological domains suitable for peer-referenced assessment and the different measurement strategies are the focus of this chapter.

The main reason for using peer-referenced assessment is that it provides important information that cannot be obtained from other sources. The importance of peer perceptions has both an intuitive and empirical basis. A child or adolescent's social milieu is considered a major influence on a child's psychological adjustment in most develop-

P.J. Frick et al., *Clinical Assessment of Child and Adolescent Personality and Behavior*,
DOI 10.1007/978-1-4419-0641-0_9, © Springer Science+Business Media, LLC 2010

mental theories. Therefore, one of the most devastating effects of a child's behavioral disturbance is the effect that it may have on his or her social environment (Mayeux, Bellmore, & Cillessen, 2007). Also, interventions that change many aspects of the child's behavior may not result in changes in the child's peer relationships (Hoza et al., 2005).

For these reasons, understanding how a child is viewed by peers is critical in developing a complete picture of a child's or adolescent's overall psychological adjustment. Peer-referenced assessment, whether it focuses specifically on a child's social relationships or indirectly assess a child's social milieu by determining how peers perceive a child's emotional and behavioral functioning, allows for a better understanding of a child's social network.

The empirical literature supports this theoretical emphasis on peer relationships. Parker and Asher (1987) conducted a meta-analytic review of studies that have tested the utility of peer relationships (primarily acceptance and aggression) in predicting later outcomes (dropping out of school, criminality, and psychopathology). Two of the major findings of this review were that low peer acceptance was consistently related to dropping out of school and that peer-rated aggression was consistently related to delinquency. Similarly, in another study of 445 girls who were first studied at ages 10 to 13, rejected peer status was related to increased risk for criminal offending and alcohol abuse almost 40 years later (Zettergren, Bergman, & Wangby, 2006).

This literature, therefore, clearly supports the importance of peer perceptions in predicting the negative outcomes of a child and, hence, it illustrates the need to assess and to intervene in a child's social milieu. Box 9.1 summarizes several other interesting findings from the Parker and Asher's review that have implications for the use of peer-referenced techniques in clinical assessments.

The assertion that peer perceptions cannot be obtained by other methods comes from the meta-analysis conducted by Achenbach, McConaughy, and Howell (1987). These authors calculated the average correlations across the studies between peer reports of social, emotional, or behavior functioning with the reports of teachers and with the child's self-report. Across 23 studies reviewed, the average correlation across all psychological domains was .44 between peer and teacher ratings, with the correlation being somewhat higher for behavioral (.47) problems than for emotional (.35) problems. Similarly, across 20 studies in which the correlation between peer ratings and the child's self-report of adjustment was determined, the average correlation was .26, again with the correlation for behavioral difficulties (.44) being somewhat higher than for emotional difficulties (.31). These data suggest that there are substantial differences between how peers rate children and how teachers rate children and how children describe themselves. Therefore, to understand a child's peer network that is heavily influenced by peer perceptions, these perceptions must be assessed directly.

Ethics of Peer-Referenced Strategies

Despite research on the unique and important contributions that peer-referenced techniques can make to clinical assessments, these techniques are probably one of the least used assessment techniques of any reviewed in this book. The failure to include peer-referenced techniques in many assessment batteries could be, in part, due to the paucity of standardized, well-normed, and readily available assessment procedures. This exclusion could also be due to the time-consuming nature of many of the peer-referenced techniques used in the research literature. However, as we discuss later in this chapter, there

Box 9.1

Research Note: Meta-Analysis of the Association Between Peer Relationships and Later Psychological Adjustment

Parker and Asher (1987) completed a comprehensive meta-analytic review of the predictive association between poor relationships in early to middle childhood and later (adolescent and adult) psychological adjustment. As mentioned in the text, this review clearly supported the importance of a child's social context in general, and peer perceptions of a child specifically, in terms of predicting later adjustment.

However, in addition to illustrating the overall importance of peer relationships to clinical assessments of children, this review had several other interesting results that can guide the assessment process. For example, in terms of predictive accuracy, a consistent pattern of errors emerged in which peer-referenced procedures tended to make few false-negative errors in predicting which children would have poor outcomes, but there were many false-positive errors. That is, most children who have problems later in life had peer relationship problems. However, a large number of children with relationship problems do not show later difficulties. Knowledge of this type of predictive relationship can be quite helpful in interpreting peer-referenced assessments.

The authors of this review also caution users of the literature to be aware of the fact that, despite knowing that there is a predictive relationship between early peer relations and later adjustment, we do not know *why* this relationship exists. For example, it could be that because these children are excluded from normal patterns of peer interactions, they may also be excluded from normal socialization experiences and deprived of important sources of support. However, it is also possible that early forms of a pathological process that may emerge more fully in adulthood may have a negative influence on early peer relationships. In essence, peer relationships could be an accidental by-product of a pathological process and not really have a causal relationship with later adjustment.

A final relevant point made by the authors of this review is the fact that future research should attempt to obtain a more comprehensive picture of children's social relationships. For example, the authors found very limited data on shyness and social withdrawal in predicting later outcomes, with most studies relying on indices of acceptance and aggression as the primary aspects of social relationship to be studied. Other aspects of peer relationships that could be studied systematically include impulsive/hyperactive behavior, bossy and demanding behaviors, and behaviors that define attributes that approximate how children choose their friends (e.g., Is this child fun to play with?).

Source: Parker, J. G., & Asher, S. R. (1987). Peer relations and later personal adjustment: Are low-accepted children at risk? *Psychological Bulletin*, 102, 357–389.

are several relatively time-efficient peer-referenced procedures that have been used extensively in research which could add to a clinical assessment battery. Therefore, the low frequency of use is probably the result of other considerations.

One such consideration could be the intrusiveness of peer ratings. Peer-referenced assessment typically involves the use of many peer raters, making it more intrusive than many other assessment techniques. For example, asking a teacher to complete a behavior rating scale adds only one person to the assessment process. In contrast, having a child's class participate in a sociometric exercise involves 15–30 additional people in the assessment process.

In addition to the sheer number of people that must be involved, the people involved are typically children who may not appreciate the need for discretion and confidentiality. Therefore, special precautions to limit the intrusiveness of this intervention are essential. There are several necessary precautions for the use of any peer-referenced strategy. First, it is important that both the parent and the child being assessed are clearly informed and give their consent to the peer-referenced assessment (Gresham & Little, 1993). Second, peer-referenced techniques should be designed to ensure that the child's classmates do not know that the assessment is focused on any one individual (see Box 9.2 for an example of instructions provided in a sociometric exercise). Finally, administration of peer-referenced techniques should be carefully monitored to ensure that answers are not shared, and those involved in the assessment should be instructed on the importance of the confidentiality of their responses after the assessment (McConnell & Odom, 1986).

One of the most controversial aspects of peer-referenced strategies is the use of negative ratings from peers (e.g., nominations of children who are not liked or who are aggressive). Teachers and parents are often concerned about the possibility that these negative ratings will lead to social rejection and other negative reactive effects. Fortunately, over 50 years of research using peer-referenced strategies has not found any evidence for these negative effects (McConnell & Odom, 1986). In fact, the potential for negative effects has been specifically tested (Hayvren & Hymel, 1984; Mayeux, Underwood, & Risser, 2007). For example, Mayeux, Underwood, and Risser (2007) completed a sociometric exercise with 91 third graders and then interviewed them and their teachers. Their results indicated that children were not hurt or upset by the procedures nor did the participants feel that their peers treated them differently following the testing.

Despite the lack of evidence for reactive effects of negative ratings, it would be nice to be able to use only positive ratings. Unfortunately, research has clearly shown that negative ratings are not simply the opposite of positive ratings. Negative ratings add crucial additional information to the assessment. For example, rejected children are not simply unaccepted children in terms of peer status, but they are actively disliked by their classmates (Coie, Dodge, & Copotelli, 1982). Therefore, one cannot simply assess peer acceptance and then consider those low on acceptance as being rejected by peers. As we discuss later in this chapter, this rejected status, which requires negative ratings to assess, is one of the most important indices of a child's social status. Therefore, negative ratings appear to be an important part of a peer-referenced assessment strategy. However, clinical assessors should be sensitive to concerns about negative ratings and assure parents and teachers that appropriate safe-guards are being used in the assessment procedures and explain to them the critical need for this information in the evaluation.

Types of Peer-Referenced Techniques

Peer Nominations

Peer nominations are the oldest and most commonly used form of peer-referenced assessment (Asher & Hymel, 1981). The procedure involves asking children in a classroom to select one or more of their peers who display a certain characteristic (e.g., liked, fights, cooperates, shy, leader). Although this procedure is relatively simple and straightforward, there are several variations of peer nomination procedures. For example, there can be a predetermined number of children that can be selected in each category (*fixed-choice format*). Alternatively, the number of peers nominated in each category can

Box 9.2

Instructions for Two Peer-Referenced Techniques

Assessor-Administered Exercise with Unlimited-Choice Format (Carlson, Lahey, & Neeper, 1984)

After discussing the importance of confidentiality, sheets are provided to each child with the class role and each of 30 nomination categories.

Now we're ready to begin. We have written down lots of things kids do, and we would like you to check which kids in your class do these things. Look across the list of names along the top of the page until you find your name. We'll ask you to tell us about what things you do later, but for now put a line through your name and draw a line down the column your name is in so you will remember not to check these things for yourself. Go to the other page and do this every time you see your name.

Now go back to the first page. See the number one? After the number one, it says, "Those who are tall." Now look across the names. Who is tall? Put an "X" under their name. Who isn't tall? Put a "0" under their name. Go through every name one at a time and put an "X" under it if they are tall, and a "0" under it if *they* aren't tall. Be sure to read every name on the top so you don't forget to check anyone. When you finish with number one, you may turn back to the first page and wait for the rest of the group to finish.

Following the completion of item one, all subsequent items were completed in a similar manner, with each item read aloud.

Items

1. Those who are tall
2. Those who say they can beat everybody up
3. Those who complain a lot
4. Those who bother people when they are trying to work
5. Those who stand back and just watch others who are playing
6. Those who get mad when they don't get their way
7. Those who start a fight over nothing
8. Those who act like a baby
9. Those who do not follow the rules when they play games
10. Those who tell other children what to do
11. Those who try to change the game when they join in
12. Those who help others
13. Those who speak softly and are difficult to understand
14. Those who do not pay attention when someone is talking to them
15. Those who daydream a lot
16. Those who keep talking even when someone is talking to them
17. Those who ask a lot of questions when they join a group
18. Those who always talk about themselves when they join the group
19. Those who do not want your help even if you offer it
20. Those who do not know how to join in the group
21. Those who show off in front of the class
22. Those who share their things
23. Those who give in to others too much
24. Those who are afraid to ask for help
25. Those who often change the subject
26. Those who are honest
27. Those who do not try again when they lose
28. Those who can not wait their turn
29. Those who never seem to be happy
30. Those who let others boss them around a lot

Teacher-Administered Exercise with Fixed-Choice Format (Strauss et al., 1988)

A. Pass out paper to all of the children in the class.

(Continues)

Box 9.2 (Continued)

B. Read the following statement to the children: "Class, I want us to do an exercise now that will help me learn more about you as people and about your friendships. It will just take a couple of minutes and should be fun, but if anyone does not want to take part, you may feel free to sit quietly while the rest of us do the exercise. Because the questions that I will ask are about private feelings, I want to ask you not to discuss your answers with each other and not to let your neighbors see your paper."

C. Then ask the children to list the *three* children in the class that you...
   1. Like the most
   2. Like the least
   3. Think fight the most
   4. Think are the meanest
   5. Think are the most shy

D. After the exercise is completed, collect the papers. To protect the feelings of the children, you may wish to briefly look through the collected papers and state, "I haven't had a chance to look carefully at these, but it looks like everybody was named as most liked by at least one person. That's really nice." Reiterate the need for the children not to discuss their responses with each other.

E. Count the total number of children who participated in the exercise, and the number of times the child being evaluated was named in response to each of the five questions. Please write this information on the back of the page and mail it in the self-addressed stamped envelope provided.

F. Thank you again for your assistance. If the parent gives us permission to do so, a copy of the evaluation results will be sent to you. It is important to note that the fact that this child is being evaluated does not necessarily mean that he or she has psychological problems; many of the children that we evaluate turn out to be perfectly normal.

Note: Procedures are provided with permission of the authors.

be left entirely to the child providing the nominations (*unlimited-choice format*). An example of instructions for both a fixed-choice and an unlimited-choice format is provided in Box 9.2. Although some authors prefer the unlimited-choice format to avoid forcing a set number of children into categories, especially negative categories (McConnell & Odom, 1986), there is little empirical evidence for any clear advantage of one format over the other.

A second dimension on which peer nomination procedures can vary is the degree of explicitness that defines the nominating pool. For example, some procedures simply instruct the children to consider any child in their class (Strauss, Lahey, Frick, Frame, & Hynd, 1988). In contrast, other nomination strategies provide children with a roster of names from which to choose (Coie & Kupersmidt, 1983) or may even provide pictures of classmates from which the rater selects nominees for the individual categories (Moore & Updegraff, 1964). The rule of thumb is that the younger the rater, the more explicit the definition of the nominating pool should be. Also, if the pool of potential nominees is not within a well-defined group (e.g., only part of a class is participating in the procedure), then more explicit definitions are required.

Because of the difficulty and level of intrusiveness involved in collecting peer nominations from entire classrooms, Prinstein (2007) compared two alternative methods for obtaining peer perceptions. That is, this author compared nominations obtained from a full sample of 232 adolescents ages 15–17 years old, with those obtained (a) using only a randomly selected subsample of 26 students and (b) using only two students in each class to rate other students. These students were chosen by their teachers as "social experts." The correlations between nominations obtained in the full classroom and those completed by experts were generally quite high (*r*'s ranging from .55 to 93). Similar correlations were found between the full classroom procedure and the nominations completed by a random subsample (*r*'s ranging from .49 to 90). Thus, these results suggest that there may be some less cost intensive alternatives to obtaining peer nominations, at least in classrooms with adolescent students.

The typical level of interpretation of a peer nomination procedure is the number of times a child was nominated in a given category. This number is then compared to a normative base for that particular procedure to see if the child was nominated at a level that is atypical for children his or her age. However, there are some instances where more complex combinations or adjustments of peer nominations are desired. For some purposes it may be useful to compare the number of nominations obtained by a child in one area with the number of nominations that the same child received in another area. For example, in sociometric techniques, one often compares the number of times a child was nominated as Liked Least with the number of times he or she was nominated as Liked Most by classmates. This allows one to determine the relative balance of two nomination categories. However, to make such comparisons, the two scores should first be converted to standard scores (e.g., Z-scores; Coie et al., 1982) to equate for possible differences in the variance of the raw scores.

A second type of conversion is warranted if one wishes to compare nominations of one child with the nominations of another child from another nominating pool (e.g., different class). To make this comparison the number of nominations must be adjusted to equate scores for differing class sizes. For example, 5 nominations of Most Cooperative in a class of 12 should be interpreted differently than 5 nominations in a class of 30. As an example of this conversion, Strauss et al. (1988) divided the number of nominations obtained by a child by the number of children participating in the assessment. The quotient was multiplied by 23, so that the nominations were all expressed in terms of a common class size of 23.

Sociometrics

Sociometric techniques focus on a specific, important aspect of a child's peer relationships: a child's social status. It answers the question of whether or not a child is liked and accepted by his or her peer group. Sociometrics do not assess specific behaviors of the child. It answers the question of whether the child is liked and not what is the child like or why the child is liked (Asher & Hymel, 1981). Sociometric exercises have appeared in the research literature since the 1930s (see Gresham & Little, 1993; Hughes, 1990), and the most commonly used procedure has changed very little over this time. An example of this basic technique from Strauss et al. (1988) is provided in Box 9.2.

Sociometric exercises can take the form of peer ratings, whereby peers rate a child on a Likert scale as to how well liked or disliked he or she is (Hamilton, Fuchs, Fuchs, & Roberts, 2000). However, the more common method of obtaining sociometrics is through peer nominations. In this technique, children can be nominated by peers as a child who is *Liked Most* (sometimes defined as Most like to have as a best friend or Most like to play with) and/or they can be nominated by peers as a child who is *Liked Least* (or alternatively, Least like to have as a friend or Least like to play with). Although there is no definitive normative study that specifies exact cut-offs for when nominations are considered indicative of problems, in a fixed response format allowing three nominations in each category in a class size of approximately 20 students, Liked Most (LM) nominations of less than two and nominations of Liked Least (LL) of greater than four are generally considered indicative of problems in peer relations (Dodge, Coie, & Brakke, 1982; Green, Vosk, Forehand, & Beck, 1981; Strauss et al., 1988).

A common way of interpreting sociometric nominations is by combining the LM and LL nominations into five distinct social status groups (Hughes, 1990). As mentioned previously, when combining LM and LL nominations, the nominations should first be converted to standard scores to equate for potential differences in the variance of the two categories. The five groups are based on two difference scores. The social preference score is the difference between LM and LL scores (LM – LL = Social Preference). High social preference scores indicate substantially more LM nominations than LL nominations. The social impact score is the sum of the LM and LL scores (LM + LL = Social Impact). High social impact scores simply determine the number of nominations a child receives, regardless of whether they are negative or positive. A combination of these scores leads to a child being considered in one of several social status groups: Popular, Rejected, Neglected, Controversial, and Average. The method of combining these scores to determine a child's social status and two computational formulas that have been used in research are provided in Box 9.3.

Although there have been several variations in the formulas for determining a

Box 9.3

Determining Social Status from Sociometric Nominations

Category	Description	Computational Formula Using Standard Scores (Coie, Dodge, & Coppotelli, 1982)	Computational Formula Using Raw Scores (Strauss et al., 1988)
Popular	High social preference scores (LM – LL) but few LL nominations	(1) ZLM – ZLL > 1 (2) ZLM > 0 (3) ZLL < 0	(1). LM > 4.5 (2) LL < 1.5
Rejected	Low social preference scores with few LM nominations	(1) ZLM – ZLL < –1 (2) ZLM < 0 (3) ZLL > 0	(1) LM < 1 (2) LL > 4.5
Neglected	Low social impact scores (LM + LL) and few nominations in LM category	(1) ZLM + ZLL < –1 (2) LM = 0	(1) LM < 1.5 (2) LL < 1.5
Controversial	High social impact scores and above-average LM and LL scores	(1) ZLM + ZLL > 1 (2) ZLM > 0 (3) ZLL > 0	
Average	Average social preference scores	(1) ZLM – ZLL > –.5 (2) ZLM – ZLL < .5	

NOTE: .Both computational formulas are based on a fixed-choice format allowing for three nominations in both the Like Most (LM) and Like Least (LL) categories. ZLM refers to LM nominations converted to standard Z-scores and ZLL refers to LL nominations converted to standard Z-scores. The unstandardized formulas are based on scores adjusted to a class size of 23.

child's social status, the validity of these groupings has been consistently shown in research (see Gresham & Little, 1993), including showing good convergence with statistical methods for clustering children based on peer nominations (Zettergren, 2007). Further research has suggested that these nominations are quite stable over time. Jiang and Cillessen (2005) conducted a meta-analysis of 77 studies of over 18,339 participants and reported that the average level of stability for social status over periods of less than 3 months ranged from r = .70 to r = .80. For periods of over 3 months, the average ratings ranged from .52 to .58.

Importantly, research has suggested that sociometric nominations can be influenced by the racial composition of a classroom with social preference scores being higher when nominations are obtained from same-race peers (Singleton & Asher, 1979). Jackson, Barth, Powell, and Lochman (2006) reported on 1,268 sociometric nominations from children ages 9 to 11 years old across 57 classrooms that ranged from 3 to 95% African-American. The results indicated that African-American students nominations were more sensitive to the racial composition of the classroom than for Caucasian students. Specifically, African-American students' social preference scores and nominations for fighting and being a leader improved as the percentage of African-American students in the classroom increased. The effects for Caucasian students was less clear, although there was a small effect of Caucasian students having lower preference scores if the classroom was less than 33% Caucasian.

Social status has also been associated with emotional and behavioral characteristics of the child. One of the most consistent findings is that rejected children show higher levels of aggressive and acting-out behavior than nonrejected classmates (e.g., Dodge, 1983). However, neglected status is also associated with problems in adjustment, most notably with anxiety (Strauss et al., 1988). Several behavioral characteristics are associated with popular children, including being more likely to contribute to conversations during play, being more likely to engage in parallel play, receiving and initiating more positive social behavior, and using effective peer-entry strategies (Gresham & Little, 1993). Children in the controversial status group have been less well studied. However, one study suggests that children in this social status group tend to exhibit aggressive and disruptive behaviors, like the rejected children, but also tend to be viewed as socially skilled and as leaders, like the popular children (Coie et al., 1982).

A distinction that research has increasingly shown to be important is between whether a child is well liked by their peers (i.e., accepted) and whether the child is viewed as "popular" (Prinstein, 2007). First, these ratings have only been modestly correlated with each other (Prinstein, 2007; Vaillancourt & Hymal, 2006). Second, ratings of greater peer acceptance have consistently been related to more positive behavioral (e.g., less aggression; more prosocial behavior) and emotional (e.g., higher self-esteem) functioning (Gresham & Little, 1993; Sandstrom & Cillessen, 2006). However, children perceived by their peers as popular often show more physical and relational forms of aggression (McDonald, Putallaz, Grimes, Kupersmidt, & Coie, 2007; Vaillancourt & Hymel, 2006). Third, peer popularity seems to be more strongly related to peer-valued characteristics such as power, physical attractiveness, athleticism, and dress than peer acceptance (Prinstein & Cillessen, 2003; Vaillancourt & Hymel, 2006).

From this research, it is clear that a child's social status is intertwined with his or her behavioral and emotional functioning, both in terms of current and future functioning. Therefore, sociometrics can contribute important information to many clinical assessments by providing a reliable method of assessing a crucial aspect of a child's social functioning.

Most sociometric exercises are conducted in school classrooms because they provide a very clear and well-defined reference group of peers from which to judge a child's social acceptance or rejection. However, an important consideration in the usefulness of data obtained from sociometric exercises conducted in classrooms is the level of student participation in the exercise. That is, there is evidence that even moderate declines in full classroom participation in the sociometric exercise can have a major influence on the results. For example, Hamilton et al. (2000) compared sociometric results using a peer-rating procedure across varying levels of classroom participation. These authors reported that, even with a 75% rate of classroom participation, there were substantial differences in the results compared to those obtained from the full classroom. The results for 25 and 50% participation rates were even more divergent from those obtained with full participation. Importantly, the instability in the results across the varying levels of participation was greatest for children with adjustment problems compared to well-adjusted children. Therefore, for children with problems, who are often of most interest in sociometric exercises, participation rates seem to be especially important for interpreting the results. These findings highlight the need to interpret information from sociometric techniques in the context of the level of classroom participation in the exercise. In Box 9.4 additional findings from the Hamilton et al. (2000) study that have potentially important implications for interpreting information from sociometric exercises are summarized.

Box 9.4

Research Note: A Comparison of Sociometric Results Across Varying Levels of Classroom Participation

Hamilton et al. (2000) investigated the effects of different rates of classroom participation on peer ratings of social acceptance. These authors reviewed 26 studies using sociometric ratings to assess the social acceptance of children with learning or behavioral disorders and found that the vast majority of studies did not report the rate of participation in the sociometric exercise and, for those studies that did, the rates varied from 67 to 100%. The potential effects of these varying rates was investigated in 14 classrooms (grades 3 through 6) with full, or nearly full, rates of participation (i.e., 92 to 100%). The authors used a group sociometric procedure in which each student was provided with a class roster. Each student's name was accompanied by four circles closing (1) a smiling face to indicate that the student is liked, (2) a straight-mouthed face to designate that the rater is indifferent to the student, (3) a frowning face to indicate that the student is disliked, and (4) a question mark to indicate that the rater is unsure of the student's likability. Each student received a percentage score for each of the four categories by dividing the number of responses (e.g., smiles) by the number of student raters minus one, thereby creating percentage scores for each type of acceptance rating.

To assess the effects of classroom participation rates, the classrooms were then sampled randomly and repeatedly three times for each level) so that 25, 50, and 75% of students were involved in the exercise. At each participation level, peer ratings were compared against those obtained at the full level of participation. The results were quite consistent indicating that, as the rate of classroom participation decreased, ratings tended to be increasingly divergent from those obtained at full participation. Even the ratings at the 75% level were significantly different from the ratings obtained at full participation (ranging from 3 to 18%). Importantly, the authors compared the ratings of students with learning

(Continues)

Box 9.4 (Continued)

disabilities and nondisabled students that were underachieving to average and high-achieving students. The decline in participation rates was especially problematic for the ratings of the two groups with learning problems.

The authors noted that the effects of classroom participation on this peer-rating procedure may not generalize to the more common peer nomination procedure, although they make the important point that participation effects on nomination procedures need to be tested in light of their results. They also offer an interesting explanation for why participation rates may affect the ratings of less well-adjusted children to a greater degree. The authors suggest that the better-adjusted children may be viewed more similarly across classmates, with a general consensus across students on their likeability. In contrast, students may have more "polarized" views of children with problems in adjustment, with some classmates liking them, others disliking them, and still others having a neutral view. As a result of this polarization, the ratings of these children may be more dependent on which children are participating in the sociometric exercise. In actual practice, the problems in the accuracy in the peer ratings of disturbed children at lower levels of participation may be exacerbated if these children tend to have disturbed friends who may be less likely to volunteer to participate in the exercise. The authors conclude by noting that it is impossible to identify a specific "minimum rate" of participation that should be obtained before the results of a peer-rating sociometric exercise are uninterpretable. However, they suggest that these data clearly indicate that assessors using sociometric ratings need to recognize the potential effect of participation rates on the results of these exercises, especially when assessing children with adjustment problems.

Aggression

Another common aspect of a child's functioning that is assessed by peer nominations is aggression. The typical format is to have a class nominate the children in the class who "Fights most." As with other nomination techniques, the format can either be in a fixed-choice or unlimited-choice format. Peer nominations of aggression have been shown to be correlated with a psychiatric diagnosis of conduct disorder and therefore can be considered an important indicator of the impairment associated with this syndrome (Walker et al., 1991). However, one of the most interesting and troubling characteristics of peer-nominated aggression is its stability. In their 5-year study, Coie et al., and Dodge (1983) found that peer nominations of "Starts Fights" showed the most stability across the5 years of any of the peer-nomination categories that were obtained, exhibiting correlations of .83 between third and fourth grades and .84 across fifth and sixth grades. Huesmann, Eron, Lefkowitz, & Walder (1984) provide even more dramatic evidence for the stability of peer nominations of aggression. These authors found that peer nominations of aggression at age 8 significantly predicted aggression *30 years later.* Therefore, peer nominations of aggression assess an aspect of problematic interpersonal functioning that can be highly stable for a child and is thus an important target for intervention.

Hyperactivity

Assessment of inattention and motor hyperactivity, behaviors typically associated with ADHD, has relied primarily on information obtained from parents and teachers (Loeber, Green, Lahey, & Stouthamer-Loeber, 1991). However, Schaughency and Rothlind (1991) provide some interesting data to suggest that peer nominations of inattentive and hyperactive behavior could aid in the assessment of ADHD. Specifically, these authors reported that peer nominations of "Can't pay attention," "Can't wait turn," and "Can't sit still" correlated with teacher and observer measures of inattention and hyperactivity. In a second study, these authors reported that peer nominations of "Doesn't pay attention" and "Can't sit still" significantly discriminated between youngsters diagnosed with ADHD from other clinic-referred children.

Although these results are promising and suggest that peer nominations can aid in the assessment of ADHD behaviors, there is no evidence that these peer nominations should take the place of parent and teacher ratings as a primary information source for these behavioral domains. Also, it is unclear whether or not peer nominations add anything to the assessment of ADHD behaviors over the information provided by other assessment techniques.

Depression

Lefkowitz and Tesiny (1980) developed the Peer Nomination Inventory of Depression (PNID) to aid in the assessment of childhood depression. A list of 13 depression-related categories was developed by nine expert judges. These nomination categories are provided in Box 9.5. Lefkowitz and Tesiny found that the 2-month test-retest reliability of the individual depression items (mean r = .66) and the depression composite for all 13 items (r = .79) were acceptable. More importantly, the PNID Depression composite was significantly associated with teacher (r = .41) and child (r = .23) ratings of depression. As was the case with peer nominations of inattention

Box 9.5

Depression Items on the Peer Nomination Inventory of Depression

Procedures

Children were provided a class roster. Each item was read aloud twice, and children were instructed to draw a line through all the names on their class roster "which best fit the question" (Lefkowitz & Tesiny, 1980, p. 45). Self-nominations were not permitted, but children could choose not to nominate anyone in a category.

Depression Items

Who often plays alone?
Who thinks they are bad?
Who doesn't try again when they lose?
Who often sleeps in class?
Who often looks lonely?
Who often says they don't feel well?
Who says they can't do things?
Who often cries?
Who does not play?
Who does not take part in things?
Who does not have much fun?
Who thinks others do not like them?
Who often looks sad?

The 13 items are only the depression items on the PNID. The PNID includes 20 items, with additional items measuring happiness and popularity.

SOURCE: Lefsowitz, M. M., & Testiny, E. P. (1980). Assessment of childhood depression. *Journal of Consulting and Clinical Psychology*, *48*, 43–50.

and hyperactivity, peer assessment of depression is promising as a component to a comprehensive evaluation but has not been sufficiently tested to determine its contribution relative to more traditional measures of depression.

Other Peer-Referenced Techniques

Although we have focused most of our discussion on peer nomination techniques, there are other peer-referenced assessment strategies that have been used in research that may be applicable to some clinical settings. *Peer ratings* require children to rate on a Likert-type scale each member of their class or peer group (Gresham & Little, 1993; McConnell & Odom, 1986). Like any rating scale, peer scales vary on the behavioral dimensions included on the scale, the number of points on the scale, and the behavioral descriptions used as anchors on the scale. For example, a rating scale for young children used a happy face to anchor the positive end of the continuum, a neutral face to anchor the middle, and a sad face to anchor the negative end of the continuum (Asher, Singleton, Tinsley, & Hymel, 1979).

One of the most reliable forms of peer assessment, especially for very young children McConnell & Odom, 1986), is the *paired comparison technique*. In this procedure, photographs are taken of all the children in the class and photographs of each possible classmate dyad are paired. The rater is then asked to choose between the two children in each dyad in reference to some criterion (e.g., Fights, Liked, Shy, Cooperative, etc.). The salient cues used in making the choices between peers make this procedure much more reliable for young children, especially of preschool age. However, it is so labor-intensive that it is not feasible for use in most clinical assessments. As McConnell and Odom (1986) point out, for a class of 20 children, each child will have to make 171 selections for each criterion.

Conclusions

Peer-referenced assessment strategies share the common characteristic of having a child or adolescent evaluated on important psychological dimensions by his or her peers. Due to several practical and ethical considerations, peer-referenced strategies are not commonplace in many clinical assessments. This is unfortunate because, if designed appropriately and with precautions taken to ensure safe administration, peer-referenced assessment can provide an invaluable picture of child's social context. This picture of a child's social relationships is essential for treatment planning given the importance of social relationships for a child's current and future psychological adjustment.

One of the most commonly used peer-referenced techniques is the sociometric exercise. This peer nomination technique allows one to determine whether or not a child is accepted, rejected, or ignored (neglected) by his or her peer group. These dimensions of social status cannot be adequately assessed by other methods of assessment, such as teacher ratings or a child's self-report. In addition, this crucial aspect of a child's social context has been highly related to emotional and behavioral disturbances. Therefore, sociometric assessment is a type of peer-referenced assessment that could be an especially important component of many clinical evaluations.

Chapter Summary

1. Peer-referenced assessments provide information on how a child or adolescent is viewed by his or her peers and, thereby, provide important insights into a child's social milieu.

2. Peer-referenced assessments must be conducted in light of two important ethical issues: the importance of minimizing the intrusiveness of the assessment and the need to minimize potential reactive effects of negative ratings by peers.
3. Peer nominations are the most commonly used forms of peer-referenced assessments. They involve having a child's or adolescent's peers select one or more children who display certain characteristics.
4. Sociometric exercises are a type of peer nomination that determines whether a child is accepted, rejected, or neglected by his or her peers.
5. Aggression, hyperactivity, and depression have also been assessed through peer nomination procedures. Unfortunately, the relative utility of peer-referenced assessments of these psychological dimensions, in comparison to other assessment modalities, has not been tested.
6. In addition to peer nominations, perceptions of a child's peers can be obtained by having children rate each other along certain dimensions on a Likert-type scale.

CHAPTER 10

Projective Techniques

Chapter Questions

- What are some of the key issues in the debate over whether and how projectives should be used in clinical assessments?
- What are some of the strengths and limitations of the clinical and psychometric approaches to interpretation of projectives?
- How would viewing projective techniques from either a traditional projection approach or as a behavioral sample influence the type of technique that would be used and the interpretations that would be made?
- What are the basic interpretive strategies for inkblot techniques, thematic techniques, sentence-completion techniques, and projective drawing techniques?
- What are some specific examples of administration, scoring, and interpretive systems for each type of projective technique?

The Controversy Surrounding Projective Techniques

No type of assessment has engendered as much controversy as projective techniques. For some, projectives are synonymous with personality testing and provide some of the richest sources of clinical information on children and adolescents (Hughes, Gacono, & Owen, 2007; Rabin, 1986; Weiner, 1986). For others, projective techniques typically

P.J. Frick et al., *Clinical Assessment of Child and Adolescent Personality and Behavior*,
DOI 10.1007/978-1-4419-0641-0_10,

do not meet even the minimum of basic psychometric standards, and their use, therefore, detracts from the assessment process and tarnishes the image that psychological testing has with other professionals and with the general public (Anastasi, 1988; Gittelman-Klein, 1986; Hunsley & Bailey, 2001). In Box 10.1, we have attempted to summarize some of the major arguments made on either side of this debate.

Our philosophy in writing this chapter was not to espouse either of the strong views on projective testing. Instead, our goal was to provide the reader with an overview of this method of assessment that would allow for an informed view of the appropriate role of projective techniques in clinical assessments. Too often in the past the debate over projectives has focused on ideological arguments, or even on personal beliefs, without a critical and scholarly examination of the actual issues involved. Therefore, the first part of this chapter focuses on what we feel are the major issues in the use of projectives that determine *whether* they should be used and *how* they should be used in clinical assessments.

Irrespective of one's eventual stand on the projective controversy, projective techniques remain one of the most commonly used methods of clinical assessment by psychologists in general (Watkins, Campbell, Neiberding, & Hallmark, 1995) and by child psychologists specifically (Hojnoski, Morrison, Brown, & Matthews, 2006). This fact is

Box 10.1

The Projective Debate

Pro	Con
Less structured format allows clinician greater flexibility in administration and interpretation and places fewer demand characteristics that would prompt socially desirable responses from an informant.	The reliability of many techniques is questionable. As a result, the interpretations are more related to characteristics of the clinician than to characteristics of the person being tested.
Allows for the assessment of drives, motivations, desires, and conflicts that can affect a person's perceptual experiences but are often unconscious.	Even some techniques that have good reliability have questionable validity, especially in making diagnoses and predicting overt behavior.
Provides a deeper understanding of a person than would be obtained by simply describing behavioral patterns.	Although we can at times predict things we cannot understand, it is rarely the case that understanding does not enhance prediction (Gittelman-Klein, 1986).
Adds to an overall assessment picture.	Adding an unreliable piece of information to an assessment battery simply decreases the overall reliability of the battery.
Helps to generate hypotheses regarding a person's functioning.	Leads one to pursue erroneous avenues in testing or to place undue confidence in a finding.
Non-threatening and good for rapport building.	Detracts from the time an assessor could better spend collecting more detailed, objective information.
Many techniques have a long and rich clinical tradition.	Assessment techniques are based on an evolving knowledge base and must continually evolve to reflect this knowledge.

not cited to defend their use. It is cited simply to indicate that projective techniques are a firmly entrenched part of the clinical assessment process that shows no signs of changing in the near future.

Clinical Technique or Psychometric Test?

Much of the debate over the use of projective techniques comes from a confusion as to the most appropriate criteria with which to judge the usefulness of projectives. Traditional methods of evaluating psychological tests are grounded in measurement theory, which, as was discussed in Chap. 2, relies primarily on indexes of the reliability and validity of the scores that result from the test (Anastasi, 1988). When evaluated on these terms, most projective techniques have not fared well (Hunsley & Bailey, 2001). As Rabin (1986) states:

> "An aspect of projective tests that is not to be overlooked is the frequent disappointment and disaffection with the adequacy, reliability, and validity of several projective methods. The psychologist, reared in the atmosphere of respect for science and for the psychometric purity of his instruments, often finds them wanting" (p. 8).

One way in which these criticisms have been addressed has been through the development of standardized administration, scoring, and interpretive procedures for certain projective techniques which are designed to provide scores that meet traditional psychometric standards (Weiner, 2001). Two examples of such approaches that are frequently used for testing children and adolescents are the Rorschach Comprehensive System (Exner, 1974) and the Roberts Apperception Test for Children (McArthur & Roberts, 1982). Both of these approaches to projective testing are discussed in more detail later in this chapter. However, it is important to note that both systems share the goal of providing very clear and explicit guidelines on how the tests are to be given, scored, and interpreted. Such standardization is a prerequisite to further psychometric evaluation.

This method of addressing the criticisms of projective tests has not met with unanimous approval. Instead, it has been argued that projective tests should not be evaluated by traditional measurement theory and that any attempt at standardization will limit the clinical utility of the technique. For example, Haak (1990) has argued that:

> "The problem with all of these standardization efforts is the amount of destruction they wreak on the essential nature of projectives. All such approaches result in a huge loss of the rich and complex information that is obtained by using the technique in the first place" (p. 149).

This argument is based on the contention that projectives are part of the older clinical tradition that seeks to describe the individual person in depth, capturing all of his or her unique dispositions, motivations, conflicts, and desires. This is an idiographic approach that is not concerned with how the individual differs from the norm or how his or her scores compare to those of some other reference group (e.g., those with diagnoses of depression). Instead, the goal is simply to understand the person's unique qualities. In this conceptualization, "validity" takes on a very different meaning than the one that is typically used in measurement theory. One is not concerned with how a score compares to some objective criterion outside the person being tested.

For some psychologists this clinical approach might seem unscientific. However, all clinicians rely on intuition at some point in an evaluation to understand the nuances of an individual case. Our science of human behavior is not at a point where every clinical decision can be guided by well-established principles, and, given the complexity of psychological functioning, such pure empiricism may never be possible. Therefore, the clinical view of projectives considers these techniques as a structured way of obtaining these intuitions. By using this structure, one can use the judgments of other experienced clinicians as a guide to making interpretations.

The importance of understanding this debate is not to decide which view is right. What is more crucial is for one to recognize the two disparate ways of using projective techniques and the unique strengths and weaknesses of both. For example, using projectives as a psychometric technique allows one to compare a person's score with those from a normative group, or with those from some relevant clinic group, or with some other clinically important criterion (e.g., response to treatment). However, to use the scores in this way, one must maintain rigorous standardization in procedures and be willing to live within the confines of the data that are available. A frustrating aspect of clinical assessments is realizing the limitations of what our assessments can provide.

On the other hand, using projectives as a clinical tool allows one greater flexibility in administration and interpretation. However, with this flexibility, the interpretations that result from the assessment are much more susceptible to influences that are indiosyncratic to the assessor. Interpretations of the same case material may vary widely across clinicians. As such, interpretations should be clearly viewed as *clinical impressions* and not be evaluated in the same way as empirically derived interpretations. In Box 10.2 we have provided a more detailed discussion of the importance of clearly defining one's approach to projective assessment and then recognizing the limitations inherent in either method.

Projection or Behavioral Sample?

Even more basic than the debate over the method of interpretation is confusion over what psychological processes projective techniques are supposed to measure. The critical nature of this question is obvious from a psychometric viewpoint. Validity is the critical property of a test and it is often defined as evidence that the test is measuring what it is supposed to measure (Anastasi, 1988). Therefore, if it is unclear what a test is supposed to measure then it will be unclear as to what are the most appropriate methods of determining its validity.

One dominant view of projective tests, which is the view that led to the name *projective*, is best described by Murray (1943): "There is the tendency for people to interpret an ambiguous human situation in conformity with their past experiences and present wants" (p. 1). This forms the basis of the *projective hypothesis*. The projective hypothesis rests on the assumption that people, in the absence of clear environmental demands, will project basic aspects of themselves in their interpretations of environmental stimuli. Freudian theory, which dominated clinical psychology for decades, heavily emphasized unconscious conflict as the basic element of human personality. Projection is seen by many as being a window to these unconscious dynamics (Rabin, 1986).

However, there is a second view of projectives. Rather than seeing them as windows to hidden or unconscious motives and drives, many assessors view projectives as *a behavioral sample*. For example, Knoff (1983) writes:

> "A student completes an incomplete sentence blank with '*I* hate myself' or '*My* father beats me up all the time,' and these hypotheses are confirmed through self-injurious behavior or a physically abusive father, is this a hidden aspect of personality? Or how is a student's

Box 10.2

Two Approaches to Projective Testing: You Cannot Have It Both Ways

The divergent approaches to the interpretation of projectives can be descriptively labeled as the psychometric approach and the clinical approach. The problem that arises in the use of projectives is that many clinical assessors aren't aware of the approach that they are using and therefore, do not recognize the limitations of their approach. To put it bluntly, many assessors want the best of both worlds. They want the flexibility and the rich clinical information afforded by the clinical approach, but they do not want to recognize the potential biases in interpretation that are inherent in such usage. In contrast, many psychologists have found new promise in projective assessments with the advent of standardized administration and scoring procedures for some techniques. However, users of these systems are frustrated by the limited and often confusing data-bases on which to base interpretations and often slip back into making interpretations that are better considered clinical intuitions. In this box we provide two examples of the confusion resulting from these differing approaches to interpretation.

In the clinical tradition, interpretations are based on clinical judgment and experience. This is often considered bad practice, but we feel that such clinical intuition is unavoidable and even desirable in any assessment enterprise. The problem arises when users fail to recognize the potential unreliability of their clinical judgments. In fact, justification for their interpretation is often based on research on the Exner Comprehensive System for Rorschach interpretation, which has demonstrated acceptable levels of reliability for many scores (Hiller et al., 1999). Unfortunately, they use this argument to justify the reliability of *any* interpretation they make from the Exner system or to justify the reliability of their interpretations from *any* projective technique. This latter practice would be analogous to assuming that all self-report measures of anxiety have the same psychometric properties and therefore can be interpreted in the same way.

A second example comes from a common practice in using one of the newer standardized systems, like the Exner system for Rorschach interpretation. Psychologists have enjoyed the increase in reliability that such systems provide and which sets the stage for more empirically based interpretations. However, studies have not always been able to show empirical support for some of the interpretations that have been well established in the clinical tradition (Carter & Daccy, 1996; Finch & Belter, 1993; Stredney & Ball, 2005). This has led some to the conclusion that the richness of the Rorschach record is simply too complex for current methodology (Finch & Belter, 1993). This implies that the scores cannot be tested adequately with current research methodology. Because of this fact, these authors and others have recommended that one should use both the psychometric *and* clinical method of interpretation of Rorschach when using the Exner system.

The problem arises when assessors make a clinical interpretation that does not have empirical support but place undue confidence in this interpretation because they are using a "reliable and valid system." This goes back to a basic psychometric principle. Tests or interpretive systems are not themselves reliable and/or valid. The individual interpretations that one makes from them can be reliable and/or valid. Unfortunately, the Exner system, like most of the interpretive systems for the projective techniques, encourages interpretations based on the clinical tradition, some of which have been supported in research and others of which have not garnered much research support. Users then are often unaware of the basis of their interpretations.

---

response to a thematic approach which uses real photographs depicting significant interpersonal situations (i.e., peer group acceptance, attitudes toward school-work, reactions to new sibling) different from an interview question asking how she/he is getting along with peers on the playground?" (p. 448).

It is evident from this quotation that one can view responses to projective tests as samples of behaviors from which one would like to generalize to behaviors in other situations, outside of the testing environment. In fact, this type of interpretation underlies Rorschach's original development of the inkblot test and has been the guiding principle for Exner's more recent system of interpretation. Rorschach, and later Exner (see Exner & Martin, 1983; Exner & Weiner, 1994), describe the inkblot tests as a "perceptual test," meaning that a person's perception of the inkblot is used as a sample of behavior with which to generalize to the person's perception of other, more clinically relevant, stimuli.

These two competing views of what is measured by projectives have several important implications for the assessment process. As already mentioned, how one views the process will determine what evidence is used to establish the test's validity. For example, if one views the test as a behavioral sample, then one would want evidence that the behaviors obtained from the test are associated with behaviors outside the testing situation. Alternatively, if one views projectives as tapping unconscious conflicts, then the relationship to overt behavior is not expected to be one-to-one, because the same conflicts can be manifested in different behaviors (Koppitz, 1983). In this case, validity would be best established by showing that responses on a projective technique are associated with other indicators of unconscious conflicts.

Implicit in this discussion is the important point that the way one views the psychological process that is being measured by projective tests will determine the types of interpretations that will be made from a child's or adolescent's responses. A person viewing the results in terms of projection will make interpretations about drives and motivations. It is these types of predictions that one wishes to make. In contrast, a person viewing the results in terms of a sample of behavior will make interpretations about behavioral tendencies that are likely to be manifested in situations outside of the testing situation. For example, if the Rorschach is used as a sample of perceptions, one would wish to make predictions about how these perceptual tendencies will be manifested in other situations.

The final impact of viewing projective techniques as either projection or a behavioral sample is its influence on the selection of the type of stimulus used. Specifically, if one is operating from the projective hypothesis, one would want as ambiguous a situation as possible. For example, the Thematic Apperception Test (Murray, 1943) contains a blank card that has no picture on it and the person is required to make up a story about this card. This is an example of a very ambiguous situation with few demand characteristics, or very little stimulus pull, that would guide a person's response. This stimulus allows for the purest form of projection.

In contrast, if one wishes to obtain a behavioral sample from the projective technique, high levels of stimulus pull may actually be beneficial. If one knows the demand characteristics that promoted the response, then one would have some clue as to what situations one might generalize (i.e., ones with similar demand characteristics). For example, cards from the Roberts Apperception Test for Children (McArthur & Roberts, 1982) were designed to pull for specific themes (e.g., peer conflict, school problems, marital discord in parents). This is not a desirable property from the pure projection viewpoint because it increases the demand characteristics of the stimulus and thereby limits the degree of projection required.

Summary

Our approach to the debate over the use of projective techniques is that assessors should use or not use projective testing based on a careful consideration of critical assessment issues. Assessors are often unclear about what approach to measurement they are using (i.e., clinical or psychometric), and often make inappropriate interpretations based on this confusion. Further, assessors are often unclear about what they are trying to measure with projectives, and again, this leads to confusion in interpretations or to the selection of a technique that is not well-suited for their purpose. The rest of this chapter will highlight characteristics of specific projective techniques. However, these general issues are paramount in understanding and using these techniques; therefore, these issues are revisited throughout this chapter with reference to specific techniques.

Inkblot Techniques

One of the most commonly used projective techniques is the ink-blot technique. The stimulus is simply an inkblot, and the child is asked to interpret this ambiguous stimulus in some way. The best known of the inkblot techniques, the Rorschach, consists of ten cards with standardized inkblots. Although the Rorschach is often considered synonymous with inkblot techniques, a notable alternative is the Holtzman Inkblot Technique (HIT). This technique was developed to overcome psychometric limitations in the Rorschach by constructing a completely new set of inkblots (Holtzman & Swartz, 2003). The HIT consists of two parallel forms, each of which contains 45 inkblots.

Volumes have been written on the different interpretive systems for inkblot techniques for children (e.g., Ames et al., 1974; Exner & Weiner, 1994; Holtzman & Swartz, 2003). The primary variations among these systems are along the dimensions discussed in the introduction to this chapter: whether the inkblot test is viewed as a projective approach or as a behavioral sample, and whether a clinical or psychometric approach to interpretation is taken. Rather than giving a superficial overview of the different approaches to interpretation, we will focus on one of the most commonly used methods of interpretation for children: Exner's Comprehensive System (ECS) for Rorschach interpretation. This system attempts to integrate five major approaches to Rorschach interpretation into a single Rorschach approach (Exner & Martin, 1983). Even limiting our focus to one system of interpretation does not allow us to do justice to the intricacies of Rorschach interpretation using the ECS; accordingly, the reader is referred to Exner and Weiner (1994) for a more in-depth discussion of this system of interpretation for assessing children and adolescents.

The Exner Comprehensive System for Rorschach Interpretation

Process Measured

The ECS treats the Rorschach as *a perceptual-cognitive task*. When viewed in this way:

> "The Rorschach becomes a task to which people respond by exercising their perceptual-cognitive abilities and preferences. To articulate their answers, they must select parts of these variegated stimulus fields to which they wish to attend, use some mixture of the features of the stimulus and their own needs to guide formulations, and identify objects that will give substance to their impressions. In short, they decide how to scan the stimulus, how to translate the stimulus input, and what to report" (Exner & Weiner, 1982, p. 3).

Weiner (1986) outlines four basic factors that influence a child's response to the inkblot. First, the nature of the stimulus itself may lead the child to classify a blot in a certain way. Although the inkblots were designed to minimize stimulus pull, there are clearly some common or typical answers that are based on the specific features of the blots. Second, responses may be influenced by concerns about making a particular impression which could lead to some censoring of responses in a socially desirable manner. Third, responses are influenced by personality traits that predispose a person to perceive the blots in idiosyncratic ways. Fourth, responses are partly a function of situational psychological states that affect a person's perceptual experience. Each of these factors provides an important context for interpreting a child's response to the Rorschach inkblots.

Administration and Scoring

In contrast to the complexity of Rorschach interpretation, administration of the task is relatively simple. The subject is handed the individual cards with the inkblot stimuli and merely asked, "What might this be?" The only unacceptable response is, "It's an inkblot." If the child provides this answer, then he or she is encouraged to see it as something it's not. All ten cards are administered in this way, and the subject's responses during this *free association phase* are recorded verbatim for later scoring. After the child responds to all ten cards, the examiner enters the *inquiry phase*. The assessor readministers each card and reads to the child his or her initial responses. The child is instructed to show the examiner which part of the blot led to the response and what made him or her think it looked that way. The child is informed that the assessor would like to see it "just the way you did" and several standardized prompts are provided (e.g., "What in the blot makes it look like that to you?" Exner & Wiener, 1994). The child's responses during this inquiry phase are also coded verbatim to use in later scoring.

The heart of the ECS is the extensive and detailed scoring procedure of a child's test protocol (i.e., verbatim responses to Rorschach cards). This system includes approximately 90 possible scores. There are seven major categories of codes, which are described in Table 10.1: Location, Determinants, Form Quality, Organizational Activity, Popularity, Content, and Special Scores. The ECS utilizes a Structural Summary, which shows all of the possible scores, plus various summary scores that are ratios, percentages, and other derivations of the individual scores that provide important information for interpretation.

Norming

The best normative data on the Exner system come from a large (n = 1,870) nationwide sample of children between the ages of 5 and 16 (Exner & Weiner, 1994). At each age in this 12-year age range, there were at least 105 children. There was also fairly equal gender representation at each age, and the inclusion of minority children was at a proportion that approximated national census data. The only weakness evident in this normative data base was the overrepresentation of children from higher socio-economic strata (Exner & Weiner, 1994). From this normative sample, Exner and Weiner (1994) documented several age-related trends in scores. These trends are summarized in Table 10.2. Users of the ECS with children should be aware of these developmental changes in the Rorschach responses and interpret scores within a normative perspective.

The extensive normative database for children available with the ECS aids in such interpretations. This normative base is one of the major reasons for the popularity of the ECS for use with children. However, it is important to note that the adequacy and consistency of the normative scores across different samples of children and adolescents has been questioned (Hunsley & DiGiulio, 2001; Meyer, Erdberg, & Shaffer, 2007).

TABLE 10.1 Summary of Scores Used in Exner's Comprehensive System to Rorschach Interpretation

Categories	Description	Examples of Scores
Location	Part of the blot used by respondent	W = Whole blot D = Common area Dd = Uncommon Area S = White space
Determinant	Features of the blot that contributed to the formation of the response	F = Form C = Color T = Texture/Shading M = Human Movement
Form Quality	Measures the perceptual accuracy of the response (i.e., does the area of the blot really conform to the child's perception)	+ = Superior–overelaborated 0 = Ordinary–common U = Unusual–rare but easy to see - = Minus-distorted, arbitrary, and unrealistic
Content	Places into categories the various persons, places, and things that form the child's response	H = Whole Human An = Anatomy Bl = Blood Fi = Fire Fd = Food Hh = Household items
Popular	Codes the number of times the child gave a high-frequency (very common) response to a blot	P = Number of popular responses given in the entire protocol
Organizational Activity	Provides an estimate of the efficiency of a child's organization of the stimulus field	Z score = Higher scores indicate greater organizational effort
Special Scores	Denotes unusual verbal material in a child's response	INCOM = Incongruous Combination-merges details or images in unrealistically way MOR = Morbid-response includes references to death or clear dysphoric feeling AG = Aggressive Movement-response includes action that is clearly aggressive

Reliability

Because of its explicit and standardized administration and scoring procedure, it is not surprising that the ECS has proven to be more reliable than many other inkblot interpretive systems, showing high inter-rater and high test-retest reliability (Hiller et al., 1999). For example, in a sample of 25 8-year-old children, one-week test-retest coefficients for individual and summary

Table 10.2 Age Trends in the Normative Data for the Exner Comprehensive System for Rorschach Interpretation

Score	Age Trend
Length of Record	Younger children tend to give fewer responses than older children. Protocols of less than 17 are not uncommon before age 15 and records of more than 25 are unusual prior to age 13.
Location	Younger children (less than 11) give more responses that include the whole blot rather than a specific area. More children, and especially very young children, give at least one response that uses an infrequently identified area of the blot.
Developmental Quality	Younger children frequently give many vague responses in which diffuse impressions of the blot or blot area are given without clearly articulating specific outlines or structural features. Such vague responses account for one-third of the responses of children ages 5, 6, and 7.
Movement Determinants	Younger children give few human movement responses. It is not unusual for the responses of 5-, 6-, and 7-year-olds to have few or none such determinants, whereas it is uncommon for this to occur after age 11.
Chromatic Color Determinants	It is not uncommon for children to give color responses that are *not* created based on the form features of the blot. The presence of such pure color responses is often interpreted as indicative of poor affective regulation. About 70% of 5-year-olds, 35% of 8-year olds, 23% of 12-year olds, and 8% of 16-year olds give at least one pure color response.
Form Dimension	Answers that include the impression of depth, distance, or dimensionality increase with age such that, by age 8, they appear at least once in over half of all subjects' records.
Reflection Responses	In contrast to responses of adults, images reported as reflections or mirror images, because of the symmetry of the blot are quite common in child protocols. Such responses appear in about half of the protocols of children under the age of 8. Although the incidence of such responses declines over time, they are still found in about 25% of the protocols of 15-year olds.
Popular Responses	There is a steady increase in the number of popular responses with age, with adolescents giving approximately one-third more popular responses than children under age 8.
Special Scores	Many of the special scores that document unusual verbalizations and cognitive slippage are more common in young children than in adolescents and adults

scores ranged from $r = .49$ to $r = .95$, with a mean coefficient of $r = .84$ (Exner & Weiner, 1994). In fact, the only coefficient to drop below $r = .70$ was the coefficient for Inanimate Movement ($r = .49$).

Validity and Interpretations

While Rorschach scores are reliable over short time intervals, the stability of the scores over longer periods is lower than the stability of adult scores. Specifically, Exner, Thomas, and Mason (1985) tested 57 children at 2-year intervals from age 8 to 16. In general, most scores showed only moderate consistency over each two-year interval until the interval between the ages of 14 and 16. Some notable exceptions were the fairly stable coefficients for the use of good form, the use of popular responses, the number of active movement responses, and the use of shading features for making depth and dimension responses.

The modest stability of Rorschach scores is not unique to this type of assessment, but is characteristic of most assessment techniques in children (e.g., McConaughy, Stanger, & Achenbach, 1992). In fact, this is probably a positive attribute of the scores because it suggests that the scores capture the rapid developmental changes experienced by children and adolescents. However, there is a tendency to equate Rorschach responses with personality assessment, and to equate personality with stable dispositions. These findings on the low stability of Rorschach scores clearly argue against making strong dispositional statements based on a child's Rorschach protocol.

One common use of the ECS has been to assess childhood depression. Exner (1983) initially developed a Depression Index (DEPI) based on six scores from a child's protocol. Unfortunately, the DEPI, based primarily on research in adults, showed very poor agreement with other measures of depression in children, which led Exner to revise the DEPI (Exner, 1990) in an effort to increase its correspondence with other measures of depression. Tests of the revised DEPI index have also failed to find consistent associations with other measures of depression (Archer & Krishamurthy, 1997; Ball et al., 1991; Carter & Dacy, 1996). These findings could be a function of inadequate methods of assessing childhood depression in general, which results in the failure to have an appropriate standard with which to judge the Rorschach. Alternatively, Weiner (1986) has argued that the Rorschach: "is a measure of personality processes, not diagnostic categories… it can help to identify forms of psychopathology only to the extent that they identify personality characteristics associated with the types of disorder" (p. 155). However, these findings suggest that users of the DEPI from the ECS should not expect the scores to be highly related to other indexes of depression.

An even more extreme caution is in order for the Suicide Constellation for Children, a set of scores based on an index used to assess for suicidal tendencies in adults (Exner, 1978). The suicide constellation was developed by selecting the eight best predictors of suicide from the ECS in a small sample ($n = 39$) of children who had attempted or committed suicide within fewer than 60 days after the Rorschach was taken (Exner & Weiner, 1994). Unfortunately, the predictive validity of this index has not been replicated in other samples, making the interpretation of this index questionable at present (Allen & Hollifield, 2003).

Another common use of the Rorschach is in the detection of cognitive and perceptual irregularities that could be associated with schizophrenia (Weiner, 1986). Exner and Weiner (1994) outline four sets of Rorschach scores that can aid in this detection. First, disordered and illogical thought processes are the focus of several special scores in the Exner system. For example, the Incongruous Combination score identifies responses that condense blot details or images into a single incongruous percept in which the parts or attributes do not belong together: "a person with the head of a chicken" (Weiner, 1986, p. 217). Second, perceptual inaccuracies are suggested when the child has a protocol with many responses that do not correspond closely to the form structure of the blot (i.e., poor form quality) or protocols with few common or popular responses. Third, interpersonal inadequacies that are often associated with schizophrenia can be assessed in responses involving human movement. Movement responses with poor form quality are considered indicative of inaccurate or unrealistic interpretations of interpersonal situations (Exner & Weiner, 1994).

Fourth, the irregular content of a protocol, such as one with very violent (e.g., two boys stabbing each other in the chest) or very bizarre (e.g., flowers squirting poisonous gas) content can be considered suggestive of disturbed ideation that is often associated with schizophrenia.

Exner and Weiner (1982) reported data on 20 children (ages 9–16) reliably diagnosed with schizophrenia and 23 nonschizophrenic children. These data indicated that the use of these indexes produced a high correct classification rate (90.7%). These positive findings must be interpreted with three cautions, however. First, indicators of perceptual disturbances for the Rorschach have not always shown high correlations with other behavioral indicators of thought disorders (Smith, Baity, Knowles, & Hilsenroth, 2001). Second, while these indexes appear to be correlated with a diagnosis of schizophrenia, it is unclear how much utility these indexes possess over the actual behavioral symptoms of the disorder (Gittelman-Klein, 1986). In other words, there is no evidence to suggest that children who show elevations on these indexes, but who do not show overt behavioral manifestations of the disorder, are at risk for developing schizophrenia. Second, Gallucci (1989) studied a sample of 72 intellectually gifted children and found elevated rates on these indexes, compared to age norms, but no other signs of maladjustment in the children. Intellectually superior children may process the Rorschach stimuli in nonconventional ways, but these differences should not be considered indicative of a psychotic process. Similarly, Holaday (2000) reported that children and adolescents diagnosed with post-traumatic stress disorder also reported significantly higher scores on the Rorschach indicators of schizophrenia. Thus, indicators of schizophrenia on the Rorschach appear to have a high rate of false-positives for thought disorders (i.e., many children score high who do not have other indicators of psychosis).

Evaluation

These examples are only a small sample of the common uses of the ECS in clinical assessments of children and adolescents. However, these examples illustrate two issues that are important for using the Rorschach in the assessment of children and adolescents. In general, Rorschach responses do not typically correspond closely to behaviorally based diagnoses; therefore, use of the Rorschach for diagnostic purposes is not recommended. Second, many of the Rorschach scores and indexes were developed and validated on adults. Unfortunately, the extension to children has not met with great success, as is evident from studies on the Children's Depression Index and Suicide Constellation of Children. Therefore, users should be wary about using adult-oriented systems for interpreting the Rorschach responses of children.

Thematic (Storytelling) Techniques

The second type of projective technique for children is the storytelling or thematic approach. In this technique a child is shown a moderately ambiguous picture or photograph and asked to tell a story about it. For example, the instructions to the Roberts Apperception Test for Children (McArthur & Roberts, 1982) are:

> "I have a number of pictures I am going to show you one at a time. I want you to make up a story about each picture. Please tell me what is happening in the picture, what led up to this scene, and how the story ends. Tell me what the people are talking about and feeling. Use your imagination and remember that there are no right or wrong answers for the picture" (p. 7).

Thematic tests have been a popular type of projective technique with children because the storytelling format is usually non-threatening and fun for them. However, it does require a significant level of verbal ability in the child.

There are many different thematic techniques that have been used with children and adolescents, which vary in the types of pictures that are used to promote children's stories (see Kroon, Goudena, & Rispens, 1998 for a review). One of the most commonly used techniques for children and adolescents is the Thematic Apperception Technique (TAT; Murray, 1943). The TAT consists of 31 cards with black-and-white pictures of primarily adult figures involved in some relatively ambiguous action or interaction. Because the TAT was designed primarily for use with adults and contained adult pictures, the Children's Apperception Test (CAT; Bellak & Bellak, 1949) was developed especially for children. The original CAT contains ten cards with pictures depicting animal figures, although a later CAT-H was developed with human figures. The pictures on both the CAT and the CAT-H were designed to elicit typical childhood conflicts that are predicted from psychodynamic theory (e.g., sibling rivalry, oedipal urges, toileting concerns). Another thematic test heavily influenced by psychodynamic theory is the Blacky Picture Test (Blum, 1950). The Blacky Picture Test consists of 11 cartoons whose central figure is a dog named Blacky. Like the CAT, the pictures were designed to depict psychosexual conflicts common in children.

Two apperception tests, the School Apperception Method (Solomon & Starr, 1968) and the Michigan Picture Test-Revised (Hutt, 1980), were designed more specifically for use in educational settings. Another apperception test designed specifically for use with children is the Roberts Apperception Test for Children (RATC; McArthur & Roberts, 1982). The RATC is quite explicit in the themes assessed by the stimulus pictures. Unlike many other thematic techniques, the themes the pictures were designed to assess are not specific to psychodynamic theory. Also, the RATC is one of the few thematic techniques that includes an explicit scoring system. The RATC is reviewed in greater detail later in this chapter.

Several thematic approaches have specific sets of pictorial stimuli for specific groups of children. This is based on research showing that children provide greater verbalization on thematic apperception techniques when the stimulus material more closely matches their ethnicity, gender, and age (Constantino & Malgady, 1983). For example, the TAT and RATC contain some pictures that are gender-specific and the RATC contains supplementary pictures depicting African American children (McArthur & Roberts, 1982). Of particular note, the Tell-Me-A-Story technique (TEMAS: Constantino, Malgady, & Rogler, 1988) is a thematic apperception test that was specifically designed to be a culturally sensitive test for inner-city children and adolescents. The TEMAS involves 23 brightly colored cards depicting inner-city themes involving peer and family interactions. There are 11 sex-specific cards and two parallel sets for minority (depicting Hispanic and African-American characters) and nonminority children. Also, unique to the TEMAS are separate norms for Caucasian, African-American, Puerto Rican, and other Hispanic children across three age groups (5–7, 8–10, 11–13). However, these norms are based on a rather limited sample (n = 642) of children from public schools in New York City (see Flanagan & DiGiuseppe, 1999).

General Interpretation of Thematic Techniques

One important issue in the use of thematic techniques is the lack of standardized administration or scoring procedures for most systems. Of the 12 thematic apperception tests used for children and adolescents reviewed by Kroon et al. (1998), only 5 had standardized and objective methods of scoring children's responses. For example, assessors administering the TAT often select certain cards to administer. Further, there are many different systems for obtaining scores but most assessors do not use any systematic scoring system. Given the lack of consistency in administration and scoring, it is not surprising that evidence for the reliability and validity of thematic techniques is limited. Thematic techniques are often interpreted within an idiographic or clinical tradition in which clinical impressions of an individual child are obtained through an analysis of the child's stories.

Clinical interpretation of a child's story is typically based on two broad aspects of a child's response. The first step is *a process* interpretation. In this part of the interpretation, one notes such characteristics of the stories as how elaborate the stories were, whether the stories were coherent and tied to the stimulus card, and whether there were any specific cards for which the child had difficulty formulating a story. This type of interpretation can be used to determine how invested the child or adolescent was in the assessment process, whether there were any potential disturbances or idiosyncrasies in thought processes, and whether there were any specific types of stimuli that elicited defensive reactions from the child.

The second part of the interpretive process is a *content* analysis. Children's stories are typically analyzed for (1) the characteristics of the hero or main character (e.g., motives, needs, emotions, self-image), (2) forces that affect the hero in his or her environment (e.g., rejection by peers, punitiveness from parents, frightening forces, support by parent, affection from sibling), (3) the coping or problem-solving strategies used by the hero (e.g., aggression, compromise, nurturance), and (4) the outcomes of the story (e.g., positive or negative, outcomes brought about by hero or someone in his or environment, outcomes are realistic). The content analysis should determine whether there are any consistent themes in a child's story, especially themes that transcend the stimulus pull of a card. For example, an aggressive story provided for a card that shows two children fighting is less diagnostic than a story with an aggressive theme based on a picture of two people sitting next to each other in a park.

Roberts Apperception Technique for Children

The Roberts Apperception Techniques for Children (RATC; McArthur & Roberts, 1982) is one example of a thematic technique that was explicitly designed for use with children and is one of the few storytelling procedures with an explicit and standardized scoring system. This instrument illustrates some major components in the interpretive process of thematic techniques.

Content

The RATC is intended for use with children and adolescents of ages 6–15. There is a standard set of 27 stimulus cards depicting common situations, conflicts, and stresses in children's lives (McArthur & Roberts, 1982). Eleven cards have parallel male and female versions, and there is a supplementary set of stimulus cards featuring African-American children. A description of the RATC cards and the themes the cards were designed to elicit are provided in Table 10.3.

Administration and Scoring

The administration procedures of the RATC are quite simple (the instructions given to the child were provided earlier in this chapter). The RATC provides

TABLE 10.3 Depictions in the Stimulus Cards from the Roberts Apperception Test for Children

Card Number	Description	Common Themes
1 (B & G)	Both parents discussing something with child	Elicits themes of family confrontation and stories in which parents are giving advice or punishing a child
2 (B & G)	Mother hugging child	Elicits themes of maternal support and dependency needs in relation to a material figure
3 (B & G)	Child working on homework	Elicits themes related to child's attitude to school, teachers, tests, and homework
4	One child standing over another child in prone position	Elicits themes with aggression, accidents, and illnesses
5 (B & G)	Parents are shown in an embrace with child looking on	Elicits themes related to a child's attitude toward parental displays of affection
6 (B & G)	Two white children are shown interacting with a black child	Elicits themes related to peer interactions and racial attitudes
7 (B & G)	Child sitting up in bed awake	Elicits themes of anxiety and bad dreams
8	Both parents speaking to male and female child	Elicits themes related to family discussions, such as around discipline or planning a family activity
9	Child standing with clenched fists over a child sitting on the ground	Elicits themes related to peer aggression
10 (B & G)	Mother holding baby with child looking on	Elicits themes of sibling rivalry and attitudes toward the birth of a new sibling
11	Child cowering with hands in front of face	Elicits themes of fear and anxiety
12 (B & G)	Adult male glaring at a distressed adult female with child looking on	Elicits themes of parental conflict and parental depression
13 (B & G)	Child preparing to throw chair onto the ground	Elicits themes of anger and aggressive feelings
14 (B & G)	Child with paint on hands has put handprints on wall with mother looking on in distress	Elicits themes of maternal limit setting and child wrongdoing
15	Adult female in bathtub with male child looking through door	Elicits attitudes toward sexuality and nudity
16 (B & G)	Child and father in a discussion while father looks at a paper	Elicits themes of father-child relationships and paternal approval

Note: B & G = Separate cards for girls and boys.
Source: McArthur, D. S., & Roberts, G. E. (1982). *Roberts Apperception Test for Children*. Los Angeles: Western Psychological Service.

explicit instructions for scoring the stories provided by a child. Each story is scored on 16 coding categories. There are 8 Adaptive categories, 5 Clinical categories, and 3 categories labeled Indicators. A description of these categories is provided in Table 10.4. As evident from this box, the RATC coding categories are quite similar to traditional content areas used to interpret other thematic techniques. Scores used in interpretations from the RATC are the total number of times a given code was present across all stories. This allows one to determine consistent themes (high scores within a category) across stories.

Norming

One objective of the authors of the RATC was to develop a standardized scoring system so that normative data could be generated and used by other users of the system (McArthur & Roberts, 1982). The importance of age-specific normative data in the interpretation of projective tests was already discussed in the previous section on the Rorschach. Unfortunately, the normative data provided in the RATC manual are minimal. The normative sample on which norm-referenced scores are based consisted of 200 school children: 20 boys and 20 girls in the age ranges of 6–7 and 8–9 and 30 boys and 30 girls in the age ranges of 10–12 and 13–15. Not only is the size of the sample small, but its representativeness is also questionable. The sample was taken from three school districts in southern California. Although the manual states that an effort was made to select children from lower, middle, and upper socioeconomic family backgrounds (McArthur & Roberts, 1982), there is no evidence to show that this goal was met, nor is there any information given on the ethnic makeup of the sample. Finally, comparisons of scores from this normative sample to other non-referred samples of children have shown very different distributions of scores (Bell & Nagle, 1999). Therefore, the norm-referenced scores provided in the RATC manual are of questionable utility.

Reliability

A positive outcome of the explicit scoring system was an increase in reliability compared to other thematic approaches without standardized administration or scoring procedures. The manual reports that 17 doctoral-level raters averaged 89% agreement on three RATC protocols, and 8 master's-level clinicians reached 84% agreement. Evidence for the split-half reliability of the RATC was less impressive, however. Acceptable reliability (above .70) was found for only 6 of the 13 adaptive and clinical scales: Limit Setting, Unresolved, Resolution 2, Resolution 3, Problem Identification, and Support.

Validity and Interpretations

The increase in reliability afforded by the RATC scoring system has set the stage for the development of a database with which to judge the instrument's validity. However, the extent of this database is presently quite limited and the findings mixed. For example, the manual reported comparisons between 200 clinic-referred children and the 200 well-adjusted children in the standardization sample (McArthur & Roberts, 1982). In this broad test, all eight of the adaptive scales and all three indicators differed between the two groups. In contrast, the only clinical scale to show differences between groups was the Rejection scale. Thus, the clinical scales failed to differentiate maladjusted from well-adjusted children, which does not bode well for the likelihood of these scales accomplishing the more difficult task of differentiating types of problems within clinic-referred children.

Table 10.4 Profile Scales and Indicators from the Roberts Apperception Test for Children

Description of Scale	Purpose	Scoring Criteria
Reliance on Others (A)	Designed to measure the adaptive capacity to use help to overcome problem	Main character (1) seeks assistance for handling problem or completing tasks, (2) asks permission, or (3) asks for approval or material objects
Support-Other (A)	Reflects tendency to support others	Main character (1) gives object or does something requested or (2) gives emotional support or encouragement
Support-Child (A)	Measures self-sufficiency, maturity, assertiveness, and positive affect	Main character (1) shows appropriate self-confidence, assertiveness, self-reliance, perseverance, or delay of gratification or (2) experiences positive emotions
Limit Setting (A)	Measures the extent to which parent places reasonable and appropriate limits on child	Story describes some appropriate disciplinary action or constructive discussion following child wrongdoing
Problem Identification (A)	Measures child's ability to articulate problem situations	Character in story states a problem or obstacle or experiences contradictory feelings
Resolution-1 (A)	Measures child's tendency to seek easy or unrealistic solutions to problems	Story involves a situation in which a problem is solved without any clear mediating process or by some unrealistic or imaginary process
Resolution-2 (A)	Measures a child's tendency to use constructive resolutions to problems	Story involves constructive resolution of internal feelings, external problem, or conflicted interpersonal relationship; solution is limited to present situation without an explanation of the process involved in working through the problem
Resolution-3 (A)	Measures a child's tendency to use constructive resolutions to problems	Same as Resolution-2, except the story explains how the character worked through problem
Anxiety (C)	Measures a child's tendency to interpret situations as dangerous and fearful	Story involves (1) character showing apprehension, self-doubt, or guilt or (2) themes of illness, death, or accidents
Aggression (C)	Measures a child's aggressive impulses	Story involves angry feelings, physical or verbal attack, or destruction of objects
Depression (C)	Measures a child's tendency to depression	Story involves dysphoric feelings, giving up, or vegetative symptoms of depression

(Continues)

TABLE 10.4 (Continued)

Description of Scale	Purpose	Scoring Criteria
Rejection (C)	Measures issues that a child might have concerning separation and rejection	Story involves physical separation, rejection, dislike of another person, needs unmet by others, or racial discrimination
Unresolved (C)	Measures a tendency toward having an external locus of control or an inability to control one's emotions	Story involves an emotional reaction without a resolution
Atypical Response	Measures distortions in a child's thought processes or unusual ideation	Story involves a distortion of stimulus card, is an illogical story, involves homicidal or suicidal ideation/action, involves death, or involves child abuse
Maladaptive Outcome (I)	Measures poor problem-solving abilities or the presence of a pessimistic or hopeless cognitive style	Story involves characters that behave inappropriately to solve a problem or when the story ends with the main character dying
Refusal (I)	Measures a lack of investment in the task or extreme defensiveness to certain stimuli	Child refuses to respond or stops in the middle of a story and refuses to go on

Note: Descriptions of scoring criteria are not full criteria and should not be used in place of the explicit criteria provided in the RATC manual. Manual also provides concrete examples of each criterion. (A) = Adaptive scale, (C) = Clinical scale, (I) = Indicator.
Source: McArthur, D. S., & Roberts, G. E. (1982). *Roberts Apperception Test for Children*. Los Angeles: Western Psychological Services.

Evaluation

Because of the lack of validity evidence, the RATC should not be used in diagnostic decision-making, as is the case for other thematic approaches. Instead, the RATC should be used as a method of obtaining clinical impressions, with a consideration of all the strengths and weaknesses of this method of interpretation. However, unlike many other thematic techniques, the explicit scoring system of the RATC has led to a reliable scoring procedure that sets the stage for further validation to guide interpretations. Another caution in interpreting the RATC stems from the poor normative base from which norm-referenced scores provided in the RATC are derived (Bell & Nagle, 1999). These scores should he regarded as suspect until further information becomes available from larger and more representative samples of children and adolescents.

Sentence Completion Techniques

Another type of projective technique that is frequently used in the clinical assessment of children is the sentence-completion technique (SCT). The sentence-completion method involves providing the child, either orally or in writing, with a number of incomplete sentence stems such as, "My family is..." or "I am most ashamed of...." As is evident from these examples, the stimulus employed in sentence-completion techniques is much less subjective than the other projective methods reviewed in this chapter. That is, the sentence stems have a high degree of stimulus pull in prompting certain types of answers. As a result, many have debated whether sentence-completion methods should even be considered projective, given their more objective nature (Hart, 1986).

Although SCTs clearly require a different level of inference than other projectives, they probably are closer to other projectives in design and interpretation than to self-report rating scales. However, a decision as to whether or not to use an SCT in a clinical assessment goes back to our initial discussion of projective techniques in general. If one wishes to interpret projectives as a behavioral sample, then the objective nature of the SCT and the lower level of inference required is a distinct advantage. In contrast, if one wishes to enhance projection, then the strong stimulus pull of the SCT is less desirable.

To illustrate the diversity in how SCTs are used, Holaday, Smith, and Sherry (2000) surveyed a random sample ($n = 100$) of members of the Society for Personality Assessment and they obtained a 60% response rate to their survey. On questions related to why and how they used SCTs in their clinical practice; the only response endorsed by the majority of respondents (67%) was as "part of a more comprehensive assessment battery." A substantial minority were split in endorsing "to determine personality structure" (i.e., as a projective test) and in endorsing "as a structured interview" (i.e., as a behavioral sample) to describe their use of SCTs, with 30% and 25%, respectively, endorsing these uses. Interestingly, 28% endorsed the use "to obtain quotable quotes" as a justification for inclusion of SCTs in their assessment battery, suggesting that the information provided by the SCT is often used to obtain examples to illustrate findings from other assessment procedures (e.g., clinical diagnoses).

Features of SCTs

Content

Despite a common format, there are numerous SCTs available that vary in their content, length, complexity, and purpose. The Rotter Incomplete Sentence Blank

(Rotter & Rafferty, 1950) is one of the oldest and most common of the SCTs. It was originally developed for use with adults and consists of 40 items designed to elicit information on psychosexual conflicts. It is available in three forms, and the authors provide a quantitative scoring procedure that can be used to determine the degree of conflict present in each response. Another commonly used SCT is the Hart Sentence Completion Test for Children (HSCT). The 40-item HSCT was developed specifically for use with children, and the content was designed to elicit children's perceptions of family, peers, school, and self (Hart, 1986). There are numerous other SCT procedures that are beyond the scope of this chapter to discuss in detail (see Haak, 2003; Holaday et al., 2000 for reviews).

Administration

Administration of SCTs is straightforward and typically includes instructions which inform children that they are to complete the sentences in whatever manner they choose, and that there are no right or wrong answers.

There are three important dimensions on which the administration procedures of SCTs differ (Hart, 1986). First, SCTs and users of SCTs can differ on whether the sentence stems are to be read aloud to the child or adolescent or whether the child being assessed is to be asked to read the questions and respond privately. The choice of which administration format to use is partly a function of the child's reading level and age, with assessors tending to read sentence stems to children more often than to adolescents (Holaday et al., 2000). However, the verbal interchange that results from the reading of questions to a child can also provide an assessor with additional information (e.g., a child's affective response to a sentence stem, a child's apparent motivation toward the task) on which to evaluate his or her responses.

Second, some users of SCTs request that the child answer as quickly as possible by saying the first thing that comes to his or her mind in an effort to elicit spontaneous and unguarded responses. In contrast, other users attempt to promote deliberation by telling the subjects that they can complete the sentences in any way they like and that the purpose of the test is to better understand their *real* feelings. The first use of the SCT is typically preferred if the goal of administration is projection. The second administration procedure is typically preferred if the goal is to obtain a behavioral sample.

Third, SCTs differ in whether or not they include an inquiry process. In the inquiry phase, children are asked to explain their responses in more depth. This questioning helps the assessor determine why a child may have completed the sentence in a particular way. This information is especially useful for responses that are unusual, ambiguous, or diagnostically important (Hart, 1986). Because of the important clinical information obtained by this inquiry, it is often an integral part of the administration of SCTs for many assessors (Haak, 2003).

Interpretation

As with most projective techniques, there is great variability in how SCTs are scored and interpreted. Many SCTs do not have explicit scoring or interpretive guidelines and, even for those that do, many users do not follow them in practice. For example, of the 60 respondents from the survey of users of SCTs conducted by Holaday et al. (2000), only 17% of those respondents who said they use SCTs in the assessment of children stated that they score the test according to a manual or according to the authors' instruction, and 27% of those respondents who said they use SCTs with adolescents reported doing so. In fact, 25% of respondents did not even know the name of the SCT that they used in practice and 13% reported that they write their own sentence stems to address their client's needs.

However, interpretation of SCTs typically relies on an analysis of the manifest content of a child's responses. As was the case with the thematic techniques, an assessor would analyze a child's response for consistent themes that might provide clues to the child's emotional adjustment or his or her perceptions of certain persons or situations. For example, positive responses to stems designed to assess perceptions of parents (My father is the best; What I like best about my father is he is nice) are thought to be an indication of a positive father-child relationship. This is an example of the low level of inference that is often applied to the interpretation of SCTs.

Some assessors also analyze the *process* of a child's responses, such as whether they are complex, whether they are perseverative, whether they are expressive and imaginative, and whether they are coherent and related to the sentence stem (Haak, 2003). This type of analysis can provide the assessor with insight as to how invested a child was in the task and some possible clues about a child's thought processes. Box 10.3 provides an overview of the most common approaches to interpreting responses on SCTs.

Evaluation

As is evident from the discussion of SCTs to this point, most systems do not have explicit and standardized administration, scoring, and interpretive procedures. These decisions are often left to the judgment of the assessor, who can be guided by the advice of the authors of the SCT or other experienced clinicians (e.g., Haak, 2003). As a result, most SCTs can be considered to fall in the clinical tradition of projectives, with most techniques failing to have well-established psychometric properties (Anastasi, 1988). Of particular concern is the lack of a normative base to guide the interpretation of SCTs in children and adolescents. Also, most SCTs were initially developed for adults, so the content is often inappropriate for children.

Drawing Techniques

A final popular approach to projective testing with children is through the interpretation of children's drawings. The popularity of drawing techniques in the assessment of children can be attributed to two factors. First, unlike other projective techniques that require substantial verbal ability often exceeding the capacity of some very young children, drawing techniques are primarily nonverbal. Second, most children are familiar and comfortable with drawing, so it is an enjoyable assessment context for a child. Koppitz (1983) writes:

> "Drawing is a natural mode of expression for boys and girls. It is a nonverbal language and form of communication; like any other language, it can be analyzed for structure, quality, and content" (p. 426).

From this description, it is evident that the interpretation of children's drawings is based on the same assumptions that underlie the interpretation of other projective approaches; namely, that drawings contain nonverbal clues and symbolic messages about a child's self-concept, motivations, concerns, attitudes, and desires (Cummings, 1986).

Knoff (2003) provides a general framework for administering and interpreting drawings. Specifically, administration involves two phases. During the performance phase, the child is provided with the necessary materials to complete the task (e.g., paper; crayons) and asked to draw

Box 10.3

Research Note: Interpretive Approaches to Sentence Completion Techniques

The author of the Hart Sentence Completion Test for Children (Hart, 1986) provided an interesting summary of various interpretive approaches to sentence completion techniques (SCTs) in the clinical assessment of children and adolescents.

Strategy 1

The most common interpretive approach to SCT is to review each item's content and obtain clinical impressions about a child's personality dynamics. The assessor searches for patterns, clues, and thought processes and generates hypotheses consistent with the assessor's view of human behavior. This approach often leads to different interpretations of the same set of responses by different clinicians. What is viewed as important or diagnostic will depend on the assessor's theoretical orientation.

Strategy 2

The next approach places sentence stems into clusters with similar item content that are judged to elicit similar psychological information. The assessor determines if there are important patterns of responses within a cluster of items. However, like the first strategy, the interpretations are heavily dependent on the assessor's orientation. Which items determine a meaningful cluster and what constitutes an important pattern of responses within a cluster are based on an assessor's theoretical orientation.

Strategy 3

The third approach is exemplified by the Rotter Incomplete Sentence Blank (Rotter & Rafferty, 1950) and is based on psychodynamic theory. Each response is analyzed according to the degree of intrapsychic conflict evident in the response. It is a quantitative scoring system in which the severity of the conflict is rated as negative, neutral, or positive.

Strategy 4

The fourth approach involves comparing responses on an SCT to some predetermined criteria. This approach attempts to limit the unreliability inherent in the other strategies by minimizing the reliance on the assessor's theoretical orientation. An example of this approach is the Hart Sentence Completion Test for Children (Hart, 1972). In a standardization sample, a large pool of responses was obtained for each sentence stem. The responses were placed into positive, negative, and neutral categories by expert judges. In each rating category, representative responses were identified for each sentence stem to aid assessors in making their determination of the valence of a child's response.

Source: Hart, D. H. (1986). "The Sentence Completion Techniques," in H. M. Knoff (Ed.), *The Assessment of Child and Adolescent Personality*, New York: Guilford.

specific pictures. During the inquiry phase, a series of questions are asked to clarify the persons and objects in the picture, to understand their actions and motives, and to have the child describe in more detail why he or she chose to draw the picture in the way he or she did. Both the drawing itself and the child's description of it are used to generate hypotheses about potential themes that may provide insight into the child's emotional (e.g., anxiety) and social (e.g., family relations) functioning.

Draw-a-Person Technique

One of the most popular drawing techniques for children is the Draw-a-Person Technique (DAPT), made popular by a seminal publication by Koppitz (1968). In this technique a child is simply given a paper and lead pencil and asked to draw a picture of a whole person. It is left up to the child the type of person to be drawn (e.g., age, gender, race, context of figure). After finishing this first drawing, the child is given another sheet of paper and asked to draw another person of the opposite sex from the first drawing.

Koppitz (1968) provides one of the most explicit guides to interpreting children's figure drawings. She organizes her approach around three basic questions. The first question is, *How did the child draw the figure?* Such content analysis is the focus not only of the Koppitz system, but of most interpretive systems of children's drawing. In the Koppitz system, the figure is viewed as reflecting a child's self-concept. Koppitz developed a series of 30 Emotional Indicators (EI) that were rare in children's drawings, that were independent of age, and that differentiated undisturbed from maladjusted children. Examples of EI in the Koppitz system include poor integration of parts, slanting of figure by 15° or more, omission of mouth, body, or limbs, and monster or grotesque figures. Figure size is another EI that is not only a part of the Koppitz system, but is included in many interpretive systems and is considered to be a key indicator of a child's self-esteem. Small figures are interpreted as indicating low self-esteem (2 in. or less in height) and large expansive figures (9 in. or more in height) are interpreted as indicating high levels of self-esteem. Box 10.4 summarizes, in more detail, Koppitz's EI.

Box 10.4

Further Discussion of the Koppitz Emotional Indicators for Human Figure Drawings

As mentioned in the text, the writings of Koppitz (1968, 1983) have been quite influential in the interpretation of human figure drawings for children and adolescents. A key element to her projective interpretation of drawings is the presence or absence of 30 Emotional Indicators (EI). Koppitz's El were chosen based on (1) their utility in differentiating disturbed from nondisturbed children, (2) their low prevalence (less than 6%) in the drawings of nondisturbed children, and (3) their occurring independent of age.

The EIs can be divided into three broad categories: Quality Signs, Special Features, and Omissions

Quality Signs	Special Features	Omissions
Poor integration of parts	Tiny head	No eyes
Shading of face	Crossed eyes	No nose
Shading of hands & neck	Presence of teeth	No mouth
Asymmetry of limbs	Short arms	No body
Slanting figures	Long arms	No arms
Tiny figure	Arms clinging to body	No legs
Big figure	Big hands	No feet
Transparencies of major body parts	Hands cut off	No neck
	Legs pressed together	
	Genitals	
	Monster/grotesque figures	
	Multiple figures drawn spontaneously	
	Clouds	

(Continues)

Box 10.4 (Continued)

Koppitz explains that the EI are not scores but are clinical signs that may reveal underlying attitudes and characteristics of the child (Koppitz, 1983). There is evidence that the EIs occur at a greater frequency in the drawings of emotionally disturbed than nondisturbed children (see Finch & Belter, 1991). However, Koppitz describes the difficulty in interpreting EIs for the individual child:

> "There is no relationship between an EI and overt behavior. For instance, long arms and big hands both reflect aggressiveness and anger, yet children who show these two EI on their drawings may act very differently. One boy may reveal his anger by refusing to do his homework or by truanting from school, another child may be physically aggressive to peers, while a third child may withdraw and soil himself when angry. The Human Figure Drawings indicate that all three pupils are angry; the youngsters' behaviors demonstrate how they express this anger. It is also important to recognize that different EI can reflect the same attitude. Thus, a girl may show acute anxiety by shading the body and face of her Human Figure Drawing and by omitting the arms. When she makes another drawing some time later, she may omit the figure's nose and hands and may draw a dark cloud above the figure. Similarly, a single EI may have different meanings depending on the situation. For example, a tiny figure may reflect underlying timidity or shyness, or it may indicate withdrawal or depression. The true meaning of a given EI can only be determined by other aspects of the personality battery, from observing the child in different settings, and from studying his or her developmental and social background" (Koppitz 1983, p. 423).

The second question around which the Koppitz interpretation is organized is, *Whom does the child draw?* Most children tend to draw figures that are of the same gender as themselves (Cummings, 1986; Finch & Belter, 1993). Based on these findings, Koppitz considered a child's drawing an opposite-sex figure on his or her first drawing to be diagnostic, either of problems in gender identity or as a reflection of loneliness and isolation. There is also a tendency to view the figure as an indicator of the child's image of his or her own body (Cummings, 1986).

The final question in the Koppitz interpretive system is, *What is the child trying to express via the drawing?* A child's self-figure may reflect his or her self-perceptions, or a drawing of someone else may reflect attitudes or conflicts toward this person. Koppitz notes that a child's drawing may (1) be a reflection of a child's wish, fantasy, or ideal; (2) be an expression of real attitudes or conflicts; or (3) be a mixture of both. To help clarify this issue, many assessors note either a child's spontaneous verbalizations about a figure or ask the child to tell a story about the figure. As noted above, the assessor may follow up with an inquiry phase in which he or she asks specific questions about the figure such as, Who is he/she? or Whom were you thinking about while you were drawing? or What is he/she thinking about? or How does he/she feel?

House–Tree–Person

A second projective drawing technique is the House-Tree-Person (HTP) technique (Cummings, 1986). In this technique the child is asked to draw a house, a tree, and a person. The order is always the same and the drawings are done on separate sheets of paper. After the drawing, children are asked a series of questions to give them an opportunity to describe and interpret the objects that were drawn (Cummings, 1986; Koppitz, 1983). According to one of the originators of the HTP technique, the three figures give insight into different facets of a child's functioning (Hammer, 1958). The house is thought to elicit feelings associated with the child's home situation and familial relationship. In contrast, the tree is thought to elicit deeper and unconscious feelings about the child and his or her relationships with the environment. Unlike the self-portrait, the tree is thought to have less pull for conscious self-descriptions and therefore to involve a greater level of projection. And, finally, the drawing of a person is thought to reflect more of a conscious or semiconscious view of the child's self, the child's ideal self, or a significant other.

Kinetic Family Drawing

A third common projective drawing technique that is used in the assessment of children and adolescents is the Kinetic Family Drawing. In this technique a child is asked to "Draw a picture of everyone in your family, including you, doing something" (Burns & Kaufman, 1970, p. 5). These instructions emphasize the family engaging in some activity, hence the term *kinetic*. As was the case for the HTP technique, there is an inquiry phase in which a child is asked to describe and explain his or her drawing (Cummings, 1986). The first part of the inquiry typically involves the child explaining who each figure is (e.g., name, relationship to the child, age). The child is then asked to describe all the figures, what they are doing in the picture, how they are feeling, and what they are thinking about. After these initial descriptive questions, the child is asked to tell a story about the drawing, saying what happened immediately before the actions depicted in the drawing took place and what happens next. Finally, the child is asked to describe anything that he or she would change about the picture if he or she could.

The popularity of the KFD lies in its ability to assess a child's perceptions of his or her family in a fun and nonthreatening way. Burns and Kaufman (1970) outline a three-part interpretive process that is heavily dependent, not just on the drawing, but on the inquiry phase that follows. The first part of the interpretive process is the analysis of the actions portrayed in the drawing. They not only refer to the movements between people but the energy (e.g., avoidance, conflict, nurturance) and emotion (e.g., love, anxiety, anger) captured in the picture. The next part of the interpretive process deals with the style of the family drawing. Style refers to the patterns of interactions among significant family members and often reflects a child's defense system (e.g., denial, isolation). The final stage of the interpretation is the symbolic interpretation, which is analogous to the content interpretations of other projective drawing techniques.

Psychometric Cautions for Drawing Techniques

As with most other projective techniques, the best method of validating projective drawings has been hotly debated. In a review of the psychometric properties of drawing techniques, Cummings (1986) found that the lack of explicit scoring and interpretive guidelines for projective drawings has caused most systems to have poor reliability. Even for those systems in which high reliability estimates have been obtained, correlations between drawings and other measures of a child's adjustment have not been consistently shown (Joiner, Schmidt, & Barnett, 1996). Most studies have found that clinicians are unable to distinguish clinically identified children from nonclinical controls using projective drawings. Of great concern is the use of projective drawings to detect child sexual abuse. Summaries of this research have not been able to find indicators from drawings that have consistently and reliably differentiated abused from non-abused children across multiple samples (Garb, Wood, & Nezworski, 2000).

This inability to demonstrate the validity of projective drawings has led some authors to suggest that the use of drawings in clinical assessments of children is unethical (Martin, 1983). This strong stance has sparked a lively debate (Knoff, 1983). It is clear that content analyses of drawings have rarely been shown to predict overt behavior, yet many users still try to make behavioral predictions (e.g., aggression, anxiety, history of sexual abuse) from drawing techniques. A quote from Cummings's (1986) review of projective drawing research seems to summarize a sensible way to view assessment with projective drawings and possibly a good way to view projective testing in general:

> "The greatest value associated with projective drawings does not lie in the graphic symbols represented on the paper. Rather, the value of the technique may be in the practitioner's opportunity to observe the examinee's behavior while drawing. Drawings provide a nonthreatening beginning point which should lead to an in-depth exploration of attitudes, feelings, and beliefs via the synthesis of direct interviews, third-party interviews, observations, and test data" (pp. 238–239).

Conclusions

In this chapter we have outlined some of the major issues in the debate of when and how to use projective testing in the clinical assessment of children and adolescents. As with most assessment techniques, the problem with projective testing lies not in the techniques themselves, but in the inappropriate purposes for which they are often employed. This issue is exacerbated in the use of projective techniques because of wide-spread disagreement over the basic nature of these techniques. There is considerable debate over which psychological processes they are designed to measure, and there is lack of agreement over what method of interpretation (e.g., clinical or psychometric) is most appropriate for a given technique. The most important goal of this chapter was to provide the reader with a clear discussion of these issues so that projectives can be used appropriately, with the assessor clearly recognizing the limitations of whichever interpretive approach is used.

We have also summarized some of the major methods of projective testing that are used with children. We have discussed inkblot techniques, story-telling techniques, sentence-completion techniques, and projective drawings. Space limitations prevent an exhaustive review of specific techniques and interpretive systems. However, we have attempted to provide selected examples of each type of projective method as a basis for developing greater expertise in the use and interpretation of these techniques through further didactic and clinical training.

Chapter Summary

1. Projective techniques have been the focus of much controversy. However, they remain the most frequently used method of psychological assessment.
2. Much of the debate over projective techniques stems from the confusion over what the projective techniques were designed to measure and how to best evaluate their usefulness.
   (a) The first area of confusion is whether projective techniques obtain samples of behavior or whether they assess unconscious personality dynamics.

(b) The second focus of debate is whether projectives are ways of obtaining highly individualized clinical impressions or whether they are psychometric tests that should be evaluated by traditional indexes of reliability and validity.

3. The Exner Comprehensive System provides a structured method for administering, scoring, and interpreting responses to Rorschach inkblots.
   (a) The inkblots are administered in two phases: a free association phase and an inquiry phase.
   (b) Detailed scoring of responses provides 90 possible scores to be used in interpretation.
   (c) Normative samples of children have documented several age trends in children's Rorschach responses.
   (d) Scores from the Exner system have proven to be reliable.
   (e) The validity of scores for children has not been well established, although it has been difficult to determine the most appropriate way of testing the validity of Rorschach scores.
4. Thematic story-telling techniques provide a child with a relatively ambiguous picture and require that the child "make up a story" about the picture.
5. Most interpretive systems of thematic tests use a two-part interpretation of a child's stories. The first step interprets the process of a child's stories (e.g., coherence of stories) and the second step interprets the content of the stories.
6. A popular thematic test for use with preadolescent children is the RATC.
   (a) The RATC contains pictures depicting common situations that children experience and provides a standard scoring system for children's responses.
   (b) The explicit scoring instructions allow for reliable scoring of children's responses.
   (c) The standardization sample on which norm-referenced scores are based is quite small and its representativeness is questionable.
   (d) Existing evidence for the validity of RATC scores is quite limited.
7. Sentence-completion techniques provide the child with a sentence stem and require the child to complete the sentence.
8. Most sentence-completion techniques do not have standardized scoring procedures for interpreting children's responses. It is left to clinical judgment how to interpret the content of the responses.
9. Drawing techniques, such as the Draw-a-Person Technique, the House-Tree-Person, and the Kinetic Family Drawings are popular for assessing children because drawing is a familiar and enjoyable exercise for children.
10. Despite their popularity, scores derived from children's drawings have not been highly associated with other indicators of a child's emotional, behavioral, or social functioning.

Chapter 11

Structured Diagnostic Interviews

Chapter Questions

- What are the major differences between structured and unstructured interviews?
- What are the major similarities and differences among the most common structured diagnostic interviews used to assess children?
- What information can diagnostic interviews provide that cannot be obtained from other assessment techniques?
- What are some important guidelines for the appropriate use of diagnostic interviews in the assessment of children and adolescents?

History

Clinical interviews have a prominent place in the history of psychological assessment. The face-to-face verbal dialog between assessor and client is the prototypical format for most clinical enterprises. Historically, the most common type of clinical interview has been the unstructured interview. In the unstructured interview, the interviewer determines what questions should be asked, how the questions should be framed, what follow-up questions should be asked, and what are acceptable responses from the client. This unstructured format is quite consistent with the clinical approach to assessment, which was discussed in the previous chapter on projective techniques. It allows the assessment to be tailored to the individual needs of the client and relies heavily on the individual clinician's orientation and expertise.

However, the unreliability inherent in unstructured interviews generates some significant problems. The results and interpretation of such interviews tend to be highly idiosyncratic to the clinician conducting the interview. This unreliability is especially problematic for research. Hence, many clinical assessors have developed more

P.J. Frick et al., *Clinical Assessment of Child and Adolescent Personality and Behavior*,
DOI 10.1007/978-1-4419-0641-0_11, © Springer Science+Business Media, LLC 2010

structured diagnostic interview schedules that provide a clear and standardized format from which to conduct the clinical interview. This standardization helps address the key problems associated with unstructured interviews; however, one must recall that these interviews are valid only for certain purposes (e.g., collecting data on specific symptoms) and relatively less valid for others (e.g., treatment planning for a specific client; Mash & Hunsley, 2005).

Initially, most of these instruments were designed for use with adults and were primarily used in research. Two of the better known early interview schedules were the Feighner Research Diagnostic Criteria (Feighner et al., 1972), which later became the NIMH Diagnostic Interview Schedule (DIS; Robins et al., 1981), and the Schedule for Affective Disorders and Schizophrenia (SADS; Endicott & Spitzer, 1978).

Over the past two decades, structured diagnostic interviews have moved from being strictly research instruments to being a part of many clinical assessments. In addition, several interview schedules have been developed for use with children and adolescents. This chapter focuses on these interview schedules and their potential role in the clinical assessment of children and adolescents.

Overview

Structured diagnostic interviews consist of a set of questions that the assessor asks the informant (e.g., parent or child). There are explicit guidelines on how responses are to be scored. Interview questions generally start with a stem question (e.g., Have you been involved in many physical fights?). If the stem is answered affirmatively, then follow-up questions are asked to determine other relevant parameters such as frequency (e.g., How many fights have you been in, in the past year?), severity (e.g., Have you ever used a weapon in a fight?), onset (e.g., When was the first time you got into a fight?), and impairment (e.g., Has fighting caused problems for you at school, home, or with kids your age?). An example of the question format from the NIMH Diagnostic Interview Schedule for Children-Version 4 (DISC-IV; Shaffer et al., 2000) is provided in Box 11.1.

Box 11.1

Example of the DISC-IV Question Format

The following is an example of the stem/follow-up question format used by most diagnostic interview schedules. This question was taken from the questions assessing Major Depressive Disorder from the DISC-IV (Shaffer et al., 2000).

"I'm now going to ask some questions about feeling sad and unhappy."

1. In the last year, was there a time when you often felt sad or depressed for a long time each day?

   IF YES,

   A. Was there a time in the last year when you felt sad or depressed for a long time each day?
   IF NO, GO TO QUESTION 2

   B. Would you say that you felt that way for *most of the day?*

   C. Was there a time when you felt sad or depressed *almost every day*?
   IF NO, GO TO QUESTION 2
   IF YES,

   D. In the last year, were there two weeks in a row when you felt sad or depressed almost every day?
   IF NO, GO TO QUESTION 2

   E. When you were sad or depressed, did you feel better if something good happened or was about to happen to you?

   F. Now, what about the *last four weeks?* Have you felt sad or depressed?

Commonalities Across Interview Schedules

In Table 11.1, we summarize the basic characteristics of some of the most commonly used diagnostic interviews for children. It should be noted that the interviews are continuously updated to keep up with changing diagnostic criteria or modified for some specific application (e.g., outcome measure for treatment of childhood depression, screening device for an epidemiological study of child disorders). Therefore, many of the interviews have multiple versions and are continually being revised. The contents of these interviews are all based on the criteria specified in the *Diagnostic and Statistical Manual of Mental Disorders*, starting with the third edition (*DSM-III;* American Psychiatric Association, 1980) and continuing through its most recent revision (*DSM-IV-TR;* American Psychiatric Association, 2000).

Which *DSM* disorders are assessed is generally quite similar across the different interview schedules. All of the interviews can be used to assess for the disruptive behavior disorders, affective disorders, and anxiety disorders in children and adolescents. Each of these interviews also allows for at least a brief screening for schizophrenia. The majority of structured interviews also allow for an assessment of substance use, elimination, and eating disorders. Tic disorders are covered exclusively by CAPA, DISC-IV, and K-SADS, whereas the ADIS contains unique screening questions for mental retardation, learning disorder, and somatoform symptomatology. The CAPA is unique in its detailed assessment of sleep disorder symptoms. Most interviews organize questions by diagnosis. However, the Interview Schedule for Children and Adolescents (ISCA; Sherrill & Kovacs, 2000) provides a symptom-oriented interview format with items clustered by content (e.g., impaired concentration) and topic area (e.g., mental status) rather than specific diagnostic criteria.

In order to promote multi-informant assessments, most interviews contain parallel forms to ask identical questions to both the child and a parent. There is even an experimental teacher version of the DISC 2.3, an earlier version of the DISC, that was used in the *DSM-IV* field trials for the disruptive behavior disorders (Frick et al., 1994).

A recent trend in the most widely used structured interview schedules is the development of computer-administered versions. Currently, the DISC-IV, the DICA, the CAPA, and the Dominic-R all have formats that can be administered by computer. The computer format was designed to enhance the reliability of the interviews by increasing the ease of administration and data collection. Similar to the pencil-and-paper version, the computer format is designed to be administered by an examiner. The examiner reads items from the computer screen and enters the patient's responses. The computer quickly scores and stores responses, selects the appropriate follow-up questions, and skips out of diagnostic sections when the respondent fails to meet a certain threshold of severity. Also, the computer-administered interviews have programs that quickly score the interview and provide various summary scores (e.g., symptom indexes, number of diagnostic thresholds met) that aid in the interpretation of the results.

Most of the interviews were designed to assess children and adolescents between the ages of 8 and 17. Some interviews report applicability to younger children with parents as informants (e.g., Valla et al., 2000). However, there is some evidence that the reliability of children's self-report on diagnostic interviews is low before age 9 (Edelbrock et al., 1985; Hodges & Zeman, 1993). The length of time that it takes to administer a diagnostic interview is heavily dependent on the child being assessed. Because of the stem/ follow-up question format, children with

Table 11.1 Overview of Structured Diagnostic Interviews for Children

Interview	Time	Ages	Time Frame	Informants	Comments
Anxiety Diagnostic Interview for *DSM-IV* (ADIS; Albano & Silverman, 1996; Silverman, Saavedra, & Pina, 2001)	60–90 min	7–17	Present	Child and Parent	Semi-structured interview focusing on childhood anxiety disorders. Categorical and dimensional symptom assessment with diagnostic summary that places diagnoses in hierarchical format. Support for reliability and validity for anxiety disorder diagnoses. Limited validity data for other diagnostic categories.
Child and Adolescent Psychiatric Assessment (CAPA; Angold & Costello, 2000)	60–120 min	9–17	Present	Child and Parent	Semi-structured interview with flexibility in wording and in probing for relevant symptoms. Can be used by trained lay interviewers. Includes Likert-type symptom severity scores. Separate section for impairment. Good reliability except for modest estimates for ODD and CD. Some validity evidence for diagnoses relative to external criteria.
Children's Interview for Psychiatric Symptoms (ChIPS; Weller et al., 2000)	30–60 min	6–18	Present	Child and Parent	Highly structured format. Can be used by trained lay interviewers. Brief with broad symptom coverage. Simplified language for use with younger children. Limited research, but some evidence of good sensitivity and specificity.
Diagnostic Interview for Children and Adolescents (DICA; Reich, 2000; Reich et al., 1982)	60–120 min	6–18	Lifetime	Child and Parent	Structured with changes toward more flexible format. Good reliability with some evidence of validity. Evidence supporting use categorically and dimensionally. Used cross-culturally and with a variety of populations.
Diagnostic Interview Schedule for Children (DISC-IV; Shaffer et al., 1993, 2000)	90–120 min	6–17	Present (separate lifetime module)	Child and parent (experimental teacher version available)	Highly structured format designed for use by trained lay interviewers. Good reliability at symptom and diagnosis level. Covers many diagnostic domains. Frequently used in epidemiological studies. Diagnoses from parent version related to greater impairment.

Dominic-R (Valla, Bergeron, & Smolla, 2000)	15–25 min	6–11	Present	Child	Highly structured pictorial interview with verbal symptom descriptions. Designed for use by lay interviewers with minimal training. Promising reliability and validity data. Should be interpreted with caution if used with young children.
Pictorial Instrument for Children and Adolescents (PICA-III-R; Ernst, Cookus, & Moravec, 2000)	40–60 min	6–16	Present	Child	Semi-structured pictorial interview with verbal symptom descriptors. Designed for use by experienced clinicians. Categorical and dimensional symptom assessment of 14 diagnostic categories. Should be interpreted with caution if used with young children. Limited psychometric data. Authors note the need for update to reflect *DSM-IV* criteria.
Schedule for Affective Disorders and Schizophrenia for School-Aged Children (K-SADS; Ambrosini, 2000; Chambers et al., 1985; Tillman et al., 2003)	90 min	6–18	Present and lifetime (in separate and combined interview formats)	Child and Parent	Semi-structured interview originally designed to focus on depression. Variety of versions that vary in length. Low level of structure necessitates use by clinicians. Includes ratings of symptom severity. Widely used in a variety of populations with good psychometric evidence.

more symptoms will require more interview time because of the need to ask more follow-up questions. However, as is evident from Box 11.1, the average time to administer the interviews does not vary much across the different schedules and lasts typically from 60 to 90 min.

Major Sources of Variation Across Interview Schedules

From the previous discussion it is clear that the various interview schedules probably have more similarities than differences. However, one of the major differences across schedules is the *degree of structure* inherent in the interview format. All of the interviews provide some degree of structure and give guidelines for standardized administration and scoring. However, there is substantial variation in the amount of "leeway" given the assessor across the various interviews. For example, the K-SADS is one of the least structured of the interviews. The original manual for administration includes the following instructions:

> "The K-SADS supplies a series of questions addressed to the child for each item to be rated. The aim is not to oblige the rater to ask all of the questions. They serve as a guide for questions which have been found most helpful and informative. The rater should ask as many questions as necessary to arrive at a well-documented rating. Needless to say, probing should be as neutral as possible and leading questions should be avoided" (Puig-Antich & Chambers, 1978, p. 2).

In contrast, the DISC was designed to have a high degree of structure in administration. The manual for its administration includes the following instructions:

> "The DISC symptom questions are designed to be read *exactly* as written. There is very limited scope for independent questioning. DO NOT deviate from the prescribed question sequence. DO NOT make up your own questions because you think you have a better way of getting at the same information, or because you think the question is poorly worded" (Fisher et al., 1992, p. 31).

The trade-off between leeway and structure is obvious. Less structure allows the assessor to tailor the interview according to the needs of the individual client. However, these interviews generally require a greater degree of experience to administer and often have lower levels of reliability (Gutterman, O'Brien, & Young, 1987; Hodges & Zeman, 1993).

Another major variation among the structured interviews for children is the time frame used to assess symptoms and diagnoses. All of the interviews assess whether problems are currently evident. This is called *a present episode* frame of reference. Most interviews consider present episodes to be within the previous six months, although in some instances the time frame may be as short as within the last two weeks (e.g., ISCA for emotional disorders) or as long as within the last year (e.g., DISC-IV for Conduct Disorder). Of note, the CAPA restricts the assessment of symptoms to the previous three months due to concerns with the reliability of memory in children and adults over longer time intervals. Similarly, the Dominic-R does not obtain any temporal information, such as onset and duration of symptoms, given concerns as to the validity of such information in young children. Nevertheless, the major source of variation is whether or not interview schedules are limited to present episodes. A number of interviews restrict the focus of assessment to the present episode time frame (e.g., CAPA and ChIPS). However, an increasing number of interviews provide for the assessment of both present and *lifetime* diagnoses. For example, the DISC-IV provides a more recently incorporated whole-life module assessing for whether or not a child has exhibited symptoms of diagnoses since age five but prior to the current year (Shaffer et al., 2000). Similarly, there are lifetime formats for both the ISCA and K-SADS. The DICA is unique in its exclusive focus on lifetime diagnoses.

A third source of variation within the interview schedules is the answer format. For most interviews, the interview responses are coded into a categorical format (yes, no). This categorical format is consistent with the *DSM* orientation in which symptoms are considered either present or absent. In contrast, the ADIS, CAPA, ISCA, PICA-III-R, and K-SADS have answer formats that can be placed on a Likert-type scale that allows one to rate the severity of a symptom. While this format makes it more difficult to translate responses into *DSM* diagnoses, it does not create an artificial dichotomy between the presence or absence of a symptom and allows symptom scores to reflect gradations in severity.

Evaluation of Diagnostic Interviews

Advantages

Structured interviews share with behavior rating scales the goal of obtaining a detailed description of a child's emotions and behaviors from multiple informants. The logical question is: what advantages do the time-consuming structured interviews offer in comparison to the more time-efficient behavior rating scales? Some of the more important advantages of structured diagnostic interviews follow.

(1) Structured interviews are useful in obtaining important parameters of a child's behavior that are not typically assessed by most behavior rating scales. Specifically, most interview schedules provide questions that elicit information on the duration of a child's behavioral difficulties and the age at which the problems began to emerge. This temporal information allows one to take a developmental perspective in understanding a case, a perspective that has proven to be crucial for assessing many forms of childhood psychopathology (e.g., Silverthorn & Frick, 1999).

(2) Interviews also allow one to determine the *temporal sequencing* among behaviors. For example, it is important in the assessment of childhood depression to determine whether periods of sadness occurred contiguously with other behaviors associated with depression, such as sleep disturbances, eating disturbances, or thoughts of death (Kazdin, 1988).

(3) Most structured interviews assess the *level of impairment* associated with behaviors being reported. Most interviews have questions that elicit information on the degree to which a child's difficulties are affecting his or her functioning in major life arenas (e.g., at home, at school, and with peers).

(4) Diagnostic interviews also enhance the *correspondence between assessment techniques and diagnostic criteria*. As mentioned previously, the most common structured interviews were specifically designed and revised to correspond to the changing *DSM* system. Therefore, the usefulness of the interview is, in part, dependent on the usefulness of the diagnostic definitions that are being assessed.

This tie between assessment and diagnosis can be advantageous for several reasons. First, it promotes revisions of the interviews to correspond with advances in our knowledge of the basic characteristics of child and adolescent psychological disorders. Second, it allows one to make a diagnosis based on strict adherence to diagnostic criteria. Either due to theoretical, empirical, or practical reasons (e.g., insurance reimbursement), many clinicians attempt to make *DSM* diagnoses as a result of their assessments. Too often, diagnoses are made based on information (e.g., rating scales, projective tests) that do not directly assess the diagnostic criteria or through techniques that are unsystematic in their assessment of symptomatology and associated features (e.g., unstructured interviews; Klein et al., 2005). As a result, the meaning of the diagnosis is ambiguous. Structured diagnostic interviews do not have this problem. They tend to result in more reliable diagnoses (Silverman & Ollendick, 2005) and can actually provide important information that may alter diagnostic impressions and treatment recommendations (Kashner et al., 2003).

(5) Diagnostic interviews are also helpful in *training* clinical assessors. As assessors are developing their competence in interviewing, it is often helpful to have an explicit format from which to conduct the interview. It gives the assessor a good way to learn the basic characteristics of childhood emotional and behavioral disorders. After being trained in administration procedures and after conducting several interviews with actual clients, assessors often begin to internalize the diagnostic criteria for the most common disorders of childhood. This knowledge can then be applied in situations in which a structured interview is not possible.

Disadvantages

Diagnostic interviews also have a number of weaknesses of which the clinician should be aware.

(1) The time consuming nature of the interviews coupled with some question as to whether they provide incremental validity in the assessment of some disorders such as ADHD (Pelham et al., 2005) suggest that structured interviews may not be practical or useful in many situations.

(2) In addition, structured interviews depend on DSM criteria, which is a strength for assessing well-validated syndromes but a weakness for assessing disorders with a weak empirical basis.

(3) Diagnostic interviews are subject to the same potential *reporter biases* that were discussed in previous chapters on self-report inventories and parent and teacher behavior rating scales.

(4) Making differential diagnoses with the assistance of structured interviews still does not directly translate to plans for intervention (Mash & Hunsley, 2005).

(5) There is great difficulty in making *norm-referenced interpretations* from interviews. Clinically significant levels of symptoms are often based on *DSM* criteria rather than based on a comparison with a representative normative sample. Therefore, the appropriateness of clinical elevations for a given age depends on the appropriateness of the diagnostic criteria for that age. For example, Barkley (1997) has questioned the validity of applying the same diagnostic criteria (i.e., the same number of symptoms) for ADHD across the early-childhood and adolescent years based on a documented decline in hyperactivity and impulsivity symptoms as children move into adolescence. As a result, the uniform diagnostic threshold, while appropriate for elementary school-aged children, may be too conservative for adolescents.

Several community studies using an early version of DISC (e.g., Anderson, et al., 1987; Costello, 1989) allow one to view the base rates of disorders assessed by the DISC in community samples of school-age children. Such work has continued with the current version with various populations (e.g., Roberts,

Roberts, & Xing, 2007). Although these studies provide some information on how a child who meets criteria would compare to others in the general population, this type of normative information is still much more limited than the type provided by other assessment techniques, most notably behavior rating scales.

(6) Another weakness of most diagnostic interviews is the failure to provide a format for obtaining information from a child's teacher. This source of information is crucial in the clinical assessment of elementary school-aged children (Loeber et al., 1991). As a result, information from teachers must be obtained by some other method, thereby making it difficult to determine if discrepancies between a teacher's report and the report of others are due to real differences in a child's classroom behavior or whether they are due to differences in the assessment format.

Recommendations for Use of Structured Interviews

Based on the strengths and weaknesses of structured interviews, several recommendations can be made on their appropriate use in the clinical assessment of children and adolescents. First, like any assessment technique, the diagnostic interview should never be used alone in a clinical evaluation. It should be one part of a comprehensive assessment battery. For example, information from diagnostic interviews should be supplemented by assessment techniques that provide better norm-referenced scores (e.g., behavior rating scales) and by assessment techniques that provide information on a child's classroom functioning (e.g., behavioral observations in the school).

In addition, the diagnoses derived from the diagnostic interviews should be viewed within the context of the overall assessment. A diagnosis can be viewed similarly to the way an elevation on a behavior rating scale is interpreted. Specifically, it is one piece of information that needs to be integrated with other sources of information to develop a good case formulation. Stated simply, diagnoses based solely on diagnostic interviews should not be considered final clinical diagnoses. Such final diagnoses should be based on an assessor's integration of multiple sources of. A case example in which a diagnostic interview was used as part of a comprehensive assessment battery is provided in Box 11.2.

The child's age is also an important consideration in the use of structured interviews. Generally, the reliability for most interview schedules is low before the age of 9 for child self-report (Hodges & Zeman, 1993). It seems that the structured, face-to-face dialogue is not appropriate for assessing very young children. Several interviews have been developed using pictorial stimuli, rather than relying purely on question-and-answer format, in an effort to increase the reliability of the interview for younger children.

A description of two such pictorial interviews is provided in Box 11.3.

Another important issue in interpreting information obtained from standardized interview schedules is the consistent finding that, if the interview is repeated, parents and children uniformly report fewer symptoms on the second administration (Jensen, Watanabe, & Richters, 1999; Piacentini, et al., 1999). For example, Piacentini, et al. (1999) found that when the DISC-IV was readministered to the same sample of 245 parent–child pairs (age 9–18) 12 days later, parent-reported symptoms dropped 42%, and child-reported symptoms dropped 58%,

The reasons for this symptom attenuation have not been conclusively shown. However, they can include (1) sensitization to clinical

Box 11.2

Case Example: The DISC-IV in the Evaluation of a 9-Year-Old Girl with Attention-Deficit Hyperactivity Disorder

Alexis who is 9 years and 3 months old was referred for a comprehensive psychological evaluation by her parents upon the recommendation of her teachers. Her teachers had reported to Alexis' parents that she was having difficulty paying attention and was daydreaming, interrupting others, and making careless mistakes in her work. Her parents requested a comprehensive evaluation to determine the severity and possible cause of these difficulties and to get recommendations for possible interventions to aid in her school adjustment.

Alexis's background, developmental, and medical history were unremarkable. During the testing, Alexis had great difficulty concentrating and was easily distracted. She was also very fidgety and restless. Intellectually, Alexis had much better verbal comprehension abilities, especially in the area of verbal reasoning, than nonverbal perceptual-organizational abilities. Consistent with her verbal abilities, Alexis scored in the above average range on measures of reading and math achievement.

Alexis's emotional and behavioral functioning were assessed through the use of structured interviews con-ducted with Alexis, her parents, and her teachers as well as through rating scales completed by her parents and teacher. The structured interviews were the parent version of the DISC-IV and the experimental teacher version used in the DSM-IV field trials (Frick et al., 1994). The child version was given to Alexis.

The following is an excerpt from the report of Alexis's evaluation that illustrates how information from the DISC-IV was integrated with other assessment information.

The only problematic areas that emerged from this assessment of Alexis' emotional and behavioral functioning were significant problems of inattention, disorganization, impulsivity, and overactivity that seem to be causing her significant problems in the classroom. On the DISC-IV, Alexis's parents agreed that such difficulties were noticeable by the time she was age 5. Alexis herself endorsed many symptoms of inattention, but not overactivity, on the DISC-IV. Alexis's teachers described her as being very restless and fidgety, being easily distractible, having very disorganized and messy work habits, having a hard time completing tasks, and making many careless mistakes. Results from teacher rating scales further suggested that these behaviors are more severe than would be typical for children Alexis's age. These behaviors are consistent with a diagnosis of Attention-Deficit Hyperactivity Disorder (ADHD). Also consistent with this diagnosis were the age of onset of these symptoms as reported by Alexis's parents. These behaviors associated with ADHD seem to be causing significant problems for Alexis in school, affecting the amount and accuracy of her schoolwork.

issues leading to a heightened threshold for symptom reporting, (2) a circumscribed focus on only the interval between assessment periods, (3) statistical regression to the mean, and (4) knowledge that brevity of responding will shorten the duration of the interview (Piacentini et al., 1999). This symptom attenuation is not much of an issue in most clinical uses of structured interviews that do not involve multiple administrations. However, there is also evidence that the number of symptoms reported declines *within* an interview schedule, such that parents and child tend to report more symptoms for diagnoses assessed early in the interview, even if the order of assessment is varied (Jensen et al., 1999).

This type of symptom attenuation within an interview is of much greater concern because it clearly can influence the results from a typical clinical use of structured interviews. In an attempt to solve this problem, Edelbrock, Crnic, and Bohnert (1999) modified the administration of DISC-2.3

Box 11.3

Research Note: Developing Structured Interviews for Young Children

To increase the usefulness of structured interviews for assessing younger children, several authors have attempted to develop interviews that involve pictorial content to either replace or augment the typical question-and-answer format for structured interviews. One example of this approach is the Dominic-R by Valla et al. (2000). The Dominic-R is designed to assess *DSM-III-R* criteria for anxiety disorders, mood disorders, and the disruptive behavior disorders in children ages 6–11.

The interview involves pictures of a child named Dominic facing situations that are common in children's daily lives. The pictures are accompanied by questions about the visual image (e.g., "Do you feel sad and depressed most of the time, like Dominic?"). There is a version of the Dominic-R, the "Terry Questionnaire," that employs an African American character named "Terry," and there are translations of the Dominic-R in French, Spanish, and German. There is also an Interactive Dominic Questionnaire that is a CD-ROM-based interactive cartoon. The Dominic-R takes about 15 to 25 minutes to complete and is highly structured, which allows it to be administered by lay interviewers. The reliability of the Dominic-R was assessed in a sample of 340 community children aged 6 to 11, and it revealed reliability coefficients that were much improved over other structured interviews with very young children. An adolescent version has also been developed (Smolla et al., 2004).

For the child version, test-retest reliability over 7 to 12 days for diagnoses from the Dominic-R ranged from a kappa of .44 to a kappa of .69, with most being above .60 (Valla et al., 1997). Also, the diagnoses based on the Dominic-R were strongly associated with diagnoses made by experienced clinicians with kappa values ranging from .64 to .88 (Valla et al., 2000). Furthermore, research has shown the Dominic-R to accurately designated children meeting *DSM-IV* criteria for Conduct Disorder (Arseneault et al., 2005). Therefore, it appears that the combination of pictorial stimuli and verbal stimuli can enhance the reliability and validity of responses in young children.

A similar assessment system, described by Ernst, Cookus, and Moravec (2000), is called the Pictorial Instrument for Children and Adolescents (PICA-III-R). The PICA-III-R is a semi-structured interview that includes 137 pictures assessing anxiety disorders, mood disorders, disruptive behavior disorders, psychotic disorders, and substance abuse. Therefore, the content of the PICA-III-R is somewhat broader than that of the Dominic-R. Like the Dominic-R, the PICA-III-R combines pictorial stimuli with verbal questions. However, the verbal questions on the PICA-III-R are more extensive, often including many follow-up questions (e.g., "Do you ever get like him (e.g., sad)?" "How much?" "Do people tell you that you look sad?"). Also, the PICA-III-R verbal questions are not meant to be read verbatim. The type and degree of questioning is left somewhat up to the interviewer. Because of all of these characteristics, the PICA-III-R may be more useful for older children with more severe forms of psychopathology compared to the Dominic-R, and it must be administered by a experienced clinician. Ernst et al. (2000) reported that, in a sample of 51 inpatient children and adolescents (aged 6 to 15), the PICA-III-R scales were generally internally consistent (i.e., most over .80), although the internal consistency of the Mania (.69) and Obsessive-Compulsive symptoms (.54) were somewhat low. There is minimal information on the validity of the PICA-III-R other than the fact that scores from this interview changed over the course of hospitalization for the inpatients, which presumably reflected improvement brought about by treatment.

Both the Dominic-R and PICA-III-R provide examples of ways to enhance the usefulness of structured interviews in obtaining child self-report. It is important to note, however, that both of these interviews are in the very early stages of development, and much more information is needed on their

(Continues)

Box 11.3 (Continued)

reliability across samples and their validity for assessing *DSM* diagnoses.

Finally, another example of a unique approach to the assessment of young children is the Berkeley Puppet Interview (see Measelle, Ablow, Cowan, & Cowan, 1998). This interview calls for two puppets to make statements about themselves and then ask the ask the child a question with two choices based on the same attribute (e.g., "Are you good at making friends or are you not good at making friends?"). This interview includes academic, social, and symptom-related (i.e., aggression-hostility and depression-anxiety) domains. Some evidence of convergent validity has been found based on ratings by parents and teachers (Measelle et al., 1998) and the interview has been able to differentiate clinic-referred from community samples of children (Ablow et al., 1999). However, much more research on the validity, feasibility, and utility of this assessment tool is needed.

to produce more stable symptom endorsements that are less susceptible to attenuation effects. They included a more detailed introduction with an overview of all areas to be covered on the interview, and they provided definitions of key concepts used throughout the interview. Furthermore, they employed a flexible order of administration that allowed parents to select the order in which the various diagnoses were assessed. Using this methodology in a sample of 24 parent-child pairs with children ranging in age from 6 to 15, there was very minimal reduction in the number of symptoms reported when the interviews were repeated one week later. However, none of the standardized administration procedures that accompany structured interview schedules provide for this type of administration, and therefore, the possible drop in number of symptoms reported for disorders assessed later in the interviews must be considered when interpreting the results for individual children and adolescents.

A final consideration in using structured interviews concerns when to administer diagnostic interviews in the assessment battery. There is no research on this issue, and these recommendations come from clinical experience. Diagnostic interviews should not be the first assessment administered to parents. The structured format does not facilitate the development of rapport between the interviewer and parent, and some parents become frustrated in trying to fit their main concerns and descriptions of their child's behavior into the confines of the interview. Therefore, it is often helpful to precede diagnostic interviews with less structured questions that allow parents to express, in their own words, their concerns for their child. However, for children and adolescents, we actually find that the structured format enhances rapport in many cases. Children often enter the assessment situation nervous because they are unsure about what is expected of them. The clear and explicit response format of diagnostic interviews makes the demands of the situation apparent for the child and thereby reduces his or her anxiety in many cases.

Up to this point, we have tried to give an overview of structured interviews, looking at the various formats that are available, highlighting some of the advantages and disadvantages of using interview schedules in a clinical assessment, and providing guidelines for appropriate use. In the next section, we provide a more in-depth look at one particular interview schedule, the DISC-IV. We chose the DISC-IV as a prototypical example of a structured interview because it is one of the most widely used interview schedules for children and adolescents, and it has been one of the most systematically developed. However, one must be aware that the DISC-IV is one of the most structured interview schedules, and therefore, it has all of the advantages and disadvantages that accompany a high degree of structure.

Focus on the NIMH Diagnostic Interview Schedule for Children (DISC-IV)

Development

The original version of the DISC (DISC-1; Costello, 1983; Costello et al., 1984) was designed to be a downward extension of the adult-oriented Diagnostic Interview Schedule (Robins et al., 1981). The DISC-1 was developed as part of an initiative by the NIMH Division of Biometry and Epidemiology that focused on obtaining a greater understanding of the prevalence of childhood mental disorders (Shaffer et al., 2000). The DISC-1 was designed for use in epidemiological studies and was explicitly tied to the version of the *DSM* being used at the time (*DSM-III*; American Psychiatric Association, 1980).

In 1985, Dr. David Shaffer at the New York State Psychiatric Institute and his colleagues undertook a revision of the interview to (1) improve its reliability for use with children and for use by lay interviewers and (2) provide diagnostic compatibility with the *DSM-III-R* (American Psychiatric Association, 1987) and anticipated *DSM-IV* and ICD-10 criteria (Fisher et al., 1992). Modifications to the DISC have been greatly informed by field-testing conducted as part of a large NIMH-funded multisite study titled the Methods for the Epidemiology of Child and Adolescent Mental Disorders (MECA) study.

The current version of the DISC, the DISC-IV (Shaffer et al., 2000), assesses approximately 30 diagnoses of childhood and adolescence and is fully compatible with the *DSM-IV* (American Psychiatric Association, 2000) and ICD-10 (World Health Organization, 1993) classification systems. The development of the DISC has expanded to other languages and to alternative administration formats (i.e., computerized).

Structure and Content

The DISC-IV (Shaffer et al., 2000) contains 358 core questions and approximately 1,300 questions that are asked contingent on a child's responses to the core questions. There are two parallel versions of the DISC-IV, the youth version (DISC-Y), to be administered to children of ages of 9–17, and the parent version (DISC-P), to be administered to the parents of children of ages 6–17. There is also an experimental teacher version (DISC-T), which was developed for use in the *DSM-IV* field trials (Frick et al., 1994). The DISC-IV was designed with a primary focus on current psychological functioning. It assesses for symptoms occurring within two overlapping time intervals: the past twelve months and the past four weeks. The DISC-IV contains an optional whole life module designed to measure symptoms occurring as early as age 5. An alternative present-state version has been developed targeting only the four-week time interval (see Shaffer et al., 2000).

The DISC-IV is organized in "diagnostic modules." There are six modules that comprise sets of related disorders. A summary of the modules is provided in Box 11.4. For each diagnosis, DISC-IV is designed to obtain information about the presence of symptoms included in *DSM*

Box 11.4

Organization and Content of the DISC-1V

Module	Disorders Covered
Anxiety	Social Phobia Separation Anxiety Specific Phobia Panic Agoraphobia Generalized Anxiety Selective Mutism Obsessive-Compulsive Posttraumatic Stress
Mood	Major Depressive/Dysthymic Mania/Hypomania
Psychosis	Schizophrenia
Disruptive	Attention-Deficit/Hyperactivity
Behavior	Disorder Oppositional Defiant Disorder Conduct Disorder
Substance	Alcohol Abuse/Dependence
Use	Nicotine Dependence Marijuana Abuse/Dependence Other Substance Abuse/ Dependence
Miscellaneous	Anorexia Nervosa/Bulimia Nervosa Elimination Disorders Tic Disorders Pica

Source: Shaffer et al., 2000.

criteria. If a certain threshold, usually below *DSM* diagnostic threshold, is met, the questions regarding the age of first onset, impairment, and past treatment are asked. (See Box 11.1 for an example of the DISC-IV question format.)

Administration

The DISC-IV was designed to be administered by interviewers without clinical experience after approximately two to six days of training. Use of the computerized DISC-IV is accompanied by less stringent training requirements. Training includes (1) instruction on standard DISC-IV administration procedures, (2) viewing an actual administration of the DISC-IV, and (3) supervised practice in administration with a confederate in a controlled situation.

At the beginning of the interview, the interviewer completes an introductory module consisting of several pieces of demographic information (e.g., age and sex of child) that are necessary to properly administer the interview. The interviewer also establishes a time line with the interviewee to assist in his or her recall for the onset and duration criteria contained in the interview. The time line establishes salient events (e.g., birthdays, vacations, start of the school year, holidays) that occurred in the year preceding the interview. These anchors help the child or parent remember the time frame for diagnostic questions.

The verbal instructions given to the respondent are semi-structured. That is, several points that must be covered are provided, but verbatim instructions are not required. The points include:

1. There are no right or wrong answers. The best answer is the one that tells the most about the child.
2. The informant should try to answer "yes" or "no" to each question.
3. The time frame is within the last year, unless otherwise specified.
4. Some of the questions on the form will be left out.
5. Some questions maybe asked more than once.
6. It is possible to take breaks, if needed.

Unlike the instructions, the administration of the actual DISC-IV questions is quite structured. The questions are designed to be read exactly as written and in the sequence prescribed. Interviewers are explicitly instructed not to make up their own questions or to ask for an example unless it is requested in the interview format. If a respondent does not understand the question, the interviewer should repeat the question, emphasizing the words that seemed to cause confusion. The interviewer is not allowed to answer interpretive questions for the respondent (e.g., "What do you mean by often?" *or* "Is one or two times considered frequent?"). The interviewer is instructed to simply ask the respondent to interpret the question "whichever way s/he thinks is best."

Reliability

The DISC-IV (and other interview schedules) relies heavily on psychometric data derived from prior versions of the instrument. Initial reliability data on the DISC-2.3 was obtained from a series of articles by Shaffer and colleagues (Piacentini et al., 1993; Schwab-Stone et al., 1993; Shaffer et al., 1993). These authors tested the psychometric properties of the DISC-2.3 in a sample of 75 clinic-referred children ages 11–17. In 41 cases, the child and/or parent were re-interviewed one to three weeks later by a second interviewer. There were sufficient cases to calculate the test-retest reliability for five *DSM-III-R* diagnoses (i.e., Attention-Deficit Hyperactivity Disorder, Oppositional Defiant Disorder, Conduct Disorder, Major Depression, and Separation Anxiety Disorder). The kappa statistics for the test-retest agreement are reported in Table 11.2. Also reported in this table are the intraclass correlations, which provide an estimate of the test-retest reliability of the symptom clusters that form the criteria for *DSM-III-R* diagnoses. Importantly, the tendency for parents and children to report substantially fewer symptoms on repeated administrations of structured interview can substantially reduce test-retest coefficients. Therefore, Table 11.2 also includes another index of reliability, the Cronbach's alpha, as an estimate of the internal consistency of the symptom clusters.

TABLE 11.2 Test–Retest and Internal Consistency Estimates from the DISC-2.3

	Kappa	ICC	Alpha
Parent only (*n* = 39)			
Attention-Deficit Hyperactivity	.55	.87	.87
Oppositional Defiant	.88	.82	.75
Conduct	.87	.86	.56
Major Depression	.72	.82	.88
Separation Anxiety		.77	.61
Child Only (*n* = 41)			
Attention-Deficit Hyperactivity		.72	.83
Oppositional Defiant	.16	.44	.67
Conduct	.55	.60	.59
Major Depression	.77	.68	.85
Separation Anxiety	.72	.66	.71
Combined Parent and Child (*n* = 37)			
Attention-Deficit Hyperactivity	.56	.84	
Oppositional Defiant	.59	.65	
Conduct	.50	.80	
Major Depression	.71	.66	
Separation Anxiety	.80	.72	

NOTE: Kappa is the agreement between diagnoses at Time 1 and diagnoses at Time 2 with a 1- to 3-week interval between interviews. ICC is the intraclass correlation between symptoms at Time 1 and Time 2. Alpha is Chronbach's alpha calculated for the symptom at Time 1.SOURCE: M. Schwab-Stone, P. Fisher, J. Piacentini, D. Shaffer, M. Davies, & M. Briggs (1993). "The Diagnostic Interview Schedule for Children-Revised Version (DISC-R): II. Test–Retest Reliability," *Journal of the American Academy of Child and Adolescent Psychiatry*, *32*, 651–657.

On a diagnostic level, all diagnoses showed relatively high test-retest agreement for the parent interview, the child interview, and the combined parent and child interview. When combining a parent and child report, a symptom was considered present if either parent or child endorsed it. The one exception to the generally good reliability was the low reliability of the Oppositional Defiant Disorder diagnosis by child report. Another exception was the low internal consistency of the Conduct Disorder symptoms. However, the low internal consistency of these symptoms is not surprising for two reasons. First, only three symptoms are required for the diagnosis of Conduct Disorder and most of these symptoms tend to have a relatively low base rate. Second, these symptoms tend to be indicative of discrete—perhaps independent—problem behaviors or delinquent acts, making internal consistency estimates a less than optimal method of determining the reliability of this symptom domain.

Although these reliability data are based on an earlier version of the DISC, the DISC 2.3, Shaffer et al. (2000) provide initial reliability estimates for the DISC-IV from a sample of 84 parents and 82 children, ages 9–17, selected from several outpatient psychiatric clinics. These data were derived from the computer-administered version of the DISC-IV, the C-DISC-IV. Interviews were conducted by lay interviewers with an average retest interval of seven days. The preliminary findings are consistent with the results for the DISC-2.3, with kappa coefficients ranging from .43 (Conduct Disorder) to .96 (Specific Phobia) for the parent report and from .25 (Simple Phobia) to .92 (Major Depressive Episode) for the child report.

Validity

The validity of diagnostic interviews is often assessed by comparing the results of structured interviews to diagnoses made by experienced clinicians. For example, Piacentini et al. (1993) reported moderate to strong agreement between the results of DISC interviews and clinician diagnoses when the Parent DISC-2.3 was used (average kappa = .50) but low agreement based on the Child DISC-2.3 (average kappa = .34). Combining the two interviews gave agreement estimates between those of either informant alone (average kappa = .41). These authors reported that most of the cases with disagreements between clinician diagnoses and the DISC-2.3 were cases that were close to the diagnostic threshold. For example, several disagreements emerged in which children had seven symptoms of ADHD (rather than the required eight symptoms in *DSM-III-R* criteria) and were not given the diagnosis according to the DISC-2.3 but were given the diagnosis of ADHD by the clinician.

However, another study (Lewczyk et al., 2003) found relatively poor correspondence between diagnoses based on the DISC-IV and diagnoses by clinicians. The DISC-IV yielded higher rates of diagnoses on anxiety disorders, ODD, CD, and ADHD, but clinician diagnoses of depression were more common.

Friman et al. (2000) provided a unique investigation of the predictive validity of the DISC by comparing interview data to behavioral observations recorded in a residential treatment program. The researchers examined both convergent and discriminant validity across a lengthy time interval (i.e., one year). Validity data were obtained on 369 children, aged 9–17, who were administered a computerized version of the DISC-Y 2.3, the C-DISC-Y 2.3, upon enrollment in the residential program and at a one year follow-up. Diagnoses of both Oppositional Defiant Disorder and Conduct Disorder were compared to daily observations of disruptive behavior that were coded by program staff and summed to form monthly behavior ratings of both oppositional and conduct problem behaviors. Youth meeting criteria for a DISC-2.3 diagnosis of ODD or CD upon enrollment exhibited significantly greater observed behavioral difficulties on program entry than youth not meeting a diagnosis for either disorder. Furthermore, change in diagnostic status across the two assessment periods predicted changes in observed disrupted behavior across the same time interval. For example, youth who met criteria for an ODD/CD diagnosis at Time

1 but not at Time 2 were characterized by a downward pattern of observed antisocial behavior in the months separating the interviews. This is contrasted with youth whose observed antisocial behavior increased as they moved from no diagnosis at Time 1 to diagnosis at Time 2.

As further evidence for the validity of the DISC interview, Edelbrock and Costello (1988) found strong associations between the diagnoses of ADHD, Conduct Disorder, and Depression/Dysthymia from the DISC-P and the Hyperactive, Delinquent, and Depressed scales of a previous version of the Child Behavior Checklist (Achenbach & Edelbrock, 1983) in a sample of 270 clinic-referred children between the ages of 6 and 16. High rates of agreement were also found between the original DISC-P and the CBCL in another study of 40 psychiatric referrals and 40 pediatric referrals (Costello, Edelbrock, & Costello, 1985). In contrast, the relation between the CBCL and the child version of the DISC tended to be much lower. However, it is impossible to determine whether the low correlations with the DISC-C were due to differences in informants (i.e., parent-completed CBCL and child-respondent DISC) or to differences in the assessment instruments themselves.

Conclusions

Structured diagnostic interviews have become an important part of many clinical assessments of children and adolescents. Like behavior rating scales, diagnostic interviews provide a reliable means of assessing a child's emotional and behavioral functioning. In this chapter, we have attempted to highlight the advantages and disadvantages of using diagnostic interviews. Diagnostic interviews enhance clinical assessments by providing a format for determining how long a child's problems have been occurring, for determining the temporal sequencing of behaviors, and for estimating the degree of impairment associated with a child's emotional or behavioral problems. These important parameters of a child's emotional and behavioral functioning are often not assessed by other assessment modalities. In addition, diagnostic interviews are typically tied to the most recent revisions of the *DSM*, which closely links assessment with this system of classification.

On the negative side, diagnostic interviews are often time intensive, and they typically do not provide any norm-referenced information on a child's functioning above that which is accorded by *DSM* criteria. In addition, diagnostic interviews typically do not include a format for obtaining information from a child's teacher, and their reliability in obtaining self-report information for young children (i.e., below age 9) is somewhat questionable, although pictorial or other formats provide a promising method of enhancing their usefulness in this young age group. As a result of these weaknesses, diagnostic interviews are best used as part of a more comprehensive assessment battery. We have attempted to provide guidelines for their use in this capacity. We have also attempted to provide an overview of the most commonly used diagnostic interviews for assessing children and adolescents, highlighting the major commonalities and differences across interviews. We concluded the chapter with a more detailed discussion of the DISC-IV as an example of a typical diagnostic interview schedule designed for use with children and adolescents.

Chapter Summary

1. Structured diagnostic interviews consist of a set of questions to be asked of a child or adolescent with explicit guidelines on how the youth's responses are to be scored.

2. Most of the commonly used structured interviews are designed to assess diagnostic criteria from one of the recent versions of the *Diagnostic and Statistical Manual of Mental Disorders*. Therefore, if a goal of the evaluation is to make or clarify a *DSM* diagnosis, structured interviews are an important assessment tool.
3. Interviews vary on the degree of structure inherent in the interview format and whether or not the interview assesses only current episodes of the disorders.
4. Structured interviews, like behavior rating scales, obtain detailed descriptions of a child's emotions and behaviors from multiple informants.
5. Unlike rating scales, however, structured interviews allow for the assessment of important parameters of a child's behavior, such as the duration of the behavioral difficulties, the temporal sequencing among problems, and the degree of impairment associated with the difficulties.
6. Most structured interviews are time consuming and are not good for making norm-referenced interpretations.
7. Diagnoses derived from structured interviews should be viewed within the context of other assessment instruments.
8. Child self-report from diagnostic interviews is typically not reliable before age 9.
9. The NIMH Diagnostic Interview Schedule for Children-Version IV (DISC-IV) is a prototypical structured diagnostic interview for use with children and adolescents.
   a. The DISC is highly structured so that it can be administered by trained lay interviewers.
   b. There are child, parent, and experimental teacher versions of the DISC.
   c. The DISC contains 358 core questions and 1,800 follow-up questions that are asked contingent on a child's responses to the core questions.
   d. The DISC is organized in six modules: (1) Anxiety Disorders, (2) Mood Disorders, (3) Psychosis, (4) Disruptive Behavior Disorders, (5) Alcohol and Substance User Disorders, and (6) Miscellaneous Disorders (i.e., Eating Disorders, Elimination Disorders, Tic Disorders).
10. Diagnostic interviews should only be used as part of a more comprehensive assessment battery.

CHAPTER 12

Assessing Family Context

Chapter Questions

- Why is assessing a child's family context important in the clinical assessment of children's emotional and behavioral functioning?
- What dimensions of a child's family context are most important to the assessment process?
- How can one assess these important dimensions of family functioning?

Introduction

In the summary of research on childhood psychopathology provided in Chap. 3, one of the more important findings was that children's and adolescents' emotional and behavioral functioning was heavily influenced by the demands and stressors they experienced in their environment. As a result, to truly understand a child's or adolescent's psychological adjustment, one must not limit the assessment to obtaining characteristics of the youth but must also assess the important contexts that shape a child's or adolescent's behavior. There is no context more important to understanding a child or adolescent than the family context.

Causal Role of Familial Influences

Research on childhood psychopathology consistently suggests that factors within the family play a major causal role in the development of personality and psychopathology (Erickson, 1998). At times the causal role of

P.J. Frick et al., *Clinical Assessment of Child and Adolescent Personality and Behavior*,
DOI 10.1007/978-1-4419-0641-0_12,

a child's family has been overemphasized, either by ignoring the potential effects that a child or adolescent can have on the family (Pardini, 2008), or by ignoring the factors that can influence both the family and child (Frick & Jackson, 1993). These caveats indicate that a child's family context is only one piece of a very complex puzzle in understanding the psychological adjustment of a child or adolescent. However, research also suggests that it is a very important piece of the puzzle. Family factors play an integral role in the causal theories of many types of problems across many theoretical orientations. Box 12.1 provides examples of three different types of childhood problems from three different theoretical perspectives, all of which emphasize the family context as a causal agent in a child's adjustment problems. Therefore, if the goal of an assessment is to uncover the possible causes of a child's or adolescent's emotional or behavioral difficulties and, thereby, point the way to important treatment goals, the assessment of family functioning is critical to the assessment process.

Box 12.1

Childhood Problems in a Family Context: Examples of Three Problems and Three Theoretical Orientations

Childhood Anxiety: An Operant Perspective

One way of conceptualizing the causes of childhood anxiety has been from an operant perspective. In this model a child receives reinforcement from his or her environment that functions to maintain and increase the anxious behavior. Often this reinforcement is provided in the family context. A good example is provided by Ross (1981) of an 8-year-old girl, Valerie, with school phobia. Valerie refused to attend school, and an assessment of her home context revealed that the consequences of her refusal to go to school were indeed quite positive. Instead of going to school, Valerie was able to sleep an hour later than her three siblings who were attending school. Until her mother left for work, she was allowed to follow the mother around the house and then was taken to a neighbor's house for the day. At the neighbor's house Valerie was free to do whatever she pleased for the rest of the day, such as playing games and making occasional trips to a corner store where she bought candy, gum, and soft drinks. It was clearly a comfortable routine for both child and mother, who thereby avoided Valerie's temper tantrums.

Childhood Aggression: A Social Learning Perspective

Gerald Patterson (Patterson, 1982) and his colleagues at the Oregon Social Learning Center have developed a social learning model for the development of aggression. In this model, family interactions provide a training ground for a child to learn coercive methods of controlling interactions with others. Through analyses of micro-social interactions between parents and children, Patterson outlines the development of a coercive cycle that develops between parent and child and which escalates through aversive conditioning. The cycle starts when a parent makes a demand of a child and a child reacts aversively (e.g., whines, becomes defiant). Rather than pushing the child, the parent withdraws the demand, which reinforces the child's aversive response. During the next phase of the cycle, the parent again makes a demand of the child but decides not to give in to the child's aversive behaviors. As the child becomes more aversive (e.g., temper tantrum), the parent becomes more aversive (e.g., yelling, spanking). As the parent becomes more aversive, the child eventually complies, which reinforces the parent's increase in aversive behavior.

(Continues)

Box 12.1 (Continued)

This cycle repeats itself over and over again, leading to each party reinforcing increasing levels of aversiveness in the other. This training in coercive responses is then carried over by the child into other settings with other people (e.g., teachers, peers). It is evident that the cycle is transactional: that is, both the child and the parent contribute to the escalating cycle. However, for the purpose of the current discussion, it is evident how important the child's family environment, especially parent–child interactions, is to the development of aggression within this theoretical framework.

Eating Disorders: A Family Systems Perspective

Sargent, Liebman, and Silver (1985) describe family characteristics that provide a context in which the psychological features of anorexia nervosa fit and are adaptive.

Families of a person with anorexia have been found to have parents who are overinvolved in their child's life. This overinvolvement prevents the child with anorexia from perceiving her own sensations, including hunger. It also prevents the child from developing a sense of self-competence and the ability to use problem-solving skills. As the anorexia worsens, the family becomes more protective and involved and further inhibits the affected child from acting more maturely and adaptively. Families of a child with anorexia also tend to have difficulty resolving conflict. As a result of unresolved marital conflict, the parents have difficulty collaborating to handle the child's symptoms and actually counteract each other in their attempts. These are just a few of the family dynamics that family system theorists have proposed to explain the development and maintenance of anorexia nervosa in a child. However, it clearly illustrates the primary role of the family context for understanding a child with an eating disorder.

Family History and Differential Diagnoses

Two other facts emerge from research on childhood psychopathology that point to the importance of assessing a child's family context in clinical assessments. First, childhood emotional and behavioral problems tend to be rather amorphous, lacking clear boundaries, more so than is the case in adult psychopathology (see Lilienfeld, 2003). Stated another way, children with problems often have multiple types of problems, and it is often difficult to know what is primary and what might be secondary. Second, there seems to be a parent–child link to many types of psychopathology, with parents and children showing similar patterns of adjustment (McMahon & Dev Peters, 2002). Taking these two facts together, assessment of the adjustment of parents in whom the type of problem may be more clearly defined may provide clues to the primary problem of the child.

An example from research on childhood affective disorders illustrates the use of family history data in making a differential diagnosis. Prior to adolescence, the diagnosis of a bipolar affective disorder is difficult to make. But research suggests that a significant proportion of children with a depressive disorder will develop a bipolar disorder later in life (Geller, Fox, & Fletcher, 1993). Geller et al. found that obtaining a family psychiatric history helped to predict which children with a depressive disorder were at most risk for developing a bipolar disorder. Specifically, the presence of a family history of a bipolar disorder significantly predicted which of the children with depression would later begin to cycle between manic and depressive states. This study also illustrates the important treatment implications for making differential diagnoses. Children who were depressed and had a family history of bipolar disorders were more likely to have manic behaviors develop following treatment with anti-depressant medication than were the depressed children without a family history of bipolar disorder. A case study in which family history information was used in making a differential diagnosis is provided in Box 12.2.

Interpreting Information Provided by the Parent

Many of the assessment techniques discussed throughout this book rely on the report of family members in the assessment of child or adolescent adjustment. As a result, another important reason for assessing a child's family context is that factors within the family can affect the

Box 12.2

Family History and Differential Diagnosis: A Case Study of a 7-Year-Old Girl with Social Phobia

Claire is a 7-year, 2 month-old girl who was in the middle of the first grade when her teacher recommended that she be tested at an outpatient mental health clinic. Her teacher was concerned that she might have Attention Deficit Hyperactivity Disorder. Claire seemed bright and capable of learning and, in fact, performed quite well in one-on-one situations with the teacher or teacher's aide. However, in the general classroom setting, Claire rarely finished her work. She was often noted to be staring off into space and she had to be constantly redirected back to her work. Her teacher emphatically stated that Claire was not a behavior problem. In fact, Claire was quite quiet and reserved and even had difficulty asking for help when it was needed.

There were several differential diagnoses that were considered in the psychological evaluation of Claire. A psychoeducational evaluation that included an intelligence test and an academic screener indicated that Claire was quite capable of learning at or above a level expected for her age. Therefore, her problems in school did not seem to be caused by the presence of an intellectual deficit or a learning disability. However, the differential diagnosis between an attention deficit disorder and an anxiety disorder was more difficult, as she exhibited many behaviors consistent with both types of problems. Several pieces of information helped make the decision that Claire's primary problem was one of anxiety, and particularly, social anxiety.

First, Claire's attentional difficulties tended to be much milder than would be expected for children with attention deficit hyperactivity disorder, as indicated by structured interviews conducted with Claire's mother and teacher and rating scales completed by her mother and teacher. Second, Claire showed a number of other symptoms of anxiety in social situations. For example, she refused to go to Sunday school at church and to other social activities (e.g., parties) and she had one good friend in the neighborhood but would only spend time with her if they were alone. Third, Claire's mother had a history of agoraphobia that had led to several lengthy periods in which she could not leave the house because of her fears.

In this example a family history of anxiety was just one piece of the assessment that helped to make the differential diagnosis. However, it seemed to be an important piece. The diagnosis itself ended up being important because rather than treatment focusing on Claire's attentional problems, a treatment strategy that used systematic desensitization to social situations was implemented, with Claire's teacher reporting dramatic improvements in Claire's school performance by the end of the year.

information provided by family members on the child's adjustment. To appropriately interpret the information obtained from parents and other family members, one must understand those factors that could influence a parent's accuracy in providing information on a child. For example, a noncustodial parent involved in a custody dispute may try to inflate the problems of a child in an effort to get a more favorable court decision. In contrast, the custodial parent may have motivations to present the child in a more positive light. A second example would be parents who are trying to have their child placed in a residential treatment center and who may inflate problems in an effort to justify this placement. These are just two examples of a myriad of familial factors that can affect how one interprets the information provided by family members.

De Los Reyes and Kazdin (2005) provide a review of several family factors that can influence parent ratings of the child including family stress, the parent–child relationship, and the level of marital discord. De Los Reyes and Kazdin (2005) also note several aspects of parental adjustment that can influence how parents rate their children's adjustment. One area that has been the focus of substantial research is on the effects of depression on parents' report of their child's adjustment. There have been numerous studies that have called into question the accuracy of depressed mothers' reports about their children's behavior (see De Los Reyes & Kazdin, 2005 and Richters, 1992 for reviews). This research has suggested that depressed mothers report more problems in their children than are reported by nondepressed parents and teachers and more than are detected using direct behavioral observations of the children. These findings have led many authors to conclude that parents' depression leads to a distorted view of the children's behavior. We summarize Richter's (1992) review and critique of this literature in Box 12.3.

Box 12.3

Research Note: Depressed Mothers as Informants About Their Children: A Critical Review

John Richters (1992) conducted a critical review of the research on the effects of depression on a parent's rating of a child's behavior. Richters cited 17 studies that have been published calling into question the accuracy of depressed mothers' reports. In general, depressed mothers have tended to report more behavior problems in their children than the level reported by teachers, fathers, or children and greater than that observed in behavioral observations. All of these studies led researchers to the conclusion that depressed mothers' perceptions of their children's behavior were biased by their own level of depression. However, Richters's critical review of several methodological and interpretive problems that have plagued this body of research calls into question this depressive bias theory.

The first major problem in these studies was the fact that most of the comparisons between mothers and other informants used measures that were discordant on either the types of behaviors assessed or the situation in which the behaviors were assessed. The best example was the frequent comparison between mothers' and teachers' ratings on a behavior rating scale that had a different item content. In this case, both the behaviors assessed and the situation in which the behaviors were being observed were discordant. As a result, it is unclear whether the differences between mothers and the other raters were due to maternal depression or to differences in the behaviors and/or situations being assessed. Only 27% of the comparisons between depressed mothers and

(Continues)

Box 12.3 (Continued)

other informants used ratings that were both behaviorally and situationally concordant.

The second pervasive problem in this literature is the fact that most of the studies (94%) did not demonstrate that the mothers' overreporting was systematically related to maternal depression. Twenty-four percent of the studies simply documented that depressed mothers reported more behavior problems in their children than did nondepressed mothers. Seventy-one percent indicated that maternal depression predicted variance in mothers' ratings of their children that was not accounted for by criterion ratings provided by other informants. Richters argues that the most direct evidence for the depression distortion hypothesis would be if mother-criterion disagreements were systematically related (correlated) with measures of maternal depression.

The third problem discussed by Richters is that most of the studies (94%) focused only on maternal depression. It is well established that depression is related to other factors within the individual (e.g., other forms of psychopathology) and the environment (e.g., marital satisfaction). Therefore, it is unclear whether or not mothers' disagreements with informants were due to the depression or to other aspects of the mothers' adjustment and/or concomitant stressors in the family environment.

As a result of these problems, Richters suggested that we must be cautious in accepting the depression distortion hypothesis until more refined research is conducted. In fact, Richters cites five studies that used better methodology and found that depressed mothers agreed with other informants as well or even better than nondepressed mothers. However, these are only a few studies, and they are not without flaws themselves. At this point, however, clinical assessors should at least be aware of the issues, many of which are unresolved, in this very important body of research.

SOURCE: Richters, J. E. (1992). Depressed mothers as informants about their children: A critical review of the evidence for distortion. *Psychological Bulletin, 112*, 485–499.

Like parental depression, there is also evidence that parental anxiety may influence a parent's report of childhood problems (Briggs-Gowan, Carter, & Schwab-Stone, 1996). Frick and colleagues (Frick, Silverthorn, & Evans, 1994) found that in a sample of 41 clinic-referred children between the ages of 9 and 13, mothers tended to report more symptoms of anxiety disorders than did the child. This overreporting was systematically related to anxiety in the mother. Specifically, the more anxious the mother, the greater the overreporting of anxiety in the child. These authors also reported that maternal anxiety was not associated with overreporting of other types of maladjustment but seemed to be more specifically related to anxiety. This pattern of results would be consistent with the possibility that anxious mothers project their anxiety symptoms onto their reports of anxiety in their children.

Assessing Family Functioning: General Issues

To this point we have discussed several reasons why assessing the family is an important part of clinical assessments of a child or adolescent. In this section we discuss more specifically *what* areas of family functioning should be assessed and *how* this can be accomplished. However, before discussing specific areas and techniques, two general points deserve mention.

First, many of the behavior rating scales that were reviewed in previous chapters have subscales that assess various aspects of a child's family context. For example, the parent-completed Personality Inventory for Children-2 (PIC-2; Lachar & Gruber, 2001) and the child self-report Personality Inventory for Youth (PIY; Lachar & Gruber,

1994) both include a Family Relations scale. Included in this scale are items assessing marital stability, consistency in discipline, emotional tone of family, community connectedness, and parental adjustment. The MMPI-A contains a supplementary content scale, the Adolescent-Family Problems scale (Archer, 1992), which includes 35 items assessing an adolescent's perceptions of family conflict, level of love and acceptance in the home, family communication, and emotional support provided by the family. The BASC-2 Self-Report Scale (Reynolds & Kamphaus, 2004) contains a Relations with Parents scale that assesses a child's perceptions of being important in the family, the quality of parent–child interactions, and the degree of parental trust and concern. All of these scales provide a time-efficient screening of many important aspects of a child's family environment. The main drawback is that each scale combines many different aspects of a child's family environment, making it impossible to uncover specific areas of strength and/or dysfunction that could be important in understanding a child and in making treatment recommendations.

This criticism leads to our next general comment for assessing a child's family context. What areas to assess and how rigorous the assessment should be within these areas will vary depending on the purpose of the evaluation. In the sections that follow we make the case that several aspects of the family should be routinely assessed: parenting style and parenting practices, parenting stress, marital conflict, and parental adjustment. The depth of the assessment in each area and which additional areas of family functioning should be assessed will vary depending on the individual case. For example, the assessment of a child by a school psychologist to document emotional and behavioral factors that might be impairing academic performance may include only minimal assessment of the child's perception of the family environment and only as it may influence his or her behavior in the classroom. In contrast, an assessment designed to assess a child's adjustment to a recent parental divorce in order to make treatment recommendations on factors that could aid in the child's post-divorce adjustment may include a substantial family component. This assessment will most likely include obtaining extensive information on the level of parental conflict and level of parental cooperation in child-related issues, as these factors are crucial to understanding a child's adjustment to divorce (Amato & Keith, 1991).

Another type of assessment that requires very detailed and somewhat specialized assessment of family functioning is in the case of known or suspected child abuse. A recommended assessment strategy for cases of child abuse is summarized in Box 12.4. These examples illustrate the point that how intensive the assessment of family factors will be and which familial factors will be assessed may vary somewhat from case to case.

General Considerations in Assessing Family Functioning

In the subsequent sections, we review several critical areas of family functioning that we feel are particularly important in the clinical assessments of children and adolescents. In each case, we provide a brief overview of the research supporting the importance of each aspect of family functioning for understanding a child's adjustment. This is followed by a summary of some commonly used measures to assess that domain of functioning. It is important to note that most of the assessment methods that were chosen for review were parent-report or child-report measures of family functioning. This was done for several reasons. First, these methods typically are the most time

Box 12.4

Research Note: A Child Abuse and Neglect Assessment Strategy

Crooks and Wolfe (2007) outline a conceptual model to guide assessments of child abuse and neglect. Their model emphasizes the need to understand, not only the abusive behavior of the parent, but the family context in which the abuse takes place. They note that "the impact of maltreatment depends on not only the severity and chronicity of the abusive events themselves but also how such events interact with the child's individual and family characteristics" (p. 646). As result, an assessment must focus on a myriad of individual, familial, and cultural factors that research has related to child abuse and neglect, as well as the possible protective factors that can reduce the impact of these risk factors.

On the basis of this view of child abuse and neglect, Crooks and Wolfe suggest that most assessments need to be comprehensive and need to address the following general purposes: (1) identify the general strengths and needs of the family system; (2) assess parental responses to the demands of child-rearing; (3) identify the needs of the child; and (4) assess parent–child relationship and abuse dynamics. A summary of the important assessment objectives that follow from these overall goals is provided below. Interested readers are referred to the Crooks and Wolfe chapter in which they provide recommendations for specific techniques to accomplish each of these goals. Many of these techniques are reviewed in other chapters of this text.

Goal 1: Identify General Strengths and Problem Areas of Family System

A. Family Background
1. Parental history of rejection and abuse during own childhood.
2. Discipline experienced by parents during own childhood.
3. Family planning and effect of children on the marital relationship.
4. Parents' preparedness for and sense of competence in child rearing.

B. Marital Relationship
1. Length, stability, and quality of marital relationship.
2. Degree of conflict and physical violence in marital relationship.
3. Support from partner in child rearing.

C. Areas of Perceived Stress and Supports
1. Employment history and satisfaction of parents.
2. Economic stability of family.
3. Social support for parents, both within and outside the family (e.g., number and quality of contacts with extended family, neighbors, social workers, and church members).

D. Parental Physical and Mental Health
1. Recent or chronic health problems
2. Drug and alcohol use
3. Emotional disturbance and social dysfunction

Goal 2: Assess Parental Responses to Child-Rearing Demands

A. Emotional Reactivity of Parent
1. Parents' perception of how abused child differs from siblings and other children.
2. Parents' feelings of anger and loss of control when interacting with child.
3. Typical methods of coping with arousal during stressful episodes.

B. Child-Rearing Methods
1. Appropriateness of parental expectations for child behavior, given child's developmental level.
2. Typical methods used by parents for controlling/disciplining the child.
3. Willingness of parents to learn new methods of discipline.
4. Parents' perception of effectiveness of discipline strategies.
5. Child's response to discipline attempts.

(Continues)

Box 12.4 (Continued)

Goal 3: Identify Needs of the Child

A. Child Social, Emotional and Behavioral Functioning
   1. Behaviors that may place this child at risk for abuse.
   2. Problems in adjustment resulting from abuse and living in family with multiple stressors.

B. Child Cognitive and Adaptive Abilities
   1. Identify child's developmental level and coping capacity to determine most appropriate method and level of intervention.
   2. Determine if abuse or chronic family stressors have led to cognitive delays or delays in the child's development of adaptive behaviors.
   3. Child's attributions for the abuse and reaction to family difficulties.

Goal 4: Assessing Parent–Child Relationship and Abuse Dynamics

A. Risk of parent for future abuse and neglect.
B. The quality of the parent-relationships.
C. Parental empathy toward children's feelings

SOURCE: Crooks, C. V., & Wolfe, D. A. (2004). Child abuse and neglect. In E. J. Mash & R.A. Barkley (Eds.), *Assessment of childhood disorders* (4th ed., pp. 639–684). New York: Guilford Press.

efficient method for collecting information on the child's family. Second, these measures are often standardized and easily obtainable. Third, these rating scales tend to have the best normative data that allow for interpretations of scores based on some comparison group. Thus, these rating scales tend to be the most useful in many clinical assessments.

However, such assessment methods are not without limitations. Morsbach and Prinz (2006) reviewed eight measures that use parent-report of their own parenting behaviors. Their evaluation of these measures suggests that most demonstrated acceptable internal consistency (.70 and above). Further, most measures showed moderate concordance between parent and child ratings of parenting (.23–37) with somewhat higher concordance between reports of the two parents and between parent report and observations of parenting behavior. However, these authors noted that parents are often asked to make estimates of high-frequency behaviors (e.g., yelling) over long periods of time (e.g., 6 months) which may make accurate reports difficult. Further, they noted that many of the questions deal with sensitive issues that may not be socially desirable and may be considered intrusive by parents. As a result, such questions could result in biases in their responses. Finally, these authors also noted that many scales often include vague quantifiers (e.g., frequently, sometimes, never) that may also influence the accuracy of parents' responses.

Thus, although we have chosen to focus largely on ratings scales for the assessment of family functioning for the reasons noted above, it is important to recognize the limitations in the information obtained by this assessment format. As noted by McMahon and Frick (2007), information obtained by these measures should be interpreted with other assessment information, such as interviews and behavioral observations, whenever possible.

Parenting Styles and Practices

There is broad consensus that parenting behaviors exert a significant influence on child development. There is less consensus regarding the specific aspects of parenting that are most crucial to child adjustment. However, Darling and Steinberg (1993) provide a good context for conceptualizing parenting and its effect on child and adolescent adjustment.

Darling and Steinberg (1993) divide parenting into two main components: parenting styles and parenting practices. These authors define parenting styles as "a constellation of attitudes toward the child that are communicated to the child and create an emotional climate in which the parents' behaviors are expressed" (p. 493). These authors use Baumrind's (1971) typology to exemplify parenting style. Baumrind divides parenting styles into three types. The *authoritarian* style is characterized by a rule-adherence orientation that de-emphasizes autonomy and emotional support. The *permissive* style is a child-centered style in which child autonomy is of primary importance and rules and demands are minimal. The *authoritative* style is characterized by emotional support and respect for appropriate autonomy in the child but in the context of clearly defined and consistently enforced rules. It is this last parenting style, Authoritative, that research has consistently linked to healthier child adjustment.

In contrast to parenting style, parenting practices are defined as the techniques used by the parent to socialize their child and enforce rules. For example, a specific discipline practice (e.g., degree of corporal punishment), use of positive parenting strategies (e.g., praise and reward for appropriate behavior), consistency in parenting, and appropriate supervision and monitoring of a child's behavior by a parent are all examples of parenting practices that have been linked to child adjustment (Frick, 1994).

The unique contribution of Darling and Steinberg's model of parenting is not only its explicit distinction between parenting style and parenting behaviors but also its clear specification of how these factors interact to influence child development. Specifically, parenting style provides a context in which parenting behaviors influence a child's development. As a result, the same parenting behavior may have different effects on a child depending on the parenting style. For example, there is a generally accepted association between adolescents' school performance and their parents' involvement in their schooling. However, the effectiveness of parents' school involvement in facilitating academic achievement has been found to be greater among parents who have an authoritative parenting style than among parents who show an authoritarian parenting style (Steinberg, Lamborn, Dornbusch, & Darling, 1992).

The implications of this model of parenting are important for clinical assessments of children and adolescents. It suggests that, to understand the effects of parenting on a child or adolescent's development, one must assess both parenting style and parenting practices. In the following sections, we provide a review of some measures that have been used to assess both parenting style (The Family Environment Scale – Moos & Moos, 1986) and parenting practices (Alabama Parenting Questionnaire – Shelton, Frick, & Wootton, 1996; the Parenting Scale – Arnold, O'Leary, Wolff, & Acker, 1993; Dyadic Parent–Child Interaction Coding System; Eyberg, Nelson, Duke, & Boggs, 2005).

Family Environment Scale-Second Edition (FES)

The FES (Moos & Moos, 1986) is a 90-item true-false questionnaire that is widely used to assess persons' perceptions of their family environment. It is one of the most widely used instruments for assessing family processes (Piotrowski, 1999). It has been used to assess family functioning in a wide variety of cultures (Bao-Yu & Lin-Yan, 2004; Teufel-Shone et al., 2005) and in families of children with a range of adjustment problems including Attention Deficit Hyperactivity Disorder (Pressman et al., 2006), anxiety disorders (Suveg, Zeman, Flannery-Schroeder, & Cassoano, 2005) and affective disorders (Belardinelli et al., 2008).

The FES can be completed by the parent and/or child (over 11 years). There are three forms of the FES. We focus on the Real Form (Form R) of the FES, which measures the respondent's actual perceptions of the family environment. However, there are also two special forms of the FES. The Ideal Form (Form I) allows the respondent to answer items in terms of the type of family he or she would ideally like. The Expectations Form (Form E) allows the respondent to answer items in terms of what he or she expects family environments to be like.

Content

The FES is divided into ten subscales from three domains: Relationships, Personal Growth, and System Maintenance. A description of the ten subscales within these domains is provided in Table 12.1. The item content was primarily developed on the basis of family systems theory. This is evident from the emphasis on family structure and organization and the focus on the transactional patterns between members of

Table 12.1 Subscales of the Family Environment Scale

Dimension	Subscale	Description of Item Content
Relationship	Cohesion	Commitment, help, and support provided by family members
	Expressiveness	Extent to which family members are encouraged to express feelings
	Conflict	Amount of anger, aggression, and conflict among family members
Personal growth	Independence	Extent to which self-sufficiency, assertiveness, and independence are encouraged in the family
	Achievement orientation	Extent to which activities of family members are achievement-oriented and competitive
	Intellectual-cultural orientation	Degree of interest in political, social, and cultural activities
	Active-recreational orientation	Emphasis placed on participation in social and recreational activities
	Moral-religious emphasis	Importance placed on ethical and religious issues
System maintenance	Organization	Importance placed on having a clear family structure and well-defined roles
	Control	Degree to which rules and procedure for family are explicit

Source: Moos & Moos (1986).

the family in the FES item content. Also, as evident from the content, the FES is best thought of as a measure of parenting style or family climate, rather than of specific parenting practices.

Norms

The FES manual reports information on a large normative sample that included 1,125 families from all regions of the country, single-parent and multi-generational families, families drawn from ethnic minority groups, and families of all age groups (Moos & Moos, 1986). It is unclear how representative the sample is on each of these variables. However, the authors note that 294 families from the normative sample were drawn randomly from specified census tracts in the San Francisco area, and the means and standard deviations of FES scales did not differ between this group and the rest of the normative sample.

Although the normative group includes families of all age groups, it is notable that the majority of the normative samples was based on the reports of adults, with much less data available on the reports of children and adolescents. This is important because the authors found small but systematic differences between the scales completed by parents and adolescents (Moos & Moos, 1986). Specifically, adolescents perceived less emphasis on cohesion, expressiveness, independence, and intellectual/religious orientation and more emphasis on conflict and achievement than did their parents.

Reliability and Validity

The ten subscales of the FES generally have been shown to have acceptable levels of reliability in many samples. The manual reports internal consistency estimates in a large community sample (n = 1,067) ranging from α = 61 to α = 78 (Moos & Moos, 1986). Two-month test-retest reliability in a smaller community sample (n = 47) ranged from r = 68 to r = 86. One note of caution for the reliability of the FES is finding that the reliability of the scales may be lower in adolescent samples (Boyd, Gullone, Needleman, & Burt, 1997).

Moos and Moos (1986) provide a good summary of over 100 research articles using the FES, which attests to its correlation with other measures of family functioning, its ability to differentiate distressed from nondistressed families, and its sensitivity to treatment effects. Many more studies have been published since this review (Piotrowski, 1999).

As noted above, the FES has been widely used with several different clinical populations of children and adolescents. For example, using the FES, Suveg et al. (2005) noted that mothers of children with an anxiety disorder showed less emotional expressiveness than non-clinic referred children (ages 8–12). As another example, Pressman et al. (2006) found that families of children and adolescents with Attention Deficit Hyperactivity disorder reported higher rates of family conflict on the FES. Finally, Lucia and Breslau (2006) reported that higher levels of family cohesion, as measured by the FES when children were age 6, were associated with fewer emotional and attentional problems in the children at age 11.

Probably the biggest threat to the validity of the FES is the failure to validate the scale structure through factor analyses. The scales were designed primarily on the basis of content and face validity. Unfortunately, factor analyses have generally isolated anywhere from two (e.g., Fowler, 1982) to six (Sanford, Bingham, & Zucker, 1999) or seven (Robertson & Hyde, 1982) factors on the FES. No study has provided convincing evidence supporting the ten-scale structure that is the basis for most interpretations from the FES.

Alabama Parenting Questionnaire (APQ)

The APQ (Shelton et al., 1996) is a measure of parenting behavior that was developed for use with parents of elementary-school-aged children and adolescents (6 to 17 years old). However, it has been used in samples as young as ages 3 and 4 (Clerkin, Marks, Policaro, & Halperin, 2007; Dadds, Maujean, & Fraser, 2003) with some modification of its content. It consists of 42 items that are presented in both global report (i.e., questionnaire) and telephone interview formats, and there are separate versions of each format for parents and children. Also, Elgar, Waschbusch, Dadds, and Sivaldason (2007) have developed a 9-item short version of the scale for use as a brief screener.

Most of the research using the APQ has used the questionnaire formats. Items on this format are rated on a five-point Likert-type frequency scale and ask the informant how frequently each of the various parenting practices typically occurs in the home. On the telephone interview format, four interviews are conducted with parents and children with at least 3 days between each interview. The informant is asked to report the frequency with which each parenting practice has occurred over the previous 3 days and responses for each item are averaged across the four interviews.

Content

The content of the APQ was developed to assess the five dimensions of parenting that have been most consistently related to behavior problems in youth: Involvement, Positive Parenting, Poor Monitoring/Supervision, Inconsistent Discipline, and Corporal Punishment (Shelton et al., 1996). It also includes several other items assessing "other discipline practices," such as use of time out or taking away privileges. The items on the APQ and its subscales are provided in Table 12.2. The items used on the 9-item short version are also designated in this table (Clerkin et al., 2007). Studies using the APQ often have used scores from the individual scales (e.g., Frick, Christian, & Wootton, 1999) or they have used composites of these scales (e.g., Frick, Kimonis, Dandreaux, & Farrell, 2003). There

Table 12.2 Subscales of the Alabama Parenting Questionnaire

Involvement

1. You have a friendly talk with your child
4. You volunteer to help with special activities that your child is involved in (such as sports, boy/girl scouts, church youth groups)
7. You play games or do other fun things with your child
9. You ask your child about his/her day in school
11. You help your child with his/her homework
14. You ask your child what his/her plans are for the coming day
15. You drive your child to a special activity
20. You talk to your child about his/her friends
23. Your child helps plan family activities
26. You attend PTA meetings, parent/teacher conferences, or other meetings at your child's school

(Continues)

Table 12.2 (Continued)

Positive parenting
2. You let your child know when he/she is doing a good job with something[a]
5. You reward or give something extra to your child for obeying you or behaving well
13. You compliment your child when he/she does something well[a]
16. You praise your child if he/she behaves well[a]
18. You hug or kiss your child when he/she has done something well
27. You tell your child that you like it when he/she helps around the house

Poor monitoring/supervision
6. Your child fails to leave a note or to let you know where he/she is going[a]
10. Your child stays out in the evening past the time he/she is supposed to be home[a]
17. Your child is out with friends you do not know[a]
19. Your child goes out without a set time to be home
21. Your child is out after dark without an adult with him/her
24. You get so busy that you forget where your child is and what he/she is doing
28. You don't check that your child comes home from school when he/she is supposed to
29. You don't tell your child where you are going
30. Your child comes home from school more than an hour past the time you expect him/her
32. Your child is at home without adult supervision

Inconsistent discipline
3. You threaten to punish your child and then do not actually punish him/her[a]
8. Your child talks you out of being punished after he/she has done something wrong[a]
12. You feel that getting your child to obey you is more trouble than it's worth
22. You let your child out of a punishment early (like lift restrictions earlier than you originally said)[a]
25. Your child is not punished when he/she has done something wrong
31. The punishment you give your child depends on your mood

Corporal punishment
33. You spank your child with your hand when he/she has done something wrong
35. You slap your child when he/she has done something wrong
38. You hit your child with a belt, switch, or other object when he/she has done something wrong

Other discipline practices
34. You ignore your child when he/she is misbehaving
36. You take away privileges or money from your child as a punishment
37. You send your child to his/her room as a punishment
39. You yell or scream at your child when he/she has done something wrong
40. You calmly explain to your child why his/her behavior was wrong when he/she misbehaves
41. You use time out (make him/her sit or stand in corner) as a punishment
42. You give your child extra chores as a punishment

[a]Items that are included in the 9-item short screening version of the APQ (Clerkin et al., 2007).

are two common ways of forming composite scores. The first way is to standardize the scores (e.g., create z-scores) and then combine the Involvement and Positive Parenting scales into a Positive Parenting Composite and the Poor Monitoring/Supervision, Inconsistent Discipline, and Corporal Punishment scales into a Negative Parenting Composite. The second method for forming composites from the APQ is to create a single Dysfunctional Parenting composite by standardizing all five scales, inversely scoring the positive parenting scales, and summing all five dimensions.

Norms

One of main limitations in the APQ is the lack of norm-referenced scores that can be used to interpret the scales. However, there are now two studies that provide scores from fairly large samples of non-referred children, from which cut-scores can be developed. The first study was conducted with 1,402 children ages 4 to 9 (Elgar et al., 2007) in Australia and the second study was conducted with 1,219 German school children ages 10 to 12 (Essau, Sasagawa, & Frick, 2006).

Reliability and Validity

As noted previously, most of the published research using the APQ to date has utilized the global report formats of the scale, with the exception of Shelton et al. (1996). Across studies, the reliability and stability of APQ scores have generally been acceptable with several notable exceptions. First, the internal consistency of the short three-item Corporal punishment scale has often been quite low on all formats. Second, the internal consistency of the Poor Monitoring/Supervision scale has been low in the interview format (all alphas below .50 – Shelton et al., 1996). Third, Frick et al. (1999) showed poor reliability of the child-report formats in very young children (below age 9) (see also Shelton et al., 1996).

Several studies have provided factorial support for the five dimensions around which the scale was developed (Elgar et al., 2007; Essau et al., 2006). Also, parent ratings on the APQ are significantly associated with observations of parenting behavior in 4- to 8-year-old boys (Hawes & Dadds, 2006). However, the most common use of the APQ has been to study parenting in families of children with conduct problems. An association between APQ scales and conduct problems has been reported in community (Dadds et al., 2003), clinic-referred (Frick et al., 1999; Hawes & Dadds, 2006), and inpatient samples (Blader, 2004), as well as in families with deaf children (Brubaker & Szakowski, 2000) and families with substance-abusing parents (Stanger, Dumenci, Kamon, & Burstein, 2004). Also, these studies have documented this relationship in samples as young as age 4 (Dadds et al., 2003; Hawes & Dadds, 2006) and as old as age 17 (Frick et al., 1999).

Importantly, Frick et al. (1999) reported some differences in which dimensions of parenting were most strongly associated with conduct problems at different ages, with Inconsistent Discipline being most strongly associated in young children (ages 6–8), Corporal Punishment being most strongly associated in older children (ages 9–12), and Involvement and Poor Monitoring/Supervision being most strongly related in adolescents (ages 13–17).

Although the most common use of the APQ has been to assess parenting in families of youth with conduct problems, it has been used to assess family correlates to anxiety disorders (Pfiffner & McBurnett, 2006) and to assess parenting in families of depressed parents (Cummings, Keller, & Davies, 2005). Finally, several studies have used the APQ scales to test changes in parenting behaviors following treatment (e.g., Feinfield & Baker, 2004; Hawes & Dadds, 2006).

Parenting Scale (PS)

The PS (Arnold et al., 1993) is another commonly used measure of parenting. It is a 30-item parent report scale that focuses specifically on parents' attitudes and beliefs about discipline. The items are all rated on a seven-point scale in which the parent is asked to estimate the probability with which they would use a particular discipline strategy (e.g., when my child misbehaves, I spank, slap, grab, or hit my child). It was originally developed for use with young children (ages 18–48 months; Arnold et al., 1993) and has primarily been used to assess parenting in preschool children. However, there is evidence for its utility in samples of children as old as 11 years of age (Prinzie, Onghena, & Hellinckx, 2007; Steele, Nesbitt-Daly, Daniel, & Forehand, 2005).

Content

The PS items can be grouped into three dimensions: Laxness, Overreactivity, and Verbosity. There has been some debate over the appropriateness of this three scale structure because it has obtained factor analytic support in some studies (i.e., Arney, Rogers, Baghurst, Sawyer, & Prior, 2008; Arnold et al., 1993; Rhoades & O'Leary, 2007) but not in others (Prinzie et al., 2007; Reitman et al., 2001; Steele et al., 2005). The difference in the factor analyses typically involves whether the Verbosity factor emerges as a separate dimension. Also, Rhoades and O'Leary (2007) developed a PS-Should scale that was designed to assess how parents believe they "should discipline their children," rather than assessing their report of actual discipline practices.

Norms

One of main limitations in the PS is the lack of norm-referenced scores that can be used to interpret the scales. However, there are several studies that provide scores from fairly large samples of non-referred children from which cut-scores can be developed. Arney et al. (2008) provided data from 1,656 mothers of children (ages 3–5) from South Australia and Prinzie et al. (2007) provided data from 596 mothers and 559 fathers of children ages 5 to 11 years in Belgium. Finally, Rhoades and O'Leary (2007) provided data on 453 families of children ages 3 to 7 years from the northeast United States.

Reliability and Validity

Most studies of the PS show adequate internal consistency and test-retest reliability for the PS (e.g., Arnold et al., 1993; Rhoades & O'Leary, 2007) with the exception of the Verbosity scale (Arney et al., 2008). Further, the PS has been shown to be correlated with other measures of parenting practices (Rhoades & O'Leary, 2007; Steele et al., 2005) and has been associated with measures of adjustment problems in children (Arney et al., 2008; Prinzie et al., 2007). Scores on the PS have also been shown to be sensitive to effects of interventions designed to improve parenting behaviors (Sanders, Markie-Dadds, Tully, & Bor, 2000).

Dyadic Parent–Child Interaction Coding System (DPICS)

The DPICS (Eyberg et al., 2005) is a highly structured coding system designed to assess maternal behaviors and parent–child interactions in several standard settings. In contrast to the other measures of parenting that have been reviewed, the DPICS is an observational system. It has typically been used to code parent–child interactions of preschool children (e.g., Eisenstadt, Eyberg, McNeil, Newcomb, & Funderbunk, 1993; Robinson & Eyberg, 1981). Parents and children are observed in two 5-min periods, typically in a clinic playroom setting. In the Child Directed Interaction (CDI) the parent is instructed to allow the child to choose any activity and to play along with the child. In the Parent Directed Interaction (PDI) the parent is instructed to select an activity and to keep the child playing according to parental rules.

Content

The 5-min interactions are videotaped for later coding. The DPICS includes a detailed manual for coding several parent and child behaviors. The system codes 12 parent and 14 child behaviors. A summary of these behaviors included in the DPICS is provided in Table 12.3. In addition to discrete behaviors, several additional categories are included in the DPICS to code sequences of behaviors. Parental responses (i.e., ignores or responds) to child's defiant behavior and child responses (i.e., compliances, non-compliances, or no opportunity) to parental commands are coded. The coding system is a continuous frequency count of all behaviors observed during the 5-min interaction periods.

TABLE 12.3 Categories from the Dyadic Parent–Child Interaction Coding System

Maternal behaviors
1. Praise
(a) Labeled praise
(b) Unlabeled praise
2. Command
(a) Direct commands
(b) Indirect commands
3. Other verbalizations
(a) Descriptive/reflective questions
(b) Descriptive/reflective statements
(c) Irrelevant verbalization
(d) Verbal acknowledgment
4. Responses to child behavior
(a) Physical positive
(b) Ignore
(c) Critical statement
(d) Physical negative
Child behaviors
1. Deviant
(a) Whine
(b) Cry
(c) Smart talk
(d) Yell
(e) Destructive
(f) Physical negative
2. Response to commands
(a) Compliance
(b) Noncompliance
(c) No opportunity

SOURCE: Eyberg & Robinson (1983).

Norms

The normative information available on the DPICS is quite limited. Robinson and Eyberg (1983) provide data on 22 families with children between the ages of 2 and 7. The sample was primarily two-parent families (73%) and highly educated (mean of 15.2 years of education for parents). As a result, the generalizability of this information to other samples is questionable.

Reliability and Validity

Not surprisingly, given the very detailed behavioral descriptions provided by the DPICS manual, trained observers have been able to achieve quite high interrater reliability with the DPICS. In a sample of 42 families (20 clinic-referred and 22 normal control) the mean interrater reliability for parent behaviors was .91 and for child behaviors was .92 (Robinson & Eyberg, 1981). In addition, DPICS scores have been shown to differentiate families of clinic-referred children with conduct problems from families of normal control children (Eyberg et al., 2005; Robinson & Eyberg, 1981). Scores from the DPICS have also been shown to be sensitive to interventions for families of children with behavior problems (Eisenstadt et al., 1993; Eyberg & Robinson, 1982; Hembree-Kigin & McNeil, 1995).

Parenting Stress

The second dimension of family functioning that is critical to assess in most clinical assessment of children and adolescents is parental stress. A high level of stress can influence children's adjustment in a number of ways, one of which is by making it more difficult for a parent to use optimal parenting strategies (Whiteside-Mansell et al., 2007). For example, elevated stress can lead to lower levels of parental warmth and higher rates of harsh parenting (Dopke, Lundahl, Dunsterville, & Lovejoy, 2003; Haskett, Ahern, Ward, & Allaire, 2006).

There are two types of measures that can be used in clinical assessment of children and adolescents. The first are measures of general life stress (e.g., life event scales) and the second are measures of stress specific to parenting. Examples of general measures of stress include the Life Experiences Survey (Sarason, Johnson, & Siegel, 1978) and the Family Events List (Patterson, 1982). Such measures of general stress have proven to be important for understanding children with behavior problems (Johnston, 1996; Snyder, 1991) and they have been related to abusive behavior in parents (Whipple & Webster-Stratton, 1991). However, in the sections below, we focus on two measures of stress more specifically related to parenting.

Child Abuse Potential Inventory-Second Edition

The CAPI (Milner, 1986) is a 160-item rating scale completed by a child's parent. As the name implies, the CAPI was originally developed to assess dimensions of parental behavior that have proven to be risk factors for physical abuse of children. However, the CAPI assesses multiple areas of family functioning that are important in many clinical assessments. Further, several of the scales focus directly on stressors related to parenting a child or adolescent. The items require a third-grade reading level to complete and each item is presented in a forced-choice, agree-disagree format. The full form takes approximately 15 min to complete. However, a brief 24-item version of the scale has been developed and has proven to be highly correlated with the full version (Ondersma, Chaffin, Mullins, & LeBreton, 2005).

Content

The CAPI contains three validity scales: Lie, Random Response, and Inconsistency. The Lie scale was designed to detect tendencies to distort responses in a socially desirable manner. Both the Random Response and Inconsistency scales were designed to detect haphazard or random responses to items without regard to item content. To test the usefulness of these validity scales, Milner and Crouch (1997) had two groups of parents, 106 community volunteer parents and 80 parents attending a program for parents at risk for abuse, complete the CAPI in several different ways: answering honestly, answering in a way to make themselves "look good," answering in a way to make themselves "look bad," and answering inconsistently. These differing instructions did affect how parents answered the CAPI questions, suggesting that parents can intentionally distort their ratings. With the exception of detecting the faking-bad condition (58% correct identification), the CAPI validity indexes were good at detecting most of the other response conditions, ranging from 82 to 100% correct identification across both samples of parents.

There are six primary scales of the CAPI that are combined into a composite Abuse scale. The items were developed from an extensive review of the child abuse and neglect literature. The Distress scale assesses parental anger, frustration, impulse control, anxiety, and depression. The Rigidity scale assesses parents' flexibility and realism in their expectations of children's behavior. It includes such items as "A child should never disobey," "A child should always be neat," and "A child should never talk back." The Unhappiness scale assesses a parent's degree of personal fulfillment as an individual, as a parent, as a marital/sex partner, and as a friend. Problems with Child and Self is a scale with items tapping parents' perceptions of their child's behavior and their perceptions of their own self-concept as a parent. The last two scales, Problems with Family and Problems with Others, assess the level of family conflict in the extended family and the level of conflict with persons outside the family or community agencies.

Norms

Normative information is available in the CAPI manual (Milner, 1986) from a sample of 836 parents, child care workers, and parent aides from Florida, California, North Carolina, Hawaii, Oklahoma, Illinois, New York, and West Germany. It is unclear how this normative sample was selected, and the representativeness of this sample in terms of parental education, socio-economic status, and ethnicity is also unclear. This is crucial information because there is evidence that family functioning can vary as a function of these variables (Maccoby & Martin, 1983). As a result, lack of accessible information on the normative sample hinders the ability to make norm-referenced interpretations from the CAPI scales.

Reliability and Validity

The CAPI manual provides evidence that the composite Abuse scale and the Distress and Rigidity scales exhibit acceptable internal consistency and temporal stability. The reliability of the four other individual scales tends to be more inconsistent across samples. In terms of validity, there is evidence that CAPI scores are associated with documented risk factors for child abuse (Budd, Heilman, & Kane, 2000; Grietens, De Haene, & Uyteeborek, 2007; Haskett, Scott, & Fann, 1995). Also there is evidence that the composite Abuse scale can successfully discriminate between proven abusers and control subjects (Milner & Wimberley, 1980), and this extends across cultural groups (Haz & Ramirez, 1998). Finally, the Abuse scale has proven to be sensitive to the effects of intervention with high-risk parents (Wolfe, Edwards, Manion, & Koverola, 1988). Therefore, it appears that the CAPI provides a reliable method of assessing dysfunctional elements of a child's family environment, including several aspects of parental stress that are associated with child abuse. In addition, the composite Abuse scale does seem to be an index of risk for abuse, although it is important to recognize that many parents who score high on the CAPI have no documented evidence of abuse in the home (i.e., false positive) (Haz & Ramirez, 1998).

Parenting Stress Index-Second Edition (PSI)

The PSI (Abidin, 1986) is unique in its focus specifically on stressors related to parenting. It was primarily designed to assess the family context of preschool children between the ages of 1 and 4, although it has been used in older samples of pre-adolescent children. Completion of the PSI requires at least a fifth-grade education. It contains 151 items and generally takes 20–30 min to complete. A short-form of the PSI has been developed with 36 items (Abidin, 1995).

Content

The items of the full PSI are divided into two main categories: Child Domain (47 items) and Parent Domain (54 items). The Child Domain consists of items that assess qualities of a child that make it difficult for parents to fulfill their parental role. The Parent Domain assesses sources of stress and disability related to parental functioning. Table 12.4 provides a summary of the scales that constitute the Child and Parent domains. The PSI also allows for the computation of a composite score that provides an overall indicator of the amount of stress in the parent–child system.

TABLE 12.4 Item Content of the Parenting Stress Index-Second Edition

Scale	Items	Characteristics of High Scorers
Child domain	47	Child displays qualities that make it difficult for the parent to fulfill parenting roles
Adaptability	11	Child shows inability to change from one task to another without emotional upset, avoids strangers, is overreactive to changes in routine and difficult to calm
Acceptability	7	Child is not as attractive, intelligent, or pleasant as the parent had hoped or expected
Demandingness	9	Child is very demanding of parents' time and energy, with patterns such as frequent crying, frequent requests for help, and frequent minor problem behaviors
Mood	5	Child is frequently unhappy, sad, and crying
Distractibility/ Hyperactivity	9	Child displays overactivity, restlessness, distractibility, and short attention span, fails to finish things, and shifts from one activity to another
Reinforces parent	6	Interactions between child and parent fail to produce good feelings in the parent; associated with parental feelings of rejection and poor self-concept as parent
Parent domain	54	Indicates significant stress on the parent–child system that is related to dimensions of parental functioning
Depression	9	Parent reports significant feelings of depression and guilt. High scores may prevent parent from mobilizing sufficient levels of psychic and physical energy to fulfill parenting responsibilities
Attachment	7	Parent does not feel emotional closeness to child and parent perceives an inability to accurately read and understand child's feelings and needs
Restriction of role	7	Parents feel that parental role restricts their freedom and impairs their attempts to maintain own identity
Sense of competence	13	Parents do not feel that they can adequately fulfill their parental roles either because of a lack of knowledge of child development or a limited range of child-management skills
Social isolation	6	Parents perceive themselves as socially isolated from their peers, relatives, and other social support systems
Relationship with spouse	7	Parents perceive that they do not receive emotional and physical support from their spouse in area of child management
Parent health	5	Parents report a deterioration in physical health that is impacting their ability to fulfill parental responsibilities

SOURCE: Abidin (1986).

The 36-item short form of the scale has been tested and items form two relatively distinct factors of parental distress and dysfunctional parent child interactions (Haskett et al., 2006). Importantly, the correlation between the total scores on the short and long form is generally quite high (e.g., $r = 87$; Abidin, 1995).

Norms

The normative sample for the PSI consisted of 534 parents of children referred to a small group of pediatric clinics in Virginia; the median age of the children was 9 months (SD = 23.2 months). The representativeness of the normative sample is one of the major weaknesses of the scale. The sample consisted of primarily White (92%), highly educated (1/3 with college degrees) parents from central Virginia. Thus, the use of norm-referenced scores for families that do not match these characteristics is questionable.

Reliability and Validity

The manual of the PSI provides convincing evidence for the internal consistency and temporal stability of the three composite scores: Total Stress, Parent Domain, and Child Domain. The reliability coefficients for the individual scales, however, are much more variable and typically exhibit relatively low reliability estimates. The manual provides one of the best summaries of the extensive use of the PSI in research on the family context of preschoolers (see also Abidin, Flens, & Austin, 2006 for an updated review). In general, the PSI scales have been correlated with other measures of family functioning (Pinderhughes, Dodge, Bates, Petit, & Zelli, 2000), including correlations with observations of parenting behavior (Bigras, LaFreniere, & Dumas, 1996). Also, the PSI has differentiated families who are experiencing major stressors from nonstressed families (Holden & Banez, 1996; Whiteside-Mansell et al., 2007) and has proven sensitive to treatment effects (Nixon, Sweeney, Erickson, & Touyz, 2003).

Also, factor analyses generally support the broad Parent and Child Domains for grouping the various PSI subscales, although some studies have provided support for a third Parent–Child Interaction Domain, which includes the subscales of Child Acceptability, Child Reinforces Parent, and Parent Attachment to Child (Hutcheson & Black, 1996; Solis & Abidin, 1991). Further, Bigras et al. (1996) reported that, in a sample of 218 mothers of preschoolers, the Parent and Child Domains predicted parental, familial, and child outcomes different from those obtained from other sources. Specifically, the Parent Domain was more strongly and independently associated with measures of marital adjustment and maternal depression, whereas the Child Domain was more strongly and independently associated with child difficulties reported by the mother and children's problems observed during parent–child interactions. These results are important in suggesting that the two domains are valid in assessing somewhat independent dimensions of family functioning.

Marital Conflict

There is a long history of research showing a link between divorce and child behavior problems. The most comprehensive summary of this research comes from Amato and Keith (1991). These authors conducted a meta-analysis of 92 published studies of the impact of divorce on a child's psychological well-being. The combined samples from the 92 studies involved over 13,000 children. This meta-analysis revealed that divorce consistently had a negative impact on several types of child well-being (e.g., conduct problems, school achievement, social adjustment, and self-concept). These studies suggested that the relationship between divorce and psychological difficulties in children was greatest within the 2 years immediately following a divorce.

The meta-analysis also provided intriguing data in support of the theory that it is the conflict that occurs between parents before and during the separation that has the most detrimental impact on a child's adjustment (see also Emery, 1982). Whereas children of divorced families tended to have poorer adjustment than children in low-conflict, intact families, children in *intact, high-conflict* homes tended to have the poorest adjustment of all three groups. Also consistent with this perspective, several studies found that less conflict and better divorce cooperation between parents predicted better post-divorce adjustment for children.

The implications of these findings are important to clinical assessments of children and adolescents. They suggest that it is not simply enough to determine the marital status of a child's parents for understanding the potential impact of the parents' marital relationship on the child. A more important focus of assessment is the overt conflict between parents that is witnessed by the child.

There are several marital inventories that are frequently used in research and clinical practice, and often included in the clinical assessment of children and adolescents (McMahon & Frick, 2007). The Marital Adjustment Test (MAT; Locke & Wallace, 1959) and the Dyadic Adjustment Scale (DAS; Spanier, 1976) are two self-report instruments that have been shown to produce reliable scores and differentiate persons in distressed and nondistressed marriages. However, these inventories tend to focus on general marital satisfaction rather than on overt conflict per se. The O'Leary-Porter Scale (OPS; Porter & O'Leary, 1980) is a brief rating scale that focuses on overt marital conflict and, even more specifically, on marital conflict that is witnessed by the child or adolescent. As a result, the OPS is uniquely suited for use in clinical assessments of children and adolescents.

O'Leary-Porter Scale (OPS)

The OPS (Porter & O'Leary, 1980) was developed specifically for studying the association between marital adjustment and child behavior problems. The OPS is a 20-item self-report inventory within which are embedded nine items that assess the degree of marital conflict witnessed by the child. A parent rates on a five-point frequency scale (Never to Very Often) how often the child witnesses arguments between himself or herself and the spouse over money, discipline, wife's role in family, and personal habits of the spouse. Two questions also ask for overall estimates of the amount of verbal and physical hostility between spouses that is witnessed by the child.

There is little normative data on the OPS. However, 2-week test-retest reliability in a sample of 14 families was found to be quite high (r = 92) (Porter & O'Leary, 1980). These authors also reported that the OPS was correlated with several types of maladjustment in children. Highlighting the importance of focusing specifically on overt conflict, these authors found that the OPS was more consistently associated with child adjustment difficulties than was a measure of general marital satisfaction (i.e., the MAT). This association between scores on the OPS has been replicated in other studies (Forehand, Long, & Hedrick, 1987; Mann & MacKenzie, 1996). Thus, it appears that the OPS captures the critical component of marital discord in terms of its detrimental effect on child adjustment.

Parental Adjustment

In the introduction to this chapter, we discussed several ways in which assessing parental psychiatric adjustment is critical to the clinical assessment of children. We discussed two areas of research, one on parental depression and another on parental anxiety, that suggest that information obtained from a parent must be interpreted in light of the parent's level of emotional distress. We also discussed the importance of obtaining a family psychiatric history for making differential diagnoses and treatment recommendations. In this section, we provide a brief overview of basic research showing the link between parent and child adjustment difficulties that can aid the clinical assessor in structuring assessments and making appropriate interpretations from the assessment information.

Parental Depression

One type of parental adjustment that has a well-documented link to child development is parental depression. Studies have found that between 40% (Orvaschel, Walsh-Allis, & Ye, 1988) and 74% (Hammen et al., 1987) of the children of depressed parents exhibit significant adjustment problems. Depression in parents places children at risk for a number of problems spanning academic, social, emotional, and behavioral domains (Downey & Coyne, 1990). Therefore, it seems that parental depression is a *nonspecific* risk factor for problems in children. That is, it is not specifically related to the development of a single type of child behavior problem.

There are two possible exceptions to this non-specific relationship, both related to subtypes within affective disorders. First, Weissman, Warner, Wickramaratne, & Prusoff (1988) found some preliminary evidence that *early-onset* recurrent depression (depression that has its initial onset before adulthood) might have a more specific link with childhood depression. Second, family histories of bipolar disorders in parents predict a risk for subsequent bipolar disorder in adolescents with a childhood-onset of depressive symptoms (Geller et al., 1993).

Goodman and Gotlib (1999) reviewed the literature on the risk for problems in adjustment in children of depressed mothers. They outline four possible mechanisms to explain this risk: (a) an inherited predisposition transmitted from parent to child; (b) failure of the child to develop appropriate emotional regulation strategies; (c) exposure to negative maternal moods, thoughts, and behaviors; and (d) exposure to a high rate of stressors associated with mother's depression (e.g., higher rates of marital conflict). These links clearly illustrate the need to assess parental depression to understand several potential causal factors that could help to explain a child's or adolescent's problems in adjustment.

Parental Substance Abuse

A comprehensive review of the literature found that, like parental depression, parental alcoholism is associated with a number of child adjustment problems. West and Prinz (1987) reported studies finding an association between parental alcohol abuse and the following problems in their children: hyperactivity, conduct problems, delinquency, substance abuse, intellectual impairment, somatic problems, anxiety, depression, and social deficits. Like depression, some of the lack of specificity in its effect on child adjustment may be due to a failure to define subgroups within parents who abuse substances (Frick, 1993). Alternatively, West and Prinz reviewed several studies suggesting that the effects of having a substance-abusing parent on a child's adjustment may be mediated through the impact on the home environment and the impact on parent and child interactions. Consistent with this view, parental substance use has been linked to a host of problematic parent practices, including higher rates of abuse (Ondersma, 2007; Walsh, MacMillan, & Jamieson, 2003).

Parental Antisocial Behavior

The intergenerational link to antisocial behavior is a consistent finding in research and one that has long intrigued social scientists and policy-makers alike (see Frick & Loney, 2002, for a review). Early studies tended to focus on the intergenerational link to criminality. This research found that the link was independent of socioeconomic status, neighborhood, and intelligence (Glueck & Glueck, 1968). More recent studies have focused on psychiatric definitions of antisocial disorders. As in studies of criminality, children diagnosed with antisocial disorders are significantly more likely to have parents with antisocial disorders than are children without conduct problems (Frick et al., 1992; Monuteaux, Faraone, Gross, & Biederman, 2007).

An important methodological point in the more recent family history studies was the fact that each used clinic control groups and found that histories of antisocial disorders in parents were specific to conduct problems in children. That is, children with conduct problems not only had higher rates of parental antisocial disorder (APD) than normal controls, but they also had higher rates of parental APD than clinic-referred children with other problems in adjustment (Frick et al., 1992). Therefore, unlike parental depression and substance abuse, parent antisocial behavior appears to have a more specific relationship to a particular child problem (i.e., conduct problems).

Frick and Loney (2002) reviewed data supporting several potential mechanisms to explain this link including an inherited disposition passed from parent to child, parental modeling of antisocial behaviors, and disruptions in the family caused by the parent's antisocial behavior. In support of at least some inherited predisposition, Tapscott, Frick, Wootton, and Kruh (1996) showed that a paternal history of antisocial personality disorder was associated with a higher rate of Conduct Disorder in their biological offspring, even if the father had no contact with the child since the first year of life.

Parental ADHD

There is evidence that parents and other biological relatives of children with ADHD show more attentional problems (Albert-Corush, Firestone, & Goodman, 1986) and a higher rate of ADHD (Faraone, Biederman, Keenan, & Tsuang, 1991). However, these studies may have underestimated the link between parent and child ADHD by studying the parents' *current* adjustment. Given that 30–50% of children with ADHD may not be diagnosed with this disorder as adults (Barkley, Fischer, Smallish, & Fletcher, 2002), it may be that many of the parents of ADHD children exhibited ADHD as a child but are not currently showing symptoms.

To test this possibility, Frick et al. (1991) studied the childhood histories of parents of clinic-referred children. A child's biological parent reported on whether or not he or she had problems associated with ADHD before the age of 18 and then completed a similar family history questionnaire for all first-degree relatives. Children with ADHD were more likely to have mothers, fathers, and other biological relatives who also exhibited ADHD as children than were other clinic-referred children. In fact, approximately 75% of the 103 children with ADHD had one biological relative with a significant history of ADHD (27% of mothers and 44% of fathers) and 46% had two biological relatives with a significant history of ADHD. This study suggests that an assessment of parents' childhood histories of behavior problems could aid in the assessment of ADHD in children.

Parental Anxiety

Another type of problem that appears to have a familial link is anxiety. Last, Hersen, Kazdin, Francis, and Grubb (1987) reported that in their sample of children with an anxiety disorder (n = 58), 83% of the children had a mother with a lifetime history of anxiety disorders. Furthermore, 57% had a mother experiencing significant levels of anxiety concurrently with the child. Both of these proportions were significantly greater than what was found in parents of clinically referred children without anxiety disorders.

Importantly, Frick et al. (1994) found similar results but also found that the link between mother and child anxiety could not solely be attributed to anxious mothers *reporting* more anxiety in their children. All of the children in the Frick et al. study who self-reported an anxiety disorder had a mother with a history of an anxiety disorder. Further, there are a number of studies suggesting that parental anxiety can influence the attachment between the parent and child (Costa & Weems, 2005) and can lead to parenting behaviors (e.g., overprotectiveness, failure to encourage independence) (Dadds, Barrett, Rapee, & Ryan, 1996) that can place a child at risk for anxiety and other problems in adjustment. Thus, it is clear from these findings that parental anxiety is an important area to be assessed in clinical assessments of anxious children.

Parental Schizophrenia

Another type of maladjustment with a clear familial link is schizophrenia. Children of one schizophrenic parent appear to have a 10 to 15% likelihood of developing schizophrenia; the children of two schizophrenic parents have about a 25 to 46% risk (Gottesman, McGuffin, & Farmer, 1987). These rates of disorder in offsprings of schizophrenic parents are striking given that the prevalence of schizophrenia in the general population is between 1 and 10 per 1,000 individuals (Helzer & Pryzbeck, 1988). However, parents who have another relative with schizophrenia are often quite concerned over the risk for their children, on the basis of the evidence for a familial transmission. Therefore, it is often important for clinical assessors to also view these risks from the point of view that the vast majority of children with a schizophrenic relative, even if that relative is a parent, do not develop schizophrenia.

Assessment of Family History

From this very brief overview of the familial link to childhood disorders it is evident that obtaining a family history is a critical component of most clinical assessments of children and adolescents. However, like all aspects of the assessment process, what areas to be assessed and the depth at which they will be assessed depend on the individual case. In some cases a screening for psychiatric disorders in a child's relatives can be conducted as part of an unstructured interview followed by a more in-depth family history assessment only if this is judged to be warranted from the initial screening. In other cases a more detailed and structured assessment may be needed from the outset.

It is beyond the scope of this book to cover assessment of adult psychopathology in great detail. However, it is important to note that one can assess a wide range of problems in parents or other relatives through omnibus rating scales or structured interviews. For example, the NEO-Personality Inventory (NEO-PI; Costa & McCrae, 1985) and the Minnesota

Multiphasic Personality Inventory-Second Edition (MMPI-2; Hathaway & McKinley, 1989) are two widely used and readily available objective personality inventories that cover a number of areas of psychological functioning. There are also numerous structured diagnostic interviews that are available, like the NIMH Diagnostic Interview Schedule-Third Edition (DIS-IIIA: Helzer & Robins, 1988) and the Structured Interview for DSM-IV (SCID; First, Spitzer, Gibbon, & Williams, 1995).

When considering what type of assessment may be needed, it is important to note that structured interviews tend to focus on more severe pathology, assessing for diagnosable disorders, than the objective personality inventories do. In addition, the structured interviews tend to be more amenable to the family history method of assessment, in which a family member reports on him- or herself and other relatives who cannot be assessed directly.

There may be some assessments when a more focused family history is deemed appropriate, such as when one wants to focus on some specific domain of parental adjustment. For example, the Beck Depression Inventory (BDI; Beck, Steer, & Garbin, 1988) and the State-Trait Anxiety Inventory (Spielberger, Gorsuch, & Lushene, 1970) are brief screening measures for depression and anxiety, respectively that are often used to assess parental adjustment in clinic-referred children. These are just a few of a host of domain-specific rating scales that can be used to assess a specific area of adjustment in a child's parent or other relatives (see McMahon & Frick, 2007 for others).

Conclusions

In this chapter we discussed several reasons why the assessment of the family environment is critical to most clinical assessments of children and adolescents. Family factors often play a critical causal role in child maladjustment and familial factors can aid in making differential diagnoses and treatment recommendations, two important goals of many clinical assessments. Further, factors within the family are often important for interpreting information provided by members of the family on a child's or adolescent's adjustment.

There are a large number of dimensions of family functioning that can influence child adjustment. We focused on four dimensions that we think are especially important to assess in most clinical assessments of children and adolescents: parenting styles and practices, parenting stress, marital conflict, and parental adjustment. For each of these dimensions, we reviewed the research linking them to child adjustment and then provided several methods for assessing them in clinical assessments.

Chapter Summary

1. There is no context more important to understanding a child's emotional and behavioral functioning than understanding the child's family context. This is because of the following factors:
   (a) Familial influences often play major causal roles in a child's or adolescent's psychological difficulties.
   (b) A family psychiatric history can be instrumental in making differential diagnoses.
   (c) Understanding a child's or adolescent's family context can help to interpret information provided by members of the family.
   (d) Understanding a child's family context can help to determine the most important targets for intervention.
2. Many behavior rating scales reviewed in previous chapters, such as the PIC-2, the PIY, the MMPI-A, and the BASC-

2-SRP, have scales that assess various aspects of a child's family context.

3. Research suggests that two critical dimensions of family functioning related to child adjustment are parenting style, which is the emotional climate provided by the parents, and parenting practices, which are techniques used by parents to socialize their children and enforce rules.
4. The Family Environment Scale-Second Edition (FES) is a commonly used measure of parenting style and the emotional climate of the family. The FES is divided into subscales from three domains: Relationships, Personal Growth, and Systems Maintenance.
5. The Alabama Parenting Questionnaire (APQ) and the Parenting Scale (PS) are measures that focus more specifically on parenting behaviors, such as parents' discipline strategies.
6. The Dyadic Parent Child Interaction Coding System (DPICS) is an observational coding system designed to assess parent and child behaviors in two standardized parent–child interaction tasks.
7. The amount of stress experienced by parents is also important to child adjustment. Scales can assess general stressors or stressors specific to parenting.
8. The Child Abuse Potential Inventory-Second Edition (CAPI) was developed to assess parents' risk for abusing their children and includes several scales related to family stress.
9. The Parenting Stress Index-Second Edition (PSI) focuses specifically on stressors related to parenting.
10. The level of marital discord and overt marital conflict in the home has proven to be important in understanding children's functioning.
11. Assessing parental adjustment can provide critical information in clinical assessments, especially family histories of depression, anxiety, antisocial behavior, attention deficit disorder, substance abuse, and schizophrenia.

Chapter 13

History Taking

Chapter Questions

- What are the unique contributions of historical information to the child assessment process?
- What are the typical domains, variables, or behaviors, assessed by such strategies?
- What structured and unstructured history taking methods are available?
- How should clinicians go about collecting comprehensive historical information efficiently?

The Role of History Taking in Child Assessment

History taking, often through a clinical interview is central to the purpose of child assessment. Indeed, it is perhaps the essential component of child psychological assessment, as a good history enables the clinician to conceptualize a case by providing information about the developmental course of the child's difficulties, the specific presentation of the individual child's difficulties, risk and protective factors, and the important contextual influences on the child's functioning. Such factors are not routinely assessed by rating scales, self-report inventories, or other widely used measures. Indeed, it is impossible to conceive of a competent assessment that would not include history taking in some form.

Although it is at least as crucial as other types of information for child assessment, historical information is often underutilized by clinical assessors. This oversight is especially regrettable given the widespread availability of history-taking measures or guides and the ease with which they can be used. It appears that history taking is simply not as well entrenched in child behavioral

P.J. Frick et al., *Clinical Assessment of Child and Adolescent Personality and Behavior*,
DOI 10.1007/978-1-4419-0641-0_13, © Springer Science+Business Media, LLC 2010

assessment, as it is in medical assessment, where history taking (interviewing) is central to making initial diagnostic decisions. Instead, many clinicians may focus on the current presentation of symptoms or problems, as well as behavioral observations (which is important information), to the exclusion of gathering information about the child's developmental history.

On the other hand, clinicians may center an entire assessment around history taking through an unstructured clinical interview which is necessarily idiosyncratic by child and clinician. Such approaches to assessment fail to gather specific information on the symptomatology and the child's functioning relative to developmental norms through norm-referenced assessment.

Therefore, as with every other method discussed in this text, history taking should be considered part, but not all, of a comprehensive assessment. In short, we consider history taking necessary but not sufficient. There are numerous reasons for taking histories as part of any child assessment. A few of the variables that are uniquely assessed by history taking include age of onset, course/prognosis, etiology, previous treatment history, and other relevant background information.

Age of Onset

Most rating scales and self-report inventories do not directly assess the age of onset of problems. Age of onset is particularly important in child assessment as it affects diagnosis directly. In the case of mental retardation, for example, age of onset must occur during the developmental period (i.e., prior to age 18). Furthermore, the age of onset is crucial for the diagnosis of ADHD, autistic disorder, learning disabilities, and many other childhood disorders (APA, 2000).

Most psychologists have seen cases of suspected mental retardation with a reported age of onset in the early 20s. Similarly, children are often referred for ADHD with an age of onset after age 7. Sometimes, however, the age of onset is unclear or disputed, and the typically less structured format of history taking is ideal for clarifying the onset issue for a particular child.

As one example, a mother may bring in a college freshman because he is suddenly having problems in school. On a rating scale or other more structured assessment format, the clinician may be tempted to accept this current time as the age of onset. In the less structured history-taking interview, one can pursue the issue of onset more thoroughly by asking the mother if her son had ever received special education services, had a history of difficulty concentrating or finishing tasks, had been prescribed medication for attention problems, or had received tutoring in an early grade. The clinician may also ask if there were any teacher complaints in early elementary school concerning attention problems.

It is not unusual for a clinician to find a much earlier age of onset than that initially stated by a child, teacher, parent, or other informant. If, in this sample case, the college student did experience some difficulties in the first grade that were associated with inattention and hyperactivity, and he also struggled to pass both the ninth and twelfth grades, then the clinician may investigate more carefully the diagnosis of ADHD with its associated early age of onset. A more extended case study is provided in Box 13.1.

Course/Prognosis

The *course* of a child's difficulties refers to the assessment of the developmental trajectory of symptomatology. Differences in the stability of symptoms can have substantial implications for differential diagnosis. For example, if a parent describes a child as having had severe hyperactivity in first grade that was not apparent in second

Box 13.1

Case Example of the Use of History Taking

James is a 15-year-old male who was referred by his father for suspected ADHD. The referral for evaluation was also supported by his high school teachers.

According to James's father, his school difficulties became pronounced about 3 years ago. He rarely does homework and is described by his teachers as exhibiting hyperactivity, impulsivity, and inattention. He is also described as the class clown by his teachers. A recent classroom observation found that James was grossly inattentive in comparison to the other children. He, for example, was the only one who briefly rolled around on the floor in the rear of the room during part of a teacher's lecture. Previously, norm-referenced behavior ratings by four of his teachers identified him as highly hyperactive and inattentive.

Being mindful of the late onset of James' symptoms, the clinician asked James's father for more detail about the onset of his problems. His father could not identify significant symptomatology prior to age 12. It was also discovered that James's parents went through a contentious divorce concurrently with the onset of symptoms. It was further disclosed that James recently has threatened to attempt suicide on several occasions. An interview with James subsequently revealed significant evidence of depression with suicidal ideation.

In this case, history taking, by clarifying the age of onset, made a significant contribution to the conceptualization of James's difficulties and intervention design. Failure to use history taking to rule out ADHD in this case could have been disastrous, as poor history taking could have resulted in perhaps no assessment of suicidality and in a failure to treat his depression.

grade but then emerged again in the fourth grade, the diagnosis of ADHD may be called into question. Such a pattern would signal that contextual variables or other difficulties might be related to the emergence of symptoms. Similarly, if a child displays symptoms of autism that seem to spontaneously remit and reappear, then the diagnosis of autism becomes questionable. Furthermore, a previous history of episodes of depression place an individual at significantly greater risk for future such episodes (Klein, Dougherty, & Olino, 2005). Thus, history taking is critical for understanding an individual's risk for depression and to plan for the most appropriate interventions.

Evaluation of course also provides evidence of the effectiveness of previous intervention strategies. A child's, or family's, failure to respond to previous interventions suggests that different and/or more intensive interventions may be warranted. The trajectory of behavioral excesses or deficits is uniquely accessed via history taking. Subtleties of this nature are difficult to assess even with many of the structured diagnostic interviews. However, clinicians who are aware of the influence of course on case conceptualization, treatment planning, and prognosis are more likely to be adept at gathering and integrating such information into their assessments.

Etiology

Etiology refers to the likely presumed cause of a child's difficulties. The assessment of etiology is crucial in that it has important implications for treatment. The discovery that a child's learning difficulties in mathematics did not begin until the ninth grade may very well rule out a learning disability, depending on other aspects of the client's history. If the clinician then discovers that the child was for the first time placed in the advanced section of a mathematics class, then curriculum placement becomes a potential etiological agent. A simple change in classes may be an effective intervention for this suspected mathematics learning disability. Such a parsimonious intervention may not have been tried, however, without important historical information that led the clinician to a potential etiology.

Knowledge of etiology, in general, is of potential importance for at least four reasons (AAMR, 1992).

1. The etiology may be associated with other problems (e.g., Down Syndrome) that may impair other aspects of functioning - physical, social, etc.
2. The etiology may be amenable to treatment/intervention.
3. Knowledge of etiology may lead to the design of prevention programs for certain etiologies.
4. Etiologies may be useful for forming homogeneous groups for research or treatment.

It is apparent that part of this assessment should include a history of other symptomatology to assess for comorbidity, as well as issues that could have actually precipitated current difficulties (e.g., a history of depression that now manifests partly as difficulty concentrating).

In addition, attempting to determine etiology for a specific client helps clarify both case conceptualization to answer the referral question and the recommended interventions targeting the presumed etiologies. After all, these activities are the primary purpose of child assessment, and history taking is valuable to these ends.

Unfortunately, for most childhood problems the range of potential single and multiple etiologies is often extensive. The potential etiologies associated with depression, for instance, are multitudinous. A non-exhaustive list of these factors is shown in Table 13.1. Moreover, multiple etiologies may be interacting to produce symptoms of a problem such as depression. It would not be unusual, for example, for a depressed child to be affected by parental depression, poverty, and the death of a friend, all of which may require simultaneous and/or coordinated intervention.

Commonly used history-taking forms may not fully address the various etiologies associated with a problem or set of problems. Clinicians often have to use their knowledge of child development, psychopathology, and other areas of psychological research to go beyond the standard questions included on a history form (i.e., branching) to rule out important high-frequency etiologies.

This process of branching from a history form is difficult for even the most savvy clinician. For the majority of examiners, the most realistic option will be to assess history over the course of two or more assessment sessions. A second session could be as simple as a telephone call that allows the clinician to rule out an etiology that has been hypothesized based on previous history, assessment data, or other information. As Green (1992) notes: "Time between sessions is often an important diagnostic and therapeutic ally" (p. 460), and taking such time would allow the clinician to be more accurate in his/her case conceptualization. However, it is acknowledged that many practitioners are working in settings or under circumstances in which assessments are expected to be completed very quickly. Therefore, it is important that the clinician be highly knowledgeable about etiology at the outset of the assessment, approach the history taking interview accordingly, and still take the necessary time to not hastily attempt to answer a referral question.

TABLE 13.1 Selected Etiologies of Depression

Medical disorders associated with depression

Autoimmune disorders: systemic lupus, rheumatoid disease, sarcoidosis

Cancers: head, pancreas, gastrointestinal, lung, renal

Central nervous system diseases: Parkinson's disease, degenerative dementias, normal-pressure hydrocephalus, subarachnoid hemorrhages. Huntington's disease, reversible dementias, focal lesions (nondominant), stroke, head trauma

Endocrinopathies/metabolic disorders: hypothyroidism, Addison's disease, Cushing's disease, pituitary tremors, diabetes, hyperparathyroidism, porphyria

Intoxications: lead, mercury, thallium

Occult infections: genitourinary tract, liver

Viral infections: influenza, viral pneumonia, mononucleosis, hepatitis

Drugs associated with major depression or dysthymia

Anticancer: vincristine, vinglastine

Antihypertensives: reserpine, methyldopa, propanolol, guanethidine, hydralazine, clonidine

Anti-infectives: cycloserine

Anti-Parkinson agents: levodopa, arnantadine, carbidopa

Corticosteroids

Hormones: estrogens, progesterone

Psychotropics

Other psychiatric disorders that may confound the diagnosis of depression

Anxiety disorders: panic disorders, phobic disorders

Obsessive-Compulsive Disorder

Sleep disorders: narcolepsy, sleep apnea

Psychotic disorders

Eating Disorders: Anorexia Nervosa, bulimia

Vague somatic complaints

Dementia

Sexual dysfunctions

Family Psychiatric History

As noted in the previous chapter, a specific etiological agent of increasing importance is familial psychiatric history. Research has underscored the importance of family psychiatric history as a risk factor for similar problems in offspring and as a variable that may contraindicate some treatment options (see Klein et al., 2005). School screening is an example of the application of family psychiatric history taking. Prekindergarten screening programs often ask questions about child behavior, and the inclusion of family history information may trigger prevention or intervention efforts. If, for example, a father reports a history of separation anxiety as a young child, then follow-up could be planned to monitor this father's offspring upon entry into kindergarten. While some minor separation anxiety symptoms are common at this age, if a child with family resemblance for such problems displays some difficulties, then earlier and more aggressive intervention may be warranted. The importance of family history is illustrated in the case study provided in Box 13.2.

Box 13.2

A Case Study Illustrating the Importance of Family History

Bradford is a 10-year-old male who was referred for school difficulties. He has reportedly always had school problems, but they have worsened in the fifth grade. His teachers complain that he is unmotivated, moody, irritable, and oppositional.

His father stated that he has had difficulty getting Bradford to complete homework. These homework sessions usually turn into power struggles, and Bradford ends up crying. He also reportedly seems unusually emotional in comparison to his younger brother. According to his mother, he angers quickly and cries easily.

Bradford's developmental history is unremarkable, with the exception of the continuing problems with work completion. Recently, however, he has had problems interacting with his peers. He cannot identify a best friend, and he is less frequently invited over to other children's homes, according to his mother.

Assessment results did not reveal any problems of note. His intelligence and academic achievement scores ranged from average to above average, with his scores in math in the Low Average range. From his teachers' report, it appears that Bradford's difficulty with completing work has contributed to his falling behind somewhat in math.

Parent and teacher rating scales did not produce any significant T-scores. His self-report scores on internalizing scales such as anxiety and depression were slightly elevated (in the 60s).

Bradford's developmental history and test results make his case conceptualization difficult. The results suggest that he has internalizing problems, but he does not display symptomatology that approaches the severity necessary to meet diagnostic criteria for depression, dysthymia, or anxiety disorders. The clinician began to question the parents' reason for the referral. In particular, it was difficult to discern why the parents were so concerned about what appears to be a circumscribed problem with homework completion and achievement motivation. The clinician discovered the real reason for the parents' referral at the feedback session.

After the clinician presented the findings, recommended behavioral intervention for homework incompletion, and did not make a diagnosis, Bradford's father (who had not attended the previous assessment session) disclosed his concern about Bradford's internalizing symptoms, saying that Bradford had inherited his father's susceptibility to depression. Bradford's father then disclosed that he had not wanted the clinician to know about his previous and ongoing treatment, so as to not bias the clinician. Bradford's dad then revealed that he has suffered from depression since childhood and has found it difficult to control. He has reportedly been involved in psychotherapy at various times, including currently. He has also received pharmacological treatment for depression and is currently taking Prozac. He reported that he has been hospitalized previously because of suicidal ideation. He also said that although he is a successful businessman, he has difficulty functioning without ongoing psychotherapy and medical management. He also revealed that his father suffered from depression and eventually committed suicide.

These belated but important historical findings certainly affected the clinician's conceptualization of the case and intervention planning. The clinician changed his recommendations to include psychotherapy as a further assessment tool and as a means for designing preventive interventions.

One of the methodological problems associated with family health and psychiatric history taking is that of underreporting of illness. More reliable information may be obtained by directly interviewing each family member, a method known as family study (Rende & Weissman, 1999). Numerous interview methods exist for conducting a family study of adults including the Diagnostic Interview for Genetic Studies (DIGS; Nurnberger et al., 1994) and the Family History Screen (Weissman et al., 2000). Apart from a specific focus on family psychiatric history, some methods exist that may help a clinician organize information about the child's family structure and history. A brief discussion of genograms as one such method is presented in Box 13.3.

Box 13.3

Genograms, not unlike profile plots on measures such as the MMPI-A or intelligence tests, present information graphically in a manner that can be quickly interpreted by the trained professional. In its most widely used form, the genogram is essentially a family tree that allows the professional to document the client's family structure (i.e., parents, siblings, grandparents, etc.), the relationships among family members, critical events, as well as any particular variables of interest (e.g., psychiatric history, genetic history).

Several volumes on genograms exist (e.g., McGoldrick, Gerson, & Shellenberger, 2008). The uses of genograms vary widely including as a means for obtaining medical history (see Papadopoulos, Bor, & Stanion, 1997), for understanding an individual's cultural context (Shellenberger et al., 2007), and to aid in clinical supervision (Aten, Madson, & Kruse, 2008). For clinical assessment, Papadopoulos et al. (1997) emphasize that genograms are not a quantitative technique with an objective interpretative strategy. Instead, genograms provide a visual representation of family history that can be used, in conjunction with other information, to allow the clinician to develop hypotheses about the case.

In addition to gathering information to aid in case conceptualization and answering a referral question, genograms may also be useful to convey etiological theories to the client/parent about the presenting problems (Papadopoulos et al., 1997). For example, visually depicting an extensive family history of depression (or depicting protective factors in the family context) may help parents reconceptualize their child's problems.

Of course, to take advantage of the presumed benefits of genograms, including efficiency of information gathering, one must be well-trained at constructing and interpreting genograms and must still conduct a clinical interview in a manner that will obtain the desired information. Genograms are not amenable to the same tests of reliability, validity, and utility of many of the other tools described in this text. Therefore, the decision of whether or not to routinely employ such a strategy comes down to the clinician's training, comfort, and perception of a genogram's usefulness.

A common set of symbols, and a very basic genogram example is given below:

Common Genogram Symbols

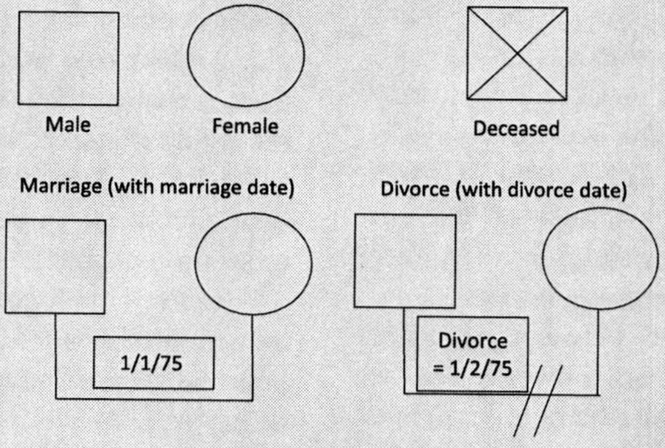

Two Generations of a Family with Three Children and a First-born Male Child

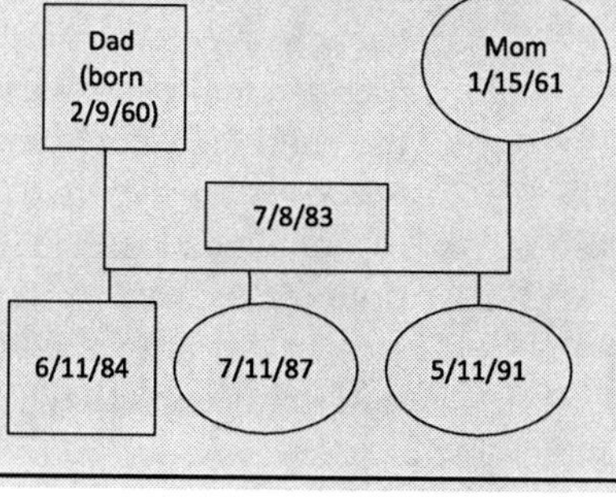

Previous Assessment/ Treatment/Intervention

A child's history of previous intervention/ treatment and assessment of these factors is primarily available through history taking. Similarly, previous assessment results may affect interpretation of current findings.

A clinician, for example, may encounter a child who has received psychotherapy for depression for 2 years, pharmacological treatment for 3 months, and partial hospitalization for 6 months prior to the current evaluation. If the child is demonstrating symptomatology during the current evaluation that is more severe than previously noted, the child's clinician is more likely to advise aggressive treatment, perhaps even hospitalization. The need for aggressive treatment, however, may not appear compelling without the knowledge of the previous intervention failures.

Information about previous assessment also allows clinicians to gauge the accuracy of their current findings. A clinician can validate their current findings by comparing them to the previous assessment results. A child, who was diagnosed with an anxiety disorder 2 months earlier, may demonstrate significant anxiety as indicated by current MMPI-A and RCMAS results. This congruence between current and recent findings may lend some validity to the psychologist's current results.

A lack of congruence between the recent and current test findings, however, can be equally insightful. In this situation, an advised first step would be to check the scoring of the current measures. Previous diagnoses may also help guide further assessment. If a child has been diagnosed previously with ADHD, then the examiner may wish to expand the assessment to other forms of disruptive behavior, given the high comorbidity among such problems (American Psychiatric Association, 2000). Knowledge of the ADHD diagnosis and its associated features and comorbidities gives the clinician a specific hypothesis totest with further assessment results and a potentially valuable set of targets for intervention planning.

Contextual Factors

As noted above, clinicians should be prepared to branch off of standard history questions or forms to assess issues that are client-specific and highly important to a comprehensive case conceptualization.

For even a novice clinician, it is readily apparent that contextual factors in a child's history may exert great influence on his/ her present functioning. Such factors include family relationships, divorce, moves, socioeconomic status, ethnicity, culture, neighborhood environment, and traumatic events (see Dodge & Pettit, 2003). For example, it is one thing to determine that a child's present academic difficulties are the cause of a parent's concerns and the reason for referral. It is quite another to learn that there were no such difficulties for the child until after his/her parents divorced.

A more complex contextual factor that may play a direct role in the design of interventions is that of the goodness-of-fit between the child's characteristics and the contexts in which he/she is expected to function. In particular, contexts in which the child spends more time or that are more proximal likely will exert a stronger positive or negative influence (Cicchetti & Toth, 1998). If a child is prone to problems with anxiety and his or her parents likewise openly worry about many things and interact with the child in an emotional manner, the child's anxiety is likely to be exacerbated. Being in the same class as another anxious student with whom the child does not interact will not have an influence on the child's anxiety. Treatment recommendations will likely include suggestions for the parents in managing their own anxiety and/or in altering their communication strategies with the child.

These contextual factors should be routinely included as part of history taking even if there is no indication of adverse contextual factors at the outset of the assessment. The influence of context can also be protective, and thus, these variables may also serve as strengths around which interventions can be built.

Content

There is considerable overlapping content among history measures although varying degrees of emphasis exist. Some of the most common areas of inquiry include (adapted from the Department of Psychiatry and Child Psychiatry, The Institute of Psychiatry, and the Maudesley Hospital of London, 1987):

Complaints
Present illness
Family history
Mother
Father
Siblings
Other relatives
Family atmosphere
Personal history
Early development
Behavior and temperament
School
Occupation
Adolescence
Sexual history
Medical history
Previous psychiatric problems
Alcohol, tobacco, and drug use
Antisocial behavior
Current life situation
Developmental delays or disabilities
Personality

Attitudes toward others in social, family, and sexual relationships
Attitudes toward self
Moral and religious attitudes and standards
Mood
Leisure activities and interests
Fantasy life
Reaction pattern to stress

A history that is of interest to a certain specialty practice may have a differing emphasis. The content of a history that may be taken by a neurologist or neuropsychologist is described by Teodori (1993) as including the following topics:

Birth history
Developmental history
School history
IQ test results
Social history
Nutritional history
History of exposure to chemicals or toxins
History of other family illnesses
Other medical illnesses
Medications
Hospitalizations
Surgery
Review of systems inquiring about all other aspects of the child's physical functioning
Previous records

Formats

History taking is typically conducted via two formats: an interview and a written form. While history taking research has focused on the interview, there are often occasions where a written form may be used, particularly with the parents of children. Parents are already accustomed to completing such forms while waiting in physicians' offices. Increasingly, parents are also accustomed to completing rating scales in psychologists' offices.

Most history-taking forms, however, require considerable English language fluency on the part of parents. Technical topics, such as the type of special education program that their child attends or a previous medical condition, are difficult for even the most sophisticated parents. Regardless, parents may be able to complete part of the history and thereby save the examiner interviewing time. Assessment systems such as the BASC (Reynolds & Kamphaus, 2004) which was discussed in previous chapters on rating scales, also include forms for history taking (e.g., BASC-2 Structured Developmental History; SDH). An example of a history form is shown in Fig. 13.1. Of course, history forms will vary greatly in their depth and breadth.

Figure 13.1- Sample History Form

USM PSYCHOLOGY CLINIC
(For Child & Adolescent Cases)
FAMILY DATA

Child's Name ______________________ Today's Date______________
Last First Middle

Date of Birth: ____________________ Age_____________ Sex (circle one): Male 0 Female 1

Parent's Name________________________________ Phone __________________

Mailing Address: ____

____

____

School: ____ Grade: ____________

Teacher's name: ____

Person filling out this form (circle one) Mother Father Stepmother Stepfather Grandparent

Other: ____________________________

In case of emergency, notify: ________________________________ Phone: _________________

Relationship to child __________________________

Child's physician ____ Phone: _________________

Referred to this clinic by ____

Reason for seeking services: ____

____

- -

Marital Status of Parents: Married Divorced Separated Widowed Never Married

If separated, divorced, or widowed, age of child when occurred _________________________

If separated or divorced, who has legal custody? _____________________________________

Parents' occupation(s) ____

____

Primary language spoken in the home: ____________________

Is the child on any medication at this time? Yes No

If yes, type of medication ___________________________

Social and Behavioral Information (circle one)

My child:

Engages in behavior that could be dangerous to self or others Describe: ______________________	Yes	No	
Has specific fears Describe: ______________________	Yes	No	
Has unusual habits (e.g., thumbsucking, pulling hair, etc.) Describe: ______________________	Yes	No	
Has difficulty with language	Yes	No	
Has difficulty with coordination	Yes	No	
Does not get along well with siblings	Yes	No	N/A
Does not get along well with other children	Yes	No	
Has trouble sleeping Describe: ______________________	Yes	No	
Has trouble with appetite Describe: ______________________	Yes	No	
Shows daredevil behavior Describe: ______________________	Yes	No	
Has difficulty with change Describe: ______________________	Yes	No	
Gives up easily	Yes	No	
Is likable	Yes	No	

Academic Information

Is your child in a special education class? If yes, describe: ______________________ If yes, when began? ______________________	Yes	No
Has your child been held back a grade? If yes, which one(s)? ______________________	Yes	No
Has your child ever been suspended from school?	Yes	No
If yes, please describe: ______________________		
Has your child ever received in-school suspension? If yes, please describe: ______________________	Yes	No

Developmental and Medical Information

During pregnancy, was the child's mother on medication? Yes No
If yes, describe: ______________________________

During pregnancy did the child's mother smoke? Yes No

During pregnancy did the child's mother drink alcoholic beverages? Yes No
During pregnancy, did the child's mother use drugs? Yes No
If yes, what type? ______________________________

Was the child born prematurely? Yes No

Number of weeks gestation ______________
Birth weight ______________________

Were there any complications during the pregnancy or birth? Yes No
If yes, describe: ______________________________
____

As a baby, did your child have any difficulty feeding? Yes No
If yes, describe: ______________________________
____

As a baby, did your child have any difficulty sleeping? Yes No
If yes, describe: ______________________________
____

As a baby, did your child like being held? Yes No

As a baby, was your child overly fussy? Yes No

At what age, did your child first....

Walk alone? ______________ Speak first word? __________

Become toilet trained? ____________

Has your child had any significant illnesses? Yes No
If yes, describe illnesses and give the ages at which they occurred:
____

Has your child had any significant accidents or injuries? Yes No
If yes, describe and the ages at which they occurred:
____

Has your child had any hospitalizations for medical reasons? Yes No
If yes, describe and give the ages at which they occurred:
____

Does your child have a history of:

Ear infections Yes No
Problems with vision Yes No

Dizzy or fainting spells	Yes	No
Seizures	Yes	No
Asthma	Yes	No
Other medical problems	Yes	No

If yes, please describe: ____
____

Family History

Is there a family history of:

Alcoholism Yes No
If yes, relationship to child ______________________________

Drug Abuse Yes No
Relationship to child ______________________________

Schizophrenia Yes No
Relationship to child ______________________________

Manic Depression (Bipolar Disorder) Yes No
Relationship to child ______________________________

Depression Yes No
Relationship to child ______________________________

Anxiety Yes No
Relationship to child ______________________________

Suicide attempt Yes No
Relationship to child ______________________________

Antisocial behavior Yes No
Relationship to child ______________________________

Attention problems Yes No
Relationship to child ______________________________

Learning problems Yes No
Relationship to child ______________________________
Describe: ______________________________

Psychological History

Has your child been in counseling or therapy before Yes No
If yes, please describe and give age at which occurred:
____

Has your child been on medication for emotional or behavioral problems? Yes No
If yes, when and what kind?
____

Has your child ever used drugs? Yes No
If yes, please describe: ______________________________

Has your child ever been arrested or had contact with the police?	Yes	No
If yes, please describe: ____________________		
Has your child ever been hospitalized for emotional or behavioral problems?	Yes	No
If yes, please describe: ____________________		

Other Information

Is your child helpful toward adults?	Yes	No
Is your child helpful toward other children?	Yes	No
Is your child responsible?	Yes	No
Does your child learn quickly from his/her mistakes?	Yes	No

Please list your child's other assets/strengths:

____

____

____

Please provide any other information that may be useful to us in getting to know and in helping your child:

____

____

____

The important issue is to cover essential history information as part of the assessment and to ideally do so in an efficient manner. Forms, such as the one shown in Fig. 13.1, allow the clinician to gain such information but also require the clinician to follow up based on the parent's responses.

Many clinicians, however, prefer a completely interview format because it allows them to use a branching procedure to pursue topics that are of particular relevance to issues of onset, course, etiology, and previous treatment history among other factors without a potentially cumbersome form that includes some irrelevant information for a particular child. A sample scenario is a case where an 8-year-old child is referred because of a decline in academic achievement. The examiner may discover that the child's performance in school was exemplary until the current academic year, when the child missed 35 days of school because of an automobile accident. The examiner, in this case, will likely branch to ask questions about the child's length of absence from the school and the extent of documented head injury. New and detailed information about these problems may profoundly influence intervention planning. Special education may be placed in abeyance in favor of remedial coursework and monitoring to see if the child recovers his premorbid level of functioning with little intervention, as would often be predicted. Hence, the interview or partial interview format allows the clinician the flexibility necessary for thorough exploration of variables that may impact intervention rather than have the parent spend time on a number of history questions that are not central to the referral concern. It must be emphasized that such interviews are, by nature, clinician- and client-specific, so psychometric properties, particularly reliability, are not meaningful in evaluating a clinician's interview as part of the assessment process. Despite their lack of amenability to empirical evaluations, as noted above, interviews are indispensable in psychological assessment. History forms may be quite useful for efficiency and research purposes, but in clinical assessment they should be augmented by a direct clinical interview.

The face-to-face approach of the interview format may offer additional advantages beyond the possibility for branching. See, for example, Green's (1992) advice on observing nonverbal cues during history taking given in Box 13.4.

Conclusions

This chapter puts forth the argument that history taking is a central, but often overlooked component, of child assessment. Various reasons for making history taking more central to the child assessment process are offered with the focus on the unique contributions that history taking makes to the process. Specifically, history taking is ideal for assessing factors such as age of onset, etiology, course, and previous assessment/intervention outcomes.

Psychologists are advised to select appropriate history forms and practice the branching procedures necessary for integrating psychological science with child history. In fact, history taking provides an ideal venue for the integration of psychopathology, child development, and cognitive science literatures, among others, with child characteristics. Empirical evidence should shape the domains covered in standard history-taking procedures; however, the process will, by nature, be client-specific.

Box 13.4

Observing Nonverbal Cues During History Taking

Green (1992) provides some advice to pediatricians regarding behaviors to observe during the interviewing process. This compendium is equally useful to the psychologist who, while interviewing, is developing hypotheses about family dynamics and other factors that impact child development. The following is an adapted list of behaviors for which psychologists should observe during history taking with a caregiver informant or set of informants.

- Perspiration, blushing. or paling; controlled, uneven, or blocked speech; plaintive voice; talking in a whisper; gait; posture; tics; affirmative nodding; negative shaking of the head
- Frequent swallowing tenseness, fidgeting, preoccupied air, avoidance of eye contact, social distance
- A sudden glance at the interviewer or someone else in the family precipitated by a statement or question
- Clenching, rubbing, wringing hands, searching or nail biting
- Dress and personal grooming
- Reddening of eyes or crying
- Frowns, smiles
- Affect inappropriate to ideation (e.g., a parent smiles when talking about a child's severe behavior problems)
- Interactions among parents, child, and examiner
- Developmentally inappropriate behavior (e.g., older child on parent's lap)
- The way in which the infant or young child is held or helped during the interview
- The parent's ability to have child respond to a parent's request
- Adopted from Green (1992), p. 455.

Chapter Summary

1. Most rating scales and self-report inventories do not directly assess the age of onset of problems as well as do history taking methods.
2. The use of history taking to clarify age of onset is crucial for the diagnosis and conceptualization of a number of childhood disorders.
3. Etiology refers to the likely presumed cause of a child's difficulties.
4. Knowledge of etiology is of potential importance for at least four reasons:
   (a) The etiology may be associated with other problems (e.g., Down Syndrome) that may impair other aspects of functioning - physical, social, or other domains.
   (b) The etiology may be amenable to treatment/intervention.
   (c) Knowledge of etiology may lead to the design of prevention programs.
   (d) Etiologies may be useful for forming homogeneous groups for research or administrative purposes.
5. Research indicates a number of important areas to cover in child and adolescent history taking. Clinicians should be aware of these areas and use the "branching" technique to appropriately follow up on any areas of concern for the client.

CHAPTER 14

Adaptive Behavior Scales

CHAPTER QUESTIONS

- What is meant by the term *adaptive behavior?*
- What are the typical domains of adaptive behavior scales?
- How is adaptive behavior different from other constructs such as personality or intelligence?
- What are some of the most popular adaptive behavior scales?

HISTORY OF THE CONSTRUCT

The adaptive behavior construct traces its roots to early work in mental retardation, which, in turn, is linked to the roots of intellectual assessment (Kamphaus, 2001). Although intelligence tests contributed mightily to the recognition of the mental retardation syndrome, Doll (1940) noted that intelligence measures lacked sufficient breadth for assessing all of the relevant domains of behavior that needed to be considered in treatment of individuals with mental retardation.

Doll drew on his experience as a psychologist at the Vineland State Training School in New Jersey, where he was charged with the assessment and rehabilitation of individuals with mental retardation. He noted that such individuals not only lacked intellectual abilities necessary for academic attainment, but they also often appeared to lack day-to-day living skills needed for independent functioning. In Doll's terminology, they lacked social maturity.

In order to intervene and improve a child's social maturity, Doll created a scale to assess specific behaviors that were

P.J. Frick et al., *Clinical Assessment of Child and Adolescent Personality and Behavior*,
DOI 10.1007/978-1-4419-0641-0_14,

deemed necessary for successful living. The Vineland Social Maturity Scale (Doll, 1953) was the first of its genre. It included several sets of items that assessed various aspects of social maturity including locomotion, social skills, and grooming. The Vineland yielded a score that was roughly parallel to a composite score offered by many intelligence tests of the day. His total score was dubbed a "Social Quotient." The Vineland became the premier measure of adaptive behavior up to the present day, and Doll's pioneering work became the basis for all subsequent measures.

The AAIDD Criteria

The American Association on Intellectual and Developmental Disabilities (AAIDD), formerly the AAMR, bases its criteria for an intellectual disability, or mental retardation, on deficits in both intellectual functioning and adaptive behavior (see Luckasson et al., 2002), similar to previous criteria (e.g., AAMR, 1992). The current criteria that indicate that three broad areas of adaptive behavior should be assessed list ten domains of adaptive behavior that should be assessed for the purposes of mental retardation diagnosis and intervention planning. These domains are: conceptual skills (e.g., language, reading, writing, money skills), social skills (e.g., interpersonal, responsibility, avoiding victimization, obeying rules), and practical skills (e.g., maintaining a safe environment, self-care such as dressing, eating meals, hygiene).

It should be noted that competence in these areas of function may provide a basis of intervention for children with other problems such as autism, ADHD, learning problems, or anxiety. In fact, the assessment of adaptive behavior has been referred to as an essential part of assessments for autism (Ozonoff, Goodlin-Jones, & Solomon, 2005). Adaptive functioning has also been described as one factor that can help differentiate mental retardation from learning disabilities, in that the former would be marked by broad deficits in adaptive functioning, and the latter would be marked by more specific deficits (Fletcher, Francis, Morris, & Lyon, 2005). The acquisition and demonstration of adaptive skills have also been identified as an important buffer against the development of psychopathology. For example, social competencies may allow a child to resist being overwhelmed by negative life stressors (Tanaka & Westerman, 1988). In this context, adaptive behavior scales may serve an important function in the assessment of all children referred for evaluation, not just those who are suspected of having an intellectual disability

Defining Adaptive Behavior

Adaptive behavior has been defined as "the performance of the daily activities that are required for social and personal sufficiency" (Sparrow, Cicchetti, & Balla, 2005, p. 6). Hence, adaptive behavior is the antithesis of most of the behavioral constructs discussed in this book in that it deals with behavioral competencies and their absence as opposed to assessing behavioral problems.

Most definitions of *adaptive behavior* have some core similarities including the premise that it is an age-related construct. Specifically, adaptive behavior increases with age in the absence of interfering circumstances, much as academic achievements accrue over time. Adaptive behaviors are identified by the standards of others and the social context in which the child functions (DeStefano & Thompson, 1990). Finally, adaptive behavior assessment focuses on typical behavior as opposed to ability. This assessment emphasis is also consistent with the assessment of other developmental accomplishments such as academic achievements.

Relationship to Intelligence

The choice of informant is apparently a moderator variable affecting the correlation of measures of adaptive behavior and intelligence (Kamphaus, 2001).

Correlations between intelligence and adaptive behavior measures are modest, .40 to .60 (DeStefano & Thompson, 1990) indicating some overlap but independence. This modest relation, however, is an oversimplification. The correspondence between the two constructs has been found to be higher in individuals with pervasive developmental disorders who also have deficits in intelligence than in individuals with pervasive developmental disorders who do not have intellectual deficits (Bolte & Poustka, 2002). In both groups, adaptive behavior across domains was below average. In addition, moderate correlations between adaptive behavior and intelligence have been found for juvenile offenders (Hayes, 2005). The informant and domain of adaptive behavior assessed also seem to affect the relation. Specifically, when teachers are used as informants, the correlation between intelligence and adaptive behavior increases, and domains that assess communication and functional academic skills tend to correlate higher with intelligence test results (Kamphaus, 1987).

Hence, if one sees a stronger relationship between intelligence and adaptive behavior as desirable, an emphasis on the assessment of functional academics rated by teachers will provide adaptive behavior results of desired value. If, however, one views the adaptive behavior construct as separate or complementary to intelligence assessment, parent ratings of less academically related skills (e.g., socialization) should be sought. In essence, where possible, an evaluator should seek information from both parents and teachers in a variety of adaptive behavior domains.

Otherwise, Harrison (1990), who has made numerous contributions to the adaptive behavior assessment literature, favors the use of parents as informants. She observes:

> "The third-party method of administration is particularly appropriate for the assessment of adaptive behavior. Because adaptive behavior is generally conceptualized as the daily activities in which a per-son engages to take care of himself or herself and get along with other people, the information sup-plied by a third party will be more valid than the direct administration of tasks. The third-party method also allows for the assessment of individuals who cannot participate in the administration of many tests, such as the severely handicapped and young children" (pp. 472–473).

The modest to small relation of adaptive behavior to intelligence is punctuated in a study by Szatmari et al. (1993). This study followed 129 children of extremely low birthweight (501–1,000 g) to the ages of 7 or 8 years and compared their performance to that of a control group. They found significant decrements in intelligence for the low birthweight group but no significant deficits for adaptive behavior. Such results indicate that different mechanisms affect the development of intelligence and adaptive behavior skills.

While the low to moderate relation between intelligence and adaptive behavior scales is well documented (Kamphaus, 2001), the relation between adaptive behavior and academic achievement is of considerable importance given that academic achievement is often the criterion variable of interest to child clinicians. di Sibio (1993) examined the relation of adaptive behavior to achievement after the variance attributable to intelligence was removed.

While intelligence scores were more highly correlated with achievement, the measure of adaptive behavior in that study added 11% of the variance to the prediction of achievement beyond that predicted by intelligence. The results of this study support the importance of assessing adaptive behavior and intervening in order to enhance a child's behavioral competencies which, in turn, provide another approach to enhancing academic achievement.

Uses of Adaptive Behavior Scales

Traditionally, adaptive behavior scales have been considered central to the diagnosis of mental retardation (DeStefano & Thompson, 1990). Although this use is circumscribed, it is an important one given the epidemiology of mental retardation and the importance of accurate diagnosis that includes a comprehensive assessment of adaptive functioning. It has also been argued that assessment of adaptive behavior has been included in order to reduce the number of false positive diagnoses of mental retardation occurring based solely on IQ scores (see Greenspan, 2006).

Perhaps as importantly, as the counterpoint of behavior problem scales, adaptive behavior scales hold unique potential for intervention design based on assessment results. Adaptive behavior scales measure key skills that contribute to a child's successful functioning in a variety of environments. That is, adaptive behavior scales serve a valuable function for the clinician in that they pinpoint specific skills that a child has not acquired, which then may serve as the focus of treatment efforts.

Adaptive behavior scales are particularly useful in educational settings where their results can be integrated with the objectives of individualized educational plans (IEPs). For instance, adaptive behavior scales can be used to identify social skills and other target behaviors for classroom intervention planning.

Characteristics of Adaptive Behavior Scales

Domains Assessed

Adaptive behavior scales are analogous to measures of behavior problems in that the domains assessed vary somewhat from test to test. In Table 14.1 we illustrate the content for three measures of adaptive behavior. Domains assessing various aspects of independent functioning/daily living, social skills, and communication skills are common to many tests. These domains are reflective of those in the intellectual disability criteria described above. The domains of behavior that are assessed by a particular test are influenced by its age range. Children's tests, for example, may place less emphasis on occupational skills, independent living, and interpersonal relationships than measures that are more concerned with assessing adult adaptation. Measures of adult functioning require domains aimed at assessing occupational skills, whereas the child's analog is school functioning. The domains of an adaptive behavior scale, thus, become an important consideration in test selection. A client's age, the institution's treatment program, and other factors may also influence test selection.

In a 1993 study, Widaman, Stacy, and Borthwick-Duffy applied multitrait/multimethod matrix procedures to the identification of major domains of adaptive behavior. The participants for this study were 157 persons with moderate, severe, and profound mental retardation. The authors found clear evidence for the existence of four major domains: cognitive competence, social competence, social maladaptation, and personal maladaptation. These results suggest that, when assessing individuals with mental retardation, measures of at least these four domains would be desirable. Fortunately, the majority of adaptive

Table 14.1 Overview of Three Measures of Adaptive Behavior

Test Name	Age Range	Scales/Domains	Administration Time
Vineland Adaptive Behavior Scales, 2nd edition	Birth through 90 Parent/caretaker and classroom Rating forms; survey and expanded interview forms	Communication (receptive, expressive, written); daily living skills (personal, domestic, community); socialization (interpersonal relationships, play and leisure time, coping skills); motor (gross, fine); maladaptive behavior (internalizing, externalizing, other)	20–60 min
Scales of Independent Behavior: Revised	Infancy through adulthood	Motor skills (gross motor, fine motor); social interaction and communication skills (social interaction, language comprehension, language personal expression); personal living skills (eating and meal preparation, toileting, dressing, personal self-care, domestic skills); community living skills (time and punctuality, money and value, work skills, home/community orientation)	Broad independence scale, 45–60 min; short form scale, 10–15 min; early development scale, 10–15 min
Adaptive Behavior Assessment System-II	Birth to 89 years Separate forms for 0–5; 5–21; and 16–89	Communication, community use, functional academics, home living, health and safety, leisure, self-care, self-direction, social, work	15–20 min to administer

behavior scales measure these domains and, in many cases, additional areas as well.

Norm vs. Criterion Referencing

Prior to the publication of the revised Vineland in 1984, there were no nationally normed adaptive behavior scales. Several scales possessed local or regional norms, and many were created locally and interpreted informally. Unfortunately, many of these scales were used for making norm-referenced decisions such as determining whether or not a child had adaptive behavior deficits that were significant enough to warrant the diagnosis of mental retardation.

Among the adaptive behavior assessment questions most frequently posed by psychologists are the following:

1. Does the child have adaptive behavior deficits that are significant enough to warrant the diagnosis of mental retardation?
2. What are the adaptive behavior deficits that most influence the child's adjustment and therefore, require intervention?
3. What are the adaptive behavior strengths displayed by the child?

Questions 2 and 3 are less likely to require norm referencing, although it may still be of some benefit. In order to answer these questions, the clinician could make intraindividual comparisons and/or gauge deficits on the basis of how the deficits impair adaptation to particular environments (e.g., failure to follow rules in games).

Choice of Informant

The Vineland Social Maturity Scale represents one of the first scales in psychology to place a premium on parents as informants. This approach stood in stark contrast to the popularity at the time of using direct measures of child behavior, such as intelligence tests.

Modern adaptive behavior scales such as the Vineland-2 (Sparrow, Cicchetti, & Balla, 2005) and Scales of Independent Behavior-Revised (Bruininks, Woodcock, Weatherman, & Hill, 1996) still emphasize the use of parents as informants. For most scales in which parents serve as informants, maternal reports are used nearly exclusively for item development, scaling, and norming. Although fathers are used less frequently, there are no systematic data currently available that clarify the differences between mothers and fathers as informants regarding adaptive behavior.

Secondarily, teachers often serve as raters of adaptive behavior. However, teachers have different views of a child's adaptive behavior because of the varied demands of school and home settings. Domains that are commonly included on parent scales of adaptive behavior, such as toileting, bathing, dressing, budgeting, and health care are impractical for teachers. Likewise, parents have difficulty reporting on functional academics in reading, writing, calculation, and some vocational skills. The differing demands of school and home environments virtually ensure that a clinician will have an incomplete understanding of a child's adaptive behavior if either teacher or parent adaptive behavior ratings are not used.

Other caregivers also serve as important informants regarding a child's adaptive behavior. Caregivers may include psychiatric aides in hospitals, nurses, mental health assistants, nannies, grandparents, teacher aides, work supervisors, or others who have sustained nearly daily contact with a child or adolescent. These individuals may, in some circumstances, fulfill parent or teacher roles and therefore may be competent primary or secondary informants for such scales. Even when parents or teachers complete an adaptive behavior scale, other caregiver information may be of value. An adolescent's work supervisor is one example of an informant who may contribute unique and important information to the pool of assessment data gathered on adaptive functioning.

Finally, the child as an informant should not be overlooked. In other words, the child may be tested directly in order to assess adaptive behavior, although this is a less popular option with many clinicians. Perhaps one reason for its lack of popularity is a dearth of available instruments. The Children's Adaptive Behavior Scale (CABS; Richmond & Kicklighter, 1979) is one of the few direct measures of adaptive behavior available. The CABS uses an individual testing format to assess Language Development, Independent Functioning, Family Role Performance, Economic/Vocational Activity, and Socialization. Obviously, these domains are common to many types of adaptive behavior measures.

As is the case with behavior rating scales, there is often a high level of disagreement between the informants who give information or adaptive behavior scales. Parents and teachers have been found to generally agree on overall adaptive behavior estimates (e.g., Harrison & Oakland, 2003). However, they may disagree considerably at the scale or domain levels (Shaw, Hammer, & Leland, 1991). Self- and caregiver reports have been found to sometimes agree on adaptive behavior ratings but to disagree considerably on ratings of maladaptive behavior (Voelker et al., 1990). Factors such as child age and length of involvement in a treatment program may also affect agreement between informants (see Shaw et al., 1991).

Administration Format

Adaptive behavior scales are commonly administered using a checklist or semi-structured interview technique, except, of course, in the case of direct assessment of the child. The checklist format is equivalent to the approach used for parent or teacher ratings of behavior problems discussed in previous chapters. The semi-structured interview method espoused by Doll (1953) and popularized by Sparrow, Balla, and Cicchetti (1984) differs substantially from rating scale methods.

The semi-structured interview technique, however, requires a high level of clinical skill. The clinician has to make the interview conversation-like, topical, and empathic, while at the same time collecting the necessary information to allow for accurate rating (scoring) of individual items. In addition, younger children could have a difficult time articulating their skills in various adaptive behavior domains. Therefore, when using self-report procedures for adaptive behavior, a semi-structured interview format is not recommended. The rating scale method is more time-efficient and practical in that the clinician does not even need to be present for the administration of the scale.

However, the semi-structured interview technique has many virtues, including the following:

- Allowing the examiner to clarify questions for the informant by providing examples, and so forth
- Contributing to the establishment of rapport between clinician and parent because of the conversation-like nature of the interaction
- Mitigating against response sets such as fake good or fake bad
- Permitting the assessment of adaptive behavior, despite poor English-language reading skills

The semi-structured interview technique can be easily mastered with practice. Some techniques for mastering the technique follow.

1. Begin by asking general questions and then proceed to the specific information needed to score items. If one started with the Communication domain of the Vineland-2, for example, a good starting question for a parent of a toddler might be something like, "Tell me about some of the things that Tom is saying these days."
2. Ask for examples of day-to-day behavior because adaptive behavior scales are designed to assess typical behavior rather than ability (see Sparrow et al., 2005). A follow-up expressive language question might be, "Tell me the words that you can remember Tom saying today."
3. Become very familiar with the interview items and scoring criteria for specific items in order to ensure that adequate clarification is sought.
4. Conduct the interview topically. For example, ask all of the items regarding telephone skills (answering appropriately, states telephone number, uses pay phone, etc.) before proceeding to the next topic.
5. Pursue questioning until you have a clear picture of the child's day-to-day behavior. Once you have achieved this portrait, you can confidently rate the child's behavior on individual items.

Omnibus Adaptive Behavior Scales

Vineland Adaptive Behavior Scales, 2nd edition (The Vineland-2; Sparrow, Cicchetti, & Balla, 2005)

The Vineland-2 (Sparrow et al., 2005) is the latest version of an assessment tool for adaptive behavior that traces its roots to the originator of the adaptive behavior construct, Edgar Doll. Doll created the first widely used scale of adaptive behavior, the Vineland Social Maturity Scale. The Vineland-2 and its predecessor (Sparrow, Balla, & Cicchetti, 1984) represent a substantial revision, adaptation, and extension of Doll's original scale.

The Vineland-2 consists of a family of scales each of which possesses characteristics that make it well-suited for particular purposes. The Vineland components include the following: The Teacher Rating Form assesses adaptive functioning in the classroom for children ages 3½ through 18. The Survey Interview Form is administered to parent/caretakers of individual from birth to age 90 in semi-structured interview format (an Expanded Interview Form is also available). New to the Vineland-2 is a Parent/Caregiver Rating Form that allows parents to rate adaptive behavior items in a rating scale format.

The Vineland-2 has many uses in addition to its popularity as a tool in assessments and diagnoses of mental retardation. The Vineland-2 provides a rather comprehensive assessment of an individual's behavioral competencies and can be used to assess treatment progress, as well as to determine treatment goals.

Content

Aside from re-standardization, the most substantial change in the Vineland-2 from the previous Vineland is in the expansion of the number of items in each domain and the inclusion of the Parent/Caretaker Rating Form (Sparrow et al., 2005). The Vineland-2 includes the same domains as its predecessor: Communication, Daily Living Skills, Socialization, Motor Skills, and Maladaptive Behavior. The Motor Skills domain is designed for ages from birth through 6 years and for older individuals with motor handicaps. The Maladaptive Behavior domain is essentially a behavior problems checklist that assesses very severe difficulties such as problems in public, sexual misbehavior, self-injurious behavior, bedwetting, and truancy. Each of the domains consists of following content:

- Communication
  - Receptive
  - Expressive
  - Written
- Daily Living Skills
  - Personal
  - Domestic
  - Community
- Socialization
  - Interpersonal Relationships
  - Play and Leisure Time
  - Coping Skills
- Motor Skills
  - Gross
  - Fine
- Maladaptive Behavior
  - Internalizing
  - Externalizing
  - Other (e.g., wets bed)

Administration and Scoring

The Vineland Survey form uses Doll's well-known semi-structured interview technique, a method that is often not followed loyally by Vineland users. The technique has many advantages; unfortunately, its disadvantages are more salient. Said simply, mastering the semi-structured interview technique is not easy.

A central problem with the method is the necessity of organizing the interview topically, while the items are placed on the response form by difficulty order. For example, several items of the Daily Living Skills domain of the Survey Form have to do with telephone skills – answering, dialing, and so on. The semi-structured interview technique involves obtaining adequate information to score these items, even though they are scattered throughout the record form. This central contradiction of simultaneously interviewing topically as well as having items ordered by increasing difficulty undoubtedly leads to routine usage of the Vineland as a rating scale despite the fact that this is a violation of standardized procedure. Two aspects of the Vineland-2 speak to the tendency for clinicians to have difficulty with the semi-structured interview approach: (a) icons are now shown on the record form such that interviewers can more easily spot items that go together (e.g., a book icon signals items that have to do with reading skills); and (b) the Parent/Caretaker Rating Form and the Teacher Rating Form now make it possible for the clinician to obtain Vineland ratings without the use of an interview. Nevertheless, given the many advantages of the semi-structured interview technique cited earlier, it behooves clinicians to acquire this unique skill.

Vineland interpretation features standard scores based on a mean of 100 and standard deviation of 15 for the Adaptive Behavior Composite and for each of the Domain scores. A new feature is the use of "v-scale" scores for subdomains. These scores have a mean of 15 and standard deviation of 3.

Norming

The Survey Form norming sample of the Vineland was collected on the basis of 2001 US Census Bureau statistics (Current Population Survey, 2001). The sample was made up of 3,687 subjects from birth through 90 years. The sample appears to be representative of the larger population in terms of ethnicity, SES, geographic region, and disability status. Clinical samples of individuals with ADHD, autism (both with and without language), hearing impairment, and "emotional or behavioral disturbance" were included in the standardization and subsequent studies (Sparrow et al., 2005, p. 91).

Reliability

Reliability analyses indicate good internal consistency for the Adaptive Behavior Composite and the domain scores, with coefficients generally .90 and higher for the former and .80 and higher for the latter. Subdomain internal consistency coefficients likewise tended to be .80 and higher, with the exception of the Receptive (communication), Personal (daily living skills), and Play and Leisure time (socialization) which were somewhat lower (see Sparrow et al., 2005).

Test-retest reliability (approximately 2–5-week interval) coefficients were also good, and the parent forms of the Vineland-2 demonstrated adequate interviewer agreement on the Survey Interview Form and adequate interrater reliability across parents on the Parent/Caregiver Form (Sparrow et al.).

Validity

Many aspects of validity are addressed by the authors of the Vineland-2 (Sparrow et al., 2005). The content of the Vineland-2 was designed to be reflective of AAIDD and *DSM-IV-TR* criteria for adaptive functioning, as outlined for diagnoses of intellectual disabilities or mental retardation. In addition, the raw scores increase lawfully from age to age lending credence to the argument that the Vineland measures adaptive behavior as a developmental phenomenon. In other words, with development, an individual should acquire more adaptive skills, and this phenomenon is reflected in the Vineland-2 raw score data.

Differential validity studies described by the authors note that the Vineland-2 Adaptive Behavior Composite and domain scores differentiated among individuals with mild, moderate, or severe mental retardation. Similarly, the scores for individuals with autism who also had verbal skills were higher than those for individuals with autism without verbal skills (Sparrow et al.).

Convergent validity was examined by the associations between Vineland-2 domains and analogous scales on the BASC-2. In general, parent reported Vineland-2 domains were moderately correlated with similar parent report BASC-2 scales (e.g., Communication with Functional Communication). These coefficients were generally higher for individuals ages 12–18 than for younger subjects. Similar results were found for analyses of the Vineland-2 and the Adaptive Behavior Assessment System-II (ABAS-II; see below), with moderate correlations found across age groups for analogous domains and subdomains.

Strengths and Weaknesses

The Vineland-2 and its predecessors benefit from a long history of successful use and numerous research investigations. The Vineland's noteworthy strengths include the following:

1. Multiple components that are useful for a variety of diagnostic and intervention planning purposes
2. A supportive research base that suggests that the Vineland-2 possesses expected correlations with measures of similar (convergent validity) constructs
3. An exhaustive item pool which allows for the ready identification of treatment goals and objectives
4. A large national normative sample and several local norm samples, which make it particularly well suited for diagnostic decision making
5. Modifications of the new version which eases administration in either semi-structured interview or rating scale formats

Among the Vineland's weaknesses are the following:

1. The considerable training that is required to properly use the semi-structured interview technique
2. Relatively little research on the Vineland-2 which is offset to some extent by research on its predecessors and its familiarity to many clinicians.
3. More limited research on the classroom version, particularly regarding its utility for educational interventions.

In Box 14.1 we provide a case example illustrating the use of the Vineland-2.

Box 14.1

A Case Example Use in the Vineland-2

Name: Joan
Age: 12 years
Grade: 6
Evaluation Procedures
Differential Abilities Scale (DAS)
Woodcock Johnson Tests of Achievement, 3rd edition (WJ-III)
Behavior Assessment System for Children (BASC-2): Parent Rating Scales (PRS), Teacher Rating Scales (TRS), and Self-Report of Personality (SRP)
Vineland Adaptive Behavior Scales, 2nd edition (Vineland-2): Classroom Rating Scale, Parent/Caretaker Rating Scale

Reason for Referral

Joan, a 12-year-old girl, was referred for evaluation by her father to determine if she is receiving the education services that she needs in school. Joan is a sixth-grade special education student who is currently in a fifth-grade inclusion classroom where she reportedly is receiving extra help from her teacher and an aide throughout the day. Her reading skills are reportedly well below what would be expected for her grade level. According to Joan's mother, her school has recommended retaining Joan in the sixth grade next year, and Joan's father would like a second opinion.

Background Information

According to her mother, Joan has lived with her biological parents and paternal grandparents for the last 10 years. Joan's mother is a legal secretary, and her father works at a lumberyard. Joan reportedly has no other siblings. At birth, Joan weighed 7 lb, 11 oz and was described as a healthy baby. Joan's development during infancy was reportedly normal, and she did not have any serious diseases or other difficulties.

Mrs. Jordan indicated that Joan is involved with her church youth group and the local 4H Club. She enjoys caring for her pets which include a rabbit, goat, and two dogs. Joan also reportedly enjoys making crafts with her grandmother.

Joan's teacher and aide were interviewed. Both stated that they are impressed and pleased with Joan's progress, since the beginning of the school year. She was described as a nice kid who works hard. Reading reportedly continues to be Joan's weakest area, and math is a relative strength. According to her teacher, Joan is easily frustrated with reading assignments. She is described as a sight reader. Joan's socialization skills in the classroom and the community have reportedly improved. Her teachers and mother noted that she gets along well with her peers and adults in her environment.

According to her mother, the school team has recommended placing Joan in a sixth-grade inclusion class next year in order to give her another year to develop before starting middle school. Although her socialization skills have improved, they reportedly believe that she needs the additional year to mature. Joan's father reports that Joan would prefer to go to the middle school next year with her friends.

Previous Evaluation

Joan was reportedly in a speech program until third grade for fluency and articulation difficulties. She continues to have problems with expressive speech, but her teachers report that this is not a significant problem. Joan is described as speaking relatively clearly in class. Joan was recently prescribed glasses, but reportedly she fails to wear them in class, and she did not wear them during this evaluation.

Joan was initially evaluated when she was in the first grade. From that evaluation, she was diagnosed as mildly intellectually delayed and placed in a self-contained classroom. Joan's Mental Processing Composite on the Kaufman Assessment Battery for Children, 2nd edition (KABC-2) at that time was in the Borderline range (MPC = 70). She was re-evaluated three years later, and her Full Scale score on the Wechsler Intelligence Scale for Children-Fourth Edition (WISC-IV) was also in the Borderline range (FSIQ = 74). Her Adaptive Behavior Composite on the Vineland Adaptive Behavior Scale was also in the Below Average range (ABC = 72).

Behavioral Observations During Testing

Joan was appropriately dressed and well-groomed during the evaluation. No auditory or motor abnormalities were noted. She also did not appear to have any visual difficulties, but she was not wearing her prescribed corrective lenses. Rapport was easily established; however, Joan was not talkative during the evaluation, and she did not initiate conversation. At times, she was difficult to understand because she mumbled. However, she willingly answered the examiner's questions and smiled frequently. She appeared to be nervous in the beginning, but she became more relaxed, as suggested by more frequent smiling and relaxed body posture, as testing progressed. Joan was cooperative and polite. Although Joan worked hard during testing, she became frustrated easily, especially during reading exercises. When frustrated, Joan tended to respond more impulsively, shift often in her seat, rub her face, avoid eye contact, and adopt a flat affect.

Observations during testing suggest that Joan's self-report personality test results are somewhat suspect. Her limited reading abilities and verbal expression skills, as well as her impulsivity on tasks requiring reading limits the potential value of those findings.

Test Results and Interpretation

Psychoeducational Assessment: Cognitive functioning was assessed using the DAS. She obtained a General Conceptual Ability score on the DAS of 59. There is a 90% probability that Joan's DAS General Conceptual Ability score falls between 54 and 64, indicating that her performance meets or exceeds less than 1% of her peers. Both her Verbal and Nonverbal scores were also in the Significantly Below Average range, but her Spatial score was somewhat higher, falling in the Significantly Below Average to Moderately Below Average range. These results indicate that her intellectual functioning is below that of her same-aged peers.

These results are also highly consistent with Joan's performance on academic achievement measures. Standard scores on the Kaufman Tests of Educational Achievement (KTEA) ranged from 48 (Reading Comprehension) to 64 (Math Applications), which correspond to percentile ranks of less than 1. All of the academic skill areas assessed were significantly below average. In general, these results are supported by

Joan's prior evaluations, curriculum-based measures taken at her school, and teacher reports.

Adaptive Behavior: The Vineland-2 was completed by Joan's mother, who indicated that Joan's overall adaptive behavior is significantly below average for her age. Her Socialization and Daily Living Skills domain scores were in the Below Average range, suggesting that Joan has some difficulty communicating her needs and ideas and caring for herself relative to her same-aged peers. Her rating for the Communication Domain, which was well below average, suggests that Joan has substantial difficulty expressing her ideas verbally or in written form and in understanding what she reads or hears from others. Her teacher's ratings on the Vineland-2 were higher in each domain, indicating that her overall adaptive behavior in the classroom is slightly below that of her same-aged peers. Joan's teacher rated her in the Average range in Daily Living Skills and Socialization. Her rating in the Communication Domain was in the Below Average range.

The results of the Vineland-2 suggest that the following behaviors should be considered as objectives for intervention:

Communication: Reading simple stories, printing three- and four-word sentences, reading vocabulary of at least ten words, and writing vocabulary of at least ten words

Daily Living Skills: Dressing appropriately for the weather, avoiding individuals with contagious diseases, telling time by 5-min segments, caring for her hair and fingernails, and using household cleaning products

Socialization: Controlling anger when denied own way and attending after school or evening activities with same age/grade peers

The results suggest that Joan's adaptive functioning may be better at school than at home. However, her overall adaptive functioning is still below what would be expected for her age, particularly in the area of Communication. Her intellectual functioning and academic achievement are substantially below what is expected for her age. The results indicate that Joan meets criteria for a diagnosis of Mild Mental Retardation.

Reports by Joan's mother and teacher on the BASC-2 of poor functional communication, poor adaptability to change, and difficulties with self-care (parent report) are consistent with their reports of Joan's adaptive functioning on the Vineland-2 and with her diagnosis of Mild Mental Retardation. Joan's teacher reported on a moderate level of concerns on the Learning Problems scale of the TRS, which is consistent with Joan's history of academic difficulties.

General Recommendations

1. From the results of the current evaluation, it is apparent that Joan should receive resource educational services through her school. Joan should not be expected to make one year of academic progress for each year of attendance in school. Therefore, slow academic attainment by itself may not warrant retention in grade. Joan's parents and school officials should communicate regularly as to the appropriate placement and accommodations for Joan.
2. Joan's parents are advised to read some literature on other children functioning at Joan's intellectual level to understand how she learns, what expectations are reasonable for her, what her needs are, and how to meet those needs.
3. The focus of academics for Joan should be to help her develop minimal competency in independent living skills, including vocational skills.
4. Joan should receive vocational counseling to guide her educational program.

5. Joan may need to be reevaluated for the speech program at school given her continued difficulties with communication and the difficulty of understanding her at times during the present evaluation.
6. If a computer is available, Joan could use software designed to increase her reading, math, and spelling skills. She could work on the computer alone or with a teacher. Computer usage would increase her independence, give her the attention that she needs, and provide individualized instruction.
7. Joan should be allowed as much as possible to be around her regular classroom peers (i.e., education in the least restrictive environment possible), so that she can learn socialization, coping, and behavioral skills by observing and interacting with them.

Scales of Independent Behavior: Revised (SIB-R; Bruininks, Woodcock, Weatherman, & Hill, 1996)

The SIB-R in many ways resembles the Vineland. It is a broad-based assessment of adaptive behavior spanning an age range of infancy through adulthood.

Content

The SIB-R includes 14 subscales that are subsumed under four clusters (i.e., Motor Skills, Social Interaction and Communication Skills, Personal Living Skills, and Community Living Skills). These clusters are summarized by a Broad Independence scale composite score. The clusters and their subscales are the following:

- Motor Skills
    - Gross Motor
    - Fine Motor
- Social Interaction and Communication Skills
    - Social Interaction
    - Language Comprehension
    - Language Expression
- Personal Living Skills
    - Eating and Meal Preparation
    - Toileting
    - Dressing
    - Personal Self-Care
    - Domestic Skills
- Community Living Skills
    - Time and Punctuality
    - Money and Value
    - Work Skills
    - Home/Community Orientation

An Early Development scale is provided on the SIB-R for assessing the adaptive skills of infants and young children. This scale may also be of benefit for the assessment of significantly impaired individuals with developmental ages of 8 or lower.

Flexible use of the SIB-R is further enhanced by the availability of an Individual Plan Recommendation form. This form aids the process of intervention planning through needs identification and progress monitoring.

Another valuable feature of the SIB-R is the provision of a short form that can be administered in 10–15 min. The short form consists of items from the longer scale that give a quick indication of the overall presence or absence of adaptive behavior deficits. A low score on this scale would trigger the administration of the complete form or another adaptive behavior scale.

A Problem Behaviors scale is also included. This scale measures eight areas of problem behavior:

- Hurtful to Self
- Hurtful to Others
- Destructive to Property
- Disruptive Behavior
- Unusual or Repetitive Habits
- Socially Offensive Behavior

Withdrawal or Inattentive Behavior; Uncooperative Behavior

An additional advantage of this scale is that problem behaviors are not only rated according to frequency but also by severity. The severity ratings provide the clinician with more guidance to follow in a problem-solving assessment paradigm (Bruininks et al., 1996).

Administration and Scoring

The SIB-R is administered via structured interview or checklist in approximately 45–60 min. The questions are merely posed to a parent, teacher, or other caregiver as they are written. Respondents are given four response options for each item:

1. Never or rarely, even if asked
2. Does, but not well, or about 1/4 of the time; may need to be asked
3. Does fairly well, or about 3/4 of the time; may need to be asked
4. Does very well, or always or almost always; without being asked

The items are worded as precise behavioral objectives that require little comprehension on the part of the informant.

The SIB-R offers a large and useful variety of derived scores including standard scores, percentile ranks, and age equivalents. The more novel scores include training implication ranges, a relative mastery index, and a support score, although more traditional scores of different adaptive behavior domains are also available.

Norming

A sample of 2,182 subjects was used for norming the SIB-R (Bruininks et al., 1996). The age range of the sample extended from infancy through adulthood.

Reliability

Split-half coefficients for the clusters are reported in the test manual to be in the .80s to low .90s (Bruininks et al., 1996). The Broad Independence scale reliability estimates were commonly in the mid to high .90s. Test–retest reliabilities for the clusters and the Broad Independence scale were similarly high.

Validity

DeStefano and Thompson (1990) lauded the original SIB for its evidence of content validity by the observation: "The SIB shows good content validity, in that its structure and content cover a broad range of skills and traits included in current models of adaptive and maladaptive behavior" (p. 461).

Roberts et al. (1993) conducted a correlational study of the previous SIB and Vineland Survey Form that demonstrates considerable criterion related validity for both instruments. This study involved 128 4-year olds to 7-year olds with developmental disabilities. Both tests were found to produce one large factor. Similarly, McGrew, Bruininks, and Thurlow (1992) found the SIB to correlate significantly with community adjustment for 239 adults with mild to severe levels of mental retardation. While the SIB-R is not as well-researched as its predecessor or the Vineland, the few studies available show good evidence of criterion-related validity.

Interpretation

As with the other adaptive behavior scales reviewed in this chapter, we recommend interpretation of the SIB-R first at the composite level and then at the cluster level. In most cases, the composite will give an accurate overall picture of the individual's adaptive functioning. However, there may be relative strengths or weaknesses across clusters (and perhaps on specific items/skills) that would inform intervention in a meaningful way. It is good practice for clinicians to consider what specific sets of skills led to particular strengths or weaknesses in areas of adaptive functioning to illustrate the skills that the client has acquired or struggled to acquire.

Strengths and Weaknesses

The SIB-R possesses many admirable traits that make it a very practical tool. Its strengths include the following:

1. Flexibility of administration with the availability of both short and long forms
2. An objective item-scoring scheme that eases scoring
3. Its link to other Woodcock-Johnson tests, which foster transfer of training to the SIB-R.
4. Broad item coverage (i.e., content validity)

The weaknesses of the SIB-R include the following:

1. Relatively complex scoring algorithms (which are eased considerably by the use of its accompanying Compuscore software program)
2. A lack of factor-analytic and criterion-related validity studies conducted by those other than the test developers

Adaptive Behavior Assessment System, 2nd edition (ABAS-II; Harrison & Oakland, 2003)

The ABAS-II, a newer adaptive behavior scale, is organized in a manner that is closely related to *DSM* and AAIDD criteria. It is a comprehensive system that is designed to assess individuals from 5 to 89 years of age (Harrison & Oakland).

Content

The ABAS assesses ten constructs including:

Communication
Community Use
Functional Academics
Home/School Living (denoted as "Home" on the Parent Form and "School" on the Teacher Form)
Health and Safety
Leisure
Self-Care
Self-Direction
Social Work (only completed if the individual has a full or part-time job)

The ABAS-II includes various forms that assess the ten skill areas. Specifically the ABAS-II consists of a parent and a teacher/daycare provider form for ages 0–5, separate parent and teacher forms for ages 5–21, and an adult form, completed by a caregiver, for ages 16 through 89 years.

Administration and Scoring

The ABAS-II is a rating scale that appears to be straightforward to use. According to the manual (Harrison & Oakland, 2003), an informant can rate the child in 15–20 min. Items are organized by skill area in order of difficulty, which probably reduces administration time. The work area is skipped for most children, for example, and many skills listed are so far beyond the competencies of most children that they can quickly be answered with zero.

The item response scale is 0 = is not able; 1 = never when needed; 2 = sometimes when needed; 3 = always or "almost always" when needed; and a last category is "check if you guessed." This latter category may help examiners determine the amount of confidence to place in a rater's responses.

Item scores merely need to be summed to produce raw scores by skill area. The raw scores are then transferred to the back of the record form to conduct table conversions to standard scores for each scale (M = 10, SD = 3) and a "General Adaptive Composite" (M = 100, SD = 15). Percentile ranks and confidence intervals are also offered.

Norming

The ABAS was normed on a total sample of 7,370 individuals with demographic sampling based on 1999 US Census estimates. General national norms are offered as well as numerous validity studies of individuals with disabilities. Stratification variables for the sample included geographic region, parental educational attainment, sex, and race/ethnicity. The norming sample may have included a slight under-representation of children with disabilities (see Richardson & Burns, 2005).

Reliability

Reliability of the ABAS-II was evaluated via internal consistency, test–retest, and inter-rater reliability. Reliability coefficients were generally quite high with the internal consistency coefficients for the General Adaptive Composite and the skill areas being all around .90 and the inter-rater reliability coefficients were generally in the .80s. In addition, cross-informant coefficients across forms and skill areas were good (i.e., approximately .70; Harrison & Oakland, 2003).

Validity

The ABAS-II has been described as having good content validity on the basis of its theoretical foundation in diagnostic criteria for mental retardation (Richardson & Burns, 2005). Confirmatory factor analyses support the factor structure of the ABAS-II, and the manual presents good evidence of both convergent and divergent validity (Harrision and Oakland, 2003). In addition, the differential validity of the ABAS-II was demonstrated for children in a variety of diagnostic categories compared to matched controls. Richardson and Burns (2005) suggest that more research is needed concerning the applicability of various items of the ABAS-II cross-culturally. The same could be said for other measures of adaptive functioning.

Interpretation

ABAS-II interpretive guidelines are offered in the manual along with a few case studies. The interpretive suggestions are basic, clear, and sensible. We again recommend a top-down approach to interpretation (i.e., composite to items) with skill examples being provided to illustrate the client's relative strengths and weaknesses. In addition, corroborating evidence is needed on adaptive functioning such that clinicians do not hastily use a profile of scores to make a diagnostic decision (Harrison & Oakland, 2003).

Strengths and Weaknesses

The ABAS-II is a viable alternative to the Vineland and SIB-R given its ease of use and linkage to the AAIDD and *DSM-IV* criteria. Noteworthy strengths include the following:

1. A close link to diagnostic criteria
2. Ease of administration and hand scoring
3. Inclusion of numerous validity studies in the manual

Some potential weaknesses of the ABAS-II may include the following:

1. Inability to gather unsolicited clinical information as it is often available in a semi-structured interview
2. Lack of validation research by others than the test developers
3. Slight underrepresentation of children with disabilities in the norming sample.

Measuring Social Skills

A universally accepted definition of adaptive behavior remains elusive resulting in scales that may have a variety of domains (Merrell & Popinga, 1994). The development and revision of adaptive behavior instruments of late have resulted in measures that reflect AAIDD criteria for mental retardation. However, any one of those domains (e.g., daily living skills, social skills) can be assessed in a more detailed fashion than is typically the case with adaptive behavior scales. One aspect of adaptive behavior, social competence, or social skills is of such importance for a variety of child outcomes that scales which measure this construct exclusively are available.

Social Skills Rating System

The SSRS (Gresham & Elliott, 1990) is a comprehensive measure of social skills that incorporates multiple domains and raters. Teacher, parent, and student forms are provided for measuring a variety of social skills across settings. Although the SSRS also measures externalizing, internalizing, and hyperactivity problem behaviors, social skills are the focus of the system. The teacher form of the SSRS also includes a rating of academic competence.

Content

The SSRS differs from other crude assessments of social skills or omnibus rating scales (e.g., BASC-2) by assessing multiple domains of social skills. The domains corresponding to each form are shown in Table 14.2. A total score is also available for each form.

Administration and Scoring

Each of the SSRS forms is straightforward to use. The parent and teacher forms are somewhat unique rating scales in comparison to many of the measures reviewed thus far. In addition to requiring the rater to assess the frequency of a behavior, the rater is also asked to indicate the importance of the behavior for a child's development. The availability of these importance ratings allows the clinician to better prioritize behaviors for intervention.

A full range of scores are offered by the SSRS, including standard scores, percentile ranks, and a behavior level. Behavior levels are somewhat like stanines in that they divide up portions of the distribution of scores into three levels where > + 1 *sd* = more, <–1 *sd* = fewer, and the middle of the distribution =

Table 14.2 Domains Assessed by SSRS Forms

	Cooperation	Assertion	Responsibility	Empathy	Self-Control
Teacher Form					
Preschool	x	x			x
Elementary	x	x			x
Secondary	x	x			x
Parent Form					
Preschool	x	x	x		x
Elementary	x	x	x		x
Secondary	x	x	x		x
Student Form					
Elementary	x	x		x	x
Secondary	x	x		x	x

average. Such indices are available for each domain and the total score.

Norming

The SSRS norming samples consisted of 4,170 children, 1,027 parents, and 259 teachers who completed forms in 1988 (Gresham & Elliott, 1990). The sample used for the Student Form is well-described in the manual. On the other hand, the Parent and Teacher Form samples are described in only a few paragraphs. The characteristics of the children rated on the Teacher Form, such as their SES and ethnicity, are not given. The SES of the parent sample is heavily skewed toward high levels of SES. The lack of detailed information given for norming of the Teacher and Parent Forms makes it difficult to evaluate the quality of the norms and to make recommendations for their use.

Reliability

The reliability estimates for the Teacher and Parent forms reported in the SSRS manual are generally adequate. Mean coefficient alpha reliability estimates for the Teacher Form subscales were in the high .80s and .90s. Parent Form coefficients are slightly lower with more coefficients in the .70s. Student Form reliabilities were generally low. Coefficients for the Cooperation, Assertion, and Self-Control scales did not exceed .70. The test-retest coefficients for the Student Form were even more disappointing, with none of the values exceeding .70, including the Total Scale value, which was only .68 (Gresham & Elliott, 1990). Moderate correlations between parent and teacher ratings on the SSRS have been found (Ruffalo & Elliott, 1997).

Validity

Conducting criterion-related validity studies with the SSRS may be difficult because of debate about the appropriate criterion. There is not a clear criterion in the assessment of social skills. Some sense of criterion-related validity may be gained from the studies reported in the manual (Gresham & Elliott, 1990).

A study of the SSRS Teacher Form correlations with the Social Behavior Assessment (SBA) lends some criterion-related validation to the Teacher Form. The majority of correlations were significant for a sample of 79 cases, suggesting that the two measures share considerable overlap. The Cooperation subscale of the Teacher Form was most highly correlated with scores from the SBA. This scale correlated -.70 with the Interpersonal domain of the SBA and -.73 with the Task-Related domain of the SBA.

A study of the relation of the Teacher Form to the Achenbach Child Behavior Checklist-Teacher Report Form (CBCL-TRF) provided mixed support for the Problem Behavior scales. The Externalizing Scale correlated .69 with its counterpart on the CBCL, but the Teacher Form correlated only .33 with its CBCL counterpart (Gresham & Elliott, 1990).

Similar results were obtained for the SSRS Parent Form. In a study of 45 parent ratings of children, the Externalizing Scale correlated .70 with the Externalizing score of the CBCL-PRF. Again, however, the Internalizing Scale correlated only .50 with the Internalizing Scale of the CBCL-PRF (Gresham & Elliott, 1990). These studies of the Problem Behaviors scales of the SSRS suggest that the Internalizing Scale measures something different from the corresponding scale of the widely used Achenbach.

The factor analyses provided in the SSRS manual provide limited insights into the underlying traits assessed by the SSRS primarily because of the methods used. Principal components were extracted, but factor analysis was not conducted. Furthermore, the components were apparently derived solely on the basis of empirical methods. Subsequent research has found a poor fit of the factor structure described in the manual for parent ratings of elementary school-aged children (Van Horn et al.,

2007). In particular, Van Horn et al. (2007) found better support for a shorter version of the SSRS with the same domains as traditionally used in the SSRS (Gresham & Elliott, 1990). Importantly, that longitudinal study also suggested that the structure of the SSRS may vary across ethnic groups and that the SSRS may evaluate a somewhat different construct for 3rd grade children than for children in kindergarten. In other words, SSRS scores may not be a good way to track changes in social skills over time because the scores may change in meaning over time (Van Horn et al., 2007). Similarly, Whiteside, McCarthy, and Miller (2007) found a lack of support for the proposed factor structure of the SSRS for elementary school-aged children. However, in support of the SSRS's overall construct validity, they found that scores on the SSRS were significantly related to a history of peer problems.

Strengths and Weaknesses

The SSRS provides a unique assessment tool for child clinicians in that it is a thorough method for assessing behaviors that are often labeled as social skills. Furthermore, although the norming of the SSRS is not ideal, it is far superior to other measures that do not possess adequate norms and yet are used to make norm-referenced decisions. Other strengths of the SSRS include the following:

1. An attempt at a multi-domain assessment of social skills
2. The use of multiple informants
3. An integrated method of interpretation and intervention planning

Some of the weaknesses of the SSRS include the following:

1. Inadequately described norm samples for the Teacher and Parent Forms
2. Poor reliabilities for some of the subscales, especially those on the Student Form
3. Potential differences in meanings of scores across ethnic groups and developmental stages (Van Horn et al., 2007)
4. Emerging research that does not support the SSRS factor structure described in the manual
5. Less than adequate criterion-related validity for the Internalizing scale of the Problem Behaviors domain

Conclusions

Adaptive functioning is increasingly being recognized as an important, if not essential, aspect of child assessments. Although Doll introduced this intuitive concept in the 1930s, adaptive behavior was not formally included as central to the mental retardation diagnostic process until the 1950s.

In addition to its inclusion in diagnostic criteria, adaptive functioning also has an important role in intervention planning. To this end, components of adaptive behavior scales are now included on many behavior rating scales, such as the Achenbach and BASC-2, and these components are summarized in Box 14.2.Another interesting trend is for adaptive behavior scales to be single-domain measures. The SSRS is an excellent example of the trend toward developing assessment measures of what may be called sub-constructs of adaptive behavior.

This chapter highlighted several of the most popular adaptive behavior scales, but the reader should be aware that there are a substantial number of such scales available.

Chapter Summary

1. Edgar Doll first discussed the construct of adaptive behavior by drawing on his experience as a psychologist at

Box 14.2

Adaptive Behavior as a Component of Omnibus Rating Scales

With recent research and development in the assessment of adaptive behavior, it is sufficient to say that this construct is no longer considered a mere afterthought in child assessment or as a secondary component of evaluations for mental retardation. Instead, adaptive behavior is viewed as an important target of assessment for describing an individual's strengths and weaknesses and for designed skill-based interventions. This increased recognition of adaptive behavior as a central aspect of child assessments is evident in recent changes to omnibus rating scales. For example, although the original BASC (Reynolds & Kamphaus, 1992) was unique at the time in its multi-domain assessment of adaptive behavior, the BASC-2 (Reynolds & Kamphaus, 2004) has an expanded set of adaptive behavior domains. The BASC-2 saw the addition of a Functional Communication (parent and teacher) and Activities of Daily Living (parent) scale. The reader will note that these scales in particular seem consistent with adaptive behavior domains included in the measures reviewed in this chapter. The other adaptive scales (i.e., Adaptability – parent and teacher; Study Skills – teacher; Social Skills – parent and teacher; Leadership – parent and teacher; Self-reliance – self; Self-esteem – self; Relations with Parents – self; Interpersonal Relations – self) may overlap to some extent with Socialization, but they may also provide some unique information (e.g., one's ability to adjust to change in the case of the Adaptability scale). Research is quite scant on these scales to date. Initial validation of the BASC-2 found that the adaptive scales were generally negatively correlated with clinical scales of the BASC-2, as well as other measures (Reynolds & Kamphaus, 2004). Such results do not provide information as to the potential clinical utility of each individual scale. That is, although the psychometric properties of these scales are adequate, interpretation and clinical use might be best at the item level in terms of pinpointing specific behavioral concerns in the areas of adaptability, communication, self-care, and social skills. On the basis of state of the relevant research, a clinician cannot say with much confidence, for example, what a low (or high) score on the Leadership scale of the BASC-2-PRS really means. However, some items (e.g., "Is creative;" "Is good at getting people to work together.") may highlight specific strengths of the child or areas that may need some improvement.

The BASC-2 is not the only omnibus scale that directly assesses adaptive behavior. The Achenbach and PIC/SBS/PIY (see Chaps. 6 and 7) systems also have strategies for assessing strengths and socialization. In the case of the former, these are limited to a few screener-type items regarding overall competencies. In the case of the latter, these are framed in terms of social problems, the absence of which would imply adaptive social functioning. Therefore, the assessment of adaptive behavior offered on scales such as the BASC-2 or Achenbach cannot be considered substitutes for more detailed evaluations such as through the Vineland-2 or ABAS-II. If clinicians are routinely using omnibus rating scales as part of comprehensive assessments, then at the very least they will now have the ability to efficiently screen for deficits in adaptive functioning that can be more thoroughly evaluated through means such as those described in this chapter.

the Vineland State Training School, where he was charged with the assessment and rehabilitation of individuals with mental retardation. He noted that such individuals not only lacked intellectual abilities that were necessary for academic attainment, but they also often appeared to lack day-to-day living skills needed for independent functioning.

2. The American Association on Intellectual and Developmental Disabilities (AAIDD), formerly the AAMR, lists three broad domains (i.e., conceptual skills, social skills, and practical skills) of adaptive behavior that should be evaluated in assessments of mental retardation (see Luckasson et al., 2002). In addition, adaptive functioning is an important construct for case conceptualization and treatment planning for a number of problems (e.g., autism, ADHD).
3. Adaptive behavior has been defined as the performance of the daily activities that are required for social and personal sufficiency.
4. Adaptive behavior scales serve a valuable function for child clinicians in that they pin-point specific deficits that a child has not acquired, which in turn may serve as the focus of treatment efforts.
5. Widaman, Stacy, and Borthwick-Duffy (1993) found clear evidence for the existence of four major adaptive behavior domains: cognitive competence, social competence, social maladaptation, and personal maladaptation. Most present day measures of adaptive behavior include domains consistent with these findings.
6. Parents, teachers, and other caregivers are most often used as informants for adaptive behavior scales. Children may also be used as self-informants for some adaptive behavior scales, although such a strategy has some obvious limitations.
7. Correlations between intelligence and adaptive behavior measures are modest (i.e., .40 to .60), indicating some overlap but also substantial independence.
8. Adaptive behavior scales are commonly administered using a checklist or semi-structured interview technique.
9. The semi-structured interview technique requires a high level of clinical skill. The clinician has to make the interview conversation-like, topical, and empathic, while at the same time collecting the necessary information to allow for accurate rating (scoring) of individual items.
10. The Vineland-2 is probably the most well-known and widely used tool for assessing adaptive behavior for individuals from birth through adulthood. There is an extensive body of research on its predecessor, and a number of changes were made to the present version to facilitate administration, scoring, and interpretation.
11. The Scale of Independent Behavior (SIB-R) in many ways resembles the Vineland. It is a broad-based assessment of adaptive behavior spanning an age range of infancy through adulthood.
12. The ABAS-II is closely aligned with *DSM* and AAIDD criteria. So far, it has demonstrated good reliability and validity.
13. One aspect of adaptive behavior, social competence or social skills, is of such importance that scales that measure this construct exclusively are available.
14. The Social Skills Rating System (SSRS) is a comprehensive measure of social skills which incorporates multiple domains and raters. Teacher, parent, and student forms are provided for measuring a variety of social skills across settings.
15. The assessment of adaptive behavior is increasingly being viewed as a central component of child assessment. Expanded components of adaptive behavior scales are now being included on omnibus rating scales such as the Achenbach and BASC-2.

Part III

Advanced Topics

CHAPTER 15

Integrating and Interpreting Assessment Information

Chapter Questions

- What are some reasons why assessment information may differ depending on who is providing it?
- What are the issues involved in using simple (equal weighing) or complex (unequal weighing) methods for combining information from different sources?
- How might age of the child and type of behavior affect the agreement between different sources on a child's or adolescent's adjustment?
- What steps should one go through to integrate information from different sources, from different methods, and across different areas of functioning?

Introduction

Throughout this book we have emphasized the need for a comprehensive evaluation when testing children and adolescents in most circumstances. Comprehensive means that (1) many areas of functioning should be assessed, (2) assessments should be conducted using multiple techniques, and (3) assessments should obtain information from many sources (e.g., child, parent, teachers, peers). If one follows this advice, one is confronted with a dizzying array of information gathered during the assessment. In the previous chapters we discussed each individual component of the assessment in isolation. However, the

P.J. Frick et al., *Clinical Assessment of Child and Adolescent Personality and Behavior*,
DOI 10.1007/978-1-4419-0641-0_15,

most important and most difficult part of the evaluation is the integration of this information into a clear case formulation that answers the referral questions and points the way to the most appropriate intervention.

Although we discuss integrating information across multiple domains of functioning and across multiple assessment techniques, a main focus of this chapter is on integrating information from different informants. This is a particularly difficult endeavor because one is theoretically obtaining the same information on a child's adjustment from different sources. One might expect that there would be a high degree of correlation between information provided by different informants. Unfortunately, this is not the case. A large body of research has indicated that there are generally quite small correlations between different informants providing the same type of information (Achenbach, McConaughy, & Howell, 1987; De Los Reyes & Kazdin, 2005).

One explanation for this low rate of agreement between informants is that different people see a child in different settings. That is, the low correlations between informants may reflect real differences in a child's behavior across different settings. The meta-analysis conducted by Achenbach et al. (1987) provides some support for this possibility. Across the 119 studies that they reviewed, the average correlation in ratings between informants who see a child in different settings (e.g., parent/teacher) was .28. In contrast, the average correlation between informants who see a child in the same setting (e.g., pairs of parents or pairs of teachers) was .60. This substantial increase in agreement between informants who see a child in the same setting provides evidence that the lack of informant agreement reflects, at least in part, real *situational variability* in children's behavior.

Konold, Walthall, and Pianta (2004) also provide evidence to support the contention that much of the cross-informant disagreement is due to situational specific behaviors in children across settings. Specifically, these authors obtained parent and teacher ratings of young children's behavior. They reported that the general form and factor loadings for the ratings were very similar across mother, father, and teacher ratings, even though the correlations among the ratings from each informant were fairly low. Thus, the low level of agreement appeared to be more likely due to situation-specific behavior, than due to the manner in which the behaviors were measured.

This situational variability has important implications for clinical assessments. It suggests that to make sense of information on a child's emotional and behavioral functioning, a clinical assessor must also assess the contextual demands that might influence a child's behavior and, thereby, account for the discrepant information one is obtaining. For example, a clinical assessor might be quite puzzled over a teacher's report of significant problems of inattention, disorganization, and hyperactivity at school, when it appears to be in stark contrast to only minimal problems being reported by a child's parent. However, further assessment of the home context may indicate that the parents do not put many demands for sustained attention, organization, or sitting still on the child at home. As a result, the behaviors are not problematic in this setting.

Another important aspect of the lack of agreement between informants is determining the *level of analysis* at which agreement is being measured. Individual behaviors tend to show less consistency across informants than broader dimensions or composites of multiple behaviors. A good example of this phenomenon comes from a study by Biederman, Keenan, and Faraone (1990). In a clinic sample of children and adolescents, the average correlation between parent and teacher reports of individual symptoms of Attention-Deficit Hyperactivity Disorder

(ADHD) on a structured interview was quite low ($r = .21$). However, these authors found that, if one looked at the diagnostic level, the level of agreement between parents and teachers was quite high. If a parent reported that a child had ADHD on the structured interview, there was a 90% probability that the child's teacher would report the presence of the disorder.

There are two ways one can conceptualize this issue. On a psychometric level, classic measurement theory states that an aggregate measure shows higher reliability than its individual components (Peterson, Kolen, & Hoover, 1989). Alternatively, the same issue can be framed as another aspect of the situational specificity of behavior. That is, the same underlying construct or psychological dimension may be present across situations, but the behavioral manifestation may change, depending on the situational demands. If one frames it in this way, the implication for clinical assessment is the same as that discussed previously. To understand the different behavioral manifestations, one must understand the demands of the different contexts under consideration.

Karver (2006) provided data to suggest that some of the disagreement between informants is related to the types of behaviors being assessed. Using 20 judges for ratings of 59 child behaviors on 11 dimensions, three primary dimensions of behavior accounted for 43% of the level agreement between parent and child ratings. The first two dimensions relate to the saliency of the behavior to the parent or child (e.g., ease of recall of the behavior, objective nature of the behavior, perceived seriousness of the behavior). The third dimension involved how observable the behavior was and how willing the parent or child would be to report the behavior accurately because of social desirability.

One final issue on informant disagreement is the fact that some apparent disagreement may be an artifact of *different measurement techniques* used across informants. An example is a case in which a child is showing indications of depression on a projective technique but this is not reported by parent and teacher on rating scales. A clinical assessor may consider this a disagreement across informants. In fact, this is more a function of the lack of agreement across methods, because studies have shown that the agreement between projective and objective self-report measures is generally low (Ball, et al., 1991). However, even within the same method, what is assessed may differ across informants. For example, some rating scales include very different items for parents and teachers (Richters, 1992). As a result, it becomes unclear whether disagreements are due to actual differences in perceptions between parents and teachers or whether they are due to different questions being asked of the two informants.

Considering these issues, clinical assessors should first try to determine if seemingly discrepant information can be attributed solely to varying situational demands, the level of analysis, the types of behaviors being assessed, or to differences in the assessment strategy. If the discrepant information can be explained by these factors, one has gone a long way in explaining the reasons for a child's problems and one usually has obtained important information for designing treatment. For example, if a child is displaying highly anxious behavior in the school setting only, one should look for what aspects of the school environment are leading to the anxiety (e.g., social-evaluative situations). In doing this, one has pointed the way to one route of intervention. That is, to systematically desensitize the child to the anxiety-provoking stimuli. Unfortunately, in many situations one cannot be confident that any of these factors are contributing to the discrepant information. In such cases, one is confronted with the difficult decision of what to do with conflicting information in developing a case formulation.

Integrating Information across Informants

Simpler May be Better

To deal with this issue of conflicting information, clinical assessors have often developed their own algorithm or methods of deciding how to weigh the reports of different informants. In Box 15.1 we summarize the results of a survey of child mental health professionals in which respondents rated the importance of different informants for assessing various types of childhood psychopathology. This provides a good illustration of common practice in weighing different informants. In Box 15.2 we summarize an explicit diagnostic decision tree that was developed to standardize the diagnostic decision-making process. This decision tree was designed for use with structured diagnostic interviews. We feel that these two pieces of research illustrate the problems one faces when attempting to systematically integrate discrepant

Box 15.1

A Survey of Mental Health Professionals' Use of Different Informants to Assess Childhood Psychopathology

Loeber, Green, and Lahey (1990) conducted a survey of 105 members of the Society for Research in Child and Adolescent Psychopathology assessing their perceptions of the relative usefulness of pre-pubertal children, their mothers, and their teachers as informants on emotional and behavioral problems in children. Two-thirds of the respondents had Ph.D's and one-third had M.D.'s. Fifty-nine percent described themselves as child researchers and clinicians, 34% described themselves as researchers only, 1.9% described themselves as clinicians only, and 5% described themselves in an "other" category. Respondents rated the utility of information provided by mothers, teachers, and 7–12-year-old children on a 0 (not useful) to 3 (very useful) scale. There were 44 behaviors rated covering the domains of inattention/hyperactivity, oppositional problems, conduct problems, anxiety, and depression.

These authors found that the perceived relative usefulness of children, mothers, and teachers varied as a function of the domain being assessed. Specifically, teachers were rated as more useful than both parents and children in the assessment of inattention/hyperactivity. In contrast, parents were rated as more useful than teachers and children in assessing severe antisocial behavior and aggression. Both parents and teachers were rated as more useful in assessing children's oppositional behavior than children themselves, although there was no difference in the perceived usefulness of parents and teachers within this domain. In general, parents and children were judged more useful in assessing internalizing problems (anxiety and depression) than teachers. Somewhat surprisingly, parents were judged significantly more useful than children in assessing internalizing problems.

In sum, these authors found that there were systematic preferences for certain informants over others in assessing childhood psychopathology, and these preferences varied as a function of the behavioral domain being assessed. These authors correctly point out that the results were limited to mental health professionals' perceptions of pre-pubertal (ages 7–12) children. The results may have been different, especially in the relative importance placed on child self-report, if the assessment of psychopathology in adolescents had been the focus of the survey (see for example Cantwell, Lewinsohn, Rhode, & Seeley, 1997).

Source: Loeber, R., Green, S. M., & Lahey, B. B. (1990). Mental health professionals' perception of the utility of children, mothers, and teachers as informants on childhood psychopathology. *Journal of Clinical Child Psychology, 19*, 136–143.

Box 15.2

An Attempt to Develop Rules for Combining Multiple Sources of Information on Childhood Psychopathology

The struggle to develop standardized methods of integrating information from multiple informants is exemplified in an article by Reich and Earls (1987). These researchers set out to develop "a replicable strategy to make psychiatric diagnoses when reports are obtainable independently from parents and children" (p. 601). The authors clearly state that the goal was not to achieve perfect parent-child agreement but to learn how to evaluate these different sources of information. The following is a summary (see appendix of research article for full criteria) of the decision tree used by these authors to make diagnoses according to the *DSM-III* (American Psychiatric Association, 1980). We present this approach not so much as a recommended decision tree, but as an example of strategies that assessors have developed to resolve the problem of discrepant information.

1. Attention-Deficit Disorder
   (a) Minimum of eight symptoms from parent report, at least six symptoms from child report, and an age of onset before 7.
   (b) Evidence of impairment in school from teacher's report either of significant inattention, disruptive behavior, academic underachievement, or peer difficulties.
   (c) If parent reports six or seven symptoms and child report shows four or five, diagnosis can be made with compelling evidence from teacher.
2. Oppositional Disorder
   (a) Minimum of two symptoms from both parent and child and a report of at least 6 months duration.
   (b) Teacher indicates a pattern of negative and defiant behavior.
3. Conduct Disorder
   (a) Two or more symptoms from either parent or child.
   (b) Confirmation of antisocial behavior from at least one other source.
4. Major Depression
   (a) For children over 13, a diagnosis can be made from child report alone if (1) child reports dysphoric mood or anhedonia for 2 weeks or longer; (2) at least four vegetative symptoms from *DSM-III* criteria are present for 2 weeks or longer; (3) there is evidence of impairment, such as grades dropping, irritability, social withdrawal, etc.
   (b) A diagnosis of depression would normally not be made by parents report alone unless child report was just under threshold.
5. Separation Anxiety and Overanxious Disorder
   (a) Diagnosis can be made from either parent or child report alone only if the other informant provides some evidence of anxiety and/or depressive symptoms.

SOURCE: Reich, W., & Earls, E. (1987). Rules for making psychiatric diagnoses in children on the basis of multiple sources of information: Preliminary strategies. *Journal of Abnormal Child Psychology, 15*, 601–616.

assessment information either in clinical practice or in clinical research (see also Smith, 2007).

Piacentini, Cohen, and Cohen (1992) provide an interesting discussion on developing ideal weighing systems for combining information across multiple informants. These authors label systems in which one source of information is weighed more heavily than others (e.g., teachers' report of inattention given more weight than parents' report) as *complex schemes*. In contrast, *simple schemes* are those where information from all sources is weighed equally. These simple schemes can also be called the *either/or rule*, since a finding is considered significant if it is reported by any informant (e.g., parent, child, or teacher).

These authors provide both a theoretical and an empirical rationale for why simple schemes are either as good as or better than complex schemes. First, these authors argue that most weighing systems rely on clinical judgment, in the absence of any clear research base to guide decisions. They cite numerous findings that "expert judgments" are "almost always inferior to equal weighing in predicting outcomes based on multiple variables" (p. 54). This rationale, however, would only hold for weighing systems based on clinical judgment. What about empirically derived weighing systems?

The authors cite a study in which a complex method of combining information was developed on the basis of logistic regression analyses. When Bird, Gould, and Staghezza (1992) compared their empirically derived weighing procedure with a simple either/or scheme, there were no differences in how well either system predicted clinicians' diagnoses. Moreover, weighing systems based on regression analyses from one sample are likely to underperform simple schemes when applied in a different sample, as the weighing system is at least partially dependent on the idiosyncratic characteristics of the sample. In summary, Piacentini, Cohen, and Cohen (1992) provide compelling arguments for the use of simple schemes in combining discrepant reports.

Although in principle this approach seems sound and we advocate that it should be the primary or default option for most clinicians, there are several issues that one needs to consider when using this approach. First, this approach assumes that false positives (i.e., a clinically significant finding from an informant that is not true) are rarer and less harmful than false negatives. For many clinical situations, this emphasis on ensuring that children in need of treatment are not missed is appropriate. However, we also feel that such a decision should not be made blindly. Clinicians should always be careful in diagnosing and classifying childhood problems and carefully consider both positive and negative consequences of any decision (see Chap. 3 for issues in diagnosis and classification). Therefore, one must carefully consider the risks and benefits of both false positives and false negatives when developing case formulations.

A second issue was raised by Piacentini, Cohen, and Cohen (1992), who noted that simple schemes are better only if informants are asked to provide "only that information they would ordinarily be expected to know" (p. 59). In essence, this implies that there will be certain informants who have better knowledge of a child's adjustment than others. For example, teachers may not have knowledge about certain behaviors that occur outside of the school setting, such as firesetting, cruelty to animals, or needing to sleep with parents. In addition to the type of adjustment being assessed, we feel that there are other factors that may make some informants better than others in a given case. In the next several sections we discuss these factors that may affect the quality of information obtained from specific sources. From the outset we should note that most of these factors largely will affect the planning of the evaluation rather than the interpretation. Specifically, many of the factors will affect the choice of informant and of the method used to obtain information.

Informant Discrepancies and the Type of Problem

The survey by Loeber, Green, and Lahey (1990), cited in Box 15.1, indicated that clinicians tend to weigh adult informants (e.g., parents, teachers) more heavily for observable behaviors and tend to weigh child self-report more heavily for emotional problems. The logical basis to this argument is that emotional distress is largely an internal subjective event that is more difficult to tie to behavioral referents that can be observed by others. However, there is a growing body of research that has largely supported this method of clinical practice.

For example, mothers and fathers show a higher level of agreement in rating children's objective, observable, behavior problems than in rating less observable emotional problems (Christensen, Mergolin, & Sullaway, 1992). Also, research has found that adults tend to report more conduct problems and overactivity than is reported by child self-report (Kashani, et al., 1985; Reich & Earls, 1987), and children tend to report more emotional symptoms than do parents or teachers (Bird, Gould, & Stagheeza, 1992; Cantwell et al., 1997; Edelbrock et al., 1986). This differential prevalence in reporting would support the common clinical practice of emphasizing adult informants in the assessment of externalizing problems and emphasizing children in the assessment of internalizing problems, if one assumes that false positives are rare. This view is consistent with the either/or approach discussed in the previous section.

However, there are other studies that have attempted to go beyond simply documenting differences in prevalence to test the differential validity of various informants on child adjustment. These studies test the *differential validity* of various informants across behavioral domains using some external and clinically important criteria. A good example of this approach is a study by Loeber et al. (1991). In a clinic referred sample of boys between the ages of 6 and 13, these authors tested the correlations among parent, child, and teacher reports of disruptive behaviors and several important impairment criteria (e.g., school suspensions, police contacts, grade retention, special education placement) assessed one year later. Supporting common clinical practice, teachers' report of inattentive/hyperactive behaviors were the best predictors of impairment one year later. For conduct problem behaviors, parental report tended to show the most consistent prediction of impairment, although teachers' and children's information also had utility in predicting school suspensions. These findings should be interpreted in light of the age of the sample studied. Specifically, this study focused on elementary school-age children. As we will discuss in more detail in the next section, there is some evidence that the age of the child may influence the importance of different sources of information. For example, the importance of child report for assessing antisocial behavior, especially covert antisocial behavior (e.g., lying, stealing), may increase in adolescents, while the importance of parental report may decrease as parents' knowledge of their child's behaviors decreases (e.g., Cantwell, et al., 1997; Elliott, Huizinga, & Ageton, 1985).

The validation of different informants requires the measurement of some independent and clinically important criteria against which to judge the usefulness of information provided. This has been very problematic for testing the differential validity of informants' reports of internalizing child behavior because it is difficult to determine what should be the validating criteria. One notable exception was a study by Frick, Silverthorn, and Evans (1994) that used a maternal history of anxiety as a way of validating informants' reports of childhood anxiety. Specifically, these authors studied the correlations among parent, child, and teacher reports of anxiety in children and a history of an anxiety disorder in mother. In the sample of children ages 9–13, these authors found that teacher report of anxiety was not related to a family history of anxiety, but both parent and child reports of anxiety were.

However, there was additional support for the relative importance of children's self-report of anxiety. Children's self-reports of anxiety disorders were always accompanied by confirmation by their parents. However, parental report was not always confirmed by the child, and parent–child disagreements on the presence of an anxiety disorder were systematically related to the parents' own level of anxiety. These authors concluded that there was evidence for parental projection of their own anxiety onto their reports of anxiety in their children. This provides some preliminary support for the relative emphasis on children's self-report of anxiety, at least in this age group (9–13 years) of children.

Informant Discrepancies and Age of Child

Another factor that might affect the quality of information provided by different informants is the age of the child or adolescent being assessed. First, one would expect that, as a child grows older, parents would have less knowledge of the child's emotions and behaviors, especially as parent–child relationships change in adolescence (Paikoff & Brooks-Gunn, 1991). Similarly, as a child leaves early elementary school, the likelihood of a single teacher spending a great deal of time with a child decreases. Third, as a child develops cognitively, he or she may become better able to report on such abstract concepts as emotions and thoughts. As a result of these factors, one would expect that the importance of parents and teachers as informants would decrease with age and the importance of children's self-report would increase.

Edelbrock et al. (1985) tested these hypothesized age effects on parent and child reports using structured diagnostic interviews. Using two-week test-retest correlations as the index of reliability, these authors found that the reliability of parent report decreased with age as predicted, although the reliability generally remained at an acceptable level into adolescence. Children's self-report showed a more dramatic age trend. Children's self-report on the structured interviews showed a clear increase in reliability with age. Importantly, the reliability of child self-report on the structured interviews was quite poor before age 9. Evidence for the predicted decrease in reliability of teacher's report also was obtained from another source. Specifically, in the initial development of the Behavioral Assessment System for Children, it was found that the reliability for the Teacher Report Form decreased with age (Reynolds & Kamphaus, 1992).

One question in interpreting these results is whether the changes in reliability across age are confined to structured techniques, like structured interviews and behavior rating scales. At least the findings for children's self-report are not confined to structured techniques. The reliability of children's responses to projective techniques has also been found to increase with age (Exner, Thomas, & Mason, 1985). Therefore, the hypothesized age-related changes in the reliability of various informants have generally been supported in research across a number of assessment domains. These findings on the limited reliability of child self-report for very young children may not be surprising for many clinicians who work with young children. However, clinical assessors who work largely with older children, adolescents, or adults tend to use a traditional approach to assessment that relies heavily on self-report and may be uncomfortable with a reduced role of self-report in the assessment of young children.

A final issue related to informant discrepancies and age of the child relates to the level of agreement between informants other than the child (e.g. parent and teachers). In their meta-analysis of 119 studies, Achenbach et al. (1987) reported that parent and teacher ratings were in greater agreement for younger children than for adolescents. As noted above, part of this age trend may be due to adolescents spending less time with teachers and parents and, as a result, these informants may have less complete information on the adolescent's adjustment. However, Achenbach et al. also suggest that younger children's behavior may be more cross-situationally consistent. Importantly, however, these age related findings have not always been consistently reported across samples (De Los Reyes & Kazdin, 2005).

Informant Discrepancies: Other Factors

In addition to type of behaviors and age of the child, there are other factors that might influence the report of various informants and which therefore should be considered when interpreting discrepant information. In a previous chapter we discussed factors within the family, such as *parental adjustment* and *marital conflict*, which may affect the information provided by the parent on a child's adjustment. For example, Foley et al. (2005) reported on a sample of 2,798 twins ages 8–17. They found that maternal alcoholism and marital difficulties were characteristic of cases in which an anxiety disorder was reported by mothers but not children.

Also, informants might have *differing motivations*, both conscious and unconscious, that can affect the information they provide (Karver, 2006). For example, a child may not want to admit to problem behavior or a teacher may be interested in getting a child placed outside of his class. Several rating scales discussed in previous chapters include validity scales that attempt to detect such response sets and aid in the interpretation of information provided.

It is also important to note *testing conditions* when interpreting the report of different informants. For example, a child may have been administered a self-report questionnaire after a long testing session and it is obvious in watching him complete the questionnaire that he is not reading the items carefully.

Summary

From this discussion it is clear that, although the simple scheme of equally weighing the report of different informants using an either/or approach is a good starting point, a clinical assessor cannot use this approach blindly. There are numerous factors that must be considered in trying to explain seemingly discrepant information from different sources.

The previous discussion outlines some of the more important issues that have been uncovered in research that can help guide clinical decision making. However, the final case formulation that results from the integration of multiple types of assessment information involves a number of complex clinical decisions. To aid in this process, in Box 15.3 we provide a summary of an article by Nezu and Nezu (1993) that outlines (1) some of the common cognitive strategies that are used by people in making decisions but which could lead to errors in clinical reasoning and (2) a general orientation to clinical reasoning that can minimize the effects of these errors in clinical judgment. Using this general problem orientation as a basis, the following section outlines a step-by-step strategy that can help to guide the clinician in the integration of assessment information.

A Multistep Strategy for Integrating Information

The following strategy assumes one has conducted a comprehensive clinical evaluation of the child or adolescent. The prerequisites are (1) having information on a child's adjustment from various sources

Box 15.3

Research Note: Common Errors in Clinical Reasoning and a Problem-Solving Model for Developing a Case Formulation

Nezu and Nezu (1993) conceptualize a clinical assessment as a method of translating a client's complaints of distress into a meaningful set of target problems and treatment goals. This is what we have referred to throughout this book as developing a case formulation. Nezu and Nezu conceptualize this process as delineating instrumental outcomes (target problems) that are believed to directly or indirectly relate to a desired outcome for the client (treatment goals). For clinicians to use assessment information in delineating instrumental outcomes, they must go through a complex problem-solving process. Nezu and Nezu first present several common cognitive strategies that can lead to errors in the problem-solving process. Next, these authors outline an orientation to problem-solving that should limit these errors in clinical reasoning.

Errors in Clinical Reasoning

1. The *availability heuristic* occurs when clinicians attempt to estimate the probability of an event on the basis of the ease with which examples of that event come to mind. Nezu and Nezu use the example of a clinician who may overestimate the risk of suicide in a new client, if the clinician was recently involved in the case of a client who committed suicide but was judged to be of low risk.
2. The *representative heuristic* occurs when a schema is accessed by a given characteristic to the exclusion of other schemas. For example, the symptom of sadness may automatically lead the clinician to consider major depression (i.e., diagnostic schema) to the exclusion of other possible diagnostic schemas (e.g., medically related mood disorder, personality disorders).
3. The *anchoring heuristic* occurs when predictions or decisions are overly dependent on initial impressions and later information is discounted, even if the new information is in disagreement with the initial impressions. For example, if a depressed client discusses interpersonal problems in the initial meeting with the clinician, the anchoring heuristic would lead the clinician to select poor social skills as the primary target of intervention to the exclusion of other information (e.g., presence of negative cognitions) obtained in subsequent assessment.
4. *Confirmatory search strategies* involve using procedures that seek only to confirm initial impressions and failing to seek disconfirming evidence. For example, a child referred for problems of inattention and motor restlessness is assessed only for other symptoms of ADHD, without considering other possible reasons for his or her symptoms (e.g., learning disability, depression, anxiety).

Problem Orientation

Nezu and Nezu propose that a systematic problem-solving approach to clinical decision-making helps to limit the use of these cognitive heuristics. The key to this approach is the clinician's problem orientation. This refers to the clinician's overall theoretical orientation for viewing problem behavior, which defines the proper content and methods of assessment. These authors recommend an orientation of *planned critical multiplism*, which assumes that clinical outcomes are brought about by a multiplicity of interacting factors. The basis of this problem orientation is that:

"A variety of biological (e.g., genetic, neurochemical, physical), psychological (e.g., affective, cognitive, behavioral) and social (e.g., social and physical environment) variables can serve to act and interact as casual agents or maintaining factors. Such variables can influence the pathogenesis of a symptom, disorder or both in either a proximal (e.g.,

(Continues)

Box 15.3 (Continued)

immediate antecedent stimulus) or distal (e.g., develop-mental history) manner" (p. 256).

Nezu and Nezu state that even if this model is incorrect in a given case (i.e., there is a unitary cause), by starting with the planned critical multiplism orientation, the clinician is less likely to selectively focus on any single type or class of instrumental outcomes. As a result, this problem orientation limits the potential for cognitive biases.

SOURCE: Nezu, A. M. & Nezu, C. M. (1993). Identifying and selecting target problems for clinical interventions: A problem-solving model. *Psychological Assessment*, 5, 254–263.

and using multiple methods; (2) having information on the child's developmental, medical, and psychiatric history; (3) having information on multiple areas of functioning, such as information on academic capabilities and peer relations, in addition to information on multiple areas of behavioral and emotional functioning; and (4) having information on the important contexts (e.g., home, school, work) in which a child functions. Once this information is obtained, the following multistep procedure can be used to develop a case formulation. In Boxes 15.4 and 15.5 we provide two case examples that illustrate this interpretive process.

Step 1: Document All Clinically Significant Findings Regarding the Child's Adjustment

The first step of the procedure follows the either/or rule. The assessor sifts through all of the information on a child's or adolescent's adjustment from all sources and methods and determines if there are any significant findings, such as norm-referenced elevations on rating scales, diagnoses based on structured interviews, or clinically significant material from projective tests. As discussed previously, this is a very sensitive procedure that can result in high rates of significant findings. We feel that it is a good starting point in the interpretive process. However, we also feel that stopping at this point would result in an unacceptably high rate of false positives. The subsequent steps help to increase the specificity of the process.

Step 2: Look for Convergent Findings across Sources and Methods

After noting all of the significant findings across methods and sources, the next step is to isolate areas that are consistent across the various pieces of assessment information. In looking at cross-method and cross-informant convergence, it is recommended that one takes a closer look at the assessment information and does not simply determine whether or not a score has crossed some threshold or elevation. We have discussed at several points in this book the arbitrary nature of many clinical cut-offs, such as elevations on a scale of a behavior rating scale or a diagnosis on a structured interview. How different is a child with a T-score of 69 from a child with a T-score of 70 on a given scale? How different is a child with seven symptoms of ADHD from a child with eight?

Box 15.4

Case Study to Illustrate the Multistep Interpretive Procedure: A 7-Year-Old Boy with Behavior Problems

Jake was a 7-year, 1-month-old boy who was referred to an outpatient psychological clinic for a comprehensive psychological evaluation by his mother. His mother reported that Jake was having great difficulty completing school work and that he was extremely oppositional and hard to manage at home. Jake was administered a comprehensive battery of tests that included (1) an unstructured clinical interview; (2) an extensive family background assessment; (3) a psychoeducational assessment; (4) an assessment of his emotional and behavioral functioning through structured interviews conducted with his mother and teacher and rating scales completed by his mother, his teacher, and by Jake himself; (5) a sociometric exercise conducted with his class; and (6) an objective assessment of his classroom performance (e.g., amount of work completed, accuracy of work).

Step 1: Document All Clinically Significant Findings on the Child's Adjustment

On a structured interview, the Diagnostic Interview Schedule for Children-Version 4 (DISC-IV; Shaffer et al., 2000), Jake met criteria for ADHD according to both his mother and his teacher. On the Child Behavior Checklist (CBCL: Achenbach, 2001), he had T-scores above 70 on both the Thought Problem scale and the Attention Problem scale according to the father and T-Scores of 70 and 67 on the Attention problem and Thought Problem scales, respectively, according to his mother's report. On the teacher-completed Comprehensive Behavior Rating Scale for Children (CBRSC; Neeper, Lahey, & Frick, 1990), he obtained a T-score of 71 on the Daydreams scale and a T-score of 65 on the Motor Hyperactivity scale.

Also on the DISC-IV, Jake met criteria for oppositional Defiant Disorder (ODD) according to his mother's report. Similarly, he obtained T-scores above 70 on the Aggressive Behavior scale of the CBCL by both mother and father reports.

A final significant finding was the report of a sufficient number of depressive symptoms to meet criteria for current Major Depression according to maternal report on the DISC-IV.

Step 2: Look for Convergent Findings across Sources and Methods

It was clear that there were convergent findings for significant problems of inattention–disorganization and impulsivity–hyperactivity associated with ADHD, according to parents and teachers and across structured interviews and rating scales. However, for the oppositional behaviors, the teacher report gave no indications of these behaviors in the school environment either on rating scales or on structured interviews. For the parental report of depression, although Jake's teacher did not report symptoms of depression of sufficient severity to warrant a diagnosis solely on her report, she did endorse several symptoms, such as feeling sad and irritable, feeling bad about himself, and often seeming as if he was about to cry. However, on the Children's Depression Inventory (CDI; Kovacs, 1991), Jake did not report significant feelings of depression.

Step 3: Try to Explain Discrepancies

In talking to Jake's teacher, it appeared that she had a very structured classroom with a teacher's aide who implemented behavioral programs for students. Jake's parents were divorced, and his mother seemed quite distressed over Jake's behavior. As a result, she seemed to be very unsure of how to discipline

(Continues)

Box 15.4 (Continued)

Jake, leading to a great deal of inconsistency and sometimes harshness in her discipline attempts. These differences in teacher and parent handling of Jake's behavior seemed to explain the fact that he was not showing significant oppositional behaviors at school. While there was some support for the depressive behaviors by Jake's teacher, Jake did not report such behaviors. However, given Jake's young age, there was some concern over his ability to accurately report on internal feelings using the structured CDI.

Step 4: Developing a Profile and Hierarchy of Problem Areas

Jake exhibited a common profile of showing both ADHD and ODD. However, there were several reasons why ADHD was considered primary. First, the ADHD behaviors had been present throughout Jake's life, and they were the only behaviors shown at both home and school. Second, Jake's teacher reported that Jake's grades were primarily affected by his failure to complete work or his hasty completion of work that led to careless errors. This teacher report was consistent with a psychoeducational assessment that revealed an IQ in the average range and academic achievement also in an age-appropriate range. A sociometric exercise indicated that Jake was disliked by a significant number of his classmates (5 out of a class of 17 nominated him as "liked least"). Therefore, the ADHD was considered to be causing a high level of impairment for Jake, educationally and socially. Third, Jake's biological father reported that he had had significant problems with inattention and hyperactivity as a child.

Jake's depressive features were also considered to be secondary to the ADHD. His mother reported that they started after the past semester in school, when he had received his worst grades ever which led to high rates of conflict at home.

Step 5: Determine Critical Information to Place in the Report

Jake's mother had seen a counselor for 6 months following her divorce from Jake's father, 3 years prior to the evaluation. This piece of information did not seem to be crucial for understanding our case formulation of Jake. Also, because the psychoeducational testing did not reveal many significant strengths or weaknesses in cognitive processing or in various areas of academic achievement, this information was only briefly summarized, indicating that it was not suggestive of the presence of a cognitive deficit or a learning disability.

Box 15.5

Case Study to Illustrate Multistep Interpretive Procedure: A 14-Year-Old Boy with a Language Disorder and Social Phobia

Jarrod was 14 years, 2 months old when his school referred him for a comprehensive psychological evaluation. They were concerned about Jarrod's inability to complete schoolwork and his extreme shyness. His teachers reported that Jarrod rarely initiated conversations with either peers or teachers and responded to other people with only one-word answers. Jarrod had been receiving resource help at school in a learning disabilities classroom for the past 2 years.

(Continues)

Box 15.5 (Continued)

Jarrod was administered a comprehensive battery of tests that included an unstructured clinical interview, an extensive family background assessment, a psychoeducational assessment, assessment of his emotional and behavioral functioning through structured interviews conducted with his mother and Jarrod and rating scales completed by Jarrod and his mother.

Step 1: Document All Clinically Significant Findings on the Child's Adjustment

On structured interviews, Jarrod met criteria for Social Phobia on the DISC-IV by both his own self-report and the report of his mother. In the psychoeducational assessment, Jarrod scored 25 points lower in his Verbal IQ than on his Performance IQ. This verbal deficit was consistent with previous testing conducted by his school. In addition to the verbal weakness, Jarrod scored poorly on tests of processing speed.

Step 2: Look for Convergent Findings across Sources and Methods

Although not in the clinically significant range, there was support for Jarrod's social anxiety and social withdrawal on parent- and child-completed rating scales. On the CBCL completed by Jarrod's mother, the Withdrawal scale had a T-score of 68. On the self-report Personality Inventory for Youth (PIY; Lachar & Gruber, 1994), Jarrod obtained a T-score of 65 on the Social Withdrawal scale. This was consistent with reports from his teachers and from behavioral observations during testing that indicated that Jarrod was very quiet and withdrawn. The other main areas of convergence were that Jarrod did not show significant behavioral problems and his parents seemed to provide a warm and stable home environment.

Step 3: Try to Explain Discrepancies

In this case the only discrepancy was the somewhat milder level of social withdrawal being reported at home than was being reported by teachers at school, although clearly the shyness was still evident at home. This was likely due to Jarrod's higher level of comfort with family members, which made him more willing to converse with family members.

Step 4: Developing a Profile and Hierarchy of Problem Areas

It seemed as though Jarrod had an expressive language disorder and a deficit in processing speed. As a result, Jarrod was likely to be uncomfortable conversing in social situations, leading to the high rate of social withdrawal. The language disorder and processing speed deficit were judged to be primary in this case because they had been chronic throughout his life and Jarrod did not show a high rate of anxiety in other situations that did not require a great deal of verbal expression.

Step 5: Determine Critical Information to Place in the Report

A great deal of the information on Jarrod's family background, current family functioning, and functioning in other behavioral, and emotional areas (e.g., conduct and depression) were only summarized briefly in the report. They were felt to be important to document Jarrod's many psychological strengths, but a detailed discussion of these areas was not felt to be needed in the written report.

Therefore, when looking for convergent pieces of evidence, one should look at the full range of scores, problems, or symptoms. For example, suppose a child reports a high level of anxiety on a self-report questionnaire, passing a clinical cut-off point as required in Step 1. However, on a parent-structured interview there are no diagnoses of anxiety disorders reported, but the parent has reported three symptoms of overanxious disorder and two symptoms of separation anxiety disorder. Further, a teacher rated the child with a T-score of 64 on the anxiety scale of a behavior rating scale. If one just viewed scores that exceeded a clinical cut-off, this pattern would look like the child's self-report of anxiety was unsupported by other informants, when, in fact, we would argue that there is fairly consistent support for the presence of anxious behaviors, although the anxiety is not being perceived as severe by parents and teachers.

Step 3: Try to Explain Discrepancies

The complexity of the assessment process is dramatically reduced when assessment information is consistent across methods and sources. This is the ideal case that is the dream of every clinical assessor. Unfortunately, existing research and clinical experience suggest that this is not likely to happen often. In most cases, there will be numerous discrepancies between the information provided by the different sources after steps 1 and 2. At this stage, one should take the information discussed in previous sections of this chapter and try to develop explanations for the discrepancies. Can the discrepancies be explained by different demands in the various settings in which a child is observed? Can the discrepancies be explained by differences in the measurement techniques used or by certain characteristics/motivations of the informants? Can the discrepancies be explained by differing knowledge of the child's behavior across informants? As mentioned previously, if one can answer these questions and account for discrepant information, one has gone a long way in developing a good case formulation and developing goals for treatment.

Step 4: Develop a Profile and Hierarchy of Strengths and Weaknesses

Both research and clinical practice indicate that children rarely have problems that are specific to one area. As a result, the next step in the interpretive process is to develop the profile of a child's or adolescent's strengths and weaknesses across the different domains of psychological functioning that have been assessed. In addition, we feel that this process needs to go beyond simply documenting the different areas of strengths and weaknesses, to also *prioritizing* the different areas of concern. This prioritization should be both a conceptual and practical endeavor.

Conceptually, one should consider what problematic area may be primary and which areas may be secondary, with *secondary* being defined as areas that seem to be largely a result of some other primary factor. For example, for a child who becomes depressed because of his/her frequent school suspensions and police contacts for antisocial behavior, the depression may best be considered secondary to the antisocial behavior.

Practically, one needs to consider what area should be the primary focus of intervention. This may follow closely with the determination of primary and secondary problems, where intervention targeting of primary areas (e.g., antisocial behavior) may also alleviate problems considered to be secondary (e.g., depression). However, these two levels of analysis do not necessarily have to be congruent. For example, a child with ADHD may have developed conduct problems secondary to the ADHD because of the effects of the child's behavior on parent–child interactions. However, given the current problems caused by the conduct disturbance and the relation of these problems to future problems in adjustment, intervention targeting the conduct problems may be the primary treatment recommendation, rather than treatment for ADHD.

Most assessors would agree with the need to prioritize problem areas, but most would also agree that this is difficult to accomplish with any degree of reliability and validity. We must admit that prioritizing areas of need and determining primary and secondary areas of dysfunction are often largely made on the basis of clinical judgment in the absence of a clear research base to guide this process. However, we feel that there are three primary factors to consider in prioritizing areas within a child's profile.

First, one should look at the *degree of impairment* associated with different areas of dysfunction. As a standard part of any assessment, one should measure the degree to which various behaviors are affecting a child's functioning in at least three major life areas: in school, with peers, and at home. Then several questions can be asked in an effort to determine if some problem areas are contributing more to impairment than others. Are the problematic areas differentially affecting a child's ability to learn or to perform well academically? Has one or more of the areas significantly affected a child's ability to form or maintain meaningful relationships with same-age peers? Is any problem area causing a higher level of conflict with parents and/or siblings than others? This method of prioritization is one of the most important factors clinically, because areas that cause the greatest degree of impairment typically are the most important targets of interventions.

Second, one can look at the temporal sequencing of when problem behaviors developed to help to determine what might be primary or secondary. Did symptoms of depression develop after a chronic pattern of antisocial behavior? A good example of the therapeutic implications of temporal sequencing comes from a study in which children with major depression who only showed conduct problems after the onset of the depression showed a significant reduction of conduct problems after the depression was successfully treated (Puig-Antich et al., 1978).

Third, viewing family history data can help in making a determination of primary and secondary areas of disturbance. As we discussed in Chap. 12, in the section on assessing a child's family history, information on parental psychiatric history can often aid in making differential diagnoses. This is largely due to the fact that (1) adult psychological disturbance tends to be more easily defined and (2) many forms of childhood disturbance show a familial link. As a result, assessing parental adjustment patterns can provide clues as to what is the primary area of dysfunction in their child or adolescent.

Step 5: Determine Critical Information to Place in the Report

In the next chapter we provide a detailed discussion of report writing. However, it is important to note that the last stage of integrating information is a filtering process. After one has developed a profile of the child that explains the referral problems and suggests treatment goals, it is likely that many pieces of information gathered will have either minimal or no bearing on the final case conceptualization. A good assessor will limit the amount of unessential information that is collected in an evaluation by carefully tailoring the evaluation to the needs of an individual child. However, much information cannot be determined to be irrelevant until after it is collected.

Many clinicians feel that, if information was collected, it should be included in the written and/or oral report of the assessment results. Our feeling is that too much irrelevant information detracts from the case formulation, making it unduly confusing. Therefore, we feel that the final step in the interpretive process is determining what information is essential for understanding the case formulation and subsequent recommendations for treatment and what information should be omitted or discussed only minimally in the report. This final step sets the stage for the writing of a clear, concise, and readable summary of the assessment results.

Conclusions

In this chapter we discuss some of the issues involved in integrating assessment information across informants, across methods, and across psychological domains. One of the more difficult aspects of this endeavor is integrating discrepant information from different informants on the same dimension of functioning. We discussed evidence that simple decision rules that equally weigh information given by various informants may be as good as or better than more complex methods of differentially weighing information provided by various informants. However, this simple rule needs to be qualified by whether the informant is knowledgeable about the child's behavior and whether the informant can report the information effectively. These two factors can be influenced by many factors, such as age of the child and the specific behavioral domain being assessed. We conclude the chapter by providing a multi-step procedure for integrating the various pieces information from a comprehensive evaluation into a clear case formulation that answers the referral question and points the way to a recommended course of intervention.

Chapter Summary

1. Because most clinical assessments of children and adolescents must be comprehensive, one of the most difficult parts of the assessment process is integrating assessment information into a clear case formulation that points the way to the most appropriate interventions.
2. The most difficult task is integrating information on the same behavior provided by different informants. Research indicates that poor agreement among informants is the rule, rather than the exception.
   (a) These discrepancies may reflect real differences in a child's functioning in different contexts (e.g., home, school, clinic). Therefore, assessing the characteristics of the different contexts can help to explain some discrepancies.
   (b) Some discrepancies may be an artifact of the level of analysis. For example, individual symptoms may be very discrepant across informants, whereas the presence of a disorder may show greater concordance.
   (c) The level of agreement can be related to certain characteristics of the behaviors being assessed, such as the salience of the behavior to the informant, how observable the behavior is to others, and how willing the informant is to report on the behavior.

   (d) Discrepancies can also be an artifact of different measurement techniques used to obtain information from different informants.
3. Unfortunately, in many cases it is difficult to attribute discrepant information solely to varying situational demands, to the level of analysis, to the type of behavior being assessed, or to differences in assessment strategy. In these cases there is evidence that a simple either/or system for combining information works best. That is, a finding is considered significant if reported by any informant.
   (a) This approach assumes that false positives are rarer and less harmful than false negatives.
   (b) This approach also assumes that informants are only asked to provide information that they should be expected to know.
4. The quality of information provided by different informants seems to vary depending on the domain of functioning being assessed and the age of the child being assessed.
   (a) Research suggests that teacher report of inattentive-hyperactive behaviors, parent report of conduct problems, and child report of emotional problems seem to be relatively most important in preadolescent children.
   (b) The usefulness of child self-report increases with age and the usefulness of teacher report decreases with age. Age-related changes in parental report are less consistently found, although there are some indications that the usefulness of parental report also decreases somewhat as the child enters adolescence.
5. Other factors, such as a parent's emotional adjustment, the degree of marital conflict, idiosyncratic motivations of an informant, and testing conditions, can influence informant agreement.
6. A multistep procedure for integrating diverse assessment information is recommended.
   Step 1: Document all clinically significant findings on the child's adjustment.
   Step 2: Look for convergence across sources and methods.
   Step 3: Attempt to explain discrepancies.
   Step 4: Develop a profile and hierarchy of findings.
   Step 5: Determine what critical information to place in the formal report.

CHAPTER 16

Report Writing

Chapter Questions

- How does the call for evidence-based assessment lend itself to report writing?
- How does a clinician clarify the referral question?
- What are the common mistakes made in report writing?
- How should assessment results be reported to parents in conferences?

Reporting Problems and Challenges

Presenting assessment results orally or in writing can be a foreboding task. However, this process is central to assessment. The most sophisticated, accurate, and comprehensive case conceptualization is useless if the key figures in a child's life (e.g., parents, teachers) are unaware of the results or recommendations from an assessment or do not fully understand them. Aside from appropriately and accurately conveying results and recommendations, clinicians are also often faced with fears of litigation and insecurities about their interpretive skill. Thus, a chapter on report writing is crucial for an assessment text. As clinicians know well, their written products can carry a great deal of importance, and if done well, they can facilitate positive outcomes for a child. On the other hand, if a report is faulty (i.e., inaccurate, unclear, full of errors), it will make no impact aside from being a negative reflection on the clinician who wrote it.

Effective psychological report writing is taking on increased importance for practicing psychologists. Psychological reports are made available to parents, judges, lawyers,

P.J. Frick et al., *Clinical Assessment of Child and Adolescent Personality and Behavior*,
DOI 10.1007/978-1-4419-0641-0_16,

and other non-psychologists, creating the opportunity for improper interpretation of the results by untrained individuals. More positively, psychological reports remain particularly useful to other clinicians who evaluate a child who has previously been seen by a psychologist. A previous psychological report can provide a valuable baseline against which a clinician can gauge response to treatment, the emergence of a comorbid problem, and other factors. A previous diagnosis of Conduct Disorder, for example, may encourage the evaluating psychologist to screen for depression because of known comorbidity (DeBaryshe, Patterson, & Capaldi, 1993). A clinician can significantly enhance the quality of work conducted by a successor through the production of an articulate written report.

Despite its importance, the topic of report writing is relatively neglected in the research literature (Ownby & Wallbrown, 1986). While a number of works are available on this topic (e.g., Braaten, 2007; Lichtenberger, Mather, Kaufman, & Kaufman, 2004; Tallent, 1993), little research has been conducted to assess the effects of report writing on important outcomes such as the likelihood that a recommendation will be followed (Ownby & Wallbrown, 1986).

Ownby and Wallbrown (1986) draw several discouraging conclusions. They conclude as follows on psychological reports:

- Considered useful to some extent by consumers such as psychiatrists and social workers
- Frequently criticized by these professional groups on both content and stylistic grounds
- May (or may not) make substantial contributions to patient management

In addition to the opinions of psychiatrists and social workers, a number of studies have assessed teachers' satisfaction with psychological reports and have found that they are frequently dissatisfied with them (Ownby & Wallbrown, 1986). One can get a sense of why teachers and other professionals are dissatisfied with psychological reports by reading the following excerpt that was taken verbatim from a report. All of the conclusions drawn by the evaluator in this case are on the basis of *one test* requiring the child to simply reproduce nine designs with pencil and paper.
We quote:

> The Bender-Visual Motor Gestalt test suggests delinquency and an acting out potential. He is anxious, confused, insecure and has a low self-esteem. He may have difficulties in interpersonal relationships and tends to isolate himself when problems arise.... [He] also seems to have a lot of anxiety and tension over phallic sexuality and may be in somewhat of a homosexual panic.

This clinician was apparently using a cookbook approach to interpretation, conveying no clear evidence to support his/her case conceptualization. A report like this is of no help to anyone, especially not to the child being evaluated.

One of the difficulties with report writing is that different audiences require different reports. For example, a psychometric summary (i.e., a portion of the report that presents only test scores and is usually given at the beginning or as an appendix at the end of a report) given without context is likely to be of little use to parents but of great potential use to colleagues and perhaps teachers. An important decision that each psychologist must make prior to report writing is to determine the primary audience for the report. For example, a psychometric summary may be of minimal use to parents who have contracted with the psychologist in private practice for an evaluation. In this case, it is more sensible to present test results in context in order to communicate effectively with the parents. A psychometric summary is more in order in a treatment team situation, where it is imperative that a psychologist communicate effectively with knowledgeable colleagues.

In most situations, we recommend that the clinician attempt to make his or her reports accessible and useful to all pertinent audiences so that interested parties do not have different reports for the same assessment of the same child. Our discussion will focus mainly on the expectation that one report will be made available to parents, teachers, physicians, etc., with the understanding that certain presentations of results and interpretations will be most useful to certain audiences.

Report Writing as Part of Evidence-Based Assessment

Report writing has not specifically been addressed in recent writings on evidence-based assessment of children. Instead, the discussion has focused on the use of tools and methods that are valid and that demonstrate clinical utility (see Mash & Hunsley, 2005). We feel that the move toward evidence-based assessment should, and will, be reflected in the reports that result from psychological assessments.

Mash and Hunsley (2005) point out that evidence-based assessment is not meant to replace the clinician or the clinician's judgment. Similarly, the clinician will continue to be a key figure in assessment reports. That is, it is unlikely and undesirable that reports will be completely boiler plate endeavors that do not allow for flexibility based on the particular assessment approach used, the client's particular presenting problems, or the needs of the client and allied professionals.

In contrast, not unlike a scientific manuscript, reports from an evidence-based approach to assessment can be seen as the means by which a client's history and difficulties are described, results are obtained and interpreted, and suggestions for future (treatment) approaches to the difficulties are discussed.

The main sections of most psychological reports are discussed later in this chapter, but in many ways, they are analogous to sections of journal articles in psychology and other scientific fields. For example, the "Referral Questions" section is essentially a statement of the evaluation's purpose. "Background Information" in a report is similar to a literature review in a research article, wherein the previously noted issues are mentioned and the current questions or problems are presented to the audience. The "Assessment Procedures" or Psychometric Summary provides the methods used in trying to address the referral question(s). The results of the current assessment begin to be addressed fully in the "Behavioral Observations" section. This section provides a context for the assessment results, particularly any testing that occurred directly with the client. The analogy in a scientific manuscript would be initial analyses that point to any variables that need to be controlled or any conditions that might call some results into question. Similarly, testing conditions or client factors (e.g., child was sick on the day of testing) could be important information for interpreting assessment results. The "Assessment Results and Interpretation" sections are ideally a mix of what might be found in the "Results" and "Discussion" sections of a scientific article. In the report, the clinician should not present data with no interpretation, and the clinician should not make interpretations without clearly providing the data on which they were made. Recommendations, which are critical in an assessment report, allow the clinician to suggest what should be done in the future to address the problem. Researchers routinely do this as well in their published manuscripts.

Pointing to consistencies between assessment reports and scientific manuscripts is an oversimplification of the report writing process in some ways. Nevertheless, many clinicians-in-training are also well-versed in research methodology and writing, and this analogy may serve to make report writing seem less nebulous and daunting. The collection of background information, the scoring of measures, and interpretation of results that occur in research are essentially the processes that take place in evidence-based assessment and report writing. The gathering and explaining of evidence allow the clinician to clearly present a case conceptualization (theory) of the client's difficulties that is grounded in data, as opposed to the approach evidenced in the quote earlier in this chapter.

Pitfalls of Report Writing

Complaints about psychological reports persist. Norman Tallent (1993) wrote a landmark textbook on report writing in which he summarized the literature on the strengths and weaknesses of reports as identified by psychologists' colleagues in mental health care, most notably social workers and psychiatrists. Some of the highlights of Tallent's review are outlined in the next section.

Vocabulary Problems

The problem of using vague or imprecise language in report writing is commonplace. The colloquial term used to describe such language is *psychobabble*. Siskind (1967), for example, studied the level of agreement between psychologists and psychiatrists in defining words such as the following:

Abstract	Defense
Affective	Dependent
Aggression	Depressive
Anxiety	Emotional
Bizarre	Hostility
Bright	Immaturity
Compulsive	Impulsive
Control	Normal Constriction

The results of the study showed very little correspondence between the definitions offered by the two groups of professionals. We suspect that without clear descriptors of problems (e.g., hyperactivity, depression), such disagreement among consumers of reports persists today.

Tallent (1993) refers to one aspect of this problem with language as exhibitionism, which seems to be a frequent criticism of reports, particularly on the part of other psychologists. One commentator stated, "They are written in stilted psychological terms to boost the ego of the psychologist" (p. 33).

Some other pertinent observations by Tallent (1993) on the use of language by psychologists in reports are paraphrased below:

- They include complex (meaningless) words that are often used to add length to the report.
- They are written in esoteric language understood by the psychologist only. For example, it may be said that clients manifest overt aggressive hostility in an impulsive manner – when, in fact, they punch you on the nose.
- They are not frequently enough written in lay language. In particular, scores are over-emphasized, and the fit between the results and the child's actual behavior is under-emphasized. Tallent (1993) argues that an excessive focus on multiple scores or indices may be a method to cover up the clinician's lack of true understanding of the assessment findings.
- They include language that is so vague and unclear that it cannot be falsified or considered wrong.

These latter two points are critical if reports are to address the referral question in a manner that is amenable to subsequent, appropriate intervention. Of course, psychology cannot be singled out as the only profession with a preference for its own idiosyncratic terminology, as anyone who reads a physician's report or a legal contract will attest. Perhaps psychologists can, however, lead the way toward competent reporting of findings.

Faulty Interpretation

Faulty interpretations may be made on the basis of personal ideas, biases, and idiosyncrasies (Tallent, 1993). The problem is most readily seen when the psychologist is clearly using the same theories or drawing the same conclusions in every report. A psychologist may conclude that all children's problems are due to poor ego functioning, neuropsychological problems, or family system failure. A psychologist who adheres exclusively to behavioral principles, for example, will attribute all child problems to faulty reinforcement histories. The savvy consumer of this psychologist's reports will eventually become wary of the psychologist's conclusions, as the relevance of the favored theory to some cases is questionable. One can imagine the skepticism that may be engendered by a psychologist who concludes that a child whose school performance has just deteriorated subsequent to a traumatic head injury merely needs more positive reinforcement to bring his grades up to pre-trauma levels.

Problems may also occur if a psychologist draws conclusions that are clearly in conflict with the data collected for a child. A psychologist may decide not to make a diagnosis, in seeming contrast to rating scale findings of significant T-scores on the majority of scales. If a clear argument for resolving this incongruity is not made, the consumer of the report may well suspect biases. The psychologist who routinely does not reconcile high T-scores with a lack of a diagnosis may soon be labeled as unwilling to diagnose regardless of assessment results. The reverse situation can also be problematic, wherein the psychologist makes a diagnosis without any clear indications of significant symptomatology or impairment. Teachers, pediatricians, or other referral sources who receive this interpretation consistently from the same psychologist may eventually pay more attention to the data presented in the reports and ignore the psychologist's conclusions, or they may simply refer elsewhere.

Report Length

Psychologists, more so than other groups, complain about the excessive length of reports (Tallent, 1993). However, length may not be the real issue. Perhaps long reports are used to disguise incompetence, fulfill needs for accountability, or impress others. The possibility that length is a cover for other ills is offered in the following example:

> A business executive likes to relate the anecdote about the occasion when he assigned a new employee to prepare a report for him. In due time, a voluminous piece of writing was returned. Dismayed, the executive pointed out that the required information could be presented on one, certainly not more than two, pages. But sir, pleaded the young man, I don't know that much about the matter you assigned me to (Tallent, 1988, p. 72).

It may also be worth considering that the Ten Commandments are expressed in 297 words, the Declaration of Independence is in 300 words, and the Gettysburg Address is in 266 words.

Number Obsession

The clinician must always keep clearly in mind that the child is the lodestar of the evaluation, and the numbers obtained from personality tests and the like are only worthy of emphasis if they contribute to the understanding of the child being evaluated. One way to think of the scores is as a means to an end, with the end being better understanding of the child. *The same numbers for two children can mean two quite different things.* Just as a high temperature reading can be symptomatic of a host of disorders from influenza to appendicitis, so, too, a pathognomic behavioral sign can reveal a host of possible conditions.

One horrendous error often made when reporting test scores is a psychologist reporting a score and then saying that it is invalid. Then why report it (Tallent,

1993)? If a test score is invalid, how does it serve the child to have this score as part of a permanent record? Reporting apparently invalid scores is akin to a physician making a diagnostic decision on the basis of a fasting blood test when the patient violated the fasting requirements. In all likelihood, the flawed results would not be reported; rather, the patient would be required to retake the test. We suggest that *one does not have to report scores for a test just because it was administered.* This stance applies to scores that are deemed invalid or circumstances in which the psychometrics underlying the scores are questionable. In these situations, disregarding the information from the measure or providing only descriptions of the responses may better inform case conceptualization.

Failure to Address Referral Questions

Tallent (1993) points out that psychologists too often fail to demand clear referral questions, and as a result, their reports appear vague and unfocused. This very obvious point is all too frequently overlooked. Psychologists should insist that referral sources present their questions clearly, and if not, the psychologist should meet with the referring person to obtain further detail on the type of information that is expected from the evaluation (Tallent, 1993). Many agencies use referral forms to assist in this process of declaring assessment goals. A form similar to those used by hospitals is shown in Fig. 16.1, and one suitable for use by school systems is given in Fig. 16.2.

On occasion, the referral question(s) can be insidious and, consequently, place the psychologist in the position of disappointing the referral source before the evaluation is even initiated. Under these circumstances, the psychologist may feel helpless or even betrayed because of the negative reaction of the referral source to the presentation of results and recommendations. Psychologists may often need to pursue the true referral question. Some examples of stated and true referral questions are shown below:

Stated Referral Question	True Referral Question
A child's teacher wants to know if child has ADHD	The teacher is convinced that the child has ADHD and expects the psychologist to confirm it
A parent wants to know why a child is failing in school	The parent thinks the child is depressed and would like her to be on medication
A psychiatrist wants to know if a child is depressed	The psychiatrist has made the diagnosis of depression and has placed the child on medication. The referral was made simply because a second opinion is required for reimbursement purposes
A psychologist wants to know if the child is neurologically impaired	The psychologist is seeking a diagnosis of traumatic brain injury in order to bolster her court testimony

In all of these scenarios, it would behoove the psychologist to clearly determine the referral source's actual needs and/or desires early on in the referral/evaluation process and then determine the most appropriate way to proceed.

The Consumer's View

Virtually no recent research has been conducted on the consumer's view of psychological reports. One study evaluated teacher preferences for and comprehension of varying report formats (Wiener, 1985). This study required a group of elementary school teachers to read and rate their comprehension of and preferences for three different reports for the same child.

Patient Name <u>John Doe</u>

Medical Record Number <u>00071103</u>

Attending Physician <u>Lyman</u>

Type of Consultation:

Patient is a 13 year-old with Type I Diabetes who has poor adherence to treatment regimen. Parents are concerned that John is aware of the risks of this poor adherence but seems apathetic. Patient's affect is flat and may be depressed. Patient to be discharged from hospital following psych. consultation.

Results of Consultation: *Patient appears depressed and seems knowledgeable about diabetes and his diabetes regimen. In particular, his parents noted that he appears sad most of the time, lacks energy, has reduced his contact with friends, and does not seem interested in activities that he used to enjoy. Rating scales completed by patient and his mother showed moderate levels of depression. Family history of depression is significant. Outpatient therapy is recommended and has been scheduled to begin in 1 week.*

Signed ____________________ Title ____________ Date

FIGURE 16.1
Sample referral form consultation used by hospitals

The three reports used were a short form, a psychoeducational report, and a question-and-answer format. The short-form report was one page, single-spaced. It used some jargon, such as acronyms, to shorten length; conclusions were drawn without reference to a data source; and recommendations were given without elaboration. The psychoeducational report format was three and a half single-spaced pages. It used headings such as Reason for Referral, Learning Style, Mathematics, Conclusions, and Recommendations. Observations were stated in behavioral terms with examples used freely. Recommendations were given and elaborated, and acronyms and other jargon were only used when they were defined in text. The question-and-answer report was similar to the psychoeducational report in many ways, but it did not use headings per se. This report listed referral questions and then answered each question in turn. This report was four and a half pages long.

Amazingly, in this study, the participants preferred length. First, teachers comprehended the two longer reports better. Second, of the two longer reports, the teachers preferred the question-and-

Student's Name Jane Smith Date of Referral 10/11/07
Referring School Stuart Elem. Age 8 Grade 2 Grades Repeated N/A

Is the student now receiving speech therapy? ___ Yes x no

	Never	Sometimes	Often
Expressive Language (problems in grammar, limited vocabulary)			x
Receptive Language (comprehension not following directions)		x	
Speech (poor enunciation, lisps, stutters, omits sounds, infantile speech)		x	
Gross Motor Coordination (eye-hand, manual dexterity)	x		
Visual (cannot see blackboard, squints, rubs eyes, holds book too close)	x		
Hearing (unable to discriminate sounds, asks to have instructions repeated, turns ear to speaker, often has earaches)	x		
Health (example: epilepsy, respiratory problems, etc.)	x		
Medications	(yes)	**(no)**	(Type)

Overly energetic, talks out, out of seat: Sometimes

Very quiet, uncommunicative: Often

Acting out (aggressive, hostile, rebellious, destructive, cries easily): Sometimes

Inattentive (short attention span, poor on task behavior): Often

Doesn't appear to notice what is happening in the immediate environment: Sometimes

Poor Peer Relationships (few friends, rejected, ignored, abused by peers): Often

ACADEMIC PROBLEMS

Reading (word attack, comprehension): Often

Writing (illegible, reverses letters, doesn't write): Often

Spelling (cannot spell phonetically, omits or adds letters): Often

Mathematics (computation, concepts, application): Never

Social Science, Sciences (doesn't handle concepts, doesn't understand rerelationships, poor understanding of cause and effect): Never

Signature and position of referring person

FIGURE 16.2

Referral for consultation used by schools

answer report over the psychoeducational report. The short form was clearly least preferred. These are intriguing results in that they hint that length may be overrated as a problem in report writing and that teachers may prefer a question-and-answer report format. This finding is interesting because this format is rarely used in reports from clinical assessments.

Do parents have different preferences from teachers? In a follow-up study with parents using the same methodology, Wiener and Kohler (1986) found that teachers and parents have similar preferences. In this second study, the same three report formats were used. As was the case with teachers, parents comprehended the two longer reports significantly better than the short-form report. An interesting additional finding was that parents with a college education comprehended reports better than parents with only a high school diploma. Parents also tended to prefer the question-and-answer format to the other two formats, although the difference in preference scores between the psychoeducational and question-and-answer reports failed to reach statistical significance.

The results of these two studies suggest that the two most frequent consumers of child and adolescent psychological reports, parents and teachers, consider the clarity of reports to be more important than their absolute length. They also show a preference for reports that have referral questions as their focus. Cognizance of these two findings may benefit psychologists who write reports for children and adolescents.

Suggested Practices

Report Only Pertinent Information

One of the most difficult decisions to make when writing a report involves gauging the relevance of information to include (Teglasi, 1983). Clinicians happen onto a great deal of information during the course of an evaluation, some of which is tangential. Say, for example, a child is referred for an evaluation of ADHD. During the course of an interview with the child's father, he recounts at length his disappointment with his wife. He tells the clinician that she is dating other men, and he believes that she is not spending adequate time with their children. When writing the report on this case, the clinician has to determine whether or not this information is pertinent to the ADHD evaluation.

Clinicians must think critically about the in-formation that they include in reports and consider its relevance to the case. As discussed by Lichtenberger et al. (2004), the objectives of psychological reports are to "answer the referral questions; describe the person; organize the data; and recommend interventions" (p. 3). If information is not relevant to these objectives, and it is very personal, the psychologist should consider carefully the decision to invade a family's privacy by including such information in the report.

Define Abbreviations and Acronyms

Acronyms are part of the idiosyncratic language of psychological assessment. They can greatly facilitate communication among psychologists, but they hinder communication with non-psychologists. Psychologists, just like other professionals, need to use nontechnical language to communicate with parents, teachers, and other colleagues in the mental health field. A pediatrician would not ask a mother if her child had an emesis; rather, the physician would inquire whether or not the child vomited.

When writing a report, psychologists should limit their use of acronyms and should define any acronym used in a report. Use of the acronym *SAD* for separation anxiety disorder, for example, without defining, is questionable practice.

Emphasize Words Rather than Numbers

Particularly in the test results section of a report, clinicians must resist a temptation to focus exclusively on numbers (i.e., test scores). Lichtenberger et al. noted that "some evaluators spend too much time writing about the obtained test scores rather than about what these scores mean" (p. 5). Words often communicate more effectively than numbers because they communicate more directly and in a more accessible manner to a variety of audiences. The typical question of a referral source has nothing to do with the obtained T-scores but, rather, the psychologist's interpretation of these scores. Most laypersons will not understand the T-score metric but can more easily grasp clinician's interpretation of norm-referenced scores.

Reduce Difficult Words

The issue of using simple language is by now obvious. The difficult part for report writers is following through on this advice. Consider the following two paragraphs, which differ greatly. The first excerpt uses vocabulary that is unnecessarily complex for most consumers of reports. The second example is a rewrite of the first paragraph that uses a more practical vocabulary level.

> There is also evidence from the test data to suggest that Pam is obdurate in response to anxiety. She may also tend to be very concrete and not notice some of the subtleties of interpersonal discourse. Given these idiosyncrasies, she may find it difficult to generate effective social problem-solving strategies and mechanisms for coping with life's stressors.

The next paragraph tries to communicate more clearly by using, among other things, simpler language.

> Pam responds to stress by withdrawing from others (e.g., going to her room or leaving a group of friends on a social outing), which seems to be the only method she uses for dealing with stress. She also has trouble understanding and responding to messages given by others in social situations (e.g., body language or verbal hints). Because of these behavior patterns, Pam has trouble making friends.

Related to the use of difficult words is the issue of using the correct person. We have occasionally seen reports where instead of using the child's name, he or she was referred to as "the child" or "the subject." This usage sounds too mechanistic and impersonal for a psychological report. In most cases, the use of the child's name is better. It is important to also clearly differentiate among sources of information and between data gathered during the assessment and the clinician's interpretations. Jargon or convoluted writing makes these important distinctions difficult to be made out by the reader.

Briefly Describe the Instruments Used

In many cases, it is safe to assume that the reader of the report has little knowledge of the tests being used. When practical, we suggest that report writers describe the nature of the assessment devices being used.

The naive reader of a report will also be helped by descriptors of the nature of a scale or subscale that is being discussed. This observation is particularly true for scales that are not adequately described by their names. Depression scales are a good example of scales that may be perceived inappropriately. The label *depression* could conjure up a variety of images in a report reader's mind including the image of a child that is incapacitated by sadness. It may well be that a Depression score indicates significance but, de-pending on the items endorsed, may not warrant the formal diagnosis of depression. In this case, the clinician should try to describe the nature of the scale content and/or its interpretive meaning in order to discourage misuse of results.

Edit the Report

We have found that a number of our students do not take a critical eye toward editing their own work and not just in terms of grammar and spelling. Editing is necessary to ensure the most accurate communication in the least amount of space.

Tallent (1988) provides the following excellent example of how an editor (and the articulate psychologist) thinks:

> There is the tale of the young man who went into the fish business. He rented a store, erected a sign, FRESH FISH SOLD HERE, and acquired merchandise. As he was standing back admiring his market and his sign, a friend happened along. Following congratulations, the friend gazed at the sign and read aloud, FRESH FISH SOLD HERE. Of course it's here. You wouldn't sell it elsewhere, would you? Impressed with such astuteness, the young man painted over the obviously superfluous word. The next helpful comment had to do with the word *sold.* You aren't giving it away. Again impressed, he eliminated the useless word. Seemingly that was it, but the critic then focused on the word *fresh.* You wouldn't sell stale fish, would you? Once more our hero bowed to the strength of logic. But finally he was relieved that he had a logic-tight sign for his business; FISH. His ever alert friend, however, audibly sniffing the air for effect, made a final observation: You don't need a sign (p. 88).

Psychologists do not need to engage in such severe editing, but they should at least make an attempt to think critically about their word usage in order to reduce report, sentence, and paragraph length. Judicious editing can go a long way toward clarifying meaning in a report. Sometimes new clinicians are not used to critiquing their own writing. One readily available option is to have a colleague read reports. Confidentiality, however, should be kept in mind if an editor is used.

Use Headings and Lists Freely

Headings and lists can enhance the clarity of communication (Harvey, 1989). If, for example, a clinician draws a number of conclusions about a child, the conclusions can sometimes lose their impact if they are embedded in paragraphs.

As one would predict, the use of headings and lists to excess has a downside. A report that uses too many lists, for example, appears stilted, and it may not communicate all of the texture and subtleties of the child's performance. Report writers should consider using additional headings if a section of their report stretches for nearly a page (single-spaced) without a heading. Clinicians should consider lists if they want to add impact to statements and/or conclusions.

Use Examples of Behavior to Clarify Meaning

Because there is some disagreement regarding the meanings of particular words, report writers should clarify their meaning in order to ensure accuracy. Words that may conjure up a variety of interpretations include *anxiety*, *cooperation*, *dependent*, *hyperactive*, and *low self-esteem.* One way to foster clarity is to use examples (i.e., behavioral referents) of the child's behavior. Here, for example, are two ways to say that a child, Emilio, was anxious.

> Emilio exhibited considerable anxiety during the testing.

Or, alternatively:

> Emilio appeared anxious during the testing. He frequently asked whether or not he had solved an item correctly. He occasionally looked at the ticking stopwatch during an item and then hurried, and his face became flushed when it was obvious to him that he did not know the answer to a question.

An additional benefit of using examples of behavior generously is that it forces the psychologist to consider the extent of supporting evidence for a conclusion about a child's behavior. If a psychologist writes that a child is anxious but cannot think of behaviors to help explain this, then the conclusion should not be drawn, as it is insupportable by evidence.

Direct quotes, to some extent, are also helpful for clarifying meaning. If a clinician concludes that an adolescent is suicidal, a quote from the child may help clarify this statement considerably. The child may have said, "I thought about taking some pills once" or "I feel like I want to run out in front of a car tonight and if that doesn't work, I will steal my father's gun and kill myself." These statements convey varying degrees of suicidal intent that are most clearly differentiated by quotes.

Reduce Report Length

Tallent (1988) gives the following instances as indications of undue length:

- The psychologist is concerned that it took too long to write it (we might add that most reports will seem that way for beginning clinicians, but the time to write reports should decline with experience).
- The psychologist has difficulty organizing all of the details for presentation.
- Some of the content is not clear or useful.
- The detail is much greater than can be put to good use.
- Speculations are presented without a good rationale for them.
- The writing is unnecessarily repetitious.
- The organization is not tight.
- The reader is irritated by the length or reads only a few sections such as the Summary or Recommendations sections.

The issue of length is primarily a concern of other psychologists, and it is intertwined with other issues, such as clarity. Hence, the psychologist in training should not assume that shorter is better. Quality may be a more important issue than quantity. At this early point in training, the new report writer should keep the issue of length in mind while writing reports. Concerns about length, however, should never interfere with the need to portray a child's performance accurately.

Check Scores

An all-too-frequent and grievous error is to re-port scores that are incorrect. Computerized scoring represents a breakthrough that limits errors. In fact, if the facilities are available, we suggest that each test protocol that is scored by hand be checked against computer scoring. If this is not possible, the test scores should at least be double-checked prior to finalizing a report.

One way of checking scores is to be alert to in-consistencies. If, for example, an adjudicated adolescent who was referred for conduct problems obtains an elevated T-score on depression measures and no elevations on conduct problem scales, then the score should be double-checked to see if a scoring error is the source of the incongruity. If a score doesn't seem sensible, then the clinician should always check for a scoring error in order to rule out this possibility.

Check Grammar and Spelling

Another problem with reports that detracts from the credibility of the clinician is the presence of spelling errors. Clinicians are strongly advised to take the time to electronically and visually check their spelling and grammar.

Adapting Reports to Audience and Setting

There is probably no optimal report format. Psychologists often find that they have to adapt their reports to meet the needs of an ever-changing audience. Audiences have varying characteristics, such as literacy levels, and, more importantly, they have differing referral questions.

In a school setting, many referrals are for learning problems. Teachers may also be seeking information to assist them in curriculum decisions. These are very different referral questions than those that may be of interest in other settings. In a psychiatric hospital setting, issues such as suicide potential, safety, and coping strategies may be of greater concern. These questions are very different than those of the school setting, requiring a focus on topics such as diagnosis and implications for pharmacological treatment. Parents are yet another audience with specific questions. When conducting an evaluation for parents in a private practice setting, the emphasis may be on advising the parents on what they can do to effect change in their child's behavior.

The report excerpts used throughout this book were taken from a variety of settings with differing referral questions. The reader is advised to think carefully about the needs of referral sources when reading these examples and writing reports.

The Sections of the Psychological Report

Identifying Information

Most report formats provide some identifying in-formation on the top of the first page of the re-port. This section can include information such as name of the child, age, grade, birth date, and perhaps the name of the school or agency where the child is currently attending or being served. Also, most reports indicate that the report con-tent is confidential.

Assessment Procedures

This section typically lists the assessment methods (both quantitative and qualitative) and tests that were used in the evaluation. Evaluation procedures can, and frequently do, include inter-views, reviews of records, and classroom or other observations.

Referral Questions

This section is crucial because the referral questions dictate the design of the evaluation. This section is often brief but should be descriptive so that the purpose of the evaluation is clear. The referral source should also be stated (Lichtenberger et al., 2004). The lack of clear referral questions may lead to consumer or referral source dissatisfaction with the report. As noted previously, psychologists may have to speak more than once with the referral source to clarify the nature of the question(s). The referral questions should be stated in terms of specific examples of the child's difficulties rather than general labels (e.g., "hyperactivity," "academic problems," "anxiety"). This section may also indicate (briefly) the duration, severity, and/or frequency of the problem.

Background Information

This section should include all of the pertinent information that may affect interpretation of a child's scores. The key word here is *pertinent*. The clinician should report only information that is relevant to the current evaluation, not in-formation that is superfluous or an undue invasion of privacy (Teglasi, 1983). Material should only be included if it has some potential impact on the interpretation of the child's scores in order to answer the referral question(s). While parental occupation and marital status are generally private subjects, these may be important pieces of information, given what is currently known about the effects of parental variables on child functioning. Lichentenger et al. (2004) provide a user-friendly and sensible summary of the types of information to include in this section, as well as tips to provide the information clearly.

The report writer should also be clear about the sources of information. If the father views his son as lazy, then this statement should be attributed to the father.

Statements that could be used for making such attributions include the following:

According to...
His father/mother stated...
His mother'/father's opinion is...
His teacher's view of the situation
Her guidance counselor reported that...
His parole officer acknowledges that...

If care is not taken to make clear the sources of information, questions may arise at the time when feedback is given to involved parties.

Sensitive background information should also be corroborated or excluded from the report if it is inflammatory and cannot be corroborated. For example, a 5-year-old may say something like "My mother shoots people," and later, the psychologist discovers that the child's mother is a police officer.

Previous assessment results should also be included in this section (Teglasi, 1983). Also, previous experiences with psychological or educational interventions should be noted here. The clinician may also refer the reader to a previous evaluation. Referring to previous evaluations, without fully recapitulating them, can substantially reduce written report bulk.

Behavioral Observations

In this section, the behaviors that the child exhibits during the assessment are recorded. When writing this section, the number of observations made, the setting where the observations were made (e.g., school, clinic, etc.), and the person who made the observations should be identified (Teglasi, 1983). A brief description of the setting, particularly if the report writer is describing classroom observations, is also appropriate. Domains that routinely should be covered include "physical appearance, ease of establishing and maintaining rapport, response to failures/successes, response to encouragement, attention span, language style, distractibility, activity level, anxiety level, mood, impulsivity/reflectivity, problem-solving strategy, attitude toward the testing process, attitude toward examiner, attitude toward self, unusual mannerisms or habits and validity of test results in view of behaviors" (Lichtenberger et al., 2004, p. 60).

Care should be taken not to confuse observations with interpretations. In other words, it is appropriate, for example, to state that the child appeared motivated to perform well, but such a statement should be accompanied by the behaviors that led to this assertion.

Assessment Results and Interpretation

This section is where the test results for the child are reported. Some report writers prefer to integrate the results from various measures into a single section. Still others opt to divide this section into subsections according to domains assessed. The domains may include: cognitive/intellectual, academic achievement, adaptive behavior, visual/motor, and behavioral/personality. This latter section is of primary interest for this text.

Organization within the behavioral/personality section can be according to theoretical orientation, training, or other preferences of the psychologist. We happen to recommend that this section be organized from the most important construct to least important, such that all evidence from multiple tools regarding the most important domain of functioning for the client (e.g., depression) is discussed first, followed by other comorbid issues, rather than presenting information by each individual measure and then trying again to integrate the information from varied sources. This approach puts the focus, in our view, where it belongs: the constructs/domains of functioning, not the tests. Most importantly, this section should provide coherent interpretations of results that relate logically to one another and to other sections, such as sections devoted to providing diagnostic considerations. Hence, this section should not simply report numerical findings that are devoid of interpretation.

Diagnostic Considerations

The decision about whether or not to include a separate portion dealing with diagnostic issues is likely influenced by setting and referral questions. Nonmedical settings, for example, may discourage the inclusion of a discussion of this nature in the psychologist's report. The omission of such a section may be in keeping with interdisciplinary approaches to making classification/diagnostic/eligibility decisions.

The format for this section can be in lists or in paragraphs. A psychologist may simply list diagnoses in a manner consistent with the *DSM-IV* multiaxial approach. Others prefer to use a paragraph or two to more fully explain the rationale for or against making certain diagnoses.

Summary

The final section of the report is intended to give an overview of the major findings. This review helps to ensure that the reader understands the major points made in the report. A rule of thumb for writing summaries is to use one sentence to summarize each section of the report. In addition, a sentence should be devoted to each major finding presented in the test results section. In some cases, one sentence can be used to summarize multiple findings and recommendations.

One of the common pitfalls of preparing summaries is including new information in the summary section. If a clinician introduces a new finding in the summary, the reader is lost. The reader has no idea as to the source or rationale behind the conclusion. We suggest that students read their draft summaries carefully and check every conclusion made in the summary against the body of the report.

Signatures

Reports typically require signatures attesting to their authenticity. An important component of this seemingly unimportant aspect of the report is the necessity for clinicians to use titles that represent them accurately. Some states, for ex-ample, do not have specialty licensure, and the use of a title such as Licensed Pediatric Psychologist is not appropriate. In this case, a more generic term such as Licensed Psychologist should be used, especially if the psychologist lacks evidence of board certification of specialty training.

Students should also be careful to represent themselves accurately. A title such as Practicum Student, Intern, Trainee, or something similar should be used. Psychological custom also dictates the inclusion of the highest degree obtained by the clinician.

Recommendations

Recommendations should be specific and clear (Teglasi, 1983). A recommendation for individual psychotherapy may be difficult to carry out, for example, if the specific problems that need to be addressed and other aspects of the recommendation are not made explicit. Some reasons that recommendations are not subsequently followed may have to do with how they are communicated. Recommendations should be understood by the individuals who will implement them, developmentally appropriate for the child, and practical, and should avoid being unnecessarily complex (Lichtenberger et al., 2004).

Some recommendations may also be difficult to communicate succinctly in writing. Therefore, one approach may be to include hand-outs for treating certain problems that are much more specific than can be included in the typical recommendation section of a report. A handout detailing some specific recommendations for a teacher responding to inattentive behaviors in the classroom may be more valuable to the teacher than an abbreviated recommendation. In almost all cases, the clinician should relay recommendations in person to psychiatrists, teachers, parents, and other colleagues (Teglasi, 1983) in order to ensure that they are followed.

Psychometric Summary

Some clinicians include a listing of all of the child's obtained scores with the report. While this summary will be of limited value to the less knowledgeable reader, it may be of great value to another clinician who reviews the report. This summary is best placed on a separate sheet(s) of paper, which makes it convenient for the clinician to be selective about who receives the summary. Some psychologists may prefer to not send the summary to parents and virtually always send it to other psychologists.

The Report Writing Self-Test

A report-writing self-test is provided in Fig. 16.3. This checklist allows the psychologist to periodically and quickly review principles of re-port writing.

Item	True	False
1. Was the report edited?	T	F
2. Are unnecessary invasions of privacy avoided?	T	F
3. Is the referral question(s) explicitly stated?	T	F
4. Is the referral question answered?	T	F
5. Does the report emphasize words over numbers?	T	F
6. Can a person with a high school education understand the wording used?	T	F
7. Is the report brief enough that major findings are not lost?	T	F
8. Are the conclusions drawn without undue hedging?	T	F
9. Do the conclusions fit the data?	T	F
10. Are invalid results omitted?	T	F
11. Are percentile ranks included for the benefit of parents and clients?	T	F
12. Were spelling and grammar checked?	T	F
13. Are supporting data integrated with conclusions?	T	F
14. Are the recommendations clear and specific?	T	F
15. Are headings and lists added to enhance space?	T	F
16. Are acronyms defined and not overused?	T	F
17. Is the summary free of new information?	T	F
18. Were scores double-checked?	T	F
19. Are examples of behavior used to clarify meaning?	T	F
20. Are test instruments described adequately?	T	F
21. Is the rationale for diagnoses provided?	T	F
22. Is a conference scheduled to accompany the written report?	T	F
23. Was written parental consent obtained prior to releasing the report to interested agencies or parties?	T	F
24. Is a feedback session scheduled with the child or adolescent?	T	F
25. Are the type and paper of professional quality (e.g., laser-quality print)?	T	F

FIGURE 16.3

Report writing self-test

Communicating Results Orally

Parent Conferences

For the purposes of this text, *parent* is used generically to include any consistent caregiver in the child's life. Examples of such caregivers include stepparents, residential caretakers, and grandparents, among others.

Imparting assessment results to parents re-quires considerable savvy, as the individual differences between families are myriad. Because of this diversity, there is not a singular methodology that will be effective with all parents. This section will present some ideas for sharing results with parents or other caregivers. However, it is vital for the psychologist to remain flexible in order to adapt the format of the feedback session to the needs of the parent, other caregiver, or family, as well as the setting.

In an old but insightful article, Ricks (1959) summarized the heart of the parent conference dilemma.

> The audience of parents to which our test-based information is to be transmitted includes an enormous range and variety of minds and emotions. Some are ready and able to absorb what we have to say. Reaching others may be as hopeless as reaching watchers with an AM radio broadcast. Still others may hear what we say, but clothe the message with their own special needs, ideas, and predilections (p. 4).

Regardless of the potential pitfalls, parents must be informed of the results of a psychological evaluation of their child (the legal, ethical, and regulatory mandates for this practice are given in Chapter 4).

Some helpful suggestions for communicating test results to parents are given next:

1. Avoid excessive hedging or deceit. The problem with hedging or failing to report bad news is that many parents sense this deceit and respond to the psychologist with appropriate mistrust. Honesty is also easily sensed by parents, which ultimately enhances the credibility of the psychologist.
2. Use percentile ranks heavily when describing norm-referenced test results. This metric is easier for parents to understand than other norm-referenced scores.
3. Instead of lecturing, allow parents opportunities to participate by asking about topics such as their opinion of the results and how they fit with their knowledge of their child. Moreover, listening carefully to parents helps the psychologist determine the psychological needs of the parents that are relevant to the evaluation. Similarly, it is essential that the parents be given frequent opportunities to ask questions (Lichtenberger et al., 2004).
4. Anticipate questions prior to the interview and prepare responses. How would a psychologist answer the question, "Will my daughter outgrow her ADHD?" Psychologists can gauge the probability that such questions will arise by listening carefully in the intake interview and throughout the assessment process.
5. Schedule adequate time for the interview. Parent conferences often become more involved than one has planned. Adequate time allows the psychologist time to use counseling skills to bring a parent feedback conference to adequate closure. Ideally, 1–2 h could be allocated for such a parent session. If a session ends early, then the psychologist is the recipient of a precious gift – extra time.
6. It is often helpful to seek practice communicating with parents from a variety of back-grounds. Some parents can be addressed as if they are colleagues, while others may have only a limited grasp of the issues being discussed. Translators, ministers, teachers, trusted family

friends, and others may serve as allies in the feedback process.

7. Avoid questionable and/or overly explicit predictions (Kamphaus, 2001). Phrases to be avoided would be statements like, "She will never go to college," or "She will always have trouble with school." These types of statements can be offensive to parents, not to mention inaccurate.
8. Use good, basic counseling skills. Every parent likes to talk about the trials and successes of raising a child. Give parents at least some opportunity to do this, as it allows you to show interest in the child by listening to the parent's perspective.
9. Do not engage in counseling that is beyond your level of expertise. Parents are often very eager to obtain advice from a professional. It is inappropriate (and unethical by most stan-dards) for a psychologist to provide services for which he or she is not trained. If, for ex-ample, a parent requests marital counseling and you have no training in this area, you should inform the parent of this fact and offer a referral. In fact, the psychologist is wise to have referral sources readily available for such eventualities.
10. Be aware that some parents are not ready to accept some test results. Parents may impugn your skills because they cannot accept the fact that their child has a severe handicap. They may leave the session angry, and you may feel inept. The idea that every parent conference will end on a happy note is unrealistic. Examine your skills critically in response to parent feedback, but realize that some parents simply will not accept the results because of their own personal issues. An example of such a situation may involve a parent with the same handicapping condition as the child. If a parent was labeled handicapped and ridiculed by peers, he or she may become defensive and angry at the suggestion that his or her child may have a handicap. The session with such a parent will likely end on a tense note. In many of these cases, however, the parent will adapt and accept the news after developing the psychological resources to cope with the attendant stresses. The psychologist may find this same parent to interact more positively in the next encounter.
11. Maintain a positive tone throughout the session and discuss the child's strengths and competencies.

Teacher Conferences

Many of the principles used in parent conferences also apply to teachers. Several nuances, however, will be outlined in the following suggestions:

1. Do not monopolize a teacher's break from teaching. Some teachers get few breaks in a day. Most get a brief lunch, when they prefer to unwind with colleagues and prepare for the remainder of the day. A clinician is unlikely to command a teacher's undivided attention during such breaks. If a teacher has an additional free period, it may be a good time for a conference. After school is frequently the best time to get a teacher's undivided attention for a meeting. Teachers are generally very busy people, so the pace of the meeting will be quicker than is the case for parents.
2. Teachers are interested in schooling issues. The diagnosis of Conduct Disorder is of less concern to teachers than getting specific recommendations for helping the child in the classroom (Teglasi, 1983). If a psychologist is not trained and/or has little experience in teacher consultation, the assistance of someone like a qualified school psychologist should be enlisted to assist with the teacher conference.

In any assessment with a school-aged child, the clinician should be prepared to conduct a teacher conference, or at the very least be available to answer any questions and facilitate the implementation of classroom-based interventions. Such a conference is desirable because teachers are usually involved somehow in the treatment of children and adolescents.

Child Feedback

Providing assessment feedback to a child is often overlooked, but it is important to do so in most cases because the child will likely begin some interventions or experience some changes in his or her environment directly related to the assessment. The major decision that a clinician needs to make before giving feedback to a child regards the type of information that is appropriate for a child's developmental level. Clearly, the kind of feedback given to parents is inappropriate for a 5- or 6-year-old, who may have extraordinary difficulty understanding the concept of a percentile rank. A child this age, however, may be able to understand the consequences of the evaluation. In this situation, the child may be able to understand something like: "Remember those tests I gave you? Well, some of them seemed hard for you. Because of this, I suggested to your parents that you be helped after school. So now, you will be going to visit a teacher after school who will help you with schoolwork."

The older the child, the more similar the feedback session becomes to the one for parents. One dramatic difference, however, is that negative feedback to a child or adolescent can have the opposite of the intended effect. That is, in most cases, the goal is to improve variables such as peer-related social skills. A child who is told that he or she has poor social skills may decide to stop trying to interact with peers. In some cases, the clinician's honesty could harm the child. A few options are available in cases where a clinician is concerned about such negative consequences. One option is to have someone who knows the child well and has a positive relationship with him or her help the psychologist communicate the results in a non-threatening way to the child. A good person to fill this role is a teacher, other professional caregiver, or possibly a parent. A second possibility, if applicable, is to have the child's primary therapist or counselor eventually share the results with the child in a counseling session, when he or she could help the child cope with the results in a supportive setting.

In most cases involving feedback to children or adolescents, it is advisable to consult with a fellow professional (e.g., teacher, counselor, speech therapist, etc.) who knows the child extremely well. This colleague can help the psychologist gauge the ability of the child to deal appropriately with the assessment results and associated interventions.

Conclusions

Report writing and oral reporting are central, not ancillary, considerations in the assessment process. The most insightful and elegant of evaluations is lost if not translated to usable information in written reports and intervention planning meetings. Unfortunately, these central assessment skills are under-emphasized in the training of clinicians who are left to acquire these skills through trial-and- error. Clinicians are advised to seek out expert supervision in this area, if it is not readily offered. In addition, enlisting the aid of a competent editor can markedly enhance the quality of written work. Writing is not easy. Writing skills, however, can be acquired and improved with diligence and patience.

Chapter Summary

1. Psychological reports are frequently made available to parents, judges, lawyers, and other non-psychologists, creating the opportunity for improper interpretation of the results by untrained individuals.
2. Psychological reports can be useful to other clinicians who evaluate a child who has previously been seen by a psychologist.
3. Different audiences require different types of written reports.
4. Some of the common problems with report writing include the following:
   (a) Vocabulary problems
   (b) Faulty interpretation
   (c) Report length
   (d) A number emphasis
   (e) Failure to address referral questions
5. Some research has shown that teachers prefer a question-and-answer report format.
6. Parents also tend to prefer a question-and-answer format to other formats, although the difference in preference scores between the psychoeducational and question-and-answer reports in one study failed to reach statistical significance.
7. Suggested report writing practices include the following:
   (a) Report only pertinent information
   (b) Define abbreviations and acronyms
   (c) Emphasize words rather than numbers
   (d) Reduce difficult words
   (e) Describe the tests used
   (f) Edit the report at least once
   (g) Use headings and lists freely
   (h) Use examples of behavior to clarify meaning
   (i) Reduce report length
   (j) Check scores
   (k) Check spelling and grammar
8. Psychological reports often include some or all of the following headings:
   (a) Identifying Information
   (b) Assessment Procedures
   (c) Referral Question(s)
   (d) Background Information
   (e) Behavioral Observations
   (f) Assessment Results and Interpretation
   (g) Diagnostic Considerations
   (h) Summary
   (i) Signatures
   (j) Recommendations
   (k) Psychometric Summary
9. Hints for communicating test results to parents include the following:
   (a) Be direct and honest
   (b) Use percentile ranks heavily when describing test results
   (c) Allow parents opportunities to participate
   (d) Anticipate questions prior to the interview and prepare responses
   (e) Schedule adequate time for the interview
   (f) Practice communicating with parents from a variety of backgrounds
   (g) Avoid questionable predictions
   (h) Use good, basic counseling skills to convey difficult information
   (i) Do not engage in counseling that is beyond your level of expertise
   (j) Be aware that some parents are not ready to accept some of the conclusions offered
10. Teacher conferences are important for ensuring cooperation with recommendations.
11. The major decision that a clinician needs to make before giving feedback to a child regards the type of information that is appropriate for the child's developmental level.

CHAPTER 17

Assessment of Attention Deficit Hyperactivity and Disruptive Behavior Disorders

Chapter Questions

- What are some findings from research on Attention-Deficit Hyperactivity Disorder (ADHD) that have important implications for designing clinical assessments for children suspected of having ADHD?
- What are some practical guidelines for designing an assessment battery for children suspected of having ADHD and interpreting the assessment results?
- What are the implications of research on childhood conduct problems for designing clinical assessments for children with these problems?
- What basic questions should be addressed in clinical assessments of children with conduct problems?

Introduction

This chapter is the first of a series of chapters focusing on the assessment of several specific types of childhood emotional and behavioral problems. These chapters are designed to help an assessor apply information on the various assessment strategies discussed in previous chapters to the assessment of some of the more common types of psychopathology exhibited by children and adolescents. We start with the assessment of disorders, sometimes called externalizing behaviors (Achenbach & Edelbrock, 1978) or disorders of undercontrol (Quay, 1986). It is appropriate to start our syndrome-by-syndrome discussion with this class of disorders because they tend to be the most common reason for referral to child

P.J. Frick et al., *Clinical Assessment of Child and Adolescent Personality and Behavior*,
DOI 10.1007/978-1-4419-0641-0_17,

mental health clinics (Frick & Kimonis, 2008).

This predominance in clinic referrals is out of proportion to the prevalence of these disorders in the general population, where emotional difficulties are often as prevalent (Costello, Egger, & Angold, 2005). This high referral rate for disruptive behavior disorders is likely due to two factors. First, unlike adult mental health referrals, children and adolescents are rarely self-referred. Instead, they are often referred by significant others (e.g., parents, teachers, physicians) in their environment. Second, disruptive behavior disorders, as the name implies, are syndromes of behavior that cause significant disruptions in a child's environment, often directly affecting those responsible for referring a child for assessment and treatment. Thus, anyone working in a clinical setting with children and adolescents must have a firm understanding of these behavioral disorders.

To reiterate a common theme of this book, our recommendations for assessing children with ADHD and the disruptive behaviors disorders are based on research on the basic characteristics of these disorders. In each of the following sections we first provide a brief discussion of the most clinically relevant research findings and then discuss specific recommendations for assessment procedures based on these findings. We divide our discussion into two sections corresponding to the major subdivisions within the externalizing disorders. The first section involves a discussion of a syndrome of behaviors involving inattention-disorganization and impulsivity-motor hyperactivity labeled as Attention-Deficit Hyperactivity Disorder (ADHD) by the *DSM-IV-TR* (American Psychiatric Association, 2000). The second section focuses on conduct problems and aggression subsumed under the categories of Oppositional Defiant Disorder (ODD) and Conduct Disorder (CD) (American Psychiatric Association, 2000).

Attention-Deficit Hyperactivity Disorder

Classification and Subtypes

History

The syndrome of ADHD has long been recognized in the medical and psychological literature, with some descriptions dating back well over 100 years (Smith, Barkley, & Shapiro, 2007). However, over the years there has been considerable disagreement over what are the core features of the disorder. As a result of this confusion, there have been numerous changes in diagnostic definitions (see Frick & Lahey, 1991; Smith et al., 2007). This evolution in our conceptualization of ADHD is reflected in changes in the diagnostic criteria for ADHD over the most recent revisions of the *Diagnostic and Statistical Manual of Mental Disorders*.

The second edition of the *DSM* included a syndrome of the Hyperkinetic Reaction of Childhood to emphasize the belief that motor hyperactivity is the core feature of the disorder (*DSM-II*; American Psychiatric Association, 1968). In the third edition of the *DSM* the disorder was reconceptualized to emphasize deficits in sustained attention, acquiring the term Attention Deficit Disorder (*DSM-III*; American Psychiatric Association, 1980). Also in the *DSM-III*, it was explicitly recognized for the first time that children could have attention deficits in the absence of motor hyperactivity. The next revision, *DSM-III-R*, softened this emphasis on attention deficits, placing it on equal footing with motor hyperactivity in its definition of Attention Deficit Hyperactivity Disorder (American Psychiatric Association, 1987). The *DSM-III-R* criteria also did away with subtypes based on the presence or absence of motor activity.

Before discussing the most recent revision of the *DSM* (*DSM-IV-TR*; American

Psychiatric Association, 2000), it is important to highlight two main sources of variation in these conceptualizations of the disorder. First, a main source of debate has been over what are *the core features* of the disorder. For example, *DSM-III* proposed three core dimensions of behavior associated with attention deficit disorders: (1) inattention (e.g., very distractible, difficulty finishing things), (2) impulsivity (e.g., acts without thinking, interrupts others, loses things, makes careless mistakes), and (3) hyperactivity (e.g., fidgety and restless, running around and climbing excessively). In contrast, *DSM-III-R* eliminated any distinctions among these behaviors and considered all three dimensions to be indicative of a single domain of behavior.

Research has fairly consistently suggested that the best method for conceptualizing the symptoms is somewhere in between. Specifically, factor analyses have generally been able to document two partially independent dimensions of behavior: inattention/disorganization and impulsivity/overactivity (Lahey, Carlson, & Frick, 1997). The behaviors that are generally considered to be the core features of ADHD are listed in Table 17.1.

The second source of contention evident through the revisions of the DSM is the debate over whether there are valid subtypes of ADHD. *DSM-III* proposed the existence of two types of attention deficit disorder: Attention Deficit Disorder without Hyperactivity (ADD/WO) and Attention Deficit Disorder with Hyperactivity (ADD/H). These subtypes shared the core features of inattention and impulsivity but differed on the presence of motor hyperactivity. Lahey et al. (1997) summarize a significant body of research attesting to the validity of this distinction. Children with ADD/H tend to exhibit more conduct problems, to be more impulsive, and to be more socially rejected than children with ADD/WO. In contrast, children with ADD/WO tend to be more sluggish and drowsy (often described as unmotivated), to be more anxious and shy, and to be more likely to show an optimal response to low doses of stimulant medication than children with ADD/H. Based on their review of the research, these authors concluded

TABLE 17.1 Core Dimensions of Attention Deficit Hyperactivity Disorder

Inattention-Disorganization	**Impulsivity-Hyperactivity**
Difficulty organizing things[a,b]	Excessive running and climbing[a,b]
Difficulty finishing tasks[a,b]	Difficulty playing quietly[a,b]
Difficulty following through on instructions[a,b]	Excessive talking[a,b]
Often loses things[a,b]	Frequently interrupts and intrudes[a,b]
Easily distracted[a,b]	Always on the go[a,b]
Often does not listen[a,b]	Excessive fidgeting and squirming[a,b]
Difficulty concentrating and sustaining attention[a,b]	Difficulty staying in seat[a,b]
Misses details and makes careless mistakes[a]	Difficulty waiting turn[a,b]
Often avoids or dislikes tasks requiring sustained mental effort[a]	Frequently blurts out answers[a,b]
Often forgetful[a]	Frequently calls out in class[b]
Needs a lot of supervision[b]	

[a]Svmptoms included in the *DSM-IV-TR* (American Psychiatric Association, 2000) criteria for ADHD, although wording may not be exactly as that included in the manual.[b]Behaviors included in factor analyses reviewed by Lahey et al., 1997.

that the decision to eliminate the subtypes in the *DSM-III-R* was not consistent with this body of research.

DSM-IV-TR

The *DSM-IV-TR* definition of ADHD was designed to reflect research findings on both of these issues (American Psychiatric Association, 2000). First, there are two symptom lists, which closely correspond to the two dimensions of behavior described in Table 17.1. Second, the *DSM-IV-TR* recognizes the existence of subtypes based largely on the presence of hyperactivity. There is an ADHD Predominantly Inattentive Type to designate children with problems of inattention and disorganization but without problems of impulsivity and overactivity. In addition, there are the ADHD Predominantly Hyperactive Type and ADHD Combined Type to designate children with significant problems of impulsivity-hyperactivity, either in isolation from or in combination with problems of inattention and disorganization.

While these subtypes seem to match the research findings summarized previously, it is important to note that the stability of these ADHD subtypes over time is questionable. Specifically, in a sample of 118 children with ADHD who were ages 4 to 6 at the start of the study, Lahey, Pelham, Loney, Lee, and Wilcutt (2005) reported that it was not unusual for children to change in their subtype of ADHD over the 8-year study period. For example, 37% of children with Combined Type and 50% of the children with Predominantly Inattentive Type met criteria for a different subtype at least twice during the study period. Children with the Hyperactive Type were the most likely to shift subtypes, with most shifting to the Combined Type at some point during the study.

An inspection of the symptoms included in the *DSM-IV-TR* criteria for ADHD (see Table 17.1) indicate that the individual behaviors that form the diagnostic criteria for this disorder are behaviors that are quite common to some degree in normally developing children and adolescents. This is one of the issues that has led to serious concerns over the potential overdiagnosis of the disorder and concomitant overuse of stimulant medication to treat it (Angold, Erkanli, Egger, & Costello, 2000; Jensen et al., 1999). There are two critical issues related to these concerns. First, at present, there is little empirical evidence to support the concerns about overdiagnosis and overmedication, although clearly this is a very difficult issue on which to obtain good data (Jensen et al., 1999). Second, the symptoms of most childhood disorders, not just ADHD, are not qualitatively different from normal behaviors shown by children (e.g., sadness as a symptom of depression). This is not to imply that this is not an important issue in assessment but to illustrate that it is not specific to ADHD. It relates to the important issue raised in Chap. 3 that classification systems must clearly define what parameters are most important for differentiating disordered (i.e., clinically impairing) manifestations of the symptoms from more normal manifestations. The *DSM-IV-TR* includes several such parameters for the diagnosis of ADHD, and it is imperative that assessors systematically assess these parameters to avoid overdiagnosis.

The first parameter is the *frequency and severity of the symptoms.* The DSM-IV-TR sets six symptoms of either inattention-disorganization or impulsivity-hyperactivity as the diagnostic threshold for the disorder. This level of severity was chosen based on evidence that it seemed to designate a level of symptomology that predicted clinically significant levels of psychosocial impairment (e.g., poor academic performance, social rejection) for elementary school-aged children (Lahey, Applegate, McBurnett, et al., 1994). Using this diagnostic threshold, 3–7% of children would typically meet the diagnostic criteria for ADHD (American Psychiatric Association, 2000). It is important to note that the appropriateness of this threshold has been questioned for young preschool children as being too liberal, because many very young children show high rates of these behaviors and eventually outgrow them (Campbell, 1990), and for adolescents and young adults as being too conservative, because the frequency and severity of many of the symptoms seem to decline in adolescence (Barkley, 1997a).

The second parameter that differentiates normal and abnormal patterns of inattention, impulsivity, and overactivity is *the onset and duration of the symptoms. DSM-IV-TR* specifies that "some hyperactive-impulsive or inattentive symptoms must have caused impairment before age 7 years" (American Psychiatric Association, 2000, p. 92). This criterion is consistent with the conceptualization that ADHD is a lifelong pattern of maladaptive behavior and not a transient reaction to a specific stressor or to the demands of a particular developmental stage (Barkley, 1997a). While the age of onset criterion is consistent with this conceptual framework, there are several practical problems in using this criterion in clinical assessments. First, it is often difficult to gain accurate accounts of when symptoms became problematic, especially when assessing adolescents and adults, which involves recall of events over a long period of time (Barkley, 1997a).

Second, it is not uncommon for many of the symptoms of ADHD, especially the inattention ones, to only become problematic once the demands for sustained attention and organization increase in later elementary school years (Lahey et al., 2005; Loeber, Green, Lahey, Christ, & Frick, 1992). This developmental change in inattention symptoms is likely the reason that the age of 7 onset criterion may be particularly problematic for the Predominantly Inattentive Type of ADHD. Specifically, in a sample of 380 clinic-referred children (mean age 8.7 years) who met *DSM-IV* criteria for ADHD, almost all of those who met the symptom cut-off for the Predominantly Hyperactive-Impulsive Type and the Combined Type met the age of 7 onset criterion (Applegate et al., 1997). In contrast, only 48% of those children with Predominantly Inattentive Type met this age of onset criterion and those who did not meet the criterion did not differ from those that did on several important validity indexes, including level of impairment and level and type of comorbidity with other disorders. Therefore, the validity of the onset criterion for this ADHD subtype was questionable.

Third, it is important to recognize that, while the core deficits underlying the symptoms of ADHD may be stable across development, how these deficits are manifested in symptoms and secondary characteristics may change across development (Barkley, 1997a). In Table 17.2, we provide a brief summary of some of these developmental changes in the symptom patterns and secondary characteristics across development. One criticism of the *DSM-IV-TR* definition of ADHD that includes the same number and types of symptoms for children, adolescents, and adults is that this static definition may not capture these developmental changes adequately (Barkley, 1997a).

A third parameter in the *DSM-IV-TR* definition of ADHD that is important for separating normative from disordered levels of attention and overactivity is the specification of *cross-situational consistency of symptoms.* That is, to be diagnosed with ADHD, a child must show impairment related to the symptoms in two or more settings. This criterion is consistent with the conception that ADHD should not be solely a function of a single set of environmental circumstances (e.g., a disorganized classroom, a chaotic home environment) and clearly suggests that an adequate assessment of ADHD must involve an assessment

TABLE 17.2 Developmental Changes in the Core Features and Secondary Characteristics Associated with ADHD Across the Lifespan

Age	Primary Characteristics	Secondary Features
Preschool	Restlessness, excessive activity, difficulty remaining seated, and acts without thinking	Noncompliance, accidental injuries, aggression, and problems in toilet training
Elementary-school age	Poor attention span, distractibility, impulsivity, difficulty remaining seated, and can't play quietly	Difficulty following rules, immaturity, social rejection, needing a lot of supervision, failure to do household chores, and poor school performance
Adolescence	Poor attention span, distractibility, inability to finish things, careless mistakes, and lack of forethought and planning	Poor school performance (dropping out), low self-esteem, depression, substance use, delinquency, family conflict, needless risk taking, automobile accidents, teenage pregnancy, and rebelliousness
Young adults	Restlessness, distractibility, difficulty completing work, carelessness, and lack of forethought and planning	Poor educational and occupational performance, depression, substance use, poor social/marital adjustment, and poor anger management

SOURCES: Summarized from Barkley, 1997a; Barkley, Guevremont, Anastopoulos, & Fletcher, 1993; DuPaul & Stoner, 1994; Nadeau, 1995; Smith et al., 2007; Wender, 1995.

of the child in several different settings. However, although this criterion appears quite basic, it is difficult to use in clinical assessments for several reasons. For example, it is clear that children with ADHD will show variations in the level and severity of their behavior problems depending on the demands of the situation (e.g., time of day, level of structure, and complexity of the task) (Barkley, 1997a). Therefore, an assessor should not interpret the cross-situational criterion to imply that a child with ADHD must show the same level and severity symptoms across different settings with different demands. Instead, one must consider whether the child shows similar behaviors in situations with equivalent demands, and such judgments are very difficult to make. For example, if a child is having trouble associated with ADHD at school but not at home, the clinical assessor must judge whether or not this is due to the fact that demands for sustained attention and sitting still are not placed on the child at home.

Taken together, the level and severity of symptoms, their presence over extended periods of time, and their cross-situational consistency all are critical components of defining ADHD and must be systematically assessed in making this diagnosis. Inherent in each of these criteria is that they designate children who show some significant level of impairment in their psychosocial functioning due to the symptoms associated with ADHD. On the simplest, but possibly the most important level, it is this *significant impairment in functioning* (e.g., causing problems in school work, causing social rejection) that is most important in differentiating normative and disordered levels of the symptoms that are part of the ADHD definition. Furthermore, the degree of impairment in family functioning, peer relationships, and academic functioning, are often the main reasons that a child with ADHD is referred for an evaluation and they are some of the best predictors of a child's long-term adjustment (Pelham, Fabiano, & Massetti, 2005).

Comorbidities

Children with ADHD are an excellent example of the fact that children with problems in one area of adjustment are at risk for problems in other areas as well. Problems that often co-occur with ADHD are quite important clinically. They often cause more disruptions for the child and predict poorer outcomes than the primary ADHD symptoms themselves (Frick & Lahey, 1991). As a result, the secondary features are often a major focus of intervention (Pelham et al., 2005).

Conduct Problems/Aggression

The most common co-occurring problems experienced by children with ADHD are conduct problems and aggression, with research suggesting that 60–75% of children referred to clinics with ADHD show significant levels of these problems (Hinshaw, 1987). It is often these conduct problems that lead to a great deal of disruption for children with ADHD, leading to multiple disciplinary confrontations with parents and teachers, school suspensions, and problems in peer relations. In addition, these conduct problems are often predictive of poor outcomes in adolescence and young adulthood, especially for predicting delinquency and substance abuse (Fischer, Barkley, Fletcher, & Smallish, 1993; Mannuzza, Gittelman-Klein, Konig, & Giampino, 1989).

Other Comorbidities

Another condition that often occurs with ADHD is academic underachievement or a learning disability, both of which are frequently defined as school achievement below a level predicted by a child's age and intellectual level. Approximately 30% of children with ADHD show such learning problems (Frick, Lahey, Christ, Loeber, & Green, 1991; Massetti et al., 2008). In addition, children with ADHD tend to show a high rate of conflict with peers (Mikami & Hinshaw, 2003), with parents (Johnston & Mash, 2001), and with teachers (Cunningham & Boyle, 2002). And not surprisingly, given the amount of difficulty and conflict the ADHD child often experiences in his or her environment, children with ADHD often show high rates of anxiety (Tannock, 2000) and low self-esteem that persist throughout childhood and into adolescence (Fischer et al., 1993).

Conceptual Model

There have been numerous theories of ADHD that differ in terms of identifying the "core deficit" that underlies the symptoms of ADHD and the etiological factors that lead to this deficit. A growing number of researchers in this area have begun to focus on a failure in a child's inhibition system that influences his or her ability to regulate attention, actions, and emotions (e.g., Nigg, 2006; Whalen & Henker, 1998). One of the more influential and best articulated of such theories is one proposed by Barkley (1997b), which defines "behavioral inhibition" as the capacity to inhibit motivated behaviors, either prior to their initiation or once they are initiated, which creates a delay between an impulse and action. This delay allows the child to "think through" his or her actions and allows the behavior to be self-directed and guided by the demands of any given situation. A deficit in this inhibition system would make it difficult for a child to sustain his or her attention on a single task, it would make foresight and planning difficult, and it would make it difficult for the child to inhibit impulses for motor movement, thereby accounting for the core symptoms of the disorder. Barkley also outlines how such a deficit could account for many of the other characteristics typically found in people with ADHD, such as a poor sense of time, poor emotional self-control, deficits in problem solving, and an inability to modulate behavior based on changing situational demands.

While there is a growing consensus that a deficit in the inhibitory control of behavior may be a primary or at least an important deficit in children in ADHD, it is less clear what could cause this deficit to develop. Many theories focus on structural neurological abnormalities in parts of the nervous system involved in inhibitory control of behavior (Castellanos et al., 2002). Other theories focus on abnormalities in the functioning of these neurological regions with studies examining the cerebral blood flow of children and adults with ADHD consistently showing areas of decreased activity in the prefrontal regions of the brain (Hendren, DeBacker, & Pandina, 2000).

There is evidence that these neurological abnormalities can result from a number of different influences. Specifically, there is evidence that ADHD symptoms are highly heritable and, as a result, these neurological abnormalities may be inherited (Waldman & Gizer, 2006). In addition, the neurological abnormalities could result from trauma to the developing nervous system such a prenatal exposure to alcohol or other drugs, birth trauma, or exposure to environmental toxins (e.g., lead) (Smith et al., 2007). It is important to note that, although most theories of ADHD emphasize potential neurological underpinnings to the disorder, there is currently no neurological test that has proven to be useful in diagnosing ADHD. Instead, the diagnosis relies on a careful assessment of the behaviorally based diagnostic criteria using a process outlined in the next section of this chapter. Although social experiences can influence the development of behavioral inhibition and can change brain functioning (Cicchetti & Walker, 2001), most theories have not emphasized environmental factors as primary causal agents in the development of the core symptoms of ADHD. Instead, most theories emphasize the role of environmental factors in determining how the core deficit is expressed. For example, a child with problems in behavioral inhibition will be very difficult to socialize but some parents will be better than others in working with such a child to develop compensatory strategies to minimize the effects that the inhibitory deficit may have on the child's academic and psychosocial functioning.

As a result, environmental factors can play a large role in the development of some of the problems (e.g., poor school performance, social rejection, conduct problems) that can develop secondarily to the ADHD symptoms (Frick, 1994; Johnston & Mash, 2001). Therefore, although psychosocial influences may not be integral to many causal theories of ADHD, it is still important to carefully assess a child's psychosocial context to (1) determine the degree to which the problems associated with ADHD have negatively impacted a child's functioning and (2) guide interventions designed to reduce or prevent many of the secondary characteristics and co-occurring problems in adjustment that often develop in children with ADHD (Pelham et al., 2005).

Implications for Assessment

In Table 17.3, we summarize the main implications of research on ADHD for designing an appropriate assessment battery for children or adolescents suspected of having ADHD. In addition, in Boxes 17.1 and 17.2, we provide two case examples of a typical ADHD assessment battery, with Box 17.1 describing the assessment of a child with ADHD-Combined Type and Box 17.2 describing the assessment of a child with ADHD-Predominantly Inattentive Type.

TABLE 17.3 The Nature of ADHD and Implications for Assessment

Focus of Research	Implications for Assessment
Classification and presence of subtypes	Assess for presence of two core dimensions of behavior inattention/disorganization and impulsivity/overactivity
	Assess for subtypes based on the presence of impulsivity/overactivity
	Assess duration to determine if behaviors are chronic and stable
	Assess situational variability of behaviors
	Assess level of impairment associated with symptoms
Presence of multiple comorbidities	Assess for the presence of conduct problems/aggression
	Assess for the presence of learning problems
	Assess anxiety
	Assess self-esteem
	Assess social relationships and peer social status
	Assess level of parent–child and teacher–child conflicts
Potential alternative causes	Obtain a developmental and medical history
	Assess for intellectual and learning deficits
	Assess for emotional difficulties

Box 17.1

Case Study: Evaluation of an 8-Year-Old Girl with Attention-Deficit Hyperactivity Disorder-Combined Type

Claire was 8 years, 9 months old when her mother referred her to an outpatient mental health clinic for a comprehensive psychological evaluation. Claire's mother was concerned about Claire's aggressive behavior, describing Claire as having an "uncontrollable temper" and being very defiant. Maternal report also indicated that Claire has had very inconsistent academic performance throughout her first 3 years of school, primarily because she failed to complete work and made a lot of careless mistakes. To illustrate the effect of Claire's carelessness on her school performance, her mother described an incident the previous school year in which Claire rushed through an arithmetic test and completed all the questions as addition, even though half of the problems were subtraction. Claire reportedly knew how to do subtraction problems.

Assessment of Core Symptoms

The core symptoms of ADHD were assessed through a structured diagnostic interview conducted with Claire's mother and her teacher (DISC-IV; Shaffer et al., 2000 and behavior rating scales completed by her mother (CBCL; Achenbach, 2001) and her teacher (CBRSC; Neeper, Lahey, & Frick, 1990). On the DISC-IV, Claire's mother and teacher both reported significant problems of inattention-disorganization, such as difficulty sustaining attention, having difficulty finishing tasks, often losing things, frequently making careless mistakes, and having very messy work habits. In addition, these problems in attention were accompanied by significant problems of impulsivity and motor hyperactivity. Both mother and teacher indicated that Claire frequently interrupted others; often talked out in class; was very fidgety and restless in class; and could not stay in her seat, either in class or at home to eat dinner.

Consistent with a diagnosis of ADHD-Combined Type, Claire's mother reported on the structured interview that these problems have been evident since very early in Claire's life, especially the motor overactivity. In fact, maternal report indicated that Claire had been asked to leave two preschools because she was too "rambunctious" and could not sit still. Claire's teacher indicated that these symptoms of ADHD were currently interfering with her school performance to a substantial degree. On the Academic Performance Rating Scale (APRS: DuPaul, Rapport, & Perriello, 1991). Claire's teacher indicated that she was turning in less than half of the work required by the class and it often was inaccurate, despite Claire knowing the material.

Finally, parent and teacher report on the omnibus rating scales suggested that the core ADHD behaviors were more severe than would be expected in children her age. Using the age- and gender-specific norms of CBCL, Claire had elevations on both the Attention Problems (T-score of 75) and Thought Problems (T-score of 76) scales. Similarly, Claire's teacher on the CBRSC rated her as elevated on the Motor Hyperactivity scale, with a T-score of 79 based on the entire normative sample (across ages and gender). Whereas the CBCL elevations may have been spuriously high due to comparisons restricted to girls, the elevation on the CBRSC based on a comparison to both boys and girls clearly indicated that her behavior was more severe than is typical for children her age.

Assessment of Comorbidities

Like many children with ADHD-Combined Type, Claire also exhibited significant conduct problems. On the DISC-IV, her parent and teacher described Claire as showing frequent temper tantrums, often arguing with adults, often refusing adults' requests, blaming others for her mistakes, and being grouchy and easily annoyed. These behaviors were rated as severe on both parent and teacher rating scales, with T-scores above 70 being obtained on the Delinquent and Aggressive Behavior scales of the parent-completed CBCL and the

(Continues)

Box 17.1 (Continued)

Oppositional-Conduct Disorders scale of the teacher-completed CBRSC.

On the CBCL Social Problems scale and the CBRSC Social Competence scale, mother and teacher also indicated that Claire's behavioral problems seemed to be affecting her peer relations. She was described by parent and teacher as being bossy and domineering in peer interactions, which had led to difficulties in making friends. However, a sociometric exercise did not indicate that Claire's social status was negatively affected by this behavior. In a class of 13, she was nominated as "Liked most" by 3 children and "Liked least" by only 2 children.

A psychoeducational evaluation did not reveal any significant learning problems. Claire's intelligence scores were in the average to high average range in both verbal and nonverbal abilities. She also obtained age-standard scores in the high average range on the individually administered achievement test. Thus, there were no indications of cognitive deficits, and her achievement scores indicated that she seemed to be learning at or above a level expected for her age.

Ruling Out Alternative Causes

Claire's birth, medical, and developmental history did not suggest the presence of any medical or neurological disorder. As mentioned previously, the psychoeducational evaluation did not reveal any cognitive or learning problems that could account for the behaviors. An unstructured clinical interview did reveal that Claire reported being sexually abused over a period of 1 month during the previous summer by a paternal uncle. This alleged abuse had been reported to the local child protection agency, and Claire had been seen at the community mental health center for 3 months following the incident. However, it did not appear that Claire's difficulties could be solely accounted for by an emotional reaction to sexual abuse, for several reasons. First, the ADHD behaviors were more severe than would be expected from such a reaction, and they clearly predated the alleged abuse incident. Second, she did not show any other signs of anxiety and depression that would suggest a significant degree of emotional distress.

Box 17.2

Case Study: Evaluation of an 8-Year-Old Boy with Attention-Deficit Hyperactivity Disorder-Predominantly Inattentive Type

Sean was 8 years, 1 month when his teacher referred him to a child mental health clinic for a comprehensive psychological evaluation. Sean was failing most subjects in the third grade and his teacher attributed this poor performance primarily to problems in concentration. At home, Sean's mother also reported that he had difficulty completing things, was often daydreaming, and seemed to have little motivation for anything.

Assessment of Core Symptoms

The core ADHD behaviors were assessed by structured interviews (DISC-IV) completed by Sean's parent and teacher and by parent (CBCL) and teacher (CBRSC, APRS) behavior rating scales. On structured interviews, both parent and teacher reported that Sean showed significant problems of inattention and disorganization, such as being very distractible, frequently daydreaming, having difficulty finishing tasks, often seeming unmotivated, and seeming very sluggish and drowsy. Although Sean was described by his mother as somewhat fidgety, neither his mother nor his teacher reported significant problems of impulsivity or overactivity.

Consistent with these reports on the structured interviews, Sean was rated as showing

(Continues)

Box 17.2 (Continued)

attentional problems on parent and teacher rating scales out of a normative range. On the CBCL completed by his mother, Sean had a T-score of 69 on the Attention Problems scale. On the teacher-completed CBRSC, he had T-scores of 76 and 71 on the Sluggish Tempo and Daydreams scales, respectively. He also had a T-score of 69 on the Inattention-Disorganization scale of the CBRSC. Consistent with a diagnosis of ADHD-Inattentive Type, his teacher's rating of Motor Hyperactivity on the CBRSC was within a normative range (T-score of 57).

Assessment of Comorbidities

On parent and teacher structured interviews, Sean was reported as having some signs of mild anxiety, including frequent stomachaches, self-conscious behaviors, and concerns about his appearance. These symptoms did not seem severe enough to warrant a diagnosis of an anxiety disorder and they did not appear out of age-normative ranges on the CBCL, on the CBRSC, or on the self-report Revised Children's Manifest Anxiety Scale (Reynolds & Richmond, 1985).

A psychoeducational assessment did not reveal any evidence of a learning disability. Sean's scores on both in standardized intelligence test and achievement test were all within age-appropriate limits. An assessment of Sean's peer relations did not indicate any problems in this psychological domain, based on parent and teacher rating scales and a sociometric exercise conducted with Sean's classmates. Similarly, there were no indications from any assessment source that Sean exhibited significant conduct problems.

Ruling Out Alternative Causes

A birth, medical, and developmental history obtained from Sean's mother did not reveal any indications of significant medical or neurological problems. He reportedly had some difficulties breathing immediately following birth, but he was quickly stabilized with oxygen. Also, he had some mild allergies to dust and pollen, but these were not severe enough to warrant medication.

Although Sean exhibited some anxiety symptoms, they did not seem severe enough to be causing his problems in attention. Also, his anxiety seemed to be focused largely around school (e.g., stomachaches on school days, worry about tests). Therefore, it seemed more likely that Sean's anxiety was secondary to the academic problems caused by his attentional difficulties.

Assessing Core Behaviors

Guided by the research on classification of ADHD, the first goal of the assessment is to assess the core features of ADHD. Many of the behavior rating scales (Chaps. 6 and 7) and structured interviews (Chap. 11) discussed in previous chapters provide scales or sections that assess for these core behaviors. These behaviors can also be assessed through behavioral observations (Chap. 8; see also Pelham et al., 2005; Smith et al., 2007).

In selecting specific scales to assess the core features of ADHD, several key factors should be considered. First, one should pay close attention to item content. Many measures are based on outdated conceptualizations of ADHD or the scales were formed strictly on the basis of statistical covariation, without any guiding theory to help in scale definition. As a result, many scales that purport to measure behaviors associated with ADHD also include behaviors that are not currently viewed as being part of the primary symptom clusters. Unfortunately, these less relevant behaviors are intermixed with core behaviors, and, as a result, many measures have no pure indicator of ADHD symptoms. Examples of several commonly used omnibus rating scales with subscales that assess ADHD behaviors are presented in Box 17.3 to illustrate this point. Evident from this table is the fact that a child may have elevations on many scales that purport to measure ADHD without actually showing the core features of the disorder. Therefore, when selecting a scale to use in an assessment of possible ADHD, an important consideration is whether it contains scales that are largely composed of ADHD symptoms. Further, when interpreting scale elevations on a given rating scale, one must be sure that the elevations were actually due to the behaviors associated with ADHD.

Second, many measures simply do not have sufficient coverage of the core ADHD behaviors to aid in the differentiation of the two subtypes of ADHD. Often behaviors indicative of inattention-disorganization are intermixed with impulsive and overactive behaviors, providing no method of determining subtypes. For example, from Box 17.3 one notices that the ASEBA (Achenbach, 2001) Attention Problems scale includes items associated with inattention-disorganization and impulsivity-motor hyperactivity. As a result, use of this overall clinical scale does not aid in distinguishing subtypes of ADHD. Typically, structured interviews that are tied to diagnostic classification systems and are updated as the classification system is updated have the best symptom coverage. Structured interviews also allow one to determine the duration and stability of ADHD behaviors, which, as discussed previously, is crucial in the assessment of ADHD.

Box 17.3

Commonly Used Behavior Rating Scales with Subscales Related to ADHD: An Illustration of Item Heterogeneity

Many of the more commonly used parent and teacher rating scales have very heterogeneous item content with respect to ADHD. Most of the scales that purport to measure constructs related to ADHD contain a large number of behaviors not considered to be part of the core symptoms of ADHD (see Table 17.1). To illustrate this, we list the item content of relevant subscales from a few commonly used behavior ratings scales and highlight in boldface type the items that are not directly tied to the two core dimensions of ADHD.

Achenbach System for Empirically Based Assessment (Achenbach, 2001)

Cross Informant Scales

Attention Problems	**Attention Deficit Hyperactivity Problems**
(9 items)	(7 items)
Acts too young	Fails to finish things
Fails to finish things	Difficulty concentrating
Difficulty concentrating	Can't sit still
Can't sit still	Acts impulsively
Often confused	Innattentive
Daydreams	Talks too much
Acts impulsively	**Loud**
Poor school performance	----------------------
Innattentive	14% not part of core ADHD symptoms

44% not part of core ADHD symptoms	

Behavior Assessment System for Children – 2nd Edition (Reynolds & Kamphaus, 2004)

Parent Rating Scale		Teacher Rating Scale	
Attention Problems (6 items)	**Hyperactivity (8-items)**	**Attention Problems (7 items)**	**Hyperactivity (11 items)**
Pays attention	Cannot wait turn	Pays attention	Cannot wait turn
Has a short attention span	Acts without thinking	Has a short attention span	Acts without thinking
Listens to directions	**Has poor self-control**	Listens to directions	**Has poor self-control**
Pays attention when spoken to	Interrupts parents when they are on the phone	Does not pay attention to lectures	**Seeks attention while doing schoolwork**
Listens carefully	**Acts out of control**	Listens carefully	**Acts out of control**
Is easily distracted	Interrupts others when they are speaking	Is easily distracted	Interrupts others when they are speaking
------------------	**Fiddles with things while at meals**	Is easily distracted from class work	**Disrupts the schoolwork of other children**
0% not pare of core ADHD symptoms	**Disrupts other children's activities**	------------------	**Disrupts other children's activities**
	------------------	0% not part of core ADHD symptoms	Has trouble staying seated
	50% not part of core ADHD symptoms		Is overly active
			Calls out in class

			45% not part of core ADHD symptoms

Conners Rating Scales – 3rd Edition (Conners, 2008)

Parent	Teacher
Inattention (10 items)	**Inattention (11 items)**
Has trouble staying focused on one thing at a time	Has a short attention span
Has a short attention span	Doesn't pay attention to details; makes careless mistakes
Avoids or dislikes things that take a lot of effort and are not fun	Gives up easily on difficult tasks
Has trouble concentrating	Is sidetracked easily
Doesn't pay attention to details; makes careless mistakes	Avoids or dislikes things that take a lot of effort and are not fun
Has trouble changing from one activity to another	

(Continues)

Conners Rating Scales – 3 (Continued)

Parent	Teacher
Inattention (10 items) cont.	**Inattention (11 items) cont.**
Inattentive, easily distracted	**Gets bored**
Gives up easily on difficult tasks	Has trouble concentrating
Has trouble keeping his/her mind on work or play for long	Inattentive, easily distracted
10% not part of core ADHD symptoms	**Has trouble changing from one task to another**
	Has trouble keeping his/her mind on work or play
	for long 18% not part of core ADHD symptoms
Hyperactivity/Impulsivity (14 items)	**Hyperactivity/Impulsivity (18 items)**
Fidgeting	Leaves seat when he/she should stay seated
Blurts out answers before the question has been completed	**Gets overly excited**
Is constantly moving	Fidgets or squirms in seat
Excitable, impulsive	Restless or overactive
Gets over-stimulated	Blurts out answers before the question has been completed
Blurts out the first thing that comes to mind	Excitable, impulsive
Has difficulty waiting for his/her turn	Acts as if driven by a motor
Runs or climbs when he/she is not supposed to	Runs or climbs when he/she is not supposed to
Is noisy and loud when playing our using free time	Talks out of turn
Leaves seat when he/she should stay seated	Interrupts others (e.g., butts into conversations or games)
Fidgets or squirms in seat	
Restless or overactive	Is noisy and loud when playing or using free time
Interrupts others (for example, butts into conversations or games)	
	Gets over-stimulated or "wound up"
	Talks too much
	Fidgeting
7% not part of core ADHD symptoms	Is constantly moving
	Gets up and moves around during lessons
	Has difficulty waiting for his/her turn
	Talks non-stop
	11% not part of core ADHD symptoms

(Continues)

Personality Inventory for Children -2 (Lachar & Gruber, 2001)	Student Behavior Survey (Lachar, Wingenfeld, Kline, & Gruber, 2000)
Impulsivity and Distractibility (27 items)	**Attention Deficit Hyperactivity** (16 items)
My child's manners sometimes embarrass me	Completes class assignments
Schoolteachers complain that my child cannot sit still	**Demonstrates logical approach to learning**
My child's behavior often makes others angry	
My child often does not finish things that he/she starts	Follows teacher's directions
My child jumps from one activity to another	Maintains alert and focused attention
My child often acts without thinking	Persists even when activity is difficult
My child is often restless	Remembers teacher's directions
I cannot get my child to do his/her school lessons	Stays seated
My child often forgets to do things	Waits for turn
My child often nags and bothers other people	**Works independently without disturbing others**
My child cannot wait for things like other children do	
My child cannot keep attention on anything	Listens to other students
My child does not learn from his/her mistakes	**Daydreams**
My child is almost always on time and remembers what he/she is supposed to do	Interrupts others
My child cannot sit still in school because of nervousness	Impulsive
The school says that my child needs help in getting along with other children	**Misbehaviors unless closely supervised**
My child usually runs rather than walks	Overactive
My child tends to swallow food without chewing it	Talks excessively
Recently the school has sent home notes about my child's bad behavior	--
My child seems more clumsy than other children his/her age	25% not part of core ADHD symptoms
My child will do anything on a dare	
My child brags about being sent to the principal at school	
Nothing seems to scare my child	
My child likes to show off	
My child tends to brag	
Money seems to be my child's biggest interest	
--	
63% not part of core ADHD symptoms	

There are several ratings scales that have been designed solely to assess behaviors associated with ADHD and provide much more extensive coverage of behaviors associated with this disorder. They include the ADHD Rating Scale IV (DuPaul, Power, Anastopoulos, & Reid, 1998) and the Disruptive Behavior Disorders Rating Scale (Pelham et al., 2005), both of which were designed to provide a complete coverage of the diagnostic criteria for ADHD. The Brown Attention Deficit Disorder Scales for Children (Brown, 2001) and the Attention Deficit Disorder Evaluation Scales (ADDES-3; McCarney, 2004) also provide extensive coverage of ADHD symptoms, although they were not explicitly tied to *DSM-IV-TR* criteria.

Third, when selecting measures to assess the core features of ADHD, one must obtain information from multiple sources (parents and teachers). This helps one determine the situational variability of behaviors. Also, if the core features of ADHD can be assessed through multiple modalities (e.g., rating scales and behavioral observations), this negates the need to rely on any single imperfect assessment instrument. Therefore, one must choose a set of assessment instruments that provides a multi-informant and multi-method assessment of the core ADHD behaviors.

Fourth, one should have information that allows comparison to age norms. Most definitions of ADHD either implicitly or explicitly state that the symptoms should be inconsistent with a child's developmental level (American Psychiatric Association, 2000). Therefore, an assessment must provide information that allows one to compare a child's behaviors to the behaviors of other children of a similar developmental level. Typically, behavior rating scales are best suited for this task because of their extensive normative base. However, one important caution is in order in using norm-referenced rating scales. Many scales (e.g., ASEBA) often only provide norm-referenced scores broken down by *age and gender*. Definitions of ADHD do not make the restriction that the behaviors be inconsistent for a child's gender. In fact, it is well accepted that boys are four to six times more likely to show ADHD than girls (American Psychiatric Association, 2000). Using gender-specific norms ignores this widely found and accepted gender ratio and artificially equates the number of girls and boys with significant levels of ADHD behaviors. This will lead to more girls and fewer boys being considered to have significant ADHD behaviors than if cross-gender norms are used.

Fifth, researchers studying children with ADHD and attempting to define the core deficit that may underlie this disorder (e.g., response inhibition, sustained attention) have frequently used *laboratory measures* of inattention and impulsivity in their assessments. These measures place children in standardized conditions and attempt to quantitatively measure their inattentiveness, impulsiveness, or related behaviors under these conditions. For example, one of the most frequently used laboratory measures for the assessment of ADHD is the Continuous Performance Test (CPT). There are many variations of the CPT but a prototypical CPT is the one developed by Gordon (1983). In the Gordon CPT, a child is told to view a screen on which numbers are presented. The child is instructed to press a button each time a predetermined number is presented. Two responses are measured. *Omissions* are the number of times the designated number is presented to the child and the child fails to press the button. Number of omissions is considered to be a measure of sustained attention, especially increases in omissions over time. *Commissions* occur when the child incorrectly presses the button when the designated number is not presented and are considered a measure of impulsivity.

There are many variations of the CPT (e.g., Conners, 1995), with some CPT tasks presenting auditory rather than visual stimuli and other tasks presenting distracters (e.g., numbers flashing on either side of the target stimuli that need to be ignored). Also, in addition to the CPT, there are many other laboratory measures that have been used in research with children who have ADHD. Rapport, Chung, Shore, Denney, and Isaacs (2000) review 142 studies using over 40 different laboratory measures to assess characteristics associated with ADHD. They identify several characteristics of the tasks that most consistently differentiate children with ADHD from other children. First, the tasks that most consistently show group differences rely on recognition, recall, or both (e.g., the letter or word that a child is supposed to look for is not continuously displayed for the child), and they often involve some speed of processing component. Also, most of the tasks that reliably differentiate children with ADHD from other children place special demands on a child's working memory and each of the tasks is experimentally paced, not allowing the child to control the speed at which stimuli are presented. Rapport et al. (2000) provide an interesting discussion as to how these different task parameters may provide clues to the specific deficits displayed by children with ADHD.

It is evident from this rather extensive literature that these tasks have been quite useful in studying children with ADHD. These tasks also have a number of appealing qualities for clinical assessments as well. For example, they can help bridge the gap between assessment instruments being used in research that guide our current conceptualizations of ADHD and those commonly used in clinical practice to make the diagnosis (Frick, 2000). Even more appealing, however, is that these laboratory tasks provide a potential means of assessing the symptoms of ADHD that are not based on the perceptions of others that could be biased.

Unfortunately, despite this promise for their clinical utility, there are a number of limitations in their development that make their clinical usefulness in the diagnosis of ADHD somewhat limited at present (Pelham et al., 2005; Smith et al., 2007). For example, the primary validation of these tasks has been to differentiate ADHD children from non-ADHD children or to show the effects of stimulant medication on the task performance of children with ADHD (Rapport et al., 2000). Unfortunately, both types of studies rely on group-level data that are difficult to translate into findings that are meaningful for interpreting an individual child's score (e.g., How many children with ADHD do not score high on the laboratory measure? What percentage of treated children show the response to medication on the task?). Furthermore, it is not clear whether performance differences on these tasks are specific to children with ADHD or whether children with other types of behavioral or emotional disturbances also show similar problems in performance. Without such information, it is difficult to use these measures to make differential diagnoses between ADHD and other forms of psychopathology.

Finally, scores from the laboratory measures generally show low correlations with behavioral observations and parent and teacher reports (e.g., interviews and rating scales) of ADHD symptoms (Barkley, 1991; DuPaul, Anastopoulos, Shelton, Guevremont, & Metevia, 1992). Furthermore, there is very little information as to whether or not the laboratory measures add any clinically useful information to these more ecologically valid measures of behavior (Pelham et al., 2005; Rapport et al., 2000). For example, if a child is reported as showing significant problems with ADHD symptoms according to parent and teacher reports and based on behavioral observations in the classroom, interventions for his behavioral problems in his natural environment will likely be the same, irrespective of his performance on the laboratory task. Because treatment decisions are largely based on the more ecologically valid measures, the role of laboratory measures in clinical assessments is uncertain at this point. In Box 17.4, we summarize Barkley's (1991) review of laboratory measures of ADHD symptoms, which provide a more in-depth discussion of these measures' ecological and incremental validity.

Box 17.4

Research Note: Ecological Validity of Laboratory Measures of Attention and Impulsivity

Barkley (1991) provides a critical discussion of laboratory measures (LM) used to assess attention and impulsivity, two aspects of the core symptoms of ADHD. The focus of much of Barkley's discussion is on reaction time tasks (RTT), continuous performance tasks (CPT), and the Matching Familiar Figures Test (MFFT). Although Barkley also discusses analogue observations of motor activity, these were discussed previously in Chap. 8.

Concept of Ecological Validity

The first issue addressed in this article is the concept of ecological validity. Barkley defined ecological validity as "the degree to which LMs represent the actual behaviors of interest (i.e., inattention and impulsivity) as they occur in naturalistic settings" (p. 150). This aspect of validity is crucial for clinical assessments. In contrast, most research projects have the goal of determining the "core deficit" in ADHD, which may not be manifested in the natural setting. Therefore, a LM "need not be ecologically valid to be useful in research on ADHD" (p. 151).

Evidence for Ecological Validity

One type of research on the ecological validity of LMs consists of studies testing group differences on LMs between ADHD and control children. In general, Barkley's review suggested that all of the LMs have consistently differentiated ADHD from normal control children. However, most studies indicate that these effects are weakened or altogether eliminated when differences in intellectual level are controlled. Also, LMs do not differentiate ADHD children from other clinic-referred children. As a result, scores on the LMs are not useful in making differential diagnoses within clinic referrals.

A second type of research investigates the effect of stimulant medication on a child's performance on the LMs. Barkley's conclusion was that the research evidence was mixed. Several studies found significant effects for stimulant medication on commonly used LMs, whereas many studies found no such reliable effect.

A third type of research investigates the correlations between scores on LMs and parent and teacher ratings of ADHD behavior. Studies have generally found significant but modest (.21–.51) correlations between LM measures of attention and impulsivity and parent and teacher ratings of behaviors considered to be indicative of these constructs.

Conclusions

Barkley concludes that the ecological validity of LMs should be considered limited based on the existing research. As a result, clinical research should avoid using LMs as the "gold standard" against which other measures of attention and impulsivity are judged. For clinical assessments, one should recognize the limited usefulness of LMs in a battery of assessment tests. Most clinical decisions are based on the more ecologically valid measures of parent and teacher report of a child's behavior in the naturalistic setting. Barkley concludes, "Where LM results conflict with those obtained from other sources, such as parent and teacher behavior ratings, history, and observations in natural settings, the LM results should probably be disregarded in favor of these more ecologically valid sources" (p. 173). As a result, the incremental benefit of adding LMs to an assessment battery seems to be minimal.

SOURCE: Barkley, R. A. (1991). The ecological validity of laboratory and analogue assessment methods of ADHD. *Journal of Abnormal Child Psychology, 19*, 149–178.

One final note is in order for assessing the core features of ADHD. Despite widespread cautions against the practice (e.g., Barkley, 1990; Kamphaus, 2001; Kaufman, 1994), clinical assessors continue to use the Freedom from Distractibility (FD) factor from the Wechsler Intelligence Scales for Children (Wechsler, 1991) as an indicator of the presence of ADHD symptoms. This inappropriate use of FD is largely maintained simply because of the name given to the factor, which is a significant source of distress to the person who first applied the FD label to the WISC subtests. Alan Kaufman states, "The label should have been trashed years ago. I cringe whenever I read it" (Kaufman, 1994, p. 212).

As Kaufman goes on to explain, the use of the FD as a measure of inattention or distractibility is inappropriate because these scales are affected by multiple emotional and behavioral factors, not just distractibility. To illustrate the point, Kaufman reviewed 19 studies in which the FD was lower in samples of children with learning disabilities, children with leukemia, children with emotional difficulties, heterogeneous psychiatric samples of inpatient or outpatient children, children with autism, children with schizophrenia, children with Conduct Disorder, and children with muscular dystrophy. The author then makes the cogent point that the FD factor is important because of its robust ability to differentiate the abnormal (medically, behaviorally, and educationally) from the normal population, but it is basically meaningless for identifying a specific type of exceptionality, such as ADHD.

Assessing Comorbid Problems

Many of the problems that often co-occur with ADHD can be assessed in conjunction with the assessment of the core ADHD behaviors. For example, many of the omnibus rating scales and structured interviews discussed in previous chapters include items that assess for conduct problems, anxiety, depression, self-esteem, and social competence. Like the ADHD behaviors themselves, potential co-occurring problems are best assessed through multiple informants and using multiple formats. Given the overlap with learning problems, psycho-educational testing should also be a part of most ADHD assessments. Learning difficulties are not reliably assessed through rating scales, interviews, behavioral observations, or projective testing. As a result, standardized intelligence and achievement tests are often required as part of a comprehensive evaluation for ADHD.

Some omnibus behavior rating scales include items that assess the degree of family conflict and other aspects of a child's family context. However, as discussed in Chap. 12, some assessments may require a more in-depth assessment of specific areas of family functioning that are better obtained through methods that specifically focus on the child's family context. Each aspect of family functioning that was highlighted in Chap. 12 (parenting styles and behaviors, parenting stress, marital conflict, and parental adjustment) is important in understanding the family context of a child with ADHD.

Assessing Potential Alternative Causes

One of the most difficult aspects of assessing for ADHD is ruling out alternative causes for the symptoms. Probably, the most important piece of information for this purpose has already been discussed. If one has adequately determined that the symptoms of ADHD are of sufficient number, severity, and duration and cause enough impairment to warrant a diagnosis, most of the alternative explanations for symptoms can be ruled out as a *sole* explanation for the behaviors. Many of the alternative explanations for ADHD symptoms result in behaviors similar to ADHD, but of lower intensity and of shorter duration than is typical for children with ADHD.

Given that some medical and neurological disorders can manifest in problems of inattention-disorganization and impulsivity-hyperactivity, and given that such behaviors can be side effects of certain medications, it is important that a thorough developmental and medical history be obtained on a child when assessing for ADHD. When the history is suggestive of the possible presence of a medical or neurological disorder, the child can be referred to a physician for a more comprehensive medical and/or neurological exam. However, most experts on ADHD feel that a full medical exam need not be a standard part of a diagnostic assessment of ADHD, because the diagnosis is primarily based on behavioral data (Barkley, 1997a; Pelham et al., 2005).

The greatest difficulty in ruling out alternative explanations for ADHD symptoms is the problem of determining what is primary and what is secondary. Based on the research on comorbidities, we know that ADHD children are at risk for many other problems in adjustment, most of which can also mask as ADHD (e.g., learning disabilities, emotional disorders). The distinction between primary and secondary is largely a clinical one, based on a complex weighing of various pieces of assessment information. To summarize our suggestions from Chap. 15, several types of information may be helpful in making this difficult case formulation. Considering the level of impairment associated with different areas of dysfunction (i.e., which problem areas seem to be causing the most problems for the child) and the temporal sequencing of problem behaviors (i.e., which problems seem to predate others) can help in distinguishing primary or secondary areas of dysfunction. In addition, viewing family history data and determining if a child might be at risk for a certain type of problem given its occurrence in relatives may also aid in making differential diagnoses. Specifically, for ADHD, determining if a child's parents or other first-degree relatives had childhood histories of ADHD symptoms can provide valuable information in making an ADHD diagnosis. In contrast, a positive family history for bipolar illness might warrant further assessment to determine if a child's motor restlessness and problems of impulsive control are early indicators of an affective disturbance (Smith et al., 2007).

ADHD in the Schools: Special Education Placement

ADHD is a psychological syndrome that requires collaboration between professionals across multiple specialties (i.e., psychology, education, medicine) for assessment and treatment. Clinical assessors must be able to effectively utilize the expertise of other professionals and tailor their assessments to provide useful information to many different disciplines. Because ADHD often has its most dramatic and noticeable effect on a child in the school setting, collaboration with educators is particularly crucial. It is essential that assessments for ADHD be designed to provide information helpful to educators in developing appropriate interventions.

We feel strongly that not all children with ADHD require special education placement. There is ample evidence that some children with ADHD can successfully function in a regular education classroom with medication, with specific modifications of the classroom environment, and/or with structured behavioral interventions designed to reduce the disruptive behaviors (see Abramowitz & O'Leary, 1991). However, designing a successful intervention program for a child with ADHD requires a clear documentation of a child's strengths and weaknesses (behaviorally, emotionally, cognitively, and academically). Simply knowing that a child has ADHD gives educators only limited information on which to base interventions, given the great diversity within children with ADHD. As a result, clinical assessments should clearly outline an individual child's competencies and deficits, with suggestions on how these abilities will influence a child's functioning in a classroom setting.

Unfortunately, some children with ADHD may require more intensive educational services, such as those offered in special education programs. To serve children in special education programs, school systems must operate under federal and state guidelines, the former of which may vary in implementation from state to state and the latter of which may vary both in content and implementation. It is imperative that clinical assessors understand the guidelines under which a school system is operating, in order to design assessments and make recommendations that enhance a school's ability to appropriately meet the educational needs of a child.

The primary piece of federal legislation that guides provision of special education services to children and adolescents is the Individuals with Disabilities Act (IDEA), which was originally passed in 1975 as Public Law 94–142 and amended and renamed in 1990 and 2004. IDEA, and the more recent IDEIA, mandates that children with disabilities be provided specially designed instruction and related services in the least restrictive environment (i.e., close contact with children without disabilities) necessary for a child to learn. Providing services to children with ADHD under IDEA has been a source of contention in many school systems, because ADHD is not listed as one of the disabilities explicitly covered under IDEA. However, many children with ADHD have secondary features that may allow them to be served under IDEA guidelines, such as speech or language impairments, emotional disturbance, or specific learning disabilities. In fact, most of the children with ADHD who require intensive special education services do so, not because of the ADHD itself, but because of the additional disruptions caused by these secondary features.

However, it is possible that some children with ADHD may need special education services but do not qualify under IDEA guidelines. These children can be served under a civil rights law, Section 504. Section 504 is part of the Rehabilitation Act Amendments of 1973 (PL93–112) and was designed to protect individuals with handicaps. Section 504 specifically mandates that,

> No otherwise qualified individual with handicaps in the United States, shall, solely by reason of her or his handicap, be excluded from participation in, denied the benefits of, or be subjected to, discrimination under any program or activity receiving Federal financial assistance (29 U.S.C. Sec. 794).

It is generally accepted that ADHD qualifies as a handicap under Section 504 (Madsen, 1990) and, therefore, schools must make accommodations for the individual needs of children with ADHD under this statute. Unfortunately, unlike IDEA, Section 504 does not allocate federal funding for educational interventions.

This discussion of special education laws may seem irrelevant or at least peripheral for clinical assessors who operate outside of the school system. In fact, many such assessors prefer to remain ignorant of such legal guidelines, so as not to be confined to the limits delineated in such laws. However, if one wants to aid a child with ADHD in receiving needed educational services, one should understand the legal guidelines so as to be able to work collaboratively with school personnel in developing an appropriate educational plan.

Conduct Problems

Classification and Diagnosis

Like ADHD, conduct problems in children represent a critical mental health concern. These problems are highly disruptive to others in a child's environment can be predictive of problems later in life, including criminal behavior (Frick & Kimonis, 2008). Also like ADHD, there is considerable agreement that children with conduct problems are a heterogeneous group (Frick, 2006). Therefore, a substantial body of research has been directed at determining the most appropriate method of classifying conduct problems into meaningful subtypes.

The most commonly used method of classifying conduct problems in children is a two-dimensional approach originally described in *DSM-III* and continued with some modifications in the later revisions of this manual. This system divides conduct problems into two syndromes: Oppositional Defiant Disorder (ODD) and Conduct Disorder (CD). ODD refers to a pattern of negativistic, oppositional, and stubborn behaviors, whereas CD refers to more severe antisocial and aggressive behaviors that involve serious violations of others' rights (e.g., aggression, destruction of property) or deviations from major age-appropriate norms (e.g., running away from home, truancy). A summary of the behaviors indicative of these two dimensions is provided in Table 17.4.

A detailed discussion of the validity of the ODD/CD distinction is beyond the scope of this chapter (see McMahon & Frick, 2007). However, the relationship between ODD and CD behaviors is important for a number of reasons. First, there appears to be a hierarchical relationship between the two diagnoses. That is, most children with the more severe symptoms of CD also show the symptoms of ODD (Lahey & Loeber, 1994; Spitzer, Davies, & Barkley, 1990). However, the converse is not true. There are many children with ODD who do not show the more serious conduct problems associated with CD. Second, there seems to be a developmental relationship between ODD and CD. A 3-year longitudinal study of clinic-referred boys found that 82% of the new cases of CD ($n = 22$) that emerged during the study period had received a diagnosis of ODD in the preceding year (Lahey, Loeber, Quay, Frick, & Grimm, 1992). Therefore, ODD behaviors can be viewed as a risk factor for the development of the more severe CD.

TABLE 17.4 Two-Dimensional Classification of Conduct Problems

Oppositional Defiant Disorder	Conduct Disorder
Loses temper	Bullies or intimidates others
Argues with adults	Initiates physical fights
Actively defies adults	Has been physically cruel to others
Refuses adults' requests or rules	Steals things of nontrivial value
Deliberately annoys others	Forced someone into sexual activity
Blames others for mistakes	Stays out after dark without parental permission, before age 13
Is angry and resentful	Lies to obtain goods or favors
Is spiteful and vindictive	Has been physically cruel to animals
Is touchy and easily annoyed	Has deliberately destroyed others' property
	Has set fires with intention of causing serious damage
	Has run away from home overnight more than once
	Is often truant from school, beginning before age 13
	Has broken into someone's house, building, or car

Comorbidities

The most common problem co-occurring with conduct problems is ADHD. In a meta-analytic study of community studies, Waschbusch (2002) reported that 36% of boys and 57% of girls with conduct problems had comorbid ADHD. When studying pre-adolescent children and children referred to clinics, the rate is even higher and often ranges from 75 to 90% (Abikoff & Klein, 1992; Hinshaw, 1987). This degree of overlap has led to a debate as to whether or not ADHD and conduct problems should even be considered separate psychological domains (see Rutter, 1983). We feel that the research indicates that these domains are at least partially independent (Frick, 1994; Hinshaw, 1987).

Research does suggest that the development of ADHD usually precedes the development of conduct problems (Waschbusch, 2002) and it often signals the presence of a more severe and more chronic form of conduct problems in children (Frick & Loney, 1999). Also, there is growing evidence that conduct problems improve when children with ADHD have been treated with stimulant medication (Hinshaw, 1991). Therefore, clinical assessments of children with conduct problems should routinely assess for the presence of ADHD.

Children with conduct problems also frequently have a comorbid anxiety disorder, and this seems to be especially the case for girls (Loeber & Keenan, 1994). Children with conduct disorders also show a high rate of depression (Harrington, Fudge, Rutter, Pickles, & Hill, 1991). Importantly, there is evidence that children with both conduct problems and depression show a high rate of suicidal ideation (Capaldi, 1992). The combination of suicidal ideation, depression, and poor impulse control that often is present in children with conduct problems has been associated with increased risk for suicide (Shaffer, Garland, Gould, Fisher, & Trautman, 1988). Finally, children with CD are at higher risk for substance abuse, especially those children with both ADHD and CD (Lynskey & Fergusson, 1995; Thompson, Riggs, Mikulich, & Crowley, 1996).

Research also indicates that approximately 20–25% of children with CD are underachieving in school relative to a level predicted by their age and intellectual abilities (Frick et al., 1991). The reason for this association is not clear, possibly because the mechanisms involved may differ depending on the age of the sample studied (Hinshaw, 1992). For example, in elementary school-age samples, much of the overlap between CD and academic underachievement seems to be due to the presence of ADHD (Frick et al., 1991). However, learning difficulties seem to predict adolescent-onset conduct problems independent of other factors (Hinshaw, 1992). Despite the lack of a definitive explanation for the correlation between learning and conduct problems, the simple fact that they co-occur so consistently warrants the assessment of learning problems when assessing children and adolescents with conduct problems.

Correlates with Potential Causal Roles

Most researchers agree that conduct problems are the result of a complex interaction of multiple causal factors (Frick, 2006). Identifying the important causal agents and how they interact to cause conduct problems is still an area in need of more research. Past research has uncovered several factors that are *associated* with conduct disorders and that *likely* play a role in their development. These factors can be summarized in five categories: biological factors, cognitive correlates, family context, social ecology, and peers. The research on the biological correlates of conduct problems in children, while crucial for developing causal theories, is not reviewed here because the current state of knowledge is not sufficiently developed to have clear implications for assessment (see Dodge & Pettit, 2003; Lahey, Hart, Pliszka, Applegate, & McBurnett, 1993; Raine, 2002).

In contrast, there are several aspects of the child's cognitive and learning styles that have been associated with conduct problems and aggression that may be important to the assessment process (see Frick & Loney, 2000). First, in general, children with conduct disorders tend to score low on intelligence tests, especially in the area of verbal intelligence (Loney, Frick, Ellis, & McCoy, 1998; Moffitt, 1993). Second, many children with serious conduct problems tend to show a learning style that is more sensitive to rewards than punishments. This has been labeled as a reward-dominant response style that could explain why many of these children persist in their maladaptive behaviors, despite the threat of serious potential consequences (Fisher & Blair, 1998; O'Brien & Frick, 1996). Third, many children with conduct problems show deficits in their social cognition, which is the way they interpret social cues and use them to respond in social situations. For example, children with conduct problems are more likely to attribute hostile intent to the actions of peers and are less able to develop nonaggressive response alternatives in situations involving peer conflict, both of which could make the child more likely to respond aggressively in social situations (Crick & Dodge, 1996; Dodge & Pettit, 2003).

While these cognitive correlates have played an important role in many theories of how conduct disorders develop, and they are important targets of intervention for many treatment programs (e.g., Lochman, Wells, & Lenhart, 2008), there is probably no set of correlates that has been as important to theory and treatment as family dysfunction. There seem to be at least three dimensions of family functioning that are consistently related to childhood conduct problems: parental psychiatric adjustment, marital instability/divorce, and parental socialization practices (see Frick, 1994). A meta-analysis of the research on the relationship between family functioning and conduct disorders in youth found that parental socialization practices were especially important (Loeber & Stouthamer-Loeber, 1986). To be specific, parental involvement in their child's activities, parental supervision of their child, and the use of harsh or inconsistent discipline tended to show the strongest relationships with conduct problems in children of all the variables included in the meta-analysis.

Another clinically important class of correlates is comprised of factors within the child's larger social ecology that may play a causal role in the development of conduct problems. One of the most consistently documented of these correlates has been low socio-economic status (Frick, Lahey, Hartdagen, & Hynd, 1989). However, several other ecological factors, many of which are related to low socio-economic status, such as poor housing, poor schools, and disadvantaged neighborhoods, have also been linked to the development of conduct problems in children (see Frick, 1998; Peeples & Loeber, 1994). In addition, the high rate of violence, witnessed by children who live in impoverished inner-city neighborhoods, has also been linked to the development of conduct problems (Osofsky, Wewers, Hann, & Fick, 1993).

Finally, research has documented a relationship between peer rejection in elementary school and the later development of conduct problems (Roff & Wirt, 1984). In addition, peer rejection in elementary school is predictive of an association with a deviant peer group (i.e., one that shows a high rate of antisocial behavior and substance abuse) in early adolescence (Fergusson, Swain, & Horwood, 2002). This relationship is important because association with a deviant peer group leads to an increase in the frequency and severity of conduct problems (Patterson & Dishion, 1985) and it has proven to be a strong predictor of later delinquency and other negative outcomes, such as substance abuse (Dishion, Capaldi, Spracklen, & Li, 1995; Fergusson et al., 2002). Therefore, peer rejection may be directly related to the development of conduct problems but also may indirectly influence conduct problems by increasing the chance that the child or adolescent will associate with deviant peers.

Conceptual Model

From the preceding section, it is clear that there has been a great deal of research documenting many characteristics of children with severe conduct problems that are important to consider in conducting assessments with these children. Unfortunately, there has not been much agreement as to a good framework for organizing these many diverse characteristics into a clear conceptual framework for understanding how conduct problems develop. Many theorists have tended to focus on either one correlate (e.g., community violence) or one class of correlates (e.g., family dysfunction) without attempting to integrate the many diverse and potentially interacting influences that play a role in the development of conduct problems. Others have viewed these problems from a "cumulative risk" perspective, which acknowledges that any single factor will be limited for explaining the development of conduct problems and that their development in any child is likely the result of the additive influence of many different causal factors (Loeber, Burke, Lahey, Winters, & Zera, 2000).

An alternative framework that is gaining support in research is a "developmental pathway approach," which proposes that children may develop conduct problems through many different causal trajectories, each involving somewhat different interactions of causal processes (Frick, 2006). This approach recognizes that, for any child, the development of serious conduct problems is likely the result of multiple interacting causal factors. In addition, a developmental framework explicitly recognizes that there may be distinct subgroups of children with severe conduct problems with different causal processes underlying their behavior. This approach is consistent with a long history of trying to divide antisocial and delinquent youth into distinct subgroups that differ in terms of behavior, associated characteristics, outcomes, and response to treatment (see Frick & Marsee, 2006 for a review).

Consistent with this research, the *DSM-IV-TR* specifies two subtypes of Conduct Disorder (CD; American Psychiatric Association, 2000). Children in the childhood-onset subtype begin showing severe conduct problems prior to adolescence, often as early as preschool or early elementary school, and their behavioral problems increase in rate and severity over the childhood years (Lahey & Loeber, 1994). In contrast, youth in the adolescent-onset subtype do not show significant behavioral problems in childhood, but begin to exhibit significant conduct problems as they enter adolescence (Moffitt, 1993, 2003). One of the key differences between these two groups of antisocial youth is that the childhood-onset group is much more likely to continue to show antisocial and criminal behavior into adulthood compared to the adolescent-onset group (Frick & Loney, 1999; Moffitt, 2003). However, in addition to the differences in prognosis, research has uncovered several other characteristics that could suggest that the causal processes underlying the antisocial behavior of the two groups are also different.

Specifically, children in the childhood-onset group are characterized by more aggression, higher rates of cognitive (e.g., lower verbal intelligence) and neuropsychological (e.g., executive functioning deficits) dysfunction, more disturbances in their autonomic nervous system functioning, and more severe problems of impulse control, often leading to higher rates of diagnosis of Attention-Deficit Hyperactivity Disorder than children with the adolescent-onset pattern of CD (Frick, 2006; Moffitt, 1993; 2003). The fewer pathogenic background factors, as well as the better adult outcome for the adolescent-onset subtype, suggests that their conduct problems may be an exaggeration of a normative pattern of rebellious and antisocial behavior related to the important tasks involved in identity development that take place in adolescence (Frick, 2006; Moffitt, 2003; Silverthorn & Frick, 1999). In contrast, the childhood-onset group appears to show a more severe type of dysfunction that extends beyond a single developmental stage.

Importantly, research has also indicated that there are some important distinctions that can be made within this childhood-onset group in terms of the types of dysfunctional processes that may be operating. The distinction is based on differentiating between children who show a callous and unemotional interpersonal style and those who do not. Callous-unemotional traits refer to a lack of guilt over misdeeds, a lack of empathy toward others, and other deficits in their emotional responses (Frick & Dickens, 2006; Frick & White, 2008).

Children with conduct problems, who also show callous-unemotional traits, tend to show a more severe, more aggressive, and more stable pattern of conduct problems (Frick & Dickens, 2006). Further, these children with callous-unemotional traits tend to be more thrill and adventure seeking, they are less sensitive to the effects of punishment compared to the effects of rewards, and they are less reactive to emotionally distressing stimuli than other children with childhood-onset CD (Frick & White, 2008). All of these characteristics are consistent with a temperamental style associated with low emotional reactivity that can (1) place a child at risk for missing some of the early precursors to empathetic concern that involve emotional arousal evoked by the misfortune and distress of others; (2) lead a child to be relatively insensitive to the prohibitions and sanctions of parents and other socializing agents; and (3) create an interpersonal style in which the child becomes so focused on the potential rewards and gains involved in using aggression to solve interpersonal conflicts that he or she ignores the potentially harmful effects of this behavior on him- or herself and others (Frick & Morris, 2004).

In contrast to those youth with callous and unemotional traits, children within the childhood-onset group who do not show these traits tend to show the opposite extreme of emotional reactivity. They tend to be highly reactive to emotional and threatening stimuli and to respond more strongly to provocations in social situations (Frick, 2006; Frick & Morris, 2004). Also, their aggressive and antisocial behavior is more strongly associated with dysfunctional parenting practices and with deficits in verbal intelligence than the group that is high on callous-unemotional traits (Frick & White, 2008). These findings suggest that children with childhood-onset antisocial behavior, but who do not show high rates of callous-unemotional traits, may have problems more specifically associated with poor behavioral and emotional regulation, characterized by very impulsive behavior and high levels of emotional reactivity. Such poor emotional regulation can result from a number of interacting causal factors, such as inadequate socialization from families, deficits in their verbal intelligence that make it difficult for them to delay gratification and anticipate consequences, or temperamental problems in response inhibition such as those discussed in the previous section on ADHD. The problems in emotional regulation can lead to very impulsive and unplanned aggressive acts for which the child may be remorseful afterward but that he or she still has difficulty controlling. It can also lead to a child being susceptible to becoming angry (i.e., emotionally aroused) due to perceived provocations from peers, leading to violent and aggressive acts within the context of high emotional arousal.

This developmental framework has a number of implications for the assessment process for children with severe conduct problems (McMahon & Frick, 2005). It suggests that, not only do interventions for children with severe conduct problems need to be comprehensive in targeting a large number of diverse causal influences, but these interventions also need to be tailored to the unique needs of specific subgroups of children with conduct problems (see Frick, 2006 for a more a extended discussion of this issue). In order to implement such a comprehensive and individualized approach to treatment, there needs to be a comprehensive assessment of the child that identifies the most appropriate targets of treatment, given the individual child's specific developmental history.

Implications for Assessment

This body of psychological research forms the basis for designing an appropriate assessment for children with conduct problems. In Table 17.5, we summarize the critical areas of research and their relevance to the assessment process. In Box 17.5, we provide a case study of a comprehensive evaluation of a child with severe conduct problems. As is evident from Table 17.5, assessment of conduct problems shares several important characteristics with the assessment of ADHD. The complex and pervasive nature of conduct problems requires a comprehensive evaluation that assesses many aspects of the child's functioning and psychosocial environment. Further, conduct problems and other relevant aspects of a child's psychosocial functioning should be assessed using multiple informants and multiple assessment techniques.

TABLE 17.5 Key Research Findings and Their Implications for the Assessment of Children with Conduct Problems

Research Findings	Implications for Assessment
1. *Core symptoms and subtypes*: Conduct disorders represent a heterogeneous category with widely varying levels of impairment and many important subtypes	1a. Assess a wide range of conduct problems 1b. Assess the level of impairment associated with the disorder
2. *Common comorbidities*: Conduct disorders are often accompanied by several comorbid types of problems that influence the course and treatment of conduct disorders	2a. Assess for the presence of ADHD 2b. Assess for the presence of anxiety and depression (including suicidal ideation) 2c. Assess for substance use and abuse
3. *Correlates with potential causal roles*: Conduct disorders develop through a complex interaction of numerous factors within the child and his or her psychosocial environment	3a. Assess important aspects of a child's or adolescent's family environment 3b. Assess child's intellectual level, academic achievement, learning style, and social problem solving

(Continues)

TABLE 17.5 (Continued)

Research Findings	Implications for Assessment
	3c. Assess child's peer interactions, social status, and associations with a deviant peer group
	3d. Assess critical aspects of child's social ecology (e.g., economic disadvantage, witnessing of violence)
4. *Multiple developmental pathways*: Conduct disorders develop through multiple different pathways each involving distinct developmental mechanisms	4a. Assess the developmental sequence of onset of conduct problem behavior, especially whether severe conduct problems onset prior to adolescence
	4b. Assess for callous-unemotional traits

Box 17.5

Case Study: 14-Year-Old Adolescent Male with Severe Conduct Problems

Patrick was 14 years, 1 month old when his mother requested a comprehensive psychological evaluation from a university-based outpatient psychological clinic. His mother was concerned about Patrick's poor grades in school and his frequent lying. His mother also expressed concerns about his frequent fights both at school and in his neighborhood. Because of his fighting at school, Patrick had been placed in a full-time class for children with behavioral problems.

Assessment of Core Features and Subtypes

On the DISC-IV, both Patrick and his mother reported the presence of a number of severe conduct problems. They both reported repeat instances of lying, repeat instances of stealing items from stores (shoplifting), and several school suspensions for physical fights. His mother also reported several instances of truancy, and Patrick admitted to breaking into a neighbor's house to steal things and using a knife in a fight. Patrick further admitted to occasional use of marijuana. The severity of these conduct problems is supported by parental report on the CBCL, on which Patrick had T-scores of 79 on both the Delinquent Behavior and Aggressive Behavior scales. On the Personality Inventory for Youth (PIY; Lachar & Gruber, 1994), Patrick obtained a T-score of 69 on the Delinquency scale.

According to both Patrick and his mother, much of Patrick's aggressive and antisocial behavior occurred alone. In fact, Patrick reported problems in peer relations, as evident by T-scores of 68 and 75 on the PIY Social Withdrawal and Social Skills scales. Patrick's mother reported that his aggressive and antisocial behavior is of longstanding duration. He had averaged about two suspensions per year since the first grade, mostly because of fighting, indicating that his aggression started well before adolescence.

Assessment of Comorbidities

Both Patrick and his mother reported that Patrick goes through frequent periods of depression, often lasting for as long as a month. At the time of the assessment, Patrick had been experiencing significant periods of sadness for the past 3 weeks. He had also lost interest in activities, he had not been sleeping well at night, and he had lost his appetite resulting in significant weight loss. His mother had also

(Continues)

Box 17.5 (Continued)

noticed a decrease in energy and a decrease in his ability to concentrate. Patrick reported on the DISC-IV that he had, twice in the past 2 years, thought of killing himself by cutting his wrist and on one occasion had actually started to use a knife but was stopped by a classmate. Both Patrick and his mother reported that the episodes of depression seemed to coincide with disciplinary confrontations, such as being suspended from school.

Patrick and his mother reported some problems of attention and concentration, but these seemed to occur during periods of depression, and therefore, did not seem to be associated with ADHD. Also, a psychoeducational assessment revealed that Patrick was functioning in the low average range of intellectual abilities, with a particular weakness in his verbal abilities. He scored in a range commensurate with this intellectual level on an achievement screener.

Assessment of Correlates with Potential Causal Roles

Patrick lived alone with his mother, who worked full-time outside of the home as a secretary. Patrick's parents had divorced when he was 6 years old and he had had minimal contact with his father, who according to maternal report, was in and out of prison and had a substance abuse problem. Patrick's mother reportedly had limited social contacts. Her extended family mostly lived in a different region of the country and she had not developed a good network of friends. Patrick's mother also reported that she had great difficulty disciplining Patrick. Because he was so moody, she rarely tried to make him do things. Also, whenever he did something wrong (e.g., getting suspended from school), she did not punish him because it would simply make him angrier and more difficult to live with. There was no indication that Patrick was involved with a deviant peer group. In fact, his mother was concerned with his lack of connectedness with any peers.

Assessment of Multiple Developmental Pathways

Information from both the DISC-IV and an unstructured interview both suggested that Patrick's serious conduct problems have been evident, at least since the first grade. Thus, the problems clearly had a childhood-onset. Also, a measure of callous-unemotional traits (Frick & Hare, 2001) did not suggest that Patrick showed high rates of these traits. This would also be consistent with the high rate of depression, a weakness in his verbal intelligence, and the apparent association between his conduct problems and ineffective parenting practices in the home, all of which are typically more common in youth without callous-unemotional traits.

Assessment of Core Features

The first goal of the assessment is to carefully and thoroughly assess the number, types, and severity of the conduct problems and the level of impairment that the conduct problems are causing for the child or adolescent (e.g., school suspensions, police contacts, peer rejection). This assessment is important given that research has shown great variability in these dimensions among children with conduct problems, and it has shown that these dimensions may be some of the best predictors of outcome for children with conduct problems (Frick & Loney, 1999). The primary methods of assessing the core symptoms are structured interviews, behavior rating scales, and behavioral observations (see McMahon & Frick, 2005 for a summary of specific measures).

Many structured interviews and behavioral rating scales provide good coverage of the conduct problem behaviors and allow for multi-informant assessments. However, they each offer unique advantages in other respects. Behavior rating scales are more time-efficient and provide some of the best norm-referenced information for determining the severity of conduct problems. In contrast, diagnostic interviews often provide important information on the degree of impairment associated with the conduct problems and a structured means of assessing the age of onset of the problem behaviors. As discussed in Chap. 8, behavioral observations provide a third way of assessing conduct problem behaviors. Behavioral observations in a child's natural setting can make a unique contribution to the assessment process by providing an assessment of a child's behavior that is not filtered through the perceptions of an informant and by providing an assessment of the immediate environmental context of a child's behavior. Unfortunately, for older children and adolescents, many of the common conduct problems are by nature covert (e.g., lying and stealing) or only occur infrequently (e.g., fighting), which makes them difficult to capture through some observational technique.

One important advantage that many structured interviews have over behavioral rating scales and behavioral observations is that they provide a structured method for assessing when a child first began showing serious conduct problems, thereby providing an important source of information on the developmental trajectory of the child's problem behavior. For example, in the DISC-IV (Shaffer, Fisher, Lucas, Dulcan, & Schwab-Stone, 2000), any question related to the presence of a conduct problem that is answered affirmatively is followed by questions asking the parent or child to estimate at what age the first occurrence of the behavior took place. Obviously, such questions can also be integrated into an unstructured interview format as well.

Assessment of Comorbidities

Co-occurring problems can be assessed conjointly with the assessment of the conduct problems themselves, through the use of omnibus rating scales, structured interviews, or multi-domain observational systems. Given the association between conduct problems and learning disabilities, a psychoeducational evaluation that includes a standardized intelligence test and academic achievement screener should also be a part of most evaluations of children and adolescents with conduct problems.

Assessment of Correlates with Potential Causal Roles

Uncovering which of the many potential causal factors may be operating on a child referred for an evaluation could be crucial for making recommendations for treatment. Of primary importance are correlates within the child's family environment (Frick, 1994). In Chap. 12, we discussed some basic issues and methods in assessing crucial elements in a child's family environment (see also McMahon & Frick, 2007).

Research also indicates that peer rejection is predictive of the development of conduct problems and is associated with an adolescent's association with a deviant peer group. Therefore, assessing a child or adolescent's peer relationships is a critical assessment goal. Several of the omnibus rating scales discussed in previous chapters provide an assessment of a child's peer functioning. Also, several rating scales focus specifically on a child's or adolescent's social functioning (see also Cavell, Meehan, & Fiala, 2003). Social status can also be assessed directly through a sociometric exercise, if a child is in elementary school (see Chap. 9). Given that a child's association with a deviant peer group is associated with an increase in the severity of conduct problems, some method of assessing this aspect of a child's social functioning (e.g., Elliott, Huizinga, & Ageton, 1985) should also be included in a comprehensive assessment.

Another important class of potentially important correlates to severe conduct problems involves specific cognitive deficits and learning styles. Specifically, deficits in intelligence, especially verbal intelligence, have been associated with conduct problems, necessitating a standard intellectual evaluation as part of most assessment batteries for children with conduct problems. In addition, as discussed previously, many children with conduct problems, especially those who also show a callous and unemotional interpersonal style, show heightened sensitivity to rewards compared to punishments. There are computerized tasks developed to assess this learning style in young children; however, the clinical utility of such information and some major limitations in the development of these tasks make their usefulness in many clinical assessments somewhat limited at the present time (see Frick & Loney, 2000 for a review). There are also laboratory measures, typically involving a child being provided a hypothetical vignette of a social situation and asked to state how he or she would respond if the situation was real, that assess several deficits in social cognition that have been associated with conduct problems, such as a hostile attributional bias. Examples include the Intention-Cue Detection Task, the Problem-Solving Measure for Conflict, and the WALLY Game (Conduct Problems Prevention Research Group, 1999; Dodge & Coie, 1987; Webster-Stratton & Lindsay, 1999). The recently developed Social-Cognitive Assessment Profile (SCAP; Hughes, Meehan, & Cavell, 2004) shows promise as a brief (15–20 min), clinically useful interview with elementary school-age children, designed to assess social-cognitive deficits associated with conduct problems. While these measures are also not without some limitations in their clinical usefulness (Frick & Loney, 2000), interventions for the deficits that are assessed by these measures are part of many treatment programs for conduct problems (Lochman et al., 2008). Therefore, the information they provide can be useful in treatment planning.

Finally, a child's social ecology is often crucial for understanding the development of conduct problems in many cases. Therefore, it is important to assess such variables as the economic situation of the family, the level of social and community support provided to the child and his or her family, and other aspects of a child's social climate (e.g., neighborhood, quality of school and, degree of exposure to violence) (McMahon & Frick, 2007). For example, the Neighborhood Questionnaire (Greenberg, Lengua, Coie, Pinderhughes, & the Conduct Problems Prevention Research Group, 1999) is a brief parent-report measure used to assess the parent's perception of the family's neighborhood in terms of safety, violence, drug traffic, satisfaction, and stability.

Assessment of Important Developmental Pathways

A key area of research for guiding the assessment process is the research documenting various potential developmental pathways to conduct problems. As reviewed previously, children with conduct problems can fall into childhood-onset or adolescent-onset pathways, depending on when in development their level of severe antisocial and aggressive behavior started. Also, within the childhood-onset group, there seem to be important differences between those who do and do not show high levels of callous-unemotional traits. Knowledge of the characteristics of children in these different pathways, and the different causal mechanisms involved, can serve as a guide for structuring and conducting the assessment (McMahon & Frick, 2005). Further, interventions can be tailored to the unique needs of youth in these different pathways (Frick, 2006).

Specifically, knowledge of the developmental pathways can provide a set of working hypotheses concerning the nature of the conduct problems, the most likely comorbid conditions, and the most likely risk factors (McMahon & Frick, 2005). For example, for a youth whose conduct problems appear with the onset of adolescence, one would hypothesize based on the available literature that he or she is less likely to be aggressive, to have intellectual deficits, to have temperamental vulnerabilities, and to have comorbid ADHD. However, the youth's association with a deviant peer group and factors that may contribute to this deviant peer group affiliation (e.g., lack of parental monitoring and supervision) would be especially important to assess for youth in this pathway.

In contrast, for a youth whose serious conduct problems began prior to adolescence, one would expect more cognitive and temperamental vulnerabilities, comorbid ADHD, and more serious problems in family functioning. For those youths in this childhood-onset group who do not show CU traits, the cognitive deficits would more likely be verbal deficits and the temperamental vulnerabilities would more likely be problems regulating emotions, leading to higher levels of anxiety, depression, and aggression involving anger. In contrast, for a youth with childhood-onset conduct problems who shows high levels of callous-unemotional traits, the cognitive deficits are more likely to involve a lack of sensitivity to punishment and the temperamental vulnerabilities are more likely to involve a preference for dangerous and novel activities and a failure to experience many types of prosocial emotions (e.g., guilt and empathy). Further, assessing the level and severity of aggressive behavior, especially the presence of instrumental aggression, would be critical for children and adolescents in this group (Marsee & Frick, 2007).

As most clinicians recognize, people do not often fall neatly into the prototypes that are suggested by research. Therefore, these descriptions are meant to serve as hypotheses around which to organize an assessment based on the available research. They also highlight several specific important pieces of information that are needed when assessing children and adolescents with conduct problems. One of the most critical pieces of information in guiding assessment, and perhaps ultimately intervention, is determining the age at which various conduct problems began. This information provides some indication as to whether or not the youth may be on the childhood-onset pathway. As noted previously, unstructured and structured interviews are often the most common methods for obtaining this information.

Unfortunately, there has been little consistency in the literature concerning the most appropriate operational definition of childhood- vs. adolescent-onset. For example, the *DSM-IV-TR* makes the distinction between children who begin showing severe conduct problems before age 10 (i.e., childhood-onset) and those who do not show severe conduct problems before age 10 (i.e., adolescent-onset) in its definition of Conduct Disorder. However, other research studies have used age 11 (Robins 1966) or age 14 (Patterson & Yoerger, 1993; Tibbetts & Piquero, 1999) to define the start of adolescent onset. Thus, onset of severe conduct problems before age 10 seems to be clearly considered childhood-onset and onset after age 13 clearly adolescent-onset. However, how to classify children whose conduct problems onset between the ages of 11 and 13 is less clear and probably dependent on the level of physical, cognitive, and social maturity of the child.

In addition to the difficulty in determining the most appropriate way to divide children based on their age of onset, there is also concern about how accurate the parent or youth is in reporting the timing of specific behaviors. There are three findings from research that can help in interpreting such reports. First, the longer the time frame involved in the retrospective report (e.g., a parent of a 17-year-old reporting on preschool behavior vs. a parent of a 6-year-old reporting on preschool behavior), the less accurate the report is likely to be (Green, Loeber, & Lahey, 1991). Second, although a parental report of the exact age of onset may not be very reliable over time, typical variations in years are usually small (Green et al., 1991). As a result, these reports should be viewed as rough estimates of the timing of onset and not as exact dating procedures. Third, there is evidence that combining informants (e.g., such as a parent or youth) or combining sources of information (e.g., self-report and record of police contact), and taking the earliest reported age of onset from any source, provides an estimate that shows somewhat greater validity than any single source of information alone (Lahey et al., 1999).

If the youth's history of conduct problems is consistent with the childhood-onset pathway, then additional assessment to examine the extent to which callous-unemotional traits may also be present is important. There have been several reviews and critiques of the available methods for assessing these traits (Sharp & Kline, 2008; Vincent, 2006). The two most commonly used methods are the Psychopathy Checklist: Youth Version (PCL-YV; Forth, Kosson, & Hare, 2003) and the Antisocial Process Screening Device (APSD; Frick & Hare, 2001). The PCL-YV is a clinician completed checklist for adolescents ages 12 to 18 years. It is completed based on a 60 to 90 min semi-structured interview and review of all available collateral information (e.g., psychosocial histories, institutional records). The APSD includes parent and teacher ratings scales (Frick & Hare, 2001) and a self-report questionnaire (Munoz & Frick, 2007). Although there is research to support the usefulness of both the PCL-YV and APSD (see Frick & Dickens, 2006; Frick & White, 2008), both measures include only limited items specifically related to callous-unemotional traits (4 and 6 items, respectively). A scale that provides a more comprehensive assessment of these traits, the Inventory of Callous-Unemotional traits, has been developed and has shown some initial promise in a large ($n = 1443$) community sample of young adolescents in Germany (Essau, Sasagawa, & Frick, 2006) and moderate size ($n = 248$) sample of detained juvenile offenders in the United States (Kimonis et al., 2008). In Table 17.6, a summary of the items assessing CU traits from these three measures are provided.

Conclusions

In this chapter we discuss two specific applications of the assessment procedures and techniques reviewed in previous chapters. We discuss the assessment of two related types of childhood psychopathology: Attention-Deficit Hyperactivity Disorder and conduct problems. To continue our basic premise that clinical assessments should be guided by basic psychological research, we provide a brief overview of some of the more important research findings with particular relevance to the assessment process. For both domains, assessments should be structured around our current knowledge of the core features of each domain. In addition, the most frequent co-occurring problems associated with both types of psychopathology

TABLE 17.6 Items Assessing Callous-Unemotional Traits from Three Commonly Used Measures

Psychopathy Check-list-Youth Version (Forth et al., 2003)	Antisocial Process Screening Device (Frick & Hare, 2001)	Inventory of Callous-Unemotional Traits (Essau et al., 2006)
Lacks guilt and remorse	Feels bad or guilty (I)	Feels bad or guilty (I)
Shallow affect	Does not show emotion	Does not feel remorseful when doing something wrong
Callous use of others	Concerned about the feelings of others (I)	Easily admits to being wrong (I)
Fails to accept responsibility	Concerned about school work (I)	Tries not to hurt others' feelings (I)
	Keeps promises (I)	Feelings of others are unimportant
	Keeps the same friends (I)	Doesn't care who he/she hurts to get what he/she wants
		Concerned about feelings of others (I)
		Apologizes to persons he/she hurts (I)
		Does not care if he/she gets in trouble
		Seems very cold and uncaring to others
		Works hard on everything (I)
		Always tries best (I)
		Does not care about doing things well
		Cares about how well he/she does at school or work (I)
		Does things to make others feel good (I)
		Tries not to hurt others' feelings (I)
		Does not like to put the time into doing things well
		What he/she thinks is right and wrong is different from what others think
		Does not show emotions
		Expresses feelings openly (I)
		Hides feelings from others
		It is easy to tell how he/she is feeling (I)
		Very expressive and emotional (I)
		Does not care about being on time

NOTE: (I) designates items that are inversely scored.

should be routinely assessed, because these comorbidities often have important prognostic and treatment implications.

For ADHD, a difficult part of the assessment is ruling out other medical or psychological disorders that could solely account for the ADHD symptoms. Also, in assessing ADHD, one must be knowledgeable of educational laws related to legally mandated services for children with ADHD so that one can work with educators in designing a treatment plan for the child or adolescent with ADHD.

For conduct problems, the myriad of potential causal factors should be assessed to determine which ones may be operating for a given child and which ones should, therefore, be a focus of intervention. Also, different causal factors may be involved in the various subgroups of children with conduct problems. Understanding the different pathways through which children and adolescents develop serious conduct problems can be critical for designing assessments and interpreting the information provided by the evaluation.

Chapter Summary

1. Externalizing behaviors are the most common reason for referral to child mental health clinics.
2. Based on research on ADHD suggests that:
   (a) Assessments should include a multi-informant and multi-source assessment of the core ADHD behaviors: inattention-disorganization and impulsivity-hyperactivity; assessment of these core features must be placed within a developmental perspective.
   (b) Assessments should screen for the presence of the most common co-occurring problems that may accompany ADHD: conduct problems/ aggression, emotional disturbance, low self-esteem, problematic social relationships, learning difficulties, and family conflict.
   (c) Assessments should rule out alternative causes for the core symptoms: medical/ neurological disorders, mental handicaps, learning disorders, and adjustment reactions to environmental stressors.
   (d) Because ADHD often has a major impact on a child's or adolescent's school functioning, the assessment should be conducted in collaboration with school personnel and with a knowledge of local educational statutes relevant to services for students with ADHD.
3. Based on research on severe conduct problems in children and adolescents:
   (a) Assessments should provide a multi-source and multi-method assessment of conduct problems including determining the types and severity of conduct problems and the age at which they began.
   (b) Assessments should screen for the most common co-occurring problems that often accompany conduct problems: ADHD, emotional disturbance, substance abuse, and learning disabilities.
   (c) Assessments should assess known correlates to conduct problems that could play a role in causing or maintaining the problem behavior, and therefore, should be a major focus of intervention: family functioning, cognitive deficits, social ecology, peer relations, and associations with a deviant peer group.
   (d) The age at which the serious conduct problems began and the presence of callous-unemotional traits should be assessed because of their importance in designating unique pathways to the development of conduct problems.

CHAPTER 18

Assessment of Depression and Anxiety

CHAPTER QUESTIONS

- What are the core symptoms of childhood depression and anxiety?
- Which informant(s) and assessment strategies are most useful for the diagnosis of depression and anxiety?
- What developmental factors need to be considered in assessment of child/adolescent depression and anxiety?
- What factors contribute to better or worse prognosis for childhood depression and anxiety?

INTERNALIZING DISORDERS

It is commonplace to consider symptoms of depression and anxiety under the term internalizing problems, a tendency reflected in the structure of many common rating scales (e.g., Achenbach & Rescorla, 2001; Reynolds & Kamphaus, 2004). More specifically, rating scales often have an internalizing symptom composite that consists of depression, anxiety, and often, somatic complaints. Historically, children with internalizing difficulties have been described in a number of ways, including as having a personality problem syndrome with difficulties of anxiety, withdrawal, and feelings of inferiority (Peterson, 1961); anxious-fearful (Behar & Stringfield, 1974); inhibited (Miller, 1967); anxious-immature (Conners, 1970); and overcontrolled (Edelbrock, 1979). Children solely with internalizing problems are easily distinguished from children solely with externalizing problems, but this does not imply that such difficulties are easily diagnosed and treated. In fact, it can be quite the contrary.

Internalizing disorders are among the most difficult to diagnose because of the nature of the symptomatology. The child's symptoms take more of a toll on the child's

P.J. Frick et al., *Clinical Assessment of Child and Adolescent Personality and Behavior*,
DOI 10.1007/978-1-4419-0641-0_18, © Springer Science+Business Media, LLC 2010

subjective mental state than on significant others or on the child's adjustment to school or other settings. Furthermore, children with internalizing problems have been found to be better adapted than children with externalizing difficulties, achieving higher reading and intelligence test scores, and performing better in school (Cohen et al., 1985). The following quote from Reynolds (1990) eloquently summarizes the central assessment challenge that is presented by the most common internalizing syndromes of depression and anxiety.

> "Internalizing disorders, including depressive disorders, anxiety disorders, obsessive compulsive disorder, somatic disorders, and suicidal behaviors, among others, are associated with overcontrolled behaviors. Phenomenologically, internalizing disorders are characterized by covert, inner-directed symptomatology. The covert nature of these disturbances presents challenges to professionals, particularly with regard to assessment and treatment. As noted in this article, internalizing disorders as a function of their insidious nature, do not readily come to the attention of psychologists. Because of this, professionals need to be vigilant to the potential existence of internalizing disorders in children and adolescents" (p. 137).

Within the broad category of internalizing problems, depression and anxiety syndromes can be reliably differentiated, although it has been theorized that there may be a third disorder that is symptomatically and etiologically overlapping with both these disorders (see Klein et al., 2005). Still, research has supported a two-factor model of internalizing problems, one indicative of depression and one that can be conceptualized as anxiety (Ollendick et al., 2003). Klein et al. (2005) provide a clear review of the ways in which the symptoms of either problem can be mutually influential, and while it is beyond the scope of this chapter to consider the evidence for a common disorder for anxiety and depression, it is important for the reader to be aware that although this chapter will discuss these syndromes as if they differ in many respects (including etiology and course), there is substantial comorbidity between the two (Klein et al.).

The present discussion is influenced primarily by the structure of the *DSM-IV*, which focuses on anxiety and depression disorders as separate entities, although comorbidity is recognized in a little understood diagnosis of Mixed Anxiety-Depression Disorder (American Psychiatric Association, 2000). Ultimately, it will be up to the clinician to determine, through the evidence gathered, if interventions targeting both anxiety and depression are warranted. The important reminder is that both areas of concern be assessed as either primary or secondary influences on the child's functioning.

Childhood Depression

Diagnostic Criteria

In order to meet DSM-IV-TR diagnostic criteria for Major Depressive Disorder, at least five of nine symptoms must be present for at least a two-week period, and one of the symptoms must be either depressed mood or loss of interest or pleasure (American Psychiatric Association, 2000).

These symptoms include:

1. depressed or irritable mood
2. loss of interest in daily activities
3. significant weight loss or failure to make expected weight gains
4. frequent insomnia or hypersomnia
5. motor agitation or retardation
6. frequent fatigue
7. feelings of worthlessness or guilt
8. impaired concentration
9. suicidal ideation or suicide attempt.

For many years, the need for diagnostic criteria for childhood depression was not clear, as researchers debated whether or not the disorder could exist in childhood. There is increasing evidence that children and adolescents display much of the same symptomatology as adults, including cognitive distortion (Haley et al., 1985). Unfortunately, there is also increasing evidence that depression is quite persistent and impairing in childhood. In fact, the existence of childhood depression is no longer a point of contention (Kovacs, 1989). Although there are some developmental influences on the manifestation of depression (see below), most evidence points to the continuity of depression from childhood to adulthood (Klein et al., 2005).

Despite some of the previous controversy regarding the existence of childhood depression, clinicians are fairly reliable in their diagnosis of the condition. When using structured diagnostic interviews such as those described in Chap. 11, the inter-rater reliability of the diagnosis ranges from about .75 to .90 (Ambrosini, 2000; Christ, 1990). Emerging agreement regarding the existence of the depression syndrome in childhood, the widespread application of the *DSM* criteria, and evidence of inter-rater reliability have all contributed to forming a consensus that childhood depression is an important public health problem that warrants significant research attention.

Regardless of the accuracy of diagnosis, as Reynolds (1990) observes, the need to assess for the presence of depression is not always obvious. Consequently, the psychologist must develop some strategies and/or cues that trigger a search for depression. Strategies for assessing for depression can be gleaned from an understanding of the nature of the syndrome, including its risk factors and course. Some methods for identifying the need to assess for the presence of depression are discussed next.

Characteristics of Childhood Depression

Although prevalence rates are often debated, research has generally concluded that less than 3% of preadolescent children experience depression but that rates of depression increase substantially in adolescence to around 15%, although a larger proportion of youth suffer from symptoms of depression at some point (see Hankin et al., 2008 for review). A prevalence rate this large warrants vigilance for the existence of depression in referral populations. Also, a higher rate of depression may be expected in adolescence because of the attendant stressors associated with this age range (Cooper, 1990). Adolescents are presented with increasing developmental demands and stressors for which they may often be ill-prepared (Petersen et al., 1993).

Several studies have suggested that the expression of depression differs somewhat by age. While children and adolescents both report dysphoria as a central symptom of depression, younger children more frequently exhibit sleep disturbances. Less than half of children and adolescents report suicidal attempts, increased appetite, hypersomnia, hallucinations, or delusions (Christ, 1990). Adolescents are more likely than young children to experience feelings of hopelessness as part of depression (Weiss & Garber, 2003). One study found that a community sample of adolescents reported significantly more somatic complaints on the Child Depression Inventory (CDI) than preadolescents (Cooper, 1990). Further analyses revealed, however, that this finding was primarily due to gender differences: adolescent girls acknowledged more somatic complaints than preadolescents (boys and girls) and adolescent boys. However, this finding does suggest that excessive somatic complaints should trigger further assessment for depression.

Depression is also distinctive as a syndrome because of the crucial hereditary factor that has been identified. Heritability estimates vary widely, but the proportion of youth with depression who have a positive family history of depression is somewhere around one third (Rice, Harold, & Thapar, 2002). In addition, family history of depression is a significant predictor of recurrence of depression for children and adolescents (Klein et al., 2005). Therefore, to say the least, knowledge of family history is often helpful for conceptualizing cases. Family resemblance data may affect assessment and intervention planning for a child who has several symptoms of depression but does not meet diagnostic criteria. If this child's mother has a history of depression, more assessment and intervention would be warranted than if no family resemblance was present. This information indicates that the psychologist should routinely and carefully gather family history data regarding a history of depression for the child suspected of having an internalizing disorder.

The duration of a depressive disorder can be substantial. In an interesting study, 105 children who entered a special school for children who lost a parent due to death, divorce, or separation were divided into depressed and non-depressed groups based on a CDI cut score of 13 or greater indicating depression. The elevated group was found to, for the most part, exceed the cut score again four years later (Mattison et al., 1990). Mattison et al. found the depressed group to show considerable impairment over the four-year duration of the study. They concluded that:

> "They further showed significantly poorer academic performance, received significantly more counseling, and more often separated from the school under negative circumstances. The most pathological scores overall were demonstrated by the children in the original depressed group who separated from the school during the 4 years under negative circumstances" (p. 169).

This study did not consider actual diagnoses of depression, but the results point to potentially prolonged difficulties for youth with higher levels of depressive symptoms. Research has shown that episodes of major depression tend to average around seven to eight months in length for children and adolescents (Birmaher, Arbelaez, & Brent, 2002).

The chronicity of depressive symptomatology has even been documented in first-graders. In a study of 677 first-grade children from the Baltimore, Maryland public schools, CDI scores tended to be most stable for children with scores in the upper quartile of the scale. Interestingly, all of the children who scored in the upper quartile in the fall of the academic year remained in the upper quartile when retested in the spring. Children who scored below the upper quartile showed considerably more fluctuation from the fall to the spring (Edelsohn et al., 1992). Furthermore, Luby et al. (2002) have found support for a depression syndrome/diagnosis in preschool-aged children, if the duration requirement from the *DSM-IV* is reduced

As discussed elsewhere in this text, the developmental onset and course are critical areas to assess for understanding the manifestation of psychological problems, the associated features, and the potential outcomes. This issue is illustrated quite well for youth depression in a study by Hammen, Brennan, Keenan-Miller, and Herr (2008). They considered the outcomes at age 20 for individuals with an early onset of depression (i.e., by age 15) versus a late onset (i.e., after age 15), with an additional consideration of whether or not the depressive symptoms were recurrent by age 20. In general, the early onset, recurrent group had the worst outcomes in many psychological and social domains of functioning. In particular, these individuals:

- Were more likely than individuals to have had comorbid anxiety by age 20

- Were more likely to have comorbid eating disorders and externalizing problems
- Were more likely than individuals with recurrent depression to report not having a close friend, not being involved in a romantic relationship, and report having problems in family relationships
- Were less likely to have a history of close friendships and good family relationships.

These findings suggest that early onset of depression, and particularly recurrent depression during adolescence, have a significant impact on many areas of functioning. Thus, knowledge of the developmental manifestations of depression, recognition of heterogeneity of depressive presentations (Klein et al., 2005), and comprehensiveness in the assessment of depressive symptoms and associated features are essential for providing appropriate and meaningful recommendations.

Comorbidity

When a child is diagnosed with depression, there is a high probability (i.e., the majority of cases; Klein et al., 2005) that the child will also meet criteria for another disorder, especially an anxiety problem (Angold, Costello, & Erkanli, 1999). One study found that every child who was diagnosed with depression over a four-year period was at some point also diagnosed with an anxiety disorder (Christ, 1990). This overlap is striking, but it does not indicate that depression and anxiety comprise the same syndrome. In addition to being reliably differentiated with diagnostic measures, the two problems differ in family resemblance and course (Stavrakaki & Ellis, 1989).

Also of interest is the comorbidity of depression and disruptive behavior disorders. Angold et al. (1999) found a greater than chance probability that youth diagnosed with depression also meet criteria for ADHD, ODD, and CD. The pattern of comorbidity also appears somewhat different based on developmental level. More specifically, younger children with depression are likely to have comorbid anxiety disorders, whereas adolescents with depression are more likely to have comorbid substance abuse problems or eating disorders (see Hankin et al., 2008).

The comorbidity of youth depression also extends into the realm of academic functioning. Hammen and colleagues found youth depression was associated with greater academic problems and poorer school attendance (Hammen et al., 1999). As would be expected, depression is associated with greater social/peer problems (e.g., Klein, Lewinsohn, & Seeley, 1997; Marcotte, Fortin, Potvin, & Papillon, 2002) and a greater number of stressful life events, including interpersonal stressors that may have a particularly negative impact for young girls (Hankin, Mermelstein, & Roesch, 2007). Although a strong case can be made for depression being either the cause or the effect in these relations, the important issue in assessment is to approach referrals for depression comprehensively so as to determine all of the relevant targets of intervention. The research on childhood depression clearly indicates a need to assess for symptomatology and difficulties in a variety of domains, as well as to assess indicators of impairment related to depressive symptoms (e.g., truancy).

Furthermore, some research suggests that one should often screen for depression when a medical illness is present. In one study, depression and anxiety had a 41% higher prevalence rate in individuals with medical illness. Depression that is secondary to medical illness may have different outcomes, thus also requiring differing approaches to intervention (Cassen, 1990).

Issues of comorbidity can also be confused with the notions of primary and secondary conditions. The primacy of the condition can be especially important for internalizing disorders because it may be important to differentially intervene based on knowledge of primacy. A child with both depression and anxiety may require intervention for depression first, for example, if the child is presenting risk factors for suicidal behavior. Relatedly, a child suffering from anxiety and depression may require intervention for anxiety symptoms initially if compulsive hand-washing behavior has resulted in impaired functioning in school, at home, and among peers. Determining primacy of condition is fraught with problems (Winokur, 1990), and the implications of doing so are not yet entirely clear at this stage of research on the comorbidity of internalizing disorders in children. Some evidence suggests that anxiety or externalizing problems often precede depression rather than the other way around (see Hankin et al., 2007). The clinician should attempt to distinguish the primacy of anxiety and depression for the purpose of developing recommendations for targets of intervention. Some characteristics that may be useful in such work include symptomatology, course of symptoms and condition, family resemblance and background, test results, and response to prior treatment/interventions (Winokur, 1990).

Specialized Measures of Depression

Aside from a general approach (i.e., likely through clinical interview) for gathering evidence on symptomatology, family history, stressors, comorbidity, and developmental course in the assessment of depression, the clinician also has the ability to select specific tools that assess depressive symptoms in an in-depth, efficient manner. Several examples of such tools are reviewed in this section.

Children's Depression Inventory (CDI; Kovacs, 1992)

The Children's Depression Inventory (CDI; Kovacs, 1991) is a 27-item depression self-report scale for ages 7 through 17. A derivative of the Beck Depression Inventory (Semrud-Clikeman, 1990), the CDI enjoys a long history of clinical use, particularly in research investigations.

Scale Content

The 27 items of the CDI assess a wide range of depressive symptomatology, much of which is included in popular diagnostic systems such as the *DSM*. Items assess sadness, cognitive symptoms, social problems, somatic complaints, and acting-out behaviors. In addition to a total score, there are five subscales available: Negative Mood, Interpersonal Problems, Ineffectiveness, Anhedonia, and Negative Self-esteem.

Administration and Scoring

Contributing to the popularity of the CDI is its ease of administration and scoring. The scale can be completed in minutes by a competent reader. Each item is composed of three stems from which the child must choose one. The three stems typically represent differing levels of severity of depressive symptomatology. Items are assigned scores of 2, 1, or 0, where a higher raw score reflects more severe symptomatology.

Linear T-scores are available for the CDI total and subscale scores, with the author using a *T*-score of 65 or higher as indicative of clinical significance (Kovacs, 1992). Separate norms are available for 7–12-year-old boys, 7–12-year-old girls, 13–17-year-old boys, and 13–17-year-old girls

Norming

The CDI possesses essentially local norms based on a sample of 1,266 Florida school children in grades 2 through 8 (Kovacs, 1992). Seventy-seven percent of children in this normative sample were white, whereas the remaining 23% were African American, Hispanic, or Native American (specific percentages for each group were not reported). The normative sample gives little evidence of national representation; hence, the degree to which CDI norms can be recommended as a national or some other standard is not known. However, it is apparent that at least some minority groups were underrepresented.

Reliability

The reliability of the overall CDI score is good with internal consistency coefficients typically in the .80s. The coefficients for the scales are modest at best, ranging from .59 (Interpersonal Problems) to .68 (Negative Self-esteem). Test-retest coefficients for the total score are adequate based on data reported from a number of studies employing a range of time frames (i.e., 1 week to 1 year; see Kovacs, 1992).

Validity

Internal evidence of validity has been assessed via numerous factor-analytic investigations. Kovacs (1991) suggests using a five-factor solution for conceptualizing subscales. The presence of more than one factor, however, does not necessarily support the validity of the CDI. The factor studies do suggest dominance by a large first factor (Cooper, 1990).

Criterion-related studies are generally supportive of the CDI as a measure of internalizing symptomatology. The CDI correlates significantly with other measures of anxiety and depression (see Myers & Winters, 2002 for review).

Some of the validity evidence associated with the CDI has been described as "mixed." Although, for example, the CDI has shown some validity for differentiating between nonclinical children and samples of children with depression, several studies have shown that the CDI cannot accurately distinguish between samples with depression and other psychiatric groups (Myers & Winters; Silverman & Rabian, 1999).

Strengths and Weaknesses

The CDI continues to be a widely used measure. Among the CDI's strengths are:

1. A long research history that has contributed to considerable trust by the psychological re-search community
2. Ease of administration and scoring
3. Relatively low cost
4. Evidence of concurrent validity with measures of internalizing symptoms

The CDI, however, has some noteworthy weaknesses that caution against overinterpretation.

1. The wisdom of offering such rigid cut scores for screening or diagnostic purposes in the manual is questionable, as these suggestions are often applied rigidly by the user (Kamphaus, 2001).
2. The scale scores of the CDI have fairly low internal consistency for clinical purposes.
3. The norm-referenced scores from the CDI should be interpreted cautiously given their lack of representativeness. In fact, a crucial flaw such as this suggests that the CDI may be more useful for research purposes than for clinical assessment and diagnostic decisions. The CDI, in fact, does have an impressive history of research utility for which norm-referenced scores are often of little interest.
4. The ability of the CDI to assist with differential diagnosis is questionable (Silverman & Rubian, 1999).

Reynolds Adolescent Depression Scale, 2nd Edition (RADS-2; Reynolds, 2002)

The Reynolds Adolescent Depression Scale, 2nd edition (RADS-2; Reynolds) is designed to assess symptomatology associated with depression via self-report in adolescents ages 11–20. The RADS-2 is closely based on its predecessor (Reynolds, 1986), although it may be used with a slightly wider age range than was recommended for the original version. The RADS-2 is not designed provide a diagnosis of a specific depressive disorder. However, it is designed for use as a screening measure or for research.

Scale Content

The RADS-2 provides a thorough sampling of depressive symptoms that are included in the *DSM* and other nosologies and takes approximately 5–10 min to administer.

Administration and Scoring

The RADS-2 uses 30 items to which the client responds with one of four choices of frequency: almost never, hardly ever, sometimes, and most of the time. Six of these items are considered critical items. A Total Depression score, as well as scores on four scales: Dysphoric Mood, Anhedonia/Negative Affect, Negative Self-evaluation, and Somatic Complaints. The items are placed on a single page where a template is used to easily sum up item scores to obtain raw scores. Raw scores are then converted to percentile ranks based on the total sample and by gender and grade, and unlike the previous version of the RADS, T-scores are offered. The T-scores are based on the original distributions of the total score and scale scores in the norm sample (i.e., linear T scores). This change represents a significant improvement and brings the RADS-2 in line with the scores available for many other measures of child functioning. Reynolds (2002), in line with other approaches to interpreting rating scales, suggests that a *T* score of 65 or higher be considered clinically significant and worthy of close consideration (along with other assessment data) in case conceptualization.

Norming

The RADS-2 was normed on 9,052 participants from seven states and one Canadian province recruited from schools. The sample is described as socioeconomically diverse, with representation reported by age, gender, and ethnicity. The match of the sample to meaningful national criteria such as census data is not given. The author reports increased representativeness of Hispanics in the RADS-2 norm sample; however, Hispanics (i.e., 4.5% of the norm sample) and African Americans (7.4% of the norm sample) both appear to be underrepresented. A clinical sample consisting of 297 participants was also recruited. This sample was mostly female (55.6%), with the vast majority of the clinical sample being Caucasian (86.1%).

Reliability

Reliability indices for the RADS-2 total score are good, with the internal consistency coefficients of the total score and scales ranging from .86 to .93 in the norming sample (Reynolds, 2002). Two-week test-retest reliability was also good, ranging from .77 for Somatic Complaints to .85 for the Total Depression score.

Validity

Like the RADS, the RADS-2 has good content validity in that it systematically assesses many of the symptoms commonly associated with the syndrome. To date, there are limited data on the construct validity of the RADS-2, although the manual reports higher correlations between the RADS-2 and Hamilton Depression Rating Scale Clinical Interview than were enjoyed by the RADS. In addition, the RADS-2 total and scale scores showed moderate to high correlations (i.e., ranging from the mid .40s to high .70s) with the Major Depression and Dysthymic Disorder scales of the Adolescent Psychopatology Scale (Reynolds, 1998).

Many studies show reasonable correlations between the original RADS and measures of depression and similar internalizing constructs. Research (e.g., Krefetz, Steer, Gulab, & Beck, 2002) has shown good convergence between the RADS and Beck Depression Inventory (BDI), with consistently significant correlations ranging from .68 to .76.

Additional research has shown that the previous version of the RADS correlate well with a measure of suicide risk (Kaczmarek, Hagan, & Kettler, 2006) and to be predictive of later suicidality in hospitalized adolescents (Huth-Bocks et al., 2007).

Strengths and Weaknesses

The RADS-2 has many apparent strengths including:

1. A thorough assessment of depressive symptomatology rooted in content validity
2. Norm-referenced scores, unlike its predecessor
3. Ease of administration and scoring
4. Good recommendations regarding interpretation in the manual

Weaknesses may include:

1. More information of the norming sample is provided than was the case for the RADS, but it still does not appear to be representative of the U.S. population, particularly in regards to ethnicity.
2. A quite limited research based on the RADS-2, particularly in comparison to the CDI.
3. The response scale (i.e., "almost never," "hardly ever," "sometimes," "most of the time") may be difficult for some adolescent respondents to interpret.

Reynolds Child Depression Scale (RCDS; Reynolds, 1989)

The Reynolds Child Depression Scale (RCDS; Reynolds) is a downward extension of the RADS designed for ages 8 through 12. It is designed with the same rationale and intended uses as the RADS.

Scale Content

The scale includes 29 items that use a Likert-type four-choice format. The four response options measure frequency of symptomatology with the following options: almost never, sometimes, a lot of the time, and all the time. A 30th item uses a rebus response format with five faces depicting a range of happy to sad faces. As with the RADS, some items are reverse-scored in order to discourage response sets. The items were selected with diagnostic criteria clearly in mind, ensuring that the RCDS assesses a good range of depressive symptoms.

Administration and Scoring

An attempt was made to make all items readable by second-graders to enhance its utility with this younger age range. The RCDS is also self-contained on one sheet for convenience, and a scoring template is provided. A machine-scannable form is also available for group or other large-scale administration of the RCDS. Although a cut score is provided, the author cautions against its use for diagnostic purposes (Reynolds, 1989). Of course, cut scores are always questionable, even for screening purposes. Again, only percentile rank scores, with their attendant problems, are offered for the RCDS in lieu of standard scores.

Norming

The RCDS was normed with a sample of 1,620 children in the Midwest and other portions of the country. Reynolds (1989) presents data showing similar raw scores for samples tested in Sacramento, California and Beloit, Wisconsin and concludes that geographic representation is adequate for the sample. Unfortunately, SES was not specifically indicated for the norming sample, with the exception that some students had teachers estimate their SES. Gender, ethnicity, and grade data are reported for the sample. Like the RADS-2, however, the representation of the sample in comparison to criteria such as census data is not given.

Reliability

The internal consistency of the RCDS is strong, with coefficients at most grade levels of .90. A coefficient of .87 was obtained even at grade 3. Test-retest at 2- and 4-week intervals is strong, with coefficients ranging from .81 to .92 (see Myers & Winters, 2002 for review; Reynolds, 1989).

Validity

Reynolds (1989) makes a good case for content validity. In addition, five studies of the relationship of the RCDS to the CDI produced significant correlations, mostly in the .70s. The RCDS has also shown good correlations with a variety of other indicators of childhood depression (see Myers & Winters, 2002). Correlations with the RCMAS (see below) are also significant, ranging from .60 to .67 in three studies.

A five-factor solution is reported for the RCDS, with the first factor clearly dominant. The presence of a strong first factor argues (lays?) for an emphasis on total score interpretation.

Strengths and Weaknesses

The RCDS is strikingly similar to the RADS in terms of its strengths and weaknesses (see above). However, the RCDS, unlike the RADS-2, uses only percentiles as norm-referenced scores. We have some concern regarding the use of norm-referenced scores with the RCDS, given the lack of information regarding the norming sample. The RCDS may be a good way to efficiently gain self reports on depressive symptoms, but interpretation of the RCDS should be descriptive rather than reliant on ordinal scale data (i.e., percentiles).

Peer Nomination Inventory for Depression (PNID)

The PNID includes 20 items that assess three aspects of depression: depression, happiness, and popularity (Lefkowitz & Tesiny, 1980). It is designed for classroom-based assessment. The PNID is quite different from the other measures reviewed in this section in that it is based on peer nominations. A child's score on each item is the number of nominations divided by the number of students who rated the child in the classroom. The item scores are then summed to yield a total score. Normative data for the PNID have been collected for grades 3 through 5. Reliability data for the PNID are adequate, but correlations with self-report measures of depression have been low (Merrell, 1994) to moderate (Semrud-Clikeman, 1990). Although not a strong measure of clinical depression *per se*, the PNID could serve as an additional data source in the evaluation of children by gauging a child's popularity, social interaction, and happiness as perceived by peers. Information of this nature could assist in targeting for intervention classroom behaviors that improve a child's adaptation in this important setting.

An Assessment Strategy for Depression

As we have in previous chapters, we recommend a five-stage assessment process for the assessment of depression: screening, classification, co-morbidities, alternative causes, and treatment considerations (see Table 18.1).

In light of the prevalence of depression, its common comorbidity with other problems, its adverse effects on development in a variety of domains, and its less-than-flagrant symptomatology, we recommend that every child who is seen by a clinician should be screened for depression. Research findings support the need for screening all referrals that are seen not only by psychologists, but also by other professionals (e.g., pediatricians, teachers). The screening process can be time-efficient and may include:

- Administering a brief, self-report inventory to the child, who has adequate reading ability.
- Asking parents whether or not their child exhibits symptoms given in the *DSM-IV* criteria.
- Querying teachers, nurses, grandparents, or others about symptoms of depression.

Any one of these screening methods takes only a few minutes. In fact, querying both

TABLE 18.1 The Assessment Questions Related to Childhood Depression and Implications for Assessment

Assessment Question	Implications for Assessment
Screening	Administer screening measures or screen during interview. Assess for critical symptoms (i.e., suicidality, psychosis). Determine need for further assessment.
Classification	Assess for presence of symptoms that meet *DSM-IV* criteria. Determine stability and duration of symptoms.
	Determine onset.
	Determine family resemblance.
Comorbidities	Assess for presence of anxiety disorders, ADHD, LD/MR, eating disorders, or Oppositional Defiant Disorder/Conduct Disorder. Determine the influence of depression on school performance, absenteeism, etc.
	Assess social relationships and peer social status.
	Assess for presence of substance abuse, particularly in adolescents.
Alternative Causes	Obtain developmental and medical histories.
	Rule out dysthymia and Post-traumatic Stress Disorder.
	Rule out medical problems that are associated with depression.
Treatment Considerations	Assess for presence of maladaptive cognitions. Assess for presence of chronic stressors. Assess parental depression and parenting style.
	Evaluate response to previous interventions (e.g., psychotropics).

the child and a parent would take only a few minutes. Screening efforts may allow the clinician to implement intervention in order to avert considerable suffering (see Box 18.1).

Classification of a child as depressed requires meeting the *DSM-IV-TR* criteria, and by this we mean meeting all criteria based on apparently valid information. Possessing the necessary symptomatology is only a first step in meeting criteria. The psychologist has to be sure that malingering, response sets, or other threats to validity have not had an effect on the report of symptoms. An adolescent, for example, may be asked if he/she has experienced decreased appetite, fatigue, sleeplessness, agitation, and suicidal ideation. He/she may discern that it is wise to deny all of these difficulties if he/she thinks that he may be a candidate for inpatient or partial hospitalization treatment. Clinicians who treat adolescents have seen cases in which the youth denies suicidal ideation, although he/she may have been transferred from a hospital emergency room because of a suicide attempt. An array of valid assessment methods is necessary in order to ensure adequate documentation of symptoms:

- Structured and semi-structured interviews (e.g., K-SADS; see Chap. 11) with children, their parents, teachers, and other caregivers are necessary to assess for the presence of symptomatology and their effects on the child's functioning in different environments. Indeed, semi-structured interviews, because of their flexibility and comprehensive have been described as "best practice" by Klein et al. (2005; p. 427).
- Self-report inventories and parent and teacher rating scales can provide further documentation of symptoms, screen for comorbid problems, and assess for

Box 18.1

A Case of Individual Screening for Depression

Screening for depression is crucial because of the nature of internalizing symptomatology. Such screening is time-efficient in most settings. This case example illustrates the importance and practicality of screening.

Matt was referred for an evaluation because of his parents' concerns about his academic progress. He is a 16-year-old junior in high school. His parents and teacher suspect that he has a reading disability.

Matt's mother reported a long history of academic problems for Matt, including considerable speech delays as a youngster. He was reportedly enrolled in speech therapy throughout his elementary school years. He was often ridiculed by his peers for misarticulations and stuttering. His speech problems have reportedly declined somewhat in high school. He has, however, had longstanding problems with reading and spelling.

Matt's parents expressed some frustration because they feel that Matt has been passed along from grade to grade because he is very quiet and never causes any problems.

He continues to have trouble in most of his classes. He is performing adequately in math, but he complains that he has trouble taking notes in class and comprehending them after he takes them. He reportedly failed in his English class during the first semester of the current academic year. He is very distraught about these failures because of his desire to go to college following graduation and his concerns about disappointing his parents. Matt also reported some other recent stressors in his life. He recently broke off a 1-year relationship with a girlfriend, and he is receiving rehabilitation for a severe back injury that he incurred in a bicycle accident six months ago. Matt also has two sisters who were reportedly diagnosed with developmental disorders, one with a reading disability and the other with ADHD.

Matt gave the impression of being well-adjusted and socially skilled. He was impeccably groomed and a good conversationalist. He even asked the examiner questions about his interests and offered his full cooperation with the assessment process. Matt described many successes in his life, including being chosen as captain of the baseball team at his school. He apparently has an active and successful social life. Aside from athletics, he is reportedly involved in a variety of other extracurricular activities.

The results of the assessment produced clear evidence of below-average achievement in reading, even though Matt's intellectual functioning was slightly above average.

Following reports of moderate levels of depression on the parent and self-report versions of the BASC-2, Matt was asked to complete the Child Depression Inventory (CDI). Matt acknowledged enough symptoms on the CDI to fall into the mild/moderate range of depressive symptoms. He acknowledged guilt about past failures, uncontrollable sadness, insomnia, hopelessness, decreased appetite, increased fatigue, low self-esteem, concerns about his appearance, lack of interest in social activities, and occasional thoughts of hurting himself, among other symptoms. The incongruence between the symptoms endorsed on rating scales and his presentation was striking. During the feedback session, Matt and his parents were apprised of these findings and asked to verify their validity, which they did. He was then referred for follow-up assessment and intervention for his depression.

This case illustrates how time-efficient screening for depression can be of potential importance. In this scenario, depression was not suspected by the referral sources, the examining psychologist, or the client.

---

the presence of response sets or other threats to validity.

- History- taking from the child and/or parents is necessary in order to establish adequate duration and pervasiveness of symptoms as well as to obtain valuable information in areas such as family psychiatric history (Klein et al., 2005).

Anxiety disorders are especially important to consider when ruling out comorbidities of depression. Anxiety symptomatology should be assessed concurrently with all of the data collection necessary for classification. Omnibus rating scales that include a well-validated anxiety scale and interview schedules that also assess for anxiety are helpful in this regard. The full realm of anxiety problems should be routinely ruled out. Somatization problems, phobias, milder fears, obsessive-compulsive disorder, and separation anxiety disorder should be distinguished.

One of the alternative causes that looms large in cases of depression is a medical difficulty that can cause depression. We recommend that a clinician assessing a child who displays the symptoms of depression should have access to the results of a recent physical exam, or an exam should be scheduled if one has not been conducted within a few months of the psychological evaluation.

The psychological evaluation must also rule out other conditions that may appear to be a major depressive episode. In this regard, thorough history-taking is necessary in order to rule out transient states such as bereavement (e.g., depression due to a child's mother being called away to active duty in the armed forces), adjustment disorder with depressed mood, or dysthymia.

Finally, assessment methods must be selected that help direct intervention efforts. Rating scales may be used to broadly sample behavior in home, school, and other settings. A broad sampling of behavior allows the clinician to consider depressive problems and other difficulties that may in some way adversely affect the child's adaptation. If, for example, the child also shows considerable evidence of worry about school difficulties, an adjustment in the child's curriculum may have a positive effect on the child's perceived level of stress, which, in turn, could help abate depressive symptoms.

An assessment of academic achievement may also be necessary in order to determine whether or not a child is suffering from academic under-achievement associated with long-term depressive symptomatology. Teacher interviews and norm-referenced and curriculum-based measures may be helpful in this regard.

Self- and other informant ratings are also critical for initial assessment and for monitoring response to interventions. The previous research citing long-term adaptation difficulties for children with depressive problems suggests that careful monitoring of the effects of treatment is necessary, and post-treatment follow-up is warranted in order to prevent or effectively deal with indications of relapse.

A case study of an adolescent girl with depression is provided in Box 18.2, illustrating this approach to assessing depression.

Anxiety Disorders of Childhood

The term *anxiety* can be traced to the Latin root *angere*, which means to cause distress or strangle. That is, unpleasant feelings of anxiety, including potentially intense feelings of fear, dread, and worry, evoke emotions associated with strangulation (Stavrakaki & Ellis, 1989). In there, discussion of evidence-based assessment of anxiety in children, Silverman and Ollendick (2005) highlight Barlow's relatively recent definition of anxiety as being particularly useful for assessment and subsequent intervention. For Barlow (2002), anxiety can be described as being dominated by concerns about future unpredictability or loss of control which is accompanied by a "shift in attention to the focus on potentially dangerous events or one's own affective response to these events" (p. 104).

Problems that are commonly discussed under the general rubric of anxiety include

Box 18.2

Sample Case of an Adolescent with Depression

Several assessment methods are applied in the case of Corin. The report is given as it would be written in a typical psychological report, with commentary regarding interpretation.

Corin, a 16-year-old girl, was referred for a psychological evaluation by her mother due to academic problems. According to Mrs. Jacobs (mother), Corin has trouble concentrating in school and she thought that Corin's school problems may be caused by ADHD.

Corin lives with her mother and younger brother. Corin's parents are divorced, and she reportedly rarely sees her father.

Mrs. Jacobs stated that there were no difficulties during her pregnancy with Corin. During birth, however, Corin was in fetal distress, and Mrs. Jacobs had an emergency Cesarean delivery. Corin was born full-term and weighed 8 pounds, 7 ounces. Corin's mother described her development as normal in that she reached all motor and language developmental milestones at age-appropriate times. Corin is, reportedly, in very good health. She is supposed to wear contact lenses, but her mother reports that Corin rarely wears them.

Corin's parents divorced when Corin was 5 years old. In addition, Corin was reportedly very close to her maternal aunt who died earlier this year. Corin stated that her mother is constantly on her back and that she has to do too much work around the house. There is a family history of alcohol abuse on both her mother's and father's sides of the family. Corin's mother and father also both have a reported history of alcohol abuse.

Corin is currently in the 10th grade. Corin's mother noted that Corin did well in elementary school, always receiving A's or B's. Starting in the seventh grade, Corin's academic performance reportedly deteriorated. Her mother noticed that she had problems reading aloud and problems with mathematics.

Corin received her first failing grade in the ninth grade and was moved from algebra back to pre-algebra, which she had in eighth grade. According to her mother, her grades continued to deteriorate, and currently she is receiving an "F" in history and English, a "C" in science, algebra, and Spanish, and an "A" in photography.

Corin's teachers feel that she is smart but that she does not put forth significant effort. They reported that she exhibits behavioral problems in the classroom. She is reportedly constantly talking and disrupting the class. Her algebra teacher stated that she is fond of Corin but that she plays around with her classmates too much. She reportedly talks back to her teachers, which is consistent with the reports from last year's teachers. Corin's teachers also reported that she frequently sleeps through class.

According to records kept by the school for the past two years, Corin is often excessively tardy and absent from class. In the fall of this year, she served two days of suspension in study hall for being rude to a new teacher. Subsequent to this incident, a parent conference at school resulted in Mrs. Jacobs agreeing to have Corin evaluated in order to rule out ADHD.

Corin has reportedly been seen in counseling at a community clinic for two years. Her current counselor reported that Corin remains under a great deal of stress due to her parents' divorce, her aunt's death, and her continuing academic vproblems. Mrs. Jacobs mentioned that Corin also often has stomachaches and dizzy spells, which she attributes to stress. Corin complains of not being able to go to sleep; once asleep, she frequently has nightmares about dying. She reported that she worries about getting cancer. She told the examiner that one time, she felt a bump on her leg and thought that she had cancer.

Mrs. Jacobs reported that Corin drinks alcohol regularly, and that at times, she drinks quite heavily (i.e., 12–15 beers). Corin told the examiner that she sometimes blacks out on the weekends from drinking. She also admitted to frequent use of marijuana, and she reportedly smokes at least one pack of cigarettes a day. A few weeks before the evaluation, Corin was detained by police because of skipping school and being intoxicated.

In two interview sessions, Corin described herself as being depressed. She told the examiner that, for the past three weeks, she has felt angry, sad, and hopeless. Throughout the interview Corin appeared to be agitated.

Corin's intellectual functioning was estimated as being above her same-aged peers. She did well on tests that were timed and involved physical manipulation of materials and the results indicate that her nonverbal reasoning abilities are better developed than her abilities in verbal reasoning.

Generalized Anxiety Disorder, Separation Anxiety Disorder, Agoraphobia, Social Phobia, Simple Phobia, School Phobia, other fears, Obsessive-Compulsive Disorder, Post-traumatic Stress Disorder, and Panic Disorder, among others.

Although they share obvious features, these anxiety problems also comprise unique facets that have clear implications for assessment, differential diagnosis, and treatment planning. According to the *DSM-IV-TR* (2000):

(a) Generalized Anxiety Disorder is characterized by excessive, unfocused worry;
(b) Separation Anxiety Disorder is centered around significant distress when separated from primary caretakers or home;
(c) Agoraphobia features anxiety regarding being in places or situations from which escape is difficult or perceived as difficult;
(d) Social Phobia is characterized by fear of situations that involve social evaluation;
(e) Simple Phobias are marked by significant, intense fear of particular objects or stimuli, whether the exposure is direct or anticipated;
(f) Obsessive Compulsive Disorder consists of persistent, recurrent thoughts and behavioral compulsions associated with impaired functioning;
(g) Post-traumatic Stress Disorder is based on re-experiencing of a traumatic event and increased arousal; and
(h) Panic Disorder features a sudden occurrence of intense physiological and cognitive symptoms of anxiety that tend to occur unexpectedly.

The measures of anxiety that often used in child assessments typically screen aspects of all of these problem areas broadly. It is then up to the clinician to obtain the necessary information to best conceptualize the specific anxiety problem or disorder and then make recommendations accordingly.

Characteristics of Childhood Anxiety Disorders

Comparatively speaking, much less is known about childhood anxiety disorders compared to the knowledge base for depression. Classification schemes and the assessment instruments themselves are primarily based on research on adult anxiety disorders (Silverman & Ollendick, 2005). There are issues from research on children and adolescents specifically that have importance for assessment practice:

- In many respects, anxiety disorders can be conceptualized as exaggerations of normal responses to developmental demands (e.g., separation anxiety in young children; anxiety in social situations for adolescents). It is when the anxiety response is impaired that intervention is needed (Silverman & Ollendick, 2005).
- Evidence regarding the stability and prognosis of anxiety disorders in children is quite mixed (Weems & Stickle, 2005).
- Research using the Anxiety Disorders Interview Schedule for Children (ADIS) has found strong parent-child interrater reliability for individual anxiety disorder diagnostic categories (Lyneham, Abbott, & Rapee, 2007) but also substantial parent-child disagreement (Grills & Ollendick, 2003). These results should caution the clinician to attend to reasons for convergence and divergence among informants.
- The phenomenology of childhood anxiety disorders appears to be very similar to that of adults (Silverman, 1993). However, the assessment methods used to make diagnoses of childhood anxiety

disorders have often not been developed with potential developmental influences on the manifestation of anxiety in mind (Silverman & Ollendick, 2005).

- While anxiety often is apparent in cases of depression, anxiety disorders also often occur in the absence of depression (Silverman, 1993). Anxiety with comorbid problems is associated with poorer outcomes than anxiety alone (see Saavedra & Silverman, 2002).
- Separation Anxiety Disorder typically occurs in children less than 11–13 years of age (Strauss, 1993; Weems, Hammond-Laurence, Silverman, & Ginsburg, 1998); however, social phobia becomes more common in adolescence (Weems et al., 1998).
- Fears of animals, the darkness, and heights are more likely to occur at younger ages than social phobias which, in turn, occur at younger ages than agoraphobia (Strauss, 1993).
- There are two main types of school phobia: those that come on acutely in a child who has functioned reasonably normally before onset, and those that arise in a child who has had similar problems from the preschool years and has never developed the social skills that would permit normal functioning (Berg, 1993).
- The average of onset for childhood Obsessive-Compulsive Disorder (OCD) is approximately 9–12 years, with family history of OCD placing a youngster at-risk for an even younger onset of OCD symptoms (see Baldwin and Dadds, 2008 for review).
- The central symptoms of Post-traumatic Stress Disorder (PTSD), increased arousal, psychic numbing, and re-experiencing the trauma, occur in children as well as adults who are diagnosed with the condition (Last, 1993). However, the frequency and intensity of these symptoms may be important indicators of impairment due to PTSD symptoms for children (Carrion, Weems, Ray, & Reiss, 2002).

Specialized Measures of Anxiety

Rating Scales

Revised Children's Manifest Anxiety Scale (RCMAS; Reynolds & Richmond, 1985)

The Revised Children's Manifest Anxiety Scale (RCMAS; Reynolds & Richmond) measures the expression of anxiety symptomatology whether or not the construct is conceptualized as being a state or a trait. We review the RCMAS in relative depth because it is widely used and has many unique features for a single construct rating scale

Scale Content

The RCMAS includes 37 items distributed among four scales: Physiological Anxiety (10 items), Worry/Oversensitivity (11 items), Social concerns/Concentration (7 items), and Lie (L, 9 items). The content of the subscales appears diverse. Items from the physiological anxiety subscale, for example, range from "difficulty making decisions" (note that the physiological nature of this item is not apparent) to "awakening scared from sleep" to "having sweaty hands."

The L scale is a rather unique feature of a single-construct measure. The RCMAS L scale measures children's tendency to portray themselves in a favorable light with items like, "I always have good manners." To obtain a high score on this scale, children would have to deny ever getting angry and liking everyone they know. This scale is likely to be transparent to many adolescents. Research has shown that younger children tend to score higher on the RCMAS Lie scale than older youth (Pina, Silverman, Saavedra, & Weems, 2001).

Administration and Scoring

Children have simply to respond "yes" or "no" to RCMAS items that are read from a one-page response form that is accompanied by a template for scoring. Group administration is feasible for older children. A high score is indicative of higher anxiety.

The Total Anxiety score is a T-score conversion of a raw score. Standard scores with a mean of 10 and standard deviation of 3 are also provided for the subscales. A standard score of 13 on the L scale should lead the clinician to suspect the child's report (Reynolds & Richmond, 1985). Norm-referenced scores are provided by gender, age, and ethnicity, giving the user a variety of interpretive options. Nongender-based norms are not offered.

Norming

The RCMAS was normed using 4,972 children age 6 through 19 years. The sample was collected from 13 states. Age, gender, and ethnic in-formation is given in the manual (Reynolds & Richmond, 1985). The representation of Hispanic students is lacking, and no formal measure of SES is included. Consequently, while the sample size is large and the geographic representation is better than for some other single-trait measures, the representativeness of the RCMAS sample is still open to question.

Reliability

Internal consistency reliability of the composite score is good with overall coefficients in the low .80s. Subscale reliabilities are somewhat lower, particularly for the Physiological Anxiety and Social Concerns/Concentration scales. The Physiological Anxiety scale produced a coefficient of .67 for the total score in the norm sample. The Social Concerns/Concentration estimate was similar at .64. The Worry/Oversensitivity coefficient was somewhat higher at .76. Clearly, the Worry/Oversensitivity subscale is the most trustworthy and may, in some instances, be more useful for identifying children with anxiety problems *per se* than the RCMAS total score (see Silverman & Ollendick, 2005).

Validity

Considerable validity evidence is provided in the RCMAS manual. Factor studies of the standardization data do not suggest that the RCMAS is dominated by a single factor. A review of the factor loadings suggest that some of the scale placements were based on minimal loadings. The item about having difficulty making decisions, for example, had a .26 loading on both the first and second factors for the norming sample, yet the item is placed on the Physiological Anxiety factor, not Worry/Oversensitivity. Theoretical or logical considerations may have helped with the item-placement process.

The RCMAS demonstrates consistent relations with other measures of anxiety. A correlation of .65 is reported between the RCMAS Total Anxiety score and the State Trait Anxiety Inventory for Children Trait Anxiety score.

Like the CDI, the ability of the RCMAS to identify true cases of specific anxiety disorders is questionable (Silverman & Rabian, 1999). Similarly, in their review of the relevant research, Silverman and Ollendick (2005) point out that the RCMAS does not consistently distinguish children with anxiety disorders from children with other forms of psychopathology (e.g., depression, Conduct Disorder, ADHD), although it may distinguish children with anxiety from children without any significant psychological difficulties. Clinicians are, therefore, advised to use diagnostic interviews or other measures to identify disorders *per se*, with the RCMAS serving as one potential indicator of problems with anxiety.

Strengths and Weaknesses

Strengths of the RCMAS include:

1. A broad sampling of anxiety symptomatology

2. Ease of administration and scoring
3. A larger and more geographically diverse norming sample than is typical for single-construct measures
4. A reliable Total Anxiety score
5. The presence of an L scale

Weaknesses of the RCMAS include:

1. A lack of information about relevant ethnic and SES representation of the norming sample
2. Subscales with questionable external evidence of validity

Additional Self-Report Measures

In addition to the RCMAS, there is a vast array of rating scales for child anxiety. Silverman & Ollendick (2005) provide a useful review of many such measures.

Three self-report measures that have enjoyed wide use and extensive research are the Fear Survey Schedule for Children-Revised (FSSCR; Ollendick, 1978), the Multidimensional Anxiety Scale for Children (MASC; March et al., 1997), and the State-Trait Anxiety Inventory for Children (STAIC; Spielberger, 1973). The STAIC has a companion parent report version. Some of the assessment domains offered by these measures are provided in Table 18.2.

Two relatively new self-report ratings of anxiety focus on aspects of the individual's cognitions as they contribute to, or be a sign of, marked anxiety. The Anxiety Control Questionnaire for Children (Weems, Silverman, Rapee, and Pina, 2003) contains 30 items that assess the child's perceived control over threatening events or stimuli. The Children's Automatic Thoughts (Schniering & Rapee, 2002) assesses whether or not the respondent has experienced particular negative thoughts about anxiety-provoking situations. Initial research on the psychometrics of both of these scales has had promising results (see Silverman & Ollendick, 2005), and the unique focus of these scales also appears to translate well to cognitive-behavioral interventions for childhood anxiety.

Table 18.2 Domains Assessed by Several Rating Scales Assessing Anxiety

FSSC-R Domains
Total fear score
Failure/criticism
Fear of unknown
Injury/small animals
Fear of danger/death
Medical Fears
MASC Domains
Physical symptoms
Social anxiety
Harm avoidance
Separation/panic
STAIC Domains
Total State Anxiety
State-cognitive
State-somatic
Total trait anxiety
Trait-cognitive
Trait-somatic

Interviews and Clinician Ratings

The typical way for anxiety to be assessed in children is through interviews (including some of the diagnostic interviews reviewed in Chap. 11) or subscales within broad-band ratings (usually completed by parents, teachers, or youths themselves). The Anxiety Disorders Interview Schedule for Children (Albano &Silverman, 1996) is a unique-structured interview in that it provides an in-depth assessment of symptoms and impairment across anxiety disorder categories.

The Yale-Brown Obsessive Compulsive Scale for Children (Goodman et al., 1989) is but one example of a clinician rating of anxiety symptoms. The adult version of this scale is well-known and extensively used in research and practice. Such a tool may be useful if a clinician wants to zero in on specific areas of anxiety symptomatology in a quick, efficient manner (the YBOCS has ten items) rather than conducting an extensive multi-domain interview.

Cognitive-Behavioral Assessment

Kendall and Ronan (1990), among others, emphasize the importance of a child's information processing as a mediating variable in the development and expression of anxiety symptoms. Some of the cognitive variables that may mediate anxiety are self-statements, irrational beliefs, current concerns, images, problem-solving capacities, expectancies, and attributions. Methods for assessing these cognitive variables include (Kendall & Ronan, 1990):

- Self-monitoring
- Recordings of spontaneous verbalizations
- Think aloud methods
- Role playing
- Imagery assessment
- Thought sampling and thought listing techniques
- Interviews
- Endorsement measures

In addition, numerous other observational methods, including parent-child interactions and social interaction scenarios have been used in the assessment of youth anxiety (see Silverman & Ollendick, 2005).

These informal methods of assessment vary in the degree to which they have been developed for clinical use. Cognitive-behavioral methods potentially serve the clinician, even in experimental form, by providing corroborating data for test-based findings, and by providing insights that may be useful for intervention design. Still, the incremental validity obtained by incorporating such procedures into assessment batteries for childhood anxiety is uncertain (Silverman & Ollendick, 2005).

The preceding discussion in no way provides an exhaustive description of the available methods for assessing anxiety in children. Instead, we have attempted to highlight those measures that are well-known, widely used, and/or unique in their implementation or focus. The reader is encouraged to remain up-to-date on the burgeoning body of research on evidence-based assessment of anxiety (as well as other forms of psychopathology) to determine which approaches possess clinical utility.

An Assessment Strategy for Anxiety

We again recommend a five-stage assessment process for the assessment of anxiety: screening, classification, comorbidities, alternative causes, and treatment considerations (see Table 18.3). Screening for anxiety can be accomplished using both informal and formal means. A few questions about anxiety symptoms may be more appropriate for many settings than the use of self-report or other more formal psychometric devices. As noted elsewhere in this text, many omnibus rating scales provide a screening of anxiety, but they do not differentiate among different types or classes of anxiety problems. The most important screening principle to remember is to do it, because failure to screen for anxiety may result in under-serving children with less obvious problems.

Classification of anxiety difficulties is complicated by debate regarding the

Table 18.3 The Assessment Questions Related to Childhood Anxiety and Implications for Assessment

Assessment Question	Implications for Assessment
Screening	Administer time efficient assessment instruments (i.e., rating scales) Determine need for further assessment.
Classification and Subtypes	Assess for presence of symptoms that meet may *DSM-IV* criteria through specific rating scales or interviews. Determine stability and duration of symptoms. Determine onset.
Comorbidities	Assess for presence of depression, academic difficulties, externalizing problems, or other anxiety problems. Determine the influence of anxiety on school performance, absenteeism, etc. Assess social relationships and peer social status.
Alternative Causes	Obtain developmental and medical histories. Rule out stressful life events or other psychopathology as primary explanation for anxiety symptoms. Rule out medical problems that are associated with anxiety.
Treatment Considerations	Assess for presence of maladaptive cognitions. Assess parental depression and parenting style. Evaluate response to previous interventions (e.g., pharmacotherapy, counseling, etc.).

appropriateness of existing criteria, including the *DSM-IV*. These issues notwithstanding, it is critical for treatment planning purposes for the clinician to determine the phenomenology of the client's anxiety and the situations/stimuli that tend to elicit or alleviate the anxiety. Silverman and Ollendick (2005) note that some available measures are better able than others for assessing different types of anxiety.

Anxiety disorders are most likely to be comorbid with other internalizing disorders such as other anxiety disorders or depression. Moreover, the nature of the symptomatology may vary over time. A child may, for example, initially be diagnosed with SAD and not have school difficulties. School refusal and subsequent academic problems, however, may appear at a later time.

Medical problems should be ruled out as alternative causes because of the role that physical illness and medical procedures can play in initiating or exacerbating a child's anxiety symptoms. In fact, one of the first hypotheses to consider when somatic symptoms are present (e.g., headaches, stomachaches, diarrhea) is the possibility that the child is physically ill. Although it seems obvious, it should be stated that a medical evaluation should be conducted when somatic complaints are evident.

Further assessment should be conducted on the factors that may influence treatment outcome. Research on this area of assessment is limited, but an approach that incorporates behavioral observation, rating scales, and/or self-monitoring is recommended (Silverman & Ollendick, 2005). Maladaptive cognitions, family stressors, and traumatic events are but some of the variables that may play a role in the client's manifestation and maintenance of anxiety symptoms and that will undoubtedly play a role in the progress of treatment.

A sample case illustrating this assessment approach for anxiety is provided in Box 18.3.

Box 18.3

A Sample Case Illustrating the Assessment of Anxiety

Thomas is a 9-year-old male who was referred for an assessment due to academic difficulties subsequent to being transferred to a new school. He was referred in May of the school year. His grades are reportedly lower in his new school than in the previous school. He makes frequent self-deprecating statements and reportedly requires much attention and supervision to complete his homework. He tends to give up easily on academic activities, often refusing to complete them. He reportedly has trouble separating from his mother, and he often seeks attention in the classroom. On the positive side, he is described as endearing to teachers, creative, and artistically talented.

Thomas was reportedly born three months preterm and weighed approximately three pounds at birth. He was treated in neonatal intensive care for two months after delivery. His mother reported that he did not walk until 16 months, and he did not speak in single words until 24 months of age.

Thomas was reportedly diagnosed at age 5 with a motor delay, ADHD, and ODD. He continues to receive occupational therapy for his motor problems. His teachers have reportedly always indicated that he responds better in a structured classroom. His grades have usually been above grade level with the exception of mathematics. He has not been retained nor has he been served in special education. According to his mother, Thomas often complains of headaches and stomachaches at school.

Thomas's test behavior was also remarkable in that he refused testing initially. He clung to his mother in the waiting room. He cried and requested that his mother join him for the testing. During testing (with his mother in the room), he cried, tantrumed, threw objects, refused to answer questions, and responded impulsively. Several times, he remarked, "I'm an idiot." He was rescheduled to complete testing a week later.

During the second assessment session, Thomas cooperated fully. He again pleaded with his mother to join him, but she refused. He did not display any of the previous behavior problems, and he did not make self-deprecating statements.

Thomas's intellectual functioning was in the Low Average range as was his measured academic achievement in reading, math, and writing. His academic difficulties do not appear to be the result of a specific learning disability, although it is reasonable to expect that Thomas may struggle with some academic tasks, unless he is given some assistance in acquiring further academic skills.

Based on findings from rating scales and historical information, Thomas was diagnosed with Separation Anxiety Disorder. This diagnosis was based on the rationale that he displayed the minimum of three symptoms for a minimum of four weeks. His symptoms included:

1. Excessive distress when separated from family members
2. Worry about the well-being of family members
3. Somatic complaints when separated

An interesting aspect of this case is that the previous diagnoses of ADHD and ODD were not confirmed based on detailed interview information and rating scales. For example, many of Thomas's oppositional behaviors seemed better explained by his refusal to separate from his mother and his difficulty working on tasks to their completion when he was upset. His teacher reported that Thomas only seems inattentive and distracted when faced with difficult tasks. On new or difficult tasks, Thomas seems to adjust better when given some initial guidance and feedback on his performance.

Treatment recommendations were made that centered around ways for Thomas to cope with his anxiety, particularly regarding going to school and ways for his mother to facilitate his progress and not maintain his desire to avoid separation through tantruming or refusal to perform tasks. The results of the evaluation were also shared with school personnel, and a behavioral intervention plan for Thomas was developed at school.

Conclusions

The assessment of child anxiety and depression requires a well-trained clinician. The less obvious nature of their symptomatology and the range of disorders related to anxiety and depression make identification of these problems a professional challenge. The nature of the symptomatology also points to the necessity of gathering self-report information – an additional challenge in the assessment of young children.

Many child anxiety and depression measures combine the two sets of symptoms. As such, scales are not likely to differentiate between the two syndromes, necessitating efforts at scale refinement (Silverman & Rabian, 1999).

Although our understanding of child depression and anxiety has increased exponentially of late, our understanding of these problems still lags behind the available knowledge base for adults. Clinicians are advised to make a concerted effort to remain abreast of changes in the emerging research base. We recommend the discussion of evidence-based assessment of childhood depression by Klein et al. (2005) and the article on evidence-based assessment of childhood by Silverman and Ollendick (2005) as useful resources for highlighting important issues in this area of assessment.

Chapter Summary

1. Depression and anxiety difficulties can be subsumed under the more global set of adjustment difficulties of childhood commonly referred to as internalizing difficulties/disorders.
2. Internalizing disorders are among the most difficult to diagnose because of the nature of the symptomatology.
3. In order to meet the diagnostic criteria for Major Depressive Disorder, at least five of nine symptoms must be present for at least a two-week period, and one of the symptoms must be either depressed mood or loss of interest or pleasure (American Psychiatric Association, 2000). The nine symptoms include: (1) depressed or irritable mood, (2) loss of interest in daily activities, (3) significant weight loss or failure to make expected weight gains, (4) frequent insomnia or hypersomnia, (5) motor agitation or retardation, (6) frequent fatigue, (7) feelings of worthlessness or guilt, (8) impaired concentration, (9) suicidality. However, commonly used assessment tools vary in the degree to which their depression scales match these criteria (See Box 18.3.)
4. Approximately 2–3% of preadolescent children may be suffering from depression at any point in time, with rates increasing significantly in adolescence.
5. Specialized measures that may be useful for assessing childhood depression include the Children's Depression Inventory, the Reynolds Adolescent Depression Scale-2, the Reynolds Child Depression Scale, and the Peer Nomination Inventory for Depression, among many others.
6. A five-step method for assessing for depression and anxiety involves (1) screening, (2) classification, (3) comorbidities, (4) alternative causes, and (5) past treatment.
7. Each of the anxiety disorders described in the *DSM-IV* has a different set of core symptoms or problems. Thus, differential diagnosis is often quite important for optimal treatment planning.
8. Some findings regarding anxiety disorders include: many anxiety problems can be conceptualized as exaggerations of normal developmental processes (e.g., separation anxiety for young children); research is mixed on the degree

of parent-child agreement for anxiety symptoms on structured interviews; the phenomenology of childhood anxiety disorders is very similar to that of adults; anxiety disorders often occur in the absence of depression.

9. Some relatively popular self-report measures of anxiety symptomatology in children include the Revised Children's Manifest Anxiety Scale, the Fear Survey Schedule for Children-Revised, the Multidimensional Anxiety Scale for Children, and the State-Trait Anxiety Inventory for Children.

10. Cognitive-behavioral assessment, behavioral observations, and clinician ratings have also been espoused as important assessment tools for anxiety that have implications for intervention planning and that enable progress monitoring. Structured diagnostic interviews are often useful for differential diagnosis and treatment planning as well.

CHAPTER 19

Assessment of Autism Spectrum Disorders

Chapter Questions

- How are autism-spectrum disorders defined by the *DSM-IV*?
- How is autism differentiated from mental retardation?
- What types of scales or strategies are most useful for the assessment of children with these syndromes?
- What is the recommended approach for the assessment of autism spectrum disorders?

Definitional Issues

Autism is believed to affect 1 in 500 children (Bertrand et al., 2001), yet it is often not recognized until after the child is 3 years of age (Filipek et al., 2000). Hence, early screening is important for devising the most appropriate intervention strategy. In addition, because of the difficulty in recognizing autism or related problems, new assessment methods for infants and toddlers are needed. However, a discussion of the development of such tools is beyond the scope of this chapter. Importantly, the array of assessment strategies available for autism spectrum assessment referrals has greatly improved and more easily translate to treatment recommendations. This chapter will give an overview of the measures and noteworthy issues in the assessment of childhood autism.

DSM-IV-TR Criteria

In the *DSM-IV-TR*, Autistic Disorder is part of a class of problems known as Pervasive Develop-mental Disorders (PDD; American Psychiatric Association, 2000).

P.J. Frick et al., *Clinical Assessment of Child and Adolescent Personality and Behavior*,
DOI 10.1007/978-1-4419-0641-0_19, © Springer Science+Business Media, LLC 2010

However, the term "Autism Spectrum Disorders" (ASD) is now generally used in lieu of PDD (see Ozonoff, Goodlin-Jones, & Solomon, 2005). Other disorders that are included under the rubric of ASD include Childhood Disintegrative Disorder, Asperger's Disorder (often referred to as "Asperger's Syndrome"), Rett's Disorder, and PDD Not Otherwise Specified (American Psychiatric Association, 2000).

The prototypical ASD is, of course, Autistic Disorder, a condition that has long been of interest to psychologists. Autistic Disorder will be the primary focus of this chapter, with some discussion of other ASD issues, particularly regarding the assessment of Asperger's Disorder. The *DSM-IV-TR* describes Autistic Disorder as "the presence of markedly abnormal or impaired development in social interaction and communications and a markedly restricted repertoire of activity and interests."

Autistic Disorder is also known by other terms such as *autism* or *early infantile autism*. Autistic Disorder is known to be frequently comorbid with mental retardation (American Psychiatric Association, 2000). With co-morbidity estimates ranging as high as 75%, the differential diagnosis of autism and mental retardation can be challenging.

The *DSM-IV* emphasizes three classes of symptoms that are central to the disorder: social interaction problems, communication problems, and repetitive and stereotyped behaviors. The onset of these symptoms must occur by age 3. The *DSM* criteria require that a total of six symptoms with a minimum of one from each of the three classes of problems be present in order to make a diagnosis. Furthermore, at least two of the symptoms from the social interaction class of problems must be present.

The social interaction symptoms include:

1. Failure to engage in appropriate nonverbal behaviors such as appropriate eye contact, facial expressions, body postures, and social gestures
2. Poorly developed peer relationships
3. Failure to share pleasurable interests, activities, or achievements with others
4. Lack of social reciprocity

Communication symptoms include:

1. Delayed development of spoken language
2. When speech is present, inability to begin or maintain a conversation
3. Stereotyped or repetitive use of language
4. Lack of imaginative play

Problems with repetitive or stereotyped play include:

1. Preoccupation with one or more behavior patterns
2. Preoccupation with nonfunctional routines or rituals
3. Inappropriate motor movements
4. Preoccupation with specific objects

Characteristics of Autism

Autism Spectrum Disorders are often described as etiologically diverse disorders. Evidence points to genetic (e.g., Bailey et al., 1995) and neurological (e.g., Courchesne et al., 2001) underpinnings of ASDs; however, specific etiological agents have not been identified. Much remains to be learned about risk factors that may be etiologically involved in autism. The lack of scientific clarity implies that clinicians should not place undue importance on etiological agents when conceptualizing cases of autism or when providing feedback to others. Instead, the focus of assessment should be on symptomatology, developmental history (e.g., language development), strengths, and impairments.

Differentiation of autism from other ASDs and from Mental Retardation can be quite difficult. One study found that children with language disorder could be more easily differentiated from children with autism, but autism and PDD-NOS were more difficult to differentiate (Mayes, Volkmar, Hooks, & Cicchetti, 1993). Similarly, differentiation of high functioning children with autism (i.e., those with average or higher intelligence) from children with Asperger's Syndrome can be quite difficult in that such youth with autism may not appear to have communication difficulties (Howlin, 2003).

Some of the assessment tools discussed in this chapter may provide useful information in making distinctions among ASDs as well as related problems. However, there remains a relative lack of research on this issue and no measure to date has clearly shown the ability to differentiate within ASDs in meaningful ways (Ozonoff et al., 2005). Therefore, it is incumbent on the clinician to use a variety of methods to gain a comprehensive picture of the client's difficulties and history such that the most appropriate interventions can then be sought.

Comorbidity

The most frequent comorbid problem for autism is mental retardation, with the majority of children with autism also meeting criteria for mental retardation (American Psychiatric Association, 2000). On the other hand, the majority of individuals with mental retardation do not meet criteria for autism or another ASD. Needless to say, the inclusion of cognitive functioning in assessments of ASDs is critical for case conceptualization and treatment planning. The same, then, can be said for the inclusion of a measure of adaptive functioning in the assessment battery.

As noted by Ozonoff et al. (2005), new difficulties may emerge over the course of development for youth with ASDs such that initial diagnosis as well as treatment planning and progress monitoring are complicated. A common comorbid area of concern, particularly for high-functioning individuals with autism, is in the internalizing problem domain (e.g., Kim, Szatmari, Bryson, Streiner, & Wilson, 2000). However, the validity of commonly used measures of depression and anxiety – such as those discussed in the preceding chapter – for individuals with ASDs is unknown (Ozonoff et al., 2005).

Regular, comprehensive assessment across domains of functioning will aid in tracking treatment gains as well as other important areas of difficulty apart from the primary problems associated with ASDs. For example, many children with ASDs may also present with significant externalizing behavioral problems that occur when expectations are not met, routines change, or due to frustration from communication difficulties. These behaviors may themselves be a primary focus of treatment. In addition, sleep difficulties that may accompany ASDs may warrant specific interventions (Ozonoff et al., 2005).

Specialized Measures of Autism

Infant Behavioral Summarized Evaluation (IBSE)

The IBSE (Adrien, Barthelemy, Perrot, & Roux, 1992) is a unique rating scale in that it is appropriate for infants and preschoolers. One study evaluated some psychometric properties of the scale for a sample of 39 children with autism, 33 with Mental Retardation, and 17 with other handicaps (Adrien et al., 1992). Good inter-rater reliability was found. A factor analysis of 31 items found two factors, with the first factor accounting for most of the items. Adrien et al. also concluded that first factor scores were capable of differentiating the group of children with autism group from the other two groups. The IBSE was also able to differentiate among preschoolers with autism and other children with developmental delays by age 26 months (Desombre et al., 2006).

Autism Diagnostic Interview-Revised (ADI-R)

The ADI-R is a semi-structured diagnostic interview designed to be used with a child's primary caregiver and can be used for anyone with a mental age of 2 years or higher (Lord, Rutter, & Le Couteur, 1994). The ADI-R assesses behaviors relevant to the differential diagnosis of pervasive developmental disorders in individuals from 18 months to adulthood. The ADI focuses on three domains of behavior that are largely consistent with the *DSM-IV* criteria: reciprocal social interaction; communication, and repetitive, restricted, or stereotyped behavior. Scores on the ADI-R have been found to differentiate children with autism from children with other forms of delay (Mildenberger, Sitter, Noterdaeme, & Amorosa, 2001). Another study again found the ADI-R to reliably differentiate between samples of children with autism and children with mental retardation (Lord, Storoschuk, Rutter, & Pickles, 1993). This investigation, however, identified difficulties when trying to differentiate these samples among children with mental ages of less than 18 months, reflecting the continuing dilemma of diagnostic accuracy with low-functioning children.

One study evaluated inter-rater reliability of the ADI-R across seven examiners for one case (Cicchetti, Lord, Koenig, Klin, & Volkmar, 2008) and found perfect agreement for 74% of the items and "poor" agreement on less than 10% of the items. A large scale study of the ADI-R found support for a two-factor model (i.e., social communication and stereotyped behaviors) as well as a three-factor model (i.e., social communication, peer relationships/play, and stereotyped behaviors; Frazier, Youngstrom, Kubu, Sinclair, & Rezai, 2008).

The strength of the ADI-R is its strong research base, including the validity evidence of the current version and its predecessor which goes back to two decades (Le Couteur et al., 1989). However, the ADI-R is quite lengthy, taking anywhere from 90 min to 3 h to administer and score (Ozonoff et al., 2005). Therefore, it may be less practical than other tools in many clinical settings.

Parent Interview for Autism (PIA)

The PIA (see Stone, Coonrod, Pozdol, & Turner, 2003) is a newer alternative to the ADI-R. It is unique in its focus on tracking changes in symptoms over time, with parents rating the frequency of symptoms on a five-point scale. Research has shown good internal consistency and differential validity for the PIA. In addition, changes in PIA ratings, particularly in the areas of social and communicative functioning, were related to changes reflected in other ratings of the child symptomatology (Stone et al., 2003). While generally based on the three core dimensions of autism, the PIA has items that were developed and rationally/theoretically grouped into the following scales (Stone & Hogan, 1993):

- Social Relating Affective Responses Motor Imitation
- Peer Interactions Object Play
- Imaginative Play Language Understanding
- Nonverbal Communication
- Motoric Behaviors
- Sensory Responses Need for Sameness

While the PIA has shown some promise, research is limited, and the validity of the 12 subscales is not documented.

Childhood Autism Rating Scale (CARS)

The CARS (Schopler, Reichler, & Renner, 1988) is a rating form that is typically completed by an observer of the behavior of a child who has reached a developmental age of approximately 2 years or higher. In some cases, an observation period of only about 30 min is used (Sevin, Matson, Coe, & Fee, 1991). Items are rated on a 7-point continuum for the 15 subscales. The CARS is composed of nine portions. It includes items such as a puzzle-like task and a set of toy objects designed to assess make-believe play activity.

The CARS produces a moderately high correlation of.67 with the ABC (Eaves & Milner, 1993). Although this correlation is significant, the two instruments did classify children at differing rates. The CARS correctly identified 98% of the children with autism, whereas the ABC did so for 88% of the sample (Eaves & Milner, 1993).

In an investigation by Sevin et al. (1991), 24 children were assessed with the CARS. The inter-rater reliability of the CARS for these subjects was found to be highly variable. Coefficients were as low as 0.10 (Activity Level) and 0.14 (Intellectual Response), and as high as 0.85 (Relating to People). The inter-rater reliability coefficient for the total score was 0.68.

In spite of such low to modest reliability coefficients, the CARS results showed fairly good concordance with clinician diagnoses of autism (Sevin et al., 1991). The CARS classified 19 of the 24 subjects with autism correctly. Only two of the subjects were incorrectly classified with autism, although this study provided a weak test of differential validity because of the small sample of subjects without autism. Subsequent research has shown that the total score on the CARS correlates highly with the ADI-R but that it also may overidentify autism among children with mental retardation (Saemundsen, Magnusson, Smari, & Sigurdardottir, 2003).

The CARS is a well-known, widely used assessment tool for autism; however, Ozonoff et al. (2005) caution that the content is based on conceptualizations of autism dating prior to *DSM-IV*.

Autism Diagnostic Observation Schedule (ADOS)

The ADOS (Lord, Rutter, DiLavore, & Risi, 2002) is designed to assess symptoms of ASDs in a wide rang of individuals based on age and language skills. The ADOS consists of four modules, with the module selected based on the child's current expressive language and developmental level (i.e., Module 1 for no speech; Module 2 for phrase speech; Module 3 for verbally fluent children and young adolescents; Module 4 for verbally fluent adolescents and adults; Lord et al., 2002). Module 2 is described in Box 19.1.

The ADOS emphasizes the assessment of reciprocal social interaction and communication rather than restricted or repetitive behavior, and it is structured in that the environment for the observation is structured in a standardized way, and the examiner presents predefined tasks to the child in this structured setting. In this way, the examiner serves as both the stimulus for interaction in try to elicit particular responses from the subject and as the recorder of behavior.

A study on the development of the current version of the ADOS revealed strong interrater reliability, internal consistency, and (Lord et al., 2000). The differential validity of the ADOS for distinguishing children with autism vs. other delays was also good. Another study found substantial agreement between the ADOS and ADI-R in the classification of children as having autism or not in children younger

Box 19.1

A Closer View of the Autism Diagnostic Observation Schedule (ADOS)

Together with the ADI-R, the ADOS has been referred to as the current "gold standard" for the diagnosis of ASDs (Ozonoff et al., 2005, p. 524). The ADI-R, of course, allows the clinician to gain a detailed history of the child's development and symptomatology in a semi-structured interview format. This approach is not particularly unique among assessment practices. However, the structured observation format of the ADOS is unique to child assessment in that there are no well-established analogous procedures for assessment of internalizing or externalizing problems.

To further illustrate the content of the ADOS, Module 2, designed for children who speak in phrases, is described below. Module 2 consists of 14 tasks as follows (see Lord et al., 2002):

1. *Construction task*: Designed to assess how the child communicates a need for more objects to complete the task. For example, some children with ASDs may grab the examiner's hand to reach for more objects rather than making a verbal request
2. *Response to name*: Evaluates how readily the child responds to his/her name as said by the examiner or a parent or other stimuli directed to the child (e.g., phrases, touching). Children with ASDs may require more direct stimuli or prompting to response
3. *Make-believe play*: Assesses whether child's play includes imaginative use of objects beyond their usual purpose and the extent to which dolls are used to depict social interaction
4. *Joint interactive play*: Assesses the extent to which the child initiates interaction with the examiner during joint play above and beyond responding to the examiner's statements or requests
5. *Conversation*: Evaluates extent to which the child responds to the examiner's statements or questions in a way that leads to further back-and-forth conversation
6. *Response to joint attention*: The examiner shifts his/her gaze and observes the extent to which the child follows that shift (with or without pointing). Children with ASDs may have difficulty engaging in joint attention in this manner, particularly without other prompts such as pointing
7. *Demonstration task*: Designed to assess how well the child demonstrates common activities (e.g., brushing teeth, getting dressed) without the use of objects.
8. *Description of a picture*: For this task, the examiner attempts to elicit spontaneous language from the child and to observe what kinds of stimuli (from pictures) are of interest to the child
9. *Telling a story from a book*: In addition to assessing the child's spontaneous language and interest in a story, this task, in requiring the child to tell a story from a picture book, evaluates whether the child can provide continuity in the story by sequencing events in the story in a sensible manner
10. *Free play*: This task is designed to assess whether or not the child seeks interaction or involvement from the examiner during free play. In addition, the extent to which the child maintains attention to one task for an appropriate interval is observed. Repetitive behaviors – a symptom of ASDs – may also be evident during this task (Lord et al., 2002)
11. *Birthday party*: This task evaluates the child's ability to participate in a common-scripted event (i.e., birthday part for a doll). Children with ASDs may not engage in the make-believe of imagining the doll as a child or may have trouble participating, including with prompting
12. *Snack*: Assesses how readily the child communicates a preference from a choice of snacks. Other social interaction skills (e.g., gaze, facial expression) are also observed during this task.
13. *Anticipation of a routine with objects*: This task is designed to assess how well a child anticipates a routine (e.g., the response of a balloon when it is deflated or let go) and whether or not the child participates in the routine

(Continues)

Box 19.1 (Continued)

14. *Bubble play*: This task allows the examiner to observe the child's enjoyment of a play activity, social interaction skills, and motor skills in another play context

On an achievement test, Corin's performance on all areas of achievement were in the average range, indicating that her academic achievement is consistent with what would be expected for her age.

Several measures were given to assess Corin's behavioral and emotional functioning. Rating scales were completed by Mrs. Jacobs, two of Corin's teachers, and Corin. Corin's mother and a teacher completed the Achenbach Child Behavior Checklist (CBCL) and Teacher Rating Form (TRF), respectively. This teacher rated Corin as having significant attention problems, delinquent behaviors, and somatic complaints. Mrs. Jacobs did not indicate any significant problems on the CBCL. Despite the reports of attention problems, Corin's teachers stated that they do not believe that Corin has ADHD.

Corin completed several self-report measures that were used to determine her self-perceptions. She was given the Piers-Harris Self-Concept Scale (PHCSCS), and the YSR. On the PHCSCS, Corin rated herself high on anxiety, depression, somatization, and (external) locus of control. On the YSR, Corin's responses were similar to the other self-report measures. Corin also endorsed items that indicate problems with impulse control and compliance.

On the self-report measures, Corin reported some positive qualities for herself. She described herself as being good looking and has having good peer relationships. She reported that all of her friends like her because she is funny. Corin also indicated that her peer relationships and social life at school are the areas in her life that are not currently stressful for her.

As a follow-up measure, Corin was given a structured psychiatric interview on which Corin endorsed all of the items in the area of major depression with the exception of suicidal ideation. Corin described herself as being anxious, and she told the examiner that she often has stomachaches and dizzy spells that she associates with stress. Also, according the structured interview, Corin meets the *DSM* criteria for alcohol abuse. She stated that she frequently drinks large quantities of alcohol, and occasionally, she has blackouts. Corin also admitted to the examiner that she smokes marijuana quite a bit.

From the information gathered a diagnosis of ADHD does not seem appropriate. Corin's acting-out behaviors are more than likely caused by the stress and depression that she currently feels. Current diagnostic impressions are major depression, single episode, moderate, and alcohol abuse.

Recommendations for Corin include:

1. Consultation with a psychiatrist to help determine the most appropriate treatment strategies for Corin's depression.
2. It is also recommended that Corin continue receiving counseling services.
3. Corin is referred to an addictions counselor who works with adolescents who are abusing alcohol.
4. Corin may benefit from group counseling for her alcohol abuse. The best group would be one made up of other teenagers.
5. The Jacobs family should seek family counseling to improve the home situation, particularly in regards to communication and parenting monitoring. Mrs. Jacobs may also benefit from

(Continues)

Box 19.1 (Continued)

individual counseling to help alleviate some of the stress in her life.

6. Corin's teachers reportedly enjoy having Corin in their classroom and seem eager to do what they can to help her. The school psychologist can devise behavior modification plans to be implemented by Corin's teachers to increase Corin's appropriate classroom behaviors. Corin should take part in the development and implementation of the plans.
7. Communication between the school and home is necessary. Weekly reports of Corin's behaviors should be provided. Mrs. Jacobs is encouraged to work with Corin's teachers to devise solutions to any problems that may occur.
8. After six months to a year of intervention, Corin needs to be reevaluated to see if there are still issues of attention problems in the classroom.
9. Corin would benefit from tutoring in algebra.

than age 8. However, the agreement was lower for older individuals (de Bildt et al., 2004). Still, these authors suggested that an assessment battery that includes both the ADOS and ADI-R is suitable, and perhaps the best available, for the assessment of autism.

Gilliam Autism Rating Scale – 2nd Edition (GARS-2)

The GARS-2 (Gilliam, 2008) is a norm-referenced rating scale that can be completed in approximately 5–10 min by parents. The GARS-2 includes 42 items, three scales (i.e., Stereotyped Behaviors, Communication, and Social Interaction) and a total score (Autism Index). Norm-referenced scores are available for the GARS-2, and initial research indicates good internal consistency and differential validity (Gilliam, 2008).

The previous version of the GARS (Gilliam, 1995) has been the subject of much more research. A consistent finding from this research is that many youth otherwise indicated as having autism scored lower on the GARS than on other measures of autism symptoms (Mazefsky & Oswald, 2006; Sikora, Hall, Hartley, Gerrard-Morris, & Cagle, 2008; South et al., 2002). This set of findings may indicate some serious drawbacks of the GARS, although it is unclear whether or not this issue applies to the current version of the GARS. Because the GARS-2 is geared toward screening for symptoms of autism, the clinician may want to use a low threshold of reporting of symptoms on the GARS-2 to initiate further follow-up.

Functional Analysis

In the context of the assessment of ASDs, functional analysis helps the clinician determine "what the child is trying to communicate through the behavior" (Ozonoff et al., 2005, p. 534), which takes on added importance in light of the behavioral problems and communication difficulties that present with ASDs. It is difficult to imagine a comprehensive assessment of ASDs that does not include some form of behavioral observation and functional analysis as a means to determine targets of intervention. Direct observation, coupled with functional analysis, allows the clinician to also confirm or disconfirm the notions of parents, teachers, or other caretakers as to the communicative intent of the child's behavior and on appropriate ways to reduce inappropriate communicative behaviors (e.g., using another's hand to obtain a desired object; biting oneself from frustration). Functional analysis, then, is conducted squarely with behavioral interventions in mind. It is not a tool to differentially diagnose ASDs from other problems.

An Assessment Strategy for Autism

ASDs, including autism specifically, are recognized as having heterogeneous etiologies and highly variable symptomatology among those affected (Campbell et al., 1991). Such within-syndrome variability suggests that children who are either suspected of or diagnosed with autism or other ASDs should have access to multidisciplinary assessment procedures. The severity of autistic symptoms, as demonstrated by the overlap with mental retardation, further emphasizes the need for a range of professionals to be involved in assessing the affected child. Such interdisciplinary work, however, can be challenging if there are no adequate structures for encouraging interdisciplinary practice. Consequently, the psychologist may have to make a concerted effort to go beyond the typical practice regimen and communicate more frequently with colleagues who practice related specialties.

Marcus, Lansing, and Schopler (1993) described one of the better methodologies for fostering multidisciplinary assessment of autism. They described the State of North Carolina TEACCH evaluation system as follows:

> This process includes a developmental/psychoeducational assessment of the child, psychological assessment, detailed parent interviewing including assessment of adaptive functioning, and a medical screening. This integrated and multiperspective approach generates comprehensive data on diagnosis, intellectual and adaptive functioning, motor, language, and social functioning, behavior problems, medical factors, family functioning and school or community factors. The data are sufficiently detailed and objective to be organized into dimensions or axes that both overlap with and extend beyond the DSM-III-R system (p. 350).

In situations in which interdisciplinary assessment and intervention teams are not as readily available, it is still incumbent on the clinician to utilize methods that assess ASDs comprehensively and specifically, rather than rely on subjective clinical opinion or measures (e.g., IQ tests) that do not differentially diagnose ASDs from other developmental delays. Having said that, the incremental validity and clinical utility of specific ASD measures are largely unknown (Ozonoff et al., 2005). As with other areas of child assessment, more research is needed as to the most sound, parsimonious battery that would address referrals for ASDs and lend itself to useful recommendations.

Nevertheless, the severity and frankness of the symptomatology of ASDs require us to emphasize different aspects of our five-stage paradigm: screening, classification, comorbidities, alternative causes, and treatment considerations (see Table 19.1).

The screening process for ASDs is aimed primarily at the population of children with developmental delays as opposed to the general population. We advise that clinicians consider the possibility of ASDs in all samples of young children with developmental disabilities. Because the nature of ASDs usually does not allow the child to serve as a source of screening information, parent and teacher ratings are likely to be the most fruitful. The time-efficiency of such ratings

TABLE 19.1 Assessment Questions Related to Childhood Autism Spectrum Disorders and Implications for Assessment

Characteristic	Implications for Assessment
Screening	Administer screening measures; target young children with signs of developmental delay
	Determine need for further assessment
Classification	Assess for presence of symptoms that meet *DSM-IV* criteria
	Determine stability and duration of symptoms
	Determine age of onset
Comorbidities	Assess for presence of mental retardation
	Determine the influence of autism on school performance, adaptive behavior, development, etc.
	Assess social relationships and peer social status
Alternative causes	Obtain developmental and medical histories
	Differential diagnosis/rule out of Rhett's Disorder, Asperger's Syndrome, language disorders, mental retardation, and hearing impairment
Treatment considerations	Assess adaptive behavior assets and deficits
	Identify behavior problems that require intervention
	Assess caregiver stress and caregiver ability to provide adaptive behavior instruction and behavioral problem management
	Evaluate response to previous interventions

argues for their routine use with these populations.

Classification of the child as having ASDs requires meeting the *DSM-IV-TR* criteria outlined earlier. The classification process will depend heavily on caretaker information such as detailed histories/interviews, and possibly child behavior ratings. Furthermore, medical, language, and other assessment data will need to be integrated in order to make differential diagnoses.

The most likely comorbid condition for autism is mental retardation. An in-depth assessment of intelligence and adaptive behavior development is, therefore, required in every comprehensive study of a child suspected of autism or a related disorder. Sensory impairments must also be ruled out by other clinicians.

The process of ruling out alternative causes is a lengthy one requiring full participation by medical and other professionals in the assessment process. Neurological problems, in particular, should be ruled out as primary etiologies for the child's behavior. As noted above, the differentiation within types of ASDs is also often quite difficult (see Box 19.2 for a specific discussion of the assessment of Asperger's Syndrome).

A central aspect of psychological intervention for children with ASDs is skill development in a variety of domains. A structured behavioral observation (e.g., ADOS, functional analysis) and a comprehensive measure of adaptive behavior are typically very useful for defining needed skills and evaluating the effectiveness of intervention.

In Box 19.1, we provide a case example of this assessment approach for a child with autism.

Box 19.2

Issues in the Assessment of Asperger's Disorder

The most straightforward distinction between Asperger's Disorder and autism is the lack of language difficulties seen in the former (American Psychiatric Association, 2000). However, this difference is hard to pinpoint for youth who have average- to above-average intellectual functioning (and thus, typically demonstrate no impairments in verbal communication). A careful, detailed history of developmental delays is critical in differentiating ASDs from other forms of delays and for differentiating among ASDs. For example, past and present impairments in social skills and the presence of stereotypical behaviors in the absence of a history of language delays would be more indicative of Asperger's Disorder than autism. There has been an increased availability of specific screening tools for Asperger's Disorder and other ASDs. The Gilliam Asperger's Disorder Scale (GADS; Gilliam, 2001) is a 32-item screener that is meant to be completed by a parent, teacher, or clinician. Items load on to four scales: Social Interaction, Cognitive Patterns, Restricted Behavioral Patterns, and Pragmatic Skills. The Asperger Syndrome Diagnostic Scale (ASDS; Myles, Bock, & Simpson, 2001) consists of 50 items to be completed by a caretaker, teacher, or clinician with five scales: Cognitive, Language, Social, Maladaptive, and Sensorimotor. Another example is the Krug Asperger's Disorder Index (KADI; Krug & Arick, 2003) which consists of 32 items and yields a total score. Research on the differential validity is limited.

An exception is Campbell's (2005) study that compared these rating scales and two others that had been used in research. Campbell cited concerns regarding each of these measures. For the ASDS, Campbell noted that the standardization sample was weak, particularly due to the lack of there being no independent diagnosis of Asperger's Disorder in that sample. The GADS was described as having a stronger standardization sample, although the Asperger's Disorder diagnoses in this sample were unconfirmed. In addition, internal consistency was less-than-desirable (Campbell, 2005). The KADI was described as the best of these measures overall in terms of reliability (i.e., internal consistency, stability, and interrater agreement) as well as in content validity. However, the standardization of the KADI also lacked information on independent diagnoses. Additionally, for all three of these scales, the cognitive functioning of individuals in the standardization sample with autism was not provided, which is important in determining how well a measure of Aspeger's Disorder helps distinguish between children with Asperger's Disorder *vs.* high functioning children with autism (Campbell, 2005). Therefore, at present, such measures should be used as one potential component of assessments for ASDs but in no way replace detailed histories obtained through interviews and behavioral observations in determining the child's specific impairments.

A Sample Case of Autism in a Child with Neurological Impairment

Julie was a 5-year, 1-month-old girl who was referred by her parents.

Referral Information

Julie was referred for a psychological evaluation by her parents. Original referral questions included concern about delayed language development, short attention span, difficulty in her kindergarten class, and a possible learning disability. Subsequently, however, Julie had two seizures and was diagnosed as having tuberous sclerosis and seizure disorder. On learning that tuberous sclerosis often affects a child's intelligence, her parents requested a thorough evaluation to determine Julie's current level of functioning.

Background Information

Julie is a 5-year-old girl who lives with both parents. Her mother reported that she had no serious difficulties when she was pregnant with Julie. Julie was reportedly born full-term and weighed 7 pounds, 0 ounces. Both Julie and her mother were reportedly in good condition at the time of birth. Julie did, however, have an open sore on her back that was surrounded by a purple mark. The doctor remarked at the time that this type of wound was very unusual.

According to her mother, Julie has had two seizures. The first was reportedly about 6 weeks prior to this evaluation. Her mother describes these seizures as lasting about a minute and not involving severe convulsions. Julie was seen by a neurologist. According to Julie's medical reports, she was somewhat difficult to understand and hyperactive during that medical examination. Her doctor had difficulty obtaining her cooperation. Her physical condition appeared to be normal, except for a large scar on her right hip and skin lesions on her face and extremities. Based on Julie's physical condition, recent seizures, EEG results, and CAT scan results, she was diagnosed as having seizure disorder and tuberous sclerosis, a genetic disorder associated with tumors in the brain and internal organs and skin lesions on the face and body. Her doctor prescribed Tegretol for seizure control.

According to her mother, Julie has also had frequent ear infections, beginning at 8 months of age and continuing until 3 months ago. At that time, she had tubes placed in her ears. She has reportedly had no difficulties since then. She had a hearing examination 2 months ago that indicated a slight hearing loss in the right ear. Julie has also had frequent colds, according to her mother. Julie's vision is reportedly normal.

Julie's mother described Julie's development as inconsistent. She seemed to learn gross motor skills at a normal rate, but her fine motor and language development appeared to be delayed. She reportedly spoke her first words at 9 months, but by 18 months, she could still speak only four words. Her mother states that Julie did not speak in sentences until she was 2½ years old. Her speech articulation is reportedly clear, but her language is still delayed. She was reportedly in speech therapy until recently.

Her mother stated that Julie is sweet, has a good sense of humor, and enjoys singing. Julie, however, can also be stubborn and sometimes does not seem to listen to or obey her mother. Her mother noted that Julie likes to play by herself rather than with other children. She also reported that Julie can be easily overstimulated in that she seems uncomfortable in crowded or noisy places, is very energetic and active, has a short attention span, and is impulsive (e.g., not waiting for her turn, grabbing objects at stores without permission). She added that Julie seems to require a great deal of parental attention.

Julie has reportedly been in a preschool program since she was 2 years old. Her mother stated that Julie's teachers have been concerned because Julie did not communicate in school, had difficulty doing age-appropriate work, required much teacher attention, and seemed to lack self-esteem and confidence. Julie is now enrolled in a kindergarten class. Her current teacher reported that Julie is a sweet child and seems to want to please others. Julie reportedly memorizes well and knows many songs.

Julie's teacher also stated, however, that Julie shows many behaviors that make it difficult to teach her. She reportedly spends most of the day by herself, talking only to herself or inanimate objects. She seems to repeat, over and over, phrases that she has heard adults say. According to her teacher,

Julie does not interact with the other children. When called on in class, she seems embarrassed and then blurts out any answer. She reportedly has a very short attention span and also sometimes leaves the room without teacher permission. Her teacher stated that she is teased by the other children because of her behavior, which includes chewing on her mat and her clothes. According to her teacher, Julie has not learned many academic skills. She seems to have learned a few basic concepts, such as shapes. She can also make a capital "A," but it is frequently upside down. She reportedly writes and works with other objects upside down frequently and does not seem to recognize that she is doing so. She reportedly cannot complete worksheets, as she just draws lines up and down the page or colors the whole page one color. According to her teacher, Julie sometimes does better with one-on-one assistance, but at other times, she will not accept help from her teacher.

Julie was briefly observed at school during lunch. She was sitting at the end of the table by herself and did not interact with the other children. Although she had talked with the observer previously, she showed little response to her at this time. When asked if she remembered the observer, she said that she did, but she still did not interact with her. She just continued eating.

Behavioral Observations

Julie was tested over a 2-day period. Three examiners participated in her evaluation. She was brought to the first testing session by her mother. She seemed very uncomfortable meeting strangers and clung to her mother. Her mother carried her to the testing room and stayed for a while until Julie was more comfortable. Julie did not become relaxed with the examiners for some time. Adequate rapport for testing purposes was finally established.

During testing, Julie was very active and distractible. The examiners had difficulty keeping her attention on the test materials. She required much direction and attention from the examiners to stay on task. She frequently wanted to play with the other toys. At one point, she sat on the floor, facing the wall. When asked what she was doing, she said she was in time-out. On further questioning, she responded that she was put there because she did not pay attention. Later, she again sat on the floor, this time repeating "Stephanie, it's time to go to school." The examiner had difficulty redirecting her from this behavior. This type of behavior seemed to occur most when Julie was being asked to perform a task that was difficult for her. After this last time, Julie could not be enticed to pay any more attention to the test materials. She got up and left the room without the examiner's permission.

Julie was more cooperative during the second testing session. She seemed much more comfortable with the examiners and accompanied them readily to the testing room. She was, however, still very distractible and active, requiring much examiner attention for her to stay on task.

Test Results and Interpretations

Intellectual Functioning

Julie's intellectual functioning was far, to well below, that of her same-aged peers. This level of functioning is consistent with her teacher's and mother's reports of her ability and with her current school performance. Her performance across subtests was consistent, showing no relative strengths or weaknesses.

Visual Motor Integration

On a test of visual motor integration, Julie's performance was at or above that of 8% of children of her age, suggesting that her visual motor integration and fine motor skills are well below average. Her mother and teacher also reported difficulty with fine motor tasks, such as drawing and writing.

Academic Achievement

On a standardized test of academic achievement, only two subtests were able to be administered. Her performance on the subtests administered was well to far below average. On these subtests and informal assessment, Julie showed the ability to sing the alphabet and count objects with one-to-one correspondence.

Adaptive Behavior

The Vineland-2 is a measure of Julie's ability to take care of herself, get along with others, and live in the community appropriately for her age. It includes four domains: Communication, Daily Living Skills, Socialization, and Motor Skills. On the Vineland-2, Julie's mother indicated that Julie's overall ability in these domains is slightly below average for her age. Most of her scores were consistent with her overall Adaptive Composite score. Her score in the Socialization domain was slightly higher than the others. This score, however, is not consistent with teacher and parent reports or behavioral observations.

Julie's teacher completed the Vineland-2, Classroom Edition. Her teacher indicated that Julie's adaptive behavior is variable. Julie's score on the Daily Living Skills domain from her teacher's report is similar to that given by her mother and is in the Below-Average range. However, her other scores are in the Well Below-Average range, more consistent with her intelligence test scores. Her Socialization domain score is inconsistent with that of her mother's rating but more consistent with other assessment findings. It indicates far below-average socialization skills for Julie at school relative to same-aged peers.

Overall, the report of Julie's mother and teacher on the Vineland-2 indicates that Julie's adaptive behavior is below what would be expected for her age but is somewhat above her intellectual ability as assessed in this evaluation. However, it does not appear that a diagnosis of Mental Retardation is appropriate at this point, as Julie's adaptive functioning is not far enough below what would be expected for her age to warrant such a diagnosis.

Rating Scales

Julie's mother and father completed the Achenbach CBCL, whereas her teacher completed the TRF. This rating scale assesses behavioral and emotional problems of children. Although the raters reported similar behavioral patterns, only Julie's father indicated that Julie has any serious problems. He rated Julie as having problems in the areas of social withdrawal and hyperactivity. Julie's mother and teacher also rated her high in these areas, but not significantly so. These findings are consistent with teacher and parent report and behavioral observations in that Julie has some incidents of apparent overactivity in the classroom and consistently seems uncomfortable interacting with others. Based on Julie's current emotional, behavioral, social, intellectual, and adaptive functioning, as well as her history of communicative delays, a diagnosis of Pervasive Developmental Disorder, Not Otherwise Specified seems appropriate.

Summary and Conclusions

Julie is a 5-year-old girl referred by her parents to determine her current level of functioning. She has been diagnosed as having seizure disorder and tuberous sclerosis. Her mother reported that her language and fine motor development were delayed. Her teacher reported that she made little progress in adjusting to kindergarten or learning basic academic skills. Parent and teacher reports indicate that she is active and inattentive and requires much adult attention and supervision. These behaviors were also observed in the testing situation, in which examiners had much difficulty getting Julie to cooperate and attend to the tasks. She was very active and distractible. Parent and teacher reports, as well as observation during testing, also suggest that Julie displays several unusual behaviors, such as talking to herself or inanimate objects, repeating the same phrases or motions, panting heavily at times, chewing on clothes, preferring to stay by herself, and not interacting with other children.

Most of Julie's test results, including intellectual, achievement, visual motor, and some adaptive behavior areas, are in the Well Below-Average range. Other adaptive behavior scores, however, were only slightly below average for her age. Information from rating scales indicates that Julie tends to be socially withdrawn, hyperactive, distractible, slow to learn or adapt to new situations, and sometimes fussy too.

Taking all of the assessment information together, the diagnosis of Pervasive Developmental Disorder–Not Otherwise Specified seems appropriate. At this time, a diagnosis of mental retardation does not seem applicable. Although her intelligence test scores are within the mild mentally retarded range, her adaptive behavior scores lie outside the mental retardation range. Both of these areas of functioning must be significantly below average to warrant a diagnosis of Mental Retardation.

Recommendations

Julie should be evaluated again at the end of this academic year to assess her progress. At this time the following recommendations are made for Julie:

1. Julie would benefit from a highly structured educational environment where she can get the attention and supervision, she needs, to learn. Her parents should consult school personnel in order to determine the most appropriate placement for her
2. Julie will need much individual instruction, gradually moving to small-group instruction
3. Julie's classroom assignments should be within the range appropriate for her intellectual and academic levels
4. Julie should be allowed to learn and work at her own pace
5. Instructional tasks should be organized into short, structured units
6. Julie will need to be taught at a very concrete and practical level, using many manipulatives and teaching aids
7. Skills and concepts will need to be repeated and reviewed often for Julie to master them
8. Julie may be helped by being tutored by someone who has been trained in tutoring children with her set of difficulties
9. Julie's parents and teachers should continue to search for activities that she does well and enjoys and encourage her in these activities
10. Julie should be provided with increased opportunities to learn and practice age-appropriate self-care and socialization skills
11. Julie's parents and teachers should continue to use behavioral management strategies, such as positive reinforcement and time-out, to help her learn appropriate behavior. Her parents may wish to attend sessions with a mental health specialist to become more facile with these techniques
12. Inappropriate behavior should be ignored as much as possible, while appropriate behavior is rewarded with praise and other appropriate reinforcers
13. Communication between school and home should be maintained. A home-school note, in which Julie is rewarded at home and for appropriate behavior at school, may be helpful
14. Julie should be allowed as much as possible to be around other children her own age, so that she can learn socialization and develop behavioral skills by observation and interaction with them
15. Julie's parents should closely monitor her physical functioning and symptoms and maintain regular contact with her physicians regarding her seizures
16. Julie should be evaluated in approximately 1 year to determine her level

of functioning, particularly after the above strategies have been implemented.

Conclusions

Autism and its related disorders are among the most difficult of the developmental disorders to reliably classify, yet classification is central to research efforts aimed at prevention and intervention. Considerable progress has been made in defining the three core dimensions of impairment that separate this condition from other developmental disabilities and in developing assessment tools geared toward evaluating these dimensions. Many of these tools appear to be useful in devising intervention strategies for individuals with ASDs.

Many of the available instruments also differentiate ASDs from other developmental disabilities, but this differentiating is particularly difficult for very young children and those with more severe developmental delays. While new methods of assessment have made strides in terms of differential validity, considerably more progress is needed. The most promising method for assessing and classifying autism at this time is a thorough and standard interview of the child's primary caregiver along with either a structured observation that systematically evaluates symptoms of ASDs and/or a functional analysis that evaluates the communicative intent of a child's behavioral problems. Complementing the diagnostic process is the use of intelligence and adaptive behavior scale such as the Vineland-2.

In summary, current recommendations (e.g., de Bildt et al., 2004; Ozonoff et al., 2005) call for a combination of a detailed developmental history (e.g., ADI-R), behavioral observation (e.g., ADOS), assessment of cognitive functioning, and assessment of adaptive functioning.

Chapter Summary

1. Autistic Disorder is part of a class of problems known as Pervasive Developmental Disorders (PDD) or Autism Spectrum Disorders (ASDs)
2. The *DSM* emphasizes three classes of symptoms that are central to the disorder: social interaction problems, communication problems, and repetitive and stereotyped behaviors
3. Much remains to be learned about risk factors that may be etiologically involved in autism
4. Differentiation within ASDs and of autism from Pervasive Developmental Disorder – Not Otherwise Specified (PDD-NOS) and Mental Retardation is difficult
5. The most frequent comorbid problem for autism is mental retardation
6. The Autism Diagnostic Interview – Revised (ADI-R) is a semi-structured diagnostic interview that is designed to be used with a child's primary caregiver. It provides for a detailed history of the domains of functioning relevant to ASDs
7. The Autism Diagnostic Observation Schedule (ADOS) is designed for the assessment of autism through structured observation in a classroom or clinical setting. Four modules are available based on the individual's expressive communication skills and developmental level
8. Assessment strategies such as functional analysis can be useful in determining the communicative intent of problem behaviors in children with ASDs and may directly translate to intervention plans
9. There has been an increase in rating scales aimed at screening for Asperger's Disorder. However, more research on the psychometrics and utility of these measures is needed
10. The within-syndrome variability associated with autism suggests that children who are either suspected of, or diagnosed with, the disorder should have access to multidisciplinary assessment procedures

References

AAMR. (1992). *Mental retardation: Definition, classification and systems of supports* (9th ed.). Annapolis, MD: Author.

Abad, J., Forns, M., Amador, J. A., & Martorell, B. (2000). Youth self-report reliability and validity in an adolescent sample. *Psicothema, 12*(1), 49–54.

Abidin, R. R. (1986). *Parenting stress index manual* (2nd ed.). Charlottesville, VA: Pediatric Psychology Press.

Abidin, R. R. (1995). Parenting Stress Index: professional manual (3rd ed.). Odessa, FL: Psychological Assessment.

Abidin, R., Flens, J.R., & Austin, W.G. (1995). The Parenting Stress Index. In R.P. Archer (Ed.), Forensic uses of clinical assessment instruments (pp. 297-328). Mahwah, NJ: Erlbaum.

Abikoff, H., & Klein, R. G. (1992). Attention-deficit hyperactivity and conduct disorder: Comorbidity and implications for treatment. *Journal of Consulting and Clinical Psychology, 60*, 881–892.

Ablow, J. C., Measelle, J. R., Kraemer, H. C., Harrington, R., Luby, J., Smider, N., et al. (1999). The MacArthur three-city outcome study: Evaluating multi-informant measures of young children's symptomatology. *Journal of the American Academy of Child & Adolescent Psychiatry, 38*, 1580–1590.

Abramowitz, A. J., & O'Leary, S. G. (1991). Behavioral interventions for the classroom: Implications for students with ADHD. *School Psychology Review, 20*, 220–234.

Achenbach, T. M. (1982). Assessment and taxonomy of children's behavior disorders. In B. B. Lahey & A. E. Kazdin (Eds.), *Advances in clinical child psychology* (Vol. 5, pp. 1–38). New York: Plenum.

Achenbach, T. M. (1986). *Child behavior checklist-direct observation form* (rev. ed.). Burlington: University of Vermont.

Achenbach, T. M. (1991a). *Integrative guide for the 1991 CBCL/4–18, YSR, and TRF profiles.* Burlington: University of Vermont, Department of Psychiatry.

Achenbach, T. M. (1991b) *Manual for the child behavior checklist/4–18 and 1991 profile.* Burlington: University of Vermont, Department of Psychiatry.

Achenbach, T. M. (1991c). *Manual for the teacher's report form and 1991 profile.* Burlington: University of Vermont, Department of Psychiatry.

Achenbach, T. M. (1991d). *Manual for the youth self-report & 1991 profile.* Burlington: University of Vermont, Department of Psychiatry.

Achenbach, T. M. (1993). *Empirically based taxonomy: How to use syndromes and profile types derived from the CBCL/4–18, TRT & YSR.* Burlington: University of Vermont, Department of Psychiatry.

Achenbach, T. M. (1995). Empirically based assessment & taxonomy: Applications to clinical research. *Psychological Assessment, 7*, 261–274.

Achenbach, T. M. (1997). *Manual for the young adult self-report and young adult behavior checklist.* Burlington: University of Vermont, Department of Psychiatry

Achenbach, T. M., & Rescorla, L. A. (2000). *Manual for the ASEBA preschool forms and profiles.* Burlington, VT: Research Center for Children, Youth, and Families.

Achenbach, T. M. (2001). *Manual for the ASEBA school-age forms and profiles.* Burlington, VT: Research Center for Children, Youth, and Families.

Achenbach, T. M., Conners, C. K., Quay, H. C., Verhulst, F. C., & Howell, C. T. (1989). Replication of empirically derived syndromes as a basis for taxonomy of child/adolescent psychopathology. *Journal of Abnormal Child Psychology, 17*, 299–323.

Achenbach, T. M., & Edelbrock, C. (1978). The classification of child psychopathology: A review and analysis of empirical efforts. *Psychological Bulletin, 85*, 1275–1301.

Achenbach, T. M., & Edelbrock, C. (1983). *Manual for the child behavior checklist and revised child behavior profile.* Burlington: University of Vermont, Department of Psychiatry.

Achenbach, T. M., & Edelbrock, C. (1986). *Manual for the teacher's report form and teacher- version of the child*

P.J. Frick et al., *Clinical Assessment of Child and Adolescent Personality and Behavior*,
DOI 10.1007/978-1-4419-0641-0_5, © Springer Science+Business Media, LLC 2009

behavior profile. Burlington: University of Vermont, Department of Psychiatry.

Achenbach, T. M., & Edelbrock, C. (1991). *Manual for the youth self report and profile.* Burlington: University of Vermont Department of Psychiatry.

Achenbach, T. M., & Howell, C. T. (1993). Are American children's problems getting worse? A 13-year comparison. *Journal of the American Academy of Child and Adolescent Psychiatry, 32,* 1145–1154.

Achenbach, T. M., Howell, C. T., McConaughy, S. H., & Stanger, C. (1995a). Six-year predictors of problems in a national sample of children & youth: I. Cross-informant syndromes. *Journal of the American Academy of Child and Adolescent Psychiatry, 34,* 336–347.

Achenbach, T. M., Howell, C. T., McConaughy, S. H., & Stanger, C. (1995b). Six-year predictors of problems in a national sample of children & youth: II. Signs of disturbance. *Journal of the American Academy of Child and Adolescent Psychiatry, 34,* 488–498.

Achenbach, T. M., Howell, C. T., McConaughy, S. H., & Stanger, C. (1998). Six-year predictors of problems in a national sample: IV. Young adult signs of disturbance. *Journal of the American Academy of Child and Adolescent Psychiatry, 37,* 718–727.

Achenbach, T. M., Howell, C. T., Quay, H. C., & Conners, C. K. (1991). National survey of problems and competencies among four-to sixteen-year-olds: Parents' reports for normative and clinical samples. *Monographs of the Society for Research in Child Development, 56*(3), 1–131.

Achenbach, T. M., & McConaughy, S. H. (1987). *Empirically based assessment of child and adolescent psychopathology: Practical applications.* Newbury Park, CA: Sage.

Achenbach, T. M., & McConaughy, S. H. (1996). Relations between DSM-1V and empirically based assessment. *School Psychology Review, 25,* 330–342.

Achenbach, T. M., & McConaughy, S. H. (1997). *Empirically based assessment of child & adolescent psychopathology* (2nd ed.). Thousand Oaks, CA: Sage.

Achenbach, T. M., McConaughy, S. H., & Howell, C. T. (1987). Child/adolescent behavioral and emotional problems: Implications of cross-informant correlations for situational specificity. *Psychological Bulletin, 101,* 213–232.

Achenbach, T. M., & Rescorla, L. A. (2000). *Manual for the ASEBA preschool forms & profiles.* Burlington: University of Vermont, Department of Psychiatry.

Adrien, J. L., Barthelemy, C., Perrot, A., & Roux, S. (1992). Validity and reliability of the infant behavioral summarized evaluation (IBSE): A rating scale for the assessment of young children with autism and developmental disorders. *Journal of Autism and Developmental Disorders, 22,* 371–394.

AERA, APA, & NCME. (1999). *Standards for educational and psychological testing.* Washington, DC: AERA.

Agras, W. S., Chapin, H. N., & Oliveau, D. C. (1972). The natural history of phobias: Course and prognosis. *Archives of General Psychiatry, 26,* 315–317.

Albano, A. M., & Silverman, W. K. (1996). *Anxiety disorders interview schedule for DSM-IV: Clinician manual.* New York: The Psychological Corporation.

Albert-Corush, J., Firestone, P., & Goodman, J. T. (1986). Attention and impulsivity characteristics of the biological and adoptive parents of hyperactive and normal children. *American Journal of Orthopsychiatry, 56,* 413–423.

Alderman, E., & Kennedy, C. (1995). *The right to privacy.* New York: Alfred A. Knopf.

Allen, J. C., & Hollifield, J. (1990). Using the Rorschach with children and adolescents: The Exner Comprehensive System. In C. R. Reynolds & R. W. Kamphaus (Eds.), *Handbook of psychological and educational assessment of children: Personality, behavior, and context* (pp. 168–185). New York: Guilford.

Allen, J. C., & Hollifield, J. (2003). Using the Rorschach with children and adolescents: The Exner Comprehensive System. In C. R. Reynolds & R. W. Kamphaus (Eds.), *Handbook of psychological and educational assessment of children: Personality, behavior, and context – 2nd edition* (pp. 182–197). New York: Guilford.

Allen, M. J., & Yen, W. M. (1979). *Introduction to measurement theory.* Long Grove, IL: Waveland.

Altepeter, T. S., & Breen, M. J. (1989). The home situations questionnaire (HSQ) and the school situations questionnaire (SSQ): Normative data and an evaluation of psychometric properties. *Journal of Psychoeducational Assessment, 7,* 312–322.

Aman, M. G., Werry, J. S., Fitzpatrick, J., Lowe, M., & Waters, J. (1983). Factor structure and norms for the revised behavior problem checklist on New Zealand children. *Australian and New Zealand Journal of Psychiatry, 17,* 354–360.

Aman, M. G. (1994). Instruments for assessing treatment effects in developmentally delayed populations. *Assessment in Rehabilitation and Exceptionality, 1,* 1–19.

Amanat, E., & Butler, C. (1984). Oppressive behaviors in the families of depressed children. *Family Therapy, 11,* 65–77.

Amato, P. R., & Keith, B. (1991). Parental divorce and the well-being of children: A meta-analysis. *Psychological Bulletin, 110,* 26–46.

Ambrosini, P. J. (2000). Historical development and present status of the schedule for affective disorders and schizophrenia for school-age children (K-SADS). *Journal of the American Academy of Child and Adolescent Psychiatry, 39,* 39–48.

American Educational Research Association. American Psychological Association, and National Council on Measurement in Education. (1999). *Standards for educational and psychological testing.* Washington, DC: Author.

American Psychiatric Association. (1968). *The diagnostic and statistical manual of mental disorders* (2nd ed.). Washington, DC: Author.

American Psychiatric Association. (1980). *The diagnostic and statistical manual of mental disorders* (3rd ed.). Washington, DC: Author.

American Psychiatric Association. (1987). *7 he diagnostic and statistical manual of mental disorders* (3rd ed., rev.). Washington, DC: Author.

American Psychiatric Association. (1994). *The diagnostic and statistical manual of mental disorders* (4th ed.). Washington, DC: Author.

American Psychiatric Association. (2000). *The diagnostic and statistical manual of mental disorders* (4th ed., text rev.). Washington, DC: Author.

American Psychological Association. (1985). *Standards for educational and psychological testing.* Washington, DC: Author.

American Psychological Association. (1992). Ethical principles of psychologists and code of conduct. *American Psychologist, 47*, 1612–1628.

American Psychological Association. (1994). Guidelines for child custody evaluations in divorce proceedings. *American Psychologist, 49*, 677–680.

Ames, L. B., Metraux, R., Rodell, J. L., & Walker, R. (1974). *Child Rorschach responses* (rev. ed.). New York: Bruner/Mazel.

Anastasi, A. (1992). Introductory remarks. In K. F. Geisinger (Ed.), *Psychological testing of Hispanics* (pp. 1–7). Washington, DC: American Psychological Association.

Anastasi, A. (1988). Psychological testing (16th ed). New York: Macmillan.

Anastasi, A., & Urbina, S. (1998). *Psychological testing* (7th ed.). New York: Prentice-Hall.

Anderson, J. C., Williams, S., McGee, R., & Silva, P. A. (1987). *DSM-III* disorders in preadolescent children. *Archives of General Psychiatry, 44*, 69–76.

Angold, A., & Costello, J. (2000). The child and adolescent psychiatric assessment (CAPA). *Journal of the American Academy of Child and Adolescent Psychiatry, 39*, 49–58.

Angold, A., Costello, E. J., & Erkanli, A. (1999). Comorbidity. *Journal of Child Psychology and Psychiatry & Allied Disciplines, 40*, 57–87.

Angold, A., Erkanli, A., Egger, H. I., & Costello, F. J. (2000). Stimulant treatment for children: A community perspective. *Journal of the American Academy of Child and Adolescent Psychiatry, 39*, 975–983.

Applegate, B., Lahey, B. B., Hart, E. L., Waldman, I., Biederman, J., Hynd, G. W., et al. (1997). The age of onset criterion for DSM-W attention-deficit hyperactivity disorder: A report of the DSM-IV field trials. *Journal of the American Academy of Child and Adolescent Psychiatry, 36*, 1211–1221.

Archer, R. P. (1992). *MMPI-A: Assessing adolescent psychopathology.* Hillsdale, NJ: Erlbaum.

Archer, R. P. (1997). *MMPI-A: Assessing adolescent psychopathology* (2nd ed.). Mahwah: Lawrence Erlbaum.

Archer, R. P. (2005). Implications of MMPI/MMPI-A findings for understanding adolescent development and psychopathology. *Journal of Personality Assessment, 85*, 257–270.

Archer, R. P., Belevich, J. K. S., & Elkins, D. E. (1994). Item-level and scale-level factor structures of the MMPI-A. *Journal of Personality Assessment, 62*, 332–345.

Archer, R. P., & Elkins, D. E. (1999). Identification of random responding on the MMPI-A. *Journal of Personality Assessment, 73*, 407–421.

Archer, R. P., Handel, R. W., & Lynch, K. D. (2001). The effectiveness of MMPI-A items in discriminating between normative and clinical samples. *Journal of Personality Assessment, 77*, 420–435.

Archer, R. P., & Krishnamurthy, R. (1994). A structural summary approach for the MMPI-A: Development and empirical correlates. *Journal of Personality Assessment, 63*, 554–573.

Archer, R., Krishnamurthy, R., & Stredny, R. (2007). The Minnesota Multiphasic Personality Inventory-Adolescent. In S. R. Smith (Ed.), *The clinical assessment of children and adolescents: A practitioner's handbook* (pp. 237–266). Mahwah, NJ: Lawrence Erlbaum Associates.

Archer, R. P., & Krishnamurthy, R. (1997). MMPI-A and Rorschach indices related to depression and conduct disorder: An evaluation of the incremental validity hypothesis. *Journal of Personality Assessment, 69*, 517–533.

Archer, R. P., & Newsom, C. R. (2000). Psychological test usage with adolescent clients: Survey update. *Assessment, 7, 227–235.*

Archer, R. P., & Slesinger, D. (1999). MMPI-A patterns related to the endorsement of suicidal ideation. *Assessment, 6*(1), 51–59.

Arita, A. A., & Baer, R. A. (1998). Validity of selected MMPI-A content scales. *Psychological Assessment, 10*, 59–63.

Arney, F., Rogers, H., Baghurst, P., Sawyer, M., & Prior, M. (2008). The reliability and validity of the parenting scale for Australian mothers of pre-school aged children. *Australian Journal of Psychology, 60*, 44–52.

Arnold, D. S., O'Leary, S. G., Wolff, L. S., & Acker, M. M. (1993). The Parenting Scale: A measure of dysfunctional parenting in discipline situations. *Psychological Assessment, 5*, 137–144.

Aronen, E. T., Teerikangas, O. M., & Kurkela, S. A. (1999). The continuity of psychiatric symptoms from adolescence into young adulthood. *Nordic Journal of Psychiatry, 53*(5), 333–338.

Arseneault, L., Kim-Cohen, J., Taylor, A., Caspi, A., & Moffit, T. (2005). Psychometric evaluation of 5- and 7-year-old children's self-reports of conduct problems. *Journal of Abnormal Child Psychology, 33*(5), 537–550.

Asher, S. R., & Hymel, S. (1981). Children's social competence in peer relations: Sociometric and behavioral assessment. In J. D. Wine & M. D. Smye (Eds.), *Social competence* (pp. 125–157). New York: Guilford Press.

Asher, S. R., Singleton, L. C., Tinsley, B. R., & Hymel, S. (1979). A reliable sociometric measure for preschool children. *Developmental Psychology, 15*, 443–444.

Assing, R. (1998, August). *BASC parent rating scale (Spanish translation): Validity study.* Paper presented at the annual meeting of the American Psychological Association, San Francisco.

Aten, J. D., Madson, M. B., & Kruse, S. J. (2008). The supervision genogram: A tool for preparing supervisors-in-training. *Psychotherapy: Theory, Research, Practice, Training, 45*, 111–116.

Atkins, M. S., Pelham, W. E., & Licht, M. (1985). A comparison of objective classroom measures and teacher ratings of attention deficit disorder. *Journal of Abnormal Child Psychology, 13*, 155–167.

Atkinson, L. (1990). Standard errors of prediction for the Vineland adaptive behavior scales. *Journal of School Psychology, 28*, 255–259.

August, G. J., McDonald, A. W., Realmuto, G. M., & Skare, S. S. (1996). Hyperactive and aggressive pathways: Effect of demographic, family, and child characteristics on children's adaptive functioning. *Journal of Clinical Child Psychology, 25*, 341–351.

Baer, R. A., Ballenger, J., & Kroll, L. S. (1998). Detection of underreporting on the MMPI-A in clinical and community samples. *Journal of Personality Assessment, 71*, 98–113.

Bailey, A., LeCouteur, A., Gottesman, I., Bolton, P., Simonoff, E., Yuzda, E., et al. (1995). Autism as a strongly genetic disorder: Evidence from a British twin study. *Psychological Medicine, 25*, 63–77.

Baldwin, J. A., & Bell, Y. R. (1985). The African-American Self-Consciousness Scale: An Africentric personality questionnaire. *Western Journal of Black Studies, 9*, 61–68.

Baldwin, J. S., & Dadds, M. R. (2008). Anxiety disorders. In M. Hersen (Series Ed.) & D. Reitman (Vol. Ed.), *Handbook of Psychological Assessment, Case Conceptualization, and Treatment* (pp. 231–263). Hoboken, NJ: John Wiley & Sons.

Ball, J. D., Archer, R. P., Gordon, R. A., & French, J. (1991). Rorschach depression indices with children and adolescents: Concurrent validity findings. *Journal of Personality Assessment, 57*, 465–476.

Bao-Yu, W., & Lin-Yan, S. (2004). Family environment and the development of behavior in children with ADHD. *Chinese Journal of Clinical Psychology, 12*, 145–146.

Barker, P. (1990). *Clinical interviews with children and adolescents.* New York: Norton.

Barkley, R. A. (1981). *Hyperactive children: A handbook for diagnosis and treatment.* New York: Guilford Press.

Barkley, R. A. (1988). Attention-deficit disorder with hyperactivity. In E. J. Mash & L. G. Terdal (Eds.), *Behavioral assessment of childhood disorders* (2nd ed., pp. 69–104). New York: Guilford Press.

Barkley, R. A. (1990). *Attention-deficit hyperactivity disorder: A handbook to diagnosis and treatment* (2nd ed.). New York: Guilford Press.

Barkley, R. A. (1991). The ecological validity of laboratory and analogue assessment methods of ADHD. *Journal of Abnormal Child Psychology, 19*, 149–178.

Barkley, R. A. (1997a). Attention deficit hyperactivity disorder. In E. J. Mash & L. G. Terdel (Eds.), *Assessment of childhood disorders* (3rd ed., pp. 71–129). New York: Guilford Press.

Barkley, R. A. (1997b). *ADHD and the nature of self-control.* New York: Guilford Press.

Barkley, R. A., & Edelbrock, C. (1987). Assessing situational variation in children's problem behaviors: The home and school situations questionnaires. In R. J. Prinz (Ed.), *Advances in behavioral assessment of children and families* (Vol. 3, pp. 157–176). New York: JAI.

Barkley, R. A., Fischer, M., Smallish, L., Fletcher, K. (2002). The persistence of attention deficit hyperactivity disorder into adulthood as a function of reporting source and definition of disorder. *Journal of Abnormal Psychology, 111*, 279–289.

Barkley, R. A., Guevremont, D. G., Anastopoulos, A. D., & Fletcher, K. F. (1993). Driving related risks and outcomes of attention-deficit hyperactivity disorder in adolescents and young adults. *Pediatrics, 92*, 212–218.

Barlow, D. H. (2002). *Anxiety and its disorders: The nature and treatment of anxiety and panic* (2nd ed.). NewYork: Guilford.

Baron-Cohen, S., Allen, J., & Gillberg, C. (1992). Can autism he detected at 18 months? The needle, the haystack, and the CHAT. *British Journal of Psychiatry, 161*, 839–843.

Barringer, M. S. (2000). Assessment of ADHD-hyperactive sub-type using visual continuous performance, psychophysiological, and behavior measures. A dissertation submitted to the Office of Graduate Studies of Texas A & M University.

Barrios, B. A. (1988). Fears and anxiety. In E. J. Mash & L. G. Terdal (Eds.), *Behavioral assessment of childhood disorders* (2nd ed., pp. 196–264). New York: Guilford Press.

Barrios, B. A. (1993). Direct observation. In F. H. Ollendick & M. Hersen (Eds.), *Handbook of child and adolescent assessment* (pp. 140–164). Boston, MA: Allyn & Bacon.

Barrios, B. A., & Hartmann, D. P. (1988). Fears and anxiety. In E. J. Mash & L. G. Terdal (Eds.), *Behavioral assessment of child-hood disorders* (pp. 167–221). New York: Guilford Press.

Barry, C. T., Frick, P. J., & Grafeman, S. J. (in press). Child versus parent report of parenting practices: Implications for the conceptualization of child behavioral and emotional problems. *Assessment.*

Barry, T., Dunlap, S., Cotten, S., Lochman, J., & Wells, K. (2005). The influence of maternal stress and distress on disruptive behavior problems in boys. *Journal of the American Academy of Child & Adolescent Psychiatry, 44*, 265–273.

Bauer, D. H. (1976). An exploratory study of developmental changes in children's fear. *Journal of Child Psychology and Psychiatry, 17*, 69–74.

Baumrind, D. (1971). Harmonious parents and their preschool children. *Developmental Psychology, 4*, 99–102.

Beck, S. T., Steer, R. A., & Garbin, M. G. (1988). Psychometric properties of the Beck depression inventory: Twenty-five years of evaluation. *Clinical Psychology Review, 8*, 77–100.

Befera, M. S., & Barkley, R. A. (1985). Hyperactive and normal girls and boys: Mother-child interactions, parent psychiatric status, and child psychopathology. *Journal of Child Psychology and Psychiatry, 26*, 439–452.

Behar, L. B., & Stringfield, S. A. (1974). A behavior rating scale for the preschool child. *Child Development, 10*, 601–610.

Bell, N. L., & Nangle, R. J. (1999). Interpretive issues with the Roberts apperception test for children: Limitations of the standardization group. *Psychology in the Schools, 36*, 277–283.

Bellak, L., & Bellak, S. (1949a). *A manual for the children's apperception test.* Larchmont, NY: CPS.

Bellak, L., & Bellak, S. S. (1949b). *The children's apperception test.* New York: CPS.

Belter, R. W., & Piotrowski, C. (1999). Current status of master's-level training in psychological assessment. *Journal of Psychological Practice, 5*, 1–5.

Belardinelli, C., Hatch, J. P., Olvera, R. L., Fonseca, M., Caetano, S. C., Nicoletti, M., et al. (2008). Family environment patterns in families with bipolar children. *Journal of Affective Disorders, 107*, 299–305.

Bender, W. N. (1997). Medical interventions and school monitoring. In W. N. Bender (Ed.), *Understanding ADHD: A practical guide for teachers and parents* (pp. 107–122). Upper Saddle River, NJ: Merrill.

Benson, J. (1998). Developing a strong program of construct validation: A test anxiety example. *Educational Measurement: Issues and Practice, 17*, 10–22.

Berg, I. (1993). Aspects of school phobia. In C. G. Last (Ed.), *Anxiety across the lifespan: A developmental perspective* (pp. 78–93). New York: Springer.

Bergman, L. R., & Magnusson, D. (1997). A person-oriented approach in research on developmental psychopathology. *Development and Psychopathology, 9*, 291–319.

Bertrand, J., Mars, A., Boyle, C., Bove, F., Yeargin-Allsopp, M., & Decoufle, P. (2001) Prevalence of autism in the United States population: The brick township New Jersey investigation. *Pediatrics, 108*, 1155–1161.

Berument, S. K., Rutter, M., Lord, C., Pickles, A., & Bailey, A. (1999). Autism screening questionnaire: Diagnostic validity. *British Journal of Psychiatry, 175*, 441–451.

Beutler, L. E., & Malik, M. (Eds.). (2002). *Rethinking the DSM: Psychological perspectives.* Washington, DC: American Psychological Association.

Bickman, L. (2002). The death of treatment as usual: An excellent first step on a long road. *Clinical Psychology Science and Practice, 9*, 195–198.

Biederman, J., Gao, H., Rogers, A., & Spencer, T. (2006). Comparison of parent and teacher reports of attention-deficit/hyperactivity disorder symptoms from two placebo-controlled studies of atomoxetine in children. *Biological Psychiatry, 60*, 1106–1110.

Biederman, J., Keenan, K., & Faraone, S. V. (1990). Parent-based diagnosis of attention deficit disorder predicts a diagnosis based on teacher report. *Journal of the American Academy of Child and Adolescent Psychiatry, 29*, 698–701.

Bigras, M., LaFrenier, P. J., & Dumas, J. E. (1996). Discriminant validity of the parent-child scales of the parenting stress index. *Early Education and Development, 7*, 167–178.

Bird, H. R., Gould, M. S., & Stagheeza, B. (1992). Aggregating data from multiple informants in child psychiatry epidemiological research. *Journal of the American Academy of Child and Adolescent Psychiatry, 31*, 78–85.

Bird, H. R., Gould, M. S., & Staghezza, B. M. (1993) Patterns of diagnostic comorbidity in a community sample of children aged 9 through 16 years. *Journal of the American Academy. of Child and Adolescent Psychiatry, 32*, 361–368.

Bird, H. R., Yager, T. J., Staghezza, B., Gould, M. S., Canino, G., & Rubio-Stipec, M. A. (1990). Impairment in the epidemiological measurement of childhood psychopathology in the community. *Journal of the American Academy of Child and Adolescent Psychiatry, 29*, 796–803.

Birmaher, B., Arbelaez, C., & Brent, D. (2002). Course and outcome of child and adolescent major depressive disorder. *Child and Adolescent Clinics of North America, 11*, 619–638.

Black, K. (1994). A critical review of the MMPI-A. *Child Assessment News, 4*(1), 9–12.

Blader, J. C. (2004). Symptom, family, and service predictors of children's psychiatric rehospitalization within one year of discharge. *Journal of the American Academy of Child & Adolescent Psychiatry, 43*, 440–451.

Blair, R. J. R. (1999). Responsiveness to distress cues in the child with psychopathic tendencies. *Personality and Individual Differences, 27*, 135–145.

Blashfield, R. K. (1984). *The classification of psychopathology: Neo-Kraepelinian and quantitative approaches.* New York: Plenum.

Block, J. H. (1965). *The child rearing practices report.* Berkeley: Institute of Human Development, University of California-Berkeley.

Block, J. H., Block, J., & Morrison, A. (1981). Parental agreement-disagreement on child-rearing orientations and gender-related personality correlates in children. *Child Development, 52*, 965–974.

Bloomquist, M. L., August, G. J., Cohen, C., Doyle, A., & Ever-hart, K. (1997). Social problem solving in hyperactive-aggressive children: How and what they think in conditions of automatic and controlled processing. *Journal of Clinical Child Psychology, 26*, 172–180.

Blum, G. S. (1950). *The blacky pictures: Manual of instructions.* New York: The Psychological Corporation.

Bölte, S., & Poustka, F. (2002). The relation between general cognitive level and adaptive behavior domains in individuals with autism with and without co-morbid mental retardation. *Child Psychiatry & Human Development, 33*, 165–172.

Borgen, F. H., & Barnett, D. C. (1987). Applying cluster analysis in counseling psychology research. *Journal of Counseling Psychology, 34, 456–468.*

Bornstein, M. R., Bellack, A. S., & Hersen, M. (1977). Social-skills training for unassertive children: A multibaseline analysis. *Journal of Applied Behavioral Analysis, 10*, 183–195.

Bower, E. M. (1982). Severe emotional disturbance: Public policy and research. *Psychology in the Schools, 19*, 55–60.

Bowlby, J. (1969). *Attachment and loss: I. Attachment.* New York: Basic Books.

Boyd, C. P., Gullone, E., Needleman, G. L., & Burt, T. (1997). The family environment scale: Reliability and normative data for an adolescent sample. *Family Process, 36*, 369–373.

Braaten, E. (2007). *The child clinician's report writing handbook.* New York: Guilford.

Bracken, B. A., Keith, L. K., & Walker, K. C. (1994). Assessment of preschool behavior and social-emotional functioning: A review of thirteen third-party instruments. *Assessment in Rehabilitation and Exceptionality, 1*, 331–346.

Bracken, B. A., Keith, L. K., & Walker, K. C. (1998). Assessment of preschool behavior and social-emotional functioning: A review of thirteen third-party instruments. *Journal of Psychoeducational Assessment, 16*, 153–169.

Brandt, H. M., & Giebink, J. W. (1968). Concreteness and congruence in psychologists' reports to teachers. *Psychology in the Schools, 5*, 87–89.

Briggs-Gowan, M. J., Carter, A. S., & Schwab-Stone, M. (1996). Discrepancies among mother, child, and teacher reports: Examining the contributions of maternal depression and anxiety. *Journal of Abnormal Child Psychology, 24*, 749–765.

Brody, G., Stoneman, Z., & Burke, M. (1987). Family system and individual child correlates of sibling behavior. *American Journal of Orthopsychiatry, 57*, 561–569.

Brody, G., Stoneman, Z., & Burke, M. (1988). Child temperament and parental perceptions of individual child adjustment: An intrafamilial analysis. *American Journal of Orthopsychiatry, 58, 532–542.*

Brown, R. A. (1999). Assessing attitudes and behaviors of high-risk adolescents: An evaluation of the self-report method. *Adolescence, 34*, 25–32.

Brown, T. E. (2001). *Brown attention-deficit disorder scales for children and adolescents.* San Antonio, TX: Psychological Corporation.

Brubaker, R. G. & Szakowski, A. (2000). Parenting practices and behavior problems among deaf children. *Child & Family Behavior Therapy, 22*, 13–28.

Bruininks, R. J., Hill, B. K., Weatherman, R. F., & Woodcock, R. N. (1986). *Inventory for client and agency planning.* Allen, TX: DLM Teaching Resources.

Bruininks, R. J., Woodcock, R. W., Weatherman, R. F., & Hill, B. K. (1986). *Scales of independent behavior.* Allen, TX: DLM Teaching Resources.

Bruininks, R. H., Woodcock, R. W., Weatherman, R. E., & Hill, B. K. (1996). *Scales of independent behavior – revised.* Itasca, IL: Riverside.

Budd, K. S., Heilman, N. E., & Kane, D. (2000). Psychosocial correlates of child abuse potential in multiply disadvantaged adolescent mothers. *Child Abuse & Neglect, 24*, 611–625.

Burns, G. L., & Patterson, D. R. (1990). Conduct problem behaviors in a stratified random sample of children and adolescents: New standardization data on the Eyberg child behavior inventory. *Psychological Assessment: A Journal of Consulting and Clinical Psychology, 2*, 391–397.

Burns, R. C., & Kaufman, S. H. (1970). *Kinetic family drawings* (KF-D): *An introduction to understanding children through kinetic drawings.* New York: Bruner/Mazel.

Buss, A. H. (1995). *Personality: Temperament, social behavior, and the self.* Boston: Allyn and Bacon.

Bussing, R., Schumann, E., Belin, T. R., Widawski, M., & Perwien, A. R. (1998). Diagnostic utility of two commonly used ADHD screening measures among special education students. *Journal of the American Academy of Child and Adolescent Psychiatry, 37*, 74–82.

Butcher, J. N., Cabiyo, J., Lucio, E., & Garrido, M. (2007). *Assessing Hispanic clients using the MMPI-2 and MMPI-A.* Washington, DC: American Psychological Association.

Butcher, J. N., Williams, C. L., Graham, J. R., Archer, R. P., Tellegen, A., Ben-Porath, Y. S., et al. (1992). *MIJPI-A, Minnesota multiphasic personality inventory-adolescent: Manual for administration scoring, and interpretation.* Minneapolis: University of Minnesota Press.

Cai, X., Kaiser, A., & Hancock, T. (2004). Parent and teacher agreement on child behavior checklist items in a sample of preschoolers from low-income and predominantly African American families. *Journal of Clinical Child and Adolescent Psychology, 33*, 303–312.

Campbell, J. (2005). Diagnostic assessment of Asperger's disorder: A review of five third-party rating scales. *Journal of Autism and Developmental Disorders, 35*, 25–35.

Campbell, M., Kafantaris, V., Malone, R. P., & Kowalik, S. C. (1991). Diagnostic and assessment issues related to pharmacotherapy for children and adolescents with autism. Special issue: Current perspectives in the diagnosis, assessment, and treatment of child and adolescent disorders. *Behavior Modification, 15*, 326–354.

Campbell, S. B. (1986). Developmental issues in childhood anxiety. In R. Gittelman (Ed.), *Anxiety disorders of childhood* (pp. 24–57). New York: Guilford Press.

Campbell, S. B. (1990). *Behavior problems in preschool children*. New York: Guilford Press.

Canino, G., & Bravo, M. (1999). The translation and adaptation of diagnostic instruments for cross-cultural use. In D. Shaffer and C. P. Lucas (Eds.), *Diagnostic assessment in child and adolescent psychopathology* (pp. 285–298). New York: Guilford Press.

Cantwell, D. P. (1996). Classification of child and adolescent psychopathology. *Journal of Child Psychology and Psychiatry*, 37, 3–12.

Cantwell, D. P., Lewinsohn, P. M., Rohds, P., & Seeley, J. R. (1997). Correspondence between adolescent report and parent report of psychiatric diagnostic data. *Journal of the American Academy of Child and Adolescent Psychiatry, 36*, 610–619.

Capaldi, D. M. (1992). Co-occurrence of conduct problems and depressive symptoms in early adolescent boys: II. A 2-year follow-up at Grade 8. *Development and Psychopathology, 4*, 125–144.

Cardell, C. P., & Parmer, R. S. (1988). Teacher perception of temperament characteristics of children classified as learning disabled. *Journal of Learning Disabilities, 21*, 497–502.

Carlson, C. L., Lahey, B. B., & Neeper, R. (1984). Peer assessment of the social behavior of accepted, rejected, and neglected children. *Journal of Abnormal Child Psychology, 12*, 189–198.

Caron, C., & Rutter, M. (1991). Comorbidity in child psychopathology: Concepts, issues, and research strategies. *Journal of Child Psychology and Psychiatry, 32*, 1063–1080.

Carrion, V. G., Weems, C. F., Ray, R., & Reiss, A. L. (2002). Toward an empirical definition of pediatric PTSD: The phenomenology of PTSD symptoms in youth. *Journal of the American Academy of Child & Adolescent Psychiatry, 41*, 166–173.

Carroll, A., Houghton, S., Taylor, M., West, J., & List-Kerz, M. L. (2006). Responses to interpersonal and physically provoking situations: The utility and application of an observation schedule for school-aged students with and without attention deficit/hyperactivity disorder. *Educational Psychology, 26*, 483–498.

Carter, C. L., & Dacey, C. M. (1996). Validity of the Beck's depression inventory, MMPI, and Rorschach in assessing adolescent depression. *Journal of Adolescence, 19*, 223–231.

Casat, C., Norton, H., & Boyle-Whitesel, M. (1999). Identification of elementary school children at risk for disruptive behavioral disturbance: Validation of a combined screening method. *Journal of the American Academy of Child & Adolescent Psychiatry, 38*, 1246–1253.

Cassen, E. H. (1990). Depression and anxiety secondary to medical illness. In G. Winokur (Ed.), *The psychiatric clinics of North America: Anxiety and depression as secondary phenomena* (pp. 597–612). Philadelphia, PA: W. B. Saunders.

Castellanos, F. X., Lee, P. P., Sharp, W., Jeffries, N. O., Greenstein, D. K., Clasen, L. S., et al. (2002). Developmental trajectories of brain volume abnormalities in children and adolescents with attention deficit hyperactivity disorder. *Journal of the American Medical Association, 288*, 1740–1748.

Cavell, T. A., Meehan, B. T., & Fiala, S. E. (2003). Assessing social competence in children and adolescents. In C. R. Reynolds and R. W. Kamphaus (Eds.), *Handbook of psychological and educational assessment of children* (2nd ed., pp. 433–454). New York: Guilford.

Chambers, W. J., Puig-Antich, J., Hirsch, M., Paez, P., Ambrosini, P. J., Tabrizi, M. A., et al. (1985). The assessment of affective disorders in children and adolescents by semi-structured interview: Test-retest reliability of the schedule for affective disorders and schizophrenia for school-aged children, present episode. *Archives of General Psychiatry, 42*, 696–702.

Chandler, L. A. (1990). The projective hypothesis and the development of projective techniques for children. In C. R. Reynolds & R. W. Kamphaus (Eds.), *Handbook of psychological and educational assessment of children: Personality, behavior, & context* (pp. 55–69). New York: Guilford Press.

Chapieski, I., Friedman, A., & Lachar, D. (2000). Psychological functioning in children and adolescents with Sturge-Weber syndrome. *Journal of Child Neurology, 15*(10), 660–665.

Chilcoat, H. D., & Breslau, N. (1997). Does psychiatric history bias mothers' reports? An application of a new analytic approach. *Journal of the American Academy of Child and Adolescent Psychiatry, 36*, 971–979.

Christ, M. G. (1990). *A four-year longitudinal study of depression in boys: Phenomenology and comorbidity of conduct disorder.* Doctoral dissertation: University of Georgia, Athens.

Christensen, A., Margolin, G., & Sullaway, M. (1992). Inter-parental agreement on child behavior problems. *Psychological Assessment, 4*, 419–425.

Cicchetti, D., Lord, C., Koenig, K., Klin, A., & Volkmar, F. (2008). Reliability of the ADI-R: Multiple examiners evaluate a single case. *Journal of Autism and Developmental Disorders, 38*, 764–770.

Cicchetti, D., & Toth, S. L. (1998). The development of depression in children and adolescents. *American Psychologist, 53*, 221–241.

Cicchetti, D. & Walker, E. F. (2001). Stress and development: Biological and psychological consequences. *Development and Psychopathology, 13, 413–418.*

Claiborn, C. D. (1995). Review of the Minnesota multiphasic personality inventory – Adolescent. In: J. C. Conoley & J. Impara (Eds.), *Twelfth mental measurements yearbook.* Lincoln, NE: Burns Institute.

Clerkin, S. M., Marks, D. J., Policaro, K., & Halperin, J. M. (2007). Psychometric properties of the Alabama parenting questionnaire-preschool revision. *Journal of Clinical Child and Adolescent Psychology, 36*, 19–28.

Cohen, N. J., Gotlieb, H., Kershner, J., & Wehrspann, W. (1985). Concurrent validity of the internalizing and externalizing profile patterns of the Achenbach child behavior check-list. *Journal of Consulting and Clinical Psychology, 53*, 724–728.

Cohen, P., & Kasen, S. (1999). The context of assessment: Culture, race, and socioeconomic status as influences on the assessment of children. In D. Shaffer, C. P. Lucas, & J. E. Richters (Eds.), *Diagnostic assessment in child and adolescent psychopathology* (pp. 299–318). New York: Guilford Press.

Coie, J.D. & Dodge, K.A. (1983). Cotinuities and changes in children's social status: A five year longitudinal study. Merrill-Palmer Quarterly, 29, 261–282.

Coie, J. D., Dodge, K. A., & Coppotelli, H. (1982). Dimensions and types of social status: A cross-age perspective. *Developmental Psychology, 18*, 557–570.

Coie, J.D. & Kupersmidt, J.B. (1983). A behavioral analysis of emerging social status in boys' groups. Child Development, 54, 1400–1416.

Collett, B., Ohan, J., & Myers, K. (2003). Ten-year review of rating scales. VI: Scales assessing externalizing behaviors. *Journal of the American Academy of Child & Adolescent Psychiatry, 42*, 1143–1170.

Conduct Problems Prevention Research Group. (1999). Initial impact of the fast track prevention trial for conduct problems: I. The high-risk sample. *Journal of Consulting and Clinical Psychology, 67*, 631–647.

Connell, J. P. (1985). A new multidimensional measure of children's perception of control. *Child Development, S6*, 1018–1041.

Conners, C. K. (1970). Symptom patterns in hyperkinetic, neurotic, and normal children. *Child Development, 41*, 667–682.

Conners, C. K. (1995). *Conners continuous performance test.* Toronto: Multi-Health Systems.

Conners, C. K. (1997). *Conners rating scales -revised.* Toronto: Multi-Health Systems.

Conners, C. K. (2008a). *Conners* (3rd ed.). Toronto: Multi-Health Systems.

Conners, C. K. (2008b). *Conners comprehensive behavior rating scales.* Toronto: Multi-Health Systems.

Conners, C. K. (1999). Conners Rating Scales-Revised. In M. E. Maruish (Ed.), *The use of psychological testing for treatment planning and outcomes assessment* (2nd ed., pp. 467–495). Mahwah, NJ: Lawrence Erlbaum Associates, Inc.

Conoley, J. C., & Conoley, C. W. (1991). Collaboration for child adjustment: Issues for school and clinic-based child psychologists. *Journal of Consulting and Clinical Psychology, S9*, 821–829.

Constantino, G., & Malgady, R. G. (1983). Verbal fluency of Hispanic, Black, & White children on TAT and TEMAS, a new thematic apperception test. *Hispanic Journal of Behavioral Sciences, 5*, 199–206.

Constantino, G., Malgady, R. G., Rogler, L. H. (1988). *Technical manual: TEMAS thematic apperception test.* Los Angeles, CA: Western Psychological Services.

Cooper, D. K. (1990). *Developmental trends in children's depression inventory responses across age and gender.* Master's thesis, University of Georgia, Athens.

Corbett, J. A., & Trimble, M. R. (1983). Epilepsy and anticonvulsant medication. In M. Rutter (Ed.), *Developmental neuropsychiatry* (pp. 112–132). New York: Guilford Press.

Costa, P. T., & McCrae, R. R. (1985). *The NEO personality inventory manual.* New York: Psychological Assessment Resources.

Costello, A. J. (1983). *The NIMH diagnostic interview schedule for children.* Pittsburgh, PA: University of Pittsburgh.

Costa, N. M., & Weems, C. W. (2005). Maternal and child anxiety: Do attachment beliefs or children's perceptions of maternal control mediate their association? *Social Development, 14*, 574–590

Costello, A. J., Edelbrock, C. S., Dulcan, M. D., Kalas, R., & Marie, S. H. (1984). *Report of the NIMH diagnostic interview schedule for children (DISC).* Washington, DC: National Institute of Mental Health.

Costello, E. J. (1989). Child psychiatric disorders and their correlates: A primary care pediatric sample. *Journal of the American Academy of Child and Adolescent Psychiatry, 28*, 851–888.

Costello, E. J., Edelbrock, C. S., & Costello, A. J. (1985). Validity of the NIMH diagnostic interview schedule for children: A comparison between psychiatric and pediatric referrals. *Journal of Abnormal Child Psychology, 13*, 579–595.

Costello, E. J., Egger, H., & Angold, A. (2005). 10-year research update review: The epidemiology of child and adolescent psychiatric disorders: I. Methods and public health burden. *Journal of the American Academy of Child and Adolescent Psychiatry, 44*, 972–986.

Courchesne, E., Karns, C. M., Davis, B. S., Ziccardi, R., Carper, R. A., Tigue, Z. D., et al. (2001). Unusual brain growth patterns in early life in patients with autistic disorder: An MRI study. *Neurology, 57*, 245–254.

Crick, N. R., & Dodge, K. A. (1996). Social information processing mechanisms in reactive and proactive aggression. *Child Development, 67*, 993–1002.

Crijnen, A. A. M., Achenbach, T. M., & Verhulst, F. C. (1997). Comparisons of problems reported by parents of children in *12* cultures: Total problems, externalizing, and internalizing. *Journal of the American Academy of Child and Adolescent Psychiatry, 36*, 1269–1277.

Crijnen, A. A. M., Achenbach, T. M., & Verhulst, F. C. (1999). Problems reported by parents of children in multiple cultures: The child behavior checklist syndrome constructs. *American Journal of Psychiatry, 156*, 569–574.

Crnic, K. A., & Reid, M. (1989). Mental retardation. In E. J. Mash & R. A. Barkley (Eds.), *Treatment of childhood disorders* (pp. 247–346). New York: Guilford Press.

Crooks, C. V. & Wolfe, D. A. (2004). Child abuse and neglect. In E. J. Mash & R. A. Barkleyl (Eds.), *Assessment of childhood disorders* (4th ed., pp. 639–684). New York: Guilford Press.

Cuellar, L., Harris, I. C., & Jasso, R. (1980). An acculturation scale for Mexican American normal and clinical population. *Hispanic Journal of Behavioral Science, 2*, 199–217.

Cumella, E. J., Wall, A. D., & Kerr-Almcida, N. (1999). MMPI-A in the inpatient assessment of adolescents with eating disorders. *Journal of Personality Assessment, 73*, 31–44.

Current Population Survey. (2001). Washington, DC: U.S. Census Bureau.

Cummings, E. M., Keller, P. S., & Davies, P. T. (2005). Towards a family process model of maternal and paternal depressive symptoms: Exploring multiple relations with child and family functioning. *Journal of Child Psychology and Psychiatry, 46*, 479–489.

Cummings, J. A. (1986). Projective drawings. In H. M. Knoll (Ed.), *The assessment of child and adolescent personality* (pp. 199–244). New York: Guilford Press.

Cunningham, C. E. & Boyle, M. H. (2002). Preschoolers at risk for attention-deficit hyperactivity disorder and oppositional defiant disorder: Family, parenting, and behavioral correlates. *Journal of Abnormal Child Psychology, 30*, 555–569.

Curry, J. F., & Craighead, W. E. (1993). Depression. In T. H. Ollendick & M. Hersen (Eds.), *Handbook of child and adolescent assessment* (pp. 251–268) Boston, MA: Allyn and Bacon.

Cytryn, L., & McKnew, D. H. (1974). Factors influencing the changing clinical expression of the depressive process in children. *American Journal of Psychiatry, 131*, 879–881.

Dadds, M. R., Barrett, P. M., Rapee, R. M., & Ryan, S. (1996). Family process and child anxiety and aggression: An observational analysis. *Journal of Abnormal Child Psychology, 24*, 715–734.

Dadds, M. R., Maujean, A., & Fraser, J. A. (2003). Parenting and conduct problems in children: Australian data and psychometric properties of the Alabama parenting questionnaire. *Australian Psychologist, 38*, 238–241.

Dadds, M. R., & Sanders, M. R. (1992). Family interaction and child psychopathology: A comparison of two observation strategies. *Journal of Child and Family Studies, 1*, 371–391.

Dahlstrom, W. G. (1993). Small samples, large consequences. *American Psychologist, 48*, 393–399.

Dalby, J. T. (1985). Taxonomic separation of attention deficit disorders. *Contemporary Educational Psychology, 10*, 228–234.

Dalton, J. E. (1996). Juvenile male sex offenders: Mean scores and the BASC self-report of personality. *Psychological Reports, 79*, 634.

Dana, R. H. (1993). *Multicultural assessment perspectives for professional psychology*. Boston, MA: Allyn and Bacon.

Dana, R. H. (2000). *Handbook of cross-cultural and multicultural personality assessment*. Mahwah, NJ: Lawrence Erlbaum.

Danforth, J. S., & DuPaul, G. J. (1996). Interrater reliability of teacher rating scales for children with attention-deficit hyperactivity disorder. *Journal of Psychopathology and Behavioral Assessment, 18*, 227–238.

Daniel, M. H. (1992, August). *Item-level covariance structure analysis for constructing personality/behavioral scales*. Paper presented at the annual meeting of the American Psychological Association, Washington, DC.

Daniel, M. H. (1993, April). *Diagnostic specificity of parents' vs. teachers' behavior ratings*. Paper presented at the Annual Meeting of the National Association of School Psychologists, Washington, DC.

Daniel, M. H. (1993, August). *Diagnostic specificity of parents' and teachers' behavior ratings*. Paper presented at the annual meeting of the American Psychological Association, Washington, DC.

Darling, N., & Steinberg, L. (1993). Parenting style as context: An integrative model. *Psychological Bulletin, 113*, 487–496.

David, C. F., & Kistner, J. A. (2000). Do positive self-perceptions have a "dark side"? Examination of the link between perceptual bias and aggression. *Journal of Abnormal Child Psychology, 28, 327–337.*

David-Ferdon, C., & Kaslow, N. J. (2008). Evidence-based psychosocial treatments for child and adolescent depression. *Journal of Clinical Child and Adolescent Psychology, 37*, 62–104.

de Bildt, A., Sytema, S., Ketelaars, C., Kraijer, D., Mulder, E., Volkmar, F., et al. (2004). Interrelationships between the ADOS, ADI-R, and DSM-IV-TR classification in children and adolescents with mental retardation. *Journal of Autism and Developmental Disorders, 34*, 129–137.

De Groot, A., Koot, H. M., & Verhulst, F. C. (1996). Cross-cultural generalizability of the youth self-report and teacher's report form cross-informant syndromes. *Journal of Abnormal Child Psychology, 24*, 651–664.

De Los Reyes, A. & Kazdin, A. E. (2005). Informant discrepancies in the assessment of childhood psychopathology: A critical review, theoretical framework, and recommendations for further study. *Psychological Bulletin, 131*, 483–509.

Deater-Deckard, K., Reiss, D., & Hetherington, F. M. (1997). Dimensions and disorders of adolescent adjustment: A quantitative genetic analysis of unselected samples and selected extremes. *Journal of Child Psychology and Psychiatry, 38*, 515–525.

DeBaryshe, B. D., Patterson, G. R., & Capaldi, D. M. (1993). A performance model for academic achievement in early adolescent boys. *Developmental Psychology, 29*, 795–804.

Department of Health and Human Services. (2000). Standards for privacy of individually identifiable health information. *Federal Register, 65*(250), 82462–82829.

Departments of Psychiatry and Child Psychiatry, The Institute of Psychiatry, & The Maudsley Hospital London (1987). *Psychiatric examination: Notes on eliciting and recording clinical in-formation psychiatric parents.* Oxford: Oxford University Press.

Desombre, H., Malvy, J., Roux, S., de Villard, R., Sauvage, D., Dalery, J., et al. (2006). Autism and developmental delay: A comparative clinical study in very young children using IBSE scale. *European Child & Adolescent Psychiatry, 15*, 343–351.

DeStefano, L. (1998). Review of the Personality Inventory for Youth. *Thirteenth Mental Measurements Yearbook.* Lincoln, NE: Buros Institute.

DeStefano, L., & Thompson, D. S. (1990). Adaptive behavior: The construct and its measurement. In C. R. Reynolds & R. W. Kamphaus (Eds.), *Handbook of psychological and educational assessment of children: Personality, behavior, and context* (pp. 445–469). New York: Guilford Press.

Dishion, T. J., Patterson, G. R., & Skinner, M. S. (1989). *A process model for the role of peers in adolescent social adjustment.* Paper presented at the biennial meeting of the Society for Research in Child Development, Kansas City, MO.

Dishion, T. J., Capaldi, D., Spracklen, K. M., & Li, F. (1995). Peer ecology of male adolescent drug use. *Development and Psychopathology, 7*, 803–824.

DiSibio, M. (1993). Conjoint effects of intelligence and adaptive behavior on achievement in a nonreferred sample. *Journal of Psychoeducational Assessment, 11*, 304–313.

Dodge, K. A. (1983). Behavioral antecedents of peer social crams. *Child Development, 54*, 1386–1399.

Dodge, K. A., & Coie, J. D. (1987). Social-information processing factors in reactive and proactive aggression in children's peer groups. *Journal of Personality and Social Psychology, 53*, 1146–1158.

Dodge, K. A., Coie, J., Brakkc, N. (1982). Behavior patterns of socially rejected and neglected adolescents: The roles of social approach and aggression. *Journal of Abnormal Child Psychology, 10*, 389–410.

Dodge, K. A., McClaskey, C. L., & Feldman, E. (1985). Situational approach to the assessment of social competence in children. *Journal of Consulting and Clinical Psychology, 53*, 344–353.

Dodge, K. A., & Pettit, G. S. (2003). A biopsychosocial model of the development of chronic conduct problems in adolescence. *Developmental Psychology, 39*, 349–371.

Doleys, D. M. (1977). Behavioral treatments for nocturnal enuresis in children: A review of the recent literature. *Psychological Bulletin, 84*, 30–54.

Doll, B. (1998). Review of the Child Behavior Checklist. *Thirteenth Mental Measurements Yearbook.* Lincoln, NE: Buros Institute.

Doll, E. A. (1940). A social basis of mental diagnosis. *Journal of Applied Psychology, 24*, 160–169.

Doll, E. A. (1953). *Measurement of social competence: A manual for the Vineland Social Maturity Scale.* Circle Pines, MN: American Guidance Services.

Dopke, C. A., Lundahl, B. W., Dunsterville, E., & Lovejoy, M. C. (2003). Interpretations of child compliance in individuals at high- and low-risk for child physical abuse. *Child Abuse & Neglect, 27*, 285–302.

Downey, G., & Coyne, J. C. (1990). Children of depressed parents: An integrative review. *Psychological Bulletin, 108*, 50–76.

Doyle, A., Ostrander, R., Skare, S., Crosby, R. D., & August, C. (1997). Convergent and criterion-related validity of the behavior assessment system for children-parent rating scales. *Journal of Clinical Child Psychology, 26*, 276–284.

Dresden, J. (1994). *Gender, temperament, and mathematics achievement.* Doctoral dissertation, University of Georgia, Athens.

Drotar, D., Stein, R. E. K., & Perrin, E. C. (1995). Methodological issues in using the child behavior checklist and its related instruments in clinical child psychology research. *Journal of Clinical Child Psychology, 24*, 184–192.

DuBois, P. H. (1970). *A history of psychological testing.* Boston, MA: Allyn and Bacon.

Duhig, A., Renk, K., Epstein, M., & Phares, V. (2000). Interparental agreement on internalizing, externalizing, and total behavior problems: A meta-analysis. *Clinical Psychology: Science and Practice, 7*, 435–453.

Durbin, C., Hayden, E., Klein, D., & Olino, T. (2007). Stability of laboratory-assessed temperamental emotionality traits from ages 3 to 7. *Emotion, 7*, 388–399.

Dunbar, J. L. (1999). Differential item performance by gender on the externalizing scales of the behavior assessment system for children. *Dissertation Abstracts International Section A: Humanities and Social Sciences, 60*(6-A), 1902.

DuPaul, G. J., Anastopolous, A. D., Shelton, T. L., Guevremont, I. C., & Metevia, L. (1992). Multimethod assessment of attention-deficit hyperactivity disorder: The diagnostic utility of clinic-based tests. *Journal of Clinical Child Psychology, 21*, 394 402.

DuPaul, G. J., Power, T. J., Anastopolous, A. D., & Reid, R. (1998). *ADHD-IV rating scale: Checklists, norms, and clinical interpretation.* New York: Guilford.

DuPaul, G. J., Rapport, M. D., & Perrillo, L. M. (1991). Teacher ratings of academic skills: The development of the academic performance rating scale. *School Psychology Review, 20*, 284–300.

DuPaul, G.J. & Stoner, G. (1994). ADHD in the schools: Assessment and intervention strategies. New York: Guilford.

Eaves, L. J., Silberg, J. L., Hewitt, J. K., Rutter, M., Meyer, J. M., Neale, M. C., et al. (1993). Analyzing twin resemblance in multisymptom data: Genetic applications of a latent class model for symptoms of conduct disorder in juvenile boys. *Behavior Genetics, 23*, 5–19.

Eaves, R. C., & Milner, B. (1993). The criterion-related validity of the childhood autism rating scale and the autism behavior checklist. *Journal of Abnormal Child Psychology, 21*, 481–491.

Edelbrock, C. (1979). Empirical classification of children's behavior disorders: Progress based on parent and teacher ratings. *School Psychology Digest, 8*, 355–369.

Edelbrock, C. (1985). Age differences in the reliability of the psychiatric interview of the child. *Child Development, 56*, 265–275.

Edelbrock, C., & Costello, A. J. (1988). Convergence between statistically derived behavior problem syndromes and child psychiatric diagnoses. *Journal of Abnormal Child Psychology, 16*, 219–231.

Edelbrock, C., Costello, A. J., Dulcan, M. K., Conover, N. C., & Kalas, R. (1986). Parent child agreement on child psychiatric symptoms assessed via structured interview. *Journal of Child Psychology and Psychiatry, 27*, 181–190.

Edelbrock, C., Costello, A. J., Dulcan, M. K., Kalas, R., & Conover, N. C. (1985). Age differences in the reliability of the psychiatric interview of the child. *Child Development, 56*, 265–275.

Edelbrock, C., Crnic, K., & Bohnert, A. (1999). Interviewing as communication: An alternative way of administering the diagnostic interview schedule for children. *Journal of Abnormal Child Psychology, 27*, 447–453.

Edelsohn, G., Ialongo, N., Werthamer-Larrson, L. Crockett, L., & Kellam, S. (1992). Self-reported depressive symptoms in first-grade children: Developmentally transient phenomena? *Journal of the American Academy of Child and Adolescent Psychiatry, 31*, 282–290.

Education for All Handicapped Children's Act of 1975, P.L. 94–142, 20 U.S.C. Section 1401 (1975).

Eiraldi, R. B., Power, T. J., Karustis, J. L., & Goldstein, S. G. (2000). Assessing ADHD and comorbid disorders in children: The Child Behaviour Checklist and the Devereaux Scales of Mental Disorders. *Journal of Clinical Child Psychology, 29*, 3–16.

Eisenstadt, T. H., Eyberg, S., McNeil, C. B., Newcomb, K., & Funderbunk, B. (1993). Parent-child interaction therapy with behavior problem children: Relative effectiveness of two stages and overall treatment outcome. *Journal of Clinical Child Psychology, 22*, 42–51.

Elgar, F. J., Waschbusch, D. A., Dadds, M. R., & Sivaldason, N. (2007). Development and validation of a short form of the Alabama parenting questionnaire. *Journal of Child and Family Studies, 16*, 243–259.

Elliott, S., & Bretzing, B. (1980). Using and updating local norms. *Psychology in the Schools, 17*, 196–201.

Elliot, D. S., Huizinga, D., & Ageton, S. S. (1985). *Explaining delinquency and drug use.* Newbury Park, CA: Sage.

Emery, R. E. (1982). Interparental conflict and the children of discord and divorce. *Psychological Bulletin, 92*, 310–330.

Endicott, J., & Spitzer, R. L. (1978). A diagnostic interview: The schedule for affective disorders and schizophrenia. *Archives of General Psychiatry, 35*, 57–63.

Erickson, M. T. (1998). Etiological factors. In T. H. Ollendick & M. Hersen (Eds.), *Handbook of Child Psychopathology* (3rd ed., pp. 37–62). New York: Plenum Press.

Erikson, E. H. (1968). *Identity, youth, and crisis.* New York: Norton.

Ernst, M., Cookus, B. A., & Moravec, B. C. (2000). Pictorial instrument for children and adolescents (PICA-III-R). *Journal of the American Academy of Child and Adolescent Psychiatry, 39*, 94–99.

Essau, C. A., Sasagawa, S., & Frick, P. J. (2006). Psychometric properties of the Alabama parenting questionnaire. *Journal of Child and Family Studies, 15*, 597–616.

Essau, C. A., Sasagawa, S., & Frick, P. J. (2006). Callous-unemotional traits in a community sample of adolescents. *Assessment, 13*, 454–469.

Eyberg, S. M., Nelson, M. M., Duke, M., & Boggs, S. R. (2005). *Manual for the dyadic parent-child interaction coding system* (3rd ed.). Available on-line at www.PCIT.org.

Exner, J. E. (1974). *The Rorschach: A comprehensive system, I.* New York: Wiley.

Exner, J. E. (1978). *The Rorschach: A comprehensive system, II: Recent research and advanced interpretation.* New York: Wiley.

Exner, J. E. (1983, June). The depression index. *1983 Alumni Newsletter* (p. 7). Bayville, NY: Rorschach Workshops.

Exner, J. E. (1990, April). The depression index. *1990 Alumni Newsletter* (pp. 12–13). Asheville, NC: Rorschach Workshops.

Exner, J. E., & Martin, L. S. (1983). The Rorschach: A history and description of the comprehensive system. *School Psychology Review, 12*, 407–413.

Exner, J. E., Jr., & Weiner, I. B. (1982). *The Rorschach: A comprehensive system, Vol. 3: Assessment of children and adolescents.* New York: Wiley.

Exner, J. E., & Weiner, I. B. (1994). *The Rorschach: A comprehensive system, Vol. 3: Assessment of children and adolescents* (2nd ed.). New York: John Wiley and Sons.

Exner, J. E., Thomas, E. A., & Mason, B. (1985). Children's Rorschachs: Description and prediction. *Journal of Personality Assessment, 49*, 13–20.

Eyberg, S. M., & Robinson, E. A. (1982). Conduct problem behavior: Standardization of a behavioral rating scale with adolescents. *Journal of Clinical Child Psychology, 12*, 347–354.

Eyberg, S. M., Bessmer, J., Newcomb, K., Edwards, D., & Robin-son, E. (1994). *Dyadic parent-child interaction coding system 11: A manual.* Unpublished manuscript, University of Florida.

Eyberg, S. M., & Robinson, E. A. (1983). Dyadic parent-child interaction coding system: A manual. *Psychological Documents, 13,* 24 (Ms. No., 2582).

Eyberg, S. M., & Ross, A. W. (1978). Assessment of child behavior problems: The validation of a new inventory. *Journal of Clinical Child Psychology, 7,* 113–116.

Eyde, L. D., Robertson, G. J., Krug, S. E., Moreland, K. L., Robertson, A. G., Shewan, C. M., et al. (1993). *Responsible test use: Case studies for assessing human behavior.* Washington, DC: American Psychological Association.

Eysenck, H. J. (1965). Review of the Wittenborn Psychiatric Rating Scales. In O. K. Buros (Ed.), *Mental Measurements Yearbook* (5th ed.). Highland Park, NJ: Gryphon Press.

Faraone, S. V., Biederman, J., Keenan, K., & Tsuang, M. T. (1991). Separation of DSM-III attention deficit disorder and conduct disorder: Evidence from a family genetic study of American child psychiatric patients. *Psychological Medicine, 21,* 109–121.

Federal Register. (March 12, 1999). Assistance to states for the education of children with disabilities and the Early Intervention Program for infants and toddlers with disabilities; Final Regulations.

Feighner, J. P., Robins, E., Guze, S. B., Woodruff, R. A., Winokur, G., & Munoz, R. (1972). Diagnostic criteria for use in psychiatric research. *Archives of General Psychiatry, 26,* 57–63.

Feinberg, T. L., Crouse-Novak, M. A., Paulauskas, S. L., & Finkelstein, R. (1984). Depressive disorders in childhood: I. A longitudinal prospective study of characteristics and recovery. *Archives of General Psychiatry, 41,* 229–237.

Feinfield, K. A. & Baker, B. L. (2004). Empirical support for a treatment program for families of young children with externalizing problems. *Journal of Clinical Child & Adolescent Psychology, 33,* 182–195.

Ferdinand, R. (2008). Validity of the CBCL/YSR DSM-IV scales anxiety problems and affective problems. *Journal of Anxiety Disorders, 22,* 126–134.

Fergusson, D. M., & Horwood, J. (1995). Predictive validity of categorically and dimensionally scored measures of disruptive childhood behaviors. *Journal of Clinical Child and Adolescent Psychology,* 32, 396–407.

Fergusson, D. M., Swain, N. R., & Horwood, L. J. (2002). Deviant peer affiliations, crime and substance use: A fixed effects regression analysis. *Journal of Abnormal Child Psychology, 30,* 419–430.

Figueroa, R. A. (1990). Assessment of linguistic minority group children. In C. R. Reynolds & R. W. Kamphaus (Eds.), *Handbook of psychological and educational assessment of children: Intelligence and achievement* (pp. 671–696). New York: Guilford Press.

Filipek, P. A., Accardo, P. J., Ashwal, S., Baranek, G. T., Cook, E. H., Jr., Dawson, G., et al. (2000). Practice parameter: Screening and diagnosis of autism. *Neurology, 55,* 468–479.

Finch, A. J., & Belter, R. W. (1993). Projective techniques. In T. H. Ollendick & M. Hersen (Eds.), *Handbook of child and adolescent assessment* (pp. 229–238). Boston, LH : Allyn and Bacon.

Finch, A. J., Lipovsky, J. A., & Casat, C. D. (1989). Anxiety and depression in children and adolescents: Negative affectivity or separate constructs? In P. C. Kendall & D. Watson (Eds.), *Anxiety and depression: Distinctive and overlapping features* (pp. 171–202). New York: Academic Press.

First, M. B., Spitzer, R. I., Gibbon, M., & Williams, J. B. W. (1995). *Structure clinical interview for* Axis *I DSM-IV Disorders – Patient edition.* New York: New York State Psychiatric Institute.

Fischer, M., Barkley, R. A., Fletcher, K., & Smallish, L. (1993). The adolescent outcome of hyperactive children diagnosed by research criteria: V. Predictors of outcome. *Journal of the American Academy of Child and Adolescent Psychiatry, 32,* 324–332.

Fisher, L., & Blair, R. J. R. (1998). Cognitive impairment and its relationship to psychopathic tendencies in children with emotional and behavioral difficulties. *Journal of Abnormal Child Psychology, 26,* 511–519.

Fisher, P., Wicks, J., Shaffer, D., Piacentini, J., & Laplun, J. (1992). *NIMH diagnostic interview schedule for children: Users manual.* New York: New York State Psychiatric Institute.

Flanagan, D. P., Alfonso, V. C., Primavera, L. H., Povall, L., & Higgins, D. (1996). Convergent validity of the BASC and SSRS: Implications for social skills assessment. *Psychology in the Schools, 33,* 13–23.

Flanagan, R. (1995). A review of the behavior assessment system for children (BASC): Assessment consistent with the requirements of the individuals with disabilities education act (IDEA). *Journal of School Psychology, 33,* 177–186.

Flanagan, R., & DiGiuseppe, R. (1999). Critical review of the TEMAS: A step within the development of thematic apperception instruments. *Psychology in the Schools, 36,* 21–30.

Fletcher, J. M., Francis, D. J., Morris, R. D., & Lyon, G. R. (2005). Evidence-based assessment of learning disabilities in children and adolescents. *Journal of Clinical Child and Adolescent Psychology, 34,* 506–522.

Foley, D. L., Rutter, M., Agnold, A., Pickles, A., Maes, H. M., Silberg, J. L., et al. (2005). Making sense of informant disagreement for overanxious disorder. *Journal of Anxiety Disorders, 19,* 193–210.

Fombonne, F. (1992). Diagnostic assessment in a sample of autistic and developmentally impaired adolescents. Special issue: Classification and diagnosis. *Journal of Autism & Developmental Disorders, 22,* 563–581.

Forbey, J. D., Handel, R. W., & Ben-Porath, Y. S. (2000). A real-data simulation of computerized adaptive administration of the MMPI-A. *Computers in Human Behavior, 16*, 83–96.

Forehand, R., Long, N., & Hedrick, M. (1987). Family characteristics of adolescents who display overt and covert behavior problems. *Journal of Behavior Therapy and Experimental Psychiatry, 18*, 325–328.

Forness, S. R., & Kritzer, J. (1992). A new proposed definition and terminology to replace "serious emotional disturbance" in the individuals with disabilities act. *School Psychology Review, 21*, 12–20.

Forth, A. E., Kosson, D. S., & Hare, R. D. (2003). *Hare psychopathy checklist: Youth version.* Toronto: Multi-Health Systems.

Fowler, P. (1982). Factor structure of the family environment scale: Effects of social desirability. *Journal of Clinical Psychology, 38*, 285–292.

Francis, D. J., Fletcher, J. M., Sniebing, K. K., Davidson, K. C., & Thompson, N. M. (1991). Analysis of change: Modeling individual growth. *Journal of Consulting and Clinical Psychology, 59*, 27–37.

Franco, J. N. (1983). An acculturation scale for Mexican–American children. *Journal of General Psychology, 108*, 175–181.

Frazier, T. W., Youngstrom, E. A., Kubu, C. S., Sinclair, L., & Rezai, A. (2008). Exploratory and confirmatory factor analysis of the autism diagnostic interview-revised. *Journal of Autism and Developmental Disorders, 38*, 474–480.

Freeman, B. J., Ritvo, E. R., Yokota, A., & Rirvo, A. (1986). A scale for rating symptoms of patients with the syndrome of autism in real life settings. *Journal of the American Academy of Child Psychiatry, 25*, 130–136.

French, J. L., & Hale, R. L. (1990). A history of the development of psychological and educational testing. In C. R. Reynolds & R. W. Kamphaus (Eds.), *Handbook of psychological and educational assessment of children: Intelligence and achievement* (pp. 3–28). New York: Guilford Press.

Freud, S. (1936). *The Problem of anxiety.* New York: W. W. Norton & Co.

Frick, P. J. (1993). Childhood conduct problems in family context. *School Psychology Review, 22*, 376–385.

Frick, P. J. (1994). Family dysfunction and the disruptive behavior disorders: A review of recent empirical findings. In T. H. Ollendick & R. J. Prinz (Eds.), *Advances in clinical child psychology* (Vol. 16, pp. 213–226). New York: Plenum.

Frick, P. J. (1998). *Conduct disorders and severe antisocial behavior.* New York: Plenum.

Frick, P. J. (2000). Laboratory and performance-based measures of childhood disorders. *Journal of Clinical Child Psychology, 29*, 475–478.

Frick, P. J. (2004). Integrating research on temperament and childhood psychopathology. Its pitfalls and promise. *Journal of Clinical Child and Adolescent Psychology, 33*, 2–7.

Frick, P. J. (2006). Developmental pathways to conduct disorder. *Child and Adolescent Psychiatric Clinics of North America, 15*, 311–331.

Frick, P. J., Bodin, S. D., & Barry, C. T. (2000). Psychopathic traits and conduct problems in community and clinic-referred samples of children: Further development of the Psychopathy Screening Device. *Assessment*, 12, 382–393.

Frick, P. J., Christian, R. C. & Wootton, J. M. (1999). Age trends in the association between parenting practices and conduct problems. *Behavior Modification, 23*, 106–128.

Frick, P. J., & Dickens, C. (2006). Current perspectives on conduct disorder. *Current Psychiatry Reports, 8*, 59–72.

Frick, P. J. & Hare, R. D. (2001). *The antisocial process screening device.* Toronto: Multi-Health Systems.

Frick, P. J., & Jackson, Y. K. (1993). Family functioning and childhood antisocial behavior. Yet another reinterpretation. *Journal of Clinical Child Psychology, 22*, 410–419.

Frick, P. J., Kamphaus, R. W., Lahey, B. B., Loeber, R., Christ, M. A. G., Hart, E. L., et al. (1991). Academic underachievement and the disruptive behavior disorders. *Journal of Consulting and Clinical Psychology, 59*, 289–294.

Frick, P. J., Kimonis, E. R., Dandreaux, D. M., & Farell, J. M. (2003). The 4 year stability of psychopathic traits in non-referred youth. *Behavioral Sciences & the Law, 21*(6), 713–736.

Frick, P. J. & Kimonis, E. (2008). Externalizing disorders. In J. E. Maddux & B. A. Winstead (Eds.), *Psychopathology: Contemporary issues, theory, and research* (pp. 349–374). Mahwah, NJ: Erlbaum.

Frick, P. J., & Lahey, B. B. (1991). The nature and characteristics of attention-deficit hyperactivity disorder. *School Psychology Review, 20*, 163–173.

Frick, P. J., Lahey, B. B., Applegate, B., Kerdyck, L., Ollendick, T., Ilynd, G. W., et al. (1994). DSM-IV field trials for the disruptive behavior disorders. *Journal of the American Academy of Child and Adolescent Psychiatry, 33*, 529–539.

Frick, P. J., Lahey, B. B., Christ, M. G., Loeber, R., & Green, S. (1991). History of childhood behavior problems in biological relatives of boys with attention-deficit-hyperactivity disorder and conduct disorder. *Journal of Clinical Child Psychology, 20*, 445–451.

Frick, P. J., Lahey, B. B., Hartdagen, S., & Hynd, C. W. (1989). Conduct problems in boys: Relations to maternal personality, marital satisfaction, and socioeconomic status. *Journal of Clinical Child Psychology, 18*, 114–120.

Frick, P. J., Lahey, B. B., Loeber, R., Stouthamer-Loeber, M., Christ, M. G., & Hanson, K. (1992). Familial risk factors to oppositional defiant disorder and conduct disorder: Parental psychopathology and maternal parenting. *Journal of Consulting and Clinical Psychology, 60*, 49–55.

Frick, P. J., Lahey, B. B., Loeber, R., Tannenbaum, L. E., Van Horn, Y., Christ, M. A. C., et al. (1993). Oppositional defiant disorder and conduct disorder: A meta-analytic review of factor analyses and cross-validation in a clinic sample. *Clinical Psychology Review, 13*, 319–340.

Frick, P. J. & Loney, B. R. (1999). Outcomes of children and adolescents with conduct disorder and oppositional defiant disorder. In H. C. Quay & A. Hogan (Eds.), *Handbook of disruptive behavior disorders* (pp. 507–524). New York: Plenum Press.

Frick, P. J. & Loney, B. R. (2000). The use of laboratory and performance-based measures in the assessment of children and adolescents with conduct disorders. *Journal of Clinical Child Psychology, 29*, 540–554.

Frick, P. J. & Loney, B. R. (2002). Understanding the association between parent and child antisocial behavior. In R. J. McMahon & R. Dcv. Peters (Eds.), *The effects of parental dysfunction on children* (pp. 105–126). New York: Plenum Press.

Frick, P. J., & Marsee, M. A. (2006). Psychopathic traits and developmental pathways to antisocial behavior in youth. In C. J. Patrick (Ed.), *Handbook of psychopathic traits* (pp. 355–374). New York: Guilford Press.

Frick, P. J., & McMahon, R. J. (2008). Child and adolescent conduct problems. In J. Hunsley & E. J. Mash (Eds.), *A guide to assessments that work* (pp. 41–66). New York: Oxford University.

Frick, P. J., & Morris, A. S. (2004). Temperament and developmental pathways to conduct problems. *Journal of Clinical Child and Adolescent Psychology, 33*, 54–68.

Frick, P. J., & O'Brien, B. S. (1994). Conduct disorders. In R. T. Ammerman & M. Hersen (Eds.), *Handbook of child behaviour therapy in the psychiatric setting* (pp. 199–216). New York: Wiley.

Frick, P. J., & Silverthorn, P. (2001). Psychopathology in children. In H. E. Adams & P. B. Sutker (Eds.), *Comprehensive handbook of psychopathology* (3rd ed., pp. 881–920). New York: Kluwer-Plenum.

Frick, P. J., Silverthorn, P., & Evans, C. S. (1994). Assessment of childhood anxiety using structured interviews: Patterns of agreement among informants and association with maternal anxiety. *Psychological Assessment, 6*, 372–379.

Frick, P. J. & White, S. F. (2008). The importance of callous-unemotional traits for the development of aggressive and antisocial behavior. *Journal of Child Psychology and Psychiatry, 49*, 359–375.

Friedlander, S., Weiss, D. S., & Traylor, J. (1986). Assessing the influence of maternal depression on the validity of the child behavior checklist. *Journal of Abnormal Child Psychology, 14*, 123–133.

Friedman, S. L., & Waches, T. D. (1999). *Measuring environment across the life span: Emerging methods and concepts.* Washington, DC: American Psychological Association.

Friman, P. C., Handwerk, M. L., Smith, G. L., Larzelere, R. E., Lucas, C. P., & Shaffer, D. M. (2000). External validity of conduct and oppositional defiant disorders determined by the NIMH diagnostic interview schedule for children. *Journal of Abnormal Child Psychology, 28*, 277–286.

Fuchs, D. (1987). Examiner familiarity effects on test performance: Implications for training and practice. *Topics in Early Childhood Special Education, 102*, 90–104.

Fuchs, D., & Fuchs, L. S. (1986). Test procedure bias: A meta-analysis of examiner familiarity effects. *Review of Educational Research, 56*, 243–262.

Funderbunk, B. W., & Eyberg, S. M. (1989). Psychometric characteristics of the Sutter-Eyberg student behavior inventory: A school behavior rating scale for use with preschool children. *Behavioral Assessment, 11*, 297–313.

Gadow, K. D., & Sprafkin, J. (1997). *Early Childhood Inventory-4: Screening manual.* Stony Brook, NY: Checkmate Plus.

Gadow, K. D., & Sprafkin, J. (1998). *Adolescent Symptoms Inventory-4 norms manual.* Stony Brook, NY: Checkmate Plus.

Gadow, K. D., & Sprafkin, J. (2002). *Child Symptom Inventory-4 screening and norms manual.* Stony Brook, NY: Checkmate Plus.

Gadow, K. D., Sprafkin, J., Salisbury, H., Schneider, J., & Loney, J. (2004). Further validity evidence for the teacher version of the child symptom inventory-4. *School Psychology Quarterly, 19*, 50–71.

Gallucci, N. T. (1989). Personality assessment with children of superior intelligence: Divergence versus psychopathology. *Journal of Personality Assessment, 53*, 749–760.

Gallucci, N. T. (1997). On the identification of patterns of substance abuse with the MMPI-A scales. *Psychological Assessment, 9*(3), 224–232.

Galton, F. (1884). Measurement of character. *Fortnightly Review, 42*, 179–185. Reprinted in L. D. Goodstein & R. I. Lanyon (Eds.), *Readings in Personality Assessment,* New York: Wiley.

Ganmer, A. B., Graham, J. R., & Archer, R. A. (1992). Usefulness of the MAC scale in differentiating adolescents in normal, psychiatric, and substance abuse settings. *Psychological Assessment, 4*, 133–137.

Garb, H. N., Wood, J. M., & Nezworski, M. T. (2000). Projective techniques and the detection of child sexual abuse. *Child Maltreatment, 5*, 161–168.

Garber, J. (1984). Classification of childhood psychopathology: A developmental perspective. *Child Development, 55*, 30–48.

Garcia, M., & Lega, L. I. (1979). Development of a Cuban ethnic identity questionnaire. *Hispanic Journal of Behavioral Sciences, 1*, 247–261.

Geisinger, K. F. (1992). Fairness and selected psychometric issues in the psychological testing of Hispanics. In K. F. Geisinger (Ed.), *Psychological testing of Hispanics* (pp. 17–42). Washington, DC: American Psychological Association.

Gelfand, D. M., & Hartmann, D. P. (1984). *Child Behavior analysis and therapy* (2nd ed.). New York: Pergamon Press.

Geller, B., Fox, L. W., & Fletcher, M. (1993). Effect of tricyclic antidepressants on switching to mania and on the onset of bipolarity in depressed 6- to 12-year-olds. *Journal of the American Academy of Child and Adolescent Psychiatry, 32*, 43–50.

Gelman, C. F. (1998). Characteristics of a prenatally cocaine-exposed clinical population at school age. *Dissertation Abstracts International Section B: The Sciences and Engineering, 58*(11-B), 6234.

Ghiselli, E. E., Campbell, J. P., & Zedeck, S. (1981) *Measurement theory for the behavioral sciences.* San Francisco: W. H. Freeman.

Gibbs, J. T. & Huang, L. N. (1989). *Children of color: Psychological interventions with minority youth.* San Francisco: Jossey-Bass, Inc.

Gilliam, J. E. (1995). *Gilliam autism rating scale.* Austin, TX: Pro-Ed.

Gilliam, J. E. (2001). *Gilliam Asperger's Disorder scale.* Austin, Texas: Pro-Ed.

Gilliam, J. E. (2008). *Gilliam autism rating scale, 2nd edition.* Austin, TX: Pro-Ed.

Gittelman, R., Mannuzza, S., Shenker, R., & Bonegura, N. (1985). Hyperactive boys almost grown up: I. Psychiatric status. *Archives of General Psychiatry, 42*, 937–947.

Gittelman-Klein, R. (1986). Questioning the clinical usefulness of projective psychological tests for children. *Developmental and Behavioral Pediatrics, 7*, 378–382.

Glueck, S., & Glueck, E. (1968). *Delinquents and non-delinquents in perspective.* Cambridge, MA: Harvard University Press.

Glutting, J. J., & Kaplan, D. (1990). Stanford-Binet Intelligence Scale-Fourth Edition: Making the case for reasonable interpretations. In C. R. Reynolds & R. W. Kamphaus (Eds.), *Handbook of psychological and educational assessment of children: Personality, behavior, and context* (pp. 277–295). New York: Guilford Press.

Goldberg, L. R. (1992). The development of markers for the big-five factor structure. *Psychological Assessment, 4*, 26–42.

Goldsmith, H. H., & Rieser-Danner, L. A. (1990). Assessing early temperament. In C. R. Reynolds and R. W. Kamphaus (Eds.), *Handbook of psychological and educational assessment of children: Personality, behavior, and context* (pp. 245–278). New York: The Guilford Press.

Goodman, S. H. & Gotlib, I. H. (1999). Risk for psychopathology in the children of depressed mothers: A developmental model for understanding mechanisms of transmission. *Psychological Review, 106*, 458–490.

Goodman, W. K., Price, L. H., Rasmussen, S. A., Mazure, C., Fleischmann, R. L., Hill, C. L., et al. (1989). The Yale–Brown obsessive–compulsive scale: I. development, use, and reliability. *Archives of General Psychiatry, 46*, 1006–1011.

Gordon, M. (1983). *The Gordon diagnostic system.* DeWitt, NY: Gordon Systems.

Gorsuch, R. L. (1988). *Factor analysis* (3rd ed.). Hillsdale, NJ: Erlbaum.

Gottesman, I. I., McGuffin, P., & Farmer, A. E. (1987). Clinical genetics as clues to the "real" genetics of schizophrenia. *Schizophrenia Bulletin, 13*, 23–47.

Gottlieb, G. (1991). Experiential canalization of behavioral development: Theory. *Developmental Psychology, 27*(1), 4–13.

Green, K., Vosk, B., Forehand, R., & Beck, S. (1981). An examination of differences among sociometrically identified accepted, rejected, and neglected children. *Child Study Journal, 11*, 117–124.

Green, M. (1992). *Pediatric diagnosis: Interpretation of symptoms and signs in infants, children, and adolescents* (5th ed.). Philadelphia: Saunders.

Green, S. M., Loeber, R., & Lahey, B. B. (1991). Stability of mothers' recall of the age of onset of their child's attention and hyperactivity problems. *Journal of the American Academy of Child and Adolescent Psychiatry, 30*, 135–137.

Greenberg, M. T., Lengua, L. J., Coie, J., Pinderhughes, E., & the Conduct Problems Prevention Research Group. (1999). Predicting developmental outcomes at school entry using a multiple-risk model: Four American communities. *Developmental Psychology, 35*, 403–417.

Greenspan, S. (2006). Functional concepts in mental retardation: Finding the natural essence of an artificial category. *Exceptionality, 14*, 205–224.

Greenspoon, P. J., & Saklofske, D. H. (1997). Validity and reliability of the multidimensional students' life satisfaction scale with Canadian children. *Journal of Psychoeducational Assessment, 15*, 138–155.

Gresham, F. M., & Little, S. G. (1993). Peer-referenced assessment strategies. In T. H. Ollendick & M. Hersen (Eds.), *Handbook of child and adolescent assessment* (pp. 165–179). Boston, MA: Allyn and Bacon.

Gresham, R. M., & Elliott, S. N. (1990). *Social skills rating system.* Circle Pines, MN: American Guidance Service.

Grieten, H., De Haene, L., & Uyttebroek, K. (2007). Cross-cultural validation of the child abuse potential inventory in Belgium (Flanders): Relations with demographic characteristics and parenting problems. *Journal of Family Violence, 22*, 223–229.

Grills, A. E., & Ollendick, T. H. (2003). Multiple informant agreement and the Anxiety disorders interview schedule for parents and children. *Journal of the American Academy of Child & Adolescent Psychiatry, 42*, 30–40.

Gutterman, E. M., O'Brien, J. D., & Young, J. G. (1987). Structured diagnostic interviews for children and adolescents: Current status and future directions. *Journal of the American Academy of Child and Adolescent Psychiatry, 26*, 621–630.

Haak, R. A. (1990). Using the sentence completion to assess emotional disturbance. In C. R. Reynolds & R. W. Kamphaus (Eds.), *Handbook of psychological and educational assessment of children: Personality, behavior, and context* (pp. 147–167). New York: Guilford Press.

Haak, R. A. (2003). Using the sentence completion to assess emotional disturbance. In C. R. Reynolds & R. W. Kamphaus (Eds.), *Handbook of psychological and educational assessment of children: Personality, behavior, and context-2nd edition* (pp. 159–181). New York: Guilford.

Hammen, C., Rudolph, K., Weisz, J., Rao, U., & Burge, D. (1999). The context of depression in clinic-referred youth: Neglected areas in treatment. *Journal of the American Academy of Child & Adolescent Psychiatry, 38*, 64–71.

Hampson, S., Andrews, J., Barckley, M., & Peterson, M. (2007). Trait stability and continuity in childhood: Relating sociability and hostility to the five-factor model of personality. *Journal of Research in Personality, 41*, 507–523.

Hand, C., Archer, R., Handel, R., & Forbey, J. (2007). The classification accuracy of the Minnesota multiphasic personality inventory-adolescent: Effects of modifying the normative sample. *Assessment, 14*, 80–85.

Hankin, B. L., Grant, K. E., Cheeley, C., Wetter, E., Farahmand, F. K., & Westerholm, R. I. (2008). Depressive disorders. In M. Hersen (Series Ed.) & D. Reitman (Vol. Ed.), *Handbook of psychological assessment, case conceptualization, and treatment* (pp. 199–230). Hoboken, NJ: John Wiley & Sons.

Hankin, B. L., Mermelstein, R., & Roesch, L. (2007). Sex differences in adolescent depression: Stress exposure and reactivity. *Child Development, 78*, 279–295.

Harrison, P. L., & Oakland, T. (2003). *Adaptive Behavior Assessment System* (2nd ed.). San Antonio, TX: The Psychological Corporation.

Hayes, S. C. (2005). Diagnosing intellectual disability in a forensic sample: Gender and age effects on the relationship between cognitive and adaptive functioning. *Journal of Intellectual & Developmental Disability, 30*, 97–103.

Hayes, S. C., Nelson, R. O., & Jarrett, R. B. (1987). The treatment utility of assessment: A functional approach to evaluating assessment quality. *American Psychologist, 42*, 963–974.

Hays, S., & McCallum, R. (2005). A comparison of the pencil-and-paper and computer-administered Minnesota multiphasic personality inventory-adolescent. *Psychology in the Schools, 42*, 605–613.

Haynes, S.N., & O'Brien, W.H. (1988). The Gordian knot of DSM-III use: Integrating principles of behavior classification and complex causal models. *Behavioral Assessment, 10*, 95–105.

Hawes, D. J. & Dadds, M. R. (2006). Assessing parenting practices through parent-report and direct observation during parenting-training. *Journal of Child and Family Studies, 15*, 555–568.

Holaday, M. (2000). Rorschach protocols from children and adolescents diagnosed with posttraumatic stress disorder. *Journal of Personality Assessment, 75*, 143–157.

Haley, G. M. T., Fine, S., Marriage, K., Moretti, M. M., & Freeman, R. J. (1985). Cognitive bias and depression in psychiatrically disturbed children and adolescents. *Journal of Consulting and Clinical Psychology, 53*, 535–537.

Hall, C. W., & Haws, H. D. (1989). Depressive symptomatology in learning-disabled and nonlearning-disabled students. *Psychology in the Schools, 26*, 359–364.

Hamilton, C., Fuchs, D., Fuchs, L. S., & Roberts, H. (2000). Rates of classroom participation and the validity of sociometry. *School Psychology Review, 29*, 251–266.

Hammen, C., Brennan, P. A., Keenan-Miller, D., & Herr, N. R. (2008). Early onset recurrent subtype of adolescent depression: Clinical and psychosocial correlates. *Journal of Child Psychology and Psychiatry, 49*, 443–440.

Hammen, C., Gordon, G., Burge, D., Adrian, C., Jaenicke, C., & Hiroto, G. (1987). Maternal affective disorders, illness, and stress: Risk for children's psychopathology. *American Journal of Psychiatry, 144*, 736–741.

Hammer, E. F. (1958). *The clinical application of projective drawings.* Springfield, IL: Thomas.

Handfinger, A. S. (2000). *The effects of behavior problems on the development of adaptive skills in children. A* dissertation submitted to the graduate faculty of The University of Georgia.

Handwerk, M. L., Friman, P. C., & Larzelere, R. (2000). Comparing the DISC and the youth self-report. *Journal of the American Academy of Child and Adolescent Psychiatry, 39*, 807–808.

Handwerk, M. L., Larzelere, R. E., Soper, S. H., & Friman, P. C. (1999). Parent and child discrepancies in reporting severity of problem behaviors in three out-of-home settings. *Psychological Assessment, 11*, 14–23.

Harrington, R. G., & Follett, G. M. (1984). The readability of child personality assessment instruments. *Journal of Psychoeducational Assessment, 2*, 37–48.

Harrington, R. G., Fudge, H., Rutter, M., Pickles, A., & Hill, J. (1991). Adult outcomes of childhood and adolescent depression: II. Links with antisocial disorders. *Journal of the American Academy of Child and Adolescent Psychiatry, 30*, 434–439.

Harris, F. C., & Lahey, B. B. (1982a). Recording system bias in direct observational methodology: A review and critical analysis of factors causing inaccurate coding behavior. *Clinical Psychology Review, 2*, 539–556.

Harris, F. C., & Lahey, B. B. (1982b). Subject reactivity in direct observational assessment: A review and critical analysis. *Clinical Psychology Review, 2*, 523–538.

Harrison, P. L. (1990). Assessment with the Vineland Adaptive Behavior Scales. In C. R. Reynolds & R. W. Kamphaus (Eds.), *Handbook of psychological and educational assessment of children: Personality, behavior, and context.* New York: Guilford Press.

Harrison, P. L., & Oakland, T. (2000). *Adaptive Behavior Assessment System manual.* San Antonio, TX: The Psychological Corporation.

Hart, D. H. (1972). *The Hart sentence completion test for children.* Salt Lake City: Educational Support Systems.

Hart, D. H. (1986).The sentence completion techniques. In H. M. Knoff (Ed.), *The assessment of child and adolescent personality* (pp. 245–272). New York: Guilford Press.

Hart, D. H., Kehle, T. J., & Davies, M. V. (1983). Effectiveness of sentence completion techniques: A review of the hart sentence completion test for children. *School Psychology Review, 12*, 428–434.

Hart, E. L., & Lahey, B. B. (1999). General child behavior rating scales. In D. Shaffer and C. P. Lucas (Eds.), *Diagnostic assessment in child and adolescent psychopathology* (pp. 65–87). New York: Guilford Press.

Hartley, M. M. M. (1999). The relationship among disruptive behaviors, attention, and academic achievement in a clinic referral sample. *Dissertation Abstracts International Section A: Humanities and Social Sciences, 60*(2-A), 0333.

Hartmann, D. P., Roper, B. L., & Bradford, D. C. (1979). Some relationships between behavioral and traditional assessment. *Journal of Behavioral Assessment, 1*, 3–21.

Harvey, V. S. (1989, March). Eschew obfuscation: Support of clear writing. *Communique*, p. 12.

Hasegawa, C. (1989). The unmentioned minority. In C. J. Maker & L. W. Schiever (Eds.), *Defensive programs for cultural and ethnic minorities* (Vol. 2). Austin, TX: Pro-Ed.

Haskett, M. E., Ahern, L. S., Ward, C. S., & Allaire, J. C. (2006). Factor structure and validity of the parenting stress index-short form. *Journal of Clinical Child and Adolescent Psychology, 35*, 302–312.

Haskett, M. E., Scott, S. S. & Fann, K. D. (1995). Child abuse potential inventory and parenting behavior: Relationships with high-risk correlates. *Child Abuse & Neglect, 19*, 1483–1495.

Hathaway, S. R., & McKinley, J. C. (1940). A multiphasic personality schedule (Minnesota): I. Construction of the schedule. *Journal of Psychology, 10*, 249–254.

Hathaway, S. R., & McKinley, J. C. (1942). *Minnesota Multiphasic Personality Inventory.* Minneapolis: University of Minnesota Press.

Hathaway, S. R., & McKinley, J. C. (1989). *MMPI-2: Minnesota Multiphasic Personality Inventory – Second Edition.* Minneapolis: University of Minnesota Press.

Hayvren, M., & Hymnel, S. (1984). Ethical issues in sociometric testing: Impact of sociometric measures on interaction behavior. *Developmental Psychology, 20*, 849–884.

Haz, A. M., & Ramirez, V. (1998). Preliminary validation of the child abuse potential inventory in Chile. *Child Abuse & Neglect, 22*, 869–879.

Heber, R. (1959). A manual on terminology and classification in mental retardation (2nd ed.). (Monograph supplement). *American Journal of Mental Deficiency.*

Heber, R., & Helzer, J. E. (1988). Schizophrenia: Epidemiology. In R. Michels, J. O. Cavenar, A. M. Cooper, S. B. Guze, L. L. Judd, G. L. Merman, & A. J. Solnit (Eds.), *Psychiatry.* New York: Lippincott.

Helms, J. E. (1986). Expanding racial identity theory to cover counseling process. *Journal of Counseling Psychology, 33*, 62–64.

Helzer, J.E. & Pryzbeck, T.T. (1988). The co-occurrence of alcoholism with other psychiatric disorders in the general population and its impact on treatment. Journal of Studies on Alcohol, 49, 2129–224.

Helzer, J.E. & Robins, L.N. (1988). The Diagnostic Interview Schedule: Its development, evolution, and use. Social Psychiatry and Psychiatric Epidemiology, 23, 6–16.

Hembree-Kigin, T. L., & McNeil, C. B. (1995). *Parent-child interaction therapy.* New York: Plenum Press.

Hendren, R. L., DeBacker, I., & Pandina, G. J. (2000). Review of neuroimaging studies of child and adolescent psychiatric disorders from the past 10 years. *Journal of the American Academy of Child and Adolescent Psychiatry, 39*, 815–828.

Henning-Stout, M. (1998). Assessing the behavior of girls: What we see and what we miss. *Journal of School Psychology, 36*, 433–455.

Hicks, M. M., Rogers, R., & Cashel, M. (2000). Predictions of violent and total infractions among institutionalized male juvenile offenders. *Journal of the American Academy of Psychiatry and the Law, 28*, 183–190.

Hill, A. B., Kemp-Wheeler, S. M. & Jones, S. A. (1986). What does the Beck depression inventory measure in students? *Personality and Individual Differences, 7*, 39–47.

Hiller, J. B., Rosenthal, R., Bornstein, R. F., Berry, D. T. R., & Brunell-Neulieb, S. (1999). A comparative meta-analysis of Rorschach and MMPI validity. *Psychological Assessment, 11*, 278–296.

Hinshaw, S. P. (1987). On the distinction between attentional deficits/hyperactivity and conduct problems/aggression in child psychopathology. *Psychological Bulletin, 101*, 443–463.

Hinshaw, S. P. (1991). Stimulant medications and their treatment of aggression in children with attention deficits. *Journal of Clinical Child Psychology, 20*, 301–312.

Hinshaw, S. P. (1992). Externalizing behavior problems and academic underachievement in childhood and adolescence: Causal relationships and underlying mechanism. *Psychological Bulletin, 111*, 127–155.

Hodges, K. (1994). *Child and adolescent functional assessment scale.* Ypsilanti, MI: Eastern Michigan University.

Hodges, K., Cool, J., & McKnew, D. (1989). Test-retest reliability of a clinical research interview for children: The child assessment schedule (CAS). *Psychological Assessment, 1*, 317–322.

Hodges, K., Doucette-Gates, A., & Liao, Q. (1999). The relationship between the child and adolescent functional assessment scale (CAFAS) and indicators of functioning. *Journal of Child and Family Studies, 8*, 109–122.

Hodges, K., & Kim, C. (2000). Psychometric study of the child and adolescent functional assessment scale: Prediction of con-tact with the law and poor school attendance. *Journal of Abnormal Child Psychology, 28*, 287–297.

Hodges, K., & Saunders, W. (1989). Internal consistency of a diagnostic interview for children: The child assessment schedule. *Journal of Abnormal Child Psychology, 17*, 691–701.

Hodges, K., & Wong, M. M. (1996). Psychometric characteristics of a multidimensional measure to assess impairment: The child and adolescent functional assessment scale. *Journal of Child and Family Studies, 5*, 445–467.

Hodges, K., & Zeman, J. (1993). Interviewing. In T. H. Ollendick & M. Hersen (Eds.), *Handbook of child and adolescent assessment* (pp. 65–81). Boston, MA: Allyn and Bacon.

Hojnoski, R. L., Morrison, R., Brown, M., & Matthews, W. J. (2006). Projective test use among school psychologists: A survey and critique. *Journal of Psychoeducational Assessment, 24*, 145–159.

Holaday, M., Smith, D. A., & Sherry, A. (2000). Sentence completion tests: A survey of the literature and results of a survey of members of the Society for Personality Assessment. *Journal of Personality Assessment, 74*, 371–383.

Holden, E. W., & Banez, G. A. (1996). Child abuse potential and parenting stress within maltreating families. *Journal of Family Violence, 11*, 1–12.

Holtzman, W. H., & Swartz, J. D. (2003). Use of the Holtzman Inkblot Technique (HIT) with children. In C. R. Reynolds & R. W. Kamphaus (Eds.), *Handbook of psychological and educational assessment in children: Personality, behavior, and context* (2nd ed., pp. 198–2218). New York: Guilford.

Howlin, P. (2003). Outcome in high-functioning adults with autism with and without early language delays: Implications for the differentiation between autism and Asperger syndrome. *Journal of Autism and Developmental Disorders, 33*, 3–14.

Hoza, B., Gerders, A. C., Mrug, S., Hinshaw, S. P., Bukowski, W. M., Gold, J. A., et al. (2005). Peer –assessed outcomes in the multimodal treatment study of children with attention deficit hyperactivity disorder. *Journal of Clinical Child and Adolescent Psychology, 34*, 74–86.

Huberty, C. J., DiStefano, C. & Kamphaus, R. W. (1997). Behavioral clustering of school children. *Multivariate Behavioral Research, 32*, 105–143.

Huber, C. J., Kamphaus, R. W., & DiStefano, C. (1997). Behavioral clustering of school children. *Multivariate Behavioral Research, 32*, 105–134.

Hudziak, J. J., Heath, A. C., Madden, P. F., Reich, W., Bucholz, K. K., Slutske, W., et al. (1998). Latent class and factor analysis of DSM-IV ADHD: A twin study of female adolescents. *Journal of the American Academy of Child and Adolescent Psychiatry, 37*, 848–857.

Hudziak, J. J., Wadsworth, B. A., Heath, A. C., & Achenbach, T. M. (1999). Latent class analysis of child behavior checklist attention problems. *Journal of the American Academy of Child and Adolescent Psychiatry, 38*, 985–991.

Huesmann, L. R., Eron, L. D., Lefkowitz, M. M., & Walder, L. O. (1984). Stability of aggression over time and generations. *Developmental Psychology, 20*, 1120–1134.

Hughes, J. (1990). Assessment of social skills: Sociometric and behavioral approaches. In C. R. Reynolds & R. W. Kamphaus (Eds.), *Handbook of psychological and educational assessment of children: Personality, behavior, and context* (pp. 423–444). New York: Guilford Press.

Hughes, T. L., Gacono, C. B., & Owen, P. F. (2007). Current status of Rorschach assessment: Implications for the school psychologist. *Psychology in the Schools, 44*, 281–291.

Hughes, J. N., Meehan, B. T., & Cavell, T. A. (2004). Development and validation of a gender-balanced measure of aggression-relevant social cognition. *Journal of Clinical Child and Adolescent Psychology, 33*, 292–302.

Hunsley, J. & Bailey, J. M. (2001). Whither the Rorschach? An analysis of the evidence. *Psychological Assessment, 13*, 472–485.

Hunsley, J. & DiGiulio, G. (2001). Norms, norming, and clinical assessment. *Clinical Psychology: Science and Practice, 8*, 378–382.

Hutcheson, J. J. & Black, M. M. (1996). Psychometric properties of the Parenting Stress Index in a sample of low-income African-American mother of infants and toddlers. *Early Education and Development, 7*, 381–400.

Huth-Bocks, A., Kerr, D., Ivey, A., Kramer, A., & King, C. (2007). Assessment of psychiatrically hospitalized suicidal adolescents: Self-report instruments as predictors of suicidal thoughts and behavior. *Journal of the American Academy of Child & Adolescent Psychiatry, 46*, 387–395.

Hutt, M. L. (1980). *The Michigan picture test – revised.* New York: Grune & Stratton.

Hynd, G. W., Hern, K. L., Novey, E. S., Eliopulos, D., Marshall, R., Gonzales, J. J., et al. (1993). Attention-deficit hyperactivity disorder and asymmetry of the caudate nucleus. *Journal of Child Neurology, 8*, 339–347.

Hynd, G. W., & Willis, W. G. (1988). *Pediatric neuropsychology.* Boston, MA: Allyn and Bacon.

Inclan, J. E., & Herron, D. G. (1985). Puerto Rican adolescents. In G. T. Gibbs & L. N. Huang (Eds.), *Children of color* (pp. 251–277). San Francisco: Jossey-Bass.

Ivanova, M. Y., Achenbach, T. M., Rescorla, L. A., Dumenci, L., Almqvist, F., Bilenberg, N., et al. (2007). The generalizability of the youth self-report syndrome structure in 23 societies. *Journal of Consulting and Clinical Psychology, 75*, 729–738.

Jackson, M. F., Barth, J. M., Powell, N., Lochman, J. E. (2006). Classroom contextual effects of race on children's peer nominations. *Child Development, 77*, 1325–1337.

James, E. M., Reynolds, C. R., & Dunbar, J. (1994). Self-report instruments. In T. H. Ollendick & N. J. King, et al. (Eds.), *International handbook of phobic and anxiety disorders in children and adolescents: Issues in clinical child psychology* (pp. 317–329). New York: Plenum Press.

Janosz, M., Le Blanc, M., Boulerice, B., & Tremblay, R. E. (2000). Predicting different types of school dropouts: A typological approach with two longitudinal samples. *Journal of Educational Psychology, 92*, 171–190.

Janus, M. D., de Groot, C., & Toepfer, S. M. (1998). The MMPI-A and 13-year-old inpatients: How young is too young? *Assessment, 5*, 321–332.

Jensen, P. S. (2003). Comorbidity and child psychopathology: Recommendations for the next decade. *Journal of Abnormal Child Psychology, 31*, 293–300.

Jensen, P. S., Kettle, L., Roper, M. T., Sloan, M. T., Dulcan, M. K., Hoven, C., et al. (1999). Are stimulants overprescribed? Treatment of ADHD in four U.S. communities. *Journal of the American Academy of Child and Adolescent Psychiatry, 38*, 797–804.

Jensen, P. S., Rubio-Stipec, M., Canino, G., Bird, H. R., Dulcan, M. K., Schwab-Stone, M. E., et al. (1999). Parent and child contributions to diagnosis of mental disorder: Are both informants always necessary? *Journal of the American Academy of Child & Adolescent Psychiatry, 38*, 1569–1579.

Jensen, P. S., Watanabe, H. E., & Richters, J. E. (1999). Who's up first? Testing for order effects in structured interviews using a counterbalanced experimental design. *Journal of Abnormal Child Psychology, 27*, 439–446.

Jersild, A. T., & Holmes, R. (1935). *Children's fears* (Child Development Monograph No. 20). New York: Columbia University Press.

Jesness, C. F. (1988). *Jesness inventory of adolescent personality.* North Tonawanda, NY: Multi-Health Systems.

Jiang, X. L. & Cillessen, A. H. N. (2005). Stability of continuous measures of sociometric status: A meta-analysis. *Developmental Review, 25*, 1–25.

Johnson, S. B. (1988). Diabetes mellitus in childhood. In D. Routh (Ed.), *Handbook of pediatric psychology* (pp. 9–31). New York: Guilford Press.

Johnston, C. (1996). Parent charecteristics and parent-child interactions in families of nonproblem children and ADHD children with higher and lower levels of oppositional-defiant behaviour. *Journal of Abnormal Child Psychology, 24*, 85–104.

Johnston, C. & Mash, E. J. (2001). Families of children with attention-deficit/hyperactivity disorder: Review and recommendations for future research. *Clinical Child and Family Review, 4*, 183–207.

Johnston, C., Pelham, W. E., & Murphy, H. A. (1985). Peer relationships in ADHD and normal children: A developmental analysis of peer and teacher ratings. *Journal of Abnormal Child Psychology, 13*, 89–100.

Joiner, T. E., Schmidt, K. L., & Barnett, J. (1996). Size, detail, and line heaviness in children's drawings as correlates of emotional distress: (More) negative evidence. *Journal of Personality Assessment, 67*, 127–141.

Joint Committee on Testing Practices (2004). *Code of Fair Testing Practices in Education.* Washington, DC: American Psychological Association.

Jonsen, A. R., Siegler, M., & Winslade, W. J. (1992). *Clinical ethics* (3rd ed.). New York: McGraw-Hill.

Jung, C. J. (1910). The association method. *American Journal of Psychology, 21*, 219–235. Reprinted in L. D. Goodstein & R. I. Lanyon (Eds.), *Readings in personality assessment.* New York: Wiley.

Kachigan, S. K. (1982). *Multivariate statistical analysis: A conceptual introduction.* New York: Radus Press.

Kaczmarek, T., Hagan, M., & Kettler, R. (2006). Screening for suicide among juvenile delinquents: Reliability and validity evidence for the suicide screening inventory (SSI). *International Journal of Offender Therapy and Comparative Criminology, 50*, 204–217.

Kagan, J., & Snidman, N. (1991). Temperamental factors in human development. *American Psychologist, 46*, 856–862.

Kamphaus, R. W. (1987). Conceptual and psychometric issues in the assessment of adaptive behavior. *Journal of Special Education, 21*, 27–36.

Kamphaus, R. W. (1998). Intelligence test interpretation: Acting in the absence of evidence. In A. Prifitera & D. Saklofske (Eds.), *WISC-III Clinical Use and interpretation: Scientist-practitioner perspectives* (pp. 39–57). San Diego: Academic Press.

Kamphaus, R. W. (2001a). *Clinical assessment of child and adolescent intelligence.* Needham Heights, MA: Allyn & Bacon.

Kamphaus, R. W. (2001b). *Clinical assessment of children's intelligence* (2nd ed.). Boston, MA: Allyn and Bacon.

Kamphaus, R. W., & Frick, P. J. (1996). *Clinical assessment of child and adolescent personality and behavior.* Boston: Allyn and Bacon.

Kamphaus, R.W., & Campbell, J.C. (2006). Psychodiagnostic assessment of children: dimensional and categorical methods. New York, NY: Wiley.

Kamphaus, R. W., Huberty, C. J., DiStefano, C., & Petoskey, M. D. (1997). A typology of teacher rated child behavior for a national U. S. sample. *Journal of Abnormal Child Psychology, 25*, 453–463.

Kamphaus, R. W., Jimenez, M. E., Pineda, D. A., Rowe, E. W., Fleckenstein, L., Restrepo, M. A., et al. (2000). Analisis transcultural de un instrumento de dimensiones multiples en el diagnostico del deficit de atencidn. *Revista de Neuropsicologia, Neuropsygiatria y Neurociencias, 2*, 51–63.

Kamphaus, R. W., Morgan, A. W., Cox, M. R., & Powell, R. M. (1995). Personality and intelligence in the psychodiagnostic process. In D. H. Saklofske & M. Zeidner (Eds.), *International handbook of personality and intelligence* (pp. 525–544). New York: Plenum Press.

Kamphaus, R. W., Petoskey, M. D., Cody, A. H., Rowe, E. W., Huberty, C. J., & Reynolds, C. R. (1999a). A typology of parent-rated child behavior for a national U. S. sample. *Journal of Child Psychology and Psychiatry and Allied Disciplines, 40*, 1–10.

Kamphaus, R. W., Petoskey, M. D., Cody, A. H., Rowe, E. W., Huberty, C. J., & Reynolds, C. R. (1999b). A typology of parent-rated child behavior for a national U.S. sample. *Journal of Child Psychology and Psychiatry and Allied Disciplines, 40*, 607–616.

Kamphaus, R. W., Petoskey, M. D., & Rowe, E. W. (2000). Current trends in psychological testing of children. *Professional Psychology: Research and Practice, 31*, 155–164.

Kamphaus, R. W., & Reynolds, C. R. (1998). *Behavior Assessment System for Children (BASC) ADHD Monitor.* Circle Pines, MN: American Guidance Service.

Kamphaus, R. W., Reynolds, C. R., & Imperato-McCammon, C. (1998). Roles of diagnosis and classification in the schools. In T. B. Gutkin & C. R. Reynolds (Eds.), *The Handbook of School Psychology* (3rd ed., pp. 292–316). New York: Wiley.

Kandel, D. B., & Davies, M. (1988). Adult sequelae of adolescent depressive symptoms. *Archives of General Psychiatry, 43*, 255–262.

Karver, M. S. (2006). Determinants of multiple informant agreement on child and adolescent behavior. *Journal of Abnormal Child Psychology, 34*, 251–261.

Karver, M. S., Handelsman, J. B., Fields, S., & Bickman, L. (2006). Meta-analysis of therapeutic relationship variables in youth and family therapy: The evidence for different relationship variables in the child and adolescent treatment outcome literature. *Clinical Psychology Review, 26*, 50–65.

Kashani, J. H., Orvaschel, H., Burk, J. P., & Reid, J. C. (1985). Informant variance: The issue of parent-child disagreement. *Journal of the American Academy of Child and Adolescent Psychiatry, 24*, 437–441.

Kashner, T. M., Rush, A. J., Surís, A., Biggs, M. M., Gajewski, V. L.Hooker, D. J., et al. (2003). Impact of structured clinical interviews on physicians' practices in community mental health settings. *Psychiatric Services, 54*, 712–718.

Kaufman, A. S. (1994). *Intelligent testing with the WISC-III.* New York: Wiley

Kazdin, A. E. (1981). Behavioral observation. In M. Hersen & A. S. Bellack (Eds.), *Behavioral assessment: A practical handbook* (pp. 59–100). New York: Pergamon Press.

Kazdin, A. E. (1988). Childhood depression. In E. J. Mash & L. G. Terdal (Eds.), *Behavioral assessment of childhood disorders* (2nd ed., pp. 157–195). New York: Guilford Press.

Kazdin, A. E. (1989). Childhood depression. In E. J. Mash & R. A. Barkley (Eds.), *Treatment of childhood disorders* (pp. 135–166). New York: Guilford Press.

Keenan, K. (2000). Emotional dysregulation as a risk factor for child psychopathology. *Clinical Psychology: Science and Practice, 7*, 418–434.

Keiley, M. K., Bates, J. E., Dodge, K. A., & Pettit, G. S. (2000). A cross-domain growth analysis: Externalizing and internalizing behaviors during 8 years of childhood. *Journal of Abnormal Child Psychology, 28*(2), 161–179.

Keith, T. Z. (1990). Confirmatory and hierarchical confirmatory analysis of the differential ability scales. *Journal of Psychoeducational Assessment, 8*, 391–405.

Keller, H. R. (1986). Behavioral observation approaches to personality assessment. In H. M. Knoff (Ed.), *The assessment of child and adolescent personality* (pp. 353–390). New York: Guilford Press.

Kendall, P. C., & Ronan, K. R. (1990). Assessment of children's anxieties, fears, and phobias: Cognitive-behavioral models and methods. In C. R. Reynolds & R. W. Kamphaus (Eds.), *Handbook of psychological and educational assessment of children: Personality, behavior, and context* (pp. 223–244). New York: Guilford Press.

Kendall, P. C., & Clarkin, J. F. (1992). Introduction to special section: Comorbidity and treatment implications. *Journal of Consulting and Clinical Psychology, 60*, 833–834.

Keogh, B. K. (1994). A matrix of decision points in the measurement of learning disabilities. In G. R. Lyon (Ed.), *Frames of reference for the assessment of learning disabilities: New views on measurement issues* (pp. 15–26). Baltimore, MD: Paul H. Brookes.

Kerr, D., Lunkenheimer, E., & Olson, S. (2007). Assessment of child problem behaviors by multiple informants: A longitudinal study from preschool to school entry. *Journal of Child Psychology and Psychiatry, 48*, 967–975.

Kim, J. A., Szatmari, P., Bryson, S. E., Streiner, D. L., & Wilson, F. J. (2000). The prevalence of anxiety and mood problems among children with autism and Asperger syndrome. *Autism, 4*, 117–132.

Kimonis, E. R., Frick, P. J., Skeem, J. L., Marsee, M. A., Cruise, K., Muñoz, L. C., & Aucoin, K. J. (2008). Assessing callous-unemotional traits in adolescent offenders: Validation of the inventory of callous-unemotional traits. *Journal of the International Association of Psychiatry and Law. Special Issue: 'Psychopathy and risk taxation' in adolescent offenders , 31*, 241–251.

Klein, D. N., Dougherty, L. R., & Olino, T. M. (2005). Toward guidelines for evidence-based assessment of depression in children and adolescents. *Journal of Clinical Child and Adolescent Psychology, 34*, 412–432.

Klein, D. N., Lewinsohn, P. M., & Seeley, J. R. (1997). Psychosocial characteristics of adolescents with a past history of dysthymic disorder: Comparison with adolescents with past histories of major depressive and non-affective disorders, and never mentally ill controls. *Journal of Affective Disorders, 42*, 127–135.

Kleinmmntz, B. (1967). *Personality measurement: An introduction.* Homewood, IL: Dorsey Press.

Kline, R. B. (1989). Is the Fourth Edition Stanford-Binet a four-factor test? Confirmatory analysis of alternative models for ages 2 through 23. *Journal of Psychoeducational Assessment, 7*, 913.

Kline, R. B. (1994). Test review: New objective rating scales for child assessment, I. Parent- and teacher-informant inventories of the behavior assessment system for children, the child behavior checklist, and the teacher report form. *Journal of Psychoeducational Assessment, 12*, 289–306.

Kline, R. B. (1995). New objective rating scales for child assessment, II. Self-report scales for children and adolescents: Self-report of personality of the behavior assessment system for children, the youth self-report, and the personality inventory for youth. *Journal of Psychoeducational Assessment, 13*, 169–193.

Knight, L. W. (1997). The BASC parent rating scales: Patterns of behavior by gender, race, and socioeconomic status. *Dissertation Abstracts International Section A: Humanities and Social Sciences, 58*(1-A), 0084.

Knoff, H. M. (1983). Justifying projective/personality assessment in school psychology: A response to Batsch and Peterson. *School Psychology Review, 12*, 446–451.

Kochanska, G. (1993). Toward a synthesis of parental socialization and child temperament in early development of con-science. *Child Development, 64*, 325–347.

Kochanska, G., Kuczynski, L., & Radke-Yarrow, N. I. (1989). Correspondence between mothers' self-reported and observed child-rearing practices. *Child Development, 60*, 56–63.

Konold, T. R., Walthall, J. C., & Pianta, R. C. (2004). The behavior of child ratings: Measurement structure of the child behavior checklist across time, informants, and child gender. *Behavioral Disorders, 29*, 372–383.

Koocher, G. P. (1993). Ethical issues in the psychological assessment of children. In T. H. Ollendick & M. Hersen (Eds.), *Handbook of child and adolescent assessment* (pp. 51–61). Boston, MA: Allyn and Bacon.

Koppitz, E. M. (1968). *Psychological evaluation of children's human figure drawings.* New York: Grune at Stratton.

Koppitz, E. M. (1983). Projective drawings with children, and adolescents. *School Psychology Review, 12*, 421–427.

Kovacs, M. (1989). Affective disorders in children and adolescents. *American Psychologist, 44*(2), 209–215.

Kovacs, M. (1992). *The Children's Depression Inventory manual.* New York: Multi-Health Systems.

Kovacs, M. (2001). Gender and the course of major depressive disorder through adolescence in clinically-referred youngsters. *Journal of the American Academy of Child and Adolescent Psychiatry, 40*, 1079–1085.

Kovacs, M., Paulauskas, S., Gatsonis, C., & Richards, C. (1988). Depressive disorders in childhood: III. A longitudinal study of comorbidity with and risk for conduct disorders. *Journal of Affective Disorders, 15*, 205–217.

Krefetz, D., Steer, R., Gulab, N., & Beck, A. (2002). Convergent validity of the Beck depression inventory-II with the Reynolds adolescent depression scale in psychiatric inpatients. *Journal of Personality Assessment, 78*, 451–460.

Kroon, N., Goudena, P. P., & Rispens, J. (1998). Thematic apperception tests for child and adolescent assessment: A practitioner's consumer guide. *Journal of Psychoeducational Assessment, 16*, 99–117.

Krug, D. A., & Arick, J. R. (2003). *Krug Asperger's disorder index.* Austin, Texas: Pro-Ed.

Kuehne, C., Kehle, T. J., & McMahon, W. (1987). Differences between children with attention deficit disorder, children with specific learning disabilities, and normal children. *Journal of School Psychology, 25*, 161–166.

Kuramoto, H., Kanbayaski, Y., Nakata, Y., Fukui, T., Mukai, T., & Negishi, Y. (1999). Standardization of the Japanese version of the youth self report (YSR). *Japanese Journal of Child and Adolescent Psychiatry, 40*, 329–344.

Lachar, D. (1982). *Personality inventory for children-revised (PICR).* Los Angeles: Western Psychological Services.

Lachar, D. (1990). Objective assessment of child and adolescent personality: The Personality Inventory for Children. In C. R. Reynolds & R. W. Kantphaus (Eds.), *Handbook of psychological and educational assessment of children: Personality, behavior, and context* (pp. 298–323). New York: Guilford Press.

Lachar, D. (1993). Symptom checklists and personality inventories. In T. R. Kratochwill & R. J. Morris (Eds.), *Handbook of psychotherapy for children and adolescents* (pp. 38–57). Boston, MA: Allyn and Bacon.

Lachar, D. (1999). Personality inventory for Children, Second Edition (PTC-2), Personality Inventory for Youth (PM, and Student Behavior Survey (SBS). In M. Maiuish (Ed.), *The use of psychological testing for treatment planning and outcomes assessment* (2nd ed.). Mahwah, NJ: Lawrence Erlbaum.

Lachar, D., & Gruber, C. P. (1992). *Personality Inventory for Youth (P1Y).* Los Angeles: Western Psychological Services.

Lachar, D., & Gruber, C. P. (1993). Development of the personality inventory for youth: A self-report companion to the personality inventory for children. *Journal of Personality Assessment, 61*, 81–98.

Lachar, D., & Gruber, C. P. (1994). *The Personality Inventory for Youth.* Los Angeles: Western Psychological Services.

Lachar, D., & Gruber, C. P. (1997). *Personality Inventory for Youth (PIP) manual: Administration and interpretation guide.* Los Angeles: Western Psychological Services.

Lachar, D. & Gruber, C. (2001). *Personality Inventory for Children, second edition (PIC-2): Standard form and behavioral summary manual.* Los Angeles: Western Psychological Services.

Lachar, D., Harper, R. A., Green, B. A., Morgan, S. T., & Wheeler, A. C. (1996, August). *The Personality Inventory fir Youth: Contribution to diagnosis.* Poster presented at the 104th Annual Convention of the American Psychological Association, Toronto, Canada.

Lachar, D., Morgan, S. T., Espades, A., & Schomer, O. (2000, August). *Effect of defensiveness on two self-report child adjustment inventories.* Poster presented at the 108th Annual Convention of the American Psychological Association, Washington, DC.

Lachar, D., Wingenfeld, S. A., Kline, R. B., & Gruber, C. P. (2000). *Student behavior survey.* Los Angeles, CA: Western Psychological Services.

LaCombe,J.A.,Kline,R.B.,Lachar,D.,Butkus,M.,&Hillman,S.B. (1991). Case history correlates of a personality inventory for children (PIC) profile typology. *Psychological Assessment, 3*, 678–687.

Lahey, B. B., Applegate, B., Waldman, I. D., Loft, J. D., Hankin, B. L., & Rick, J. (2004). The structure of child and adolescent psychopathology: Generating new hypotheses. *Journal of Abnormal Psychology, 113*, 358–385.

Lahey, B. B., Applegate, B., Barkley, R. A., Garfinkel, B., McBurnett, K., Kerdyck, L., et al. (1994). DSM-IV field trials for oppositional defiant disorder and conduct disorder in children and adolescents. *American Journal of Psychiatry, 151*, 1163–1171.

Lahey, B. B., Applegate, B., McBurnett, K., Biederman, J., Greenhill, L., Hynd, G. W., et al. (1994). DSM-IV field trials for attention-deficit hyperactivity disorder in children and adolescents. *American Journal of Psychiatry, 151*, 1673–1685.

Lahey, B. B., Carlson, C. L. & Frick, P. J. (1997). Attention-deficit disorders: A review of research relevant to diagnostic classification. In T. A. Widiger, A. J. Frances, H. A. Pincus, R. Ross, M. B. First, & W. Davis (Eds.), *DSM-IV sourcebook* (Vol. 3, pp. 163–188). Washington, DC: American Psychiatric Association.

Lahey, B.B., Goodman, S.H., Waldman, I.D., Bird, H., Canino, G., Jenson, P., Regier, D., Leaf, P.J., Gordon, R., & Applegate, B. (1999). Relation of age of onset to the type of severity of child and adolescent conduct problems. Journal of Abnormal Child Psychology, 27, 247–260.

Lahey, B. B., Hart, E. L., Pliszka, S., Applegate, B., & McBurnett, K. (1993). Neurophysiological correlates of conduct disorder: A rationale and a review of research. *Journal of Clinical Child Psychology, 22*, 141–153.

Lahey, B. B., & Loeber, R. (1994). Framework for a developmental model of oppositional defiant disorder and conduct disorder. In D. K. Routh (Ed.), *Disruptive behavior disorders in childhood* (pp. 139–180). New York: Plenum.

Lahey, B. B., Loeber, R., Quay, H. C., Applegate, B., Shaffer, D., Waldman, I., et al. (1998). Validity of DSM-IV subtypes of conduct disorder based on age of onset. *Journal of the American Academy of Child and Adolescent Psychiatry, 37*, 435–442.

Lahey, B. B., Loeber, R., Quay, H. C., Frick, P. J., & Grimm, J. (1992). Oppositional defiant disorder and conduct disorders: Issues to be resolved for DSM-IV. *Journal of the American Academy of Child and Adolescent Psychiatry, 31*, 539–546.

Lahey, B. B., Loeber, R., Stouthamer-Loeber, M., Christ, M. A. G., Green, S. M., Russo, M. F., et al. (1990). Comparison of DSM-III and DSM-III-R diagnoses for prepubertal children: Changes in prevalence and validity. *Journal of the American Academy of Child and Adolescent Psychiatry, 29*, 620–626.

Lahey, B. B., Pelham, W. E., Loney, J., Lee, S. S., & Willcutt, E. (2005). Instability of the DSM-IV subtypes of ADHD from preschool through elementary school. *Archives of General Psychiatry, 62*, 896–902.

Lahey, B. B., Pelham, W. E., Schaughency, E. A., Atkins, M. S., Murphy, A., Hynd, G. W., et al. (1988). Dimensions and types of attention deficit disorder. *Journal of the American Academy of Child and Adolescent Psychiatry, 27*, 330–335.

Lahey, B. B., & Piacentini, J. C. (1985). An evaluation of the Quay-Peterson revised behavior problem checklist. *Journal of School Psychology, 23*, 285–289.

Lambert, M., Whipple, J., Hawkins, E., Vermeersch, D., Nielsen, S., & Smart, D. (2003). Is it time for clinicians to routinely track patient outcome? A meta-analysis. *Clinical Psychology: Science and Practice, 10*, 288–301.

Lambert, N. M. (1988). Adolescent outcomes for hyperactive children: Perspectives on general and specific patterns of child-hood risk for adolescent educational, social and mental health problems. *American Psychologist, 43*, 786–799.

Lambert, N., Nihira, K., & Leland, H. (1993). *AAMR adaptive behavior scale-school* (2nd ed.)(ABS-S:2). Austin, TX: Pro-Ed.

Lanyou, R. I. (1995). Review of the Minnesota Multiphasic Personality Inventory – Adolescent. *'Twelfth Mental Measurements Yearbook.* Lincoln, NE: Buros Institute.

Last, C. G. (1993). Introduction. In C. G. Last (Ed.), *Anxiety across the lifespan: A developmental perspective* (pp. 1–6). New York: Springer.

Last, C. G., Hersen, M., Kazdin, A. E., Francis, G., & Grubb, H. J. (1987). Psychiatric illness in the mothers of anxious children. *American Journal of Psychiatry, 144*, 1580–1583.

Le Couteur, A., Rutter, M., Lord, C., Rios, P., Robertson, S., Holdgrafer, M., et al. (1989). Autism diagnostic interview: A standardized investigator-based instrument. *Journal of Autism and Developmental Disorders, 19*, 363–387.

Lefkowitz, M. M., & Tesiny, E. P. (1980). Assessment of child-hood depression. *Journal of Consulting and Clinical Psychology, 48*, 43–50.

Lemery, K., Essex, M., & Smider, N. (2002). Revealing the relation between temperament and behavior problem symptoms by eliminating measurement confounding: Expert ratings and factor analyses. *Child Development, 73*, 867–882.

Lett, N. J. (1997). Differential validity of the BASC student observation system and the BASC teacher rating scale. *Canadian Journal of School Psychology, 13*, 1–14.

Lett, N. J., & Kamphaus, R. W. (1997). Differential validity of the BASC student observation system and the BASC teacher rating scales. *Canadian Journal of School Psychology, 13*, 1–14.

Lewczyk, C. M., Garland, A. F., Hurlburt, M. S., Gearity, J., & Hough, R. L. (2003). Comparing DISC-IV and clinician diagnoses among youths receiving public mental health services. *Journal of the American Academy of Child & Adolescent Psychiatry, 42*, 349–356.

Lichtenberger, E. O., Mather, N., Kaufman, N. L., & Kaufman, A. S. (2004). *Essentials of assessment report writing*. Hoboken, NJ: Wiley.

Lilienfeld, S. O. (2003). Comorbidity between and within childhood externalizing and internalizing disorders: Reflections and directions. *Journal of Abnormal Child Psychology, 31*, 285–291.

Lochman, J. E., Wells, K. C., & Lenhart, L. A. (2008). *Coping power: Child group program*. New York: Oxford.

Locke, H. J., & Wallace, K. M. (1959). Short marital-adjustment and prediction tests: Their reliability and validity. *Marriage and Family Living, 21*, 251–255.

Loeber, R. (1991). Antisocial behavior: More enduring than changeable? *Journal of the American Academy of Child and Adolescent Psychiatry, 30*, 393–397.

Loeber, R., Burke, J. D., Lahey, B. B., Winters, A., & Zen, M. (2000). Oppositional defiant and conduct disorder: A review of the past 10 years, Part I. *Journal of the American Academy of Child and Adolescent Psychiatry, 39*, 1468–1484.

Loeber, R., Green, S. M., & Lahey, B. B. (1990). Mental health professionals' perception of the utility of children, mothers, and teachers as informants on childhood psychopathology. *Journal of Clinical Child Psychology, 19*, 136–143.

Loeber, R., Green, S. M., Lahey, B. B., & Stouthamer-Loeber, M. (1991). Differences and similarities between children, mothers, and teachers as informants on disruptive child behavior. *Journal of Abnormal Child Psychology, 19*, 75–95.

Loeber, R., Green, S. M., Lahey, B. B., Christ, M. A. G., & Frick, P. J. (1992). Developmental sequences in the age of onset of disruptive child behaviors. *Journal of Child and Family Studies, 1*, 21–41.

Loeber, R., Green, S. M., Lahey, B. B., Christ, M. A. G., & Frick, P. J. (1992). Developmental sequences in the age of onset of disruptive child behaviors. *Journal of Child and Family Studies, 1*, 21–41.

Loeber, R., & Keenan, K. (1994). Interaction between conduct disorder and its comorbid conditions: Effects of age and gender. *Clinical Psychology Review, 14*, 497–523.

Loeber, R., & Stouthamer-Loeber, M. (1986). Family factors as correlates and predictors of juvenile conduct problems and delinquency. In M. Tonry & N. Morris (Eds.), *Crime and justice* (Vol. 7, pp. 29–149). Chicago: University of Chicago Press.

Loney, B. R., & Frick, P. J. (2003). Structured diagnostic interviewing. In C. R. Reynolds & R. W. Kamphaus (Eds.), *Handbook of educational assessment of children* (2nd ed., pp. 235–247). New York: Guilford.

Loney, B. R., Frick, P. J., Ellis, M. L., & McCoy, M. G. (1998). Intelligence, psychopathy, and antisocial behavior. *Journal of Psychopathology and Behavioral Assessment, 20*, 231–247.

Longman, Inc. (1984). *Longman dictionary of psychology and psychiatry*. New York: Author.

Lopez, S. R. (1999). Teaching culturally informed psychological assessment. In R. H. Dana (Ed.), *Handbook of cross-cultural/multicultural personality assessment* (pp. 669–687). Hillsdale, NJ: Erlbaum.

Lord, C., Rutter, M., DiLavore, P. C., & Risi, S. (1999). *Autism diagnostic observation schedule-WPS (ADOS-WPS)*. Los Angeles: Western Psychological Services.

Lord, C., Risi, S., Lambrecht, L., Cook, E. H., Jr., Leventhal, B. L., DiLavore, P. C., et al. (2000). The autism diagnostic observation schedule-generic: A standard measure of social and communication deficits associated with the spectrum of autism. *Journal of Autism and Developmental Disorders, 30*(3), 205–223.

Lord, C., Rutter, M., & Le Couteur, A. (1994). Autism diagnostic interview-revised: A revised version of a diagnostic inter-view for caregivers of individuals with possible pervasive developmental disorders. *Journal of Autism and Developmental Disorders, 24*(5), 659–685.

Lord, C., Rutter, M., DiLavore, P. C., & Risi, S. (2002). *Autism Diagnostic Observation Schedule manual*. Los Angeles: Western Psychological Services.

Lord, C., Storoschuk, S., Rutter, M., & Pickles, A. (1993). Using the ADI-R to diagnose autism in preschool children. *Infant Mental Health Journal, 14*, 234–252.

Lorr, M. (1965). Review of the Wittenborn Psychiatric Rating Scales. In O. K. Buros (Ed.), *Mental measurements yearbook* (5th ed.). Highland Park, NJ: Gryphon Press.

Lou, H. C., Henriksen, L., Bruhn, P., Borner, H., & Nielsen, J. B. (1989). Striatal dysfunction in attention deficit and hyperkinetic disorder. *Archives of Neurology, 46*, 48–52.

Love, A. S., & McIntosh, D. E. (March, 1994). *Differential diagnosis of attention deficit hyperactivity disordered and emotionally/behaviorally disordered children using the Temperament Assessment Battery for children*. Paper presented at the National Association of School Psychology annual meeting, Seattle, WA.

Lowman, M. G., Schwanz, K. A., & Kamphaus, R. W. (1996). WISC III third factor: Critical measurement issues. *Canadian Journal of School Psychology, 12*, 15–22.

Lynam, D. R., Caspi, A., Moffitt, T. E., Raine, A., Loeber, R. & Stouthamer-Loeber, M. (2005). Adolescent psychopathy and the big five: Results from two samples. *Journal of Abnormal Psychology, 33*, 431–443.

Luby, J. L., Heffelfinger, A., Mrakotsky, C., Hessler, M. J., Brown, K. M., & Hildebrand, T. (2002). Preschool major depressive disorder: Preliminary validation for developmentally modified *DSM-IV* criteria. *Journal of the American Academy of Child & Adolescent Psychiatry, 41*, 928–937.

Lucia, V. C. & Breslau, N. (2006). Family cohesion and children's behavior problems: A longitudinal investigation. *Psychiatry Research, 141*, 141–149.

Luckasson, R., Borthwick-Duffy, S., Buntinx, W. H. E., Coulter, D. L., Craig, E. M., Reeve, A., et al. (2002). *Mental retardation: Definition, classification, and systems of supports* (10th ed.). Washington, DC: American Association on Mental Retardation.

Lyneham, H. J., Abbott, M. J., & Rapee, R. M. (2007). Interrater reliability of the anxiety disorders interview schedule for DSM-IV: Child and parent version. *Journal of the American Academy of Child & Adolescent Psychiatry, 46*, 731–736.

Lynskey, M. T., & Fergusson, D. M. (1995). Childhood conduct problems, attention deficit behaviors, and adolescent alcohol, tobacco, and illicit drug use. *Journal of Abnormal Child Psychology, 23*, 281–302.

Lytton, H. (1990). Child and parent effects in boys' conduct disorder: A reinterpretation. *Developmental Psychology, 26*, 683–697.

Maccoby, E. E., & Martini, A. (1983). Socialization in the context of the family: Parent-child interaction. In P. H. Mussen & E. M. Hetherington (Eds.), *Handbook of child psychology: IV; Socialization, personality, and social development* (pp. 1–101). New York: Wiley.

Machover, K. (1949). *Personality projection in the drawing of the human figure.* Springfield, IL: Charles C. Thomas.

Madsen, C. J. (1990, September). *Attention deficit disorders and application of the EFL4 and Section* 504. Paper presented to the Seventh Annual Pacific Northwest Institute on Special Education and Law.

Malgady, R. G. & Costantino, G. (1998). Symptom severity in bilingual Hispanics as a function of clinician ethnicity and language of interview. *Psychological Assessment, 10*, 120–127.

Mann, B. J., & MacKenzie, E. P. (1996). Pathways among marital functioning, parental behaviors, and child behavior problems in school-age boys. *Journal of Clinical Child Psychology, 25*, 183–191.

Mannuzza, S., Gittelman-Klein, R., Konig, P. H., & Giampino, T. L. (1989). Hyperactive boys almost grown up: IV. Criminality and its relationship to psychiatric status. *Archives of General Psychiatry, 46*, 1073–1079.

March, J. S., Parker, J. D. A., Sullivan, K., Stallings, P., & Conners, K. (1997). The Multidimensional Anxiety Scale for Children (MASC): Factor, structure, reliability, and validity. *Journal of the American Academy of Child & Adolescent Psychiatry, 36*, 554–565.

Marchant, G. J., & Ridenour, T. A. (1998). [Review of the Personality Inventory for Youth]. *Thirteenth Mental Measurements Yearbook* (pp. 757–758). Lincoln, NE: Burns Institute.

Marcotte, D., Fortin, L., Potivin, P., & Papillon, M. (2002). Gender differences in depressive symptoms during adolescence: Role of gender-typed characteristics, self-esteem, body image, stressful life events, and pubertal status. *Journal of Emotional and Behavioral Disorders, 10*, 29–42.

Marcus, L. M., Lansing, M. D., & Schopler, E. (1993). Assessment of the autistic and pervasive developmentally disordered child. In D. J. Willis & J. L. Culbertson (Eds.), *Testing young children* (pp. 319–344). Austin, TX: Pro-Ed.

Maths, G. (1992). Issues in the measurement of acculturation among Hispanics. In K. F. Geisinger (Ed.), *Psychological testing of Hispanics* (pp. 235–252). Washington, DC: American Psychological Association.

Marin, G. (1992). Issues in the measurement of acculturation among Hispanics. In K. F. Geisinger (Ed.), *Psychological testing of Hispanics* (pp. 235–252). Washington, DC: American Psychological Association.

Marin, G., Sabogal, F., Marin, V. B., Otero-Sabogal, R., & Perez-Stable, E. J. (1987). Development of a short acculturation scale for Hispanics. *Hispanic Journal of Behavioral Sciences, 9*, 183–205.

Marin, G., Sabogal, F., VanOss Marin, B., Otero-Sabogal, R., & Perez-Stable, E. J. (1987). Development of a short acculturation scale for Hispanics. *Hispanic Journal of Behavioral Science, 9*, 183–205.

Marsee, M. A., & Frick, P. J. (2007). Exploring the cognitive and emotional correlates to proactive and reactive aggression in a sample of detained girls. *Journal of Abnormal Child Psychology, 35*, 969–981.

Martin, R. P. (1983). The ethical issues in the use and interpretation of the Draw-a-Person Test and other similar projective procedures. *The School Psychologist, 38*(6), 8.

Martin, R. P. (1988). *Assessment of personality and behavior problems: Infancy through adolescence.* New York: Guilford Press.

Martin, R. P. (1989). Activity level, distractibility, and persistence: Critical characteristics in early schooling. In G. A. Kohnstamm, J. E. Bates, & M. K. Rothbart (Eds.), *Temperament in childhood* (pp. 451–462) London: Wiley.

Martin, R. P., & Bridger, R. (1999). *Temperament Assessment Battery for Children – Revised (TABC-R).* Athens, GA: Authors.

Martin, R. P., & Holbrook, J. (1985). Relationship of temperament characteristics to the academic achievement of first grade children. *Journal of Psychoeducational Assessment, 3*, 131–140.

Martin, R. P., Nagle, R., & Paget, K. (1984). Relationships between temperament and classroom behavior, teacher attitudes and academic achievement. *Journal of Psychoeducational Assessment, 1*, 377–386.

Martin, R. P., Wisenbaker, J., Matthews-Morgan, J., Holbrook, J., Hooper, S., & Spalding, J. (1986). Stability of teacher temperament ratings over 6 and 12 months. *Journal of Abnormal Child Psychology, 14*, 167–179.

Martinez, R., Norman, R. D., & Delaney, H. D. (1984). A children's Hispanic background scale. *Hispanic Journal of Behavioral Sciences, 6*, 103–112.

Mash, E. J., & Dozois, D. J. A. (2003). Child psychopathology: A developmental-systems perspective. In E. J. Mash & R. A. Barkley (Eds.), *Child psychopathology* (2nd ed., pp. 3–71). New York: Guilford.

Mash, E., & Hunsley, J. (2005). Evidence-based assessment of child and adolescent disorders: Issues and challenges. *Journal of Clinical Child and Adolescent Psychology, 34*, 362–379.

Mash, E. J., & Terdal, L. G. (1988). Behavioral assessment of child and family disturbance. In E. J. Mash & L. G. Terdal (Eds.), *Behavioral assessment of childhood disorders* (2nd ed., pp. 3–68). New York: Guilford Press.

Massetti, G. M., Lahey, B. B., Pelham, W. E., Loney, J., Ehrhardt, A., Lee, S. S., et al. (2008). Academic achievement over 8years among children who met modified criteria for attention-deficit/hyperactivity disorder at 4–6 years of age. *Journal of Abnormal Child Psychology, 36*, 399–410.

Masuda, M., Matsumoto, G. H., & Meredith, G. M. (1970). Ethnic identity in three generations of Japanese Americans. *Journal of Social Psychology, 81*, 199–207.

Matazow, G. S., & Kamphaus, R. N. T. (in press). Behavior assessment system for children (BASC): Toward accurate diagnosis and effective treatment. In J. J. W. Andrews, H. Janzen, & D. Saklofske (Eds.), *Ability, achievement, and behavior assessment: A practical handbook.* San Diego, CA: Academic Press.

Mattison, R. E., Handford, H. A., Kales, H. C., Goodman, A. L., & McLaughlin, R. E. (1990). Four-year predictive value of the Children's Depression Inventory. *Psychological Assessment, 2*, 169–174.

Mayes, L., Volkmar, F. R., Hooks, M., & Cicchetti, D. V. (1993). Differentiating pervasive developmental disorder not otherwise specified from autism and language disorders. *Journal of Autism & Developmental Disorders, 23*, 79–90.

Mayfield, J. W. & Reynolds, C. R. (1998). Are ethnic differences in diagnosis of childhood psychopathology an artifact of psychometric methods? An experimental evaluation of Harrington's hypothesis using parent-reported symptomatology. *Journal of School Psychology, 36*, 313–334.

Mayeux, L., Bellmore, A. D., & Cillessen, A. H. N. (2007). Predicting changes in adjustment using repeated measures of sociometric status. *The Journal of Genetic Psychology, 168*, 401–424.

Mayeux, L., Underwood, M. K., & Risser, S. D. (2007). Perspectives on the ethics of sociometric research with children. *Merrill-Palmer Quarterly, 53*, 53–78.

Mazefsky, C., & Oswald, D. (2006). The discriminative ability and diagnostic utility of the ADOS-G, ADI-R, and GARS for children in a clinical setting. *Autism, 10*, 533–549.

McArthur, D. S., & Roberts, G. E. (1982). *Roberts Apperception Test for children.* Los Angeles: Western Psychological Services.

McCarney, S. B. (2004). *The attention deficit disorders evaluation scale, home and school versions: Technical manual.* Columbia, MO: Hawthorne.

McCarthy, L., & Archer, R. P. (1998). Factor structure of the MMPI-A content scales: Item-level and scale-level findings. *Journal of Personality Assessment, 71*, 84–97.

McConaughy, S. H. (2005). Direct observational assessment during test sessions. *School Psychology Review, 34*, 490–506.

McConaughy, S. H., & Achenbach, T. M. (1989). Empirically based assessment of serious emotional disturbance. *Journal of School Psychology, 27*, 91–117.

McConaughy, S. H., & Achenbach, T. M. (2004). *Manual for the Test Observation Form for ages 2–18.* Burlington, VT: Research Center for Children, Youth, and Families.

McConaughy, S. H., Achenbach, T. M., & Gent, C. L. (1988). Multiaxial empirically based assessment: Parent, teacher, observational, cognitive, and personality correlates of child behavior profile types for 6- to 11-year-old boys. *Journal of Abnormal Child Psychology, 16*, 485–509.

McConaughy, S. H., Stanger, C., & Achenbach, T. M. (1992). Three year course of behavioral emotional problems in a national sample of 4- to 16-year-olds: I. Agreement among informants. *Journal of the American Academy of Child and Adolescent Psychiatry, 31*, 932–940.

McConell, S. R., & Odom, S. L. (1986). Sociometrics: Peer-referenced measures and the assessment of social competence. In P. S. Strain, M. J. Guralnick, & H. M. Walker (Eds.), *Children's social behavior: Development, assessment, and modification* (pp. 215–286). New York: Academic Press.

McCrae, R. R., Stone, S. V., Fagan, P. J., Costa, P. T. (1998). Identifying causes and disagreement between self-reports and spouse ratings of personality. *Journal of Personality, 66*, 285–312.

McDonald, K. L., Putallaz, M., Grimes, C. L., Kupersmidt, J. B., & Coie, J. D. (2007). Girl talk: Gossip, friendship, and sociometric status. *Merrill-Palmer Quarterly, 53*, 381–411.

McGoldrick, M., Gerson, R., & Shellenberger, S. (2008). *Genograms: Assessment and intervention* (2nd ed.). New York: W. W. Norton.

McGrew, K. S., Bruininks, R. H., & Thurlow, M. L. (1992). Relationship between measures of adaptive functioning and community adjustment for adults with mental retardation. *Exceptional Children, 58*, 517–529.

McMahon, R. J., & Frick, P. J. (2005). Evidence-based assessment of conduct problems in children and adolescents. *Journal of Clinical Child and Adolescent Psychology, 34*, 477–505.

McMahon, R. J. & Frick, P. J. (2007). Conduct and oppositional disorders. In E. J. Mash & R. A. Barkley (Eds)., *Assessment of childhood disorders* (4th ed., pp. 132–183). New York: Guilford.

McMahon, R. J., & Peters, R. D. V. (2002). *The effects of parental dysfunction on children.* New York: Plenum Press.

McNally, S., Eisenberg, N., & Harris, J. D. (1991). Consistency and change in maternal child-rearing practices and values: A longitudinal study. *Child Development, 62*, 190–198.

McNamara, J. R., Hollmann, C., & Riegel, T. (1994). A preliminary study of the usefulness of the Behavior Assessment System for Children in the evaluation of mental health needs in a Head Start population. *Psychological Reports, 75*, 1195–1201.

McNeil, C. B., Eyberg, S., Eisenstadt, T. H., Newcomb, K., & Funderbunk, B. (1991). Parent-child Interaction Therapy with behavior problem children: Generalization of treatment effects to the school setting. *Journal of Clinical Child Psychology, 20*, 140–151.

McReynolds, P., Ballachey, E.L., & Ferguson, J.T. Development and evaluation of a behavioral scale for appraising the adjustment of hospitalized patients. American Psychologists, 1952, 7, 340

Measelle, J. R., Ablow, J. C., Cowan, P. A., & Cowan, C. P. (1998). Assessing young children's views of their academic, social, and emotional lives: An evaluation of the self-perception scales of the Berkeley Puppet Interview. *Child Development, 69*, 1556–1576.

Meehl, P. E. (1973). *Psychodiagnosis. Selected papers.* Minneapolis: University of Minnesota Press.

Meehl, P. E. & Hathaway, S. R. (1946). The K factor as a suppressor variable in the Minnesota Multiphasic Personality Inventory. *Journal of Applied Psychology, 30*, 525–564.

Mendoza, R. H. (1989). An empirical scale to measure type and degree of acculturation in Mexican-American adolescents and adults. *Journal of Cross Cultural Psychology, 20*, 372–385.

Merenda, P. F. (1996). BASC: Behavior Assessment System for Children. *Measurement and Evaluation in Counseling and Development, 28*, 229–232.

Merrell, K. W., & Popinga, M. R. (1994). The alliance of adaptive behavior and social competence: An examination of relationships between the Scales of Independent Behavior and the Social Skills Rating System. *Research in Developmental Disabilities, 15*, 39–47.

Merydith, S. P. (2000). Aggression Intervention Skill Training: Moral reasoning and moral emotions. *NASP Communique, 28*, 6–8.

Merydith, S. P., & Joyce, F. K. (1998, August). *Temporal stability and convergent validity of the BASC Parent and Teacher Rating Scales.* Paper presented at the Annual Meeting of the American Psychological Association, San Francisco.

Meyer, G. J., Erdberg, P., & Shaffer, T. W. (2007). Toward international normative reference data for the Comprehensive System. *Journal of Personality Assessment, 89*(Suppl. 1), S201–S216.

Mikami, A. Y. & Hinshaw, S. P. (2003). Buffers of peer rejection among girls with and without ADHD: The role of popularity with adults and goal-directed solitary play. *Journal of Abnormal Child Psychology, 31*, 381–397.

Mildenberger, K., Sitter, S., Noterdaeme, M., & Amorosa, H. (2001). The use of the ADI–R as a diagnostic tool in the differential diagnosis of children with infantile autism and children with receptive language disorder. *European Child and Adolescent Psychiatry, 10*, 248–255.

Milich, R. (1984). Cross-sectional and longitudinal observations of activity level and sustained attention in a normative sample. *Journal of Abnormal Child Psychology, 12*, 261–276.

Milich, R., Loney, J., & Landau, S. (1982). The independent dimensions of hyperactivity and aggression: A validation with play-room observations. *Journal of Abnormal Psychology, 91*, 183–198.

Miller, D. C. (1994, Winter). Behavior assessment system for children (BASC): Test critique. *Texas Association of School Psychologists Newsletter, 23–29.*

Miller, L. C. (1967). Louisville Behavior Checklist for males 6–12 years of age. *Psychological Reports, 21*, 885–896.

Milliones, J. (1980). Construction of a Black consciousness measure: Psychotherapeutic implications. *Psychotherapy: Theory, Research and Practice, 17*(2), 175–182.

Milner, J. S. (1986). *The Child Abuse Potential inventory: Manual – Second Edition.* De Kalb, IL: Psytec.

Milner, J. S., & Crouch, J. L. (1997). Impact and detection of response distortions on parenting measures used to assess risk for child physical abuse. *Journal of Personality Assessment, 69*, 633–650.

Milner, J. S., & Wimberley, R. C. (1980). Prediction and explanation of child abuse. *Journal of Psychology, 36*, 875–884.

Mintz, N. L., & Schwartz, D. T. (1964). Urban ecology and psychosis: Community factors in the incidence of schizophrenia and manic-depression among Italians in Greater Boston. *Inter-national Journal of Social Psychiatry, 10*, 101–117.

Mischel, W. (1968). *Personality and assessment.* New York: Wiley.

Moffitt, T. E. (1993). Adolescence-limited and life-course persistent antisocial behavior: A developmental taxonomy. *Psychological Reports, 100*, 674–701.

Moffitt, T. E. (2003). Life-course persistent and adolescence-limited antisocial behavior: A 10-year research review and research agenda. In B. B. Lahey, T. E. Moffitt, & A. Caspi (Eds.), *Causes of conduct disorder and juvenile delinquency* (pp. 49–75). New York: Guilford.

Monica, R. F., Poole, C., Son, L., & Murry, C. C. (1997). Effects of war trauma on Cambodian refugee adolescents' functional health and mental health stains. *Journal of the American Academy of Child & Adolescent Psychiatry, 36*, 1098–1106.

Monuteaux, M. C., Faraone, S. V., Gross, L. M., & Biederman, J. (2007). Predictors, clinical characteristics, and outcome of conduct disorder in girls with attention deficit hyperactivity disorder: A longitudinal study. *Psychological Medicine, 37*, 1731–1741.

Moore, S. G., & Updegraff, R. (1964). Sociometric status of pre-school children as related to age, sex, nurturance-giving, and dependency. *Child Development, 35*, 519–524.

Moos, R. H., & Moos, B. S. (1986). *Family Environment Scale Manual – Second Edition.* Palo Alto, CA: Consulting Psychologists Press.

Morgan, A. B. W. (1998). Childhood social withdrawal: The role of social skills in the relation of withdrawal and anxiety. *Dissertation Abstracts International Section B: The Sciences and Engineering, 59*(6-B), 3067.

Morgan, C. J., & Cauce, A. M. (1999). Predicting DSM-III-R disorders from the Youth Self-Report: Analysis of data from a field study. *Journal of the American Academy of Child and Adolescent Psychiatry, 38*, 1237–1245.

Morgenthaler, W. (1954). Hermann Rorschach, deceased, at his 70th birthday. *Schweizerische Zeitschrift fuer Psychologie and ihre Anwendungen, 13*, 315.

Morris, R. J., & Kratochwill, T. R. (1983). *Treating children's fears and phobias: A behavioral approach.* New York: Pergamon Press. Murray, H. A. (1943). *Thematic apperception test.* Cambridge, MA: Harvard University Press.

Morsbach, S. K., & Prinz, R. J. (2006). Understanding and improving the validity of self-report of parenting. *Clinical Child and Family Review, 9*, 1–21.

Munoz, L. C. & Frick, P. J. (2007). The reliability, stability, and predictive utility of the self-report version of the Antisocial Process Screening Device. *Scandinavian Journal of Psychology, 48*, 299–312.

Mussman, M. C. (1964). Teacher's evaluations of psychological reports. *Journal of School Psychology, 3*, 35–37.

Myers, K., & Winters, N. C. (2002). Ten-year review of rating scales: II. Scales for internalizing disorders. *Journal of the American Academy of Child & Adolescent Psychiatry, 41*, 634–659.

Myles, B. S., Bock, S. J., & Simpson, R. L. (2001). *Asperger syndrome diagnostic scale.* Los Angeles, CA: Western Psychological Services.

Nadeau, K. G. (1995). *Attention-deficit disorder in adults: Research, diagnosis, and treatment.* New York: Brunner & Mazel.

Naglieri, J. A., LeBuffe, P. A., & Pfeiffer, S. I. (1994). *Devereux scales of mental disorders.* New York: The Psychological Corporation.

Nail, J. M., & Evans, J. G. (1997). The emotional adjustment of gifted adolescents: A view of global functioning. *Roeper Review, 20*(1), 18–21.

Neeper, R., & Lahey, B. B. (1986). The Children's Behavior Rating Scale: A factor analytic developmental study. *School Psychology Review, 15*, 277–288.

Neeper, R., Lahey, B. B., & Frick, P. J. (1990). *Comprehensive behavior rating scale for children.* New York: The Psychological Corporation.

Negy, C., Lachar, D., Gruber, C., & Garza, N. (2001). The Personality Inventory for Youth: Validity and comparability of English and Spanish versions for regular education and juvenile justice samples. *Journal of Personality Assessment, 76*, 250–263.

Nelson, B., Martin, R. P., Hodge, S., Havill, V., & Kamphaus, R. (1999). Modeling the prediction of elementary school adjustment from preschool temperament. *Personality and Individual Differences, 26*, 687–700.

Neuman, R. J., Todd, R. D., Beath, A. C., Reich, W., Hudziak, J. J., Bucholz, K. K., et al. (1999). Evaluation of ADHD typology in three contrasting samples: A latent class approach. *Journal of the American Academy of Child and Adolescent Psychiatry, 38*(1), 25–33.

Newman, J., & Matsopoulos, A. (1994, March). *Temperament precursors of early reading ability.* Paper presented at the annual meeting of the National Association of School Psychologists, Seattle, WA.

Nezu, A. M., & Nezu, C. M. (1993). Identifying and selecting target problems for clinical interventions: A problem-solving model. *Psychological Assessment, 5*, 254–263.

Nigg, J. T. (2006). *What causes ADHD? Understanding what goes wrong and why.* New York: Guilford.

Nihira, K., Foster, R., Shellhaus, M., Leland, H., Lambert, N., & Windmiller, M. (1981). *AAMR adaptive behavior scale, school edition.* Monterey, CA: Publisher's Test Service.

Nihira, K., Leland, H., & Lambert, N. (1993). *AAMR adaptive behavior scales-residential and community* (2nd. ed.) (AAMR-RC: 2). Austin, TX: Pro-Ed.

Nitko, A. (1983). *Educational tests and measurement: An introduction.* New York: Harcourt Brace Jovanovich.

Nixon, R. D. V., Sweeney, L., Erickson, D. B., & Touyz, S. W. (2003). Parent-child interaction therapy: A comparison of standard and abbreviated treatments for oppositional defiant preschoolers. *Journal of Consulting and Clinical Psychology, 71*, 251–260

Nurnberger, J. I., Jr., Blehar, A. S. C., Kaufmann, C. A., York-Cooler, C., Simpson, S. G., Harkavy-Friedman, J., et al. (1994). Diagnostic interview for genetic studies: Rationale, unique features, and training. *Archives of General Psychiatry, 51*, 849–859.

O'Brien, B. S., & Frick, P. J. (1996). Reward dominance: Associations with anxiety, conduct problems, and psychopathy in children. *Journal of Abnormal Child Psychology, 24*, 223–240.

Oehler-Stinnett, J., & Stinnett, T. A. (1995). Teacher rating scales for attention deficit hyperactivity: A comparative review. *Journal of Psychoeducational Assessment, Monograph Series, Special Issue on Assessment of Attention-Deficit/Hyperactivity Disorders.* Cordova, TN: Psychoeducational Corporation.

Oesterheld, J. R., & Haber, J. (1997). Acceptability of the Conners Parent Rating Scale and Child Behavior Checklist to Dakotan/Lakotan parents. *Journal of the American Academy of Child and Adolescent Psychiatry, 36,* 55–64.

Offord, D. R., Boyle, M. H., Fleming, J. E., Blum, H. M., & Grant, N. I. R. (1989). Ontario child health study: Summary of selected results. *Canadian Journal of Psychiatry, 34,* 483–491.

Okiishi, J., Lambert, M., Eggett, D., Nielsen, L., Dayton, D., & Vermeersch, D. (2006). An analysis of therapist treatment effects: Toward providing feedback to individual therapists on their clients' psychotherapy outcome. *Journal of Clinical Psychology, 62,* 1157–1172.

Ollendick, T. H. (1978). *The Fear Survey Schedule for Children-Revised.* Unpublished rating scale: Indiana State University.

Ollendick, T. H., & Hersen, M. (1993). *Handbook of child and adolescent assessment.* Boston, MA: Allyn and Bacon.

Ollendick, T. H., & King, N. J. (1994). Diagnosis, assessment, and treatment of internalizing problems in children: The role of longitudinal data.. *Journal of Consulting and Clinical Psychology, 62,* 918–927.

Ollendick, T. H., Seligman, L. D., Goza, A. B., Byrd, D. A., & Singh, K. (2003). Anxiety and depression in children and adolescents: A factor-analytic examination of the tripartite model. *Journal of Child and Family Studies, 12,* 157–170.

Olmedo, E. L., Martinez, J. L., Jr., & Martinez, S. R. (1978). Measure of acculturation for Chicano adolescents. *Psychological Reports, 42,* 159–170.

Ondersma, S. J. (2007). Introduction to the special section on substance abuse and child maltreatment. *Child Maltreatment, 12,* 111–113.

Ondersma, S. J., Chaffin, M. J., Mullins, S. M., & LeBreton, J. M. (2005). A brief form of the Child Abuse Potential Inventory: Development and validation. *Journal of Clinical Child and Adolescent Psychology, 34,* 301–311.

Orvaschel, H., Ambrosini, P., & Rabinovich, H. (1993). Diagnostic issues in child assessment. In T. H. Ollendick & M. Hersen (Eds.), *Handbook of child and adolescent assessment* (pp. 26–40). Boston, MA: Allyn and Bacon.

Orvaschel, H., Welsh-Allis, G., & Ye, W. (1988). Psychopathology in children of parents with recurrent depression. *Journal of Abnormal Child Psychology, 16*(1), 17–28.

Osofsky, J. D., Wewers, S., Hann, D. M., & Fick, A. C. (1993). Chronic community violence: What is happening to our children? *Psychiatry, 56,* 36–45.

Ostrander, R., Weinfurt, K. P., Yarnold, P. R., & August, G. J. (1998). Diagnosing attention-deficit disorders with the Behavioral Assessment System for Children and the Child Behavior Checklist: Test and construct validity analyses using optimal discriminant classification trees. *Journal of Consulting and Clinical Psychology, 66,* 660–672.

Ostrov, J. M. & Keating, C. F. (2004). Gender differences in preschool aggression during free play and structured interactions: An observational study. *Social Development, 13,* 255–277.

Ownby, R. L., & Wallbrown, F. (1986). Improving report writing in school psychology. In T. R. Kratochwill (Ed.), *Advances in school psychology* (Vol. 5, pp. 7–49). Hillsdale, NJ: Erlbaum.

Ozonoff, S., Goodlin-Jones, B., & Solomon, M. (2005). Evidence-based assessment of autism spectrum disorders in children and adolescents. *Journal of Clinical Child and Adolescent Psychology, 34,* 523–540.

Paikoff, R. L., & Brooks-Gunn, J. (1991). Do parent-child relationships change during puberty? *Psychological Bulletin, 110,* 47–66.

Papadopoulos, L., Bor, R., & Stanion, P. (1997). Genograms in counselling practice: A review (part 1). *Counseling Psychology Quarterly, 10,* 17–28.

Pardini, D. A. (2008). Novel insights into longstanding theories of bidirectional parent-child influences: Introduction to the special section. *Journal of Abnormal Child Psychology, 36,* 627–632.

Parker, J. G., & Asher, S. R. (1987). Peer relations and later personal adjustment: Are low-accepted children at risk? *Psychological Bulletin, 102,* 357–389.

Patterson, G. R. (1982). *Coercive family process.* Eugene, OR: Castalia.

Patterson, G. R., & Dishion, T. J. (1985). Contributions of families and peers to delinquency. *Criminology, 23,* 63–79.

Patterson, G. R., & Yoerger, K. (1993). Developmental models for delinquent behavior. In S. Hodgins (Ed.), *Mental Disorder and Crime.* (pp. 140–172). Newbury Park: Sage.

Payne, A. F. (1928). *Sentence completions.* New York: New York Guidance Clinic.

Pearson, D. A., & Aman, M. G. (1994). Ratings of hyperactivity and developmental indices: Should clinicians correct for developmental level? *Journal of Autism and Developmental Disorders, 24,* 395–411.

Pearson, D. A., & Lachar, D. (1994). Using behavioral questionnaires to identify adaptive deficits in elementary school children. *Journal of School Psychology, 32,* 33–52.

Pearson, K. (1901). On lines and planes of closest fit to systems of points in space. *Philosophical Magazine (Series 6), 2,* 559–572.

Peeples, F., & Loeber, R. (1994). Do individual factors and neighborhood context explain ethnic differences in juvenile delinquency? *Journal of Quantitative Criminology, 10,* 141–157.

Pelham, W. E., Fabiano, G. A., & Massetti, G. M. (2005). Evidence-based assessment of Attention-

Deficit Hyperactivity Disorder in children and adolescents. *Journal of Clinical Child and Adolescent Psychology, 34*, 477–505.

Pelham, W. E., Gnabry, E. M., Greenslade, K. E., & Milich, R. (1992). Teacher ratings of DSM-III-R symptoms for the disruptive behavior disorders. *Journal of the American Academy of' Child and Adolescent Psychiatry, 31*, 210–218.

Perry, M. A. (1990). The interview in developmental assessment. In J. H. Johnson & J. Goldman (Eds.), *Developmental assessment in clinical child psychology: A handbook* (pp. 58–77). New York: Pergamon Press.

Petersen, A. C., Compas, B. E., Brooks-Gunn, J., Stemmler, M., Ey, S., & Grant, K. E. (1993). Depression in adolescence. *American Psychologist, 48*, 155–168.

Petersen, N. S., Kolen, M. J., & Hoover, H. D. (1989) Scaling, norming, and equating. In R. L. Linn (Ed.), *Educational measurement* (3rd ed., pp. 221–262). New York: Macmillan.

Peterson, D. R. (1961). Behavior problems of middle childhood. *Journal of Consulting Psychology, 25*, 205–209.

Pfiffner, L. J. & McBurnett, K. (2006). Family correlates of comorbid anxiety disorders in children with attention deficit hyperactivity disorder. *Journal of Abnormal Child Psychology, 34*, 725–736.

Phares, E. J. (1984). *Clinical psychology: Concepts, methods, and profession* (rev.). Homewood, IL: Dorsey Press.

Piacentini, J. (1993). Checklists and rating scales. In T. H. Ollendick & M. Hersen (Eds.), *Handbook of child and adolescent assessment* (pp. 82–97). Boston, MA: Allyn and Bacon.

Piacentini, J. C., Cohen, P., & Cohen, J. (1992). Combining discrepant diagnostic information from multiple sources: Are complex algorithms better than simple ones? *Journal of Abnormal Child Psychology, 20*, 51–63.

Piacentini, J., Robper, M., Jensen, P., Lucas, C., Fisher, P., Bird, H., et al. (1999). Informant-based determinants of symptom attenuation in structured child psychiatric interviews. *Journal of Abnormal Child Psychology, 27*, 417–428.

Piacentini, J., Shaffer, D., Fisher, P., Schwab-Stone, M., Davies, A. T., & Gioia, P. (1993). The Diagnostic Interview Schedule for Children – Revised Version (DISC-R): III. Concurrent criterion validity. *Journal of the American Academy of Child and Adolescent Psychiatry, 32*, 648–656.

Pinderhughes, E. E., Dodge, K. A., Bates, J. E., Pettit, G. S., & Zelli, A. (2000). Discipline responses: Influences of parents' socioeconomic status, ethnicity, beliefs about parenting, stress, and cognitive-emotional processes. *Journal of Family Psychology, 14*, 280–400.

Piotrowski, C. (1999). Use of tests and measures in marital and family research. *Psychological Reports, 84*, 1251–1252.

Pisecco, S., Lachar, D., Gruber, C. P., Gallen, R. T., Kline, R. B., & Huzinec, C. (1999). Development and validation of disruptive behavior scales for the Student Behavior Survey (SBS). *Journal of Psychoeducational Assessment, 17*, 314–331.

Pope, K. S., Butcher, J. N., & Seelen, J. (2000). *The MMPI, MMPI-2 and MMPI-A in court: A practical guide for expert witnesses and attorneys* (2nd ed.). Washington, DC: American Psychological Association.

Porter, B., & O'Leary, K. D. (1980). Marital discord and child-hood behavior problems. *Journal of Abnormal Child Psychology, 8*, 287–295.

Power, T., Doherty, B., Panichelli-Mindel, S., Karustis, J., Eiraldi, R., Anastopoulos, A., et al. (1998). The predictive validity of parent and teacher reports of ADHD symptoms. *Journal of Psychopathology and Behavioral Assessment, 20*, 57–81.

Poznanski, E. O., Cook, S. C., & Carroll, J. B. (1979). A depression rating scale for children. *Pediatrics, 64*, 442–450.

Prifitera, A., Weiss, L. G., & Saklofske, D. H. (1998). The WISC-III in context. In A. Prifitera & D. Saklofske (Eds.), *WISC-III: Clinical use and interpretation* (pp. 1–38). San Diego: Academic Press.

Pressman, L. J., Loo, S. K., Carpenter, E. M., Asarnow, J. R., Lynn, D., McCracken, J. T., et al. (2006). Relationship of family environment and parental psychiatric diagnosis to impairment in ADHD. *Journal of the American Academy of Child and Adolescent Psychiatry, 45*, 346–354.

Prinstein, M. J. (2007). Assessment of adolescents' preference- and reputation-based peer status using sociometric experts. *Merrill-Palmer Quarterly, 53*, 243–261.

Prinstein, M. J., & Cillessen, A. H. N. (2003). Forms and functions of adolescent peer aggression associated with high levels of peer status. *Merrill-Palmer Quarterly, 49*, 310–342.

Prinzie, P., Onghena, P., & Hellinckx, W. (2007). Reexamining the Parenting Scale: Reliability, factor structure, concurrent validity of a scale for assessing the discipline practices of mothers and fathers of elementary-school-aged children. *European Journal of Psychological Assessment, 23*, 24–31.

Puig-Antich, J. (1982). Major depression and conduct disorder in prepuberty. *Journal of the American Academy of Child and Adolescent Psychiatry, 21*, 118–128.

Puig-Antich, J., Blau, S., Marx, N., Greenhill, L. L., & Chambers, W. (1978). Prepubertal major depressive disorders. *Journal of the American Academy of Child and Adolescent Psychiatry, 17*, 695–707.

Puig-Antich, J., & Chambers, W. (1978). *The schedule for affective disorders and schizophrenia for school-aged children (Kiddie-SADS)*. New York: New York State Psychiatric Institute.

Quay, H. C. (1986). Classification. In H. C. Quay & J. S. Werry (Eds.), *Psychopathological disorders of childhood* (3rd ed., pp. 1–34). New York: Wiley.

Quay, H. C., & Love, C. T. (1977). The effect of a juvenile diversion program on rearrests. *Criminal Justice and Behavior, 4*, 377–396.

Quay, H. C., & Peterson, D. R. (1983). *Interim manual for the Revised Behavior Problem Checklist.* Coral Gables, FL: Author.

Rabin, A. I. (1986). Concerning projective techniques. In A. I. Rabin (Ed.), *Projective techniques for adolescents and children* (pp. 3–13). New York: Springer.

Raine, A. (2002). Biosocial studies of antisocial and violent behavior in children and adults: A review. *Journal of Abnormal Child Psychology, 30*, 311–326.

Ramirez, M. (1984). Assessing and understanding biculturalism–multiculturalism in Mexican–American adults. In J. L. Martinez, Jr. & R. H. Mendoza (Eds.), *Chicano Psychology* (pp. 77–94). Orlando, FL: Academic Press.

Rapoport, J. L., & Castellanos, F. X. (1996). Attention-deficit hyperactivity disorder. In J. M. Wiener (Ed.), *Diagnosis and psychopharmacology of childhood and adolescent disorders* (2nd ed., pp. 265–292). New York: Wiley.

Rapport, M. D., Chung, K. M., Shore, G., Denney, C. B., & Isaacs, P. (2000). Upgrading the science and technology of assessment and diagnosis: Laboratory and clinic-based assessment of children with ADHD. *Journal of Clinical Child Psychology, 29*, 555–568.

Realmuto, G. M., August, G. J., Sieler, J. D., & Pessoa-Brandao, L. (1997). Peer assessment of social reputation in community samples of disruptive and nondisruptive children: Utility of the Revised Class Play method. *Journal of Clinical Child Psychology, 26*, 67–76.

Reed, M. L., & Edelbrock, C. (1983). Reliability and validity of the direct observational form of the Child Behavior Checklist. *Journal of Abnormal Child Psychology, 11*, 521–530.

Reich, W. (2000). Diagnostic interview for children and adolescents (DICA). *Journal of the American Academy of Child and Adolescent Psychiatry, 39*, 59–66.

Reich, W., & Earls, F. (1987). Rules for making psychiatric diagnoses in children on the basis of multiple sources of information: Preliminary strategies. *Journal of Abnormal Child Psychology, 1S*, 601–616.

Reich, W., Herjanic, B., Weiner, Z., & Gandhy, P. R. (1982). Development of a structured psychiatric interview for children: Agreement in diagnosis comparing child and parent interviews. *Journal of Abnormal Child Psychology, 10*, 325–336.

Reitman, D., Currier, R. O., Hupp, S. D. A., Rhode, P. C., Murphy, M. A., & O'Callahan, P. M. (2001). Psychometric characteristics of the parenting Scale in a Head Start population. *Journal of Clinical Child Psychology, 30*, 514–524.

Rende, R., & Weissman, M. M. (1999). Assessment of family history of psychiatric disorder. In D. Shaffer, C. P. Lucas, & J. E. Richters (Eds.), *Diagnostic assessment in child and adolescent psychopathology* (pp. 230–255). New York: Guilford Press.

Renk, K., & Phares, V. (2004). Cross-informant ratings of social competence in children and adolescents. *Clinical Psychology Review, 24*, 239–254.

Reynolds, C. R., & Kaiser, S. (1990). Test Bias in psychological assessment. In C. R. Reynolds and R. W. Kamphaus (Eds.), *Handbook of psychological and educational assessment of children.* New York: Guilford.

Reynolds, C. R., & Kamphaus, R. W. (1992). *Behavior assessment system. for children (BASC).* Circle Pines, MN: American Guidance Services.

Reynolds, C. R., & Kamphaus, R. W. (2004). *Behavior assessment system for children, 2nd edition (BASC-2).* Circle Pines, MN: American Guidance Services.

Reynolds, C. R., Kamphaus, R. W., & Hatcher, N. M. (1999). Treatment planning and evaluation with the BASC: The Behavior Assessment System for Children. In M. Maruish (Ed.) (2nd ed.), *The use of psychological testing for treatment planning and outcome assessment* (pp. 563–597). Mahwah, NJ: Erlbaum.

Reynolds, C. R., & Richmond, B. O. (1985). *Revised children's manifest anxiety scale (RCMAS).* Los Angeles: Western Psychological Services.

Reynolds, W. M. (1986a). A model for screening and identification of depressed children and adolescents in school settings. *Professional School Psychology, 1*, 117–129.

Reynolds, W. M. (1986b). *Reynolds Adolescent Depression Scale.* Odessa, FL: Psychological Assessment Resources.

Reynolds, W. M. (1989). *Reynolds Child Depression Scale.* Odessa, FL: Psychological Assessment Resources.

Reynolds, W. M. (1990). Introduction to the nature and study of internalizing disorders in children and adolescents. *School Psychology Review, 19*(2), 137–141.

Reynolds, W. M. (1998). *Adolescent psychopathology scale.* Odessa, FL: Psychological Assessment Resources.

Reynolds, W. M. (2002). *Reynolds Adolescent Depression Scale, 2nd edition (RADS-2).* Lutz, FL: Psychological Assessment Resources.

Rhoades, K. A. & O'Leary, S. G. (2007). Factor structure and validity of the Parenting Scale. *Journal of Clinical Child and Adolescent Psychology, 36*, 137–146.

Rice, F., Harold, G. T., & Thapar, A. (2002). The genetic aetiology of childhood depression: A review. *Journal of Child Psychology and Psychiatry, 43*, 65–79.

Riccio, C., & Reynolds, C. (2003). The assessment of attention via continuous performance tests. *Handbook of Psychological and Educational Assessment of Children: Personality, Behavior, and Context* (2nd ed., pp. 291–319). New York: Guilford Press.

Richardson, R. D., & Burns, M. K. (2005). Adaptive Behavior Assessment System (2nd edition) by Harrison, P. L, & Oakland, T. (2002). San Antonio, TX: Psychological Corporation. *Assessment for Effective Intervention, 30*, 51–54.

Richmond, B. O., & Kicklighter, R. H. (1979). *Children's adaptive behavior scale.* Atlanta, GA: Humantics Limited.

Richters, J. E. (1992). Depressed mothers as informants about their children A critical review of the evidence of distortion. *Psychological Bulletin, 112*, 485–499.

Ricks, J. H. (1959). On telling parents about test results. *Test Service Bulletin, 54*, 1–4.

Roberts, B. W. & DelVecchio, W. F. (2000). The rank-order consistency of personality traits from childhood to old age: A quantitative review of longitudinal studies. *Psychological Bulletin, 126*, 3–25.

Roberts, C., McCoy, M., Reidy, D., & Crucitti, F. (1993). A comparison of methods of assessing adaptive behaviour in pre-school children with developmental disabilities. *Australia and New Zealand Journal of Developmental Disabilities, 18*, 261–272.

Roberts, G. C., Block, J. H., & Block, J. (1984). Continuity and change in parents' child-rearing practices. *Child Development, 55*, 586–597.

Roberts, M. A., Milich, R., & Loney, J. (1984). *Structured observations of academic and play settings (SOAPS)*. Iowa City, IA: University of Iowa.

Roberts, M. A., Ray, R. S., & Roberts, R. J. (1984). A playroom observational procedure for assessing hyperactive boys. *Journal of Pediatric Psychology, 9*, 177–191.

Roberts, R. E., Roberts, C. R., & Xing, Y. (2007). Rates of DSM-IV psychiatric disorders among adolescents in a large metropolitan area. *Journal of Psychiatric Research, 41*, 959–967.

Robertson, D., & Hyde, J. (1982). The factorial validity of the Family Environment Scale. *Educational and Psychological Measurement, 42*, 1233–1241.

Robins, L. N. (1966). *Deviant children grown up*. Baltimore, MD: Williams and Wilkins.

Robins, L. N., Helzer, J. E., Croughan, J., & Ratcliff, K. S. (1981). The National Institute of Mental Health Diagnostic Interview Schedule: Its history, characteristic and validity. *Archives of General Psychiatry, 38*, 381–389.

Robins, R. W., John, O. P., Caspi, A., Moffitt, T. E., & Stouthamer-Loeber, M. (1996). Resilient, overcontrolled, and undercontrolled boys: Three replicable personality types. *Journal of Personality and Social Psychology, 70*, 157–171.

Robinson, E. A., & Eyberg, S. M. (1981). The Dyadic Parent Child Interaction Coding System: Standardization and validation. *Journal of Consulting and Clinical Psychology, 49*, 245–250.

Rockett, J. L., Murrie, D. C., & Boccacini, M. T. (2007). Diagnostic labeling in juvenile justice settings: Do psychopathy and conduct disorder findings influence clinicians? *Psychological Services, 4*, 107–122.

Roff, J. D., & Wirt, R. D. (1984). Childhood aggression and social adjustments as antecedents of delinquency. *Journal of Abnormal Child Psychology, 12*, 111–126.

Roid, G. (2003). Stanford-Binet Intelligence Scale: Fifth Edition. Itasca, IL: Riverside.

Rorschach, H. (1921). *Psychodiagnostik*. Bern: Bircher.

Rorschach, H. (1951). *Psychodiagnostics: A diagnostic test based on perception* (P. Lemkau & B. Kronenberg, Trans.). New York: Grune & Stratton.

Rosenthal, G. (1996). The Behavior Assessment System for Children: Locus of control scale. *Child Assessment News, 5*(5), 1–5, 12.

Ross, A. O. (1981). *Child behavior therapy: Principles, procedures, and empirical basis*. New York: Wiley.

Rotter, J. B., & Rafferty, J. E. (1950). *Manual for the Rotter In-complete Sentences Blank, College Form*. New York: The Psychological Corporation.

Rourke, B. P., & Strang, J. D. (1983). Subtypes of reading and arithmetical disabilities: A neuropsychological analysis. In M. Rutter (Ed.), *Developmental neuropsychiatry* (pp. 473–488). New York: Guilford Press.

Rounsaville, B. J., Alarcon, R. D., Andrews, G., Jackson, J. S., Kendell, R. E., & Kendler, K. (2002). Basic nomenclature issues for DSM-V. In D. J. Kupfer, M. B. First, & D. E. Regier (Eds.), *A research agenda for DSM-V* (pp. 1–30). Washington, DC: American Psychiatric Association.

Routh, D. K., & Ernst, A. R. (1983). Somatization disorder in relatives of children and adolescents with functional abdominal pain. *Journal of Pediatric Psychology, 9*, 427–437.

Rowe, E. W., Circle, E. L., Reynolds, C. R., & Kamphaus, R. W. (1998). Behavior Assessment System for Children (BASC) Monitor for ADHD: An introduction to applications in practice. *The ADHD Report, 6*(6), 113–129.

Rucker, C. N. (1967). Technical language in the school psychologists' report. *Psychology in the Schools, 4*, 146–150.

Rudolph, K. D., Hammen, C., & Burge, D. (1994). Interpersonal functioning and depressive symptoms in childhood: Addressing the issues of specificity and comorbidity. *Journal of Abnormal Child Psychology, 22*, 355–373.

Ruffalo, S. L., & Elliott, S. N. (1997). Teachers' and parents' ratings of children's social skills: A closer look at cross-informant agreements through an item analysis protocol. *School Psychology Review, 26*, 489–501.

Rutter, M. (1983). Behavioral studies: Questions and findings on the concept of a distinctive syndrome. In M. Rutter (Ed.), *Developmental neuropsychiatry* (pp. 259–280). New York: Guilford.

Rutter, M. (1999). Forward. In D. Shaffer, C. P. Lucas, & J. E. Lucas (Eds.), *Diagnostic assessment in child and adolescent psychopathology* (pp. xii–xiv). New York: Guilford.

Rutter, M., & Garmezy, N. (1983). Developmental psychopathology. In E. M. Hetherington (Ed.), *Manual of child psychology, IV: Social and personality development* (pp. 775–912). New York: Wiley.

Rutter, M., & Giller, H. (1983). *Juvenile delinquency: Trends and perspectives*. London: Penguin.

Rutter, M., Chadwick, O., & Shaffer, D. (1983). Head injury. In M. Rutter (Ed.), *Developmental neuropsychiatry* (pp. 83–111). New York: Guilford.

Saavedra, L. M., & Silverman, W. K. (2002). Classification of anxiety disorders in children: What a difference two decades make. *International Review of Psychiatry, 14*, 87–100.

Saemundsen, E., Magnusson, P., Smari, J., & Sigurdardottir, S. (2003). Autism Diagnostic Interview

– Revised and the Childhood Autism Rating Scale: Convergence and discrepancy in diagnosing autism. *Journal of Autism and Developmental Disorders, 33*, 319–328.

Sandberg, S. T., Wieselberg, M., & Shaffer, D. (1980). Hyperkinetic and conduct problem children in a primary school population: Some epidemiological considerations. *Journal of Child Psychology, Psychiatry and Applied Disciplines, 21*, 293–311.

Sanders, M. R., & Dadds, M. R. (1989). *Depression observation schedule: An observers manual.* Brisbane, Australia: University of Queensland.

Sanders, M. R., Dadds, M. R., Johnston, B. M., & Cash, R. (1992). Childhood depression and conduct disorder: I. Behavioral, affective, and cognitive aspects of family problem-solving interactions. *Journal of Abnormal Psychology, 101*, 495–504.

Sanders, M. R., Markie-Dadds, C., Tully, L. A., & Bor, W. (2000). The Triple P-Positive Parenting Program: A comparison of enhanced, standard, and self-directed behavioral family intervention for parents of children with early onset conduct problems. *Journal of Consulting and Clinical Psychology, 68*, 624–640.

Sandoval, J., & Echandia, A. (1994). Behavior assessment system for children. *Journal of School Psychology,* 32, 419–425.

Sandoval, J., & Mille, M. (1979, September). *Accuracy judgments of WISC-R item difficulty for minority groups.* Paper presented at the annual meeting of the American Psychological Association, New York.

Sandstrom, M. J., & Cillessen, A. H. N. (2006). Likeable versus popular: Distinct implications for adolescent adjustment. *International Journal of Behavioral Development, 30*, 305–314.

Sanford, K., Bingham, C. R., & Zucker, R. A. (1999). Validity issues with the Family Environment Scale: Psychometric resolution and research application with alcoholic families. *Psychological Assessment, 11*, 315–325.

Sanger, M., MacLean, W., & Van Slyke, D. (1992). Relation between maternal characteristics and child behavior ratings: Implications for interpreting behavior checklists. *Clinical Pediatrics, 31*, 461–466.

Sarason, I.G., Johnson, J.H, & Siegel, J.M. (1978). Assessing the impact of life changes: Development of the Life Experiences Survey. Journal of Consulting and Clinical Psychology, 46, 932–946.

Sargent, J., Liebman, R., & Silber, M. (1985). Family therapy for anorexia nervosa. In D. M. Garner & P. E. Garfinkel (Eds.), *Handbook of psychotherapy for anorexia nervosa and bulimia* (pp. 257–279). New York: Guilford Press.

Sattler, J. M. (1988). *Assessment of children* (3rd ed.). San Diego, CA: Author.

Scahill, L., Schwab-Stone, M., Merikangas, K. R., Leckman, J. F., Zhang, H., & Kasl, S. (1999). Psychosocial and clinical correlates of ADHD in a community sample of school-age children. *Journal of the American Academy of Child and Adolescent Psychiatry, 38*, 976–984.

Schachar, R., Rutter, M., & Smith, A. (1981). The characteristics of situationally and pervasively hyperactive children: Implications for syndrome definition. *Journal of Child Psychology and Psychiatry, 22*, 375–392.

Schaughency, E. A., & Lahey, B. B. (1985). Mothers' and fathers' perceptions of child deviance: Roles of child behavior, parental depression, and marital satisfaction. *Journal of Consulting and Clinical Psychology, 53*, 718–723.

Schaughency, E. A., & Rothlind, J. (1991). Assessment and classification of attention-deficit hyperactivity disorder. *School Psychology Review, 20*, 187–202.

Schinka, J. A., Elkins, D. E., & Archer, R. P. (1998). Effects of psychopathology and demographic characteristics on MMPI-A scale scores. *Journal of Personality Assessment, 71*, 295–305.

Schniering, C. A., & Rapee, R. M. (2002). Development and validation of a measure of children's automatic thoughts: The Children's Automatic Thoughts Scale. *Behaviour Research and Therapy, 40*, 1091–1109.

Scholte, E., Van Berckelaer-Onnes, I., & Van der Ploeg, J. (2008). Rating scale to screen symptoms of psychiatric disorders in children. *European Journal of Special Needs Education, 23*, 47–62.

Schorre, B. E. H., & Vandvik, I. H. (2004). Global assessment of psychosocial functioning in child and adolescent psychiatry: A review of three unidimensional scales (CGAS, GAF, GAPD). *European Child and Adolescent Psychiatry, 13*, 273–286.

Schwab-Stone, M., Fisher, P., Piacentini, J., Shaffer, D., Davies, M., & Briggs, M. (1993). The Diagnostic Interview Schedule for Children – Revised Version (DISC-R): H. Test-retest reliability. *Journal of the American Academy of Child and Adolescent Psychiatry, 32*, 651–657.

Schwanz, K. A., & Kamphaus, R. W. (1997). Assessment and diagnosis of ADHD. In W. N. Bender (Ed.), *Understanding ADHD: A practical guide for parents and teachers.* Upper Saddle River, NJ: Merrill/Prentice-Hall.

Schwean, V. L., Burt, K., & Saklofske, D. H. (1999). Correlates of mother- and teacher-ratings of hyperactivity-impulsivity and inattention in children with AD/HD. *Canadian Journal of School Psychology, 15*, 43–62.

Scotti, J. R., Morris, T. L., McNeil, C. B., & Hawkins, R. P. (1996). *DSM–IV* and disorders of childhood and adolescence: Can structural criteria be functional? *Journal of Consulting and Clinical Psychology, 64*, 1177–1191.

Semrud-Clikeman, M. (1990). Assessment of childhood depression. In C. R. Reynolds & Kamphaus, R. W. (Ed.), *Handbook of psychological and educational assessment of children: Personality, behavior, and context* (pp. 279–297). New York: Guilford Press.

Semrud-Clikeman, M. (1991). ADHD and major depression in children and adolescents. *Child Assessment News, 1*, 6–7.

Sevin, J. A., Matson, J. L., Coe, D. A., & Fee, V. F. (1991). A comparison and evaluation of three commonly used autism scales. *Journal of Autism and Developmental Disorders, 21*, 417–432.

Shaevel, B., & Archer, R. P. (1996). Effects of PI-2 and MMPI-A norms on T-Score elevations for 18-year-olds. *Journal of Personality Assessment, 67*(1), 72–78.

Shaffer, D., Fisher, P. W., & Lucas, C. P. (1999). Respondent-based interviews. In D. Shaffer, C. P. Lucas, & J. E. Richters (Eds.), *Diagnostic assessment in child and adolescent psychopathology* (pp. 3–33). New York: Guilford.

Shaffer, D., Fisher, P., Lucas, C. P., Dulcan, M. K., & Schwab-Stone, M. E. (2000). NLMH diagnostic interview schedule for children version, IV IMH DISC-IV): Description, differences from previous versions, and reliability of some common diagnoses. *Journal of the American Academy of Child and Adolescent Psychiatry, 39*, 28–38.

Shaffer, D., Fisher, P., Piacentini, J., Schwab-Stone, M., & Wicks, J. (1991). *NIMH diagnostic interview schedule for children-version* 2.3. New York: New York State Psychiatric Institute.

Shaffer, D., Garland, A., Gould, M., Fisher, P., & Trautman, P. (1988). Preventing teenage suicide: A critical review. *Journal of the American Academy of Child and Adolescent Psychiatry, 27*, 675–687.

Shaffer, D., Gould, M. S., Brasic, J., Ambrosini, P., Fisher, P., Bird, H., et al. (1983). A children's global assessment scale (CGAS). *Archives of General Psychiatry, 40*, 1228–1231.

Shaffer, D., Schwab-Stone, M., Fisher, P., Cohen, P., Piacentini, J., Davies, M., Conners, C. K., et al. (1993). The Diagnostic Interview Schedule for Children-Revised Version (DISC-R): I. Preparation, field testing, interrater reliability, and acceptability. *Journal of the American Academy of Child and Adolescent Psychiatry, 32*, 643–650.

Shapiro, E. S. (1987). *Behavioral assessment in school psychology.* Hillsdale, NJ: Lawrence Erlbaum.

Shapiro, E. S., & Skinner, C. H. (1990). Principles of behavioral assessment. In C. R. Reynolds & R. W. Kamphaus (Eds.), *Handbook of psychological and educational assessment of children: Personality, behavior, and context* (pp. 343–363). New York: Guilford Press.

Sharp, C. & Kine, S. (2008). The assessment of juvenile psychopathy: Strengths and weaknesses of currently used questionnaire measures. *Child and Adolescent Mental Health, 13*, 85–95.

Shaw, J. G., Hammer, D., & Leland, H. (1991). Adaptive behavior of preschool children with developmental delays: Parent versus teacher ratings. *Mental Retardation, 29*, 49–53.

Shelby, M. D., Nagle, R. J., Barnett-Queen, L. L., Quattlebaum, P. D., & Wuori, D. F. (1998). Parental reports of psychosocial adjustment and social competence in child survivors of acute lymphocytic leukemia. *Children's Health Care, 27*(2), 113–129.

Shellenberger, S., Dent, M. M., Davis-Smith, M., Seale, J. P., Weintraut, R., & Wright, T. (2007). Cultural genogram: A tool for teaching and practice. *Families, Systems, & Health, 25*, 367–381.

Shelton, K. K., Frick, P. J., & Wootton, J. (1996). The assessment of parenting practices in families of elementary school-aged children. *Journal of Clinical Child Psychology, 25*, 317–327.

Sherrill, J. T., & Kovacs, M. (2000). Interview schedule for children and adolescents (ISCA). *Journal of the American Academy of Child and Adolescent Psychiatry, 39*, 67–75.

Shiner, R., & Caspi, A. (2003). Personality differences in childhood and adolescence: Measurement, development, and consequences. *Journal of Child Psychology and Psychiatry, 44*, 2–32.

Shopler, E., Reichler, R. J., & Renner, R. R. (1988). *Child autism rating scale.* Los Angeles: Western Psychological Services.

Sikora, D. M., Hall, T. A., Hartley, S. L., Gerrard-Morris, A. E., & Cagle, S. (2008). Does parent report of behavior differ across ADOS-G classifications: Analysis of scores from the CBCL and GARS. *Journal of Autism and Developmental Disorders, 38*, 440–448.

Silverman, W. K. (1993). DSM and classification of anxiety disorders in children and adults. In C. G. Last (Ed.), *Anxiety across the lifespan: A developmental perspective* (pp. 7–36). New York: Springer.

Silverman, W. K., & Albano, A. M. (1996). *Anxiety Disorders Interview Schedule for Children for DSM-IV: (Child and Parent Versions).* San Antonio, TX: Psychological Corporation/Graywind.

Silverman, W. K., & Nelles, W. B. (1989). The stability of mothers' rating of child fearfulness. *Journal of Anxiety Disorders, 3*, 1–5.

Silverman, W. K., & Ollendick, T. H. (2005). Evidence-based assessment of anxiety and its disorders in children and adolescents. *Journal of Clinical Child and Adolescent Psychology, 34*, 380–411.

Silverman, W. K., & Rabian, B. (1999). Rating scales for anxiety and mood disorders. In D. Shaffer, C. P. Lucas, & J. E. Richters (Eds.), *Diagnostic assessment in child and adolescent psychopathology* (pp. 127–166). New York: Guilford.

Silverman, W. K., Saavedra, L. M., & Pina, A. A. (2001). Test–retest reliability of anxiety symptoms and diagnoses using the Anxiety Disorders Interview Schedule for *DSM-IV:* Child and Parent Versions (ADIS for *DSM-IV:* C/P). *Journal of the American Academy of Child & Adolescent Psychiatry, 40*, 937–944.

Silverthorn, P., & Frick, P. J. (1999). Developmental pathways to antisocial behavior: The delayed-onset pathway in girls. *Development and Psychopathology, 11*, 101–126.

Singleton, L. C., & Asher, S. R. (1979). Peer preferences and social interaction among third-grade children in an integrated school district. *Journal of Educational Psychology, 69*, 330–336.

Siskind, G. (1967). Fifteen years later: A replication of a semantic study of concepts of clinical psychologists and psychiatrists. *Journal of Psychology, 65*, 3–7.

Skinner, B. F. (1963). Operant behavior. *American Psychologist,* 18, 503–515.

Smith, B. H., Barkley, R. A., & Shapiro, C. J. (2007). Attention-deficit/hyperactivity disorder. In E. J. Mash & R. A. Barkley (Eds.), *Assessment of childhood disorders* (4th ed.). New York: Guilford.

Smith, S. R. (2007). Making sense of multiple informants in child and adolescent psychopathology: A guide for clinicians. *Journal of Psychoeducational Assessment, 25*, 139–149.

Smith, S. R., Baity, M. R., Knowles, E. S., & Hilsenroth, M. J. (2001). Assessment of disordered thinking in children and adolescents: The Rorschach Perceptual-Thinking Index. *Journal of Personality Assessment, 77*, 447–463.

Smolla, N., Valla, J., Bergeron, L., Berthiaume, C., & St-Georges, M. (2004). Development and reliability of a pictorial mental disorders screen for young adolescents. *The Canadian Journal of Psychiatry, 49*, 828–837.

Snyder, J. (1991). Discipline as a mediator of the impact of maternal stress and mood on child conduct problems. *Development and Psychopathology, 3*, 263–276.

Snyder, M., Tanke, E. D., & Berscheid, F. (1977). Social perception and interpersonal behavior on the self-fulfilling nature of social stereotypes. *Journal of Personality and Social Psychology, 35*, 656–666.

Solis, M. L., & Abidin, R. R. (1991). The Spanish version of the Parenting Stress Index: A psychometric study. *Journal of Clinical Child Psychology, 20*, 372–378.

Solomon, I. L., & Starr, B. D. (1968). *School apperception method:* SAM. New York: Springer.

Sorneson, E., & Johnson, E. (1996). Subtypes of incarcerated delinquents constructed via cluster analysis. *Journal of Child Psychology, 37*, 293–303.

Sourander, A., Helstelae, L., & Helenius, H. (1999). Parent-adolescent agreement on emotional and behavioral problems. *Social Psychiatry and Psychiatric Epidemiology, 34*, 657–663.

South, M., Williams, B. J., McMahon, W. M., Owley, T., Filipek, P. A., Shernoff, E., et al. (2002). Utility of the Gilliam Autism Rating Scale in research and clinical populations. *Journal of Autism and Developmental Disorders, 32*, 593–599.

Southam-Gerow, M. A., & Chorpita, B. F. (2007). Anxiety in children and adolescents. In E. J. Mash & R. A. Barkley (Eds.), *Assessment of childhood disorders* (4th ed., pp. 347–397). New York: Guilford.

Spanier, G. B. (1976). Measuring dyadic adjustment: New scales for assessing the quality of marriage and similar dyads. *Journal of Marriage and the Family, 38*, 15–28.

Sparrow, S. S., Balla, D. A., & Cicchetti, D. V. (1984). *Vineland adaptive behavior scales.* Circle Pines, MN: American Guidance Services.

Sparrow, S. S., Cicchetti, D. V., & Balla, D. A. (2005). *Vineland adaptive behavior scales* (2nd ed.). Circle Pines, MN: American Guidance Services.

Speece, D. L., & Cooper, D. H. (1990). Ontogeny of school failure: Classification of first grade children. *American Educational Research Journal, 27*, 119–140.

Spielberger, C. D. (1973). *Manual for the State-Trait Anxiety Inventory for children.* Palo Alto, CA: Consulting Psychologists Press.

Spielberger, C. D., Gorsuch, R. L., & Lushene, R. E. (1970). *STAI manual for the State-Trait Inventory.* Palo Alto, CA: Consulting Psychologist Press.

Spitzer, R., & Cantwell, D. (1980). The DSM-III classification of psychiatric disorders of infancy, childhood, and adolescence. *Journal of the American Academy of Child and Adolescent Psychiatry, 19*, 356–370.

Spitzer, R. L., Davies, M., & Barkley, R. A. (1990). The DSM-III-R field trials of disruptive behavior disorders. *Journal of the American Academy of Child and Adolescent Psychiatry, 29*, 690–697.

Spivack, G., & Spotts, J. (1966). *Devereux child behavior rating scale.* Devon, PA: The Devereux Foundation.

Spivack, G., Spotts, J., & Haines, P. E. (1967). *Devereux adolescent behavior rating scale.* Devon, PA: The Devereux Foundation.

Stanger, C., Dumenci, L., Kamon, J., & Burstein, M. (2004). Parenting and children's externalizing problems in substance-abusing families. *Journal of Clinical Child and Adolescent Psychology, 33*, 590–600.

Strakaki, C., & Ellis, J. (1989). The relationship of anxiety to depression in children and adolescents. In C. Stavrakaki (Ed.), *The psychiatric clinics of North America: Affective disorders and anxiety in the child and adolescent* (pp. 777–789). Philadelphia, PA: W. B. Saunders.

Steele, R. G., Nesbitt-Daly, J. S., Daniel, R. C., & Forehand, R. (2005). Factor structure of the Parenting Scale in a low-income African-American sample. *Journal of Child and Family Studies, 14*, 535–549.

Stein, L. A. R., & Graham, J. R. (1999). Detecting fake-good MMPI-A profiles in a correctional facility. *Psychological Assessment, 11*(3), 386–395.

Stein, L., & Graham, J. (2005). Ability of substance abusers to escape detection on the Minnesota Multiphasic Personality Inventory-Adolescent (MMPI-A) in a juvenile correctional facility. *Assessment, 12*, 28–39.

Steinberg, L., Lamborn, S., Dornbusch, S., & Darling, N. (1992). Impact of parenting practices on adolescent achievement: Authoritative parenting, school involvement, and encouragement to succeed. *Child Development, 63*, 1266–1281.

Steinhausen, H. C., & Metzke, C. W. (1998). Youth self-report of behavioral and emotional problems in a Swiss epidemiological study. *Journal of Youth and Adolescence, 27*, 429–441.

Stone, W. L., Coonrod, E. E., Pozdol, S. L., & Turner, L. M. (2003). The Parent Interview for Autism – clinical

version (PIA-CV): A measure of behavioral change for young children with autism. *Autism, 7*, 9–30.
Stone, W. L., & Hogan, K. L. (1993). A structured parent interview for identifying young children with autism. *Journal of Autism and Developmental Disorders, 23*(4), 639–652.
Stoolmiller, M., Eddy, J. M., & Reid, J. B. (2000). Detecting and describing preventive intervention effects in a universal school-based randomized trial targeting delinquent and violent behavior. *Journal of Consulting and Clinical Psychology, 68*, 296–306
Stowers-Wright, L. E. (2000). *A behavioral cluster analysis of male juvenile defenders.* Unpublished doctoral dissertation: The University of Georgia.
Strauss, A. A., & Lehtinen, L. F. (1947). *Psychopathology and education of the brain-injured child.* New York: Grune & Stratton.
Strauss, C. C. (1990). Overanxious disorder in childhood. In M. Hersen & C. G. Last (Eds.), *Handbook of child and adult psychopathology* (pp. 237–246). New York: Pergamon Press.
Strauss, C. C. (1993). Developmental differences in expression of anxiety disorders in children and adolescents. In C. G. Last (Ed.), *Anxiety across the lifespan: A developmental perspective* (pp. 63–77). New York: Springer.
Strauss, C. C., Lahey, B. B., Frick, P. J., Frame, C. L. & Hynd, G. W. (1988). Peer social status of children with anxiety disorders. *Journal of Consulting and Clinical Psychology, 56*, 137–141.
Stredny, R. V. & Ball, J. D. (2005). The utility of the Rorschach Coping Deficit Index as a measure of depression and social skills deficits in children and adolescents. *Assessment, 12*, 295–302.
Sundberg, N. D. (1961). The practice of psychological testing in clinical settings in the United States. *American Psychologist, 16*, 79–83. Reprinted in L. D. Goodstein & R. I. Lanyon (Eds.), *Readings in Personality Assessment.* New York: Wiley.
Sundre, D. L. (1998). [Review of the Personnel Reaction Blank]. *Thirteenth Mental Measurements Yearbook.* Lincoln, NE: Buros Institute.
Sutter, J., & Eyberg, S. M. (1984). *Sutter-Eyberg student behavior inventory.* Gainesville, FL: University of Florida.
Suveg, C., Zeman, J., Flannery-Schroeder, E., & Cassano, M. (2005). Emotion socialization in families of children with an anxiety disorder. *Journal of Abnormal Child Psychology, 33*, 145–155.
Swensen, C. H. (1968). Empirical evaluations of human figure drawings: 1957–1966. *Psychological Bulletin, 70*, 20–44. Reprinted in L. D. Goodstein & R. I. Lanyon (Eds.), *Readings in Personality Assessment.* New York: Wiley.
Szapocznik, J., & Kurtines, W. (1980). Acculturation, biculturalism and adjustment among Cuban Americans. In A. M. Padilla (Ed.), *Acculturation: Theory, models and some new findings* (pp. 139–159). American Association for the Advancement of Science Selected Symposium 39. Boulder, CO: Westview.
Szapocznik, J., Scopetta, M. A., & Aranalde, M. A. (1978). Theory and measurement of acculturation. *Interamerican Journal of Psychology, 12*, 113–130.
Szatmari, P., Saigal, S., Rosenbaum, P., & Campbell, D. (1993). Psychopathology and adaptive functioning among extremely low birth weight children at eight years of age. *Development and Psychopathology, 5*, 345–357.
Tallent, N. (1988). *Psychological report writing* (3rd ed.). Englewood Cliffs, NJ: Prentice-Hall.
Tallent, N. (1993). *Psychological report writing* (4th ed.). Englewood Cliffs, NJ: Prentice-Hall.
Tanaka, J. S., & Westerman, M. A. (1988). Common dimensions in the assessment of competence in school-aged girls. *Journal of Educational Psychology, 80*, 579–584.
Tannock, R. (2000). Attention deficit disorders with anxiety disorders. In T. Brown (Ed.), *Attention deficit disorders and comorbidities in children, adolescents and adults* (pp. 125–170). Washington, DC: American Psychiatric Press
Tapscott, M., Frick, P. J., Wootton, J. & Kruh, I. (1996). The intergenerational link to antisocial behavior: Effects of paternal contact. *Journal of Child and Family Studies, 5*, 229–240.
Teglasi, H. (1983). Report of a psychological assessment in a school setting. *Psychology in the Schools, 20*, 466–479.
Tellegen, A., & Ben-Porath, Y. S. (1992). The new uniform T-scores for the A[MPI-2: Rationale, derivation, and appraisal. *Psychological Assessment, 4*, 145–155.
Teodori, J. B. (1993). Neurological assessment. In T. H. Ollendick & M. Hersen (Eds.), *Handbook of child and adolescent assessment* (pp. 41–50). Boston, MA: Allyn and Bacon.
Teufel-Shone, N., Staten, L. K., Irwin, S., Rawiel, U., Bravo, A. B., & Waykayuta, S. (2005). Family cohesion and conflict in an American Indian community. *American Journal of Health Behavior, 29*, 413–422.
Thomas, A., & Chess, S. (1977). *Temperament and development.* New York: Bruner & Mazel.
Thompson, C. E. (1949). *Manual for thematic apperception test: Thompson modification.* Cambridge, MA: Harvard University Press.
Thompson, L. L., Riggs, P. D., Mikulich, S. K., & Crowley, T. J. (1996). Contribution of ADHD symptoms to substance problems and delinquency in conduct-disordered adolescents. *Journal of Abnormal Child Psychology, 24*, 325–348.
Thurber, S., & Hollingsworth, D. K. (1992). Validity of the Achenbach and Edelbrock Youth Self-Report with hospitalized adolescents. *Journal of Clinical Child Psychology, 21*, 249–254.
Tibbetts, S. G., & Piquero, A. R. (1999). The influence of gender, low birth weight, and disadvantaged environment in predicting early onset of offending: A test

of Moffitt's interactional hypothesis. *Criminology, 37*, 843–877.

Tillman, R., Geller, B., Craney, J. L., Bolhofner, K., Williams, M., Zimerman, B., Frazier, J., et al. (2003). Temperament and character factors in a prepubertal and early adolescent bipolar disorder phenotype compared to attention deficit hyperactive and normal controls. *Journal of Child and Adolescent Psychopharmacology, 13*, 531–543.

Tripp, G., Schaughency, E., & Clarke, B. (2006). Parent and teacher rating scales in the evaluation of attention-deficit hyperactivity disorder: Contribution to diagnosis and differential diagnosis in clinically referred children. *Journal of Developmental & Behavioral Pediatrics, 27*, 209–218.

Trites, R. L., Bouin, A. G. A., & Laprade, K. (1982). Factor analysis of the Conners teacher rating scale based on a large normative sample. *Journal of Consulting and Clinical Psychology, 50*, 615–623.

Tsoubris, K. T. (1998). Relationship between prenatal cocaine exposure and behavioral patterns among preschool children with disabilities. *Dissertation Abstracts International Section B: The Sciences and Engineering, 59*(5-B), 2441.

Tuma, J. M., & Elbert, J. C. (1990). Critical issues and current practice in personality assessment of children. In C. R. Reynolds & R. W. Kamphaus (Eds.), *Handbook of psychological and educational assessment of children: Personality, behavior, and context* (pp. 3–29). New York: Guilford.

Tupes, E. C., & Christal, R. E. (1961). Recurrent personality factors based on trait ratings. *Technical Report ASD-TR-61-97.* Lackland Air Force Base, TX: U.S. Air Force.

Vaillancourt, T., & Hymel, S. (2006). Aggression and social status: The moderating roles of sex and peer-valued characteristics. *Aggressive Behavior, 32*, 396–408.

Valdez, G. M., & McNamara, J. R. (1994). Matching to prevent adoption disruption. *Child & Adolescent Social Work Journal, 11*, 391–403.

Valla, J. P., Bergeron, L., Bidaut-Russell, M., St., M., & Gaudet, N. (1997). Reliability of the Dominic-R: A young child mental health questionnaire combining visual and auditory stimuli. *Journal of Child Psychology and Psychiatry, 38*, 717–724.

Valla, J., Bergeron, L., & Smolla, N. (2000). The Dominic-R: A pictorial interview for 6- to 11-year-old children. *Journal of the American Academy of Child and Adolescent Psychiatry, 39*, 85–93.

Vance, F. I. (1965). I was an imaginary playmate. *American Psychologist, 20*, 990.

Van Hasselt, V. B., Hersen, M., Bellack, A. S., Rosenblum, N. D., & Lamparski, D. (1979). Tripartite assessment of the effects of systematic desensitization in a multi-phobic child: An experimental analysis. *Journal of Behavior Therapy and Experimental Psychiatry, 10*, 51–55.

Van Horn, M. L., Atkins-Burnett, S., Karlin, E., Ramey, S. L., & Snyder, S. (2007). Parent ratings of children's social skills: Longitudinal psychometric analyses of the Social Skills Rating System. *School Psychology Quarterly, 22*, 162–199.

Vasay, M. W., & Lonigan, C. J. (2000). Considering the clinical utility of performance-based measures of childhood anxiety. *Journal of Clinical Child Psychology, 29*, 493–508.

Vaughn, M. L., Riccio, C. A., Hynd, G. W., & Hall, J. (1997). Diagnosing ADHD subtypes: Discriminant validity of the Behavior Assessment System for Children (BASC) and the Achenbach paren and teacher rating scales. *Journal of Clinical Child Psychology, 26*, 349–357.

Verhulst, F. C., Koot, H. M., & Van der Ende, J. (1994). Differential predictive value of parents' and teachers' reports of children's problem behaviors: A longitudinal study. *Journal of Abnormal Child Psychology, 22*, 531–546.

Victor, J. B. (1994). The five-factor model applied to individual differences in school behavior. In C. F. Halverson, G. A. Kohnstamm, & R. P. Martin (Eds.), *The developing structure of temperament and personality from infancy to adulthood* (pp. 355–366). Hillsdale, NJ: Erlbaum.

Vincent, G. M. (2006). Psychopathy and violence risk assessment in youth. *Child and Adolescent Psychiatric Clinics of North America, 15*, 407–428.

Voelker, S. L., Shore, D. L., Brown-More, C., & Hill, L. C. (1990). Validity of self-report of adaptive behavior skills by adults with mental retardation. *Mental Retardation, 28*, 305–309.

Waldman, I. D. & Gizer, I. R. (2006). The genetics of attention deficit hyperactivity disorder. *Clinical Psychology Review, 26*, 396–432.

Walker, C. E., Milling, L. S., & Bonner, B. L. (1988). Incontinence disorders: Enuresis and encopresis. In D. K. Routh (Ed.), *Handbook of pediatric psychology* (pp. 363–398). New York: Guilford Press.

Walker, H. M., & McConnell, S. R. (1988). *The Walker-McConnell scale of f social competence and school adjustment.* Austin, TX: Pro-Ed.

Walker, J. L., Lahey, B. B., Ilynd, G. W., & Frame, C. L. (1987). Comparison of specific patterns of antisocial behavior in children with conduct disorder with or without coexisting hyper-activity. *Journal of Consulting and Clinical Psychology, 55*, 666–678.

Walker, J. L., Lahey, B. B., Russo, M. F., Frick, P. J., Christ, M. A. G., McBurnett, K., et al. (1991). Anxiety, inhibition, and conduct disorder in children: I. Relations to social impairment. *Journal of the American Academy of Child and Adolescent Psychiatry, 30*, 187–191.

Walsh, C., MacMillan, H. L., & Jamieson, E. (2003). The relationship between parental substance abuse and child maltreatment: Findings from the Ontario Health Supplement. *Child Abuse and Neglect, 27*, 1409–1425.

Wang, J. J. (1992, April). *An analytical approach to generating norms for skewed normative distributions.* Paper presented at the Annual Meeting of the American Educational Research Association, San Francisco.

Ward, J. H. (1963). Hierarchical grouping to optimize an objective function. *Journal of the American Statistical Association,* 58, 236–244.

Waschbusch, D. A. (2002). A meta-analytic examination of comorbid hyperactive-impulsive-attention problems and conduct problems. *Psychological Bulletin, 128,* 118–150.

Wasielewski, S. M., Gridley, B. J., & Hall, J. (1998, April). *Construct validity of the Behavior Assessment System for Correlations with the Personality Inventory for Children-Revised with a clinical sample.* Paper presented at the Annual Meeting of the National Association of School Psychologists, Orlando.

Watkins, C. E., Campbell, V. L., Nieberding, R., & Hallmark, R. (1995). Contemporary practice of psychological assessment by clinical psychologists. *Professional Psychology: Research and Practice, 26,* 54–60.

Webster-Stratton, C., & Lindsay, D. W. (1999). Social competence and conduct problems in young children: Issues in assessment. *Journal of Clinical Child and Adolescent Psychology, 28,* 25–43.

Wechsler, D. (1974). *Wechsler intelligence scale for children - revised.* New York: Psychological Corporation.

Wechsler, R. D. (1991). *Wechsler intelligence scale for children* (3rd ed.). New York: Psychological Corporation.

Weems, C. F., Hammond-Laurence, K., Silverman, W. K., & Ginsburg, G. S. (1998). Testing the utility of the anxiety sensitivity construct in children and adolescents referred for anxiety disorders. *Journal of Clinical Child Psychology, 27,* 69–77.

Weems, C. F., Silverman, W. K., Rapee, R. R., & Pina, A. A. (2003). The role of control in childhood anxiety disorders. *Cognitive Therapy and Research, 27,* 557–568.

Weems, C. F., & Stickle, T. R. (2005). Anxiety disorders in childhood: Casting a nomological net. *Clinical Child and Family Psychology Review, 8,* 107–134.

Weiner, I. B. (1986). Assessing children and adolescents with the Rorschach. In H. M. Knoff (Ed.), *The adjustment of child and adolescent personality* (pp. 141–172). New York: Guilford Press.

Weiner, I. B. (2001). Advancing the science of psychological assessment: The Rorschach Inkblot Method as exemplar. *Psychological Assessment. 13,* 423–432.

Weiss, B., & Garber, G. (2003). Developmental differences in the phenomenology of depression. *Development and Psychopathology, 15,* 403–430.

Weiss, B., & Weisz, J. R. (1988). Factor structure of self-reported depression: Clinic-referred children versus adolescents. *Journal of Abnormal Psychology, 97,* 492–495.

Weiss, G., Hechtman, L., & Perlman, T. (1978). Hyperactives as young adults: School, employer, and self rating scales obtained during ten-year follow-up evaluation. *American Journal of Orthopsychiatry, 48,* 438–445.

Weissman, M. M., Warner, V., & Fendrich, M. (1990). Applying impairment criteria to children's psychiatric diagnosis. *Journal of the American Academy of Child Adolescent Psychiatry, 29, 789–795.*

Weissman, M. M., Warner, V., Wickramaratne, P., & Prusoff, B. A. (1988). Early-onset major depression in parents and their children. *Journal of Affective Disorders, 15,* 269–277.

Weissman, M. M., Wickramaratne, P., Adams, P., Wolk, S., Verdeli, H., & Olfson, M. (2000). Brief screening for family psychiatric history: The family history screen. *Archives of General Psychiatry, 57,* 675–682.

Weller, E. B., Weller, R. A., Fristad, M. A., Rooney, M. T., & Schecter, J. (2000). Children's interview for psychiatric syndromes (ChIPS). *Journal of the American Academy of Child and Adolescent Psychiatry, 39,* 76–84.

Wender, P. H. (1995). *Attention deficit disorder in adults.* London: Oxford University.

West, M. O., & Prinz, R. J. (1987). Parental alcoholism and childhood psychopathology. *Psychological Bulletin, 102,* 204–218.

Whalen, C. K., & Henker, B. (1998). Attention-deficit hyperactivity disorder. In T. H. Ollendick & M. Hersen (Eds.), *Handbook of child psychopathology* (3rd ed., pp. 181–212). New York: Plenum Press.

Whalen, C. K., Henker, B., & Dotemoto, S. (1980). Methylphenidate and hyperactivity: Effects on teacher behaviors. *Science, 208*(4449), 1280–1282.

Whalen, D. K., Henker, B., Jamner, L. D., Ishikawa, S. S., Floro, J. N., Swindle, R., et al. (2006). Toward mapping daily challenges of living with ADHD: Maternal and child perspectives using electronic diaries. *Journal of Abnormal Child Psychology, 34,* 115–130.

Whipple, E.E. & Webster-Stratton, C. (1991). The role of parental stress in physically abusive families. Child Abuse & Neglect, 15, 2779–291.

Whiteside, S. P., McCarthy, D. M. & Miller, J. D. (2007). An examination of the factor structure of the Social Skills Rating System parent elementary form. *Assessment, 14,* 246–254.

Whiteside-Mansell, L., Ayoub, C., McKelvey, L., Faldowski, R. A., Hart, A., & Shears, J. (2007). Parenting stress of low-income parents of toddlers and preschoolers: Psychometric properties of a short form of the Parenting Stress Index. *Parenting: Science and Practice, 7,* 27–56.

Widaman, K. F., Stacy, A. W., & Borthwick-Duffy, S. A. (1993). Construct validity of dimensions of adaptive behavior: A multitrait–multimethod evaluation. *American Journal on Mental Retardation, 98,* 219–234.

Widiger, T. A., Frances, A. J., Davis, W., & First, M. (Eds.) (1994). *DSM-IV sourcebook* (Vol. 1). Washington, DC: American Psychiatric Association.

Widiger, T. A., Frances, A. J., Pincus, H. A., Davis, W. W., & First, M. B. (1991). Toward an empirical classification for the DSM-IV. *Journal of Abnormal Psychology, 100,* 280–288.

Widiger, T. A., Frances, A. J., Pincus, H. A., Ross, R., First, M. B., Davis, W., et al. (1998). *DSM-IV sourcebook: Vol. 4.* Washington, DC: American Psychiatric Association.

Wiener, J. (1985). Teachers' comprehension of psychological reports. *Psychology in the Schools, 22*, 60–64.

Wiender, I. B. (2001). Advancing the science of psychological assessment: The Rorschach Inkblot Method as exemplar. *Psychological Assessment, 13*, 423–432.

Wiener, J., & Kohler, S. (1986). Parents' comprehension of psychological reports. *Psychology in the Schools, 23*, 265–270.

Williams, C. L., Butcher, J. N., Ben-Porath, Y. S., & Graham, J. R. (1992). *MMPI-A Content Scales: Assessing psychopathology in adolescents.* Minneapolis: University of Minnesota Press.

Wingenfeld, S. A., Lachar, D., Gruber, C. P., & Kline, R. B. (1998). Development of the teacher-informant Student Behavior Survey. *Journal of Psychoeducational Assessment, 16*, 226–249.

Winokur, G. (1990). The concept of secondary depression and its relationship to comorbidity. In G. Winokur & R. B. Wesner (Eds.), *The psychiatric clinics of North America: Anxiety and depression as secondary phenomena* (pp. 567–583). Philadelphia, PA: W. B. Saunders.

Wirt, R. D., Lachar, D., Klinedinst, J. K., & Seat, P. S. (1984). *Multidimensional description of child personality: A manual for the personality inventory for children.* Los Angeles: Western Psychological Services.

Wirt, R. D., Lachar, D., Klinedinst, J. K., & Seat, P. S. (1990). *Personality inventory for children-1990 edition.* Los Angeles: Western Psychological Services.

Witt, J. C., Heffer, R. W., & Pfeiffer, J. (1990). Structured rating scales: A review of self-report and informant rating processes, procedures, and issues. In C. R. Reynolds & R. W. Kamphaus (Eds.), *Handbook of psychological and educational assessment of children: Personality, behavior and context* (pp. 364–394). New York: Guilford Press.

Witt, J. C. & Jones, K. M. (1998). Review of the Behavior Assessment System for Children. In J. C. Impara & B. S. Plake (Eds.), *The Thirteenth, Mental Measurements Yearbook* (pp. 131–133). Lincoln, NE: Buros Institute.

Wolf, T. H. (1966). Intuition and experiment: Alfred Binet's first efforts in child psychology. *Journal of History of Behavioral Sciences, 2*, 233–239.

Wolfe, D. A., Edwards, B., Manion, I., & Koverola, C. (1988). Early intervention of parents at risk for child abuse and neglect: A preliminary investigation. *Journal of Consulting and Clinical Psychology, 56*, 40–47.

Woodcock, R. W., & Johnson, M. B. (1989). *Woodcock-Johnson tests of achievement – revised.* New York: Riverside.

Woodin, M. F. (1999). Screening for the interface between attention, executive functioning, and working memory: A cluster and profile analytic study. *Dissertation Abstracts International Section B: The Sciences and Engineering, 59*(10-B), 5590.

Woodworth, R. S. (1918). *Personal data sheet.* Chicago: Stoelting.

Wootten, S. A. (1999). Attention-deficit/hyperactivity disorder. *Dissertation Abstracts International Section B: The Sciences & Engineering, 60*(1-B), 0380.

Wootton, J. M., Frick, P. J., Shelton, K. K., & Silverthorn, P. (1997). Ineffective parenting and childhood conduct problems: The moderating role of callous-unemotional traits. *Journal of Consulting and Clinical Psychology, 65*, 301–308.

Worchel, F. F., & Dupree, J. L. (1990). Projective storytelling techniques. In C. R. Reynolds & R. W. Kamphaus (Eds.), *Handbook of psychological and educational assessment of children: Personality, behavior, and context* (pp. 70–88). New York: The Guilford Press.

World Health Organization (1993). *The ICD-10 classification of mental and behavioural disorders: Diagnostic criteria for research.* Geneva: World Health Organization.

Wrobel, T. A., Lachar, D., Wrobel, N. H., Morgan, S. T., Gruber, C. P., & Neher, J. A. (1999). Performance of the Personality Inventory for Youth validity scales. *Assessment, 6*, 367–376.

Wrobel, N., Lachar, D., & Wrobel, T. (2005). Self-report problem scales and subscales and behavioral ratings provided by peers: Unique evidence of test validity. *Assessment, 12*, 255–269.

Youngstrom, E., Izard, C., & Ackerman, B. (1999). Dysphoria-related bias in maternal ratings of children. *Journal of Consulting and Clinical Psychology, 67*, 905–916.

Zettergren, P. (2007). Cluster analysis in sociometric research: A pattern-oriented approach to identifying temporally stable peer status groups of girls. *Journal of Early Adolescence, 27*, 90–114.

Zettergren, P., Bergman, L. R., & Wangby, M. (2006). Girls' stable peer status and their adult adjustment: A longitudinal study from age 10 to age 43. *International Journal of Behavioral Development, 30*, 315–325.

Zimmerman, I. L., & Woo-Sam, J. M. (1967). Reporting results. In A. J. Glasser & I. L. Zimmerman (Ed.), *Clinical interpretation of the Wechsler Intelligence Scale for Children (WISC).* New York: Grune & Stratton.

Zimmerman, I. L., & Woo-Sam, J. M. (1985). Clinical applications. In B. B. Wolman (Ed.), *Handbook of intelligence: Theories, measurements, and applications* (pp. 873–898). New York: Wiley.

Zuckerman, M. (1990). Some dubious premises in research and theory on racial differences: Scientific, social, and ethical issues. *American Psychologist, 45*, 1297–1303.

Author Index

Subject Index

CPSIA information can be obtained at www.ICGtesting.com
Printed in the USA
243128LV00007B/19/P

9 780387 896427